Chocolate in Mesoamerica

MAYA STUDIES

UNIVERSITY PRESS OF FLORIDA

Florida A&M University, Tallahassee
Florida Atlantic University, Boca Raton
Florida Gulf Coast University, Ft. Myers
Florida International University, Miami
Florida State University, Tallahassee
University of Central Florida, Orlando
University of Florida, Gainesville
University of North Florida, Jacksonville
University of South Florida, Tampa
University of West Florida, Pensacola

MAYA STUDIES

Edited by Diane Z. Chase and Arlen F. Chase

The books in this series will focus on both the ancient and the contemporary Maya peoples of Belize, Mexico, Guatemala, Honduras, and El Salvador. The goal of the series is to provide an integrated outlet for scholarly works dealing with Maya archaeology, epigraphy, ethnography, and history. The series will particularly seek cutting-edge theoretical works, methodologically sound site-reports, and tightly organized edited volumes with broad appeal.

Salt: White Gold of the Ancient Maya, by Heather McKillop (2002)

Archaeology and Ethnohistory of Iximché, by C. Roger Nance, Stephen L. Whittington, and Barbara E. Borg (2003)

The Ancient Maya of the Belize Valley: Half a Century of Archaeological Research, edited by James F. Garber (2003)

Unconquered Lacandon Maya: Ethnohistory and Archaeology of the Indigenous Culture Change, by Joel W. Palka (2005)

Chocolate in Mesoamerica: A Cultural History of Cacao, edited by Cameron L. McNeil (2006)

Chocolate in Mesoamerica

A Cultural History of Cacao

Edited by Cameron L. McNeil

FOREWORD BY DIANE Z. CHASE AND ARLEN F. CHASE

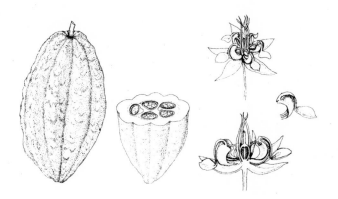

University Press of Florida

GAINESVILLE TALLAHASSEE TAMPA BOCA RATON
PENSACOLA ORLANDO MIAMI JACKSONVILLE FT. MYERS

Title page image: *Theobroma cacao*. Cut fruit showing five seeds, flower, sectioned flower, and one petal. Drawing by Samantha Tsistinas.

11 10 09 08 07   6 5 4 3 2

A record of cataloging-in-publication data is available from the Library of Congress
ISBN 0-8130-2953-8

The University Press of Florida is the scholarly publishing agency for the State University System of Florida, comprising Florida A&M University, Florida Atlantic University, Florida Gulf Coast University, Florida International University, Florida State University, University of Central Florida, University of Florida, University of North Florida, University of South Florida, and University of West Florida.

University Press of Florida
15 Northwest 15th Street
Gainesville, FL 32611-2079
http://www.upf.com

Contents

Figures

Tables

Foreword

Although broader in scope than simply the Maya area, *Chocolate in Mesoamerica: A Cultural History of Cacao* is a welcome addition to our Maya Studies series. This volume situates the Maya in a wider cultural context by combining cutting edge studies from multiple fields to consider the origin and role of cacao in ancient and contemporary Mesoamerica.

Few Native American products are as essential and omnipresent in contemporary day-to-day life as chocolate. An ancient elite Mesoamerican drink, cacao first became a limited distribution European luxury item but subsequently has been transformed into a readily available comestible to which there is global multistatus access. Today, millions of people enjoy eating chocolate on a daily basis. Thus, this contribution should be of widespread general interest.

The papers in this volume present reflections and findings on cacao from many different perspectives; each of the scholars writes with detailed knowledge of his or her own field of expertise. From an historical and archaeological perspective, this volume adds the important ingredient of time depth—the significance and function of cacao is reviewed for pre-Columbian and historic periods. There is also careful consideration of how cacao came to be absorbed into the Spanish diet and culture, eventually impacting most of Europe and then the world. Although the volume focuses largely on the Mesoamerican and, particularly, Maya use of cacao, broader geographical coverage also includes the use of this item in nearby Central America. Authors consider far-ranging topics related to cacao, including the origins and domestication; variants; environmental constraints on cultivation; processing and production; and the historic and contemporary utilization (including medicinal and ritual uses) among the Maya and other peoples of the Americas. Contributors discuss: the value of cacao; the artistic conventions concerning cacao and its use; and the archaeological identification of cacao, including the recovery of seeds in archaeological context, residue analysis from ancient ceramics, and the hieroglyphic markings on ancient ceramic containers. Exploration of the status-linked aspects of cacao consumption are also undertaken in concert with historic descriptions of cacao consumption and the significance of cacao in ancient and modern religious rituals.

In sum, this volume admirably contextualizes the use of cacao in ancient and contemporary Mesoamerica. Marshalling evidence from a wide variety of disciplines—for example, conservation biology, botany, pharmacy, ethnohistory, art history, epigraphy, anthropology, and archaeology—these scholars create a truly multidisciplinary perspective on the American origins of chocolate that will form a hallmark study for years to come in the field of Maya studies.

Diane Z. Chase and Arlen F. Chase
Series Editors

1

Introduction

The Biology, Antiquity, and Modern Uses of the Chocolate Tree
(*Theobroma cacao* L.)

Cameron L. McNeil

For people in the United States and Europe, "chocolate" summons visions of
rich desserts or boxes of sweets, and some aficionados may joke that chocolate
is their "religion." Chocolate is made from the seeds of the *Theobroma cacao*
L. tree, commonly referred to as the 'cacao tree' (Figure 1.1). For many pre-
Columbian cultures of the Americas, cacao seeds and the comestibles produced
from them were literally part of their religion and played a central role in their
spiritual beliefs and social and economic systems. In isolated areas these traditions continue to this day. Parts of this plant have been consumed in Central
and South America for thousands of years. For many of the ancient and modern cultures in these regions, cacao was not only an important part of religious
rituals, but also a component of beverages and foods, a topical cream, and an
ingredient in medicine. It reached its height of importance in pre-Columbian
Mesoamerica, whose northern limit begins in Central Mexico, and which
then encompasses Guatemala, Belize, El Salvador and western Honduras (see
Figure 1.2).[1] Mesoamerica is renowned for its myriad highly stratified societies
including the Olmecs, Maya, and Mexica (Aztecs). Cacao played a central
role in the complex elite culinary traditions and practices of these cultures,
and it also served as an important item of trade and economic wealth (Bergmann 1969; S. D. Coe and M. D. Coe 1996; Millon 1955a; J. E. S. Thompson
1956).

The origins of the cacao tree remain unknown, with scholars debating both
its natural distribution and area of domestication. The variety of comestibles
that were made from this plant in pre-Columbian times is also the subject of
disagreement. Was cacao used to produce only beverages, or was it also a com-

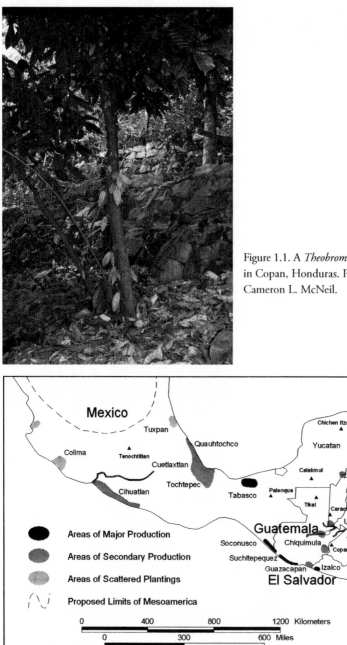

Figure 1.1. A *Theobroma cacao* tree growing in Copan, Honduras. Photograph by Cameron L. McNeil.

Figure 1.2. Map of Mesoamerica and Lower Central America with the major cacao-growing zones. The area of Mesoamerica is designated by dashes. Map by Marc Wolf after Bergmann (1969).

ponent of other types of foods? Were beverages made from the pulp of cacao pods or only from the seeds? Who consumed cacao—only members of the elite, or was it widely available to the lower socioeconomic classes? Today, some religious practices involving cacao survive in indigenous communities, especially in Mexico and Guatemala, and these practices may provide clues to ancient associations with this food. As with any ethnographic study, the difficulty is in determining which elements of the modern traditions, if any, are unchanged reflections of ancient behavior.

In this volume we use a multidisciplinary approach to explore the history of cacao in Mesoamerica. Scholars from a variety of fields provide answers to the questions posed above presenting new evidence on the domestication of cacao, its ancient use in foods other than beverages, its significance in Mesoamerican religion, and its role in elite feasts. Researchers offer theories concerning how and why cacao seeds became important and explore the survival of traditional cacao use in modern-day Mesoamerica.

The introduction presents an overview of the origins and history of cacao, providing a framework for the subsequent four sections. In Part I of the volume, experts in the fields of bio-analytical chemistry, ethnobotany, plant systematics, and anthropology explore the evolution, domestication, chemistry, and identification of *T. cacao* and its close relatives in Central and South America. In Part II, archaeologists, art historians, linguists, and epigraphers discuss the pre-Columbian use and importance of cacao from Mesoamerica down through Nicaragua. Although the majority of the chapters focus on the Maya culture, cacao use among the Mexica (Aztecs), Pipil, and Nicarao is also explored. In Part III, historians and archaeologists examine how the sixteenth-century arrival of the Spanish and the process of colonization altered the production and consumption of cacao among the peoples of Mesoamerica; it also documents the incorporation of cacao into the cuisine of the Spanish. In Part IV, archaeologists, ethnobotanists, and ethnographers discuss the continued use of cacao in Mesoamerican communities of the twentieth and twenty-first centuries.

Cacao, Its Origins and Domestication

As noted above, the word "cacao" generally refers to the species *T. cacao*, although among the Maya of Mesoamerica it is sometimes also applied to *Theobroma bicolor* Bonpl.(see Kufer and McNeil, this volume). The word cacao is a Spanish adaptation of the Nahua *kakawa-tl*.[2] The most commonly used ancient Maya term for cacao was *kakaw*. There has been some debate about the linguistic antecedent of these words. Lyle Campbell and Terrence Kaufman (1976) proposed that their origins lie in proto-Mije-Sokean and that this language was spoken by the Olmec of the southern Veracruz and the western Tabasco lowlands of Mexico. Karen Dakin and Søren Wichmann (2000) have presented arguments supporting a Uto-Aztecan origin for *kakaw-tl*, but Terrence Kaufman and John Justeson (this volume) refute the Dakin and Wichmann linguistic analysis with persuasive evidence for the previously proposed proto-Mije-Sokean source. The origin of the word *chocolatl* (the basis for "chocolate") is almost as contentious and appears to have been a late development within Nahua, possibly as late as the sixteenth century (Kaufman and Justeson, this volume). In this volume, in keeping with general practice, most authors have chosen to use "cacao" (although some use *kakaw*) when referring to the *T. cacao* tree, its seeds, and its pulp. Some authors use "chocolate" to refer to beverages made from roasted, ground cacao seeds.

Theobroma cacao is a small understory tree that produces pods containing 25–40 seeds each. The average height of the domesticated tree is 15–25 feet, although trees in wild populations may be markedly taller (Millon 1955a:10; Ogata 2002a). Cacao trees are cauliflorous; that is, flowers are produced directly on the trunk and larger branches (Figures 1.3 and 1.4). Cacao seeds are naturally dispersed by rodents (including squirrels), bats, and monkeys, who eat through the thick pod surface to reach the sweet pulp surrounding the bitter seeds (A. M. Young 1994:xi). There are numerous examples of ancient Mesoamerican artworks depicting monkeys, squirrels, and bats holding cacao pods (see this volume: Aguilar, Figure 13.5; Henderson and Joyce, Figure 7.2; Ogata, Gómez-Pompa, and Taube, Figures 3.10 and 3.12).[3] The uses of the cacao tree extend beyond culinary consumption. Fat from the seeds (better known as cocoa butter) is used in lotions and other cosmetics, and various parts of the tree are used in medicines (see Bletter and Daly, this volume; Cuatrecasas 1964).

It is generally accepted that the genus *Theobroma* evolved in South America

Figure 1.3. Flowers growing directly from the trunk
of a *Theobroma cacao* tree. Photograph by Cameron L. McNeil.

Figure 1.4. *Theobroma cacao* tree with pods growing directly from the trunk. Photograph by Cameron L. McNeil.

where both its greatest number of species and most closely related genus, *Herrania*, are found (Bletter and Daly, this volume; Young 1994). From the upper Amazon basin, *T. cacao* spread out and up through Central America and into Mexico either naturally or through human agency (Bletter and Daly, this volume; Cuatrecasas, 1964; Motamayor *et al.* 2002; Ogata, Gómez-Pompa, and Taube, this volume; Schultes 1984; Stone 1984; Young 1994). Scholars have debated not only how this tree migrated, but also in what form—wild or as a cultigen (Motamayor *et al.* 2002; Ogata 2002a; Ogata, Gomez-Pompa and Taube, this volume). Debates continue as to whether *T. cacao* has two domestication spheres, one in South America and one in Mesoamerica, or only one, located either in South America or in Mesoamerica. The concept of domestication itself further confuses this issue as scholars today recognize that domestication is a process with many steps. For example cacao could have arrived from South America as a cultigen, only to be more fully domesticated in Mesoamerica. It seems likely that if cacao was domesticated in both South America and Mesoamerica, the focus of selection for these two processes was not the same, as South Americans most commonly have used the pulp for consumption, while Mesoamericans most commonly used the seeds (Young 1994:3). The theory that *T. cacao* had a natural distribution in Mesoamerica and was independently fully domesticated there was first proposed by José Cuatrecasas (1964) and has since been supported by additional botanists and geneticists (Gómez-Pompa, Flores and Aliphat Fernandez 1990; Laurent, Risterucci and Lanaud 1994; Ogata, Gomez-Pompa and Taube, this volume). However, other researchers have posited that cacao was brought to Mesoamerica as a cultigen through human agency (Motamayor and Lanaud 2002; Schultes 1984; Stone 1984). Scientists in favor of each theory have conducted DNA analysis of *T. cacao* populations and found evidence to support their respective theories. In the quest to identify the original domestication sphere (or spheres) of cacao geneticists need to pursue DNA analysis on a significantly larger range of specimens than has been conducted to date. Samples from pre-Columbian archaeological deposits may be particularly useful for investigating the origins of *T. cacao* because they pre-date the extensive hybridization between South and Central American varieties that occurred after the arrival of the Spanish. Nonetheless, determining the origin of domestication of plant species is frequently a contentious process, and conclusive answers are rarely found.

Theobroma cacao exhibits a wide range of variability in the form of its fruit and in certain floral characteristics (Cuatrecasas 1964:504). This diversity had led botanists to separate *T. cacao* into two subspecies—*criollo* (*T. cacao* ssp. *cacao* L.) and *forastero* (*T. cacao* ssp. *sphaerocarpum* [A. Chev.] Cuatrec.), each of which contains a range of named varieties. *Criollos* have "elongated, ridged, pointed fruits and white cotyledons," and *forasteros* have "short roundish, almost smooth fruit and purplish cotyledons" (Cuatrecasas 1964:506; see Ogata, Gómez-Pompa, and Taube, Figure 3.1, this volume). Before the arrival of Europeans, *criollos* were endemic to Central America and *forasteros* were endemic to South America (A. M. Young 1994). Whether through natural evolution or human selection, the *T. cacao* species in Mesoamerica came to produce fruit and seeds distinct from those in the southern hemisphere. *Criollo* seeds are milder, that is, less bitter, than the South American members of their species and make a tastier chocolate.

Forastero-type cacao plants are hardier, and, not only do they generally produce pods two years earlier than *criollos* do (at three years), they also produce more pods per tree (Millon 1955a:11). However, the flavor of *forastero* beans is bitterer than the flavor of *criollos*. After sixteenth-century European contact, *criollos* and *forasteros* were hybridized as the Spanish tried to create breeds of cacao that produced larger amounts of pods while still retaining some of the *criollo* flavor (Young 1994).

Why Was Cacao So Much More Important in Mesoamerica Than in South America?

Most scholars believe that only the pulp, not the seeds, of *T. cacao* was consumed in pre-Columbian South America (A. M. Young 1994). The pulp, which also contains theobromine and caffeine, can be removed from the seeds and made into a fruit beverage or can be fermented to produce an alcoholic drink. It may seem surprising that the South American cultures discarded the stimulating seeds, which were so important in Mesoamerica. Nathaniel Bletter and Douglas Daly (this volume) suggest, however, that cacao seeds were not used in pre-Columbian South America because there were several other plant species containing higher levels of stimulating compounds that required far less processing. These included *mate* (*Ilex paraguariensis* A. St.-Hil.), *guaraná* (*Paullinia cupana* Kunth), and *yoco* (*Paullinia yoco* R. E. Schult. and Killip) (Weinberg and Bealer 2001:236). These caffeinated substances were not available in Mesoamerica, and their absence may explain why cacao seeds became prized in one area but not in the other (Bletter and Daly, this volume). There are many steps involved in preparing cacao seeds for use in beverages or foods. First the seeds are generally fermented in their pulp, then the pulp is removed and the seeds are dried (and sometimes roasted), and then, perhaps most significantly, the seeds must be ground (see McNeil, Chapter 17, this volume). If other species provided stronger stimulants while requiring less time investment, it is not surprising that South Americans did not find the need to create a process for using the bitter seeds as well as the pulp. The less bitter flavor of *criollo* seeds may be a product of a process of selection for seeds more appealing to the palate.

John Henderson and Rosemary Joyce (this volume) propose that Mesoamericans initially used the pulp of *T. cacao* to produce the same types of stimulating fermented beverages that are found from upper South America into at least the lower half of Mesoamerica (McNeil, Chapter 17, this volume; A. M. Young 1994). They posit that Mesoamerican people may have happened onto the technique of fermenting, drying, and grinding the seeds for "chocolate" production over time. Today, along the Pacific Coast of Guatemala, when beverages are made of the pulp the entire contents of the cacao pod are placed into a container and beaten until the sweet mesocarp loosens from the seeds. Sometimes this mixture is left to sit for several days prior to consumption, fermenting not only the fruity beverage but also the seeds (McNeil, Chapter 17, this volume). Henderson and Joyce propose that this practice may account for the initial discovery of the flavor benefits of seed fermentation.

Its sensitivity to environmental conditions limits the areas where cacao can be cultivated successfully. It "thrives on the deep, fertile alluvial soils of the river valleys in a shaded, heavily humid atmosphere (over 90 percent) with a heavy annual rainfall (70 inches [or more]) and a high average temperature (circa 80°F.—27°C.) and with a subsoil constantly moist because of the proximity of rivers" (Millon 1955a:14). In Mesoamerica, the sensitive growing conditions of cacao heightened its value because, unlike maize, it could not successfully be grown in all areas. The exploitation of the seeds as well as the pulp would have allowed people living in areas where the tree could not be cultivated to partake of its stimulating effects (Bletter and Daly, this volume) and provided inhabitants of prime cacao-growing areas with an important trade good. When the Spanish arrived on the shores of Mexico in 1519, the ideal growing areas for cacao in Mesoamerica were Tabasco, Mexico; the Soconusco region of Chiapas, Mexico, and the adjacent Pacific Coast region of Guatemala; Suchitepequez, Guatemala; the Ulua Valley, Honduras; and Izalco, El Salvador; with scattered secondary and tertiary centers in other parts of Mesoamerica and Central America (Bergmann 1969:86) (see Figure 1.2). Because of the selected areas where cacao could be grown and its socioeconomic value to Mesoamericans, wars were fought to control the ideal cacao-growing territories (Berdan and Anawalt 1997a; Caso Barerra and Aliphat F., this volume; M. J. MacLeod 1973). The conquered communities were forced to supply tribute in the form of cacao to the victors (Figure 1.5).

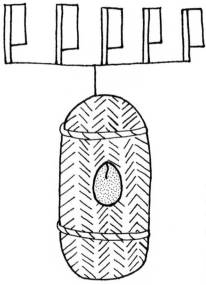

Figure 1.5. Basket with a cacao seed on the outside, marking it as a container of this precious food. The five flags, each representing the number twenty, signify that the basket contains 100 loads of cacao seeds. Drawing by Cameron L. McNeil from the Codex Mendoza (Berdan and Anawalt 1997a:99, Folio 47r).

Different varieties of cacao were developed over time, likely as a product of human selection for specific traits and because of the geographic isolation of cacao populations from one another. Francisco Hernández (2000 [1571–1615]), writing in the sixteenth century, describes the types of cacao seeds sold in the Mexica markets. The Mexica called the tree *cacahoaquahuitl* and the seeds *cacahoatl*, differentiating between each variety of cacao (Hernández 2000 [1571–1615]:108). Hernández writes:

> There are four varieties of this tree: the first called quauhcacáhoatl, is the biggest of them and has the largest fruit; the second, the mecacacáhoatl, is of medium size, spread out, and with fruit that follows the first kind in size; the third, known as xochicacáhoatl, is small, with small fruit, whose seed is reddish on the outside and like the rest inside; the fourth, which is the smallest of the four and is thus called tlalcacáhoatl, or 'little,' gives the smallest fruit, but is still the same color as the others. All of these varieties have the same nature and can be used interchangeably, although the last one is used more for drinks, just as the others are more suitable and convenient as money. (Hernández 2000 [1571–1615]:108)

Today one can find a range of colors in cacao pods, and it is difficult to know what colors originate from the varieties grown in Mesoamerica during pre-Columbian times. From pre-Columbian depictions and early Colonial descriptions, it would appear that the varieties with green pods that turned to yellow when ripe and those with red pods existed in Mesoamerica before the Conquest (G. D. Jones 1989:103–104; Winning 1985:76).

The Use of Cacao in Preclassic and Classic Period Mesoamerica

The earliest cacao iconography in the Americas may come from Peru. Nisao Ogata, Arturo Gómez-Pompa, and Karl Taube (this volume) have identified a 2500-year-old Peruvian vessel decorated with pod elements, which they propose are cacao (see Ogata, Gómez-Pompa, and Taube, Figure 3.9, this volume). The written history of cacao, however, undoubtedly begins in Mesoamerica, perhaps as early as the mid-third century A.D. (Early Classic period) in the form of glyphs on ceramic vessels (Stuart, this volume). Mexica, Maya, and Mixtec codices from later pre-Columbian periods also record the ritual significance of cacao (Figure 1.5) (see this volume: Henderson and Joyce, Figure 7.4; Stuart, Figure 9.1).

The period in which cacao was domesticated is uncertain. However, the recovery of the chemical signature for cacao in spouted vessels from Belize dating to 600–400 B.C. (Hurst et al. 2002; Powis et al. 2002:98), a vessel form known throughout Mesoamerica as well as Andean South America from at least 1000 B.C., supports a date for cacao domestication by at least this time (Henderson and Joyce, this volume; Dorie Reents-Budet, personal communication 2005). Residue analysis of the Andean spouted vessels should be pursued to determine whether these vessels also contained cacao. The identification of cacao in a vessel form found from the same period in both South and Central America might alter theories pertaining to cacao domestication.

Before the development of chemical residue testing of pottery vessels, it was difficult to determine when pre-Columbian Mesoamericans first consumed cacao (Hurst et al. 1989; see Hurst, this volume). There is a paucity of cacao macroremains from archaeological sites, and images of cacao in Mesoamerican art and material culture are unknown before the Classic period (A.D. 250–900). That cacao seeds do not frequently survive in the archaeological record further complicates our ability to trace the origins of cacao usage in ancient Mesoamerica. Although they are more durable than other types of botanical macroremains frequently recovered from middens (for example, *Phaseolus vulgaris* L., the common bean), cacao seeds are less abundant than other foods that comprised the diet of Mesoamericans. The low frequency of cacao seeds in household trash deposits is likely a product of several factors: the socioeconomic restrictions limiting cacao consumption to the sociopolitical and economic elites in at least some regions of Mesoamerica; the value of cacao seeds, which meant that they were less likely to be casually dropped on the floor and swept away during daily household cleaning; and the limited areas where the tree could be grown.

Although scarce, *Theobroma* remains have been recovered from a number of archaeological contexts. The earliest *Theobroma* macroremains found in Mesoamerica are charred wood fragments excavated from the site of Cuello, Belize (Miksicek 1991). These charcoal remains were found in strata that may be as old as 1000–900 B.C., although the AMS ^{14}C dates were secured on bone collagen from burials associated with the same levels as the recovered charcoal, not from the *Theobroma* wood itself (Norman Hammond, personal communication 2004). Charles Miksicek (1991) notes that this wood could be from either *T. cacao* or *T. bicolor*, a close relative also used for food and beverages (see Kufer and McNeil, this volume). *Theobroma* wood morphology is highly variable within different sections of the same specimen, and scholars have suggested that it is not possible to distinguish between its species on the basis of their wood structure (Chattaway 1937; Stern 1964:439).

Theobroma cacao seeds have been recovered from a number of sites in Central America: Copan, Honduras (context date not specified) (B. L. Turner et al. 1983); Uaxactun, Guatemala (Late Classic period) (Kidder 1947); Ceren, El Salvador (early Late Classic) (Lentz 1996); and Ayala, Granada, Nicaragua (A.D. 750–850) (Salgado González 1996:171; Salgado González, personal communication 2004). At least one cacao tree (in bloom) was preserved in volcanic

Figure 1.6. The trunk of a *Theobroma cacao* tree preserved in the volcanic ash at Ceren, El Salvador. Photograph courtesy of Payson Sheets.

ash at Ceren (Sheets and Woodward 2002:Figure 20.5) (see Figure 1.6). Macroremains identified as possible cacao bean fragments were found at Cuello, Cerros, and Pulltrouser Swamp (all in Belize) (Crane 1996) and Cara Sucia, El Salvador (W. R. Fowler 1987). A seed of *T. bicolor*, was found in a later Early Classic cache vessel at Tikal, Guatemala (Moholy-Nagy, Haviland, and Jones 2003). Ceramic effigy cacao seeds, identical in form and size to real ones, have been found in vessels and as adornments on censers from Pacific coastal Guatemala (Bove et al. 1993; Schmidt, de la Garza, and Nalda 1998).

In the late 1980s, W. Jeffrey Hurst created a technique for identifying the chemical signature of cacao in archaeological residues and macroremains (Hurst et al. 1989; Hurst, this volume). This development has provided a wealth of new information on cacao use in Mesoamerica. Hurst's work has identified cacao residue in the Middle Preclassic (600–300 B.C.) vessels from Belize, discussed above, as well as in Early Classic (A.D. 250–600) vessels from Río Azul, Guatemala (Hall et al. 1990; Hurst et al. 1989) and Copan, Honduras (McNeil et al. 2002). In addition, Hurst has discovered the chemical signature of *T. cacao* (and possibly *T. bicolor*) in vessels containing faunal materials excavated from a variety of elite contexts at Copan (McNeil, Hurst, and Sharer, this volume).

Cacao: The Food of the Elite

In pre-Columbian Mesoamerica to possess cacao was a sign of wealth, power, and rulership. Vessels of frothy cacao beverages are frequently represented at the foot of the king's throne on Maya vases (Reents-Budet, this volume: Figure 10.6). Similarly, a sack of cacao beans set in front of a ruler's throne, likely a gift or tribute payment, is depicted on a mural at the site of Bonampak in Mexico (Houston 1997; see Stuart, this volume: Figure 9.6). Fine vessels containing cacao or bearing cacao glyphs are frequently associated with elite Maya graves (Culbert 1993; Hall et al. 1990; Houston, Stuart, and Taube 1992; Reents-Budet, this volume; D. Stuart 1988; Stuart, this volume; Taschek and Ball 1992). Cacao iconography is present on monumental sculpture at several Mesoamerican sites (this volume: McNeil, Hurst, and Sharer; Martin; Schele and Mathews 1998; J. E. S. Thompson 1948; Tozzer 1957). Cacao seeds, as well as a prepared mixture of cacao and maize flour, often comprised tribute payments among the Postclassic (A.D. 900–1520) Mexica and other peoples of Mesoamerica (Berdan and Anawalt 1992) (see Figure 1.5). Furthermore, during Postclassic times, cacao seeds also were used as a form of money, their value, size, and durability simplifying exchange in marketplaces (Millon 1955a).

The importance of cacao during the Classic period is attested by the large number of vessels with painted or incised imagery that includes a cacao glyph and frequently the Primary Standard Sequence (PSS) (Stuart, this volume). The PSS is a hieroglyphic text, found on some Maya vessels, that contains an introductory glyph and dedication verb, the type of vessel and its contents, and sometimes the name of the vessel's owner or patron (M. D. Coe 1973). PSS inscriptions provide information on the diversity of cacao beverages available during the Classic period. During Early Classic times, vessels with cacao glyphs were concentrated around the Peten region, where they likely originated (Stuart, this volume). After A.D. 550, the production of vessels bearing cacao inscriptions spread to other Maya areas. David Stuart (this volume) finds a gradual increase in the uniformity of inscriptions during the Classic period, with certain types of ceramics and "recipes" having regional associations.

Vessels bearing cacao inscriptions are generally considered to be elite food service wares. These carefully executed containers are most commonly of ceramic, but shell examples also have been found (Reents-Budet 1994b; Reents-Budet, this volume; G. Stuart 2001). Finely made vessels had an important role as gifts to garner prestige and solidify power between leaders of polities and as rewards for loyal elites, often comprising a portion of the gifts bestowed upon guests at ritual feasting events (Landa 1941 [1566]). Such vessels reaffirmed the power of the giver, not only by the act of giving the gift but also frequently by the images portrayed on their surfaces, which reflect religious and royal themes designed to support the dominant political order (Reents-Budet, this volume). The painting style of the vessels (and sometimes the artist's signature) can provide information on the geographic location of the workshops where each originated and thereby can aid archaeologists in understanding sociopolitical relationships by tracing the distribution of these fine wares. At the Maya site of Copan, vessels bearing cacao glyphs have not been recovered from the tombs of rulers but have been found in Late Classic elite burials (McNeil, Hurst, and Sharer, this volume). These prized vessels may represent the owner's participation in important feasting events, perhaps even those organized by the ruler, and may also serve as trophies signifying the deceased's high position in the Copan political hierarchy.

Mesoamerican cacao iconography is found on censers, stelae, and sculptured building façades as well as on vessels from Classic through Postclassic times. Images of cacao become increasingly prevalent during the Classic period, reaching a peak in the Late Classic. An example of this trend is found in the art of Copan, where there was a florescence of cacao tree representations in sculpture during the Late Classic period (McNeil, Hurst, and Sharer, this volume). Mesoamerican iconography displays a complex set of associations with cacao, sometimes designating it as a sacred tree and linking it to blood, rulership, (reborn) ancestors, women (or goddesses), and the Underworld (Chinchilla Mazariegos 2005; S. D. Coe and M. D. Coe 1996; J. E. S. Thompson 1948, 1956; Tozzer 1957; see this volume: Faust and Hirose López; Kufer and Heinrich; McNeil, Hurst, and Sharer; Martin; Pugh). In addition, cacao imagery is paired with maize and the Maize God (see this volume: Kufer and Heinrich; Martin; McNeil, Hurst, and Sharer).

Cacao is sometimes portrayed as a cosmic or sacred directional tree. At Copan, cacao pods grow from the trunk of a censer in the form of the *axis mundi* (World Tree or cross). This cacao tree *axis mundi* replaces the more common representation of the World Tree as a ceiba tree or maize plant (see McNeil, Hurst, and Sharer, Figures 11.14a and 11.14b, this volume). Cacao trees as featured pictorial elements are depicted throughout Late Classic Maya art and are found as far north as Chichen Itza, Yucatan, Mexico (see Martin, Figures 8.8b and 8.15, this volume). The pivotal importance of the cacao tree is also seen in the Postclassic Mixteca-Puebla Codex Fejérváry-Mayer, where a cacao tree occupies the southern position in a diagram of the world whose cardinal directions are marked by four cosmic trees (Figure 1.7).

In pre-Columbian times cacao was associated with the South and the Underworld. In reference to the ancient Maya, Wendy Ashmore (1989:273) has noted that the southern cardinal direction can also be equated with the Underworld. In Chapter 8 of this volume, Simon Martin discusses associations between cacao and God L and the Underworld. At Copan, Late Classic censers

Figure 1.7. Cacao as the cosmic tree of the south. Drawing by Cameron L. McNeil from the Codex Fejérváry-Mayer (Postclassic Mixteca-Puebla).

in the form of cacao trees display floating faces which likely represent deceased ancestors reborn from the Underworld as cacao trees (see McNeil, Hurst, and Sharer, Figure 11.10, this volume). Lady Sak K'uk', a queen of Palenque and the mother of the ruler, Pakal, is also depicted reborn as a cacao tree in the Temple of the Inscriptions (Schele and Mathews 1998:121) (see this volume: McNeil, Hurst, and Sharer, Figure 11.9; Martin, Figure 8.6). Johanna Kufer and Michael Heinrich (this volume) suggest that cacao, possibly because its ideal growing conditions are in shaded areas, may have been associated with darkness, whereas maize, which is grown in open fields, is associated with light. Cacao's ties to the shade may also have encouraged its association with death and the Underworld. A text in the Highland Mexican Codex Magliabecchiano, placed above a scene of a person being prepared for burial, notes that the deceased was provided with cacao for his trip to the next world (J. E. S. Thompson 1956:105). At least into the mid-twentieth century, people in Mexico's Oaxaca Valley continued to provide the dead with cacao for the journey to the afterworld (E. C. Parsons 1936:147).

Cacao and maize are an important ritual pair in Mesoamerican cosmology. Both are combined in ritual beverages with sacred water to feed the gods and ancestors so that they will work to provide agricultural fertility (Girard 1995; Kufer and Heinrich, this volume). Simon Martin (this volume) proposes that in ancient Maya religion cacao was the first food to grow from the body of the maize god. Rosemary Joyce has noted that the preparation of cacao for beverages "mimics the preparation of maize for consumption" (Meskell and Joyce 2003:139–140). Kufer and Heinrich (this volume) view maize and cacao as ritually paired opposites, the former light and growing in the sun, the latter dark and favoring the shade.

Cacao may be more closely associated with women than with men. Although both female and male ancestors are depicted reborn as cacao trees, portrayals of female figures with cacao growing from their bodies are more common than similar representations of males (see McNeil, Hurst, and Sharer, Figures 11.9 and 11.15, this volume) (Chinchilla Mazariegos 2005; McNeil, Hurst, and Sharer, this volume). Various modern myths and practices also link women to cacao (see this volume: Faust and Hirose López; Kufer and Heinrich; McNeil, Chapter 17; Pugh).

Cacao was also associated with blood and sacrifice in the pre-Columbian period. For Mesoamerican peoples, blood was an important offering to the gods. Not only were animals sacrificed, but people—particularly elites and rulers—offered their own blood and that of human captives (Nájera C. 1987; Schele 1984; Wilkerson 1984). Cacao beverages were sometimes colored red with *achiote* (also called annatto), a dye from the seeds of the *Bixa orellana* L. tree. Two Colonial chroniclers, Gonzalo Oviedo y Valdez (1851–55) and Alvarado (1924 [1525]) noted the similarity between red-dyed cacao drinks and blood. The people of Cholula, Mexico, made a cacao beverage from water in which knives used in human sacrifices had been washed (Acosta 2002 [1590]:325). In the Florentine Codex, Sahagún (1950–82, Book 6, 1969:256) records that "heart" and "blood" were metaphors for "cacao . . . because it was precious." J. Eric S. Thompson (1956:100) proposed that hearts and cacao pods share associations, because both are "the repositories of precious liquids—blood and cacao." Rosemary Joyce has suggested that the frequent exchange of cacao in marriage ceremonies may signify the mixing of bloodlines (Meskell and Joyce 2003:139–140). A range of images supports the association of cacao with sacrifice and blood. A stela from the archaeological site of Santa Lucia Cotzumalhuapa on the Pacific Coast of Guatemala depicts a human figure sacrificing a cacao pod as though it were a human heart: the cacao pod spouts a liquid substance (Figure 1.8).[4] In Mixtec codices, bleeding cacao pods are depicted both on the tops and insides of temples, which were places of sacrifice (Mary E. Smith 1973:236) (Figure 1.9). In the sixteenth century, Diego García de Palacio wrote that in pre-Columbian times the Pipil people in Nicaragua marked war captives for sacrifice with strands of cacao seeds, feathers, and green stones (1985 [1576]:40). At least one ceramic figure (a whistle) of a captive with his hands bound behind his back and a necklace of cacao pods has been found in Guatemala (Chinchilla Mazariegos 2005:17, Figure 16). This figure is similar to the more common figures of monkeys with collars of cacao pods, perhaps likening them to sacrificial victims (see Figure 1.10) (Benson 1994; M. E. Miller and S. Martin 2004).

Figure 1.8. A human figure sacrifices a cacao pod. Late Classic period Monument 21. Archaeological site of Santa Lucia Cotzumalhuapa, Pacific Coast of Guatemala. Drawing by Eliud Guerra after J. E. S. Thompson (1948:Figure 6d).

Figure 1.9. Three cacao seeds rest on top of a temple; the seed on the right is bleeding. Image from the Codex Bodley. Drawing by Cameron L. McNeil after Mary E. Smith (1973:236).

Figure 1.10. Monkey wearing a collar of cacao pods. From the Museo de Sitio de Tonina, Instituto Nacional de Antropología e Historia, Chiapas, Mexico. Drawing by Eliud Guerra after M. E. Miller and S. Martin (2004:Plate 40).

Mesoamerican Cacao Use in the Contact Period

Much of what is known about cacao use in pre-Columbian times comes from accounts written by Europeans in the sixteenth century. Perhaps because the Mexica were the first great adversaries conquered by the Spanish, and their city Tenochtitlan, the greatest city in Mesoamerica at the time of the Conquest, more is known about Highland Mexican cacao use during the Contact and early Colonial periods than about other areas of Mesoamerica (Díaz del Castillo 1963 [1568]; Durán 1971 [approx. 1581]; Hernández 2000 [before 1581]; Sahagún 1950–82 [1576]). Although less was written about the Maya and cultures in areas adjacent to Mesoamerica, there are a number of good sources (Gage 1946 [1648]; García de Palacio 1985 [1576]; Landa 1941 [1566]; Oviedo y Valdes 1851–55 [1535]).

These early accounts cite prohibitions against the consumption of cacao by people other than ruling elites, warriors, and merchants among the cultures of Highland Mexico and associated Nahua groups, such as the Pipil. The Florentine Codex says of cacao beverages:

> If he who drank it were a common person, it was taken as a bad omen.
> And in times past only the ruler drank it, or a great warrior, or a commanding general . . . if perhaps two or three lived in wealth they drank it.
> Also it was hard to come by; they drank a limited amount of cacao for it was not drunk unthinkingly. (Sahagún 1950–82, Book 6, 1969:256)

In another section of the codex, however, Sahagún (1950–82, Book 4, Chapter 36, 1979:117) notes that chocolate was put aside for the servants during feasts. He also implies that Mexica women may not have drunk cacao (Sahagún

1950–82, Book 4, Chapter 36, 1979:118). Diego García de Palacio wrote of the Pipil in El Salvador that "the beverage which they prepare from the cacao was formerly so highly esteemed by the Indians, that no one was permitted to drink of it, unless he were a great personage, a cazique, or a famous warrior" (García de Palacio 1985 [1575]:21). That cacao was valuable and precious in Mesoamerica is clear, and it is understandable that it would have been more valued in areas where cacao orchards do not thrive, such as Highland Mexico. However, as René Millon (1955a:168–9) has noted, in many areas where cacao thrives there are no records of restrictions on its consumption by common-ers. In particular, less is known about the existence of pre-Columbian cacao consumption prohibitions among the Maya. While cacao's value may have pre-vented it from being commonly consumed by non-elites, Colonial accounts tying cacao use to important Maya rituals such as marriage and baptism, may imply that while more accessible to elites, it was used for important religious or ritual events by commoners (Landa 1941 [1566]; Marjil de Jesus, Mazariegos and Guillen 1984 [1695]).

The role of cacao seeds as a form of "money" is well documented by early Colonial records and appears to have continued past the mid-1800s. In the six-teenth century, José de Acosta noted that "with five *cocoa* beans one thing can be bought, and with thirty another, and with a hundred another, without hag-gling" (Acosta 2002 [1590]:210). Ephraim G. Squier wrote in 1860 that cacao seeds continued to be used for "small change" in Nicaraguan markets (Squier 1985 [1860]:21). Elsie C. Parsons noted in the 1930s that the copper money of the Oaxaca Valley was formerly cut in half and referred to as "*gabisie*"—"*bisie*" being "cacao" (E. C. Parsons 1936:147, f. 200). Although cacao is no longer used as "money," the seeds are still offered and exchanged during rituals in some areas. Bunzel (1967) noted the importance of cacao seed oblations in Maya rituals in Chichicastenango, Guatemala, in the 1930s. The modern Lenca in Honduras offer cacao seeds to deities as a way to "pay" the gods to ensure agricultural fertility (Chapman 1985:105).

From early Colonial sources we learn something about the diversity of bever-ages that were produced from the highly valued cacao. Sahagún records:

> Then in his house, the ruler was served his chocolate, with which he fin-ished [his repast]-green, made of tender cacao; honeyed chocolate made with ground-up dried flowers-with green vanilla pods; bright red choco-late; orange-red chocolate; rose-colored chocolate; black chocolate; white chocolate. (Sahagún 1950–82, Book 8, Chapter 13, 1954:39)

Beverages containing cacao may at times have included the pulp of the tree, which can be fermented to produce an alcoholic drink, or ground cacao could have been mixed into other fermented beverages (see this volume: Henderson and Joyce; McNeil, Chapter 17). A range of additives were used to flavor cacao drinks, including *achiote* paste, vanilla (*vanilla planifolia* Andrews), ground chile peppers (*Capsicum* sp.), honey, ground seeds from *Ceiba pentandra* (L.) Gaertn. or *Pouteria sapota* (Jacq.) H. E. Moore and Stearn, the fruit of *Pimenta dioica* (L.) Merr., and various spicy or aromatic flowers (*Cymbopetalum penduliflorum* [Dunal] Baill., *Piper sanctum* [Miq.] Schltdl., *Quararibea funebris* [La Llave] Vischer, *Magnolia dealbata* Zucc., *Magnolia mexicana* DC., and members of the *Bourreria*) (S. D. Coe and M. D. Coe 1996:89–92).

Bernal Díaz del Castillo noted the equally sumptuous and diverse meals of the Mexica leader Motecuhzoma, but he unfortunately did not mention whether cacao was included in sauces or other comestibles in Highland Mexico (Díaz 1963 [1568]). It is likely that a similar abundance of foods were found at the feasts of great Maya rulers, but equally detailed accounts do not exist. In funerary offerings, at sites such as Copan, some glimpse is provided into the wide diversity of prepared dishes during the Classic period, at least two of which contain cacao and faunal materials (turkey and fish) (see McNeil, Hurst, and Sharer, this volume). Diego de Landa, the Spanish friar, documented foods consumed by the Maya in the Yucatan peninsula, but the feasts that he witnessed more than forty years after the Conquest are unlikely to have equaled the feasts of the great Classic Maya kingdoms or the Postclassic kingdoms of Mayapan and the Peten Itza (Landa 1941 [1566]:90).

The accoutrements involved in the elite consumption of cacao were also developed and ornate, with different methods of mixing and production suited to the various types of cacao beverages. Sahagún, in recording the feasts of Motecuhzoma, writes:

> The chocolate was served in a painted gourd vessel, with a stopper also painted with a design, and [having] a beater; or in a painted gourd, smoky [in color], from neighboring lands, with a gourd stopper, and a jar rest of ocelot skin or of cured leather. In a small net were kept the earthen jars, the strainer with which was purified the chocolate, a large, earthen jar for making the chocolate, a large painted gourd vessel in which the hands were washed, richly designed drinking vessels. (Sahagún 1950–82, Book 8, Chapter 13, 1954:40)

Sahagún's Florentine Codex, depicts women pouring vessels of cacao back and forth to create a foam (see Henderson and Joyce, Figure 7.5, this volume). In the drawing, one can see that the vessel rests on a rounded stand. A similar more elegantly executed image can be found on the Classic period Princeton vase (see Reents-Budet, Figure 10.9, this volume). Fray Diego de Landa also documents the use (and gifting) of fine vessels and stands during feasts, but he does not mention stirring sticks, possibly because they were an invention of Highland Mexican cultures (Landa 1941 [1566]). *Batidores*, sticks to beat cacao into a froth, are used in some Maya communities today, but the use of a Spanish word for these sticks, by Mayan speakers, may reflect that they were imported after the arrival of the Spanish (see Redfield and Villa 1934:37). Landa notes that among the Maya cacao beverages were prepared and served by beautiful young women, who "turned their backs on him who took it until he had emptied it" (Landa 1941 [1566]:92).

Although the majority of information on cacao in the pre-Columbian Americas relates to its use in Mesoamerica, archaeological and ethnohistorical evidence supports a long history of use elsewhere in the Americas. Cacao seeds were likely used in beverages in pre-Columbian times at least as far south into Central America as Costa Rica (see Steinbrenner, this volume). Some scholars have written that the arboriculture of cacao was brought to Nicaragua by Mesoamerican migrants, but Steinbrenner argues that it is more likely that Mesoamerican migrants were drawn to Nicaragua by its successful cacao production. Recent finds of cacao macroremains from approximately A.D. 800 in a basement midden in Nicaragua may further support his claim that the use of cacao seeds in Nicaragua and other areas of Greater Nicoya preceded the arrival of the Pipil from Mesoamerica (Salgado 1996:171). A beverage called *pinolillo*, prepared from the pulp of *T. bicolor*, is common in Nicaragua but is rarely produced in Mesoamerica (A. M. Young 1994:15). Nicaraguan cacao beverages were and are produced from the pulp and seeds of *T. cacao*. Steinbrenner believes that unlike the large cacao-growing zones in Mesoamerica, the fertile cacao-producing areas of Nicaragua were more geared to local consumption than to trade, and he discusses the fact that cacao consumption was not prohibited to nonelites (Benzoni 1857).

Cacao in the Colonial Period

The Spanish conquest of Mesoamerica in the early sixteenth century led to the death of millions of Mesoamericans, perhaps as much as 80 percent of the population (Lovell 1992; M. J. MacLeod 1973). Although some religious officials saw the indigenous population as future converts, the primary reason behind the Conquest was economic profit. Disease was the cause of the first wave of death (and many that came after) among indigenous populations (M. J. MacLeod 1973). This was followed by warfare, exploitation through high tribute demands, conscription for various purposes, enslavement, and slave trading of native people (M. J. MacLeod 1973). In their quest to control the indigenous population, including extensive rural populations which were dispersed throughout the landscape, the Spanish forced people to live in well-laid-out towns. Under the *encomienda* system, Conquistadors were awarded rights over areas of land as well as the labor of the people living on that land for a given period of time. Tributes, frequently unreasonably high (see Fowler, this volume) were demanded by the holders of Spanish land grants, the government, and also the Spanish crown (M. J. MacLeod 1973). Religious officials also profited through offerings brought to the churches (Gage 1946 [1648]).

The Spaniards encountering Motecuhzoma's court for the first time were impressed by the lavish feasts and the strange beverage, cacao, which was consumed in large amounts. Curiously, they overlooked that cacao was sometimes mixed with blood and offered in rituals, while amaranth grain, which was also offered in a mixture with human blood, was outlawed (Balick and Cox 1996). It is likely that cacao escaped amaranth's fate because of its economic value, both as a currency within the region and as a prized comestible. As M. J. MacLeod (1973:70) noted, the Mexica had a developed cacao tribute system in place when the Spanish arrived, and the conquerors were able initially to take over this profitable system, at least until disease killed many of the growers.

The Mesoamerican people were forced to convert to Christianity by the Spanish conquerors, but they frequently retained many practices of their native religion. Fray Diego Durán, writing in the sixteenth century, noted that when Christian festivals fell on days close to ancient Mexica festivals, indigenous people used the vestments and accoutrements of the ancient festivals just as if they were celebrating those rather than the Christian ones. He notes that, in particular, during the festivals that occur in early May (a time of ancient Mesoamerican fertility festivals for the new agricultural season [see Kufer and Heinrich, this volume]) staffs or bouquets of flowers were carried as they were in pre-Conquest religious rites (Durán 1971:43, 103). The Mexica placed offerings of food and incense in front of the images of saints on their home altars as though they were idols (Durán 1971:235). In some Mesoamerican communities, offerings of incense, flowers, and food—sometimes including cacao—are still placed on home or church altars.

Despite Durán's dislike of religious syncretism, the Catholic Church in Mesoamerica benefitted from such practices. In Chapter 13 of this volume, Manuel Aguilar discusses the presence of the sixteenth-century "Christ of the Cacao" in the Mexico City cathedral where cacao seeds were left as offerings (see Aguilar, Figure 13.1, this volume). The Church was able to profit handsomely from such offerings, the gifting of which was part of the ancient religion of the region. Not all church officials took advantage of the native population, and some, like Fray Bartolomé de las Casas, actively worked to protect them. Nevertheless, unscrupulous priests and friars were able to amass substantial amounts of wealth by exploiting the native custom of making copious ritual food offerings to their deities. Fray Thomas Gage describes the All Soul's day profit of one such person in Guatemala:

> A friar that lived in Petapa boasted unto me once that upon their All Soul's Day his offerings had been about a hundred reals, two hundred chickens and fowls, half a dozen turkeys, eight bushels of maize, three hundred eggs, four sontles of cacao (every sontle being four hundred grains), twenty clusters of plantains, above a hundred wax candles, besides loaves of bread, and other trifles of fruits. (Gage 1946 [1648]:261)

All of these gifts had been brought to the church and left on the altars. Thomas Gage himself was extremely fond of "chocolate," and when he fled in secrecy from his post in Guatemala, he made certain to take a supply for the journey (Gage 1946 [1648]:332).

It is possible that religious officials did not always comprehend when elements of the old native religions entered into their places of worship. The ornate murals of the Mexican sixteenth-century Augustinian monastery of La Purificación y San Simón feature a cacao tree in a central location (see Aguilar, this volume). These murals likely meant two different things to the two groups of people (Aztecs and Europeans) inhabiting and worshipping at the monastery. For the Augustinian friars, the murals depicted a Garden of Eden composed of plants from Mexico. For the Aztec artists who painted them, however, the flowered walls likely recalled the flower-filled temples of their native religion with offerings of cacao and other sacred plants, as well as the long Mesoamerican tradition of paradisiacal gardens dating back at least as far as the age of Teotihuacan in Classic period Mexico. These murals most closely remind one of the image of Tlalocan, the land of the rain god on the Tepantitla murals (ca. A.D. 600–750) at Teotihuacan, which among other trees features one that may be cacao (Figure 1.11) (Berrin 1988:158, Figure VI.9; Pasztory 1997). But they also share a similarity with the pan-Mesoamerican concept of "Sustenance Mountain," whose interior is the source of all food (Taube 1986). The manifestation of this concept in the Maya creation story, the *Popol Vuh*, is described as containing cacao, *pataxte* (*T. bicolor*), white and yellow maize, and other delicious foods (Christenson 2003:194). Motecuhzoma had a beautiful garden called Huaxtepec, "south of the Valley of Mexico," which contained well-tended cacao trees and was likely created to emulate the mythical lands of the gods (Emmart 1940:77).

Within thirty years of their arrival, the Spanish had taken over most of the important cacao-growing areas of Mesoamerica. Two of these, the Izalcos and Soconusco, are discussed in Chapters 15 and 16 of this volume, respectively. In Chapter 15, William Fowler examines the Izalcos, a term applied to four

Figure 1.11. An unidentified flowering tree with a person leaning against it is between a maize plant (left) and what may be a cacao tree (right). Mural detail of Tlalocan. Classic period. Tepantitla, Teotihuacan, Mexico. Drawing by Cameron L. McNeil.

towns—Izalco, Naolingo, Caluco, and Tacuscalco—located along the coast of El Salvador. During the sixteenth century the majority of cacao production in this area remained in the hands of indigenous producers (Pipils) who were required to pay large amounts of cacao seeds as tribute. The tribute demanded by the Spanish was unreasonably high, impoverishing the landowners rather than ensuring their higher economic status within the community. Another important cacao-growing area in pre-Columbian times was the Soconusco (Gasco, this volume). This region, once heavily forested, provided tribute to the Mexica in the form of cacao, gourds for consuming cacao, richly colored feathers, and jaguar skins (Berdan and Anawalt 1997a:98–99, Folio 46v). Gasco (this volume) suggests that the Mexica conquered this region to gain control over its valuable cacao resources. During the Colonial period, frustrated Spaniards sought ways to transport a larger population into the area to better utilize its agricultural potential after the people were devastated by illnesses (Gasco 1989a; M. J. MacLeod 1973).

The last holdouts against Spanish imperialism in Mesoamerica were the Itza of the Peten region of Guatemala (Caso Barrera and Aliphat F., this volume). The Itza were able to turn the subjugation of surrounding cultures to their economic and acquisitive advantage during the sixteenth and seventeenth centuries. Cacao played an integral role in feasting ceremonies and was a requisite offering for esteemed visitors among the Maya as well as to people about to be sacrificed (Means 1917:63, 134). As the Spanish destroyed the once powerful

Ch'ol merchant system (G. D. Jones 1982), the Itza were able to control a large number of the Ch'ol people living in lands fertile with cacao orchards and close to salt resources. In their zeal to conquer the Itza, the Spanish devastated the cultures in the surrounding areas and ensured the death of large-scale cacao production in this region (Caso Barrera and Aliphat F., this volume). This last autonomous Maya nation was doomed after the Spanish had conquered the people of all the adjoining lands, and the priority became the subjugation of the Itza.

Cacao in Modern Mesoamerica

Cacao continues to be an important comestible and offering in some modern Mesoamerican communities, but its use has been greatly reduced from pre-Columbian times. The reasons behind this loss are many and include forces at both the regional and local levels. Since the beginning of the Colonial period, waves of disease, forced religious conversion, drastic economic changes, and environmental degradation have meant that many traditions have been compromised or all but forgotten. As independent governments in Mesoamerican countries searched for the most financially profitable agricultural products, indigenous people were forced to convert valuable arable lands into crops chosen by those in control. Perhaps most notably, coffee replaced cacao. As coffee took over fields where cacao was once planted, rendering cacao less accessible and more expensive, coffee became the more common beverage throughout Mesoamerica (McBryde 1945; Sapper 2000 [1901]). In some communities people clearly continued to reserve cacao for ritual occasions (see Bunzel 1967). Devotional offerings of cacao beverages or seeds to saints, however, may be less common because of pressure from ecclesiastical authorities, both evangelical Protestants and orthodox nonindigenous Catholic priests (Watanabe 1990).

At times, in communities that today are relatively near to one another, visitors will find a continued tradition of cacao use in one but not in the other. In these cases, the loss may be more closely tied to local history and customs. For example, a fermented beverage of *T. cacao* and *T. bicolor*, produced in Santiago Atitlan, Guatemala, until the 1970s, ceased to be made after the Guatemalan army (which murdered large numbers of community members) moved in during the counter-insurgency campaign of the Guatemalan civil war. Other causes behind the loss of traditional cacao production may be more benign, such as replacement by machine-produced goods. In the community of Salama, Guatemala, for example, which is located near large cacao groves, the only beverage containing cacao in the main market in July 2004 was a rice *atole* flavored with machine-processed cocoa powder.

The late nineteenth century and twentieth century were notable for the dramatic increase of scholarship on the lives of native people. In ethnographies from this period one can catch fleeting glimpses of the disappearance of cacao as a central ritual food and important comestible in many native communities. Charles Wisdom noted in 1940 that just fifty years earlier cacao had been used as money for trading at market. He writes, "According to a Ladino in Jocotan, the Indians would come early in the morning on market days to his house, buy seeds from him or exchange other goods, principally maize, and use the seeds later in that day in the plaza as a medium of exchange in buying from other Indians" (Wisdom 1940:34, ft. 16). Charles Wagley wrote in 1949 that cacao seeds were formerly exchanged in marriage ceremonies in the town of Santiago Chimaltenango, Guatemala, but that along with other traditional ritual gifts, they were no longer offered because the people had become too poor (Wagley 1949:129). Redfield and Villa wrote that in Chan Kom, Yucatan, Mexico, "a drink known as *x-taan chucua* used to be made as a part of the gifts offered to a girl's parents when the agreement for marriage was solemnized. Powdered cacao was beaten into water with a little corn meal, strained and mixed with Tabasco pepper and cinnamon" (1934:40).

Although these traditions were gone before ethnographers arrived, others have disappeared since they were documented. Timothy Pugh (this volume) uses twentieth-century ethnographies to explore a Lacandon god-house ritual involving cacao, a ritual which is no longer practiced in the manner he describes. In an effort to profit financially from tourism, performance modifications have been made. Patricia McAnany and Satoru Murata (this volume) trace the use of cacao in Belize from ancient to modern times. Today, cacao is once again important to indigenous farmers in this region because a foreign chocolate company engaged in fair trade practices has assured Belizean growers a fair price for their product, but in this new context cacao has been stripped of much of its ceremonial associations.

Despite the loss of many traditional practices involving cacao, some indigenous and Ladino communities continue to produce cacao comestibles the same way their ancestors did centuries ago and still use this plant in ritual practices (see this volume: Faust and Hirose; Kufer and Heinrich; McNeil, Chapter 17). In Chapter 17, I explore the continuing role of *T. cacao* and *T. bicolor* in Mesoamerican communities, with a focus on the Maya of Guatemala. In some areas of Guatemala cacao continues to be closely associated with marriage rituals, birth events, and the rebirth of Christ, who embodies many qualities of the pre-Columbian Maize God. Cacao is also an important offering during agricultural rites. For thousands of years ceremonies have been performed in Mesoamerica

Figure 1.12. Woman preparing cacao for an offering to the ritual spring. Quetzaltepeque, Guatemala. Photograph by Johanna Kufer.

to ensure a fertile growing season. To this day, for example, rain ceremonies are conducted in many traditional communities. Kufer and Heinrich (this volume) describe a ceremony involving the offering of cacao to a spring, a ritual that was also described by Raphael Girard (1966) (Figure 1.12). This ritual, occurring annually in a Ch'orti' Maya community in Quetzaltepeque, Guatemala, has not changed significantly in the last forty years.

Gifts of cacao not only ensure healthy crops, but they can also ensure healthy bodies. Betty Faust and Javier Hirose López (this volume) document the use of cacao seeds paired with chile peppers in the *k'ex* curing ceremonies of traditional Yukatek healer Pedro Ucán Itzá. They explain that the pairing of cacao and chiles has implications tied to sexuality and fertility, as well as attracting good and repelling evil, respectively. Cacao and *pataxte* seeds are also used in curing rituals in Santiago Atitlan, Guatemala (McNeil, Chapter 17, this volume). Cacao seeds or beverages are frequently offered in healing ceremonies and agricultural rituals in multiples of five (see Chapman 1985; this volume: Faust and Hirose López; Kufer and Heinrich; Pugh). The number five has a clear relationship to the continued importance of the sacred Maya quincunx, symbolizing the four corners of the world and the center which holds all of the planes of existence together.

Although cacao seeds are used to bring health to individuals in traditional healing ceremonies, and offerings of cacao beverages to sacred springs are made to encourage an ideal climate for the growing season, cacao trees themselves can promote a healthy environment. Cacao thrives in areas of abundant water and requires the shade of other trees. Encouraging cacao growth may help to preserve forests and protect the environment (Bright 2001; Gasco, this volume; Rice and Greenberg 2000; Small and Catling 2002). Ethical chocolate companies can help Mesoamerican communities by encouraging them to pursue a crop that is healthy for the ecosystem and requiring that dangerous pesticides not be used (see McAnany and Murata, this volume).

Conclusion

In this volume we explore the importance of cacao over its long history in Mesoamerica and beyond. Each chapter focuses on a specific aspect of this precious food in an attempt to augment our understanding of the role of cacao in Mesoamerican lives. Cacao is intricately intertwined with the history of this region: queens and kings were buried with it; wars were fought for it; sculptures of stone and ceramic were devoted to it; and cacao marked marriages, births, deaths, supplications to the gods, and sacrifices. Cacao continues to be an important part of the lives of many Mesoamerican people. It is not simply a "food"; it is also a tool for marking the passage of important life events and ensuring a healthy existence. At one time, the growth of cacao in the shaded valleys and coastal plains of Mesoamerica helped to preserve the environment and protected against deforestation. If this tree crop can again become common in this area, it may once more have an important role in the lives of all Mesoamericans.

Note on Orthography in the Volume

Determining the system of orthography for the volume was a challenge as many people have passionate opinions on this subject. For the most part, the spellings of the various Mesoamerican ethnic groups mentioned in the volume employ the new orthography from the *Academia de Lenguas Mayas de Guatemala*. However, this is not so in the case of Lacandon, Itza, or Lenca since some scholars in the book objected to the revised spelling on many grounds.

Acknowledgments

I thank Eric Hilt for all of his support during the editing and organizing of this volume. I also appreciate the help and encouragement provided by John Byram of the University Press of Florida. I was fortunate to have Gillian Hillis as the project editor of the volume and Myra Engelhardt as the copy editor. I am greatly indebted to Johanna Kufer, who was always there to discuss ideas and provide helpful suggestions; to Nathaniel Bletter and Douglas Daly, who gave important botanical and technical advice for the manuscript; and to Timothy Pugh who made some of the maps and provided many comments. I am grateful to the scholars who reviewed this volume: Heather McKillop, René Millon, and an anonymous reviewer; and those who provided helpful editorial comments on the introduction: Douglas Daly, Rosemary Joyce, John Justeson, Johanna Kufer, Allan Maca, and Dorie Reents-Budet. I would also like to thank all of the scholars who contributed to the volume. I extend appreciation to many people who assisted with this book: Irina Adam, Elbin Arias, Nicolas Chávez, Oswaldo Chinchilla Mazariegos, Deanna Davis, José Espinosa, Laura Flores, Reina Flores, Eliud Guerra, Nando Guerra, Fernando López, Norman Martinez, Guillermo Mata Amado, Carlos Mejia, Rufino Membraño, Claudia Monzón Sosa de Jiménez, William Parry, Fredy Rodriguez, Juan Carlos Rodriguez, Merle Greene Robertson, Ronny Reyes Rosales, Sylvia Salgado-González, Edgardo Sanabria, Julia Sandoval, David Sedat, Robert J. Sharer, Leslie H. Sheehan, Payson Sheets, Daniel Tabor, Rodolfo Yaquian Colón, Jolene Yukes, and Edgar Zelaya.

Notes

1. Today, most scholars subscribe to this geographical boundary for Mesoamerica (Joyce 2004). This area is significantly smaller than that defined by Paul Kirchhoff (1952), who first coined this term. Many ethnic groups speaking a range of languages inhabited Mesoamerica when the Spanish arrived, and these people shared numerous cultural traits: the same economic system, a stratified society, and similar beliefs concerning the origins of the world and the rituals required to inhabit it successfully (Joyce 2004:3).

2. Nahua is a group of closely related languages whose best-known members are spoken by the Mexica of the Basin of Mexico (a member of the Central branch of Nahua) and the Pipil (a member of the Eastern branch).

3. Ogata, Gómez-Pompa, and Taube (this volume) also discuss a vessel from Peru that depicts monkeys and a form which may represent cacao.

4. Some *criollo*-type cacao had scandent (vine-like) branches, which may account for the tendril-like appearance of cacao on this stela (Cuatrecasas 1964:506).

PART I

Evolution, Domestication, Chemistry,
and Identification of Cacao and
Its Close Relatives

2

Cacao and Its Relatives in South America

An Overview of Taxonomy, Ecology, Biogeography, Chemistry, and Ethnobotany

Nathaniel Bletter and Douglas C. Daly

Cacao belongs to an almost exclusively South American group of about forty species of small trees in the closely related genera *Theobroma* and *Herrania*. Along with the rest of the family Sterculiaceae, these genera have recently been subsumed into the larger Malvaceae family (Soltis et al. 2000), along with the common garden hibiscus (*Hibiscus* species), the marsh mallow (*Althaea officinalis* L.), the linden tree (*Tilia americana* L.), and the durian fruit of Southeast Asia (*Durio zibethinus* Rumph. ex Murray). Although some who know the durian and its reputable smell might now swear never to come near a cacao fruit again, the pulp of the cacao tree fruit is quite delicious, and it is enjoyed throughout South America today as it has been in the past.

It is enlightening to look at the taxonomy of all the species of *Theobroma* and *Herrania* used by people in South America, the center of diversity for both these genera, because by examining these relationships we can appreciate their diverse ecology, chemistry, and ethnobotany, including their medicinal, edible, and psychoactive uses.

Taxonomy

In the past, some taxonomists considered *Herrania* and *Theobroma* synonymous, but today the genera are considered distinct (see, for example, Whitlock and Baum 1999). Strange as it may seem for such scientifically interesting and economically important plants, it has been more than 40 years since the taxonomy of the two genera was comprehensively revised (Cuatrecasas, 1964; Schultes 1958). Some sixty-eight names have been published in *Theobroma* and twenty-three in *Herrania* (six of the latter with synonyms in *Theobroma*), but current practice recognizes twenty species in *Theobroma*, one of these with three varieties, and seventeen in *Herrania* (Laurence J. Dorr, personal communication 2004). A number of *formae*, or forms (an archaic taxonomic rank below species and variety that represents minor morphological variants) were published in both genera, but forms are rarely recognized in modern taxonomy.

Both genera traditionally have been placed along with another famous stimulant, cola nut (*Cola nitida* [Vent.] Schott & Endl.), in the family Sterculiaceae, but reorganization of this sector of the flowering plants based on molecular systematic studies is tending to group Sterculiaceae and various of its former "neighbors," including Malvaceae, Bombacaceae, and Tiliaceae, into a single family, the Malvaceae, although still within the order Malvales. The traditional Bombacaceae also includes plants with large pods containing edible seeds, such as the provision tree (*Pachira aquatica* Aubl.), the durian fruit (*D. zibethinus*), the kapok tree (*Ceiba pentandra* L.), and the baobab (*Adansonia digitalis* L.), as well as *Quararibea funebris* (La Llave) Vischer, whose flowers are often mixed into cacao beverages in Mexico.

The close relationship between *Theobroma* and *Herrania* has been recognized by traditional peoples, as evidenced by the fact that the folk generic, the grouping in a compound common name, is usually the same; an example is the Amazonian species *Herrania mariae* (Mart.) Decne. ex Goudot (see Figure 2.1), called *cacau de jacaré* or "cayman's cacao" where it occurs in Brazil, presumably because of its rough exterior. *Herrania* is distinguished from *Theobroma* by the former's palmately compound (vs. simple) leaves, the calyx usually three-lobed (vs. usually five-lobed), and the appendage on the end of the petals many times (vs. only two to three times) longer than the basal part and coiled (vs. reflexed or erect) in bud; in addition, the fruits of *Herrania* tend to be more conspicuously ribbed and have a drier husk, but this is not diagnostic (Schultes 1958).

The relatively widespread *Theobroma bicolor* Bonpl. (Figure 2.2), known as *pataxte* or *balamte* in Mesoamerica, *macambo* in Peru and Colombia, and *cacau do Peru* in Brazil, is another of the more important relatives of cacao. It was considered by Cook (1915, 1916) to represent a third genus, *Tribroma*, based on differences between it and *T. cacao* L. in its architecture, leaf venation, inflorescence structure, flower morphology, and pericarp (fruit husk), but this name is not in use. *Theobroma bicolor* has palmately veined leaves, inflorescences with finite branching on new branches, red flowers with thick club-shaped staminodes (sterile stamens), and a woody pericarp; *T. cacao* has mostly pinnately veined leaves, indeterminately branched inflorescences that are produced adventitiously on the trunk or older branches, pale flowers with pink nectar guides and slender pointed staminodes, and a more fleshy pericarp. Subsequent examination showed that these characters are independently assorted in various other species of *Theobroma*, so *T. bicolor* has been retained in the genus (Cuatrecasas 1964).

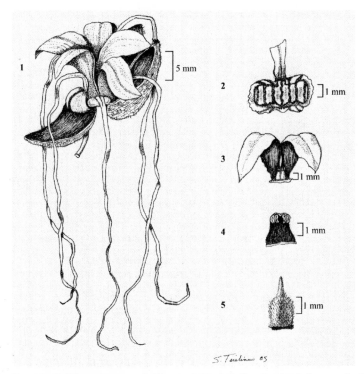

Figure 2.1. *Herrania mariae*. 1. Flower. 2. Petal. 3. Staminode. 4. Stamen. 5. Ovary. Drawing by Samantha Tsistinas after Addison and Tavares (1951).

Figure 2.2. *Theobroma* fruits from Acre, Brazil. Left: *T. cacao*. Right: *T. bicolor*. Photograph by Douglas C. Daly.

Some Aspects of Ecology

Pollination biology of the group is complex and has serious implications for management of cultivated taxa and survival of wild species where forest cover is disturbed. The little that is known about pollination in the group has been obtained from studies of a very few species under artificial conditions, that is, in cultivation and in some cases far from the natural range. The flowers of different species show distinct sizes, colors, seasonality (Erickson et al. 1987), location of glandular structures, chemistry of floral attractants, and, not surprisingly as a consequence of these factors, pollinators. Flower structure and chemistry favor pollination by midges or other small flies, although two kinds of bees can be secondary pollinators in some species; the habitats or conditions under which cacao and allies are found and grown affect the availability of these pollinators. Some cultivars of *T. cacao* have lost part of the complement of chemical attractants associated with older or "wild" populations, which may explain their poorer fruit set (A. M. Young and D. W. Severson 1994).

The stamens of these plants are hidden by the hooded petal bases (see Figures 2.1 and 2.3), so access is easiest for small flies that can enter the flower between the petal hoods, although halictid and trigonid bees force their way in. There are no fewer than three types of glandular structures on the flowers that may be the sources of chemical attractants or rewards for pollinators: "stomate"-type glands on the petal ligules or extensions (absent from *Herrania* flowers), a ring of glandular trichomes (hairs) inside the base of the sepals, and club-shaped glands on the ovaries (A. M. Young, M. Schaller, and M. Strand 1984).

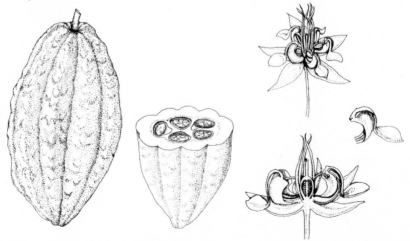

Figure 2.3. *Theobroma cacao.* Cut fruit showing five seeds, flower, sectioned flower, and one petal. Drawing by Samantha Tsistinas.

There appear to be correlations among floral chemistry, taxonomy, and pollinators for *Theobroma* and *Herrania*. An initial sampling of floral oils found those of *T. cacao* and *T. mammosum* Cuatrec. & Jorge León to consist primarily of high molecular weight, saturated and unsaturated hydrocarbons, giving them a fainter but more pungent odor. The oils of other *Theobroma* species are rich in monoterpenes with citrus-like odors, whereas the bicyclic sesquiterpenes and distinct monoterpenes in *Herrania* help separate the two genera. The heavier hydrocarbons and some of the monoterpenes are among the plant compounds in the pheromones of some kinds of bees, and in fact the flowers of *T. cacao* and some other species of *Theobroma* are visited by bees, although their principal pollinators are reported to be mostly female ceratopogonid (midges) and cecidomyiid flies (A. M. Young 1985; A. M. Young, B. J. Erickson, and E. H. Erickson 1989), in contrast to *Herrania*, whose flowers are reportedly pollinated by phorid flies (A. M. Young 1984).

The flies and midges (all dipterans) that are believed to comprise the principal pollinators of these plants require small pools of standing water for larval development; these habitats are provided by bromeliads and other water-holding plant structures such as Marantaceae (Prayer Plant family) inflorescences (Fish and Soria 1978); shady conditions and a heterogeneous canopy favor both the occurrence of these dipterans and, therefore, fruit set in *T. cacao* (A. M. Young 1982, 1983).

Possibly more so than other species in the group, *T. cacao* shows some versatility in its pollination biology; under shady conditions its flowers are pollinated mostly by midges and cecidomyiid flies, with stingless trigonid bees as pollen-robbers and only minor pollinators, whereas under sunny conditions the dipterans are mostly absent and the erstwhile pollen-robbers become the more important pollinators (A. M. Young 1985). It is uncertain whether this versatility is a result of selection or breeding over millennia, or a partial explanation for the broad distribution of the species.

Biogeography and origins

Of the forty currently accepted taxa of the *Theobroma-Herrania* group, only seven species are found in the wild (or escaped) in Mexico or Central America or both, and, of these, only *T. bicolor* Humb. & Bonpl. and *T. cacao* have been found wild (or perhaps escaped) north of Costa Rica.

Both Mesoamerica and northern South America have been proposed as the sites of origin of both the wild and cultivated *T. cacao* (Motamayor et al. 2002; Motamayor et al. 2003; Ogata, Gómez-Pompa, and Taube, this volume). Molecular techniques are available that can test hypotheses about relationships and migrations of taxa (see, for example, Zerega, Ragone, and Motley 2004), but a more complete geographic sampling is still needed to complete this for *Theo-broma* and the issue is still under debate. Cacao appears to show low genetic diversity in Mesoamerica, but this can be interpreted as representing either a relictual bottleneck or a more recent arrival via long-distance dispersal or trade. Given the multiple possible causes of genetic bottlenecks of which cacao shows evidence and the lack of archaeological and ethnobotanical evidence that Amazonian groups cultivated cacao and used the seeds in the past, this issue will probably not be settled for some time.

Other arguments about origins are circumstantial if interesting. Biogeography would indicate a South American origin for *T. cacao*, as only two species of the cacao complex occur spontaneously north of Costa Rica, and there is no proof that Mesoamerican populations of these two are wild and not escaped or relictual from cultivation. This does not preclude the possibility that the occurrence of *T. cacao* predated human interference; numerous plant groups include one species that dramatically extends the group's range (for example, the gumbo limbo tree, *Bursera simaruba* (L.) Sarg., extending into various parts of northern South America [Daly 1993]).

Patterns of traditional uses in the *Theobroma-Herrania* complex would suggest a Mesoamerican origin at least for cultivated cacao. In South America, although the seeds of the majority of species can be fermented and roasted to produce a serviceable chocolate (Cuatrecasas 1964) as seen in Figure 2.4, there is no record of chocolate that predates the plantations and commercial trade that began in the seventeenth or late sixteenth century (D. Stone 1984), although Clement (1999) has proposed that both *T. cacao* and *T. bicolor* were semi-domesticated in the Upper Amazon during late prehistoric times and their seeds consumed as stimulants. For every other species, the sweet pulp surrounding the seeds is appreciated if not prized, but *T. bicolor* is the only species whose seeds were likely a traditional foodstuff in prehistoric Amazonia, and these are roasted like a nut without fermentation and in no way resemble cacao in their flavor, chemistry, or South American uses (for example, Pinkley 1973; personal observation, Bletter, 2003). Still, the native range of *T. cacao* may have extended from Amazonia to Mesoamerica even if techniques for making chocolate—and possibly cultivars—may have originated in the northern end of its range and been brought southward in historic times. One Jesuit observer in 1699 reported what he thought were large spontaneous populations of cacao trees on islands in the Xingu River in eastern Brazilian Amazonia (Betendorf 1910). This is slightly removed from *T. cacao*'s purported origins in northern South America, but cacao was already an established commodity by then so these were not necessarily completely wild populations.

Figure 2.4. *Theobroma cacao* fruit and crude chocolate tablet from Lowland Bolivia. Photograph by Douglas C. Daly.

There is certainly conspicuous use of cacao pulp in modern Brazil, where it can be found in juice shops through much of the country (Figure 2.5). This predominance of the use of the fruit pulp in Brazil as compared to other countries where cacao grows and where the pulp is not a conspicuous commercial product (personal observations from Brazil, Peru, Ecuador, Guatemala, and Mexico) might point to origins of the use of the pulp in Amazonian Brazil which then spread to the popular culture, but it tells us little about seed use.

The etymology of the word "cacao" appears to provide strong circumstantial evidence for a Mesoamerican origin of chocolate, if not necessarily of *T. cacao* or cultivars. The use of the word in Classic period Maya culture (ca. 200 B.C.–A.D. 600) is well-established, and it is clearly derived from a Mesoamerican linguistic group (Dakin and Wichmann 2000; Kaufman and Justeson, this volume). Balée (2003) argues convincingly that "cacao" was borrowed by various Amazonian languages from *Lingua Geral Amazônica* (LGA), a Tupí-Guaraní-based creole used and propagated by the Jesuits throughout their vast sphere of influence in Amazonia, and that the early spread and prevalence of this Mesoamerican word in most of Amazonia is due to the Jesuits'

Figure 2.5. *Theobroma cacao* fruit pulp drink being sold in a Brazilian *suco* (juice) shop. Photograph by Wayt Thomas.

strong cultural and economic influence, including their involvement in cacao commerce (2003:268). He notes that the word for cacao among the Kofán of Amazonian Ecuador and other Amazonian cultures outside the historical domain of LGA is not a cognate of the Mesoamerican word (Balée 2003:266). *Theobroma cacao* and its cultivars—and perhaps chocolate—may not have been new to South America, but cacao as a trade product of overwhelming importance certainly was.

Chemistry

The chemistry of *Theobroma* and *Herrania* is extremely complex and varies significantly with the part of the plant, the maturity of the plant, and processing of the plant parts, such as fermenting and roasting. Others have thoroughly reviewed the chemistry of *T. cacao* (J. Duke 2004; Hurst, this volume), so only the other *Theobroma* and *Herrania* species and the compounds in *T. cacao* not reviewed elsewhere are listed in Table 2.1. Similarly, only the key reported medicinal activities of these chemicals are listed, given that there are 711 activities for the compounds in *T. cacao* alone listed in J. Duke (2004), so again Table 2.1 is not exhaustive.

The pharmacological activity of cacao and its relatives falls into three large categories: neuroactives, antioxidants, and stimulants. Neuroactives cause changes in brain function, often by affecting neurotransmitter activity or by

Table 2.1. Compounds and their activities found in *Theobroma* and *Herrania* species

Species	Plant part	Compound	Amount	Activities	Source
H. mariae	seeds	arachidate	high	—	(Gilabert-Escriva, Goncalves et al. 2002)
H. mariae	seeds (defatted)	tetramethyl urate	10.80 ± 0.22 mg/g	—	(Hammerstone, Romanczyk et al. 1994)
H. albiflora	seeds	caffeine	trace	stimulant, diuretic	(Hammerstone, Romanczyk et al. 1994)
H. albiflora [a]	seeds (defatted)	tetramethyl urate	2.29 ± 0.04 mg/g	—	(Hammerstone, Romanczyk et al. 1994)
H. balaënsis	seeds (defatted)	caffeine	trace	stimulant, diuretic	(Hammerstone, Romanczyk et al. 1994)
H. balaënsis [a]	seeds (defatted)	tetramethyl urate	17.7 ± 0.35 mg/g	—	(Hammerstone, Romanczyk et al. 1994)
H. columbia [a]	seeds (defatted)	tetramethyl urate	16.71 ± 0.33 mg/g	—	(Hammerstone, Romanczyk et al. 1994)
H. cuatrecasana	bark	herranone, herrantrione	—	—	(Wiedemann, Lerche et al. 1999)
H. cuatrecasana	seeds (defatted)	tetramethyl urate	19.40 ± 0.39 mg/g	—	(Hammerstone, Romanczyk et al. 1994)
H. cuatrecasana [a]	seeds (defatted)	caffeine	trace	stimulant, diuretic	(Hammerstone, Romanczyk et al. 1994)
H. nitida	seeds (defatted)	caffeine	trace	stimulant, diuretic	(Hammerstone, Romanczyk et al. 1994)
H. nitida [a]	seeds (defatted)	tetramethyl urate	10.70 ± 0.21 mg/g	—	(Hammerstone, Romanczyk et al. 1994)
H. nycterodendron [a]	seeds (defatted)	tetramethyl urate	13.02 ± 0.26 mg/g	—	(Hammerstone, Romanczyk et al. 1994)
H. purpurea	seeds (defatted)	caffeine	trace	stimulant, diuretic	(Hammerstone, Romanczyk et al. 1994)
H. purpurea [a]	seeds (defatted)	tetramethyl urate	20.20 ± 0.40 mg/g	—	(Hammerstone, Romanczyk et al. 1994)
H. umbratica [a]	seeds (defatted)	tetramethyl urate	9.59 ± 0.19 mg/g	—	(Hammerstone, Romanczyk et al. 1994)
T. angustifolium	seeds (defatted)	tetramethyl urate	0.64 ± 0.01 mg/g	—	(Hammerstone, Romanczyk et al. 1994)
T. angustifolium	leaves	tetramethyl urate	trace	—	(Hammerstone, Romanczyk et al. 1994)
T. angustifolium	leaves	caffeine	trace	stimulant, diuretic	(Hammerstone, Romanczyk et al. 1994)
T. bicolor	seeds	fatty acids and triacylglycerol	—	cocoa butter substitute	(Gilabert-Escriva, Goncalves et al. 2002)
T. bicolor	immature seeds (defatted)	caffeine	trace	stimulant, diuretic	(Hammerstone, Romanczyk et al. 1994)
T. bicolor	immature seeds (defatted)	theobromine	2.59 ± 0.05 mg/g	stimulant, diuretic	(Hammerstone, Romanczyk et al. 1994)

continued

Continued—Table 2.1. Compounds and their activities found in *Theobroma* and *Herrania* species

Species	Plant part	Compound	Amount	Activities	Source
T. bicolor	immature seeds (defatted)	tetramethyl urate	trace	—	(Hammerstone, Romanczyk et al. 1994)
T. bicolor	mature seeds (defatted)	tetramethyl urate	3.52 ± 0.07	—	(Hammerstone, Romanczyk et al. 1994)
T. bicolor	leaves	caffeine	$0.03 \pm$ trace mg/g	stimulant, diuretic	(Hammerstone, Romanczyk et al. 1994)
T. bicolor	leaves	theobromine	1.09 ± 0.06 mg/g	stimulant, diuretic	(Hammerstone, Romanczyk et al. 1994)
T. cacao	seeds	procyanidins	—	inhibits platelet activation, i.e., anti-coagulant	(Rein, Paglieroni et al. 2000)
T. cacao	seeds, cacao liquor	procyanidins	8.6–19.4 mg/g	antioxidant	(Adamson, Lazarus et al. 1999)
T. cacao	seeds	procyanidins	1960 mg/100g in commercially processed seeds	antioxidant, antihypertensive[c]	(Chevaux, Jackson et al. 2001)
T. cacao	seeds	procyanidins	3570 ± 876 mg/100g in homegrown Kuna cacao beans	antioxidant, antihypertensive[c]	(Chevaux, Jackson et al. 2001)
T. cacao	seeds	epicatechin	lower in fermented seeds	antioxidant	(Kim and Keeney 1984)
T. cacao	seeds	polyphenols including (-)-epicatechin	3% (-)-epicatechin in cacao liquor polyhphenols	antioxidant and immuno-regulatory effects	(Sanbongi, Suzuki et al. 1997)
T. cacao	seeds	flavanols including (-)-epicatechin and ($\pm$)-catechin	—	vasodilatory via increased nitric-oxide synthesis	(Fisher, Hughes et al. 2003)
T. cacao	fresh seeds	procyanidin B-1	trace, increases with fermentation	antioxidant	(Porter, Ma et al. 1991)
T. cacao	fresh seeds	procyanidin B-2	17.1%[b], decreases with fermentation	antioxidant	(Porter, Ma et al. 1991)
T. cacao	fresh seeds	procyanidin C-1	10.5%[b], decreases with fermentation	antioxidant	(Porter, Ma et al. 1991)
T. cacao	fresh seeds	procyanidin B-5	3.3%[b], decreases with fermentation	antioxidant	(Porter, Ma et al. 1991)
T. cacao	raw seeds and dark chocolate	procyanidin polymers (monomers through decamers)	—	antioxidant	(Hammerstone, Lazarus et al. 1999)
T. cacao	seeds, cacao liquor	quercetin	—	antioxidant	(Sanbongi, Osakabe et al. 1998)
T. cacao	seeds, cacao liquor	clovamide	—	antioxidant	(Sanbongi, Osakabe et al. 1998)
T. cacao	seeds, cacao liquor	dideoxyclovamide	—	antioxidant	(Sanbongi, Osakabe et al. 1998)

Species	Plant part	Compound	Amount	Activities	Source
cacao	seeds, cacao liquor	quercetin-3-glucoside	—	antioxidant	(Sanbongi, Osakabe et al. 1998)
cacao	seeds, cacao liquor	quercetin-3-arabinoside	—	antioxidant	(Sanbongi, Osakabe et al. 1998)
cacao	seeds, cacao liquor	polyphenols	27% by weight of defatted and extracted cacao liquor	antimutagen[d]	(Yamagishi, Natsume et al. 2000)
cacao	seeds, dark chocolate	serotonin	1.37–5.08 µg/g	endogenous neurotransmitter[e]	(Herraiz 2000)
cacao	seeds, dark chocolate	tryptamine	0.2–1.16 µg/g	endogenous neurotransmitter[e]	(Herraiz 2000)
cacao	seeds, dark chocolate	tetrahydro-β-carboline alkaloids	3.64–7.69 µg/g	MAO inhibitor	(Herraiz 2000)
cacao	seeds, chocolate	histamine	—	inflammatory	(Baker, Wong et al. 1987)
cacao	seeds, chocolate	2-phenylethylamine	—	neuroactive	(Baker, Wong et al. 1987)
cacao	seeds, chocolate	tyramine	—	degradeable toxin	(Baker, Wong et al. 1987)
cacao	seeds, cocoa powder	salsolinol	40 ± 4 µg/g	metabolite of neurotransmitter dopamine	(Riggin and Kissinger 1976)
cacao	seeds, unfermented and unroasted	tyramine	3.9 ± 0.1 µg/g	degradeable toxin	(Kenyhercz and Kissinger 1977)
cacao	seeds (cocoa powder and chocolate)	anandamide	0.05–57 µg/g	endogenous neurotransmitter[e]	(Tomaso, Beltramo et al. 1996)
cacao	seeds (cocoa powder and chocolate)	N-oleoylethanolamine	0.5–90 µg/g	anandamide mimic and stimulant	(Tomaso, Beltramo et al. 1996)
cacao	seeds (cocoa powder and chocolate)	N-linoleoylethanolamine	0.5–90 µg/g	anandamide mimic and stimulant	(Tomaso, Beltramo et al. 1996)
cacao	seeds	phenylethylamine	—	neuroactive	(Koehler and Eitenmiller 1978)
cacao	seeds	theobromine	—	diuretic, vasodilator	(Nuñez-Melendez 1964)
cacao	leaves	caffeine	$0.06 \pm$ trace mg/g	stimulant, diuretic	(Hammerstone, Romanczyk et al. 1994)
cacao	leaves	theobromine	1.12 ± 0.02 mg/g	stimulant, diuretic	(Hammerstone, Romanczyk et al. 1994)
cacao	pod (fruit) husk	pectin	8–11% of the dry mature fruit, 25–29% of dry immature fruits	—	(Adomako 1972)
cacao	pod (fruit) husk	galacturonic acid	—	—	(Adomako 1972)

continued

Continued—Table 2.1. Compounds and their activities found in *Theobroma* and *Herrania* species

Species	Plant part	Compound	Amount	Activities	Source
T. cacao (listed as *T. leiocarpa*)	seeds	flavanol dimer with (-)-epicatechin	0.6 mg/g	antitumor	(Oliveira, Simpãio et al. 1972)
T. grandiflorum	seeds	fatty acids and triacylglycerol	—		(Gilabert-Escriva, Goncalves et al. 2002)
T. grandiflorum	seeds	quercetin	—	antioxidant	(Yang, Protiva et al. 2003)
T. grandiflorum	seeds	kaempferol	—	antioxidant	(Yang, Protiva et al. 2003)
T. grandiflorum	seeds	(+)-catechin	—	antioxidant	(Yang, Protiva et al. 2003)
T. grandiflorum	seeds	(-)-epicatechin	—	antioxidant	(Yang, Protiva et al. 2003)
T. grandiflorum	seeds	theograndin I	—	antioxidant, anti-colon cancer	(Yang, Protiva et al. 2003)
T. grandiflorum	seeds	theograndin II	—	antioxidant, anti-colon cancer	(Yang, Protiva et al. 2003)
T. grandiflorum	fermented, roasted seeds	trimethylpyrazine, tetramethylpyrazine, 3-methylbutanal, dimethyl sulfide, dimethyl disulfide, β-linalool	—	aroma, flavor	(Oliveira, Pereira et al. 2004)
T. grandiflorum	fruit pulp	ethyl and butyl butyrate, ethyl and butyl 2-methylbutyrate, β-linalool, piperazine 2,5-dihydro-2, 5-dimethoxyfuran	—	aroma, flavor	(Oliveira, Pereira et al. 2004)
T. grandiflorum	fruit pulp	ethyl butanoate	42% of volatile compounds	aroma, flavor	(Franco and Shibamoto 2000)
T. grandiflorum	fruit pulp	ethyl hexanoate	22% of volatile compounds	aroma, flavor	(Franco and Shibamoto 2000)
T. grandiflorum	fruit pulp	hexadecanoic acid	12% of volatile compounds	aroma, flavor	(Franco and Shibamoto 2000)
T. grandiflorum	fruit pulp	1-butanol	9.17% of volatile compounds	aroma, flavor	(Franco and Shibamoto 2000)
T. grandiflorum	fruit pulp	3-hydroxy-2-butanone	3.42% of volatile compounds	aroma, flavor	(Franco and Shibamoto 2000)
T. grandiflorum	fruit pulp	2,3-butanodiol	3.29% of volatile compounds	aroma, flavor	(Franco and Shibamoto 2000)
T. grandiflorum	fruit pulp	butyl 2-methylbutanoate	3.27% of volatile compounds	aroma, flavor	(Franco and Shibamoto 2000)
T. grandiflorum	fruit pulp	butyl butyrate	2.8% of volatile compounds	aroma, flavor	(Franco and Shibamoto 2000)

Species	Plant part	Compound	Amount	Activities	Source
T. grandiflorum	fruit pulp	linalool	2.21% of volatile compounds	aroma, flavor, antiseptic	(Franco and Shibamoto 2000)
T. grandiflorum	fruit pulp	2-methyl-3-buten-2-ol	1.62% of volatile compounds	aroma, flavor	(Franco and Shibamoto 2000)
T. grandiflorum	fruit pulp	(E)-ocimene	1.15% of volatile compounds	aroma, flavor	(Franco and Shibamoto 2000)
T. grandiflorum	fruit pulp	butyl hexanoate	1.05% of volatile compounds	aroma, flavor	(Franco and Shibamoto 2000)
T. grandiflorum	fruit pulp	oleic acid, 1,3-butanodiol, acetic acid, ethyl 2-methyl-butyrate, butyl acetate, butyl 3-methylbutanoate, ethyl octanoate	trace amounts	aroma, flavor	(Franco and Shibamoto 2000)
T. grandiflorum	seeds (defatted)	tetramethyl urate	2.60 ± 0.52 mg/g	—	(Hammerstone, Romanczyk et al. 1994)
T. grandiflorum	leaves	caffeine	trace	stimulant, diuretic	(Hammerstone, Romanczyk et al. 1994)
T. grandiflorum	leaves	theobromine	trace	stimulant, diuretic	(Hammerstone, Romanczyk et al. 1994)
T. grandiflorum	leaves	tetramethyl urate	0.07 ± trace mg/g	—	(Hammerstone, Romanczyk et al. 1994)
T. grandiflorum	leaves	alkaloid tetramethyluric acid	—	—	(Schultes and Raffauf 2004)
T. grandiflorum	—	vitamin C (ascorbic acid)	38.3 mg/100g	—	(Marx and Maia 1983)
T. grandiflorum	—	beta-carotene	0.03 mg/100g	—	(Marx and Maia 1983)
T. mammosum	immature seeds (defatted)	caffeine	trace	stimulant, diuretic	(Hammerstone, Romanczyk et al. 1994)
T. mammosum	immature seeds (defatted)	theobromine	trace	stimulant, diuretic	(Hammerstone, Romanczyk et al. 1994)
T. mammosum	immature seeds (defatted)	tetramethyl urate	0.56 ± 0.02 mg/g	—	(Hammerstone, Romanczyk et al. 1994)
T. mammosum	leaves	tetramethyl urate	trace	—	(Hammerstone, Romanczyk et al. 1994)
T. microcarpum	seeds	highly unsaturated fat C18:2	—		(Gilabert-Escriva, Goncalves et al. 2002)
T. microcarpum	seeds (defatted)	tetramethyl urate	0.22 ± trace mg/g	—	(Hammerstone, Romanczyk et al. 1994)
T. obovatum	seeds	fatty acids and triacylglycerol	—	—	(Gilabert-Escriva, Goncalves et al. 2002)
T. simiarum	leaves	caffeine	trace	stimulant, diuretic	(Hammerstone, Romanczyk et al. 1994)

continued

Continued—Table 2.1. Compounds and their activities found in *Theobroma* and *Herrania* species

Species	Plant part	Compound	Amount	Activities	Source
T. speciosum	seeds	palmitate	high		(Gilabert-Escriva, Goncalves et al. 2002)
T. speciosum	seeds	fatty acids and triacylglycerol	—	cocoa butter substitute	(Gilabert-Escriva, Goncalves et al. 2002)
T. speciosum	seeds (defatted)	tetramethyl urate	1.18 ± 0.02 mg/g	—	(Hammerstone, Romanczyk et al. 1994)
T. speciosum	leaves	tetramethyl urate	trace	—	(Hammerstone, Romanczyk et al. 1994)
T. speciosum	leaves	caffeine	$0.12 \pm$ trace mg/g	stimulant, diuretic	(Hammerstone, Romanczyk et al. 1994)
T. subincanum	seeds	fatty acids and triacylglycerol	—	—	(Gilabert-Escriva, Goncalves et al. 2002)
T. subincanum	seeds (defatted)	tetramethyl urate	2.84 ± 0.06 mg/g	—	(Hammerstone, Romanczyk et al. 1994)
T. subincanum	seeds (embryo)	Tocopherols	similar to wheat germ oil	Vitamin E family, antioxidants	(Bruni, Medici et al. 2002)
T. subincanum	seeds (teguments and endosperm)	Tocopherols	lower than embryo	Vitamin E family, antioxidants	(Bruni, Medici et al. 2002)
T. subincanum	seeds (endosperm)	oleic and stearic acid	80% of fatty acid profile	—	(Bruni, Medici et al. 2002)
T. subincanum	seeds (endosperm, emrbyo, tegument)	cycloartenol	higher in endosperm than embryo and tegument	—	(Bruni, Medici et al. 2002)
T. sylvestre	seeds	palmitate	high		(Gilabert-Escriva, Goncalves et al. 2002)
T. sylvestre	seeds	fatty acids and triacylglycerol	—	cocoa butter substitute	(Gilabert-Escriva, Goncalves et al. 2002)

a. No theobromine was detected in seeds and no caffeine, theobromine, or tetramethyl urate detected in leaves of any of the *Herrania* species analyze No caffeine was detected in *H. columbia, H. mariae, H. nycterodendron,* or *H. umbratica* (Hammerstone, Romanczyk et al. 1994)

b. Percent of ethyl acetate fraction

c. antihypertensive—a compound or plant that reduces hypertension or high blood pressure.

d. antimutagen—a compound or plant that can reduce the number or severity of mutations in cell DNA that may eventually lead to cancer.

e. endogenous neurotransmitter—a neurotransmitter that is produced naturally in the human body such as anandamide, as compared to a synthe or plant-derived compound that stimulates the same receptors, such as tetrahydrocannabinol (THC) from *Cannabis sativa.*

blocking neurotransmitter receptors. Antioxidants slow the oxidation of chemicals in the body by free oxygen radicals, which can often lead to gradual loss of function of key systems such as arteries or the immune system. Stimulants increase the activity of the central nervous system and increase energy or awareness. Probably the most studied compounds in these species are the purine alkaloids or methylxanthines: caffeine, theobromine, and theophylline. Theobromine, the most abundant methylxanthine in cacao, is also the least active stimulant of these three, but it has a diuretic action greater than that of caffeine and less than that of theophylline.

The desire and the search for stimulants are almost as universal as they are for sweet substances. South American peoples had a choice of *yerba mate* (*Ilex paraguariensis* A. St.-Hil.) in the south and guayusa (*Ilex guayusa* Loes.) in the northwest (Patiño 1968), both in the holly family Aquifoliaceae, and *guaraná* (*Paullina cupana* Kunth) and *yoco* (*P. yoco* R. E. Schult. & Killip) in the soapberry family Sapindaceae in the north-northwest (Beck 1991), along with *Theobroma* as caffeine-containing stimulants. Other stimulant plants available in the Americas were *yaupon* (*Ilex vomitoria* Aiton) in the southern United States, with caffeine (Merrill 1979); *coca* (*Erythroxylum coca* Lam. and *E. novogranatense* O. E. Schulz) in the northern Andes and western Amazon, with cocaine (Plowman 1984); *ili-ga-wa-yik* (*Virola sebifera* Aubl.), from whose bark a stimulating tea is made in the Guianas (DeFilipps, Maina, and Crepin 2004), contains several tryptamine derivatives (Kawanishi, Uhara, and Hashimoto 1985); tobacco (*Nicotiana rustica* L. and *N. tabacum* L.) in the southern Andes to Argentina, with nicotine (Nee 2004); sweet flag (*Acorus calamus* L.) in the mideastern United States, with mescaline-like α-asarone (Motley 1994); *axocatzin* (*Sida acuta* Burm. f. and *S. rhombifolia* L.) smoked on the Gulf Coast of Mexico, with ephedrine (Schultes, Hofmann, and Rätsch 1998); and Mormon tea (*Ephedra* spp.) in the western United States, also with ephedrine (J. A. Duke 1992) (Figure 2.6). With most of these, the leaf, bark, root, or seed need only be steeped in water, ingested, or smoked to obtain the stimulating effects of the plant, with no need for the complex fermentation, sun drying or roasting, and grinding process necessary for cacao. Most indigenous Americans had more easily prepared caffeine-containing plants at their disposal, and, in some areas, such as the northwestern Amazon, they had a choice of several apart from cacao.

Assuming that a desire for stimulants is as inherent as that for sweet substances, examination of the map in Figure 2.6 suggests that the wide availability of easily used stimulants in all other parts of cacao's range except northern Mesoamerica may be one reason the South Americans may not have discovered the stimulant use of cacao seeds, whereas the apparent unavailability of more

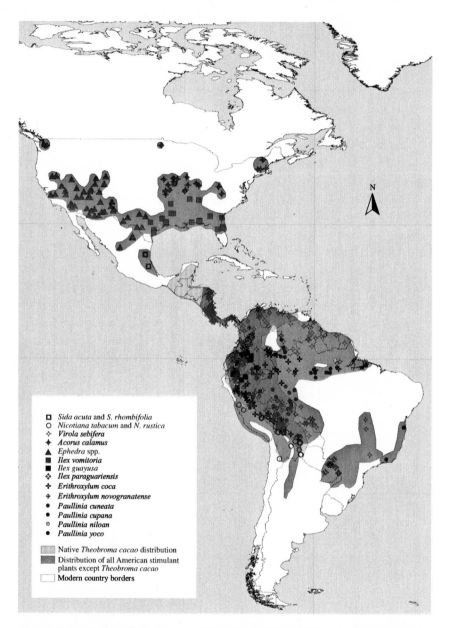

Figure 2.6. Map of hypothetical pre-Columbian distribution of stimulants in the Americas and how they overlap with that of cacao. Points for native collections of each species are derived from the Global Biodiversity Information Facility (http://www.gbif.org/) and may not completely overlap with species distributions derived from references listed in the text, such as *Ilex paraguariensis* in southern Brazil.

accessible stimulants in northern Mesoamerica may have been a driving force toward experimentation and the discovery of processes to convert cacao seeds to an edible and stimulating form. The lack of stimulant plant uses in northern Mesoamerica is especially glaring given that this area has one of the highest concentrations of nonstimulant psychoactive plant uses in the world (Schultes, Hofmann, and Rätsch 1998). If one accepts that this concentration stems from the Mesoamericans having been quite adept at discovering the psychoactive effects of the plants in their environment (and not merely from a richer psychoactive flora), it follows that they would have discovered other stimulant plants in their environment as well.

The most healthful effects of chocolate have been attributed to antioxidant procyanidins, flavonoids, tocopherols, and other compounds, leading to claims that chocolate can help fight hypertension, heart disease, and cancer. It is established that cacao contains many antioxidants and that antioxidants have beneficial health effects in stimulating the immune system and protecting against cancer and heart disease, but it is not as clear which of the antioxidants in chocolate make it through the intestinal wall and into the bloodstream to be effective. Of the highly touted procyanidins, which are polymers or interconnected chains of smaller catechin units, only the monomers (one unit) of epicatechin are absorbed through the intestine in large amounts, whereas dimers (two units) are absorbed in small amounts, and higher order polymers are not absorbed at all (Spencer et al. 2001). Ruzaidi et al. (2005), however, found that the procyanidins and other polyphenols in cacao do seem to lower blood glucose, triglycerides, and cholesterol levels in diabetic rats that ate a cacao extract-rich diet, so these compounds absorbed by the intestine may have some health benefit. Only a few of the studies on the antioxidant health benefits of chocolate have been conducted *in vivo* with humans, in an effort to determine how much of the studied active chemicals actually enter the bloodstream (Fisher et al. 2003). Thus, reports of panacea-like curative properties of chocolate must be taken with a grain of salt.

Another speculative area of research is the question of why cacao causes such strong addiction; the numerous neuroactive compounds in chocolate may provide a good clue. The neuroactive substances serotonin, tryptamine, anandamide, phenylethylamine, and dopamine interact with the brain's natural neurotransmitters by imitating them, blocking them, or slowing their destruction by enzymes to produce some psychological effect. Each of these neuroactive compounds acts on a different neurotransmitter and receptor system in the brain: anandamide and its analogs activate or block the cannabinoid receptors that are also stimulated by smoking marijuana (*Cannabis sativa* L.); tryptamine and serotonin are naturally occurring neurotransmitters that affect mood and are modified by such selective serotonin re-uptake inhibitor (SSRI) antidepressants as Prozac and Zoloft; and dopamine works in the system of the brain that controls movements and is implicated in diseases like Parkinson's. Phenylethylamine, which stimulates catecholamine neurotransmitter receptors similarly to amphetamines, is often blamed for the addictive properties of chocolate. It is also thought that although chocolate has not yet been found to contain any opiates, the combination of sugar and fats in chocolate stimulates the brain's release of natural opiates, and exogenous opiates such as heroin, opium, and morphine are notoriously addictive. The release of opiates associated with ingesting chocolate may cause addiction in a manner similar to that of heroin.

Some initially argued that cacao actually has little or no psychological effect because the concentrations of the psychoactive compounds in it are too low or their uptake by the intestine is so low that little of the compounds actually reach the appropriate sites in the brain (Smit and Rogers 2001). These authors found that the theobromine and caffeine in a regular portion of dark chocolate (50g) in fact had a positive psychopharmacological effect on reaction time, alertness, and mood (Smit, Gaffan, and Rogers 2004) and that these two methylxanthines can contribute to our liking of chocolate (Smit and Blackburn 2005). There is also great variability in the subjects' ability to perceive the effects of psychoactive components of cacao such as theobromine (Mumford, Evans et al. 1994), demonstrating that certain people may respond much more strongly than others to cacao's psychoactive compounds, and such subjects merit further study. Regardless, the neuroactive chemistry of cacao and its relatives is complex, and a new neuroactive compound is found in chocolate almost annually to confuse the issue further.

Ethnobotany

Myriad uses of the South American *Theobroma* and *Herrania* species as food, medicine, psychoactives, containers, and firewood are reported throughout the literature. We have attempted to review all this literature and compile the information, presented in Table 2.2, although it cannot be claimed to be exhaustive since often one or two uses of these two genera are scattered among many other species in papers on other topics. Still, enough uses spread across many cultures have been found to uncover some interesting patterns. Mesoamerican medicinal uses of cacao are listed in this table as well, to illustrate the broader patterns. As food, cacao is generally used as a fermented or unfermented drink made from the pulp or seeds. Medicinally it is most often used as a soothing agent, antiseptic, stimulant, snakebite remedy, or for weight gain, and it is usually used as an admixture in psychoactive preparations to enhance the effects of the main ingredients.

Table 2.2. Native uses of *Theobroma* and *Herrania* species in the Americas

cies	Group	Plant part	Common name	Use	Source
).	Colombia	pulp	—	Often left standing in cultivated areas because acid pulp is eaten.	(Schultes 1958)
ff. nitida	Tukuna of Colombia	fruit	cacao (Spanish), cha pe re (Tukuna)	Cultured in dooryard gardens, pulp of mature fruit eaten raw.	(Glenboski 1983)
biflora	Colombia	seeds	—	Mixed with commercial cacao to improve the flavor of the chocolate, and used to make a bitter febrifuge.[a]	(Schultes 1958)
spera	Colombia	seeds	—	Chocolate substitute.	(García-Barriga 1992)
alaensis	The Amazon Quichua, Shiwiar, and Zaparo of Pastaza, Ecuador	—	cambi (Pastaza), cacao monte (Spanish)	Cultivated in the fields and gardens for food.	(Garí 2001)
alaensis	Siona and Secoya, Ecuador	fruit	sunori (Siona)	Primary forest; edible fruit.	(Vickers and Plowman 1984)
reviligulata	Quichua of Napo, Ecuador	bark	sacha-cacao, cacao silvestre, cacao de monte (Quichua)	Inner bark grated, mixed with water, and drunk to treat snake bites. Outer trunk bark grated, inner bark burned to ashes in fire, ashes mixed with water or alcohol and taken by the teaspoon for dry cough, irritation of the throat, larynx, or pharynx.	(Iglesias 1985)
reviligulata	Ingano Indians of Mocoa, Colombia	bark	—	Ashes of bark used to dry up and "cure" infected wounds and ulcers.	(Schultes 1958)
reviligulata	Colombia	seeds	—	Chocolate substitute.	(García-Barriga 1992)
amargoana	Waika Indians of the Río Cauaburî	seeds	cacaurana, cacua del monte	Bitter seeds are pulverized and used as a condiment on game meat.	(Schultes and Raffauf 2004)
amargoana	Colombia	seeds	—	Chocolate substitute.	(García-Barriga 1992)
uatrecasana	Colombia	seeds	—	Chocolate substitute.	(García-Barriga 1992)
ugandii	Colombia	seeds	—	Chocolate substitute.	(García-Barriga 1992)
aciniifolia	Colombia	seeds	—	Chocolate substitute.	(García-Barriga 1992)

continued

Species	Group	Plant part	Common name	Use	Source
H. lemniscata	Guyana (formerly British Guiana)	—	—	Used to make a "beverage like chocolate."	(Schultes 1958)
H. mariae	—	seeds	—	Used as an adulterant in "Pará cacau."	(Schultes 1958)
H. mariae	Shuar and Achuar, Ecuador	fruits, bark, leaves	kushikiam (Shuar), kuchikiam (Achuar), cacohuilla (Spanish)	Fruits edible, bark and leaves used to make a wash to treat snakebites.	(Bennett, Baker et al. 2002)
H. mariae	Shuar, Eastern and Coastal Ecuador	fruit, seed, wood	kushíkiam (Shuar); pataste, cacao blanco (Spanish)	Pulp eaten raw; seeds eaten roasted; wood used for fuelwood and timber.	(Eynden, Cueva et al. 2004)
H. mariae	Colombia	seeds	—	Chocolate substitute.	(García-Barriga 1992)
H. nitida	Quichua of Upper Rio Napo, Ecuador	fruit	—	Eaten fresh.	(Friedman, Bolotin et al. 1993)
H. nitida	Karijona	seeds (Karijona),	koo-ra-tá (Karijona), cha-tê-rá (Tikuna), cacao del monte (Colombia)	Roasted and eaten as a stomach ache treatment.	(Schultes and Raffauf 2004)
H. nitida	Colombia	seeds	—	Chocolate substitute.	(García-Barriga 1992)
H. nycterodendron	Colombia	seeds	—	Chocolate substitute.	(García-Barriga 1992)
H. purpurea	Bribrí indians of Costa Rica	seeds	—	Used to make a bitter drink.	(Pittier 1908)
H. sp.	Shuar and Achuar, Ecuador	fruit, seeds, leaves, bark	kushiniap, kushikiam, kushipiak (Shuar), kuchikiam (Achuar), cacao del monte (Spanish)	Seeds and fruit pulp edible. Warmed leaves, bark, or fruit placed on snake bites as anesthetic and against swelling. Leaves, fruit husk, or part of the bark cooked with hallucinogenic natem (Banisteriopsis caapi) to increase its potency.	(Bennett, Baker et al. 2002)
H. sp.	Shuar, Eastern Ecuador	fruit, wood	kushikiam (Shuar), babaco silvestre (Spanish)	Pulp eaten raw, wood used as fuelwood.	(Eynden, Cueva et al. 2004)
H. sp.	Chamí, Colombia	wood	jimojo (Chamí) "fruit of the lizard"	Fruit pulp, resembling that of cacao, is eaten by animals called jimo (salamanders or lizards). Not eaten by humans, but wood used for firewood.	(Armella and Giraldo 1980)

Species	Group	Plant part	Common name	Use	Source
H. sp.	Quichua of Upper Rio Napo, Ecuador	seed	—	Eaten cooked.	(Friedman, Bolotin et al. 1993)
H. sp.	Chácobo Indians, Beni, Bolivia	fruits	*xaquini* (Chacobo), *ambaivillo* (Spanish)	Edible.	(Boom 1987)
H. sp.	Ketchwas	—		Believe plant treats snakebites.	(Schultes and Raffauf 2004)
H. umbratica	Colombia	seeds	—	Chocolate substitute.	(García-Barriga 1992)
H. umbratica			*puila* (Yukuna), *otonasaré* (Karijona)		(Schultes and Raffauf 2004)
H. umbratica	Colombia	fruits and seeds	*cacao del monte, cacao silvestre* (Spanish, Colombia), *puilá* (Yukuna), *beñoó* (Makuna), *otonasaré* (Karijona)	Used the same as *Theobroma* species; fruits used to make chocolate substitute because of nutritious chemicals found within.	(García-Barriga 1974)
T. bernouillii	—	seeds	—	White seeds considered a high-quality cacao.	(Cuatrecasas 1964)
T. bicolor	—	—	—	Inferior quality chocolate; "locally used to manufacture pastry and candy."	(Cuatrecasas 1964)
T. bicolor	South America	seeds	*pataste* (Central American Spanish), *bacao* (Western South America), *macambo* (Peruvian Spanish), *cacau do Peru* (Amazonian Brazilian Portuguese)	Seeds can be eaten, which roasted make a good sweet but not good for making a cacao drink; thought to cause insomnia; mixture with *T. cacao* seeds for chocolate is called *madre del cacao*.	(Patiño 1963)
T. bicolor	Tukuna of Colombia	fruit	*macambo, macambu, na* (Tukuna)	Cultured in dooryard gardens; sweet yellow pulp eaten raw.	(Glenboski 1983)
T. bicolor	Shuar and Achuar, Ecuador	fruit, seeds	*wakámpe* (Shuar), *Akágnum* (Aguaruna), *kuchi wakamp* (Achuar), *cacao blanco, patas* (Spanish)	Part of fruit surrounding seed is edible; Cofán occasionally eat the roasted seeds.	(Bennett, Baker et al. 2002)

continued

Continued—Table 2.2. Native uses of *Theobroma* and *Herrania* species in the Americas

Species	Group	Plant part	Common name	Use	Source
T. bicolor	Witoto, Colombia and Peru	fruit	—	The husk of the pod is used as a container to sweeten tobacco syrup *ambíl* applied to gums.	(Schultes and Raffat 2004)
T. bicolor			*há-ha* (Tanimuka), *ma-ra-ká* (Witoto), *heé-a* (Makú), *ao* (Makuna)	—	(Schultes and Raffat 2004)
T. bicolor	The Amazon Quichua, Shiwiar, and Zaparo of Pastaza, Ecuador	—	*quila* (Pastaza), *cacao blanco* (Spanish), *wild cacao* (English)	Cultivated in the fields and gardens for food.	(Garí 2001)
T. bicolor	Quichua of Upper Rio Napo, Ecuador	seed	*patas* (Quichua)	Cultivated and collected for seed which is eaten fried.	(Friedman, Bolotin et al. 1993)
T. bicolor	Amazon	fruit	*macambo*	Edible, cultivated.	(Duke and Vasquez 1994)
T. bicolor	Panama	fruit, seeds	*bacao* (Darian, Colombian Spanish), *patasta* (Panamanian Spanish), *culuhu* (unknown)	Pulp eaten, cocoa butter inferior chocolate made from seeds, fruit shells used as utensils.	(Duke 1972)
T. bicolor	Chamí, Colombia	fruits, seeds	*korojo, korejo, kurujo* (Chamí, "fruit of the snail," "fruit of the caiman," or "fruit of the bat or pitcher"), *bakao* (western South America, perhaps also Caribbean, "son of the thunder")	The fruits are dried over a fire for 4 days and eaten when dry; not sweet or bitter, but very tasty. Some find them sweeter than cacao. Seed eaten toasted. Cultivated by indian groups after 1850, starting in the east.	(Armella and Giraldo 1980)
T. bicolor	Bora, Peruvian Amazon	fruits	*aáhe* (Bora), *macambo* (Spanish)	A common protected plants of the Bora; "planted harvestable" in 6–12-year-old orchard fallows; one of dominant tree species in enriched 3-year-old swidden. Edible fruits and seeds; fruit shell useful. Also found in dooryard gardens and *maloca* orchards.	(Denevan and Treacy 1987)
T. cacao	Nahua, Mexico	seeds	*cacáhoatl* (Nahuatl)	Plain seeds given to people ill with "heat" or "hot" body parts such as the liver. Four roasted seeds mixed with 1 ounce roasted gum of *Castilloa elastica* is drunk to treat dysentery.	(Chabran, Chamberlin et al.)

Species	Group	Plant part	Common name	Use	Source
cacao	Nahua, Mexico	seeds	*cacáhoatl* (Nahuatl)	Drink used to treat consumption, low weight, and emaciation.	(Chabran, Chamberlin et al.)
cacao	Kuna, San Blas islands, Panama	seeds	—	Drink cacao beverages with water and sugar, and possible addition of bananas or corn.	(Chevaux, Jackson et al. 2001)
cacao	Dominican Republic	seed	—	Decoction of seeds taken orally for weakness.	(Germosén-Robineau 1995)
cacao	Caribbean	leaves	—	Used as a diuretic.	(Liogier 1974)
cacao	Venezuela	fruit, seeds	*sirú, tsirú* (Cabécar), *kau* (Tiribi), *kao* (Brunca), *ko*, kóh (Térraba), *shia*, (Cuna), *chiré* (Mirripú and Torondoy), *spiti* (Mucuchi and Muguri), *timheu* (Timote), *kiu-timheú* (Guajiro-paraujano), *oconta* (Muzo), *muselle* (Huitoto), *conocáhua* (Siona)	Fruit eaten throughout its range, chicha (fermented beverage) and vinegar made from pulp, sometimes mixed with yuca (*Manihot esculenta*).	(Patiño 1963)
cacao	South America	fruit	—	Pulp eaten; fermented drink or vinegar made from pulp.	(Friede 1953)
cacao	Venezuela	—	—	Used for burns, eruptions, cracked lips, sore breasts and genitals, vaginal and rectal irritations.	(Pompa 1974)
cacao	San Blas indians, Panama	fruit pulp	—	Decoction of the pulp and unripe fruit to aid child delivery.	(Duke 1968)
cacao	San Blas indians, Panama	young leaves	—	Antiseptic on wounds.	(Duke 1968)
cacao	Cuna indians, Panama	flowers	—	Treatment for screwworm of the eye.	(Duke 1968)
cacao	Cuna of Panama and Colombia	seeds, fruit, leaves	—	Beans often burned ceremonially, with or without hot peppers; with peppers, smoke used to treat malaria and other fevers; leaf infusions given to listless children.	(Duke 1975)
cacao	Panama	fruit, seeds	sia (Cuna), *zukurate* (unknown)	Pulp eaten, and used to make alcoholic beverages and vinegar, sometimes mixed with *Quararibea;* Cuna consume large amounts of cacao beverages including *chucula* (cacao, plantain, and cornmeal), *cuatirre* (rice flour and cacao), and *ochi* (cacao and cornmeal).	(Duke 1972)

continued

Continued—Table 2.2. Native uses of *Theobroma* and *Herrania* species in the Americas

Species	Group	Plant part	Common name	Use	Source
T. cacao	San Blas Indians, Panama	fruit, seeds	—	Widows burn cacao seeds over deceased's grave; seeds are burned on the floor during puberty rites for initiate to inhale smoke.	(Duke 1972)
T. cacao	Tukuna of Colombia	fruit	*cacao* (Spanish), *cha pe re* (Tukuna)	Second-growth forest; sweet pulp of mature fruit eaten raw.	(Glenboski 1983)
T. cacao	French Guiana Indians		*cacao* (Créole), *walapulu* (Wayãpi), *waraâru* (Palikur), *cacau* (Portuguese)	Frequently cultivated around houses; in addition to chocolate, seed mixed with various other plants by Palikur to make a remedy for extracting large splinters.	(Grenand, Moretti et al. 1987)
T. cacao	The Amazon Quichua, Shiwiar, and Zaparo of Pastaza, Ecuador	—	*cacau* (Pastaza)	—	(Garí 2001)
T. cacao	Quichua of Napo, Ecuador		*cacao-muyu* (Quichua)	Peeled and grated, mixed with yuca root (*Manihot* esculenta) and unripe banana fruit (*Musa* sp.) and applied around boils to treat them.	(Iglesias 1985)
T. cacao	—	seeds	—	Cocoa butter used in suppositories.	(Duke and Vasquez 1994)
T. cacao	throughout Colombia	leaves	*há-ha* (Tanimuka), *bai-uc'* (Makú), *aso-ya-ee* (Piratapuya), *a-ba-ca-ra-á* (Makuna), *cacao, cacao criollo, cacao dulce* (Colombia)	Infusion of leaves as a heart tonic and diuretic.	(Schultes and Raffa 2004)
T. cacao	Karijona of Colombia	seed	—	Use toasted seed with manioc squeezings for eczema-like scalp condition.	(Schultes and Raffa 2004)
T. cacao	Ingano	bark	—	Use bark decoction as a wash for cutaneous disease *sarna* (scabies).	(Schultes and Raffa 2004)
T. cacao	Colombia	leaves	*abacaraá* (Makuna), *aso-ya-ee* (Piratatuya), *baiuc* (Maku), *cacao* (Kofan), *cabecerá, ha-ha* (Tanimuca), *cacao criollo, cacao dulce* (Spanish)	The leaves are used as an infusion for theobromine diseases of the heart (cardiotonic); salts of prescribed for their action in coronary arteries.	(García-Barriga 1974)
T. cacao	Venezuela	—	—	Used to treat many diseases and to make hair grow.	(Pittier 1926)

Species	Group	Plant part	Common name	Use	Source
T. cacao	Peruvian Amazon	seeds		A cup taken three times a day of a thick chocolate drink made from the toasted seed shells is used to treat a dry cough.	(Mejia and Rengifo 1995)
T. cacao	Shuar, Quichua, Secoya-Siona and Cofán, Ecuador	fruit	*kakáu* (Shuar), *bakáu* (Aguaruna)	Cultivated as a cash crop. Fruit pulp eaten.	(Bennett, Baker et al. 2002)
T. cacao	Siona and Secoya, Ecuador	fruit	*si'e* (Siona); *cacao* (Spanish)	Cultivated in house gardens; edible pulp.	(Vickers and Plowman 1984)
T. cacao	Serin-gueiros (rubber tappers) in Acre, Brazil	fruit, bark	*cacaueiro* (Portuguese)	Planted near communities or found in "primary" forest; always spared when forest cleared. Fruit edible; also bark beaten and put into cold water, stirred, strained, and drunk; for women who just gave birth.	(Ming, Gaudêncio et al. 1997)
T. cacao ssp. *leiocarpum*	Amazon	fruit	*cacao amarillo*	Pulp edible.	(Duke and Vasquez 1994)
T. cf. *speciosum*	Shuar, Ecuador	fruit	*chukuchuk* (Shuar), *cacao de selva* (Spanish)	Fruits.	(Bennett, Baker et al. 2002)
T. cirmlinae	—	seeds	—	Occasional preparation of chocolate by natives.	(Cuatrecasas 1964)
T. gileri	—	fruit, seeds	—	Pulp sweet and aromatic, also used for chocolate.	(Cuatrecasas 1964)
T. glaucum	Eastern Nukak, Guaviare and Inírida rivers, Colombia	fruit	*ígi-jere* (Nukak), *cacao de monte* (Spanish)	Suck on seeds.	(Cárdenas and Politis 2000)
T. glaucum	Colombia	fruit, seeds	*chucú*	Seeds used as cacao by natives; fruit very much appreciated by natives.	(Karsten 1856 apud Cuatrecasas 1964)
T. grandiflorum	Amazon	fruit	*copoasu, cupuassu, cupuaçu*	Cultivated, pulp edible.	(Duke and Vasquez 1994)
T. grandiflorum	Tikunas	leaves	*taraira* (Barasana), *ñee-au* (Tanimuka), *us-per'* (Piratapuya), *cupuassú* (Brazil)	A tea of the crushed leaves used for abdominal pain.	(Schultes and Raffauf 2004)
T. grandiflorum	Tukuna of Colombia	fruit	*coca, copuassú, cupuassú* (Spanish); *ri* (Tukuna)	Cultured in dooryard gardens and in chacras; pulp eaten raw.	(Glenboski 1983)

continued

Continued—Table 2.2. Native uses of *Theobroma* and *Herrania* species in the Americas

Species	Group	Plant part	Common name	Use	Source
T. grandiflorum	Waimiri Atroari, Brazil	fruit	*aka'* (Waimiri Atroari), *cupuaçu* (Portuguese)	Recently introduced tree cultivated around villages; pulp eaten or made into refreshing drink.	(Milliken, Miller et al. 1992)
T. grandiflorum	Brazilian Amazon	leaves	*cupuaçu, cupu-assú, cupu* (Portuguese)	"Juice" of the leaves used in treatment of bronchitis and kidney infections.	(Stasi, Santos et al. 1989)
T. grandiflorum	Cabloclos of Barcarena, Para, Brazil	fruit, bark	*cupuaçu* (Portuguese)	cultivated, rural lot garden and house garden; fruit eaten, tea made from bark used to treat diarrhea.	(Amorozo and Gély 1988)
T. grandiflorum	—	fruit	—	Sweet pulp, much cultivated.	(Cuatrecasas 1964)
T. microcarpum			*metró-re-moo-eé* (Karijona)		(Schultes 2004)
T. nemorale	—	seeds	—	Said to produce a fairly good chocolate; native use not known.	(Cuatrecasas 1964)
T. nemorale	Afro-Americans, Chocó, Colombia	seeds	*chocolatillo* (Spanish)	Food (seeds made into chocolate) and used for "technology."	(Galeano 2000)
T. obovatum	Eastern Nukak, Guaviare and Inírida rivers, Colombia	fruit	*ígi* (Nukak)	Use widespread in various indigenous communities; suck on seeds.	(Cárdenas and Politis 2000)
T. obovatum	Colombia	—	*win-cheek'* (Puinave), *ma-oo-hee-reé* (Kabuyarí)	—	(Schultes and Raffa[■] 2004)
T. obovatum	Amazon	fruit	*cacahuillo, Ushpa cacao*	Pulp edible.	(Duke and Vasquez 1994)
T. purpureum	Panama	fruit	*cacao cimarron, chocolatillo* (Panamanian Spanish), *wild cocoa* (English)	Fruit pulp of pod covered with stinging hairs is eaten.	(Duke 1972)
T. simiarum	Costa Rica	seeds	—	Seeds said to give a cacao of good quality.	(Cuatrecasas 1964)
T. sinuosum	—	fruit	—	Pulp eaten.	(Cuatrecasas 1964)
T. sp.	Tukuna of Colombia	fruit	*cacao quarada* (Spanish); *ba ru* (Tukuna)	2nd growth forest, pulp eaten raw.	(Glenboski 1983)
T. sp.	Afro-Americans, Chocó, Colombia	—	*bacaillo* (Spanish)	Food.	(Galeano 2000)

Continued—Table 2.2. Native uses of *Theobroma* and *Herrania* species in the Americas

Species	Group	Plant part	Common name	Use	Source
T. sp.	Shuar and Achuar, Ecuador	fruit	*wakamp* (Shuar)	The uncooked fruit, similar to *T. cacao*, is eaten. The trees are felled to collected the fruit.	(Bennett, Baker et al. 2002)
T. speciosum	—	fruit, seeds	—	Pulp; seeds used very occasionally to make low-quality chocolate.	(Cuatrecasas 1964)
T. speciosum	Chácobo Indians, Beni, Bolivia	fruits	*nohotë* (Chacobo), *chocolate* (Spanish)	Sweet pulp of mature fruits is eaten raw.	(Boom 1987)
T. speciosum	Chácobo Indians, Beni, Bolivia	leaves	*nohotë* (Chacobo), *chocolate* (Spanish)	Reported to have an unspecified medicinal value.	(Boom 1987)
T. speciosum	Brazilian Amazon	leaves	*cacau, cacauí, cacau azul* (Portuguese)	Dried and applied near site of throat infections.	(Stasi, Santos et al. 1989)
T. speciosum	Waorani, Ecuador	fruit		Eaten.	(Davis and Yost 1983)
T. stipulatum	—	seeds	—	Said to yield a good chocolate but not used much.	(Cuatrecasas 1964)
T. subincanum	—	fruit, seeds	—	Pulp; gives an acceptable chocolate but little used.	(Cuatrecasas 1964)
T. subincanum	Venezuela	fruit	*cacao-rana* (Spanish)	—	(Patiño 1963)
T. subincanum	Shuar, Ecuador	fruit	*wakáme* (Shuar), *wakamp* (Achuar), *cacao de monte* (Spanish)	Seed pulp eaten.	(Bennett, Baker et al. 2002)
T. subincanum	Amazon	fruit	*cachuillo, cacao macambillo, macambillo, macambo sacha*	Pulp edible.	(Duke and Vasquez 1994)
T. subincanum	Amazon	bark	*cachuillo, cacao macambillo, macambillo, macambo sacha*	Powdered inner bark (of pod) mixed with tobacco as a hallucinogen.	(Duke and Vasquez 1994)
T. subincanum	Tirio, French Guyana	bark	—	Use bark as tinder for starting fires.	(Duke and Vasquez 1994)
T. subincanum	Jamamadis and Denís, Amazonian Brazil	bark	*cowadimani* (Jamamadi), *mapanahã* (Dení)	Ash of bark added to tobacco (*Nicotiana tabacum*) to make *shinã* snuff, which is said to be ineffective without the *T. cacao* ash.	(Prance 1972)

continued

Continued—Table 2.2. Native uses of *Theobroma* and *Herrania* species in the Americas

Species	Group	Plant part	Common name	Use	Source
T. subincanum	Waikas of northern Brazil and upper Orinoco of Venezuela and the Barasanas, Makunas, Taiwanos, Kabuyarís, Kuripakos, and others of Colombian Amazon	leaves and twigs	*mee-né-ro* (Witoto), *bauk* (Makú), *abe-ka-rá* (Makuna)	Ashes of leaves and twigs mixed with syrup of or used to coat pellets of *Virola theiodora* for a hallucinogenic snuff.	(Schultes and Raffa 2004)
T. subincanum	Many tribes in the Northwest amazon	—	—	Use the ash of wild cacao as the preferred admixture for tobacco (*Nicotiana tabacum*) snuff.	(Schultes and Raffa 2004)
T. subincanum	Eastern Nukak, Guaviare and Inírida rivers, Colombia	fruit	*ígi-baká* (Nukak)	Suck on seeds.	(Cárdenas and Politis 2000)
T. subincanum	Waimiri Atroari, Brazil	fruit, wood	*aka'* (Waimiri Atroari), *cupuí* (Portuguese)	Native tree of terra firme forests; fruits edible, trunks used for house posts, also for fuel; eaten by capuchin monkeys.	(Milliken, Miller et al. 1992)
T. subincanum (*T. sylvestris* Aublet)	Galibis and Garipons, French Guiana	fruit	*cacao* (Galibis and Garipon)	White and covered with a membrane that is good to eat when dry.	(Plotkin, Boom et al. 1991)
T. sylvestre	Waimiri Atroari, Brazil	fruit, wood	*srykwaba* (Waimiri Atroari), *cupuaçu* (Portuguese)	Fruits eaten by people, howler and capuchin monkeys; wood used in construction around Manaus.	(Milliken, Miller et al. 1992)
T. velutinum	—	seeds	—	Reported to yield edible seeds comparable to cacao.	(Cuatrecasas 1964)
T. velutinum	Galibis and Garipons, French Guiana	fruit and seeds	*cacao* (Galibis and Garipon), *cacao sauvage* (French)	The pod is cut open and the seeds and pulp are emptied into a vat to ferment for 24 hours, where it liquefies and turns wine-colored. This is left until fruit membranes turn brown to indicate the embryo is dead. Seeds can then be easily separated from their coat. Acidic liqueur can then be drunk.	(Plotkin, Boom et al. 1991)
T. velutinum (as *Theobroma guianensis* Aublet)	Galibis and Garipons, French Guiana	fruit	*cacao* (Galibis and Garipon), *cacao sauvage* (French)	Fruit pulp eaten.	(Plotkin, Boom et al. 1991)

a. febrifuge—a compound or plant that reduces fevers.

Food uses

A large percentage of the species in the *Theobroma-Herrania* complex are used throughout their range for food by ethnic groups in South America, but it appears that only the fruit pulp and seeds are eaten. There are a few cases of ingestion of leaf or bark preparations as medicines, but almost all of these are made as infusions (extractions of the active substances in a plant or other material made by steeping the material in hot water for five to twenty minutes), decoctions (extractions of the active substances in a plant or other material made by boiling the material in water), or tinctures (extractions of the active substances in a plant or other material made by immersing the material in cold water or alcohol for a length of time, often several weeks), which would only extract the polar or water-soluble compounds from the leaf and bark, leaving behind possibly toxic non-water-soluble compounds. Since there has been so little study of the chemistry and activities of the leaves and bark, the only compounds known from the bark or leaves that could be considered toxic are the hepatotoxic (damaging to the liver) chlorogenic acid in leaves; the hepatotoxic isopropyl acetate in the entire plant; and the methylxanthines caffeine, theobromine, theophylline, and tetramethyl urate, of which the first three are sometimes considered hepatotoxic, fetotoxic (damaging to developing fetuses), and neurotoxic (damaging to neurons and other brain tissue) in high doses. The ingestion of cacao waste, the seed shells removed after roasting, has been known to cause theobromine poisoning and death through heart failure (Lewis and Elvin-Lewis 1977). The methylxanthines are found in the seeds as well, however, and are actually a desirable component of the plant for their stimulant properties. When the leaves have been studied for methylxanthines, only theobromine has appeared in *T. cacao* and *T. bicolor* and, even then, in minute amounts compared to the seeds; thus, it is unlikely that these could be making the leaves or bark toxic. Ultimately, it is probably just the more obvious factors of taste and texture that lead people not to eat parts of the plants other than the fruit pulp and seeds.

Among South American groups, there are many documented cases of cacao-like drinks made from *Theobroma* and *Herrania* seeds; however, the time frame of these is unclear. The huge amount of knowledge exchanged between groups, the lack of information on the origins of these uses, and the few if any documented cases from the fifteenth through seventeenth centuries make it impossible to tell whether these groups had been using the seeds before the Spanish brought this use from Mesoamerica, or if they quickly picked up on this use and its name, as Balée (2003) has shown with the Ka'apor of Northeastern Amazonia. If these uses can be traced back to the earliest documented cases with trustworthy sources and if some reliable ethnohistoric studies can be conducted to trace the source of seed use, then some clarity can be brought to the origins of this widely used and celebrated food.

There are also many examples of alcohols or vinegars made from *T. cacao* pulp: in Venezuela sometimes mixed with yuca or sweet manioc (Patiño 1963), in Panama sometimes mixed with *Q. funebris* (J. A. Duke 1972), in Bolivia (personal observation 1983: see Figure 2.7), in Guatemala (McNeil, Chapter 17, this volume), in South America in general (Friede 1953), and in Nicaragua (A. M. Young 1994). Again, it is unclear when and where these uses originated and how they were transferred between Mesoamerica and South America. If the making of fermented beverages from cacao pulp is a first step towards discovering the process of fermenting the seeds for chocolate (see Henderson and Joyce, this volume), which follows logically, it seems the South Americans may have started down this road before chocolate was introduced from the north but just never took the next step of roasting the seeds and eating them without the pulp.

Tracing these origins and their biogeography may soon be necessary for other reasons: the cultivation of cacao in South America, one of its native areas and former largest producers, is in danger of collapse from pests and diseases, mainly a witch's broom fungus, *Crinipellis perniciosa* (Bright 2001). For some

Figure 2.7. Shop in Trinidad, Bolivia, selling cacao vinegar in the jar on the left. Photograph by Douglas C. Daly.

time, researchers have suggested hybridizing *T. cacao* with its wild *Theobroma* and *Herrania* relatives to create pest-resistant strains (Addison and Tavares 1951; Schultes 1958). By being obliged to find wild strains of *T. cacao* and its relatives for breeding, we will have the added benefit of being able to trace the complex's paths of speciation and migration and perhaps clarify some of the issues of where it was first cultivated. The ease of cross-species and cross-generic hybridization in the group hinders this search, however, as this makes it more difficult to find a single wild species that can create fertile hybrids with the cultivated *T. cacao*, a common method of determining the area of first cultivation of a species.

The mixed-heritage *colonos,* or *ribereños,* of Amazonia owe much of their knowledge to the indigenous people. The *colonos'* system of shade growing cacao on small farms, and similar small-farm systems, called *cabrucas* in Bahia, Brazil, may help maintain biodiversity around cacao plantations and increase cacao production in South America. On these small cacao farms, which follow the indigenous model of cacao growing, many more species of trees are grown together (Rice and Greenberg 2000), including the endangered mahogany (*Swietenia macrophylla* King) (Marina Campos, personal communication 2003), and some new plant and bird species have even been found (for example, Small and Catling 2002).

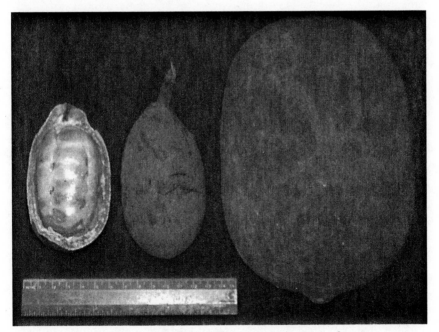

Figure 2.8. Left: Fruits of *cupuí, Theobroma subincanum.* Right: Fruits of *cupuaçu, T. grandiflorum.* Photograph by Douglas C. Daly.

Adopting traditional cultivation methods can have positive impacts such as these. Co-opting indigenous and local knowledge can, however, lead to problems, as with the recent attempts in the United States, Europe, and Japan to trademark the long-used common name *cupuaçu* for *T. grandiflorum* (Willd. ex Spreng.) K. Schum. (Asahi Foods Co. 2003) (Figure 2.8) and to trademark the name and patent the process of extracting a chocolate-like substance called *cupulate* from *T. grandiflorum*'s seeds by a Japanese company, Asahi Foods Co. (Nazaré 1992). This company has sued a German company, claiming copyright infringement, for producing a product called *cupuaçu*, which is simply a jam made of *cupuaçu* pulp. This is akin to trademarking the name *apple* for a food and claiming the trademark is valid because the patent and trademark officers in non-English-speaking countries have never heard this word before. This attempt to profit from native knowledge is also reminiscent of recent attempts to patent a variety of the widely used Indian plant neem (*Azadirachta indica* A. Juss.) and a supposed variety of the hallucinogenic Amazonian vine *ayahuasca* (*Banisteriopsis caapi* [Spruce ex Griseb.] C. V. Morton); both attempts were widely denounced and were unsuccessful.

Medicinal uses

Most of the numerous medicinal uses reported for cacao and its relatives throughout the Americas seem to fall into five common categories: stimulant or treatment for fatigue; high-calorie food for weight gain; external and internal emollient; antiseptic; and snakebite remedy. That multiple informants have reported similar uses for *Theobroma* and *Herrania* can be considered under the idea of informant consensus (Trotter and Logan 1986) to show that these uses have more validity than those uses reported only once or twice. These uses are spread throughout a closely related taxonomic group and are reported from multiple distinct cultures, making an even stronger case for these medicinal uses that should encourage further analyses of these plants. Some of the medicinal uses can be easily explained by compounds found in these plants with known corresponding medicinal activities, such as soothing or emollient compounds in plants used to treat dry skin. For some other uses to be explained, further research is required to uncover the responsible active compounds in the plants.

The stimulant and weight gain uses are the easiest to understand given the presence of the powerful methylxanthines caffeine and theobromine in cacao and the high-calorie unsaturated fats in cocoa butter. They both show the use of rational medicinal plant choices by the indigenous groups who use them, although they show effects on quite different time scales. The stimulant properties of cacao are so obvious that little deduction is necessary; one eats or drinks cacao and a few minutes later one feels stimulated and more awake. It is harder to see the connection between ingesting cacao and weight gain since the people who used cacao for this medicinally were probably ingesting quite a diversity of foods, and it could take as long as several weeks to see the weight change. This attests to the deductive powers of the Nahua of Mesoamerica, who discovered this connection (Chabran, Chamberlin, and Varey 2000). In the Dominican Republic, a cacao seed decoction being used to treat weakness (Germosén-Robineau 1995) could be considered a combination of the stimulant and weight-gain-inducing properties of cacao.

Cacao and its relatives are used to soothe many parts of the body, with preparations of the bark of *H. breviligulata* R. E. Schult. and seeds of *T. cacao* employed for cracked lips, sore throat, dry cough, and vaginal and scalp irritations. Substances that soothe irritated tissues, called emollients or demulcents, are found elsewhere in the Malvaceae family in which cacao is now placed: mallow (*Malva* sp.) leaves are often used to sooth irritations, but the mallow's emollient action is attributed to the abundant mucilage in the leaves, something that cacao lacks. Pectin, sucrose, and starch are the only compounds in cacao that are classified as demulcents or emollients (J. Duke 2004), but what else might cause cacao to be used so often to soothe irritated tissues? In addition to the three emollient compounds, there are twelve compounds in cacao that are analgesics, substances that relieve pain (ascorbic acid, caffeic acid, chlorogenic acid, coumarin, esculetin, ferulic acid, gentisic acid, pyridoxine, quercetin, quercetin-3-o-galactoside, serotonin, and thiamin), and two compounds listed as anesthetics, producing a loss of sensation (coumarin and linalool). These compounds, which probably contribute greatly to the soothing effect of the plant by easing or erasing pain, have been found mostly in cacao seeds and leaves but are likely to occur in the bark.

Explaining the use of cacao on wounds, sore throat, and vaginal irritations, at least fourteen compounds with antiseptic properties are present in *T. cacao*, *T. bicolor*, and *T. speciosum*: ascorbic acid, caffeic acid, catechol, chlorogenic acid, citric acid, esculetin, formic acid, furfural, kaempferol, linalool, oxalic acid, proanthocyanidins, protocatechuic acid, and trigonelline. The antibiotic oligomeric proanthocyanidins found in *T. cacao* would further help avoid wound and internal infections.

Herrania species figure in a number of snakebite remedies: *H. mariae* leaves are used by the Shuar of eastern Ecuador (Bennett, Baker, and Andrade 2002), *H. breviligulata* bark by the Quichua of Napo, Ecuador (Iglesias 1985), a *Herrania* sp. by the Ketchwa of Colombia (Schultes and Raffauf 2004), and warmed leaves, bark, or fruit of a *Herrania* sp. by the Shuar (Bennett, Baker, and Andrade 2002). Normally, snakebite remedies are among the most numerous, over-reported, and unverified plant treatments, but in this case there does seem to be a preponderance of evidence that this treatment could be effective given that it is concentrated in a few *Herrania* species and it is spread across several cultures. The activities we might look for in plant compounds to treat snakebites would be anti-inflammatory (to reduce the swollen bite), astringent (to absorb some of the toxins), and vasoconstrictor (to contract the blood vessels around the area and stem the spread of the snake venom), and display the antiseptic and antibiotic activities listed above to keep the wound from becoming infected. In fact, *T. cacao* contains the astringent formic acid; the vasoconstrictors quercitrin, rutin, tryptamine, dopamine, and tyramine; and no fewer than twenty-six anti-inflammatory compounds (see J. Duke, 2004, for a full list). Again, these have been found mainly in the seeds of *T. cacao* rather than in the bark or leaves of *Herrania*, but given this huge library of compounds potentially active against snakebites and given the other shared chemistry of *Herrania* and *Theobroma*, it is likely that a few of these compounds are also found in *Herrania* bark and leaves, and the use of these to treat snakebites would therefore be justified chemically, as are many of the medicinal uses of cacao and its relatives described above.

Psychoactive uses

The psychoactive uses of *Theobroma* and *Herrania*, mostly in combination with other psychoactive plants, cannot be explained as easily as the food and medicinal uses. There are many uncertainties, but many of these could be eliminated by some simple testing of the plants for these chemicals in different stages of preparation for psychoactive use. There is most likely a purpose to these combinations, as people do not usually continue to combine plants arbitrarily without any effect (Moerman 1991). This is evidenced by mixtures such as *ayahuasca* in which the Amazonian peoples found the combination of only the few possible plants that had a profound hallucinogenic effect out of the thousands of plants in their environment. These uses and the many psychoactive compounds found so far in cacao would imply that there may be more interesting compounds to be found in cacao and spread throughout *Theobroma* and *Herrania*.

Although the many psychoactive or neuroactive compounds already documented in *T. cacao* have not been sought in other species in the complex, one would assume that given their shared evolution and (to some extent) chemistry, some of these psychoactive compounds will also be found in species other than *T. cacao*. This is in keeping with the principles of chemotaxonomy, an established area of taxonomy based on the notion of shared evolution and shared chemistry (Harborne and Turner 1984). In the process of demosticating cacao, the Mesoamericans may have selected for plants with more stimulating seeds;

this explains the higher levels of compounds like the methylxanthines caffeine and theobromine in *T. cacao* than in the other *Theobroma* species analyzed. The wild or less domesticated species would be less selected and, therefore, they would most likely have lower levels of psychoactive compounds, but even small amounts of these neurotransmitter analogs would be effective. The combination of several species in psychoactive preparations may be explained by chemical synergies, in which the chemicals in one plant activate those in the other, leading to a very potent hallucinogenic effect. An example is the widespread use of hallucinogenic mixtures such as *ayahuasca,* which generally contains the *ayahuasca* vine (*Banisteriopsis caapi*) and *chacruna* (*Psychotria viridis* Ruiz and Pav.). The latter has basically no effect taken on its own, but has a synergistic effect in combination, making *ayahuasca* one of the most powerful hallucinogenic plant mixtures known (Schultes, Hofmann, and Rätsch 1998).

The insistence of the Jamamadis of the Brazilian Amazon that their tobacco snuff is not effective without the addition of *Theobroma subincanum* ash (Prance 1972) (see Figure 2.8) implies that no plant is added without reason and should prompt us to look for possible synergies in psychoactive mixtures involving *Herrania* and *Theobroma* species. In addition to this use with tobacco snuff, the uses of *T. subincanum* with *Virola theiodora* snuff (Schultes and Raffauf 2004), *T. bicolor* fruits as tobacco syrup containers as in Figure 2.9 (Schultes and Raffauf 2004), *T. subincanum* fruit husk used with tobacco (Duke and Vásquez 1994), and an unidentified *Herrania* species used in an *ayahuasca* mixture with *B. caapi* (Bennett, Baker, and Andrade 2002) should be examined closely. Although no caffeine or theobromine has been detected in the seeds or leaves of *T. subincanum* (Hammerstone, Romanczyk, and Aitken 1994), these compounds may occur in the bark, where their presence would increase the uptake during inhalation of the active 5-methoxy-N,N-dimethyltryptamine (5-MeO-DMT) found in the *Virola* snuff and the nicotine in the tobacco snuff. Alternatively, *T. subincanum* bark ash may make the pH more basic, aiding in the absorption of the 5-MeO-DMT and nicotine in the nasal cavities when used along with these snuffs.

The use of *T. subincanum* as an admixture in snuffs may be explained by examining the human neurotransmitter systems in which these different plant chemicals act. The 5-MeO-DMT in the *Virola* snuff and the harmine and harmaline in the *ayahuasca* mixture act on the serotonin neurotransmitter (or "serotonergic") system, either mimicking the natural serotonin in the body and stimulating the same neuron receptors that serotonin stimulates or increasing the amount of serotonin by blocking its destruction or reabsorption by the body. The nicotine in the tobacco acts in the nicotinic receptor system as a mimic. With the exception of the tetrahydro-β-carbolines (THBC's) in the

Figure 2.9. An indigenous Witoto man in Colombia storing tobacco syrup in a *Theobroma bicolor* fruit husk. Photograph by Richard Evans Schultes. Reprinted with permission from Synergetic Press, originally published in *Vine of the Soul* (Schultes and Raffauf 2004: Figure 33).

seeds of *T. cacao* (Herraiz 2000), the many psychoactive chemicals in cacao do not act in the serotonergic or nicotinic receptor systems. If these THBC's, which are in the same chemical class as the harmine and harmaline in *B. caapi*, are found in the leaves and bark of other *Theobroma* and *Herrania* species, and they could survive the heat when these plants are burned to ash, they would act as monoamine-oxidase inhibitors (MAOIs); that is, compounds that slow the destruction of the neurotransmitters serotonin and dimethyltryptamine (DMT) by the enzyme monoamine oxidase (MAO) in the brain. An MAOI often has the side effect of slowing the destruction of the toxin tyramine, found in fermented foods, also by MAO in the gut. THBC MAOI would slow the destruction of the *Virola*'s 5-MeO-DMT in the brain and significantly increase its activity. In the case of the *Herrania* leaves mixed with *B. caapi*, the THBC's would not have to withstand the high heat of combustion, and they would add to the MAO inhibitor effect of the harmine and harmaline in the *B. caapi* to allow the DMT in the *ayahuasca* mixture to be absorbed in the intestine and the brain without being destroyed by monoamine-oxidase.

Oddly, the normally innocuous compound tyramine found in fresh cacao seeds and many fermented foods such as chocolate (Kenyhercz and Kissinger 1977) can reach toxic levels when the action of MAO, which normally breaks it down before it can reach these levels, is blocked by MAO inhibitors such as the THBC's. That these two compounds, tyramine and MAO inhibitor THBC's, are found together in cacao seeds could possibly lead to toxic levels of tyramine when ingested. If these are both found in the *Herrania* leaves as well, along with the other MAO inhibitors harmine and harmaline found in *B. caapi* in the *ayahuasca* mixture, this would lead to a build-up of tyramine in the body of those ingesting the *ayahuasca* and cause adverse reactions such as nausea, vomiting, and diarrhea.

None of the chemicals found in cacao or its relatives seems to act in the same neurotransmitter system as the nicotine in tobacco, however. Thus, perhaps if some of the other psychoactive compounds such as the cannabinoids or phenyl-ethylamine are found in the other species, in different parts of the plant, and survive combustion, they could add a completely different layer to the effects of nicotine by activating the anandamide or catecholamine receptor system.

Given the powerful psychoactive compounds found in cacao and that Mesoamerica has the highest density of uses of psychoactive plants in the world (Schultes, Hofmann, and Rätsch 1998), it is a bit odd that there are no documented cases from Mesoamerica of cacao being used as a psychoactive on its own or in combination with other psychoactive plants. Granted there are no psychoactive plants used in Mesoamerica that act through DMT or other tryptamines that *Virola* snuff and *ayahuasca* act through and that cacao could evidently amplify, but there are some other intriguing possibilities for synergies between cacao and Mesoamerican plants.

The Mazatec of Oaxaca, Mexico, use the plant *Salvia divinorum* Montbr. and Auch. from the mint family Lamiaceae, which they call *ska maria pastora* (Wasson 1962). This plant was also possibly used by the Cuicatecs of Oaxaca (Reko 1945), the Otomi of Mexico and Veracruz states (Weitlaner 1952), and the Chinantecs of Oaxaca (Johnson 1939). *S. divinorum*'s main active compound, salvinorin A, has recently been shown to stimulate the κ-opioid receptor (Roth 2002), unrelated to any known psychoactive substance in cacao. There has been one report, however, of a cannabinoid found in *S. divinorum* (Ben-Shabat et al. 2002) that could interact with the anandamide and anandamide analogs in cacao beans (Tomaso, Beltramo, and Piomelli 1996). The cacao anandamide analogs would increase and extend the effect of the *S. divinorum* cannabinoids by in effect blocking the enzymes that naturally break down anandamide and other cannabinoids. This would essentially increase the *Cannabis*-like effect of the *S. divinorum*. It would seem that the Mazatec, Cuicatec, Otomi, or Chinantec who lived in or near the area where there was extensive cultivation of, use of, and experimentation with cacao would have discovered this effect if given the opportunity.

Investigators in Mesoamerica should search for such possible synergistic uses of cacao with other psychoactive plants among the indigenous Mesoamericans and for other possible ways to administer cacao on its own. With all these psychoactive compounds in cacao, the Mesoamericans may have found some more direct ways of delivering these compounds to their brains other than by drinking the cacao beverage, such as by smoking it, using a sublingual quid, or via an enema, this last a Maya method for administering hallucinogens (Diamond 2001). Thus, there may be something more to cacao than drinks and candies, and there may be something hiding behind all these complex chemical formulas and botanical taxonomies.

Conclusion

Because of their long history, wide geographic range, and complex chemistry, the species of *Herrania* and *Theobroma* have been adopted for myriad uses in the Americas. Although *T. cacao* is the most studied species of this group, much is still unknown about its chemistry, ecology, and actions on the human body and mind. Certainly the other species of this group will reveal many interesting new findings when they are given the same attention as cacao. As the chemical, genetic, and morphological characters of each species are made clearer, so will the taxonomy of the entire group, and these will in turn tell us more about cacao. Cacao has been used and experimented with for more than two thousand years; let us hope that it does not take two thousand more to fully understand why this plant holds such an attraction for humans.

Acknowledgments

We thank Scott Mori for help with literature acquisition, Bill Balée for allowing us to read his in-press paper, Laurence J. Dorr for a taxonomic update on *Theobroma* s.l., Wayt Thomas for photos, and Jim Duke and Dennis McKenna for background information and general advice.

3

The Domestication and Distribution of *Theobroma cacao* L. in the Neotropics

Nisao Ogata, Arturo Gómez-Pompa, and Karl A. Taube

The origins, domestication, and distribution of *Theobroma cacao* L. are controversial and difficult to discern because of its wide geographical distribution; human intervention; and interbreeding between the two taxonomic subspecies that most certainly occurred in the early Colonial period; interbreeding may also have occurred during pre-Columbian times. Although our data support Mesoamerica as a center of cacao domestication, our research also suggests that some areas in South America could have been separate centers of domestication, as well.

In Mesoamerica, trees have played an important role in the development of cultures, such as that of the Maya, who used at least 255 species (Ogata 2002a). In this environment of high diversity, Mesoamerican cultures developed a practice of domestication different from the usual "plants dependent on people" form common in Western societies. The domestication of trees in tropical forests focused not only on the species of interest but on the domestication of the forest itself (Wiersum 1998). Some examples of human-made forests in Mesoamerica are the *Te'lom* of the Huastec agroforestry system in northern Veracruz, Mexico, which are characterized as natural genetic reservoirs (Alcorn 1984), and the *Pet Kot* of the Maya, which is characterized as vegetation patches (primarily composed of useful plants) delimited by stone walls. Many "wild" forest gardens have been found in the Maya region and in other tropical areas of the world (Gómez-Pompa and Kaus 1990; Gómez-Pompa, Salvador, and Sosa 1987).

The domestication of certain tree species in Mesoamerica transformed forests for human purposes. For example, the seeds of *Brosimum alicastrum* Sw. (ramón) were substitutes for maize in the Maya area and might have been a key food source during the Classic period (Ogata 1993; Peters 1983). Other species, such as *Annona* spp. (annona, guanabana), *Spondias mambin* L.(jobo, ciruela), *Byrsonima crassifolia* (L.) H. B. K. (nance), and *Persea americana* Mill. (avocado), are products of the sophisticated domestication of species and forests.

Theobroma cacao is one of the most important economic plant species of the humid neotropics and presents an excellent model for understanding evolutionary patterns of tropical trees; centers of domestication; the origin, distribution, and migration of domesticated plants; and management in areas of high biodiversity. This understory species is distributed from South America to the Lowlands of tropical Mexico (Cuatrecasas 1964). In the wild, the trees are tall with flowers growing in a scattered manner (sometimes in clumps) out of the main stem. The number of flowers and fruit is low. The tree has a long adult life span, and it is assumed that it is self-incompatible; however, we have seen solitary wild individuals fruiting in a greenhouse. The seeds of *T. cacao* have a short dormancy period. The main dispersal vectors are monkeys and squirrels (A. M. Young 1994). In cultivation, trees are small, flowers grow out of the main stem, and there are many flowers and fruits per tree. The tree can be either self-compatible or self-incompatible, and seeds have a short dormancy period. The main dispersal vectors are humans (Hart 1911; A. M. Young 1994). Two subspecies have been described: *T. cacao* ssp. *cacao* extends from South America to southern Mexico, and *T. cacao* ssp. *sphaerocarpum* ranges from South America to Central America (Cuatrecasas 1964).

Theobroma cacao is important because in pre-Hispanic times its seeds were used as currency, medicine, and food, and today it is the source of chocolate, with almost three million tons produced in 2002 and a profit of $5.5 billion (Ogata 2002a).

Some still-unanswered questions relate to the influence of humans on the distribution of the species in the Americas and the origin of domestication. The answers to these questions are important because they may reveal new sources of cacao genetic diversity and ethnobotanical information related to ancestral ways of using cacao with other plants involved in the preparation of chocolate, food, or medicine. In this chapter, we use both genetic, ethnobotanic, and archaeological evidence to describe the origin of cacao, its domestication, and the distribution of the species.

A Range of Variation

Assessing the range of variation of *T. cacao*, which is mainly based on the structure of the fruit (Cheesman 1944; Cuatrecasas 1964), is difficult. The array of inbreeding populations ranges from trees with smooth round fruits to trees with pointed, furrowed, warty pods (Figure 3.1). The delimitation of these boundaries has led researchers to describe three different species (Pittier 1935),

Figure 3.1. *Theobroma cacao* fruits variation. Left: *T. cacao* ssp. *cacao*. Center: *Criollo* culti-vars found in Mexico. Right: *T. cacao* ssp. *sphaerocarpum*. Photograph by Nisao Ogata.

three different "groups" (Cheesman 1944), two subspecies (Cuatrecasas 1964), and an enormous number of varieties and cultivars (Cheesman 1944; Figueira, Levy, and Goldsborough 1994; Van Hall 1914).

Cacao trees with smooth round fruits are naturally distributed from South America to the Panama Isthmus, described taxonomically as subspecies *sphaero-carpum* (Cuatrecasas 1964). Those with pointed, furrowed, warty pods are dis-tributed from South America to southern Mexico and are described as subspe-cies *cacao* (Cuatrecasas 1964). *Theobroma cacao* ssp. *cacao* and *T. cacao* ssp. *sphaerocarpum* correspond to *criollo* and *forastero* cultivars, respectively, and the variants in between are generally considered *trinitario* cultivars. The color of cotyledons has also been proposed as an essential characteristic that differenti-ates subspecies and cultivars (Cheesman 1944; Cuatrecasas 1964). It has been established elsewhere that white cotyledons are characteristic for *criollo* and purple for *forastero* (Cuatrecasas 1964:506). The combination of characters, fruit shape, and cotyledon color is normally used as a yardstick to differentiate between good and bad quality cacao (Chatt 1953; Wood 1975). In theory, this combination of characters should be very useful for differentiating between types, because just by looking at the shape of a pod or cutting a seed in half one can easily see whether one is dealing with a *criollo* or *forastero* tree (Chees-man 1944; Cuatrecasas 1964; Van Hall 1914). In practice, this combination of characters is untenable because both characteristics are extremely variable, and there is no correspondence between fruit shape and cotyledon color. In the case of cotyledons, color shows a gradient (white-light gray, medium purple-dark purple, or mottled purple) that can be found in both subspecies, cultivars and wild populations, as well (J. B. Allen 1988; Bekele and Bekele 1996).

With the arrival of the Spanish to America, the importance of cacao and the transportation of plants from Mesoamerica and South America to places as far away as Africa led to an unrecorded interbreeding of the two subspecies

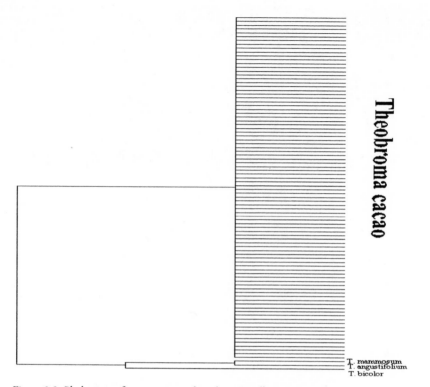

Figure 3.2. Phylogram of consensus tree based on G3pdh sequences

in many places colonized by the Spanish and others (S. D. Coe and M. D. Coe 1996). The recent use of molecular markers created the expectation that the splits could be resolved; however, the approach only led to more division (Figueira, Levy, and Goldsborough 1994). This situation remains unresolved mainly because ranking a group of organisms (that is, species, subspecies, variety, cultivar) depends on the subjective criteria (for example, taste and color [Ogata and De Luna 1998]) of the taxonomist or horticulturalist. Until now there has been no way to find an empirical criterion to uniquely and universally distinguish the species or any infraspecific rank. In systematics, it is generally agreed that there should be one consistent, general purpose reference system. Phylogeny is the best criterion for general purpose classification, both theoretically, because the tree of life is the single universal outcome of the evolutionary process, and practically, because the phylogenetic relationship is best for summarizing known data about attributes of organisms and for predicting unknown attributes (Mishler 1999). Other possible ways to classify can be used simultaneously but should be regarded as special purpose classifications and clearly distinguished from phylogenetic formal taxa. This is the case with all of the classifications of *T. cacao* that have been proposed (Cheesman 1944; Cuatrecasas 1964; Van Hall 1914).

To set the basis for a general purpose classification, we used, for the first time, a phylogenetic method involving the nuclear gene Glyceraldehyde 3-phosphatase dehydrogenase (G3pdh) to reconstruct the genealogical relationships of *T. cacao* populations and explore the monophyletic status of the species. Results of parsimony analyses supported a monophyletic origin for *T. cacao* (Figure 3.2). Hence, we searched for answers to when and how *T. cacao* ssp. *cacao* and *T. cacao* ssp. *sphaerocarpum* diverged.

Distribution of Cacao and Origin of Domestication

As mentioned above, the natural distribution of *T. cacao*, especially subspecies *cacao*, has been controversial because, contrary to the vast amount of information from Mesoamerica (the farthest area of distribution), there are few data from South America (the center of origin of the genus) (see Bletter and Daly, this volume). Thus, some proponents support subspecies *cacao* in Mesoamerica as the result of human introduction, while others suggest that the species occurs naturally throughout the neotropics. For example, Cheesman (1944) supported a human-mediated distribution of subspecies *cacao* to Mesoamerica, suggesting a center of evolutionary origin in South America. He based this on the statements F. J. Pound, who, in his 1938 expedition, claimed to have found this center near the upper waters of the Napo, Putumayo, and Caqueta rivers, tributaries of the Amazon (Pound 1938) (Figure 3.3). From this evidence, Cheesman proposed:

> that a small section of the original population on the eastern side somehow crossed the cordillera at an early time, and that from it evolved the two *criollo* groups as we know them today (Venezuela and Mesoamerica). In this view the cordillera was the barrier permitting differentiation of the well-marked characters of all *criollos*, and the Isthmus of Panama acted as a secondary barrier permitting further differentiation of a distinct Central American population out of the limited amount of material that crossed it in a westerly direction. (Cheesman 1944:155)

Cheesman refers to the possible migration of two groups of subspecies *cacao*, one towards Venezuela and the other towards Central America (this idea was also shared by Pittier [1935] for subspecies *cacao* in Venezuela before the arrival of the Spanish). Cheesman (1944) states, however, that because the species has no specialized mechanism for the natural dispersal of its seeds and the seeds quickly lose viability when removed from the pod, humans are the likely agents for transporting seeds over the Andean mountains (1944:155) (see Figure 3.3).

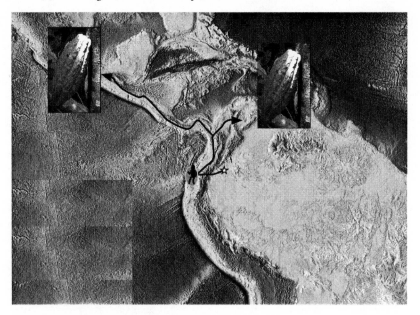

☆ = Center of origin proposed by F. J. Pound

👣 = Human-mediated migration of Cacao

──▶ = Routes of migration

Figure 3.3. Hypothesis proposed by Cheesman (1944), based on the statements of F. J. Pound, who claimed to have found the center of origin of cacao near the upper waters of the Napo, Putumayo, and Caqueta rivers, tributaries of the Amazon. Cheesman proposed a human-mediated migration of cacao.

Schultes (1984:33) supported the same human-mediated transport and suggested that *T. cacao* could have worked its way north and westward by two routes (Figure 3.4). Route A: When the cacao tree finally became established at the mouth of the Amazon, it could gradually have made its way along the humid forested Atlantic Coast of northern South America, across the Guianas and Venezuela. The Caribbean coast of Colombia, however, is arid, and cacao would not survive in that area; it would necessarily have to be taken by man to the northwesternmost corner of Colombia, the Gulf of Urabá, a highly humid region whence it could then continue on its way through Panama, Costa Rica, Nicaragua, Honduras, Guatemala, and into tropical Mexico. Route B: Another route might have been via the Orinoco. The penetration of the Río Negro of Brazil would lead directly to the Casiquiare, a canal linking the Amazon drainage area with the uppermost Orinoco. The necessary environmental continuum for this strictly tropical tree requiring abundant rainfall would have been available along this route to the coastal region of Venezuela (Figure 3.4).

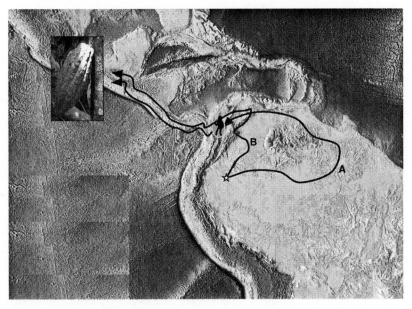

★ = Center of origin proposed by F. J. Pound

🯅 = Human-mediated migration of Cacao

➡ = Routes of migration

Figure 3.4. Schultes (1984) proposed a human-mediated migration where *Theobroma cacao* could have worked its way north and westward by two routes. Route A: Via the Amazon along coastal northern South America across to Venezuela. Then taken by man to Colombia from whence it could continue into tropical Mexico. Route B: Via the Orinoco.

More recently, Motamayor et al. (2002), using restriction fragment-length polymorphism and microsatellite markers, compared the genetic diversity of Mesoamerican cacaos with that of South American samples. They found very low diversity in the Mesoamerican samples and concluded that if the samples were wild populations, they should exhibit genetic diversity similar to that observed for geographic areas such as Peru, Colombia, and Ecuador. Therefore, they decided that the populations in the Lacandon forest (in the Mexican state of Chiapas), in Mesoamerica, should be considered neither wild nor as originating from this region (Motamayor et al. 2002). They also used as evidence the absence of *T. cacao* pollen in samples from Tertiary period deposits and the presence of ancient human settlements in the area, which suggest that Lacandon *T. cacao* populations are the remnants of cacao cultivated by the Maya.

In contrast, Pittier (1935) was one of the first proponents of a broad, natural distribution of *T. cacao* instead of a human introduction into Mesoamerica. His long experience working with *T. cacao* led to a recognition of three differ-

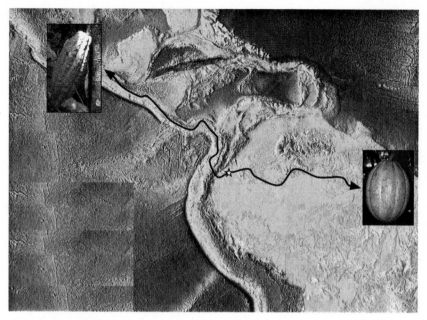

☆   = Center of origin proposed by F. J. Pound
⟶   = Routes of migration

Figure 3.5. Pittier (1935) suggested a natural distribution of *Theobroma cacao* from the northwestern part of South America to Central America. He also proposed that *T. leiocarpum* was indigenous over northeastern South America, extending far into Central America.

ent species: *T. cacao*, *T. pentagonum*, and *T. leiocarpum*. *Theobroma cacao* and *T. pentagonum* correspond to subspecies *cacao*, and *T. leiocarpum* to subspecies *sphaerocarpum*, as later described by Cuatrecasas (1964). Pittier (1935) suggested a natural distribution of "his" *T. cacao* from the northwestern part of South America to Central America, and *T. leiocarpum* as indigenous to the northeastern part of South America and extending far into Central America (1935:386). He also described *T. pentagonum* (a synonym for *T. cacao* ssp. *cacao*, according to Cuatrecasas 1964) as located in only a restricted area, including Nicaragua and perhaps part of Costa Rica, and extending north to the southern border of Guatemala (Pittier 1935:386) (Figure 3.5).

Cuatrecasas agreed with this distribution, as well (Figure 3.6), believing that formerly *T. cacao* was naturally distributed from:

> Amazonia-Guiana westward and northward to the south of Mexico; that these populations developed into two different forms geographically separated by the Panama isthmus; and that these two original forms, when isolated, had sufficiently consistent characters to be recognized as subspecies.

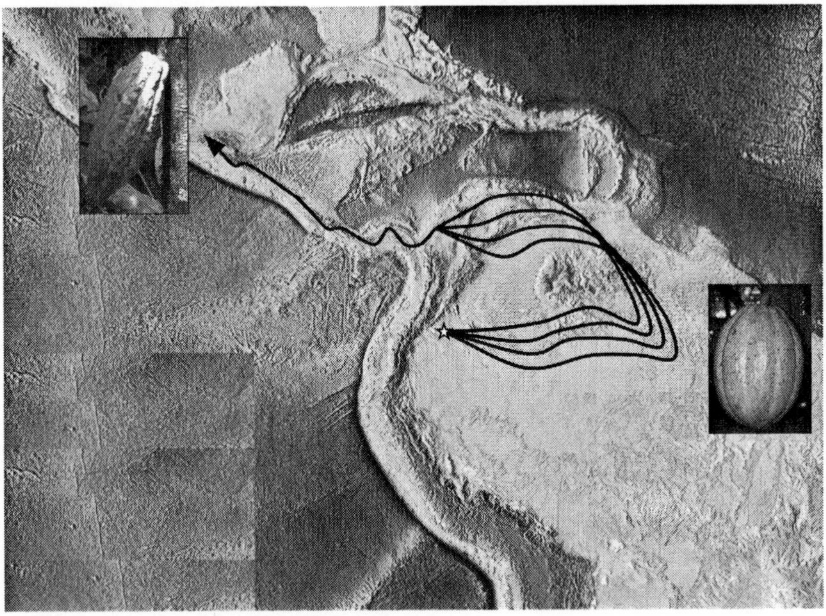

☆ = Center of origin proposed by F. J. Pound

⟶ = Routes of migration

Figure 3.6. Diagram illustrating the natural distribution of *Theobroma cacao* in the neotropics, according to Cuatrecasas (1964).

> As they intermingled readily by crossing, giving fertile and robust hybrids, they cannot be considered distinct species. (Cuatrecasas 1964:507)

More recently, Gómez-Pompa, Flores, and Aliphat-Fernandez (1990), studying sinkholes in the Yucatan Peninsula, merged the Cuatrecasas and Pittier hypotheses, suggesting that subspecies *cacao* naturally reached the southern Lowlands of Mexico and later was domesticated by early inhabitants of Mesoamerica. In the same way, De la Cruz et al. (1995) and Whitkus et al. (1998), using random amplified polymorphic DNA markers to compare the diversity of *T. cacao* in southern Mexico with that of samples from the Yucatan Peninsula and Lacandon forest, discovered a segment of genetic diversity in this part of Mesoamerica that was unique among cultivars and South American populations (De la Cruz et al. 1995:543; Whitkus et al. 1998:621).

New Research Concerning the Origins of Cacao Domestication

The authors of this chapter focused on the ecology, ethnobotany, and molecular data of the G3pdh gene in old, abandoned, and putative wild populations of cacao from southern Mexico. Samples were taken in the backyards of homes in towns mentioned in the *Suma de visitas de pueblos* (Paso y Troncoso 1905). This document consists of accounts collected between 1531 and 1544 from 907 towns in Central Mexico. From these locations, we chose towns known in the *Suma* as cacao producers in pre-Hispanic times but that currently have no traces of cacao cultivation. Other samples were taken from sinkholes in the Yucatan Peninsula (Gómez-Pompa, Salvador, and Aliphat-Fernandez 1990). Samples of putative wild populations were collected with the help of local people in the tropical rainforests of the Reserva de la Biosfera Calakmul, in the states of Campeche and Quintana Roo, and from the Lacandon forest in Chiapas. Samples of individuals from South America obtained from the Instituto Nacional de Investigaciones Forestales, Agrícolas y Pecuarias in Rosario Izapa, Chiapas, were used as outgroups.

From the *Suma*, twenty-three populations were identified, representing subspecies *cacao* in places referred to as ancient cacao-producing areas. Populations were found in backyard gardens and/or in plantations of coffee, banana, and orange in northern and southern Veracruz, northern Oaxaca, Tabasco, Chiapas, Campeche, Quintana Roo, Michoacán, Colima, northern Acapulco (in the state of Guerrero), and Yucatan.

Putative wild populations found in the forest corresponded with subspecies *cacao* and ecologically resembled wild populations J. B. Allen (1988) found in Ecuador. The main characteristics are long and slender individuals, scattered distribution in the forest, low density (about four trees per hectare), and one or no fruits for two consecutive years. Local people living in the Lacandon and Calakmul forests indicated that these plants are not cultivated.

The variation of the G3pdh gene within and between the populations sampled were explored, and coalescent theory was used to understand the stochastic processes governing evolution. Coalescent theory suggests that in the absence of selection, sampled lineages can be viewed as randomly "picking" their parents back in time. Whenever two daughter lineages pick the same parent, their lineages coalesce, until eventually all lineages coalesce into a single lineage or the Most Recent Common Ancestor (Ogata 2002a). This approach was used to test the geographic distribution and possible origin of the cacao haplotypes (a set of genes at more than one locus inherited by an individual from one of its parents) collected in Mexico.

Haplotypes were analyzed with use of statistical parsimony. Statistical parsimony estimates the maximum number of differences among haplotypes as a result of single substitutions (those that are not the result of single substitutions at a single site) with 95 percent confidence. Haplotypes differing by one change are connected, then those differing by two, by three, and so on, until all haplotypes are included in a single network or the parsimony connection limit is reached. Statistical parsimony emphasizes shared characteristics that differ minimally rather than differences among haplotypes. According to coalescent theory, the oldest ancestral haplotype is the most frequent and widely distributed (Posada and Crandall 2001).

Ninety-one individuals were connected into twenty-two different haplotypes and classified into seven main groups (Figure 3.7). Haplotype A corresponds to the outgroup *T. bicolor*. Haplotype B is the most widely distributed and is mainly represented by wild cacao from the Lacandon and Calakmul forests and old abandoned populations from northern and southern Veracruz, Oaxaca, and Tabasco, except for one individual from Venezuela. Haplotype C, one step away from B, corresponds to a wild individual from Chiapas and an old abandoned one from Oaxaca. Haplotype D, a step away from B, is represented by five individuals from old abandoned populations from southern Veracruz and Oaxaca and two individuals, two steps away from B, from Gallo

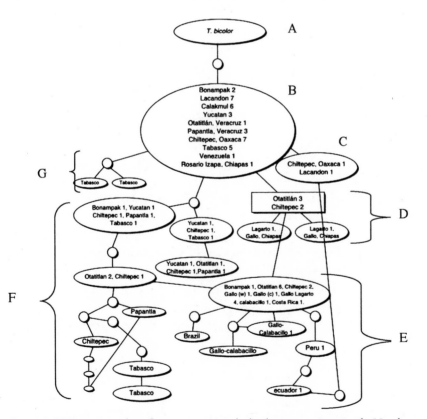

Figure 3.7. Maximum number of steps connecting the haplotypes parsimoniously. Numbers after the localities correspond to the number of individuals sampled. Letters represent the main groups of haplotypes.

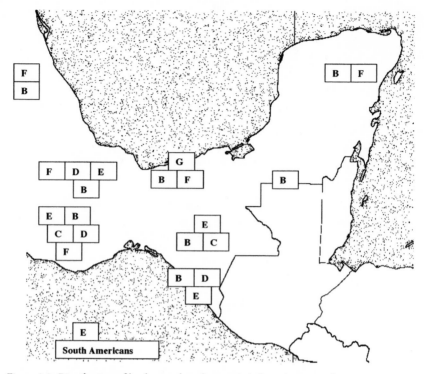

Figure 3.8. Distribution of haplotypes based on statistical parsimony analysis.

Giro, Chiapas, corresponding to the subspecies *cacao*. Haplotype E, two and three steps away from B, is represented by one wild plant from Chiapas and six from old abandoned populations in southern Veracruz, two from Oaxaca, and the rest by Central and South American individuals. Haplotype F is the most distant group from haplotype B. It includes individuals from the Lacandon forest and old abandoned populations from the Yucatan Peninsula, northern and southern Veracruz, Oaxaca, and Tabasco. Haplotype G, one step away from B, is represented by two individuals from Tabasco (Figure 3.8).

Our genetic analysis suggests that haplotype B is the oldest in the network. On the basis of the position of the outgroup *T. bicolor*, B is also closest to the root of the haplotype network. This result suggests that wild individuals from the tropical rainforests of Mexico are the source of the cacao cultivated there since pre-Hispanic times. The highest number of haplotypes may occur in Oaxaca and southern Veracruz, because at the time of Spanish arrival this area paid the highest tribute in cacao to the Mexica empire (Millon 1955a), which suggests that this region was intensively cultivated and is therefore likely to contain a diversity of cultivars. Our molecular information supports the wide natural distribution of subspecies *cacao* in the neotropics; however, still more samples are needed, especially from Central and South America.

Discussion

Theobroma cacao represents perhaps the best example in the neotropics of domestication as a multidimensional process involving a progressively closer interaction between people and plant resources (Wiersum 1998). In Mesoamerica, this interaction led not only to wild plant species becoming cultivated but also to "wild" forests becoming managed (Gómez-Pompa and Kaus 1990). One can still find evidence of domestication of cacao (and trees in general) in Mesoamerica. Wild plants were initially managed and cultivated, resulting in the modification of the basic composition of the forest vegetation. The process also involved the shift from uncontrolled utilization of the wild tree products to controlled exploitation. Subsequently, native trees were cultivated in an enriched forest or in orchard gardens; cultivation of selected varieties was the last phase of this domestication process. The final phase of the process involves breeding selected genotypes, which results in uniform tree populations with a narrow genetic base (Wiersum 1998). The Maya implemented this domestication process, which is still practiced in many areas in Mesoamerica and which may be the key to new ways to manage tropical forests.

Our genetic analysis suggests that *T. cacao*, with its morphological diversity of fruits, descends from a common ancestor. This result provided the basis for a general purpose classification based on phylogenetic relationships; any special purpose classification only requires being explicit. Therefore, whether *T. cacao* is one species, two subspecies, or three or more cultivars is a subjective problem of ranking for the taxonomist or horticulturalist, not a problem of grouping, since we have shown that *T. cacao* is monophyletic. Thus, the use of molecular information for ranking *T. cacao* (Motamayor et al. 2003) is as subjective as using color, taste, or pod shape.

Whether the distribution of subspecies *cacao* in Mesoamerica is the result of human-mediated or long-term natural distribution, our ecological, ethnobotanical, and molecular results support the hypothesis that *T. cacao* has a naturally broad distribution, as is the case for many other neotropical plants (Gentry 1982). For example, *Theobroma* is a typical neotropical genus distributed in the rainforests of the Western hemisphere between 18°N and 15°S (Cuatrecasas 1964). Although most *Theobroma* species are located on the western side of Amazonia, towards Central America, species such as *T. bicolor*, *T. speciosum*, *T. canumanense*, *T. subincanum*, *T. microcarpum*, and *T. gileri* are broadly distributed (Cuatrecasas 1964). Some species were apparently split by the elevation of the Andes in the early Tertiary period, which separated several species that were previously widespread and favored speciation through isolation (Cuatrecasas 1964). Examples of other long-term, naturally distributed species in the neotropics are *Terminalia amazonia* (J. Gmel), *Bursera simaruba* (L.) Sarg., *Cedrela odorata* L., and *Astronium graveolens* Jacq. (Ogata et al. 1999).

Our ethnobotanical results suggest that old abandoned populations in most parts of Mexico have a pre-Hispanic origin. These populations are being conserved by local people, sometimes in areas where today the use of cacao is not evident. In the case of the putative wild individuals found in the Lacandon and Calakmul forests, there were no traces of recent human settlements or recent activities related to cultivating trees.

Our genetic analysis results demonstrate that *T. cacao* populations in Mexico show nonhierarchical relationships, whereby most haplotypes exist as sets of multiple identical copies. When one of these copies mutates to a new haplotype, we expect that the ancestral haplotype is persisting in the population, and, therefore, the most widely distributed and frequent haplotype is the oldest. The same conclusion comes from the outgroup rooting of the network. Thus, the distribution of haplotypes suggests that the pre-Hispanic cacao was taken from the tropical rainforests of southern Mexico-Belize-Guatemala, where it occurs naturally even today. Our results show a pattern of congruence between the geographical distribution of haplotypes and their genealogical relationships; that is, closely related haplotypes are geographically restricted and occur in proximity to each other (Figure 3.8). Such congruence suggests a long-standing pattern of highly restricted gene flow in which novel mutation remains localized within the geographical context of origin (Templeton, Routman, and Phillips 1995).

Motamayor et al. (2002), working with Mexican populations, found low diversity and assumed that a wild population (in this case *T. cacao*) should exhibit high levels of genetic diversity similar to that observed in Peru, Colombia, and Ecuador. Furthermore, Motamayor et al. (2002) argue that the populations found in the Lacandon forest in Mesoamerica should neither be considered wild nor as originating from this region, and they advocate a human-mediated distribution in Mesoamerica. It is not clear, however, why they imply that a widespread species should show high levels of diversity along the whole range of its distribution, since most of the range of a species may contain little or no genetic variation relative to the rest of the range (Schaal et al. 1998). Certainly, such a pattern might be consistent with human introduction, but it could also be consistent with rapid expansion in regions of low diversity, especially expected for many native temperate and tropical species because of the effect of glaciations on plant distribution. The widespread distribution of individual haplotypes agrees with rapid range expansion from known refugia following Pleistocene glaciations in Europe and North America (Schaal et al. 1998). Motamayor et al. (2002) argue that the absence of palynological records of *Theobroma* in deposits from the Tertiary period supports the idea that *T. cacao* did not occur naturally in Mesoamerica before human occupation. The absence of pollen deposits, however, is not a robust argument to demonstrate the absence of a species from a region, especially when discussing *T. cacao*, which had a low density in the wild, has low flower and fruit production, and is insect pollinated. Motamayor et al. (2002) also propose to eliminate the rank of subspecies within *T. cacao* because genetic distances between subspecies are similar to those between individuals within species. They used this phenetic approach to group and rank at the same time, assuming that genetic distances indicate relationship. Distance measures, however, hide homoplasy when character by character differences are boiled down into a single difference value (Farris 1983). After all, evolution does mechanistically proceed by individual mutations not by change in some measure of overall distance (Mishler 1994). Therefore, because they did not find any discontinuity at genetic dis-

Figure 3.9. Tembladera-style ceramic vessel depicting a spider monkey and what may be a cacao tree. 1100–700 B.C. Jequetepeque Valley, northern Peru. Drawing by Kata Faust after Bonavia (1994:Photograph 6).

tances (grouping) they proposed that there should not be two subspecies but one (ranking). However, there are many kinds of discontinuities that do not necessarily correspond with each other (that is, are the same sets of organisms delimited by discontinuities when we look at morphology, as when we look at breeding or ecology?). The answer is that there is no necessary correspondence. In the case of *T. cacao* it is obvious that morphology and reproductive isolation are not correspondent. The same noncorrespondence is evident between percentage of molecular similarity and reproductive isolation, showing the subjectivity of ranking even when using molecular information.

Mesoamerica was one center of the origin and production of *T. cacao*, but recent evidence suggests that the species was domesticated as well in South America. For example, historical and ethnological information suggest that when the Spanish arrived in Venezuela, the Maracaibo Basin was already cultivated with cacao (Ogata 2003). In addition, a resin-painted Tembladera-style ceramic vessel in the Enrico Poli Bianchi collection suggests that cacao may have been cultivated in Peru thousands of years before Spanish contact (Figure 3.9).

Resembling the Early Horizon art of Chavín de Huántar, Peru, Tembladera effigy vessels derive from the middle Jequetepeque Valley of northern Peru (Alva 1987; Burger 1992:97–98). Although the great majority of these frequently elaborate items—including the piece under discussion—were looted, their similarity to Late Huacaloma ceramics in Cajamarca suggests that the Tembladera style dates to the late Initial Period and the initial portion of the Early Horizon period; that is, between 1100 and 700 B.C. (Burger 1992:98; Richard Burger, personal communication 2004). The vessel is in the form of a tree with fruits hanging directly from its trunk. With their torpedo-like forms and grooved surfaces, these fruits closely resemble cacao pods. In addition, small blossoms can be discerned growing from the upper trunk, a trait also found in cacao. However, a similar petalled element on the proximal end of each pod resembles the calyx, a fused, outer set of floral leaves absent from cacao fruit. The calyx suggests that the vessel may portray *cocona* (*Solanum sessiliflorum* Dunal) and/or *naranjilla* (*Solanum quitoense* Lam) of Solanaceae, which bears fruit with a calyx. The vessel fruits, however, are ridged, a trait lacking in both *S. sessiliflorum* and *S. quitoense*. In addition, *cocona* and *naranjilla* fruits are globular and lack the pointed tip depicted on the Tembladera-style example.

It is conceivable that the calyx-like elements on the fruits and the petalled elements on the pod stems of the Tembladera-style vessel are florid embellishments by the ancient artist. Among the Classic Maya, cacao pods have also been portrayed with elements resembling a calyx (Figure 3.10b). In addition, Cameron McNeil (personal communication 2005) has called our attention to a Teotihuacan depiction of a cacao pod (Figure 3.11). Although it appears to be

Figure 3.10. Portrayals of spider monkeys as "cacao-bringers" from Late Classic period Maya vases. a. Spider monkey with cacao growing from its tail. Detail of a vase from Chipoc, Guatemala. Drawing by Karl Taube after R. E. Smith (1952:Figure 13k). b. Spider monkey with cacao pods in its paws and atop its back; note possible excrement elements at the rear. Drawing by Karl Taube after Kerr (1994:593). c. Detail of cacao pods with calyx-like elements on previous vessel (third cacao pod is from the second vessel monkey, not illustrated in Figure 3.10b). d. Detail of vessel portraying squirrel and spider monkeys with cacao pods. Drawing by Karl Taube after Kerr (1997:768).

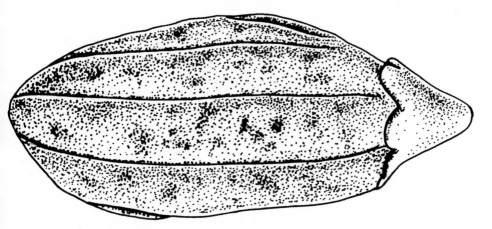

Figure 3.11. Mold-made cacao pod. Classic period. Teotihuacan, Mexico. Drawing by Karl Taube.

fashioned directly from a mold of an actual cacao pod, the piece was also provided with an explicit calyx. Consistent with cacao, the Tembladera-style vessel has flowers and hanging fruits with ridged, torpedo-like forms growing directly from the trunk. Given these shared traits, it is most likely that the Tembladera vessel portrays a fruiting cacao tree.

In the central Andes, there is one well-known fruit that has a form similar to cacao, the *pepino dulce* (*Solanum muricatum* Aiton). Botanically related to the tomato, the *pepino dulce* is native to the temperate Andean highlands (National Research Council 1989:296, 305). In general shape and proportions the *pepino dulce* fruit resembles a cacao pod, but the surface is entirely smooth rather than ridged. The whitish skin is marked with lengthwise purple striations, which appear in ancient Andean art as painted lines rather than deeply modeled grooves (for example, National Research Council 1989:305). The *pepino dulce* does appear in Tembladera-style ceramics, and the form of the fruit is quite distinct from grooved cacao pods (see Alva 1986:Figure 210). Dating to approximately 900 B.C., an Early Horizon period modeled vessel excavated at Chavín de Huántar portrays a pair of *pepino dulce* fruits, among the earliest documented examples in Andean art (see Lumbreras 1993:Plate 72, no. 578, Plate C, c-d).

The Tembladera tree is occupied by a monkey incised in an encircling band behind the hanging fruit (see Figure 3.9). Its large eye and crest of hair identify this creature as a spider monkey (*Ateles geoffroyi*). Although cacao and spider monkeys are native to the Amazon drainage rather than to the central Jequetepeque Valley, it is clear that there was extensive contact between coastal Peru and the Amazon drainage from at least the Initial period (ca. 1500–900 B.C.). Excavations at the Initial period site of Ancon, on the central coast of Peru, revealed remains of *chonta* wood and a cebus monkey, both deriving from the tropics east of the Andes (Burger 1992:73). Portrayals of spider monkeys are also relatively common in Chavín-related art of the Early Horizon period, including Tembladera ceramics (see Alva 1986:Figures 194a, 196a, 206, 273, 280, 283, 353, 359). A Cupisnique-style effigy vessel from north coastal Peru also portrays a spider monkey, its open mouth serving as the spout (see de Lavalle and Lang 1978:51). In addition, a black ceramic head from Chavín de Huántar depicts a spider monkey with its characteristic small pug nose and prominent crest of hair (see Tello 1960:Figure 172). Given the relatively low altitude of the Andes in this region, the Jequetepeque Valley is very well-suited for trade with the Marañon and greater Amazon drainage. Richard Burger (personal communication 2004) notes that Tembladera-style pottery has been reported in the Bagua region on the eastern slopes leading into the Marañon.

The presence of the spider monkey on the Tembladera vessel is significant for two reasons. First, the monkey probably reflects the tropic origins of cacao and the nearby Marañon Valley of the Amazon drainage. Second, spider monkeys naturally disperse cacao seeds during their consumption of the fruit (Aguilar, this volume; A. M. Young 1994). In Late Classic Maya art (ca. A.D. 600–900), spider monkeys are commonly depicted holding cacao pods or wearing them as pectorals or ear adornments (see Aguilar, this volume; M. E. Miller and S. Martin 1994:Plate 40; Grube and Nahm 1994:Figure 19). There is one example of a howler monkey, epigraphically labeled as *batz'*, grasping the fruit, but this is a rare exception (see Grube and Nahm 1994:696). Among the Classic Maya, spider monkeys are by far the most common animals appearing with cacao fruit. Although most Classic Maya examples derive from Late Classic vases, a crudely carved sandstone sculpture from Altar de Sacrificios, Guatemala, apparently portrays a monkey holding a cacao pod in both paws (see Willey 1972: Figure 224). Cacao pods have been depicted on the backs or even growing out of the bodies of monkeys (Figure 3.10a, b, d). Such scenes explicitly portray spider monkeys as the providers and bringers of cacao, which is their true role in the natural world. One carved vase depicts two spider monkeys carrying cacao both in their paws and on their backs (Figure 3.10b). Circular elements in the tail regions of both monkeys may portray excrement, a possible ancient folk explanation for the natural dispersal of cacao by monkeys. As has been mentioned, this vessel portrays the pods with vegetal elements resembling the calyx of certain fruit (see Figure 3.10b). Nonetheless, they display a line of dots, a convention in Maya iconography denoting rough, corrugated surfaces, including testicles and turkey wattles as well as cacao pods (for an Early Classic example, see Kerr 2000:972 [K6547]). Another Late Classic vessel depicts not only spider monkeys but also a squirrel with cacao pods (see Figure 3.10d). Squirrels are the other principal arboreal creature responsible for the natural dispersal of cacao seeds (see McNeil, Chapter 1, this volume).

The Classic Maya were by no means the only ancient Mesoamerican people that identified spider monkeys with cacao. Manuel Aguilar (this volume, Figure 13.2) notes an excellent example from the early Colonial murals in Malinalco, Mexico, in which a pair of monkeys hang from a fruit-laden cacao tree. A Classic period figurine from southern Veracruz depicts a spider monkey grasping a cacao pod in its outstretched paw (Figure 3.12a). In addition, a Classic period vessel sherd from the south coast of Oaxaca depicts a monkey hanging by its tail from a cacao tree (Figure 3.12b). The composition of this scene is notably similar to the aforementioned mural at Malinalco.

In ancient Peru, monkeys are also frequently portrayed grasping fruit, although it usually appears to be the *pepino dulce* (see Bonavia 1994:Photographs 81, 183, 198). At present, the Tembladera-style vessel is the only one in which a spider monkey appears with a ridged fruit resembling a cacao pod. A number

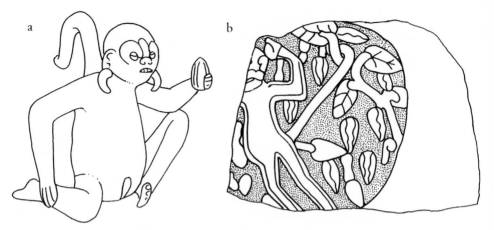

a   b

Figure 3.12. Portrayals of monkeys with cacao in Classic period Mesomerica. a. Nopiloa style spider monkey with cacao pod. Southern Veracruz, Mexico. Drawing by Karl Taube after Easby and Scott (1970: No. 138). b. Monkey in cacao tree. Sherd. Talun carved ware. South coastal Oaxaca, Mexico. Drawing by Karl Taube after Urcid (1993:Figure 26–10).

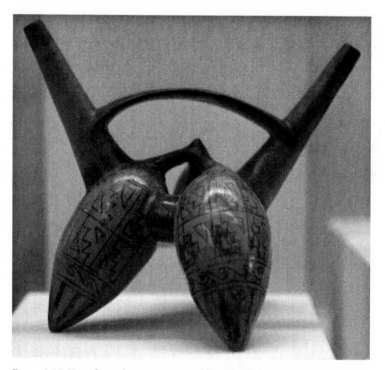

Figure 3.13. Tripod vessel portraying possible cacao pods. Late Middle Horizon period. Lambayeque Valley, northern Peru. Photograph by Nisao Ogata of vessel on display in the Museo Larco Hoyle, Lima, Peru.

of other ancient Andean vessels portray what may be cacao fruit. One possible example, in the Larco Hoyle Museum in Peru, is a Late Intermediate period bridge spout vessel with the chamber formed of three fruits (Figure 3.13). Dating to about the ninth to tenth centuries A.D., this vessel is from the Lambayeque Valley, a region slightly north of where the Tembladera-style vessel under discussion may have been made. Clearly, the documentation of cacao in ancient South America is of critical importance for understanding the origin and dispersal of this plant. Given the extremely dry conditions of coastal Peru, it is conceivable that cacao seeds may be discovered at archaeological sites in this region. As yet, however, remains of cacao have not been archaeologically documented in Peru. Aside from portrayals of cacao in ancient art and macrobotanical remains, ethnohistoric and ethnographic accounts of cacao use in South and Central America could also be of great value. Given the economic and cultural importance of this plant, the origins of cacao is a topic that will surely receive further study.

Conclusion

Our research has demonstrated that questions about the origin, distribution, and domestication processes of *T. cacao* will not be answered by splitting or clumping the group but only by describing the ancestor-descendant relations, using a robust method of inference. For example, at this point we have shown evidence suggesting the monophyletic status of *T. cacao*. This information, included in an ethnobotanical context will provide the basis for understanding causes of variation in view of natural distribution, human selection, and the way domestication processes occur in trees in the neotropics. With this approach we will be able to describe the different strategies used by different cultural groups in the domestication of a species inserted in a multispecies environment and to propose hypotheses related to causes of variation and to the existence of more than one simultaneous center of domestication. In addition, archaeological data can be used to augment genetic analysis of cacao populations.

Acknowledgments

We want to thank Laura Heraty for her professional editing and Cameron McNeil for her suggestions and comments on our chapter. We are indebted to Richard Burger and Jeffrey Quilter for generously sharing their expertise concerning Andean archaeology, and to Gene Anderson for his knowledge of native fruits of the Andes. We would also like to thank the Consejo Regional Indigena de X-Pujil for their fieldwork assistance.

4

The Jaguar Tree (*Theobroma bicolor* Bonpl.)

Johanna Kufer and Cameron L. McNeil

Theobroma cacao L. is not the only culturally important species of the genus *Theobroma* in Mesoamerica. Since prehistoric times, *T. bicolor* also has been consumed and has been used for ritual purposes. This species, commonly referred to as *pataxte* or *balamte*, has frequently been called "wild cacao," but it is not the closest relative of domesticated *T. cacao*. When Europeans first arrived in the Mexica lands, they found that *T. bicolor* was commonly sold in marketplaces, but it appeared to be appreciated less than *T. cacao*. The small amount of recorded evidence concerning the ethnobotany of *T. bicolor* indicates that it held and continues to hold a special niche in ritual life, particularly among the Maya, sometimes overlapping with and sometimes disparate from *T. cacao*. It is morphologically similar to *T. cacao*, and the use of the word cacao for both species has likely led to a lack of attention to the differences between their uses—particularly those that apply only to *T. bicolor*.

In this chapter the authors first review the botanical differences between *T. cacao* and *T. bicolor*, discussing traits of *T. bicolor* which make it appealing for ritual and comestible use. Then we examine the archaeological evidence for ancient *pataxte* use. Following this, we explore post-Contact uses, both profane and sacred, of this plant.

Botany and Biology of the Species

Although *T. cacao* and *T. bicolor* have many characteristics in common, there are a variety of significant differences in their structure, to the degree that *T. bicolor* was once moved into a separate genus, *Tribroma* (Cook 1915). *Theobroma bicolor* grows more rapidly than *T. cacao* and is a much larger tree. It has a different branching pattern; larger, more durable pods with a different surface structure; and larger seeds, lacking the bitterness of *T. cacao* (Cook 1916) (Figures 4.1, 4.2, and 4.3). The fruits have been described as "very handsome, because of the curious white and green network covering the shell, reminding one somewhat of certain varieties of muskmelons. In general appearance they are very unlike the fruits of any other cultivated species [of the genus *Theobroma*]" (Standley, Steyermark, and Williams 1949:423). As the pods dry, their surface comes to resemble the pattern on a jaguar's pelt (see Figure 4.2). This pattern has likely led to one of the common names for *T. bicolor* in Mesoamerica, *balam te'* (the Jaguar Tree). The pods emit a strong fragrance for one to two weeks after they have fallen from the tree. This fragrance is particularly aromatic in the evenings. Unlike the seeds of *T. cacao*, the mature seeds of *T. bicolor* do not contain significant amounts of caffeine, but they often contain significant amounts of theobromine (Hammerstone, Romanczyk, and Aitken 1994; Sotelo and Alvarez 1991). *Theobroma bicolor* is capable of growing at higher altitudes than *T. cacao* and has a more limited flowering season. Whereas *T. cacao* can produce flowers all year (with two main seasons) and has an indefinite number of inflorescences originating from the same bud, *T. bicolor* flowers only in the dry season and produces only one inflorescence per bud (Cook 1916:617). Whereas the pods of *T. cacao* remain on the tree even after ripening, possibly as a result of domestication (Cuatrecasas 1964), the pods of *T. bicolor* fall from the tree when ripe, facilitating natural propagation without human aid. These pods, which

Figure 4.1. Immature *Theobroma bicolor* pod on a tree. San Antonio Suchitepequez, Guatemala. Photograph by Cameron L. McNeil.

Figure 4.2. *Theobroma* pods purchased in the market. San Antonio Suchitepequez, Guatemala. Left and center: *T. cacao.* Right: *T. bicolor.* Photograph by Cameron L. McNeil.

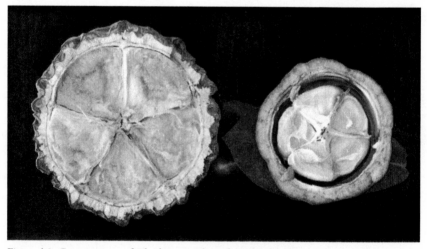

Figure 4.3. Cross sections of *Theobroma* pods. Left: *T. bicolor.* Right: *T. cacao.* Photograph by Cameron L. McNeil.

often must survive a fall from branches high in the forest canopy, have a thick woody shell and are sometimes used as containers in South America, much like the fruit of the calabash tree, *Crescentia cujete* L. (Cuatrecasas 1964:463; see Bletter and Daly, Figure 2.9, this volume).

At a time when plant domestication was discussed in terms of a simple dichotomy, "wild versus domesticated," there was some debate concerning whether *T. bicolor* has ever been "truly domesticated" or was only spared as a useful wild species when forests were cleared (Millon 1955a:13). Plant domestication is best understood, however, as an ongoing process with different degrees of interaction between people and plants. *Theobroma bicolor* is somewhere in the middle of this process and should therefore be called a managed, or semi-domesticated, species. It is distributed from Mexico to Brazil and Bolivia, sharing a range similar to that of *T. cacao* (Cuatrecasas 1964:463).

Archaeological Evidence for *T. bicolor* Use

Unfortunately, because of its morphological similarity to *T. cacao*, it is not possible to definitively document the presence of *T. bicolor* in iconography. The recovery of *T. cacao* in the archaeological record is rare (see McNeil, Chapter 1, this volume), and the identification of *T. bicolor* is even rarer. C. L. Lundell, the botanist who first brought the Classic period Maya site of Calakmul, Mexico, to worldwide attention, identified a seed recovered from a sealed late Early Classic period cache vessel at Tikal, Guatemala, as *T. bicolor* (Moholy-Nagy, Haviland, and Jones 2003:95). Unfortunately, no documentation remains to explain this identification, which could have been based on the chemical or morphological differences between the two species. Another possible reference to *T. bicolor* may appear on the well-known "lock-top" cacao vessel from Río Azul, Guatemala (see Hurst, Figure 5.7, this volume). Inscriptions on this vessel indicate that it contained two different types of cacao (D. Stuart 1988). This may refer to *T. cacao* and *T. bicolor*. Francisco Hernández, writing in the sixteenth century, reports that such a drink, made of both species of *Theobroma*, was considered particularly nutritious (Hernández 2000 [1571–1615]:109) and may have helped the deceased on the journey to the afterlife. Analysis of vessel residues at Copan, Honduras, identified two vessels which contained theobromine but not caffeine (McNeil, Hurst, and Sharer, this volume). It is possible that these vessels contained *T. bicolor* rather than *T. cacao*. One of the vessels also contained turkey bones. Although the authors are not aware of any modern uses of *pataxte* seeds in savory or meat dishes, festival *moles* in Copan are today made with peanuts, which have a flavor similar to that of *T. bicolor*. It is possible that *pataxte* seeds were formerly used in a similar way.

Local Names for *T. bicolor*

Today, local names for *T. bicolor* in Central and South America are often combinations with the word "cacao," most frequently "wild cacao," but also "white cacao" (presumably referring to the color of the seeds) and *cacao malacayo* (Cuatrecasas 1964:462). In some places, especially at higher altitudes where only *T.*

bicolor but not *T. cacao* grows, people may simply refer to *T. bicolor* as "cacao" (Breedlove and Laughlin 1993). This practice is sometimes also found in areas where both species thrive. When McNeil showed a *T. bicolor* pod to women both selling and buying produce in the marketplace next to the bus terminal in Coban, Guatemala, asking what it was called, they replied that its name was "cacao." When asked if it had another name, one of the fruit and vegetable sellers said it was also called *balam*. In Mesoamerica several variants of the Nahuatl-derived word *pataxte* are used. Francisco Hernández, writing in the sixteenth century, records that this tree is called "*quauhpatlachtli*" in Nahuatl (2000 [1571–1615]:108).[1] In different Maya languages, especially those of the K'iche' subfamily, variants of *peq* are used for *T. bicolor* today (Cuatrecasas 1964:462), just as they have been used for plants of the genus *Theobroma* since Preclassic times (Kaufman and Justeson, this volume). This term may originally have referred to *T. cacao* or to both species rather than specifically to *T. bicolor*. Other Maya groups refer to *T. bicolor* as the Jaguar Tree: among the Q'eqchi' and the Yukatek Maya it is called *balam te'* (Roys 1931:216; Standley, Steyermark, and Williams 1949:422); and among the Lacandon, *balum te'* (McGee 1990:39).

Modern Profane Uses

Like cacao, *pataxte* has continued to be an important plant for the Maya. Writing in 1916, O. F. Cook noted that cacao and *pataxte* seeds were two of the only goods that Maya people would pay money for and that, at least in the case of *T. cacao*, few of these products were still produced in Guatemala and therefore had to be brought in from the West Indies to supply the demands of workers on coffee plantations (Cook 1916:610). At that time, plantation owners had created a system of slave-like servitude, which operated by selling desired goods to workers at inflated prices that the workers could never repay.

In areas where *pataxte* is grown, the seeds are not the only part used for human consumption. The pulp of *T. bicolor* is also eaten. It is pinkish orange, with a flavor not as sweet as the pulp of *T. cacao*, reminding one of a cross between cantaloupe and papaya. It is most frequently eaten fresh (see Figure 4.4) but can also be made into a beverage (Furlan and Bressani 1999). The seeds, which lack caffeine and contain only small amounts of theobromine (Sotelo and Alvarez 1991), are less bitter than the seeds of *T. cacao*, with a pleasant, mild taste. In communities where the tree is still grown, the nutritious seeds are roasted, salted, and then eaten like nuts or ground and made into beverages.

The seeds of *T. bicolor* are known in commerce as "tiger," *wariba*, or *patashte* cacao (Standley, Steyermark, and Williams 1949:423). The name "tiger cacao" may be a translation of the indigenous name *balamte*, Jaguar

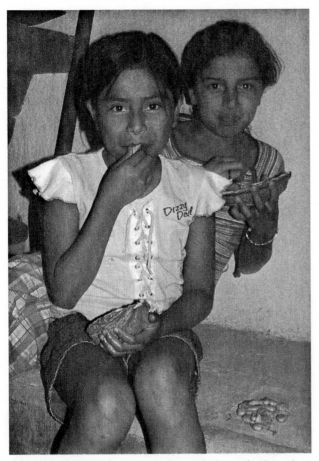

Figure 4.4. Girls enjoying the pulp from *Theobroma bicolor* pods. Copan, Honduras. Photograph by Cameron L. McNeil.

Tree (discussed above), since *tigre* is often substituted for "jaguar" in Meso-american Spanish.

On grounds of taste alone, it is unlikely that *T. bicolor* would be considered inferior to *T. cacao*. In fact, some Maya people favor *T. bicolor* seeds over those of *T. cacao*. Richard Wilk (1991:122) has written that the Q'eqchi' of southern Belize prefer *T. bicolor* for household consumption. In a trial of different *tiste* preparations (a cold drink concocted of cacao, sugar, cinnamon, *annatto*, and maize), made with either *T. bicolor* or *T. cacao*, most of the test persons preferred the drink with *T. bicolor* because it was less bitter (Furlan and Bressani 1999). Even in Mesoamerican *T. cacao* varieties, bitterness is not a desired quality. Rather, the opposite is true, and one of the main efforts of cacao breeders has been to combine the superior, less bitter taste of *criollo* cacao with the higher yields of *forastero* cacao, whose bitterness makes it inferior (see McNeil, Chapter 1, this volume).

However, when *pataxte* is used in ways analogous to cacao for the preparation of chocolate beverages from the parched seeds, it is considered inferior (see, e.g., Standley, Steyermark, and Williams 1949:423; Williams 1981:317; Wisdom 1940:61). Even in communities where *T. bicolor* is still sold in the marketplace, it is not sold in tablets, the easiest form in which to purchase *T. cacao* to create *chocolate* (see McNeil, Chapter 17, this volume).

Pataxte is most frequently sold as a complete pod or in *pinole* mixtures (see Figure 4.5). In some markets in areas of Guatemala where *pataxte* is locally grown, one can also find the seeds for sale. These seeds are a common additive in powdered *pinole* mixtures sold in Guatemalan outdoor markets. *Pinole* is a flour of maize (or rice), various spices (generally cinnamon and vanilla), sugar, and cacao and/or *pataxte*. In central and western Guatemala, *pataxte* is considered a crucial ingredient in the mixture. In some areas of western Guatemala, where *T. bicolor* is more common, *pinole* may be made only with *pataxte*. *Pinole* is viewed as a highly nutritional beverage and has a hardy flavor lacking the almost overpowering sweetness of chocolate (as it is commonly prepared in

Figure 4.5. Vendor selling *Theobroma bicolor* pods in the market. Mazatenango, Guatemala. Photograph by Cameron L. McNeil.

traditional Guatemalan communities). In the Oaxaca Valley, Mexico, *pataxte* seeds are favored for their fat content; the fat can be whipped into a "butter." The seeds are "calcified" by being buried in the ground with lime and sold in markets, where their rich fat is consumed with *atoles* (maize gruels) (Prescilla 2001:11).

At least in part, the preference for *T. cacao* may be due to the absence of caffeine and the lower amount of theobromine in mature seeds of *T. bicolor*, since these compounds enhance taste preferences for foods and drinks containing them (Smit and Blackburn 2005). Theobromine is a weak central nervous system stimulant, and its content in mature seeds of *T. bicolor*, though varying, is generally not high enough to produce a significant stimulant effect.

The Jaguar Tree

It is not only the differences in flavor and shape of the fruit and seeds that define *T. bicolor* as a distinct form of cacao. As we will discuss below, *T. bicolor* had a unique place in some ritual traditions. In the Chilam Balam of Chumayel, *T. bicolor* is mentioned as "the cacao called *balamte*," which exists in the first level of heaven (Roys 1967:111). In Yukatek Mayan, the word *balam* means both jaguar and priest (Roys 1967:111, n.3). As noted above, this name likely reflects Maya associations between the surface pattern on the pod and the pelt pattern on the jaguar. Whether this visual association actually attached the idea of *pataxte* to jaguars is unknown. Jaguars are associated with the night, caves, and the Underworld; in other words, they are associated with the same complex of symbols as cacao (see Kufer and Heinrich, this volume). The name Jaguar Tree underscores the ritual importance of *T. bicolor*. Jaguars are the strongest animals in the Maya world and are of enormous importance in Maya cosmology and ritual. The most powerful spirit companion (*way*, also called *nahual* in local Spanish, derived from Nahuatl) is the jaguar; this connection is reflected in the Yukatek usage of the word for jaguar in referring to a priest; jaguars also figure prominently in ritual dances and as guardians of sacred caves (see, e.g., Christenson 2001).

The clear visual link between *T. bicolor* and jaguars likely imbued the plant and its products with some characteristics of the sacred and awe-inspiring animal. That *T. bicolor* does not depend on humans for its propagation, and holds its pods high up in mature trees, giving them up only when ready, further distinguishes it from *T. cacao* and associates it with wild animals, such as the jaguar. Monument 4 at the archaeological site of El Baúl on the Pacific Coast of Guatemala bears a jaguar sprouting cacao or *pataxte* pods (Figure 4.6). Unfortunately, without knowing the ethnicity or language of the people who inhabited this area during the Classic period, it is not possible to say whether they

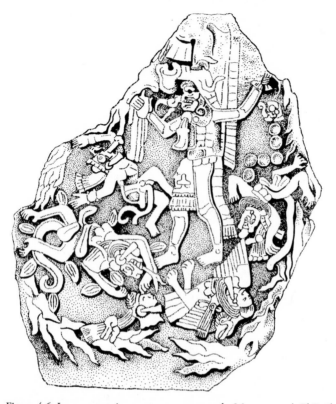

Figure 4.6. Jaguar sprouting cacao or *pataxte* pods. Monument 4, El Baúl, Guatemala. Late Classic period. Drawing by Eliud Guerra after J.E.S. Thompson (1948:Figure 5a).

associated *T. bicolor* with jaguars. J. Eric S. Thompson (1970:166) noted that some Maya hunters in Belize consumed jaguar ants—so called because of their jaguar-like markings—to "harness the prowess" of this animal. Eating the fruits of the Jaguar Tree may have held similar associations.

The differences between cacao and *pataxte* are particularly meaningful in the context of the important distinction between wild and civilized space which Maya people have emphasized in their cosmologies (Taube 2003a). Of the two *Theobroma* species, *T. bicolor* is certainly the one which better represents the wild space, the forest. On the other hand, although *T. cacao* is more domesticated than *T. bicolor*, it is not the plant which best represents civilized space for the Maya. This role belongs to maize. It is possible that the Maya prefer *T. bicolor* for certain ritual uses partly because as the "wilder" type of cacao, it makes a better counterpart to maize, the most "civilized" of all plants, which grows in the cultivated four-cornered space of the *milpa* and provides the material basis of Maya civilization.

Modern Ritual Uses of *T. bicolor*

Pataxte is sometimes used alone in Maya ritual, but it is more frequently found in conjunction with *T. cacao*. For example, in the Guatemalan departments of Solola, Quetzaltenango, and Mazatenango, *pataxte* is one of a group of fruits used for confraternity and Ladino festivals, adorning arches and Easter monuments during Holy Week (Figure 4.7) (Christenson 2001:84, 87, 98, 167; Hostnig, Hostnig, and Vásquez 1998:165; McNeil, Chapter 17, this volume). Maya poetic speech often uses the pair "*pataxte* and cacao," as in the following passage from the recorded Highland Maya dance drama Rab'inal Achi, also known as Dance of the Trumpets:

> There are some
> Shaded by quetzal feathers
>   Shaded by glistening green
> Under the golden *pataxte*
>   Under the golden cacao
> Under the golden money
>   Under the silver money
> (. . .)
> Here the only things that need care
>   are *pataxte* seeds by the score
>   cacao seeds by the score. (D. Tedlock 2003:49)

Pairing of two similar objects is a frequent feature of Maya poetic speech and may be used to emphasize the importance of what is said. In the example above, it may be a poetic feature to underscore the preciousness of cacao. In another example from the K'iche' creation story known as the *Popol Vuh*, the paired *pataxte* and cacao may also serve to make up the holy number four together with two kinds of maize.

> And so they were happy over the provisions of the good mountain, filled with sweet things, thick with yellow corn, white corn, and thick with *pataxte* and cacao. (D. Tedlock 1996:146)

Although *pataxte* and cacao are clearly a powerful ritual pair among Highland Maya groups, there are some ritual contexts in which *pataxte* is used alone. For example, in some Mam communities only *pataxte* fruits, but not *T. cacao*, are used as a ritual offering to sacred springs and for preventive health ceremonies (Hostnig, Hostnig, and Vásquez 1998:164). The Confraternity of San Juan in the town of Santiago Atitlan, Guatemala, keeps a sacred bundle of great ritual importance, called the Martín bundle, in a chest carved with depictions of two

Figure 4.7. (*Left*) Putting up the arch for Semana Santa. (*Below*) The decorated crossbeam waits to be pulled into place. San Antonio Suchitepequez, Guatemala. Photograph courtesy of Rony Romeo Reyes Rosales.

Figure 4.8. Chest containing a sacred bundle. Two *pataxte* pods are carved on the right and left front of the chest. Between them a "split-cob maize" is flanked by a deer and a bull. Confraternity of San Juan, Santiago Atitlan, Guatemala. Photograph by Cameron L. McNeil.

pataxte pods and an ear of "split-cob maize" (such maize ears have a particular ritual significance) (Christenson 2001:157; McNeil, field notes 2005) (Figure 4.8). An informant said that an earlier box bore a cacao pod on one side and a *pataxte* pod on the other. In Santiago Atitlan, where *pataxte* pods are used for many ritual occasions, the goddess of the midwives is said to have breasts of *pataxte* pods (see McNeil, Chapter 17, this volume).

In certain areas at higher altitudes, where *T. bicolor* can grow but *T. cacao* cannot, the use of the former species on its own may simply be attributable to easier availability, especially when fresh fruits and leaves are used. In addition, the particularly beautiful fruit of *T. bicolor* with its strong fragrance likely makes a better ritual adornment than does *T. cacao*.

Taste and smell preferences among humans are highly variable, however, and the fragrance of *pataxte* fruits does not appeal to everybody. In San Antonio Suchitepequez, the man in charge of the ritual adornment of the Easter arches explained to McNeil that he used *pataxte* for embellishing the arches out of respect for the tradition of his ancestors but found both the smell and taste of *pataxte* unappealing and preferred not to have it in his house (Figure 4.7).

In ritual contexts specifically related to maturing processes, such as rites of passage, there may be another reason *pataxte* is preferred over *T. cacao*. The ritual importance of this plant is explicitly stressed by Martín Prechtel (1999) in his account of Tz'utujiil youth initiations in the 1970s. The first use of *pataxte* was as an indispensable ingredient in the ritual cacao drink *qátouj*, which also contained *T. cacao*, maize, and ground *zapote* seeds (*Pouteria sapota* [Jacq.] H. E. Moore and Stearn). Prechtel (1999:288) emphasizes the very strong fragrance and the beautiful complex surface structure of the pods, which he contrasts with the comparatively plain and "prosaic" look and smell of domesticated cacao. The second use of *pataxte* in youth initiations was during the "final test of the boys' graduation," which consisted of maturing within three days a pack of five tropical fruits picked while still green, one of which was a *pataxte* pod. This process took place in the initiation hall, which was kept closed and dark during that time and was decorated with an abundance of fragrant ritual plants. The decoration of the ceiling included, among flowers and other fruit, lots of "cacao" pods, here presumably referring either to *pataxte* or to both *Theobroma* species, as the strong fragrance and more decorative pod structure make *pataxte* fruits a particularly suitable ritual adornment (Prechtel 1999: 306–307). A contemporary practice for ripening fruit both in Santiago Atitlan and along the western coast of Guatemala provides a likely explanation for this specific use of *pataxte*: Fruit growers of the Pacific Coast of Guatemala enclose a ripe fruit of *T. bicolor* with other fruits, such as bananas, which have been picked while still green, to make them mature more quickly (Ricardo Bressani, personal communication 2003; McNeil, field observation 2004). Presumably, the very fragrant fruit of *T. bicolor* produces a large amount of ethylene, a volatile plant hormone which triggers fruit ripening and also is produced in ripe fruits. The production of ethylene allows trees to synchronize the ripening of their fruits, which is particularly important for plants with a defined fruiting season, like apples or *T. bicolor*. Such plants rely on the production of an abundance of fruits at one time so that at least some seeds will survive predators. As a species with a less defined fruiting season, *T. cacao* produces less ethylene. In Santiago Atitlan, decorating the initiation hall with abundant ripe *pataxte* pods may have created ethylene concentrations sufficient for starting the ripening process even of fruits picked long before maturity.

Pataxte among the Nahua

Whereas there are numerous records from different historical and contemporary sources indicating the importance of *T. bicolor* in Maya ritual, the situation among the Nahua seems to be different. *Pataxte* was frequently used as an adulterant of cacao by unscrupulous Aztec merchants, indicating that its value was lower than that of *T. cacao* (S. D. Coe and M. D. Coe 1996:99). Francisco Hernández, writing in the sixteenth century, records that the "seeds, which are sweeter than the others [varieties of cacao] can be eaten like almonds, roasted or with sugar, although they are less suitable for making a drink" (2000 [1571–1615]:108).

In this context it is important to bear in mind that much of the symbolism derived from characteristics of the living tree, such as its "wilder" character (in comparison with *T. cacao*) and the fragrance, fruit-ripening properties, and beauty of the fresh fruit which make it particularly suitable as a ritual adornment and element of initiation rites, was less accessible to the peoples of Central Mexico, where the tree does not grow and only the seeds are available as a trade item.

The reputation of *pataxte* as an adulterant and inferior substitute for *T. cacao*, prevailing in the botanical literature and Colonial sources, is surprising in view of its prominent role in Maya ritual. It is possible that some of this reputation is due to a European misunderstanding regarding its individual significance in Mesoamerica. Colonial records, especially about plant uses, are much more detailed for the Nahua than for the Maya; thus, it would not be too surprising if the predominant interpretations of *pataxte*'s role in Mesoamerica reflected the Nahua rather than the Maya perspective. Moreover, information about ritual plant uses was and is less accessible to outsiders than information about economically important plants, which makes it easy to overlook the importance of plants like *T. bicolor*, whose main uses seem to be in the ritual domain.

A Lost Tree

Theobroma bicolor is becoming a lost tree. To an even greater degree than cacao, which has been replaced in many communities by coffee, *T. bicolor* seems to have been on a path to marginalization since the arrival of Europeans and has disappeared altogether from many areas of Mesoamerica. Even in zones where it is still appreciated, such as the west coast of Guatemala, people said that it is rarely planted and that most trees exist as relicts (McNeil, field notes 2005). Although *pataxte* is still found along the coast of Honduras, in Copan, which is located along the Honduran/Guatemalan border, it appears to have been lost. Wilson Popenoe, writing in 1919, noted that *T. bicolor* was one of the economically useful plants found in the Copan Valley (W. Popenoe 1919b). Today, however, the authors could not find anyone who grew the tree. Similarly, in the town of Jocotan, near the Guatemalan side of the border, *pataxte* was grown and used as late as the 1930s (Wisdom 1940:61), but the tree is no longer grown today.

Conclusion

Theobroma bicolor has received far less attention by researchers than its close relative *T. cacao*, and because of the frequent use of the name "cacao" for *T. bicolor*, many records may fail to distinguish between the two species. A careful review of the available information seems to indicate that *T. bicolor* was of far greater importance in pre-Columbian Mesoamerica than previously recognized, especially for the Maya. The authors hope that this chapter will encourage future study of this important plant. Clearly, *T. bicolor* is not simply the wild and inferior form of *T. cacao*, but its deeper meaning within Maya culture has been obscured by the writings and assumptions of outsiders. In a time when traditional plant uses are disappearing from indigenous communities, it is particularly important to try to understand the cultural significance of this plant while the knowledge about it is still alive.

Acknowledgments

The authors appreciate the help of Juan Carlos Rodriguez in conducting research for this chapter. Allen Christenson also generously provided assistance for this study. Many thanks to Ricardo Bressani, Universidad del Valle de Guatemala, who first drew our attention to the practice of ripening fruits with *pataxte* pods. We would also like to thank the Museo Nacional de Arqueología y Etnología, Guatemala City, and Oswaldo Chinchilla Mazariegos of the Museo Popol Vuh, Guatemala City. Many people in Santiago Atitlan, Guatemala City, Mazatenango, and San Antonio Suchitepequez provided valuable information on *T. bicolor*. They are not individually thanked here to protect their privacy.

Note

1. The suffix *-patlachtli* means 'wide' or 'broad'—possibly referring to the morphological differences in pod and seed structure between *T. bicolor* and *T. cacao*. A reliable linguistic interpretation of the term *pataxte* was not available at the time this chapter was completed, however.

5

The Determination of Cacao
in Samples of Archaeological Interest

W. Jeffrey Hurst

Although the use of cacao by Mesoamerican peoples has been discussed and documented since the early Colonial period, archaeologists have been hindered from discovering the breadth of its usage in rituals and daily life by its rare recovery from archaeological contexts. In 1989 the author was approached with the challenge of chemically determining whether cacao was present in residues from vessels recovered from Classic period tombs in Río Azul, Guatemala. Success in this endeavor has opened a new area of research into the manner in which cacao was used in pre-Columbian times and has shown that cacao was consumed in Mesoamerica at least a thousand years earlier than was previously known. In this chapter I will discuss the results of analyses on cacao samples from a range of contexts and explain the methods for chemically determining the presence of *Theobroma cacao* in decayed macrofossils and residues.

Cacao contains more than 400 discrete chemical compounds with the list continuing to grow as new analytical techniques allow researchers to detect smaller quantities of compounds. Although cacao contains a plethora of compounds, some of these, while not totally unique to cacao, are rare enough and occur in quantities that allow them to be used as marker compounds. Marker compounds are those chemical entities that are unique to the commodity in question.

One group of these compounds is the methylxanthines. The methylxanthine class contains a number of compounds based on the purine nucleus. The primary members of this class are caffeine (1,3,7-trimethylxanthine), theobromine (3,7-dimethylxanthine), and theophylline (1,3-dimethylxanthine); caffeine is the member of the class that occurs primarily in coffee. The methylxanthines have also been called purine alkaloids. Cacao is the only Mesoamerican commodity in which theobromine is the primary methylxanthine, so this compound was used for primary analytical studies. Before the advent of modern Liquid Chromatography/Mass Spectrometry (LC/MS) interface techniques and micromethods, it was necessary to perform this type of determination using wet chemical techniques that can require a substantial sample or techniques based on Gas Chromatography (GC) that require derivatization. Liquid Chromatography/Mass Spectrometry is a method in which compounds are separated from one another based on chemical differences by liquid chromatography, and the resulting compounds are identified by mass spectrometry. The data from the mass spectrometer provides information about the molecular identity of the compound. The combination of these two techniques is then used to chemically identify unknown materials. The term "micromethods" can refer to a number of analytical techniques and in this case means that determinations can now be accomplished using much smaller quantities of material than did previous methods. Gas Chromatography is another separation technique in which it is necessary for compounds to be in a volatile physical form, requiring the researcher to chemically convert compounds to a form that is suitable for the GC.

Four studies on samples of archaeological interest have been conducted using High Performance Liquid Chromatography (HPLC) with Thermospray MS, Capillary Electrophoresis (CE), and Atmospheric Pressure Chemical Ionization (APCI) LC/MS. The samples came from diverse locations in Central America, including Belize and Honduras. In this chapter I will outline the experimental protocols and techniques that have been used in each of these studies.

Collection of Archaeological Samples for Analysis

Samples were collected for analyses in a variety of ways. In ideal circumstances, preserved uncontaminated residues were recovered from tomb vessels. The recovery of vessels from largely uncontaminated contexts is rare, however, but the analysis of vessels filled with sediment or small fragments of vessels is feasible and has been shown to have productive results. Some excavators submitted samples of the lowest layer of sediments resting in vessels recovered from excavations. Others actually scraped a thin layer of ceramic from the inside bottom of the vessels. In a third case, sherds were boiled in water to extract the chemical components of foods formerly housed in the vessels. In some cases the author has been able to retrieve the chemical components of cacao from previously washed vessels.

Cacao Chemistry

The chemistry of cacao is complex. Fifteen compounds that occur in the unfermented cacao bean are listed in Table 5.1. We currently know that at least

Table 5.1. Composition of unfermented cacao bean

Water	Glucose	Tannins
Fat	Starch	Acetic Acid
Ash	Pectins	Oxalic Acid
Protein	Fiber	
Theobromine	Cellulose	
Caffeine	Pentosans	

Source: Knapp 1937

462 different volatile compounds occur in cacao. A portion of a review by Flament (1989) focused on cacao volatiles. Volatiles are chemical compounds that can be vaporized or can undergo evaporation under specific conditions such as while being analyzed by GC. The first work in this area was reported by Bainbridge and Davies in 1912. They cited the presence of thirteen compounds in cacao; this list has now grown to 462. With the advances in analytical technology, this number will likely continue to increase. Additionally, this list only covers cacao volatiles and does not include compounds such as amino acids, lipids, phospholipids, and other entities in cacao that are nonvolatile; thus, the number of compounds in cacao actually exceeds 500 (Zoumas and Smullen 1991).

Selection of Cacao Marker

From the large number of chemical compounds in cacao, it was necessary to select a marker that would satisfy a number of requirements. It had to be unique to cacao, stable, and occur at levels sufficient for trace analysis. With these parameters as a guide, a member of the methylxanthine class of compounds was chosen as the marker. The members of this class occurring in cacao are caffeine (1,3,7-trimethylxanthine), theophylline (1,3-dimethylxanthine), and theobromine (3,7-dimethylxanthine). The numbers in front of the chemical name for these compounds indicate the position of the methyl group (CH_3) on the base compound. Caffeine is the major methylxanthine in coffee, and theobromine is the major methylxanthine in cacao. Although cacao does contain caffeine, it is approximately 10 percent of the level of theobromine. Theophylline also occurs in cacao but in negligible amounts. Theobromine was the compound chosen (Figure 5.1).

Theobromine is sparsely distributed and occurs in nineteen species including *Theobroma cacao* L. (cacao), *Coffea arabica* L. (coffee), *Camellia sinensis* (L.) Kuntze (tea plant), *Cola vera* K. Schum. (kola nut), and *Ilex paraguariensis* A. St.-Hil. (*yerba mate*) (Athyade, Coelho, and Schenkel 2000; Bispo et al. 2002; Fernández et al. 2002). Research indicated that although other botanicals con-

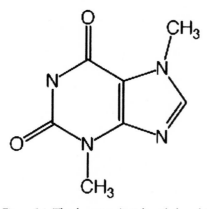

Figure 5.1. Theobromine (3,7 dimethylxanthine).

tained theobromine, cacao was the only commodity that contained theobromine as the major methylxanthine.

Overview of Methods of Analysis

The analysis of the methylxanthines is important in food- and nutrition-related research and clinical chemistry and can be accomplished using a variety of techniques. In this section I will provide an overview of the methods of analysis (for a more extensive discussion see Hurst, Martin, and Tarka 1998). Historically, methods have tended to focus on the major methylxanthine in a commodity, such as caffeine in coffee and theobromine in cacao, with the result that minor compounds such as the caffeine in cacao were either missed in the analytical scheme or included in the amount of the major methylxanthine. These determinations have been conducted through any number of analytical techniques, including spectrophotometry (measuring light absorption), gravimetric analysis (precipitating and weighing), or titrametric analysis (chemical reaction with a known amount of another compound). In early methods, the methylxanthines were extracted with hot aqueous or hot alkaline (basic) solution and then transferred to an organic solvent such as chloroform. It was also necessary to perform a preliminary separation of this extract because amino acids, polyphenols, and carbohydrates were also extracted in addition to the methylxanthines. These other compounds were known to interfere with the assay, causing incorrect results. In the case of cacao, it was also necessary to extract it with hexane, petroleum ether, or some other appropriate solvent to eliminate the large amount of lipid (commonly called cocoa butter) that would also interfere with the analysis. Thin Layer Chromatography (TLC) was the next analytical method that was used for the determination of the methylxanthines.

Thin Layer Chromatography is a valuable, inexpensive tool for both qualitative and quantitative analysis, but it does not tend to be as accurate and precise as modern Gas and Liquid Chromatography. Gas Chromatography is a popular analytical technique because of its speed, versatility, precision, and reliability. It can analyze complex mixtures through the use of a wide variety of detectors. It has been used for the analysis of methylxanthines but requires that a volatile derivative be made. High Performance Liquid Chromatography has become the technique of choice for the analysis of the methylxanthines because it has the ability to directly and selectively analyze these compounds with good accuracy and precision. The HPLC technique is the method approved by the Association of Official Analytical Chemists (AOAC) for the determination of theobromine and caffeine in chocolate and confectionery products (Kreiser and Martin 2000). In this method we use a reversed phase HPLC column with a mobile phase consisting of methanol, water, and acetic acid with UV detection. Finally, Capillary Electrophoresis has become another technique that allows for the separation of different chemicals, offering researchers the ability to perform HPLC type separations on small diameter silica tubing with minimal use of solvent. The techniques that have been used for the determination of cacao in archaeological samples have been based primarily on HPLC with one use of CE.

Method for Analysis of Archaeological Samples

Homogeneous samples of approximately 500 mg were withdrawn from the sample vials provided. They were each placed in individual flasks and 3 ml of hot distilled water at 80°C was added to solubilize any materials. Each sample was heated in a water bath at 85°C for an additional 20 minutes and was monitored to ensure there was no excess evaporation of water. Samples were then allowed to cool to room temperature and filtered through 0.45 &m filters before placing them into HPLC sample vials. The HPLC analysis involved the use of a Shimadzu 10AD VP system equipped with a variable wavelength detector and a Shimadzu QP8000 MS. The interface used was the APCI probe operated in the positive ion mode monitoring m/z 181 $(M + H)^+$ for the theobromine and 195$(M + H)^+$ for the caffeine. The m/z 181 and m/z 195 are the molecular ions for theobromine and caffeine, respectively. The UV detector was set at 270 nm. A uBondapak C18 column (3.9 mm x 150 mm) from Waters was used for the separation of the theobromine and caffeine with a mobile phase of 71/29/0.1

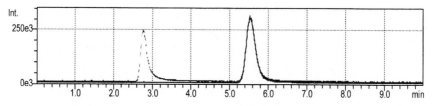

Figure 5.2. Total Ion Chromatogram (TIC) for theobromine (~2.8 min) and caffeine (~5.6 min).

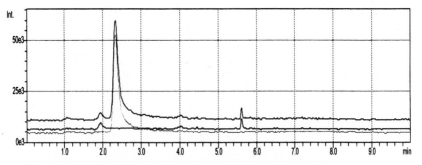

Figure 5.3. Total Ion Chromatogram (TIC) of Colha, Belize, vessel extract.

Figure 5.4. Vessel from Colha, Belize, that tested positive for cacao. Photograph courtesy of Terry Powis.

(water/methanol/acetic acid) flowing at 1 ml/min. Standards were obtained from Sigma and checked for purity using established analytical techniques in addition to MS and made up to concentrations of 50 mg/L. Two µl amounts of the standards and 25 µl volumes of the extracts were injected onto the HPLC. Figure 5.2 provides an example of the Total Ion Chromatogram (TIC) for theobromine and caffeine standard compounds. Figure 5.3 is a TIC of the theobromine and caffeine in residue from a Preclassic period vessel from Colha, Belize (see Figure 5.4).

Information from this chromatogram (Figure 5.2) shows a clear peak at the same retention time as theobromine (red trace) and also a corresponding peak for m/z 181 (green trace). Additionally, the TIC shows a smaller peak at the same retention time as caffeine with the corresponding peak for m/z 195 (blue trace). Furthermore, theobromine and caffeine occur in cacao at ~1/10 ratio, and, as this sample indicates, there is a large amount of theobromine and a much smaller amount of caffeine. High Performance Liquid Chromatography with UV detection is used routinely for the analysis of caffeine and theobromine in cacao and chocolate products and is an official AOAC method. Other modes of detection have also been used, including amperometry, but none can offer the unequivocal identity provided by MS. Although UV data are excellent for routine usage, they can be of limited value when analyzing small amounts of material because UV spectra for related compounds can be very similar. In this application, for example, the chromatograms based on UV detection are illustrated in Figures 5.5 and 5.6. Figure 5.5 is the chromatogram for the theobromine and caffeine standards, and Figure 5.6 is a chromatogram from a vessel extract. The resulting data are much less clear when compared to MS data.

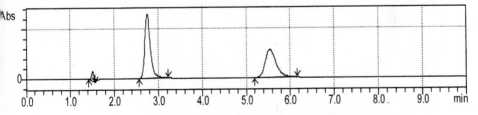

Figure 5.5. Chromatogram of theobromine and caffeine standards with UV detection.

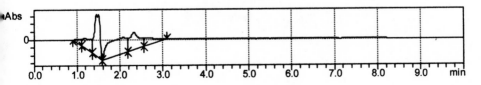

Figure 5.6. Chromatogram of vessel extract with UV detection.

Applications

The basic technique described above has been applied to samples from four different archaeological sites. In the first instance, Hurst, Martin, Tarka, and Hall (1989) successfully used HPLC coupled with Thermospray MS to identify cacao residues in the vessels at Río Azul, Guatemala (Figure 5.7). Capillary Electrophoresis with UV detection and derivative spectroscopy was used to identify cacao in samples thought to be whole cacao beans dating to the Classic period, obtained from the Maya Mountain region of southern Belize (Hurst, Tarka, and Prufer 1998; Prufer, personal communication 1997). In the last case, the sample size was minute, and although CE-MS is becoming more routine, it was not available to analyze those samples. The technique described in this chapter

Figure 5.7. Ceramic "lock-top" cacao vessel. Classic period. Río Azul, Guatemala. Museo Nacional de Arqueología y Etnología, Guatemala City. Photograph courtesy of Grant D. Hall.

was applied in the next two instances and involved samples from Colha, Belize, and from Copan, Honduras (one vessel from Colha, which tested positive for cacao, is illustrated in Figure 5.4). The results from the Colha samples have been published (Powis et al. 2002); the Copan results are described in McNeil, Hurst, and Sharer (this volume).

Conclusion

What has resulted from the studies described in this chapter and other publications is the development of a selective and sensitive analytical technique that can be used in samples from archaeological sites to determine the presence of cacao. Although there is much cultural and anecdotal information concerning the use of cacao among the Maya, this technique allows the researcher to analytically determine the presence of this material. Additionally, the technique is straightforward, making it amenable to analyzing large numbers of samples for the development of an appropriate database.

Acknowledgments

These types of endeavors are not singular activities but collaborations of many. I was honored to be chosen to head this effort. I extend thanks to The Hershey Company for its continued support of my work and to my colleagues at Hershey. I also thank Grant Hall, Terry Powis, Cameron McNeil, and Keith Prufer for their spirit of collaboration in this extremely satisfying pursuit. Finally, my deepest thanks to my wife, Deborah, who is always supportive of yet another project. I gladly share credit with all.

PART II

Cacao in Pre-Columbian Cultures

6

The History of the Word for 'Cacao' and Related Terms in Ancient Meso-America

Terrence Kaufman and John Justeson

This study addresses a problem in linguistic reconstruction that is relevant to work on lexical diffusion in Meso-America and thereby to research on intercultural interaction that probably dates to the Preclassic period. It focuses on the origin and spread of the widely diffused form *kakawa* (and variants) as a word for cacao (*Theobroma cacao* L.) in Meso-American languages.[1] It also addresses the history of the word *chokol=a:-tl*.

Cacao was a major crop in pre-Columbian Meso-America. Most commonly, the kernel was ground and beaten with water, flavorings, and usually maize to make a drink, one version of which we know as chocolate.[2] In historical times, among Meso-American Indians, the pulp that surrounds the kernels inside the husk has been and is often fermented to produce an alcoholic beverage (see McNeil, Chapter 17, this volume). Aztecs, and arguably Teotihuacanos and other pre-Columbian societies, made strong efforts to control the production and distribution of cacao. The kernel came to be used as currency—reflected, for example, by Xinka /tuwa/, meaning both 'cacao' and 'money.'

Cacao has long been grown in South America, Lower Central America, and Meso-America. In Meso-America, archaeologically recovered remains of cacao have been dated to as early as 600 B.C. in Belize (Hurst et al. 2002); the earliest dates for the associated vessel types go back to 700–1000 B.C. in the Ulua Valley, Honduras (Henderson and Joyce, this volume). Cultivated and escaped *T. cacao* is now widely distributed in lowland areas of Meso-America, and *T. bicolor* grows uncultivated in some of these areas.

There is one widely attested term for 'cacao' whose distribution is largely the result of diffusion: Mije-Sokean *kakawa* ~ *kakaw*, Nawa /kakawa-tl/, Masawa /kakawa/, general Mayan, Totonako, and Salvador Lenka /kakaw/, Paya [kaku], and Tarasko *khékua*. Boruka, Tol, and Honduras Lenka have [kaw], and

Mobe has [ku]. An antecedent form similar to [kVwa] is reflected in Amusgo and possibly in Chinanteko. A variety of other terms, none of them widespread, is found in other languages.

This study demonstrates that this word for 'cacao' originated in the Gulf Coast of southern Mexico, among speakers of an early Mije-Sokean language, as proposed by Campbell and Kaufman (1976). From there it spread to the Basin of Mexico—in the form *kakawa*—and, separately, into Mayan languages, probably, but not necessarily from Sokean. In Mayan the word came to be pronounced as *kakaw*. Probably from Mayan but perhaps from Mijean, *kakaw* spread to Honduras Lenka. From speakers of this language, most likely, it began spreading into other languages of lower Central America, as far south as Costa Rica. The term did not reach South America in pre-Columbian times.

Contrary to one recent proposal (Dakin and Wichmann 2000), Nawa had no role in the pre-Columbian development of this term.[3] However, Nawa /kakawa-tl/ is the source of the Spanish word *cacao*, which is pronounced /kakáwa/ (*cacahua*) in some regional types of Spanish; it is also the source of Spanish *cacahuate* (Iberian/Peninsular Spanish *cacahuete*) 'peanut.'

Traditionally, words for drinks made from cacao appear to have consisted either of the word for cacao itself or of that word together with modifiers. Other terms, not including the word for 'cacao,' but including a word meaning 'water, liquid' or a word meaning '(a) drink,' are known from Colonial and modern sources in various Meso-American languages. Among these is a Nawa word, attested variously as *chikol=a:-tl* and *chokol=a:-tl*, which spread to several European languages and then around the world. This term may have been coined during the sixteenth century. Contrary to persistent but uninformed speculation, Mayan languages played no role in the development of this term.

The Mije-Sokean Origin of *kakawa*

Using published materials available between 1959 and 1963, Kaufman (1963ms) reconstructed a vocabulary of about six hundred proto-Mijean (pM), proto-Sokean (pS), and proto-Mije-Sokean (pMS) words and affixes. This vocabulary included *kakawa* as the proto-Mije-Sokean word for 'cacao,' along with words for a large number of other lowland cultigens. Work by Kaufman and Campbell in the 1960s and 1970s (partly summarized in Campbell and Kaufman 1976) showed that many of these Mije-Sokean words appeared in other Meso-American language families, in which they were not reconstructible to the earliest stages. Mije-Sokean vocabulary proved to be found in every language family in Meso-America, from Tarasko in the north to Xinkan in the south, much of it early enough that the terms are reconstructible to early stages in the histories of most of those families.

The diffused words are found in a variety of semantic domains: they include words for plants, animals, tools, food preparation, the calendar and numerical calculation, and kinship and other social roles. The most numerous are names for plants and animals; more specifically, they are names for domesticated lowland plants and animals and for those wild plants and animals whose names are part of the Meso-American ritual calendar.

No other language families in Meso-America had anything like the impact that Mije-Sokean had, either in the range of linguistic families they affected or in the number of items that were borrowed from them, until late in pre-Columbian Meso-American history when Nawa loans began to be fairly widely adopted in Meso-American languages; and the number of Nawa loans does not approach the number of Mije-Sokean loans, although the former date from at least one thousand years later. Some of the Mije-Sokean loans probably go back to the influence of Olmecs, while others are attributable to a post-Olmec era of Mije-Sokean influence.

The widespread and early diffusion of the word *kakaw(a)* into a large number of Meso-American languages and language families fits the profile of these typical Mije-Sokean loans. In addition, one of the prime areas of cacao cultivation, in the lowlands of Tabasco, was part of the (Mije-Sokean-speaking) Olmec heartland, where Gulf Sokean languages are still spoken. These facts provide strong circumstantial support for Campbell and Kaufman's independently motivated hypothesis that this word is native to the Mije-Sokean family and diffused into other Meso-American languages, ultimately, from speakers of one or more Mije-Sokean languages. As a result, this hypothesis has been widely accepted. In fact, setting aside the recently contested case of *kakaw(a)*, no currently reconstructed proto-Mijean, proto-Sokean, or proto-Mije-Sokean term has a demonstrated foreign origin, so any alternative to a Mije-Sokean source requires substantial independent evidence.

This hypothesis was recently challenged, however, by Dakin and Wichmann (2000). They argue that *kakawa* developed within Nawa and from there spread to other languages in Meso-America. Here we provide additional evidence for the Mije-Sokean pedigree of the word; demonstrate that any hypothesis of Nawa origin is unlikely, given what is otherwise known of lexical diffusion from Nawa; and show that Dakin and Wichmann's own scenario for a Nawa origin is impossible.

Evidence for the development of *kakawa* in Sokean

Internal evidence that a word has been inherited by the languages of a genetic group from their common ancestor, rather than being borrowed, comes chiefly from evidence of changes that affected descendant languages in regular ways—that the forms of the words exhibit regular and recurrent sound cor-respondences. In the case of Sokean *kakawa*, such evidence comes from the rules for assigning stress, which is predictable in Sokean languages.

Stress rules can be recovered in two ways: by comparing the stress rules of the descendant languages, and by postulating stress on syllables that do not delete in words that lose syllables in some descendant languages.

All proto-Sokean words can be analyzed as having penult stress—stress on the second-to-last syllable—and as having had a weaker, secondary stress on the initial syllable of words having more than two syllables.[4] The paradigm for the disyllabic verb stem *tokoy* 'to get lost' exemplifies the penult stress rule:

category	meaning	form	pronunciation
incompletive	it gets lost	tokoy-pa	[tokóypa]
completive	it got lost	tokoy-wʉ	[tokóywʉ]
imperative	get lost!	tokoy-ʉ7	[tokóyʉ7]
optative	it should get lost	tokoy-7in	[tokóy7in]
dependent	when it gets/got lost	tokoy-e	[tokóye]
nominalized	(something) that has gotten lost	tokoy.e	[tokóye]

Probably around A.D. 500, Sokean languages split into two subgroups: Soke proper, now spoken in Chiapas and in the Chimalapa region of Oaxaca, and Gulf Sokean, now spoken in southern Veracruz in the towns of Soteapan and Texistepec and in Ayapa, Tabasco (see Figure 6.1). Soke inherited the proto-Sokean stress rule unchanged. Gulf Sokean languages also reflect this stress rule in most words. Among these are trisyllabic words, like those in the paradigm of *tokoy* cited above, whose first and/or second syllable ends in a consonant other than a glottal stop, /7/.

An innovation in the stress rule must be postulated for Gulf Sokean, how-ever: some trisyllabic words are stressed on the initial syllable and no longer on the penult syllable. The words undergoing this change are those trisyllabic words whose first and/or second syllables are either open (CV) or end in a glot-tal stop ($CV7$). This innovation affected Sokean *$CVCV7$* verb stems:

grammatical category	underlying form	pronunciation
incompletive	CVCV7-pa	[CV́:CV7pa]
completive	CVCV7-wʉ	[CV́:CV7wʉ]
imperative	CVCV7-ʉ7	[CV́:CV7ʉ7]
optative	CVCV7-7in	[CV́:CV77in]
dependent	CVCV7-e ~ CVCV7-i	[CV́:CV7e] ~ [CV́:CV7i]
nominalized	CVCV7.e ~ CVCV7.e	[CV́:CV7e] ~ [CV́:CV7i]

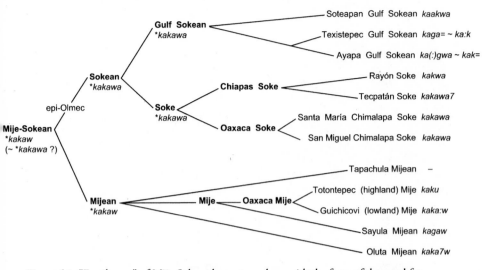

Figure 6.1. "Family tree" of Mije-Sokean languages, along with the form of the word for "cacao" in each language in which it is attested. For proto-Mije-Sokean it is possible to reconstruct either *kakaw* or *kakaw* varying with *kakawa*. For the evidence that Sayula Mijean is a form of Mije, see Kaufman (1994).

At least in SOT and TEX (the data for AYA are not yet all in), all these verb forms lost the penult syllable (including /7/); from these contracted forms a new *CV:C* stem shape was generalized.

The new rule also applied to trisyllabic roots, all of them nouns. Such roots are rare in Mije-Sokean languages, but five are attested both in Soke, where they are trisyllabic, and in Gulf Sokean, where they are disyllabic (see Table 6.1). In general, SOT and AYA stress the first syllable and lose the second, while TEX stresses the first syllable and loses the last. This shows that the first syllable was stressed in proto-Gulf Sokean; and the proto-Gulf Sokean forms must still have been trisyllabic, since TEX disagrees with SOT and AYA on which syllable is lost. Detailed discussion of the data on these and other pertinent words is provided elsewhere (Kaufman and Justeson in press).

The regularity of the results of syllable reduction and stress placement on descendants of *kakawa* shows that the form underwent regular changes in passing from proto-Sokean to proto-Gulf Sokean and from proto-Gulf Sokean to each of the modern Gulf Sokean languages: it is an incontrovertibly native Sokean word. It must have existed in this form at least since the separation of Soke and Gulf Sokean (which took place no later than about A.D. 500, according to glottochronology).

Table 6.1. Trisyllabic Sokean roots with Gulf Sokean cognates

	cacao	mamey => plantain	fire	guava	Guiana chestnut
pS	*kakawa	*sapane	*jukutʉ	*patajaC	*wakata
MIG	kakawa	xapane	jukutʉk	pataja7	
MAR	kakawa	sapane	jukutʉ	pataja	wakata
COP	kakawa7	sapane	jukʉtʉk		
TEC	kakawa7	sapane	jukʉtʉk		
RAY	kakwa [< AYA?]				
AYA	[ka(:)gwa]	xapne=	jukte	[pa:7da]	wakta
	(~ kak=)	(~ xap)	(~ pa7danh=)		(~ waktanh=)
SOT	kaakwa	saapnyi	jukti	patanh	waakta
		xapan=chay			
		'hojas secas del platanar'			
TEX	kaga=	sapun	jugut	patanh [< SOT]	
	(~ ka:k#)				

Note: The data cited here were collected by linguists working on the PDLMA, except for RAY, which is from Harrison and Harrison (1984).

*Evidence for the development of *kakaw* in Mijean*

Internal evidence of changes within Mijean establish that modern Mijean words for cacao are part of the ancient heritage of these languages. The form *kakaw* goes back at least as far as proto-Mijean: all Mijean forms are consistent with a reconstruction of pM *kakaw* (except for one Highland Mije form, Mixistlán [kaká:wa], that is irrelevant because it derives from regional Spanish *cacahua*).

The Mijean branch of Mije-Sokean consists of three subgroups (see Figure 6.1): Tapachula Mijean (extinct, and with no relevant data), Oluta Mijean, and Mije.

In Oluta, ancestral [7] is inserted before the final consonant of *CVCVC* words; since no other word shape is pronounced [CVCV7C], the word [kaka7w], for 'cacao,' must descend from *kakaw*.

In Totontepec Mije, *kakaw* yielded *káku*, with stress on the first syllable, because, in the ancestor of Totontepec Mije, words of two or three syllables were stressed on the first syllable. In all other forms of Mije, which in our subgrouping includes Sayula Mijean, descendants of *kakaw* are pronounced [kaká:w] as a result of a regular sequence of changes in these languages. First, stress shifted from the penult syllable to the final syllable in all *CVCVC* forms. In all words with stressed final syllables, including the *CVCVC* shapes as well as stressable monosyllabic words, [j] was inserted before the final consonant. Before resonants—a class of consonants that, in these languages, includes /m, n, w, y/—[j] shifted to vowel length before word-final consonants. In the case of the Mijean word for cacao, these changes led from *kakaw* through *kakáw* and then *kakájw* to the attested form *kaká:w*.

Except for one instance of borrowing from Spanish, every Mijean form is consistent with direct inheritance from proto-Mijean *kakaw*; not a single form provides evidence for a pre-Columbian disruption in the regular transmission of the word *kakaw* within the Mijean branch.[5]

Mijean *kakaw* and Sokean *kakawa*

Accordingly, the available evidence is that the word for cacao was not borrowed into either Mijean or Sokean from outside of the Mije-Sokean family; it was inherited directly from proto-Mijean and proto-Sokean. The only anomaly in the Mije-Sokean pedigree of this pan-Meso-American word for cacao is that pM *kakaw* and pS *kakawa* are not identical. Dakin and Wichmann (2000) treat this discrepancy as evidence for borrowing from one into the other after the split of Mijean and Sokean from one another. This proposal, however, would not account for the forms. A form *kakaw* would have been adopted as such in Sokean, which exhibits a large number of *CVCVC* noun roots, so such a borrowing is implausible. It is also unlikely that an ancestor of proto-Mijean would have reduced a trisyllabic noun root *kakawa* to two syllables on being borrowed into a form of Mijean predating proto-Mijean. First, although there were very few *CVCVCV* roots in proto-Mijean, there are solid examples—at a minimum, proto-Mijean *7i:tzumu* 'peccary' and proto-Mijean (also proto-Mije-Sokean) *wakata* 'Guiana chestnut' (*Pachira aquatica*) and *pu7juyu7* 'nighthawk.'[6] In addition, *many* proto-Mijean words consisting of two or more grammatical constituents had a *CVCVCV* shape—for example, *witit-u7* 'walk!' and *tokoy.e* 'lost'—and this is sufficient to make words of this shape borrowable.

The same arguments show that *any* particular foreign source for these words, such as Nawa *kakawa-tl*, cannot account for both the Mijean and Sokean form. If not by borrowing, then, how can the difference between pS *kakawa* and pM *kakaw* be explained?

Very often for a given meaning Mijean and Sokean have completely different morphemes or combinations of morphemes. Sometimes, though, the forms are clearly related phonologically but show discrepancies which forestall the reconstruction of a single phonological form to proto-Mije-Sokean, and which do not result from any regular grammatical processes otherwise attested in Mije-Sokean languages. We recognize thirty-four such forms, including pS *pok*, pM *pokok* 'bottlegourd'; pS *mun*, pM *muni* 'sweet potato'; pS *jajtzuku*, pM *tzukuC* 'ant'; pS *tzutzu*, pM *tzu7u* 'elder sister, aunt'; and pS *kakawa*, pM *kakaw* 'cacao.'

None of the differences in these thirty-four words can be explained as result-ing from borrowing between Mijean and Sokean, and no compelling case has been made that *any* of these words has been borrowed into either Mijean or Sokean from any other language.

Both between branches and within the same language, a single root may occur with both a shorter and a longer form, with the longer form having an extra vowel (plus or minus glottal stop) at the end, as in COP, TEC (Soke) *jʉpʉ* 'jaw, chin' (compare pS **jʉp* 'mouth,' pM **jʉp* 'nose') and MAR *tzusu* 'corner' (compare **tzus* in pS **kʉ(7)=tzus* 'digit nail' [lit., "under corner"]). Both in language-internal examples, and when proto-Sokean has a longer version than proto-Mijean or vice versa, there is sometimes evidence that a longer form is expanded from a shorter form, never that a shorter form is truncated. These results suggest that either **kakaw* and **kakawa* both existed in proto-Mije-Sokean or that pS **kakawa* was an expansion of an earlier pre-pS **kakaw*.

The differences between the proto-Mijean and the proto-Sokean forms for 'cacao' therefore fall within the range attested for other Mijean and Sokean roots, when, as in the case of 'cacao,' the discrepancies cannot be accounted for by borrowing.

An alternative hypothesis

Dakin and Wichmann (2000) make three claims in favor of the view that *ka-kawa*, or something similar, was borrowed into Mije-Sokean languages rather than descending from a native Mije-Sokean lexical item.

(1) Dakin and Wichmann (2000:56b) claim that "morphemes consisting of three open syllables (CV.CV.CV) are exceedingly rare" in Mije-Sokean; they state (incorrectly) that only two such stems are reconstructible within Mije-Sokean and that this in itself suggests that a word shape *kakawa* must have a foreign origin.

It is true that most Mije-Sokean noun stems are disyllabic, and most of the remainder are monosyllabic, whereas trisyllabic stems are rare. But this does not constitute evidence that trisyllabic roots in Mije-Sokean languages are likely to have a foreign source; languages admit a variety of syllable types as roots or stems, and some are much rarer than others. In fact, at least seven trisyllabic roots that begin with two open syllables are reconstructible in proto-Mijean, proto-Sokean, or proto-Mije-Sokean: to the five proto-Sokean roots in Table 6.1 may be added pMS **wakata* 'Guiana chestnut' and **pu7juyu7* 'nighthawk' and pM **7i:tzʉmʉ* 'peccary.' Empirically, setting aside the contested case of *ka-kawa*, there is no recognized foreign source for any of these trisyllabic nouns.

(2) Curiously, the evidence for stress on the first syllable of **kakawa* in Gulf Sokean—which we have shown provides strong evidence for its antiquity in

Sokean—was part of Dakin and Wichmann's (2000) argument against that antiquity. They were unaware that initial stress was a regular rule on Gulf Sokean trisyllables that begin with two open syllables, and they mistakenly assumed that any native Sokean trisyllabic root would show penult stress. They mention none of the trisyllabic vocabulary cited above, apart from *kakawa*, and argue that inherited trisyllables must have had penult stress based on a single misanalyzed word.[7]

(3) Dakin and Wichmann correctly observe that while Sokean languages point to an ancestral *kakawa*, Mijean languages point to an ancestral *kakaw*; these two forms cannot both descend normally from a single proto-Mije-Sokean form. They claim that this discrepancy points to early borrowing into Sokean or Mijean or both (Dakin and Wichmann 2000:57a). As noted above, there are numerous cases of such discrepancies (although they are hardly prevalent) between proto-Sokean and proto-Mijean reconstructions for what seem to be single etymologies, with no evidence that either was borrowed.

Why *kakawa* Cannot Have Originated in Nawa

The previous section shows that the word for 'cacao' existed in the earliest linguistically recoverable phases of the Mije-Sokean family and that the diffusion of this word in Meso-America agrees with the pattern of diffusion of other vocabulary from Mije-Sokean languages into other parts of Meso-America. It shows that Dakin and Wichmann's arguments against a Mije-Sokean source are groundless.

Mije-Sokean is one of only two language families in Meso-America that has been the source of pre-Columbian borrowings as widespread as that of *kakawa*. The other source is Nawa. Lexical diffusion from Nawa has been studied intensively and is well understood. This section shows that the pattern of diffusion of *kakawa* is inconsistent with what is known about Nawa influence on other languages; thus, any hypothesis attributing the origin of this word to Nawa is implausible. Dakin and Wichmann (2000:59–60) propose such a hypothesis, arguing that the Nawa word *kakawa-tl* has ancient roots in the Yuta-Nawan family, originating by reduplication of a Nawa descendant of proto-Sonoran *kava* 'egg'; on linguistic grounds, this proposal is simply impossible.

Lexical diffusion from Nawa

Setting aside the contested case of the word for 'cacao,' the following empirical observations can be made about borrowings from Nawa into other Meso-American languages.

(1) Nawa in general is heavily influenced by Mije-Sokean and Totonakan

and to a lesser degree by Wasteko, in its pre-Nawa stage; but neither Mije-Sokean in general nor Totonakan in general is much influenced by Nawa. Even Wasteko (a single language rather than a family), which has had Meso-Americanized Nawa as a neighbor since at least A.D. 900, has relatively few lexical borrowings from Nawa. All this makes Nawa look like a relative newcomer to Meso-America that was not in a position to provide very early loans into languages throughout Meso-America.

(2) More specifically, proto-Nawan—the common ancestor of all Nawa languages—shows substantial borrowing from Mije-Sokean languages in both vocabulary and grammar.

(3) Setting aside the contested case of pMS *kakawa*, proto-Mije-Sokean does not show a single plausible instance of a lexical borrowing from Nawa or Yuta-Nawan and neither does proto-Mijean or proto-Sokean or any other genetic subgroup of Mijean or Sokean. (Individual Mije-Sokean languages have borrowed some Nawa lexical material.)

(4) Setting aside the contested case of *kakawa*, there is no instance of a Nawa loan into any Meso-American language that clearly predates the Late Classic period. In particular, no Nawa loans have undergone sound changes characteristic of any genetic group of languages; rather, Nawa loans in Meso-American languages reflect Nawa phonology as we know it from the sixteenth century and can, therefore, not be earlier than about A.D. 1000.

Given points (2)–(4), compelling evidence is required to make a case for any word of Nawa origin having diffused into Meso-American languages at a substantially earlier time period, especially a word that was borrowed as widely as *kakawa*.

(5) Nawa words are almost always borrowed in their unpossessed form and reflect the absolute suffix -*tl* ~ -*tli* ~ -*li* when present in the Nawa model (Kaufman 2000–2006ms). In Mayan and Mije-Sokean languages in particular, then, one would expect to find something like *kakawat** rather than the attested *kakaw* if this word were indeed a borrowing from Nawa. Even the possessed forms of *kakawa* always end not in a vowel but in a suffix -*w*, as in *i:-kakawa-w* 'his cacao,' *no-kakawa-w* 'my cacao.'

(6) Cacao does not grow anywhere near the Basin of Mexico nor further north in areas from which Nawas entered Meso-America. Nawa was strongly affected by one or more Mije-Sokean languages, in its vocabulary, in its morphology, and in its syntax; it is completely plausible that Nawa would have borrowed its word for cacao from a language localized in the area in which the tree grows, which is the norm when newcomers encounter unfamiliar plants and animals, whenever they do not devise neologisms using native resources. Apart from Mije-Sokean, early forms of Nawa show substantial influence only

from Wasteko and Totonakan, whose speakers did not live in an area of cacao production.

Given these characteristics of lexical diffusion from Nawa, any proposal for a widespread lexical borrowing from Nawa in the Preclassic or Early Classic period must be approached with skepticism and requires compelling evidence to be accepted.

The alleged origin of Nawa kakawa-tl in proto-Sonoran *kava

Dakin and Wichmann (2000:59) hypothesize that Sonoran (an ancestor of Nawa) *kava 'egg' (incorrectly reconstructed by them as *kawa) is the source of Nawa /kakawa-tl/; that [kakawa] arose as a CV reduplication of a pre-Nawa *kawa 'egg'; and that [kakawa] would have originally meant 'egg-like thing.' The semantics of this hypothesis are not implausible, given the shape of the cacao pod (though sixteenth-century Nawa sources such as Molina [1571:80r] compare the pod rather to maize ears in their husks). Dakin and Wichmann acknowledge that there is no attested Nawa word kawa(-tl)* and thus no internal Nawa evidence for the analysis, which depends entirely on the plausibility of relating Nawa [kakawa] to the external Sonoran forms.

The Sonoran data they cite (Dakin and Wichmann 2000:59a) are Warijiyo ka7wá 'egg'; Taraumara ka7wá 'to lay eggs'; Kájita kava 'egg'; and Eudeve aa]kabo[ra7a 'egg.' These data are sufficient to reconstruct proto-Sonoran *kava. Contrary to Dakin and Wichmann's assumption, however, Sonoran *kava cannot be the source of Nawa kakawa-tl, because medial [v] in Sonoran, which is the allophone of single postvocalic *p, shifts to [h] in Koran and Nawa, which is subsequently lost in Nawa.

YN *sʉpʉ..	'cold' [n]	→ pSon *seve-ta	→ Naw se:-tl
	'cold' [a]	pSon *se-seve-ka [a]	→ Naw se-se:-k
YN *napo-tsi	'prickly pear'	→ pSon *navo-tsi-ta	→ Naw no:ch-tli
YN *tapun-tsi	'rabbit'	→ pSon *tavu-tsi-ta	→ Naw to:ch-tli
YN *tsi:puH	'bitter'	→ pSon *tsi-tsi:vu-ka	→ Naw chi-chi:-k
YN *pi:pah	'tobacco'	→ pSon *vi:va-ta	→ Naw i(:)ya-tl

The above data show that medial YN *p = Son *[v] does *not* survive as /w/ in Nawa, but disappears, and the resulting vowel sequence merges into a single long vowel (excepts that *iva > *ia > iya). Thus, although there is a Sonoran etymon *kava 'egg,' this would yield [ka:] rather than [kawa] in Nawa; and a hypothetical reduplicated noun deriving from Sonoran *kava would have shown up in Nawa as kaka:-tl* and not as kakawa-tl. Dakin and Wichmann's proposed Yuta-Nawan origin for the Nawa word kakawa is simply not possible.

There are two etymologies that might give the false impression that Sonoran medial [v] survives as [w] in Nawa; these are instances in which Sonoran [v] follows a rounded vowel. As usual, Sonoran medial [v] shifted to [h] in Koran and Nawa; subsequently in Nawa, after a rounded vowel this [h] became [w], after which the rounded vowel desyllabified and disappeared (this may have happened especially after /k/):

| YN *kopa | 'forehead' | → pSon *kova | → Naw kwa:(yi) 'head' |
| | | pSon *ma:kova 'five' | → Naw ma:kwi:l-li |

Unlike postvocalic Sonoran *v, which disappeared in Nawa (except as noted above), Sonoran and Yuta-Nawan medial *w survived, as w:

YN *konwa	'snake'		→ Naw kowa:-tl
YN *sunwa	'woman'		→ Naw siwa:-tl ~ sowa:-tl
YN *tʉwa	'to see'		→ Naw itwa ~ itta ~ ita
		pSon *ku7awi 'tree'	→ Naw kwawi-tl

In sum, Nawa *kakawa cannot possibly be derived from pSon *kava. This leaves no evidence either in Nawa or, more broadly, in Sonoran for a Nawa origin of Meso-American words for 'cacao.'

The Diffusion of *kakaw and *kakawa

Mije-Sokean vocabulary diffused most substantially in two areas: in southeastern Meso-America, to Mayan and Xinka, and in northern Meso-America, in and around the Basin of Mexico. In between, there is substantial diffusion into Sapoteko, but otherwise there is relatively little into Oto-Mangean.

The diffusion of 'cacao' into southeastern Meso-America

Figure 6.2 shows the location of languages addressed in this section. In the discussion that follows, "Greater Tzeltalan" refers to a group of languages consisting of the Tzeltalan languages, Tzeltal and Tzotzil, together with the Ch'olan languages, and to the common ancestor of all these languages.

A Mije-Sokean word for cacao was borrowed into a number of Mayan languages. Throughout Mayan, /kakaw/ is the typical form; it is borrowed, not native, because a proto-Mayan kakaw* would not have preserved [k] in all languages. Mayan tolerates disyllabic noun roots (though they are relatively few) but does not have native trisyllabic roots or roots ending in vowels. The model for the diffused forms could therefore have been either [kakaw] or [kakawa].

When Greater Tzeltalans adopted the word kakaw, we know that it replaced an existing word for cacao, Greater Tzeltalan *pe:k (from proto-Mayan *pe:q), since its descendant survived with a shift of meaning as pre-Ch'olan *pi:k 'eight thousand' (the semantic association comes from the use of gunny sacks to store large numbers of cacao beans and is reflected in the borrowing of *pi:k into

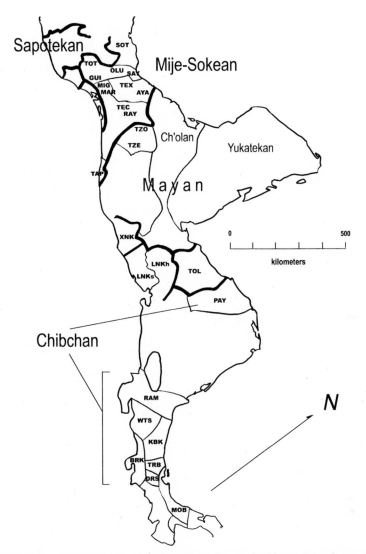

Figure 6.2. Linguistic geography of southern Meso-America and lower Central America at the time of European contact, marking those languages that have words for cacao derived, ultimately, from Mije-Sokean. To provide a sense of the linguistic geography when the word for cacao was diffusing, intrusive groups that reached their Contact-period location after ca. A.D. 500 (Nawa, Chinanteko, Chorotegan, Sutiaba) have been removed, and their territory has been divided among remaining adjacent groups. We have no data on words for cacao from Misumalpan languages, which divide Paya from the rest of the Chibchan family. Codes: *Chibchan*: BRK Boruka; DRS Doraske; MOB Mobe; PAY Paya; RAM Rama; TRB Térraba; WTS Watuso. *Mayan*: TZE Tzeltal; TZO Tzotzil. *Mije-Sokean*: AYA Ayapa Gulf Sokean; GUI San Juan Guichicovi (lowland) Mije; MAR Santa María Chimalapa Soke; MIG San Miguel Chimalapa Soke; OLU Oluta Mijean; RAY Rayón Chiapas Soke; SAY Sayula Mijean; SOT Soteapan Gulf Sokean; TEC Tecpatán Chiapas Soke; TEX Texistepec Gulf Sokean; TOT Totontepec (highland) Mije. *Other groups*: LNKh Honduras Lenka; LNKs Salvador Lenka; TOL Tol.

Yukatekan as 'skirt'; similarly in Sapoteko, the word *kwe+ (s)su:7ti 'bag, eight thousand' comes to mean 'skirt'). This, then, was a culturally motivated change in vocabulary, not the adoption of a new product. The Lowland Mayan use of cacao beverages goes back to at least 600 B.C. (Hurst et al. 2002), while the adoption of kakaw can be shown to have reached Greater Tzeltalan probably between 300 B.C. and A.D. 400 (see Kaufman and Justeson in press for detailed argumentation).

This term spread further south, into lower Central America, at an unknown date; it is probably a Mayan form like kakaw that was the ultimate source of most of these borrowings. In geographical order, these further borrowings are:

West to east in El Salvador and Honduras: Mayan kakaw; Tol [khaw] (Dennis Holt, personal communication 1993); Honduras Lenka *[kaɣaw] > /kaw/ (Lehmann 1920); Pipil kakawa-t (Campbell 1985); Salvador Lenka /k'akaw/ (Lehmann 1920).

North to south on the Atlantic Coast (Chibchan languages): Paya kaku (Dennis Holt, personal communication 2004); Rama kuk (Colette Grinevald, personal communication 1990).

West to east in Costa Rica and western Panama (all Chibchan languages): proto-Watuso-Boruka *ˈkə́hú7 (Constenla 1981:373); Watuso kaxu: (Constenla 1981:373); Térraba kó (Dakin and Wichmann 2000:75); Boruka kaw7 (Constenla 1981:373); Doraske koa (Dakin and Wichmann 2000:74); Mobe (Waymí) ku (Dakin and Wichmann 2000:74).

Pipil kakawa-t was not borrowed in Central America; rather, it was inherited from proto-Nawa, which had borrowed *kakawa from Mije-Sokean by about A.D. 500. Salvador Lenka, Paya, and Rama reflect the typical Mayan pronunciation [kakaw], and this is plausibly their immediate source.

Most of the remaining forms are Chibchan. Although the cited forms come from most of the branches of the Chibchan stock, they are limited geographically to Central America; there is no "cacao"-like form in any South American language. The forms must therefore be the result of diffusion; Constenla's reconstruction *ˈkə́hú7 may more properly be treated as a formula subsuming the phonological regularities between the Watuso and the Boruka forms as if they were cognate.

With the exception of the Rama form, which can not be fully accounted for, we can postulate that the phonological antecedent for all the forms cited above is something like [kahaw]. Central American Chibchan languages show the development [káhaw] (with first syllable "stress") > [*kə́hú7] > kaxu:, káw7, kó, ku, kuk; Tol may have developed [kaháw] (with second syllable "stress") to [khaw], or borrowed its word from one of the Chibchan languages with a (possibly intermediate) Boruka-like form [káw7]; Honduras Lenka may have done something similar.

The postulated Central American antecedent [kahaw] would have been borrowed from the general Mayan form /kakaw/. If the first intermediary into Central America from the Mayan area had been Honduras Lenka, there would be an explanation of the shift of medial /k/ to [h], because in Honduras Lenka single intervocalic /k/ is pronounced [γ], a sound which does not sound like [k] in a language having only [k] and [h] but not [γ] or [g]. If Honduras Lenka is the intermediary, why it should have simplified [kaγaw] to [kaw] is not crystal clear, but it may be observed that Spanish *vacas* yielded Honduras Lenka /waš/ 'cattle,' through an intermediate form [waγaš], so this is a plausible internal development in Honduras Lenka.

Salvador Lenka /k'akaw/ and Paya /kaku/ could be direct borrowings from Mayan with no Honduras Lenka intermediary, but Mayan languages are quite far away from Paya and there are viable alternative explanations.[8] The [g] of Salvador Lenca [k'á:gaw] could reflect the [γ] of an earlier Honduras Lenka [kaγaw] rather than Mayan [k]. Similarly, since Paya borrows proto-Mije-Sokean **pa:ju7* 'coyote,' as /paku/, it is more likely that it borrowed an antecedent Central American form [kahaw] as /kaku/ than that it made a far more distant borrowing from Mayan.

Altogether, the evidence from Central American languages suggests an antecedent form like [kahaw], borrowed from Mayan /kakaw/, maybe specifically via Honduras Lenka. From there, no specific path of diffusion can be determined.

Diffusion into the intermediate (Oto-Mangean) area

Two Oto-Mangean words for cacao have a form that might derive from **kakaw* or **kakawa*. Dakin and Wichmann (2000:74) cite Chocho /ka:kaú7/ from C. Mock (1977), but this could be borrowed from Spanish. A plausible pre-Columbian borrowing is Amusgo /tɛhšuah/ (lit., "bean cacao") (tone pattern is low, mid) 'cocoa bean' (Tapia García 1999:216) (plural /tɛh nguah/). There is a class of nouns in Amusgo that take the prefix {tz-} in the singular and {n-} in the plural; given this, and given that the underlying sequence //tz-k// is realized as š in Amusgo, the underlying form of the word for 'cacao' can be seen to be //-kuah//, with the singular //tz-kuah// realized as /šuah/ and the plural //n-kuah// realized as /nguah/.

Another possibly related Oto-Mangean form is proto-Chinanteko **kwá:7* 'case; peeling; pod; shell' (Rensch 1989:50 n. 163); compare also **kwé:7* 'bark, peeling' (Rensch 1989:50 n. 160). In no Chinanteko language, however, does a form like [kwa] or [kwe] actually mean 'cacao.'

The Amusgo and Chinanteko forms can derive from an antecedent [kVwa]. The identity of the first V can not be determined, but these forms seem as if they could reflect specifically [kawá]; both of these forms lack the initial syllable [ka] of *kakawa, and an antecedent *kawa could yield both of them. The [kawá] form has stress, or prominence, on the second vowel. This may reflect habitual accentual patterns: in Oto-Mangean languages (apart from the Mije-Sokean-influenced Sapoteko, Misteko, and Kwikateko), polysyllabic words have highest prominence on the last syllable. In the earliest stages of Oto-Mangean languages, lexical stems had one or two syllables; any lexical material in antepenult position is a clitic or a classifier. Hence, if a form like proto-Sokean *kakawa were taken into an early stage of an Oto-Mangean language (at least two thousand years ago), something would have to be done with the first /ka/; if it did not correspond in a meaningful way with an existing proclitic or classifier in the target language, it might be eliminated. We suggest that this is indeed what happened to *kakawa in Amusgo, and what might have happened in Chinanteko if proto-Chinanteko *kwá:7 ~ *kwé:7 (dating about fifteen hundred years ago) is a borrowed word (pre-proto-Chinanteko underwent sound changes whereby antecedent CVCV forms were reduced to CCV, and the initial cluster was subject to simplification in certain cases).

Northern diffusion of 'cacao'

Kaufman (2001; 2000–2006ms) shows that there was a massive diffusion of Mije-Sokean vocabulary into languages in the Basin of Mexico and its immediate surroundings (Figure 6.3). The borrowing into Totonakan was truly massive, about forty-eight items. By current count, between eight and seventeen Mije-Sokean words were borrowed into each of Nawa, Tarasko, Otomian, Matlatzinkan, and possibly Chorotegan. Further afield, eleven words were borrowed into Wasteko.

From the locations of the languages with the greatest numbers of loans, the center of this diffusion can be localized among or adjacent to Totonakans and more involved with speakers of Tarasko and Nawa than with speakers of Wasteko. This places them in or near the eastern half of the Basin of Mexico, thus in the vicinity of Teotihuacan.

This geographic analysis of the northern Mije-Sokean loans leads us to propose that one of the languages of Teotihuacan was a northern branch of the Mije-Sokean family. It probably left Olmec country no later than the time of the separation of Mijean and Sokean, since the loans now unique either to Mijean or to Sokean are proportionally (10–20 percent) about equal. These immigrant populations may be recognized at Early Preclassic sites in the Basin of Mexico starting around 1200 B.C.; at Coapexco, in the southeast, Olmec features occur in all contexts and all functional components of the assemblage, including utilitarian artifacts (Tolstoy 1989:98). Tolstoy makes their immigrant status clear: the Olmec features "(1) appear suddenly; (2) appear early; (3) ap-

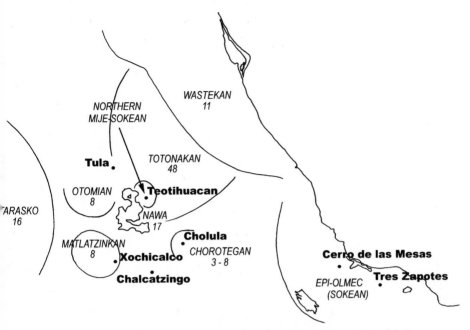

Figure 6.3. Approximate linguistic geography of northern Meso-America around A.D. 500. Numerals indicate the number of Mije-Sokean loans from each language group. The inferred region of Northern Mije-Sokean also included speakers of Totonakan, which surrounds it; the localization of Nawa, which probably arrived in Meso-America during the Early Classic period, is less secure than the locations of the other groups. Matlatzinkan becomes Matlatzinka and Tlawika (Ocuilteco); Otomian becomes Otomí and Masawa; Totonakan becomes Totonako and Tepewa.

pear together; (4) pervade general refuse, all households, and many sectors of activity; and (5) seem most abundant at the time of their first appearance. Their subsequent history, in fact, is one of fairly rapid fading or transformation and replacement by new elements" (Tolstoy 1989:98).

Despite their assimilation to local material culture practices, these Mije-Sokeans evidently remained linguistically and probably socially distinct. Centuries later, at Teotihuacan, the loan word evidence suggests that they were the elite at the site and probably coexisted there with speakers of a Totonakan language (Mije-Sokean had a more massive impact on Totonakan than on any other language or language group in Meso-America).

One of the words that was diffused into several of these languages was *kakawa*. It shows up in Totonakan, Nawa, Tarasko, and Masawa.

The word *kakawa*, then, is a quintessential representative of the distribution of Mije-Sokean loans into Meso-American languages: with substantial borrowing into Mayan languages in the south; few borrowings by Oto-Mangean languages in Oaxaca; and borrowing into several languages in and around the Basin of Mexico. This pattern provides further support for the Mije-Sokean origin of this term. Given the localization of the center of diffusion of northern Mije-Sokean loans, it is quite probable that the word *kakawa* diffused in this area in association with the regional influence of Teotihuacan. Our dating for the borrowing of the term into Greater Tzeltalan between 300 B.C. and A.D. 400 is broadly consistent with a Teotihuacanoid source for this loan, but it could instead have been associated with epi-Olmecs, who lived in the areas of cacao production.

Previous linguistic studies have drawn unsubstantiated conclusions about the nature of the intercultural interaction that was the basis for the adoption of this word by foreigners. It is plausible that the term diffused in association with the cultivation of cacao (compare Justeson et al. 1985:59); in the Mayan case, this would account for the shift in K'ichee'an of **pe:q*, the old Mayan word for 'cacao,' to mean 'uncultivated cacao.' However, it is also possible that the word diffused in connection with the processing of cacao or, more likely, with a rising importance of its use—perhaps in a ritual context, or perhaps through an economic importance, for example as money).

Nawa *chikol=a:-tl ~ chokol=a:-tl*

In Meso-America there is a related set of words for chocolate, the drink made from ground cacao kernels mixed with water and seasonings, that come from four sources: Nawa *chokola:tl*, its borrowing into Spanish as *chocolate*, Nawa *chikola:tl*, and its borrowing into regional/substandard Spanish as *chicolate*. The Nawa form is made up of a first element of uncertain origin, "chokol" or "chikol," plus {a:} 'water.'

All suggestions thus far offered for the origin of the first element are unsatisfactory. Nawa *ch* in native words should occur only before *i* (Campbell and Langacker 1978a–c). If the earliest Nawa form was *chikola:tl*, the form *chokola:tl* could have developed from it by assimilation of the first vowel to the second. If the earliest form was *chokola:tl*, {chokol=} is perhaps borrowed. Evidence for either of these two possibilities is lacking, though the first is more likely, and Dakin and Wichmann (2000:62–63) argue for it, adding the consideration of additional data which may not be relevant. This is not to say that we have a satisfactory etymology for *chikola:tl ~ chokola:tl*, because we do not.

Dakin and Wichmann argue plausibly that *chikola:tl* was the original pronunciation of this word. They cite (2000:62b) *chikola:tl* for the Nawa towns of Ocotepec (Morelos), Ameyaltepec (Guerrero), Cuetzalan (Veracruz), and Rafael Delgado = San Juan del Río (Veracruz). This form is also found in North Puebla Nawa (Una Canger, personal communication 1989), a type of Central

Nawa. In the case of Cuetzalan Nawa, Dakin and Wichmann (2000:62b) point out that *chokola:t* is said now but that the older form is reputed to have been *chikola:t*. While Dakin and Wichmann cite Tuggy's data from Rafael Delgado as having *chikola:tl*, the more recent PDLMA (Project for the Documentation of the Languages of Meso-America) data from Rafael Delgado (Romero 1999–2002) has both *chokola:tl* and, puzzlingly, *xikola:tl* (not *chikola:tl*).

The form *chokola:tl* was documented by Kaufman in 1978 for Santa María Izhuatlán. Huasteca Nawa, both West and East (Kaufman 1969, 1984–1993), has *chokola:tl* 'chocolate'; but in Chontla Huasteca Nawa the word means 'caldo de tripa de puerco' (soup/broth made from swine gut). This suggests that a Nawa morpheme {chokol=} (or {chikol=}) combined with {a:} 'water' has a generic meaning with at least two applications. Unfortunately, the more generic meaning of {chokol=} is not easy to divine. Pipil, which has been separate from other forms of Nawa since ca. A.D. 900, has *chukula:t* (Campbell 1985:200). This raises the possibility that the form *chokola:tl* is at least one thousand years old, but it could also be a borrowing from the Central Nawa speakers ("mejicanos") brought into Guatemala by the Spanish after 1525. In light of the other data discussed in this study the latter possibility seems more likely.

Even if {chokol=} is assimilated from {chikol=}, the closest comparanda in Nawa are *chiko* 'bent in a half-circle', and *chihkol-li* 'thing bent in a half-circle,' neither of which is, in fact, {chikol}. Dakin and Wichmann's hypothesis (2000:63–66) is that *chihkol-li* meant 'cacao-beater' in some kinds of Nawa, but *chihkol-li* has a preconsonantal /h/ and *chikol=a:-tl* does not. On the one hand, there is no straightforward evidence for a Nawa word *chikol-li**; on the other hand, *chiko* and *chihkol-li* must be related, both reflecting the meaning 'bent, hooked,' and this is not consistent with Dakin and Wichmann's hypothesis, which derives *chihkol-li* and their hypothetical *chikol-li** from a supposed Yuta-Nawan **tsi=* 'small/pointed stick' (Dakin and Wichmann 2000:63–64) plus **ku* 'tree, pole' (Dakin and Wichmann 2000:64–65). These difficulties render their proposed etymology unconvincing. If there were a Nawa word *chikol-li** 'stirring stick,' then Dakin and Wichmann's hypothesis that *chikol=a:-tl* meant 'stirring stick water' (their term is 'beater-drink') would be plausible; it would not support their main claim, that **kakawa* and the name for chocolate were diffused at the same time.

Nawa *chikola:tl* yields Sayula Mijean *chikúla:t*, Kora *tzikura:*, Chayuco Misteko *sikula*, San Mateo del Mar Wavi *chikolt* (the Wavi word perhaps via Spanish). In addition to the forms listed here, Dakin and Wichmann (2000:62b) cite i-forms for San Juan Colorado Misteko, Tlaxiaco Misteko, Warijiyo, Chamorro, Asturian Spanish, Catalan, and Dutch. Nawa *chokola:-tl* 'chocolate,' yields Zinacantán Tzotzil *chukul 7at* 'chocolate drink,' Oaxaca

Chontal -*tzugulalh*. From the forms of these borrowings, it appears highly likely that the languages that have it received the loan from Nawa.

The pre-Columbian diffusion of this Nawa word, in either form, was extremely limited compared to that of *kakaw(a)* in pre-Columbian times; it is simply not true that they diffused together. It is also extremely unlikely that the term for chocolate and the term for cacao diffused through Meso-America in the same time period: **kakaw(a)* was borrowed into lowland Mayan languages before A.D. 400 and then underwent various sound changes; in contrast, the Nawa word for chocolate was borrowed in diverse forms into a variety of Meso-American languages, with no internal evidence in any instance for substantial antiquity.

A further wrinkle is that neither form of the Nawa word is attested from the first decades of the Spanish colonization: it may not even be a pre-Columbian word. It is not found in Molina (either in the 1551 edition or in the expanded 1571 edition), in Sahagún (1577, 1558–1561), in the *Cantares mejicanos* (ca. 1582), or in the *Romances de los señores de la Nueva España* (from 1582). Instead, the works of Sahagún, the *Cantares*, and the *Romances* all report the use of *kakawa-tl* to refer to the drink made from cacao; Sahagún and Molina report several different cacao-based drinks with different names composed of one or more modifiers + *kakawa-tl*; and Molina (1571) reports *kakawa=a:-tl* ("cacao water": <cacauaatl> 'beuida de cacao,' Nawa to Spanish section 10v; 'beuida de cacao y mayz,' <cacaua atl>, Spanish to Nawa section 19r). Even today in some Mayan languages, such as Tzotzil (Laughlin 1975:176) and Q'anjobal (Balam, personal communication 2005), the word for cacao is used to name a drink made from it.

The earliest sources in Spanish also use *cacao* and not *chocolate* to refer to the same drink(s). Molina's (1571) Spanish to Nawa section (22r, column a) lists 'cacao, beuida,' meaning by this "cacao—a drink," "the drink called cacao," showing that for Molina chocolate was called simply *cacao* in his use of Spanish. The *Relación de Juan Bautista de Pomar (Tezcoco, 1582)* contains the passage, "Su bebida de los poderosos era cacao." ('The drink of the powerful was cacao'; Garibay 1993:193). In Durán's *Historia de las Indias de Nueva España* and his *Islas de la tierra firme*, written before 1586, the word *chocolate* is not used, while the word *cacao* is used repeatedly in reference to the drink (Durán 1965). Ruíz de Alarcón (1629; compare Andrews and Hassig 1984:132; M. D. Coe and G. Whittaker 1982:188) uses the Spanish word *cacao* to refer to the drink made from cacao. The kind of Nawa found in Ruíz de Alarcón is from Central Nawa, the same general dialect group as the Nawa of the Basin of Mexico.

The foregoing is evidence suggesting that in the Nawa of the Basin of Mexico, and perhaps in Central Nawa generally, no word *chikola:tl* or *chokola:tl* existed in the sixteenth century or before, and that drinks made from cacao were referred to as *kakawatl* or by expressions including it. The words *chikola:tl* and *chokola:tl* may not have existed in pre-Columbian times, or they may have arisen in a peripheral type of Nawa, at an undeterminable date, and only spread later to Central Nawa.

The first known use of the Nawa word *chokola:tl* is cited in Corominas (1980–1983, v. 2:385–386) from Francisco Hernández ca. 1580 as <chocol-latl>. The next known citation of the word *chokola:tl* in Nawa is from Clavijero 1780, who cites Nawa <chocolatl> glossed in Spanish translation (Clavijero 1826) as "alimento hecho con almendras de cacao y semilla del árbol llamado *pochotl*, en partes iguales" ('a food made from cacao seeds ["almonds"] and the seed of a tree called *po:cho:tl* [Ceiba, silk-cotton tree], in equal parts' [Siméon 1977:107]).

Etymologists of Spanish (see especially Corominas 1980–1983, v. 2:385–386) seem universally to agree that *chokola:tl* is not a genuine Nawa word, apparently because it is not attested in the earliest sixteenth-century sources; rather, they think *chocolate* is a Spanish word created by Spanish speakers through the mangling of a Nawa word or expression. However, Nawa *chokola:tl* and *chikola:tl* are not plausibly the re-Nawatizations of Spanish *chocolate* and *chicolate*. There is no evidence that any Spanish word of shape /..Vte#/ was ever borrowed into Nawa ending with /..V:tl/; and it is clear from the discussions by both Hernández and Clavijero that they thought that *chocola:tl* was just as much a Nawa word as all other Nawa terms they brought under discussion.

The first occurrence of the Spanish word *chocolate* is in Book 4, Chapter 22, of *Historia natural y moral de las Indias*, which was published in 1590 by Joseph (José) de Acosta.

The above evidence also shows that in the Spanish spoken in Central Mexico, chocolate was called *cacao* until well into the seventeenth century, and we know of no evidence of the word *chocolate* or *chicolate* being used there at this time. José de Acosta, however, who lived in both Mexico and Peru, was using the word *chocolate* by 1590; we must suppose that his usage in Spanish was simply different, for reasons which we are not at the moment able to determine, though his place of writing, his place of origin, and his social group affiliation are all possibly relevant.

The use by Francisco Hernández of Nawa *chokola:tl* (spelled <chocollatl>) shows that the word existed in Nawa by 1580, but it does not show where in the Nawa-speaking world it was used. Hernández collected information in various parts of Mexico, as well as Peru and the Philippines. That the next known citation of this Nawa word is Clavijero (1780) shows that there are serious gaps in our documentation of this Nawa word.

Acknowledgments

This study is a summary and extract of a larger work published in *Ancient Meso-america*, appearing here by permission of the editor, William Fowler. It was written in large part to correct both the mistaken efforts to revise long-standing results and many errors of interpretation put forward by Dakin and Wichmann (2000). Una Canger and Thomas Smith-Stark read an earlier draft and offered helpful comments. Louise Burkhart helped us track down sixteenth-century references to drinks made from cacao.

Notes

1. Language names and words in Meso-American Indian languages are cited according to the orthographic practices of the Project for the Documentation of the Languages of Meso-America (PDLMA), which in turn derive from those of the Proyecto Lingüístico "Francisco Marroquín" (PLFM). This spelling system uses only ASCII symbols, spells phonemically (one phoneme per grapheme [which may consist of a group of ASCII symbols]), and follows Spanish and traditional Meso-American orthographic practice when it is not inconsistent. This means, for example, that /q/ is <q>, /k/ is <k>, /w/ is <w>, /š/ is <x>, /c/ is <tz>, /č/ is <ch>, /ʔ/ is <7>, /ŋ/ "eng" is <nh>, /x/ is <j>, vowel length is <V:> or <VV>. Phonemic spellings found in sources not employing the PDLMA's orthographic practices are respelled; premodern citations are presented in faithful transcriptions of the original spellings. The only forms that are not respelled are those whose pronunciation is not unambiguously or adequately indicated by their symbols: such forms are cited within angle brackets <abc>. Morpheme boundaries are marked by - for inflexional affixes, . for derivational affixes, = for elements of a compound, and + for clitics (see note 4); # marks word boundaries. In historical comparisons, the format *abc]pqr[xyz* means that *pqr* is the part to be compared. In spellings of word shapes, V means vowel and C means consonant.

Unless otherwise noted, all linguistic forms cited in this study have been collected by members of the PDLMA or verified by the authors, even when these forms are also cited in Dakin and Wichmann 2000.

Language abbreviations and linguists producing the PDLMA's databases are: AYA Ayapa Gulf Sokean (Daniel Suslak, Giulia Oliverio, and James Fox); COP Copainalá Chiapas Soke (Clifton Pye); GUI San Juan Guichicovi Mije (Giulia Oliverio); MAR Santa María Chimalapa Oaxaca Soke (Terrence Kaufman and Loretta O'Connor); MIG San Miguel Chimalapa Oaxaca Soke (Terrence Kaufman and Heidi Anna Johnson); OLU Oluta Mijean (Roberto Zavala Maldonado); SAY Sayula Mijean (Richard Rhodes and Dennis Holt); SOT Soteapan Gulf Sokean (Terrence Kaufman and Valerie Himes); TEC Tecpatán Chiapas Soke (Roberto Zavala Maldonado); TEX Texistepec Gulf Sokean (Ehren Reilly and Catherine Bereznak); TOT Totontepec Mije (Daniel Suslak). The PDLMA's research has been supported by the National Science Foundation (SBR-9411247, 9511713, and 9809985), the Salus Mundi Foundation, and the

National Geographic Society (4190–92 and 5319–94), together with small grants from the State University of New York at Albany and the University of Pittsburgh.

2. In scholarly writings by botanists, the technical term for the cacao bean is "seed"; the word "kernel" as a scientific term in this literature applies only to members of the genus *Graminaceae* (grasses). In ordinary English, however, the vernacular sense of the word "seed" carries the suggestion of being planted by human agency. To avoid this suggestion, instead of "seed" we use the vernacular term "kernel," which captures the notion of the most valuable part and the angular shape, as it also does for the maize kernel; this term is frequent (though not predominant) in the nontechnical literature for describing cacao.

3. Nawa is the name of a set of closely related languages. Its main branches are Central Nawa (which includes the speech of the Basin of Mexico) and Eastern Nawa (which includes Huasteca Nawa, Gulf Coast Nawa, and Pipil).

4. Sokean languages have a class of *clitics*—words and other morphemes that cannot bear stress and so attach phonologically to a preceding or following word. Clitics are not counted when applying stress rules.

5. It was Wichmann (1995) who first recognized that the proto-Mijean form of this word was *kakaw*. He argues (1995: 343–344) that the proto-Oaxaca Mije form corresponding to proto-Sokean *kakawa* is *kakaw*, but he assumes that the Highland and Lowland Mije forms of approximate shape [kaká:w] must have been borrowings from Spanish. His evidence is that the final vowel is long and stressed; he is apparently unaware of the developments outlined here, whereby proto-Mijean *CVCVR* forms regularly appear as [CVCV́:R]. Dakin and Wichmann (2000:57a) go further than Wichmann (1995) in erroneously suggesting that the [kaká:w] forms do not develop from the same form as Totontepec Mije /kaku/.

6. Forms supporting the reconstruction of pMS *wakata* 'Guiana chestnut' and *puʔjuyuʔ* 'nighthawk' and pM *ʔitzɨmɨ* 'peccary' are cited in Kaufman and Justeson (in press).

7. Wichmann (1995) mistakenly reconstructs *makokoʔ* 'cockroach.' This lexical item should be reconstructed as *ma+ kokoʔ*: *ma+* is a proclitic and is therefore unstressable; the root *kokoʔ* is disyllabic and takes penult stress. (Evidence that *ma+* is not part of the root in *ma+ kokoʔ* is its absence in AYA *ko:ʔko*.)

8. Salvador Lenka [k'á:gaw] /k'akaw/ is recorded by Lehmann (1920:item 372n) with an anomalous initial /k'/; this may well be an error on Lehmann's part.

7

Brewing Distinction

The Development of Cacao Beverages in Formative Mesoamerica

John S. Henderson and Rosemary A. Joyce

The fact that no pre-Columbian inhabitant of South America used *T. cacao* for anything beyond manufacturing a wine from the white pulp surrounding the seeds, and using the same pulp as a nibble, would seem a convincing argument against a South American origin and subsequent transportation to Mesoamerica (S. D. Coe and M. D. Coe 1996:26).

In making this statement in their authoritative social history of cacao, Sophie and Michael Coe made an assumption shared by generations of scholars interested in the economic and ritual significance of cacao in pre-Hispanic Mesoamerica, ourselves included. This assumption was that cacao was originally cultivated for the purpose of producing the kind of drink described in the sixteenth century, made by fermenting the cacao seeds, drying them, optionally toasting them, grinding them, and mixing them with water in a thick, bitter suspension. But what if this use of *Theobroma* did not provide the original impetus for the cultivation and domestication of *Theobroma cacao* L.? What if, instead, the original cultivators—whether in Central or South America—used the wild relatives of *T. cacao* in ways analogous to those ethnographically documented for other members of the genus—for the pulp, eaten fresh or fermented to form a beverage, cacao *chicha*, or chocolate beer?

Our suggestion that this possibility be considered is based on a number of lines of argument, which will be sketched out briefly below. Fundamentally, however, it rests on a concern to avoid arguing teleologically. The complexity of the steps involved in producing the familiar chocolate beverage, if taken as the goal of the cultivation of *T. cacao*, invokes *a posteriori* logic. The original cultivators of the plant should have seen advantages to it that did not require the wholesale invention of a sequence of processing. Instead, this production process should be open to modeling as an outcome of likely actions of early plant cultivators, elaborated over time into the form we take as normative today. When we hold ourselves to this requirement, the fact that stands out in the production process of chocolate (the term we will use for the beverage highlighting ground cacao seeds, familiar to all Mesoamericanists, and taken as the norm by S. D. Coe and M. D. Coe [1996]) is that it begins with fermentation and produces precisely the product rejected as evidence for connections between South and Central American practices related to *Theobroma*: a fermented, alcoholic beverage (which we will call cacao *chicha*). Accepting that cacao may originally have been one among a wider range of plants used to produce fermented beverages, we then propose a rationale—admittedly speculative, but consistent with later Mesoamerican practices—for the conversion of interest in cacao beverages from their intoxicating properties to the potential they provided for the performance of serving.

Several authors (Blake and Clark 1999; Clark and Blake 1994; Clark and Gosser 1995; Hill and Clark 2001; Hoopes 1995) have suggested that presentation of drinks, particularly fermented beverages, in elaborately decorated containers was an important strategy employed by "aggrandizers" in early Central American societies. These authors all propose that drinking was one of the activities that could legitimately be sponsored in non-hierarchical societies to create forms of social debt, binding people in asymmetric social relations. We have previously proposed that in the recently documented early villages of Caribbean coastal Honduras, similar social events might have involved early use of cacao (Henderson and Joyce 2001), a product critical in the later history of the region and still cultivated today.

The Ulua River Valley of Honduras (Figure 7.1) was among the major documented zones of cacao cultivation in the sixteenth century (Bergmann 1969). When the Spaniards invaded the region, the ruler of Chetumal, some 200 miles distant up the coast of Yucatan, so valued his interests in Ulua cacao plantations that he sent a fleet of war canoes commanded by Gonzalo Guerrero to defend the valley against the newcomers (Henderson 1979). To date, archaeological evidence for earlier cultivation of cacao in the region has been indirect, consisting of modeled cacao pods that formed ornaments on Classic period cache vessels and figurines made and recovered in the valley (Figure 7.2; compare D. Stone 1984). Production of cacao beverages involving frothing of cacao suspension may date to the early Middle Formative, when spouted bottles with flaring necks were produced, including those Terry Powis identified as containing cacao in Belize (Powis et al. 2002).[1] The dates of such vessels in the Ulua Valley

Figure 7.1. Map showing location of lower Ulua River Valley, Honduras. Map by John S. Henderson.

Figure 7.2. Ceramic figurine of a monkey holding a cacao pod. Classic period. Ulua Valley, Honduras. Photograph courtesy of Peabody Museum, Harvard University (Photo 45–13–20/15068 N17851).

(ca. 1000–700 B.C.) appear to be the earliest reported (Powis et al. 2002:88), suggesting that the Ulua Valley may have been an early locale for production of standard Mesoamerican chocolate.

The Many Forms of Drinking Cacao

Theobroma pentagona, *T.leiocarpa*, and *T. grandiflorum*, wild relatives of cacao, are prized in northern South America for the sweet pulp that surrounds the seeds (A. M. Young 1994:3; see Bletter and Daly, this volume). South American use of the pods included the production of a drink from the fermented pulp (A. M. Young 1994:14–15). These indigenous South American practices suggest a potential route toward the elaborate processing of cacao seeds required for their consumption in the Mesoamerican fashion as chocolate, since the first step in that process is fermenting the contents of cacao pods. This indigenous tradition of production of cacao *chicha* also provides a precedent, otherwise lacking in the ethnographic accounts of use of the genus, for consuming cacao as a beverage.

The South American pattern of using members of the genus for their pulp is commonly practiced as far north as Nicaragua, where *T. bicolor* has long been used to make *pinolillo*, while people southward used the fresh pulp to make "a refreshing, frothy beverage with a citrus-like flavor" (A. M. Young 1994:15). A close relative of the *Theobroma* genus, *Herrania purpurea* (formerly *Theobroma purpurea*), was used by the Bri Bri of Costa Rica to produce a more bitter drink (P. H. Allen 1956:112, 221–222). In South America, the Andaki allowed the pulp of *Theobroma* to ferment, producing an alcoholic drink (Friede 1953). Bletter and Daly (this volume) document use of *Theobroma* spp. in fermented drinks in Panama, Venezuela, and French Guiana.

There are good grounds for thinking that even during the period when cacao was consumed as nonalcoholic chocolate in Mesoamerica, an intoxicating cacao beverage was also produced there, as it still is today. Recent research by Cameron McNeil (Chapter 17, this volume) confirms that contemporary Highland Maya people occasionally make fermented beverages from cacao pulp. Inscriptions on Classic Maya polychrome vases include references to *k'ab kakaw*, literally honey-cacao, described as "a possibly fermented cacao juice using honey" (Reents-Budet 1994c:75). The cacao foods recorded on Classic Maya polychrome pots include records of "tree-fresh" cacao, thought to be a reference to the pulp (B. MacLeod and D. Reents-Budet 1994:115–119), which is the material central to the production of fermented cacao drinks.

But the strongest evidence for use of fermented cacao beverages comes from the Late Postclassic Mexica (Aztecs), as recorded in the work of Bernardino de Sahagún (1950–82). The Nahuatl-speaking informants, describing the food consumed by the lords of Tenochtitlan, the Mexica capital, enumerated a wide range of cacao beverages, including some that recall the "tree fresh" cacao of the Classic Maya and the honey-cacao identified as possibly a fermented drink:

> Then, in his house, the ruler was served his chocolate, with which he finished [his repast]—green, made up of tender cacao; honeyed chocolate made with ground up dried flowers—with green vanilla pods; bright red chocolate; orange-colored chocolate; black chocolate; white chocolate. (Sahagún 1950–82, Book 8, Chapter 13, 1954:39).

A fermented beverage produced from members of the genus *Theobroma* apparently exhibits a distinctive taste when contrasted with other fermented beverages. The adjective that comes up repeatedly in descriptions of cacao pulp beverages is "refreshing," a term also applied to the unfermented pulp itself. The "tree-fresh cacao" of the Classic Maya is intriguingly echoed in the botanical description provided to Sahagún of a form of cacao that is clearly described as an intoxicating beverage:

> [Green cacao] makes one drunk, takes effect on one, makes one dizzy, confuses one, makes one sick, deranges one. When an ordinary amount is drunk, it gladdens one, refreshes one, consoles one, invigorates one. Thus it is said: 'I take cacao. I wet my lips. I refresh myself.' (Sahagún 1950–82, Book 11, Chapter 6, 1963:119–120)

The description is clearly of a fermented beverage and suggests that the "green cacao" described as one of the beverages served to the ruler may also have been intoxicating. The word translated as "green" here is *xoxouhqui*, which means green in color but also means unripe and potentially sour (in reference to fruit trees, the main subject of this section of the text; Susan Gillespie, personal communication 2002). The Spanish gloss on the Nahuatl text attributes the intoxicating character of "green cacao" to being "new," writing "Cuando es nuevo, si se bebe mucho emborracha, y si se bebe templadamente refrigera y refresca" ["When it is new, if one drinks much one becomes drunk, and if one drinks temperately it cools and refreshes"]. The Spanish text directly substitutes "nuevo," "new," for the Nahuatl text's "green/immature/sour."

The only way a person would become intoxicated on new cacao would be by drinking the liquid of fermentation, which is otherwise a waste product of the production of seeds to be dried for later preparation as standard Mesoamerican chocolate. The product of fermentation is a clear liquid (unlike the dense suspension of ground cacao) that is lighter in color than chocolate. References to "fresh" cacao could mark the distinction between the primary fermented beverage and the secondary, unfermented chocolate. The fermented beverage would have to be consumed new, or fresh, as soon as it was produced, since it would continue to ferment and get sour. Rather than a characterization of drinking immoderately or in moderation, the passage from Sahagún's Florentine Codex may better be read as distinguishing two forms of cacao beverage, requiring different drinking approaches.

This passage surely demonstrates that among the forms of cacao consumption in the sixteenth century, there was at least one means of drinking cacao as a fermented, intoxicating beverage. It is impossible to produce the conventional form of chocolate without producing a fermented cacao drink as one stage in the process.

Brewing Cacao *Chicha*

The quality highlighted in the Nahuatl text, and perhaps also in Classic Maya texts, is freshness versus sourness, a register of taste relevant for fermented drinks in a way it is not relevant to what we know today as chocolate. As A. M. Young (1994:74–79) describes the conventional production process, seeds and pulp are placed in a vessel (often a wooden box or even a canoe; personal observation, Henderson and Joyce) and left to ferment for several days. The conversion of the pulp to alcohol accompanies changes in polyphenols in the seeds, cutting the bitterness of the seeds and turning them a lovely pale violet. Significantly, A. M. Young (1994:74) notes that the Mesoamerican-selected "*criollo*-derived cacao seeds require less time to ferment than *forastero* seeds," the South American cultivar. This implies that the conversion of seeds to a form acceptable for Mesoamerican use could take place early in the fermentation process. This is important because after the available sugars in the seeds and pulp are converted into alcohol, a second stage of fermentation starts, which converts alcohol to acetic acid. In order to recoup drinkable cacao *chicha*, fermentation could not be allowed to continue too long, or the product would be effectively undrinkable, cacao vinegar.

The final development of the chocolate flavor of the seeds is accompanied by a change in color from purple to brown and shrinkage of the fermented seeds. The fermented seeds must be completely dried (Figure 7.3) to prevent the growth of mold, still a problem in contemporary chocolate production (Robert Steinberg, personal communication 2001). The degree of fermentation accomplished before the beans are dried can be quite varied.

The sequence of processes that result in the fermented seeds that fuel the

Figure 7.3. Cacao seeds drying in the northern Ulua Valley, Honduras, in 1982. Photograph courtesy of Kevin O. Pope.

modern chocolate industry cannot have been developed solely for the purpose of inducing the changes that make cacao seeds suitable for chocolate production. But they could easily have developed from an initial desire to produce a lightly fermented beverage from cacao pulp. We suggest that it is possible that in Mesoamerica the original use of cacao was as a form of *chicha*. Bitter chocolate is an acquired taste, with relatively subtle stimulant effects and none of the attraction of intoxicants that Hoopes (1995) persuasively argues contributed to the effectiveness of feasts in early Central American societies.

From this perspective, cacao seeds were a by-product, and their conversion to a tasty food was an unanticipated side effect of the primary fermentation of cacao pulp, perhaps more effective because of the characteristics of *criollo* cacao. A. M. Young (1994:11) suggests, based on ethnographic observations in Central America, that the seeds of plants in the genus might have been important sources of dietary fat. Bletter and Daly (this volume) document examples of cultivation of *T. bicolor* and relatives for seeds, eaten toasted, in a number of Colombian and Ecuadorian societies. We suggest that cacao seeds, a by-product of alcohol production, would have been appreciated in early Mesoamerica just as palm seeds were, for their rich fat. Ground seeds could have been added to cacao as a condiment at the time of service. The use of ground *sapote* seeds (most likely *Pouteria sapota*) as a condiment in cacao beverages has been described ethnographically among the Lacandon, making it clear that adding ground seeds to cacao is as much a part of the process as the more widely studied step of adding flowers (S. D. Coe and M. D. Coe 1996:61–66; compare Gillespie and MacVean 2002; Reents-Budet 1994c:75–79). Because of the glue-like texture of the pulp, it would have been impossible to separate cacao seeds from the pulp in advance of fermentation. Strained out of the fermented liquid, they need only have been tested for taste by food processors already accustomed to drying, toasting, and grinding seeds—practices that probably can be traced to the Mesoamerican Archaic period (ca. 8000–2000 B.C.).

Serving Cacao as Social Performance

Although most of the equipment used in processing cacao in traditional Mesoamerican style is perishable, pottery vessels do provide a possibility for tracing patterns of food serving specific to the cacao complex (see Hurst, this volume). Transport of cacao beans presumably involved soft, perishable containers. Processing of cacao pods involved equally perishable wooden troughs. It is only at the stage of preparation and consumption that specialized paraphernalia in imperishable materials, specifically grinding stones and serving vessels, were employed.

As described in the sixteenth century, the presentation of cacao required the use of specialized vessels for preparation and serving. Sahagún recorded the following description of the vessels used to serve cacao to the rulers of Tenochtitlan:

> The chocolate was served in a painted gourd vessel, with a stopper also painted with a design, and [having] a beater; or in a painted gourd, smoky [in color], from neighboring lands, with a gourd stopper, and a jar rest of ocelot skin or of cured leather. In a small net were kept the earthen jars, the strainer with which was purified the chocolate, a large, earthen jar for making the chocolate, a large painted gourd vessel in which the hands were washed, richly designed drinking vessels; [there were] large food baskets, sauce dishes, polished dishes, and wooden dishes (Sahagún 1950–82, Book 8, 1954:40).

Postclassic period (A.D. 1000–1521) vessels illustrated in the Central Mexican Codex Nuttall (1975) (Figure 7.4) would have facilitated frothing of the cacao, a crucial step required to force the chocolate sediment into suspension, enclosing the liquid within a restricted body with a flaring neck that contained the developing foam. The fundamental requirement for drinking chocolate as normally described in late periods in Mesoamerica appears to have been some form of drinking cup and some way to raise a froth on the cacao suspension (Figure 7.5).

Figure 7.4. A woman seated on a jaguar-skin throne in front of a palace (right) passes a vessel containing frothed cacao to the Mixtec Lord 8 Deer Jaguar Claw, also seated on a jaguar-skin throne (left). Note the constricted neck of the vessel. Codex Nuttall 1975 [1902]:26.

Figure 7.5. Early Colonial drawing of a Mexica woman frothing cacao by pouring it from a vase into cups. Illustration from the Florentine Codex (Sagahún 1950–82, Book 10, 1963:ill. 144a).

Bottles that are part of the earliest ceramic complexes of the lower Ulua Valley region have tall narrow necks (Figure 7.6) and seem ill-suited to this specific process of Mesoamerican cacao consumption (Healy 1974; Joyce and Henderson 2001). Vessel forms similar to those in the Codex Nuttall are not found until the advent of Middle Formative ceramic complexes, including that associated with the Ulua Valley archaeological site Playa de los Muertos (Kennedy 1981; D. Popenoe 1934). In these complexes, for which we have obtained consistent radiocarbon dates ca. 900–700 B.C. (Hendon and Joyce 1993; Joyce 1992; Joyce and Henderson 2001), new bottle forms develop. These feature both a narrow spout and a flaring neck (Figure 7.7). They would have allowed frothing of cacao by pouring from one vessel to another. We note with interest the report by Powis, Valdez, Hester, Hurst, and Tarka (2002) of the identification of chemical signatures of *Theobroma* in similar vessels dating to ca. 600 B.C. in Belize.

The suite of decorated vessel forms shared by complexes in the earlier Formative Ulua Valley (Joyce and Henderson 2001) and Soconusco (Blake and

Figure 7.6. Early Formative bottle. Barraca Brown Burnished type, Cusuco ceramic complex, Ocotillo phase, 1100–900 B.C. Honduras. Collection of the Instituto Hondureño de Antropología e Historia, Museo de San Pedro Sula, Honduras. Drawing by Yolanda Tovar.

Figure 7.7. Middle Formative bottle. Bodega Burnished type, Playa phase. Honduras. Collection of the Instituto Hondureño de Antropología e Historia, Museo de San Pedro Sula, Honduras. Photograph by John S. Henderson.

Clark 1999; Clark and Gosser 1995), both areas of probable production of cacao, includes forms appropriate for other required steps of cacao preparation, not including the last step of frothing. The small red-rimmed tecomates from Puerto Escondido would have been suitable for short-term storage of a small quantity of highly valuable consumables such as cacao beans and for transport of quantities of cacao beans sufficient for individual servings to a grinding platform. Ground cacao could have been mixed with water and other additives in pattern-burnished necked jars, whose size and formal characteristics are similar to jars shown in scenes involving presentation of cacao in Late Postclassic Central Mexican codices (see Figure 7.4). Cacao drinking would have required cups or small bowls (see, for example, Codex Nuttall 1975:30, lower right), like the pattern-burnished bowls that form the final component of the suite of vessels at Puerto Escondido.

We have proposed that drinking rituals that were the likely arena for the use of new, highly decorated pottery forms in early Mesoamerica would have been part of ceremonies entailed by social relationships contracted through marriage and fostering of children (Henderson and Joyce 2001; Joyce 1996b). The symbolic dimensions of cacao would have made it particularly appropriate to these ceremonies. In later Mesoamerican societies for which we have data on social alliances, cacao was a primary object of exchanges between social groups, marking betrothal, marriage, and children's life cycle rituals (S. D. Coe and M. D. Coe 1996:61–65; Gillespie and Joyce 1997; Marcus 1992). In the Codex Nuttall (1975), scenes showing vessels containing a brown foamy beverage are found in contexts of marriage, betrothal, children's life-cycle rituals, funerary, and ancestor veneration ceremonies.

A similar range of social ceremonies has been documented for Formative period Mesoamerican societies. Figurines have been taken as evidence for age-graded rites of passage in a number of Formative period societies, including the Playa de los Muertos society of Middle Formative Honduras (Joyce 2001: Chapter 2; compare Cyphers 1993; Lesure 1997). Although material traces of marriage or betrothal ceremonies themselves have not been identified, Cyphers (1984) has noted the likely representation in sculpture of a marital alliance between Chalcatzingo, Mexico, and another locality. Burials, including secondary mortuary treatment, can be seen as the material residues of funerary rites in Formative period villages, including sites in Honduras (Joyce 1999).

In the context of such social ceremonies, hosts could create social debts by matching preparation of feasts to the presence of particular visitors. But for fermented beverages, the work of production would have been under way in advance of such ceremonial visits, so serving fermented drinks would not as effectively be credited to relations with particular visitors as would preparing feast foods to order for the visit. One way for hosts to create specific debt and honor specific visitors would be to transform the serving of drinks into a performance aimed at particular visitors. In the case of cacao, it is clear that it was common practice in later Mesoamerican societies to add condiments at the time of serving. The addition of ground cacao seeds to an alcoholic cacao beverage, of which they were a by-product, would have lent itself to such a performative distinction at the time of serving.

The processing of cacao seeds—grinding into a fine nut meal—could have taken place as a performance of preparing a feast food for specially honored guests, creating a higher level of distinction and consequently greater social debt. The performance dimension of serving chocolate, as described in later Mesoamerican sources, is remarkable. Adding ground cacao seeds to liquid and frothing it to make a suspension was, by necessity, a last-minute action, the one depicted in the famous Classic Maya polychrome vase showing cacao being poured out of a cylinder in a palace setting (see Reents-Budet, Figure 10.10, this volume). Ethnographic accounts of the formal grinding of cacao by Lacandon women, co-sponsors of ceremonies, involving the use of archaic stone tools, precisely capture the sense of grinding as performance that we suggest may have been relevant in the early history of cacao (S. D. Coe and M. D. Coe 1996:65, citing Baer and Merrifield 1971:209–210). In this case, the ground cacao seeds are sometimes mixed into a fermented beverage—*balché*—echoing what we suggest may have been the original point of serving cacao in its early Mesoamerican history.

Implications for the Study of Ancient Cacao

The performance of cacao preparation was a means of formalizing hosting and marking the occasion of drinking as special. Ethnographic accounts of South American *chicha* drinking ceremonies (for example, Whitten 1986), in which the pots themselves—made to order and subsequently smashed—enhance the event, are a model for introducing performative actions, not strictly necessary, to increase the drama of the drinking event, making it more memorable and distinguishing one event from another. We suggest that as serving of cacao became increasingly formalized throughout the history of Mesoamerica, the emphasis shifted from the alcoholic nature of the medium to the performative preparation of a rare drink to mark a special event.

By developing a formal model for the use of cacao in early Mesoamerica that emphasizes the social setting for preparation and consumption, and that takes into account the actual vessel forms present in our excavations, we have been led to make a series of interlinked proposals. We suggest that cacao was most likely prepared originally as an alcoholic beverage, one among a suite of such drinks. This suggestion makes sense of the elaborate preparation sequence, is consistent with modern uses of wild relatives of cacao, and is supported by the description in sixteenth-century Nahuatl sources of a form of cacao that was intoxicating. The recovery of theobromine from necked bottles dating to the earliest periods of occupation at Puerto Escondido, Honduras, is consistent with the consumption of a cacao beverage that was not frothed.

Theobromine was also present in examples of typical spouted, wide-mouthed bottles that were developed slightly later, like those described from Belize, which would have facilitated frothing. Thus, between the Early and Middle Formative periods there was a shift in how cacao beverages were prepared and presented. We suggest that frothing cacao drinks and adding such condiments as flowers and ground seeds (including ground cacao seeds), must be seen as adding an element of performance to serving cacao that would have helped to underline publicly the social debt assumed by those to whom these beverages were served.

Like others interested in the social uses of cacao, we emphasize that over the long span of time during which cacao was used—now pushed a further seven-hundred years earlier by our analyses—we should expect that historical change in social organization, cuisine, and politics would have led to changes in the ways cacao was prepared, presented, and consumed.

Note

1. The alternative term "Preclassic," which is not used here, is specific to the archaeology of the Maya area, where it is defined as the development of Classic societies. The term "Formative" is used here instead because the research context for Puerto Escondido is the wider literature on early complexity in Mesoamerica. In this literature, concerning the Gulf Coast Olmec and related peoples, the time periods are referred to as Early and Middle Formative, and beginning and ending dates are different from those for the Preclassic period.

8

Cacao in Ancient Maya Religion

First Fruit from the Maize Tree and other Tales from the Underworld

Simon Martin

Like all agrarian societies, the ancient Maya had an abiding and intimate relationship with the natural world. All manner of trees, plants, leaves, flowers, fruits, and roots found a place in their symbol system, and the flora that
surrounded them, both wild and cultivated, were embedded in their spiritual
outlook. The crops that fed and enriched them were especially charged with
religious sentiment and took pivotal roles in their mythic narratives.

In recent years we have gained notable insights into the past use of cacao,
Theobroma cacao L., as a status marker and elite consumable, as well as into
some aspects of its ritual use and function as a rudimentary currency (a literal
"cash crop").[1] But it is fair to say that we have yet to establish its place in Maya
theology. I address this issue here, focusing on the art and writing of the Classic
period (A.D. 250–900), with forays into the Postclassic (A.D. 900–ca. 1542)
and Colonial eras (A.D. ca. 1542–1820). The themes encountered—fertility
and sustenance, sacrifice and regeneration, embodiment and transformation—
are pan-Mesoamerican in scope, and we can usefully draw on descriptions of
Central Mexican religion made shortly after the Spanish Conquest. Moreover,
since certain pre-Columbian ideas survive in traditional Maya communities to
this day, modern ethnographies are fertile sources of complementary data.

Cacao and Corn

We will begin with a revealing relationship between text and image on a small
stone bowl from the Early Classic era (A.D. 250–600), now in the Dumbarton
Oaks Collection in Washington D.C. (M. D. Coe 1975:11–12; Kerr 1992:470
[K4331—K-prefixed numbers refer to the Kerr Photographic Archive, accessible at <www.mayavase.com>]). It was originally carved with three roundels,
each containing a figural scene accompanied by a hieroglyphic caption, with

Figure 8.1. The Maize God as an embodied cacao tree. a. The seated god points to what may be a chocolate pot. b. The Maize God points to an open codex. c. Text naming the human protagonist as a "Maize Tree" (F2). Unprovenienced stone bowl. (K4331). Early Classic period. The Dumbarton Oaks collection, Washington, D.C. Drawings by Simon Martin after a painting by Felipe Dávalos in Coe 1975 and a photograph by Justin Kerr.

additional columns of text between each roundel. The two surviving scenes feature a male figure variously sitting or lying on a mat-decorated seat (Figure 8.1). His limbs are studded with ripe cacao pods, and his skin is marked with wavy "wood" motifs. Clearly, an anthropomorphic cacao tree is at hand. In one scene he points to what may be a chocolate pot (see Figure 8.1a); in another he examines an open book (see Figure 8.1b). Although much of the third scene is now missing, enough remains of the telltale pods to show that it was a similar portrait.

Not unnaturally, this young lord has been dubbed a "Cacao God" (S. D.

Coe and M. D. Coe 1996:45). Yet his physical characteristics—his sloping brow, tonsured hairstyle, and prominent forehead jewel—all ally him with the Maize God (see Taube 1985). Thus, despite his chocolate coating, this is not a cacao deity as such but the familiar Maize God in the guise of, or, more accurately, as the embodiment of a cacao tree (Martin 2002a; M. E. Miller and S. Martin 2004:78).

Confirmation of what seems, at first, an odd fusion comes from the captions to the scenes. In both surviving passages the second glyph joins the head of the Maize God to the sign for **TE'** 'tree' (at A2, E2). In one case, they are conflated into a single sign, as if mimicking the god-tree fusion in the scene (E2).[2] David Stuart (personal communication 1999; this volume) has proposed a reading of **IXIM** for this particular portrait of the maize deity; *ixim/ixi'im* is the word for 'maize' in almost every Mayan language spoken today. This would make the depicted figure the *iximte'* 'Maize God Tree' or simply 'Maize Tree.'[3]

In each case, *iximte'* is preceded by a term describing the posture or activity engaged in, while a subsequent glyph names the human actor who impersonates this entity.[4] Only one of these names is legible today, but it is the same male who forms the subject of the inter-roundel columns. Here again he is linked to an *iximte'* glyph (at F2), further emphasizing that he has assumed the identity of this supernatural, cacao-sprouting arbor (see Figure 8.1c).[5]

But how are we to understand "Maize Tree" in this context, and what is the nature of its connection to cacao? Since Karl Taube's fundamental work on the Maya Maize God, we have understood much of the supernatural narrative of corn (Taube 1985, 1986).[6] This tale of sacrifice and resurrection, reflecting the seasonal cycle, finds its fullest expression in the sixteenth-century K'iche' Maya epic the *Popol Vuh*—a work that draws on myths of far greater antiquity (Christenson 2003; D. Tedlock 1985). Although several episodes in the Maize God's complex journey remain to be explained (Quenon and Le Fort 1997), we can say with confidence that the corn cycle was the central metaphor of life and death for the Maya and the nucleus around which much of their religiosity was formed. If we are to appreciate the meaning of the cacao-maize relationship we must investigate this story still further.

Within the Mountain

One remarkable blackware vessel (known as the Berlin vase) illuminates key stages in the bodily transubstantiation of man, maize, and cacao (Figure 8.2). Produced in the Early Classic period, most likely in the central Peten region, it currently resides in the Ethnologisches Museum in Berlin (Eberl 2001:312; Schele and Mathews 1998:122–123; Taube 2004a:79–81). The subject matter is simultaneously an account of divine passage—the death and transformation of the Maize God—and the mortuary progress of the human lord who is follow-

Figure 8.2. The burial and transformation of the Maize God within Sustenance Mountain. a. The dead god lies on a bier. b. His body is reduced to a skeleton surmounted by anthropomorphic trees. Details. Unprovenienced vase (K6547). Early Classic period. Ethnologisches Museum, Berlin. Drawing by Simon Martin after a photograph by Justin Kerr.

ing in his footsteps. Two vignettes on the incised surface offer a sequential story, both set in the kind of watery environment that marks Underworld locales.

In the first scene the outstretched body of the dead lord is flanked by supernatural mourners in varied poses of distress. He lies on a funerary bier, his bejeweled head and feet protruding from an elaborately knotted shroud (see Figure 8.2a). The left leg of the bier carries the hieroglyph *och bih* 'road-enter.' This is a metaphor for death, describing, as it does, one stage in the mortuary odyssey of the Maize God (D. Stuart 1998:387–389). The whole assemblage is set within the rolling volutes of a personified mountain marked with maize kernels and the sign for *ak'ab* 'darkness,' identifying it as the Maya version

Figure 8.3. Sustenance Mountain in Maya art. Detail. Late Classic period. Tablet of the Foliated Cross, Palenque, Mexico. Drawing by Simon Martin after David Stuart (Stuart 1987:Figure 27).

of the Central Mexican *tonacatepetl*, or 'Sustenance Mountain.'[7] This primeval origin of maize and other important foodstuffs is a recurring feature of Mesoamerican mythologies, and the idea survives in many traditional societies today. One seventh-century representation at Palenque, Mexico, labels it **YAX-ha-li wi-tzi-na-la** *yax ? witznal* 'First ? Mountain Place' (Freidel, Schele, and Parker 1993:138) (Figure 8.3).[8] In the *Popol Vuh* this peak is called *paxil* 'Clefted (Place),' which presumably describes the lightning-carved fissure at its summit from which maize will be reborn. In modern belief it is a realm of the honored dead, with a cavernous interior in which clouds are born and with a surface covered with verdant life, especially wild game and fruit trees (Fischer 1999:483; Christenson 2001:78, 84–85).

Above the mountain on the Berlin vase appears the scalloped frame of a solar cartouche. Here it encloses an image of the Sun God within a lunar crescent, his head crowned by an undeciphered sign that has the sense of "seed" or the like.[9] Solar cartouches are elaborated glyphs for *yaxk'in* 'first sun' and often contain ancestral portraits in place of the sun deity (Tate 1992:59–62; Taube 2004b:286–287). In Mayan languages as widely separated as Yukatek in the north and Ch'orti' in the south, *yaxk'in* refers to the onset of the dry season, when the harvest is over. Between the cartouche and shrouded body there is a "wing" hieroglyph, recognizable as the sign **K'A'** in this context (David Stuart in Freidel, Schele, and Parker 1993:440). We currently lack a secure translation for it, but it forms the verbal root of the most common death expression in Maya inscriptions: *k'a'ay u-? sak ik'il*, which refers to the loss of a variety of *ik'* 'breath-essence' (Houston and Taube 2000:267).[10] This particular *ik'*, whose name includes the same "seed" glyph observed on the Sun God's head (the query mark in the translation), constitutes some inner life-force, or essence, of the Maize God.

Numerous ethnographic sources describe the soul or spirit of corn (for example, J. E. S. Thompson 1930:48–49; Wilson 1990:Chapters 1–3), and even the idea that such a spirit must leave the cob before it is harvested (Girard 1962:307–308). As we shall see, death produces a separation of body and soul in which the former is not simply an empty and discarded vessel but one that harbors the germ and material for future reproduction. In Mesoamerican ideology, humans are composed of a variety of soul-essences—each with its own nature and, on their division and release at death, their own afterlife destination (see López Austin 1988:203–236, 313–343; Vogt 1976:23). The scene on the Berlin vase depicts the flight of the Maize God's soul and its union with, or even formation of, the great celestial bodies (Figure 8.2a). In one modern story, Jesus Christ—almost universally considered a god of maize and fertility in traditional Maya societies—rises to the heavens after his crucifixion and becomes the sun

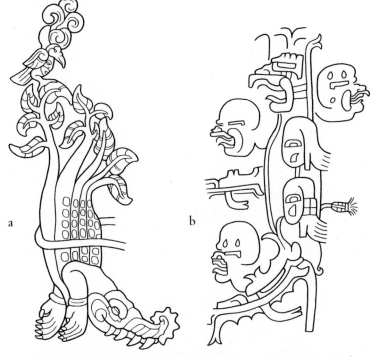

Figure 8.4. Crocodilian World Trees. a. Detail. Stela 25, Izapa, Mexico. Preclassic period. Drawing by Simon Martin after an unpublished drawing by Ayax Moreno. b. Detail of an incised design on "The Young Lord." Olmec jadite sculpture. Unprovenienced. Drawing by Simon Martin after Gillet Griffen in *The Olmec World: Ritual and Kingship* 1996:240.

(Sosa 1985:429–430). The same source says that Jesus traverses the sky on "his road," and that the souls of the dead travel with him.

The second scene depicts the body, now reduced to a skeleton, buried beneath a stepped pyramid (Figure 8.2b). The surrounding stony volutes and their animated covering of life (omitted in the illustration for the sake of clarity) emphasize that we are still within Sustenance Mountain, the conceptual prototype for funerary pyramids. Three anthropomorphic trees surmount the cadaver. Fertilized by, or erupting directly from it, their bodies are inverted, with fingers spreading to form sinuous roots, their torsos and legs transformed into trunks and leafy branches. The model for this posture is clear, the sky-supporting "World Trees" that are manifested as inverted crocodilians—a topic we will return to (Figure 8.4a, b).

Of the three tree figures in Figure 8.2b, the central one sprouts cacao pods, the one on the left bears a spiked fruit that may be *guanabana (Annona muricata* L.), and the one on the right has a snake-like design that may represent a vine or creeper (Judith Strupp Green, personal communication 2005; Schele and Mathews 1998:123). Each is identified by a hieroglyph in its headdress. The central figure is the owner of the vessel, as named in an incised text that runs over its three slab feet. This is the lord who now follows the Maize God's path through death and on to the afterlife. His companion trees—one male, one female—most likely represent his parents.

The best-known anthropomorphic trees in Maya art, those that ring the sarcophagus of Pakal of Palenque, Mexico (Robertson 1983; Ruz 1973), present an almost identical theme. Set inside a tomb chamber deep within the Temple of the Inscriptions—a symbolic cave within a mountain—the great slab of its lid shows a reclining Pakal wearing the net kilt of the Maize God, with the fiery torch of the lightning deity K'awiil set in his forehead (Figure 8.5a).

The lid scene famously illustrates Pakal's "rebirth," although it is a regeneration of a particular kind. Much debate has centered on whether Pakal emerges from or falls into the Underworld—whose entrance is symbolized here by the great pincers of an infernal centipede (Grube and Nahm 1994:702; Taube 2003b). Yet the key event is his transformation into an ascending World Tree, a mythical arbor marked with **TE'** 'tree/wood' signs and bearing bejeweled, serpent-headed flowers. Similar ideas are found in certain Maya communities today, where trees are planted over newly laid graves as tokens of future resurrection (Christenson 2001:206). J. Eric S. Thompson (1970:337) long ago noted the relationship of the lid scene to those in the Central Mexican codices Borgia (1993:49–53) and Vatican B (1972:17–18) in which recumbent deities give rise to directional World Trees (Figure 8.5b).[11] The reclining, flexed-limb pose of infancy fixes the Pakal/Maize God as a child of sacrificial death (Martin 2002b; Taube 1994b). Here he is immolated in an offering brazier so that new

a

b

Figure 8.5. Maize and the World Tree. a. Detail from the lid of Pakal's sarcophagus. Late Classic period. Palenque, Mexico. Drawing by Simon Martin after a photograph by Merle Greene Robertson (Robertson 1983:Figure 98). b. Detail from the Codex Borgia, page 53. Drawing by Simon Martin.

life might take his place; the potency of fire in transformative events is a recurring theme in Mesoamerican belief (López Austin 1988:324).

On the sarcophagus sides, ten fruit-laden saplings emerging from cracks in the ground can be identified from the shape of their progeny as cacao, guayaba, avocado, zapote, and nance (Robertson 1983:67–72) (Figure 8.6a). Each tree is fused with a human portrait, identified by its headdress and adjacent glyphic caption as a particular forebear of Pakal (with his parents shown twice, on either end of the sarcophagus). On both of its appearances the cacao tree is associated with Pakal's deceased mother, Ix Sak K'uk', 'Lady Resplendent Quetzal,' the person believed to represent his closest blood connection to the ruling line of Palenque (Figure 8.6b).

This four-sided tableau has memorably been dubbed an "orchard of the ancestral dead" (Schele and Freidel 1990:221), and links have been drawn between the cultivated landscape of life-sustaining tree crops and an animistic understanding of personified forebears (Carlsen and Prechtel 1991; McAnany 1995: 75–76). But we should also note the connection of this bounteous grove to its context; that is, its relationship to the body inside the stone coffin. Like

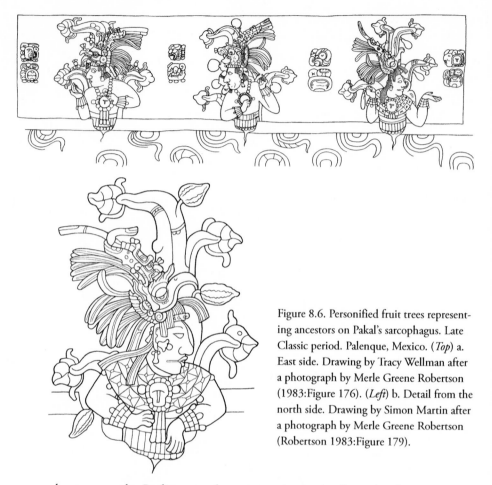

Figure 8.6. Personified fruit trees representing ancestors on Pakal's sarcophagus. Late Classic period. Palenque, Mexico. (*Top*) a. East side. Drawing by Tracy Wellman after a photograph by Merle Greene Robertson (1983:Figure 176). (*Left*) b. Detail from the north side. Drawing by Simon Martin after a photograph by Merle Greene Robertson (Robertson 1983:Figure 179).

the trees on the Berlin vase, these trees take succor from the decomposing corpse and represent a further allusion to Pakal's like-in-kind relationship with the Maize God.[12]

The themes of decomposition and transformation on both the Berlin vase and Palenque sarcophagus resonate strongly with the mythology of Central Mexico and a description in the sixteenth-century *Histoyre du Mechique* (Jonge 1905). Here the Maize God Centeotl buries himself in the floor of a cavern and from his body grows corn, as well as the fruits and seeds of other useful plants:

> [Centeotl] put himself under the ground, and from his hair emerged cotton, and from an eye a very good seed which they eat gladly, called *cacatzli*. . . From the nose, another seed called *chia*. . . From the fingers came a fruit called *camotli*. . . From the fingernails another kind of broad maize, which is the kind they eat today. And from the rest of the

body emerged many other fruits, which the men gather and sow. (Jonghe 1905:31–32)[13]

Similar ideas survive in contemporary Maya groups such as the Tzotzil (Gossen 1974:327, 335), while among the K'iche' of Chichicastenango, Guatemala, the concept has been incorporated into the Christian story. Here it is the crucified body of Christ, the latter-day Maize God, from which corn and other crops first emerge: "While nailed to the cross, Jesus miraculously turned around completely, exposing his back, and from his back came maize—white, yellow, and black—and beans and potatoes and all the other food plants" (Tax 1949:127).

All the Classic Maya sources discussed thus far give cacao a privileged position as the first or most prominent among the fruit trees grown from the Maize God's body. This no doubt reflects the special economic and status-reinforcing role this crop had in ancient times. Equally clearly, cacao was but one among many products of the Maize God's "death," an event of universal fruitfulness with greater implications for human sustenance than corn or cacao alone. As such, he is the provider of all food plants and the center of wider concepts of fecundity and abundance.

The ancestral fruit trees make it plain that this new growth encompasses the notion of generational rebirth. Robert Carlsen and Martin Prechtel (1991) have explored the themes of transformation, replacement, and regeneration among the modern Tz'utujiil and their neighbors, tracing antecedents in earlier art. They join James Mondloch (1980:9) in arguing that the human desire for immortality is satisfied in Maya religion less by removal to a heavenly paradise than by reincarnation in future generations, specifically as grandchildren. Mesoamerican religions are as one in believing humanity to be composed of corn dough, and the life cycle of the Maize God serves to "re-process" the material from which all people are made. Youngsters both in ancient and modern times are referred to as "sprouts" because they represent the fresh growth of the human seed.

The Embodied Tree

Just as this regeneration could be conceived of as an orchard of trees, it also could be condensed into the idea of a singular great arbor weighted with all the fruits of the earth except maize (see, for example, Carlsen and Prechtel 1991:27; J. E. S. Thompson 1930:134–135). The relationship between the single fruit tree and the Maize God is explicit in the *Popol Vuh*. The sacrifice of the Maize God (there called One Hunahpu) by his Underworld enemies, One Death and Seven Death, is followed by his decapitation, with the severed head then set into a barren tree:

Now when they went to place his head in the midst of the tree, the tree bore fruit. The tree had never borne fruit until the head of One Hunahpu was placed in it. This was the tree that we now call the calabash. It is said to be the head of One Hunahpu. One Death and Seven Death marveled at the fruit of the tree, for its round fruit was everywhere. Neither could be seen clearly the head of One Hunahpu, for his face had become identical in appearance with the calabashes. (Christenson 2003: 126)

Earlier in the same K'iche' tale in which the crucified Jesus was transformed into food plants, we are told of a tree which he climbed to hide from pursuers:

Jesus came down from the tree and lay down in its shade. Then he blessed the tree that it might serve for cacao. Instantly there was cacao. He told the people . . . that the cacao should serve in *cofradías* in marriages, and for borrowing money and maize. (Tax 1949:126–127)

Although adapted to the new religion, this is a recognizable reference to the miraculous tree of the Underworld engendered by the Maize God. It sets out the divine origin of cacao, as well as its role as a means of exchange. In narrative terms, the *Popol Vuh* episode provides the means by which One Hunahpu reproduces himself, impregnating an Underworld maiden with his spittle and thereby giving rise to his sons and avengers, the Hero Twins. Here the fruit serves the purpose it has in nature: a means of generational descent.

The closest visual analog for these passages in ancient Maya art is on a small polychrome cylinder vase now in the Museo Popol Vuh, Guatemala City (Kerr 1997:816 [K5615]; Taube 1985:175). Two stylized cacao trees on opposing sides of the vessel sprout heads bearing the distinctive sloping brow, tonsured hair, and jewels of the Maize God (Figure 8.7). At the base of each tree are large flowers, a feature also seen in the Madrid Codex (1967:69), where the blossom serves as glyphic *nik* in *nikte'* 'Flower.'[14] Flowers, specifically the frangipani (*Plumeria*), were viewed as sources of divine birth in some Maya lore (J. E. S. Thompson 1970:202–203). Flowering trees and mountains also symbolized paradisiacal locations of beauty and abundance in the afterlife (Taube 2004a), and one attested name for Sustenance Mountain in Tz'utujiil Maya is *kotsej juyu ruchiliew* 'Flowering Mountain Earth' (Carlsen and Prechtel 1991:27). On one of our painted trees a smaller, immature head emerges, its eyes closed as if in a fetal sleep. This is most easily explained by regarding all fruit as symbolic heads of the Maize God, as the *Popol Vuh* text clearly implies we should. Monument 21 at the Cotzumalhuapan site of Bilbao, Guatemala, shows a tree of abundance bearing cacao in which each pod is also a human face (L. A. Parsons 1969:101–

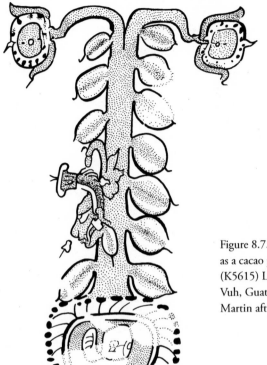

Figure 8.7. The head of the Maize God as a cacao pod. Unprovenienced vase. (K5615) Late Classic period. Museo Popol Vuh, Guatemala City. Drawing by Simon Martin after a photograph by Justin Kerr.

103, Plate 31). This association was so close that in many Maya languages the words for "fruit" and "face" are homonyms.

At this point we need to touch on the wider concept of World Trees and their relationship to the Maize God. The Maya *axis mundi* is usually described as a ceiba tree (*Ceiba pentandra* [L.] Gaertn.), and its names include *yax che'el kab* 'First/Green Earth Tree' among the Lacandon and Itza (Means 1917:135; Tozzer 1907:154) and *yax imix che'* 'First/Green *Imix* Tree' in the Colonial-era Chilam Balam documents of Yucatan (*che'* is a cognate form for *te*) (Roys 1933:64).[15] *Imix* was the Maya counterpart to the Mexican *cipactli*, a supernatural crocodile and the name for the first of the twenty days of the *tonalpohualli* (calendar) (Seler 1902–23: 1:499). *Cipactli* symbolized the surface of the earth in which plants grow, as well as the trunks of trees.[16] The Chilam Balams call the four trees that define the limits of the cosmos *imix yaxche'* or "*imix* ceiba," each prefixed by the color assigned to its relevant cardinal direction.[17] In the Maya calendar, major cycles conclude on the day *ajaw*, with the first day of any new era falling on the next *imix*. In accord with this, all five *imix* trees in the Chilam Balams were set up directly after the destruction of the previous world—the most recent in a recurring cycle of cataclysms to re-shape the earth, a fundamental Mesoamerican concept of annihilation and renewal.

The iconography of crocodilian trees is applied to the Maize God's rebirth, stressing his transformation into a World Tree (Taube 2005:25). Some images picture his lower body as the saurian's inverted snout or label him *juun ixim ahiin* 'One Maize Crocodile.'[18] The same visual metaphor was applied to cacao at Classic period Copan, Honduras, where now-fragmentary sculpted containers were originally shaped like inverted crocodiles sprouting cacao pods from their tails (Lara 1996) (Figure 8.8a).[19] A similar motif appears on a carved block newly recovered from the Osario Temple at Chichen Itza, Yucatan, Mexico (Schmidt 2003) (Figure 8.8b).

An association between World Trees and the Maize God survives in certain *loh* and *ch'a chaak* ceremonies still performed in rural Yucatan. Both rites involve a model of the world whose corners and sky-defining arches are made from bent sprigs of *Citharexylum schottii* Greenm., one of several shrubs known today as *iximche'* (Sosa 1985:379–380). It may be the long use of such plants to symbolize the incorporeal *iximte'/iximche'* that explains how at least some of

Figure 8.8. Crocodilian cacao trees. a. Reconstruction of a sculpted stone container. Late Classic period. Copan, Honduras. Drawing by Simon Martin. b. Panel fragment. Late Classic or Postclassic period. Osario Temple, Chichen Itza, Yucatan, Mexico. Drawing by Simon Martin after a field sketch by the Proyecto Arqueológico Chichen Itza, courtesy of Peter Schmidt.

them got this name. Ruud van Akkeren (1999:291–292) has previously argued that references to *iximche'* in the Rabinal Achi document of Highland Guatemala refer not to the Kaqchikel Maya citadel of that name but to the central World Tree.

Inversion alone was an attenuated reference to the crocodile tree. Karl Taube has recently identified many of the "acrobats" and "contortionists" in Maya art as images of the Maize God adopting the tree posture (2003a:461).[20] In one jade cache at Copan, such a figurine was placed at the center of a quincunx— the world-directional model in its most abstract form. This observation has implications that go beyond this, not least for cacao.

The lid of one ceramic censer from Copan depicts an arched "acrobat" with a cacao pod in his headdress (see Schmidt, de la Garza, and Nalda 1998:603), and Peter Schmidt has reassembled a fragmentary censer—perhaps from the Río Bec region in Mexico—showing an inverted body peppered with cacao pods (Figure 8.9a). Although the object is badly broken today, one can see that

Figure 8.9. The Maize God in the inverted posture and bearing cacao. a. Censer lid, possibly from Río Bec, Mexico. Ceramic. Late Classic period. Currently at the regional headquarters of the Instituto Nacional de Antropología y Historia, Merida. Drawing by Simon Martin after a photograph courtesy of Peter Schmidt. b. Censer pot. Unprovenienced (K1504b). Ceramic. Postclassic period. Unknown private collection. Drawing by Simon Martin after a photograph by Justin Kerr.

precisely the same motif was carved in stone at Copan (McNeil, Hurst, and Sharer, this volume, Figure 11.13), and is presumably analogous to the upright figurines from Highland Guatemala that are similarly festooned with pods (see this volume McNeil, Hurst and Sharer, Figure 11.15a).

The "diving" figures that become prevalent in the Postclassic era also allude to the Maize God as an embodied tree, and on small appliquéd censers we see him carrying corncobs, seeds, or cacao pods (see Figure 8.9b). Yet the bird headdress he often wears on these occasions signals that he is also flying. This seemingly incongruous conflation of ideas is made explicit in some architectural stuccoes, where leaves sprout from the divers' legs as well as wings from their arms (Taube 1992a:41, Figure 18a). The downward motion may symbolize heaven-sent beneficence in general, but it could refer to something more specific, such as the fall of seeds in planting.[21]

Four inverted deities on page 15 of the Dresden Codex (1975) also appear to combine tree personification with the act of falling or flying (Figure 8.10). Three sprout cacao pods whereas the limbs of the fourth, a skeletal Death God, transform into barren branches. Accompanying texts share the verbal root *pak'* 'to plant, sow' (Bricker 1986:147), which an early Yukatek lexicon, the *Vienna Dictionary*, elaborates as "sembrar aguacates y demás frutas; plantar árboles (to sow avocados and other fruits; to plant trees)" (Barrera Vásquez 1980:624). These gods seem to be the presiding patrons of auspicious and inauspicious days for the planting of fruit trees.[22]

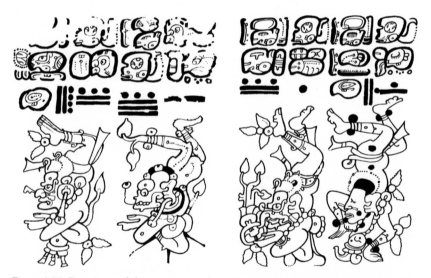

Figure 8.10. Four inverted deities in a tree-planting augury. Dresden Codex, page 15. Drawing by Simon Martin.

Out of the Underworld

Although the transformation of the Maize God into a World Tree represents his final revelation as a pillar of the sky, many of the fruitful examples, including cacao, leave us at an earlier stage, still encased within Sustenance Mountain. This is the situation that prevails in the *Popol Vuh*, where the tree of One Hunahpu grows not on the surface of the earth but in the Underworld. We must go through a further narrative turn before cacao and the other gifts of the *iximte'* reach the earth's surface.

A relatively rare appearance of cacao pods in a painted ceramic scene, on a vessel known as K631, provides important information (Kerr 1989:29; M. E. Miller and S. Martin 2004:62) (Figure 8.11). Seated in a throne room is God L—identified by the owl avatar, or familiar, in his broad hat—the most senior and powerful lord of the Maya Underworld. An aged figure with jaguar characteristics, he is often shown with a decorated cape, a staff, and a cigar.[23] On K631 he converses with the fiery, torch-headed K'awiil, who gestures toward an anthropomorphic tree weighted with cacao pods. Essentially the same inverted figure depicted on the Berlin vase (see Figure 8.2b), this character, in turn, interacts with a standing companion dressed in a scarlet macaw headdress and feathered "back-rack."[24]

Like the corresponding gods in the *Popol Vuh*, One Death and Seven Death, God L would have presided over the demise of the Maize God and possessed the resulting Maize Tree. This would explain why he is associated with the wealth of cacao. In his palace on the Princeton vase (see Reents-Budet, Figure 10.9, this volume) we see, uniquely in Maya art, a female attendant pouring a chocolate

Figure 8.11. A palace scene in the Underworld, featuring God L, K'awiil, and the Maize Tree. Unprovenienced vessel (K631). Late Classic period. Drawing by Simon Martin after a photograph by Justin Kerr.

Figure 8.12. God L with merchant's pack and cacao tree. Mural detail. Late Classic period. Red Temple, Cacaxtla, Mexico. Drawing by Simon Martin after a photograph by Enrico Ferorelli in M. E. Miller and S. Martin 2004:Figure 24.

drink from height—the traditional technique for producing a frothy surface (S. D. Coe and M. D. Coe 1996:50). The use of cacao as monetary exchange would similarly explain God L's ties to commerce and long-distance transport. In the murals of Cacaxtla, Mexico, we see him as a trader, his hat resting atop a large merchant's pack (Figure 8.12). Interestingly, this scene seems to be another version of the transformation story. Set in a symbolic netherworld at the foot of a stairway (omitted from the drawing), God L faces a cacao tree. But the scene continues up the steps, toward the earth's surface, where the tree is replaced by a series of cornstalks on which each cob is the head of the reborn Maize God.

A supernatural patron of cacao described by Diego de Landa for Colonial Yucatan was Ek Chuah, who similarly oversaw trade and long-distance travel (Landa 1941 [1566]:107, 164). In Yukatek, *ek' chuah* means 'black scorpion,' and two deities in the Madrid Codex, Gods L and M, are shown with scorpion tails and black body color (pages 79a–84a) (Seler 1902–23, v. 1:413, 451), suggesting that this was a euphemistic term for them both in late times.[25]

In the *Popol Vuh* it is the sons of the Maize God, the Hero Twins, who ultimately topple the Underworld gods from power. This is depicted on a vase painted some six or seven centuries earlier, portraying the brothers stripping God L of his fine clothes and insignia—hat, jewels, cape, and staff—and sacrificing his companion or former co-ruler (M. E. Miller and S. Martin 2004:60,

Figure 21). Mortal kings and queens sometimes brandish God L's staff as a scepter, perhaps in commemoration of this victory.[26] His undoing paves the way for the resurrection of the twins' father who, returned to bodily form in another vase scene, gives the now-naked God L a kick (M. E. Miller and S. Martin 2004:Figure 22 [K1560]). In these Classic period versions God L survives the ordeal (which the *Popol Vuh* gods do not), but he must now pay homage and tribute to the sun (David Stuart in G. S. Stuart and G. E. Stuart 1993:170–171). This obligation evidently served as a key paradigm for tribute payment in the mortal world.

A vestige of God L survives in Highland Guatemala in the complex character of Maximon, or more properly Rilaj Mam 'Ancient Grandfather' (Christenson 1998, 2001:176–190). Known as the Lord of Merchants, his effigy sports a broad-brimmed hat, fancy clothes, and a cigar. In Santiago Atitlan, Guatemala, he presides over the death of Christ and rules in his place for five days of Holy Week. For this he is brought to a special chapel symbolically set in the earth's interior, where he receives offerings of liquor, money, tobacco, and heaps of fruit (including cacao brought from the coast). On Easter Saturday he meets the resurrected Christ in ceremonial combat, and his inevitable defeat means banishment and, until lately, disrobing and disarticulation for the rest of the year. In Chichicastenango the Rilaj Mam (identified as Judas there) is publicly stripped of his clothes at the end of his reign and beaten, kicked, and burned by boys (Bunzel 1952:223). In Yucatan very similar ceremonies were once held to mark Wayeb, the last five days of the ancient Maya year (Pérez 1843:437). Here called simply Mam 'Grandfather,' the effigy was also feted for five days, then denuded and tossed to the ground (López de Cogolludo 1957[1688], v. 4:197).

A similar episode is in the Chilam Balams, the previously cited group of part-annals, part-prophesies, written in Yukatek Maya during the Colonial period. These documents combine indigenous and imported ideas, often in mystical, elliptical prose that defies easy comprehension. In a section of the Chumayel version that declares itself a history of the world before the coming of the Christian God, we find close affinities to the smiting of God L (Barrera Vásquez and Rendón 1948:153–155; Roys 1933:98–99): "Then Oxlahun-ti-ku was seized, his head was wounded, his face was slapped, he was spat upon, and he was thrown on his back as well. After that he was despoiled of his insignia and smut."[27]

Soon after, the narrative turns to the destruction of the world, first by flood and then by a collapse of the sky. God L is featured in flood scenes in the Dresden (page 74), Madrid (page 52), and Paris (1968:21) codices, where he is the recipient of a deluge poured from the water jars and open mouths of other deities and from an eclipsed sun and moon. No such image is known for the

Classic period, although his defeat on one of the aforementioned vases also takes place under an eclipsed moon (M. E. Miller and S. Martin 2004:Figure 21 [K5359]). It could also be relevant that the "Vase of the Seven Gods" shows him presiding over his infernal court on the final day of the previous "Great Cycle" in 3114 B.C. (Freidel, Schele, and Parker 1993:68; M. E. Miller and S. Martin 2004:82–83, Plate 35). The accompanying text describes a formal ordering, or re-ordering, of the gods—perhaps establishing God L's Underworld realm in the current world era.

Returning to K631 (see Figure 8.11), we might begin to explain this scene by considering the nature of the enigmatic K'awiil and comparing this with wider Mesoamerican myths about Sustenance Mountain. K'awiil has long been linked to ideas of fertility and abundance, and, significantly, he often shares the tonsured hairstyle of the Maize God (an emblem of the ripe corncob) and can be fused with the Maize God, or even Sustenance Mountain itself (Taube 1992a: 48, 78, Figure 48b).[28] K'awiil's strongest tie, however, is with lightning, and he evidently originated as the personified axe of the Maya storm god Chaak (Coggins 1988:127–128; Taube 1992a: 69–79).[29] Although often referred to as a "lineage god," this seems to be the weakest of his associations—if the term is appropriate at all. Rulers take a K'awiil scepter at their inauguration and other important points in their careers, but here it allies them with Chaak, and thus to his powers as a thunderous rainmaker and nurturer of crops. In some scenes on painted ceramics Chaak and what is probably Yopaat, a closely related god of storms, are shown splitting open the back of a great turtle with their fiery axes, making the cleft from which the Maize God will be reborn on earth (Taube 1986:57).

The link between lightning and human sustenance recurs with regularity in both Central Mexican mythology and accounts from across the Maya world. Indeed, so many native legends describe maize and other seeds as coming from under a rock or from within a mountain and freed by the agency of lightning that it can be considered a core Mesoamerican belief (see Bierhorst 1990:215 and J. E. S. Thompson 1970:348–354). To cite one of the more famous examples, in the Mexican Codex Chimalpopoca (*Leyenda de los Soles*) the god Quetzalcoatl uses lightning to recover maize from its original home within *tonacatepetl* 'Sustenance Mountain' (see Bierhorst 1992:146–147). Here maize is not only the future food of humans, it will be ground into dough by the gods to create the first people on earth. A version of this earth-shattering event appears on some Maya vessels (Taube 1986:57; 1992b:55–58).[30] Crucially, it is Chaak and his weapon, the bolt of lightning embodied in the serpentine leg of K'awiil, which splits the "house of the earth" with a tremendous crack.

The meaning of the conference depicted on K631 (see Figure 8.11) is lost to us, although we can imagine a dialogue well known to a contemporary audience.[31] In whatever way K'awiil acquires the precious cacao, the next time we see him he has it as his cargo. A series of painted capstones that decorated the vaults of buildings in Campeche, Mexico—most dating to the eighth or ninth centuries A.D.—supply this narrative connection. One of these, now in the Museo Amparo, Puebla, Mexico, is particularly explicit (Arrellano 2002:351; M. E. Miller and S. Martin 2004:75) (Figure 8.13a). The bursting bag K'awiil carries has been mistaken for a sack of maize, but the mention of *kakaw* 'cacao' in the lower glyph-band (here in the under-spelling **ka-ka**) makes it clear that cacao is the intended subject (Arrellano 2002:351). A painted glyph on the bag spells **9-PIK** *bolon pik* for 'nine eight-thousands.' This could describe the unfeasibly large and unworldly quantity of beans it contains (seventy-two thousand), although "nine" is also used as a synonym for "many" in Mayan languages and that is probably the intention here. In any case, numeration of this kind is typical of the cacao sacks presented in scenes of tribute payment and is additional evidence that these are the seeds in question. The text on a second capstone, this one from the site of Dzibilnocac, Mexico, mentions an *ox wi'il* 'abundance of food' and lists bread, water, and cacao (here rendered as **ka-wa**), which are shown stacked in plates, sacks, and baskets (Figure 8.13b).

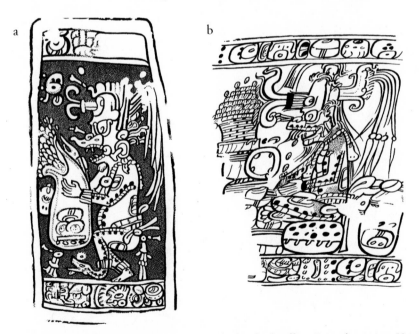

Figure 8.13. K'awiil gathering cacao beans and other foodstuffs. a. Painted capstone. Unprovenienced. Late Classic period. Museo Amparo, Puebla, Mexico. Drawing by Simon Martin after a photograph in M. E. Miller and S. Martin 2004:Plate 31. b. Painted capstone. Dzibilnocac, Mexico. Late Classic period. Drawing by Simon Martin after a photograph by Gallen N. Charles in Fuente 1999:Plate 140.

The theme is further amplified on a now-destroyed capstone from the Temple of the Owls at Chichen Itza, Yucatan, Mexico (Taube 1994a:226–228; Winning 1985:74–80) (Figure 8.14). Here a winged K'awiil emerges from the mouth of a coiled serpent, a motif that regularly encapsulates notions of rebirth and transport between worlds. In so doing he passes through the same crescent-shaped "Jaws of the Underworld" depicted on the Palenque sarcophagus lid, a motif that also denotes real portals in the earth such as cenotes and the mouths of caves. His destination is the heavens, represented by an enclosing sky-band that emits beams of radiance. In one hand he carries a plate loaded with spherical beads surmounted by jade earspools.[32] Significantly, ripe cacao pods (painted yellow in the original) hang both from the heavens and the Underworld, as if growing naturally from them.

Figure 8.14. K'awiil's flight from the Underworld. Reconstruction of a painted capstone. Late Classic or Postclassic period. Temple of the Owls, Chichen Itza, Yucatan, Mexico. Drawing by Simon Martin after a photograph by T. A. Willard in Winning 1985:Figure 95.

This image has previously been linked to cacao production in cenotes (Gó-mez-Pompa, Flores, and Aliphat Fernández 1990:253). Doubtless the Maya of Yucatan were impressed by the affinity cacao trees have for the sheltered and humid microclimates of cave mouths and sinkholes, but the association here is rather more profound in placing the origin of cacao in the Underworld. The scene expresses the rescue of the seeds—here pictured as precious jewels—from the infernal depths and their gifting to heaven and earth (M. E. Miller and S. Martin 2004:63).

K'awiil has long been identified with Bolon Tz'akab of the Colonial sources. This connection comes from the Maya New Year ceremonies, where each of four cycling "year-bearers" is ascribed its own divine patron. The two lists we have differ in only one major regard, the patron of the "Kan Years," a role the Dres-den Codex assigns to K'awiil and Diego de Landa gives to Bolon Tz'akab (Seler 1902–23, v. 1:377). In view of this, the passage in the Chumayel that directly follows the defeat and robbery of Oxlahun-ti-ku reads rather like a summary of our three capstones: "Also taken [from Oxlahun-ti-ku] were lima beans, our bread, ground hearts of small squash seeds, ground large seeds of the *ca* squash, ground kidney beans. He wrapped up the seeds, this first Bolon Tz'akab, and went to the thirteenth heaven" (Barrera Vásquez and Rendón 1948:153–155; Roys 1933:99; J.E.S. Thompson 1970:281).[33] But there is a greater connec-tion between the Temple of the Owls and K631. We must first understand the capstone not as an isolated element but as part of an integrated architec-tural program. The two piers that once supported the wide central doorway of the temple sanctuary carry relief carving on each of their four faces (Winning 1985:44–58) (Figure 8.15). Three show alternating panels of mat symbols and the horned owls that give the building its name. But the remaining, outward-facing side shows a trunk weighted with cacao pods and motifs that resemble both long-pistiled flowers and jade earspools. These are closely connected in Maya art, with the latter simply a representation of the former in greenstone (D. Stuart 1992). As we have seen, the same objects appear in K'awiil's bowl on the capstone. At the foot of this tree is a beaded semicircular motif, most likely another flower-jewel. Beneath this is an open socket into which is set a three-dimensional sculpture of a humanoid in a crossed-arm pose, creating a match for the anthropomorphic cacao tree on K631 (Taube 1994a:227).

The iconography of the Temple of the Owls largely replicates that on K631 and should encode the same narrative thread. The fruiting *iximte'* places the temple in a symbolic Underworld, while the emblematic owls invite thoughts of God L's owl familiar. In combination with the "royal" mat symbols, these features suggest we are looking at a physical reproduction of the same palace pictured on K631. The location of the capstone image is far from incidental,

Figure 8.15. The Maize Tree as an architectural motif. Reconstruction. Late Classic or Postclassic period. West pier of the Temple of the Owls, Chichen Itza, Yucatan, Mexico. Drawing by Simon Martin.

since converging vaults were perceived as the jaws of the infernal centipede, with the flat line of ceiling capstones a conceptually open gateway to the sky (M. D. Carrasco and K. Hull 2002). Together, the Temple of the Owls appears to be a shrine celebrating the maize-cacao story and the setting for appropriate rituals and reenactments by the Chichen Itza elite (Martin 2004). We might wonder if the chapel of Rilaj Mam in Santiago Atitlan is the modern descendant of such a structure.

Drink of the Gods

The only context in which the word *iximte'* appears in Maya inscriptions apart from the Dumbarton Oaks bowl (see Figure 8.1) is in the Primary Standard Sequence that encircles many ceramic vessels (M. D. Coe 1973:18–22; Grube 1990; Houston, Stuart, and Taube 1989; B. MacLeod 1990; D. Stuart 1988, 1989, this volume). Such texts formally dedicate the vessel and detail the food or drink for which it was intended. Here, *iximte'* always appears in descriptions of cacao beverages in the form *iximte'el kakaw* (Stuart, this volume) (Figure 8.16a). The literal reading here would be 'Maize Tree-like cacao,' or, more sim-

Figure 8.16. The Maize Tree and chocolate pots. a. **IXIM TE'-e-le ka-ka-wa** *iximte'el kakaw* 'Maize Tree-like cacao.' Detail of a text on a Late Classic period vessel. Burial 196, Tikal, Guatemala (K8008). Drawing by Virginia Greene in Culbert 1993:Figure 84. b. **yu-k'i-bi IXIM[TE']** *yuk'ib iximte'* 'his drinking vessel (for) Maize Tree.' Unprovenienced vessel. (K5514) Early Classic period. The Brooklyn Museum of Art, New York. Drawing by Simon Martin after a photograph by Justin Kerr. c. Jade mosaic vessel. Late Classic period (K4887) Burial 196, Tikal, Guatemala. Drawing by Simon Martin after a photograph by Justin Kerr.

ply, 'Maize Tree cacao.' The *ixim* component is sometimes omitted, providing *te'el kakaw* 'tree-like cacao'; in very attenuated versions, *kakaw* is left out and *iximte'* becomes the sole description of vessel content (Figure 8.16b).

Structurally, the *iximte'el kakaw* section might seem to form a particular "recipe," one among several in the Primary Standard Sequence. We know that maize was commonly added to Mesoamerican chocolate drinks (see Landa 1941 [1566]:90), and this could help explain the Maize God portrait here. Alternatively, since *iximte'/iximche'* refers to a number of different plants, one of these could be an ingredient or flavoring. Yet the mythological entwining of maize and cacao we have established thus far points in another direction—to 'Maize Tree Cacao' as more of a compound term. If so, the cacao they are talking about was directly compared to the magical bounty that grew from the flesh of the

Maize God—with the traditional mixing with corn no doubt having symbolic as well as culinary significance. Some support for this might be seen in the "embodied" cacao pots whose lids bear humanoid portraits (Houston, Stuart, and Taube in press). The more elaborate versions, such as the jade mosaic vessel from Tikal Burial 196, can be identified as Maize Gods (Figure 8.16c).[34] Like the other images we have discussed, they are manifestations of the deity as a cacao tree further transformed here into a chocolate pot.[35]

Discussion

This study has drawn together representations of cacao in ancient Maya art and writing in search of their symbolic purpose and place in mythic narrative. We must be alert to the difficulties inherent in any such endeavor. Representations always have lives independent of the concepts that first inspire them, and plot points can be replayed from different viewpoints or realized in equally valid metaphors. In seeking a single "meta-narrative" we might easily miss essential details or unwittingly combine distinct ideas. The fragmentary nature of our sources means that any reconstruction is provisional. Nonetheless, with these caveats in mind, we are in a position to recognize some important episodes and draw viable inferences about the significance of cacao in Maya religion.

Sources from across Mesoamerica agree that the sacrificial death of the Maize God at harvest-time—for the Maya at the hands of Underworld deities—was followed by his burial in a cave within a mountain. At least part of his soul or spirit left his body and rose to the heavens. In the *Popol Vuh* it is the Hero Twins who ascend to become the sun and moon, but in earlier versions it may be the Maize God whose apotheosized spirit joins or forms these celestial bodies. His abandoned corpse, by contrast, gives rise to trees bearing edible fruits and seeds. This takes place while he is entombed within Sustenance Mountain and symbolizes the process of germination, which occurs out of sight underground. Cacao, the most coveted product of the mortal orchard, was emblematic of all prized and sustaining vegetal growth—with the exception of maize—and the myth served to explain how it and other foodstuffs came into being. Cross-culturally, trees supply a rich collection of metaphorical meanings appropriate to generational descent, and in Maya ideology they evidently constitute a bridge between death and rebirth. It is the Maize God's manifestation as a fruit tree that allows him to pass on his procreative seed and to eventually triumph through the heroic deeds of his offspring.

The cacao of the Maize Tree grows in the domain of the Underworld's paramount lord, God L, where it is evidently the source of his wealth. He enjoys the good life, drinking and trading, unaware of his forthcoming punishment at the hands of the next generation. The task of rescuing cacao and all the other foods that will sustain humanity falls to the lightning bolt, K'awiil. His special power was to penetrate different worlds, with the awe-inspiring phenomenon of nature's electromagnetism making him a great energizer and catalyst (there are interesting overlaps here with scientific understandings, in which lightning fixes nitrogen—nature's fundamental fertilizer—in the soil, and electricity is harnessed to power all manner of different processes). The fusion of the Maize God with K'awiil, as on the Palenque sarcophagus, may suggest a shoot empowered in its struggle to reach the surface. Embarked on analogous journeys skyward, the torch-headed Maize God and the tonsure-coiffured K'awiil are partly synonymous entities.

The story builds to a climax with the Maize God's rebirth. On various painted vessels he is dressed in jade jewels and quetzal feathers symbolizing maize foliation and watered by the Hero Twins, before emerging from the cleft made by Chaak and K'awiil. The Maize God's realization as a World Tree is the ultimate expression of his resurrection, with his ascent to the sky implicated in a reconfiguration of the universe, the creation of humanity, and an end to earthly darkness and chaos.

This great life and death cycle was no remote paradigm for the Maya elite but one that seems to have made even a sip of chocolate a sacramental act. More particularly, the images on the Dumbarton Oaks bowl, the Berlin vase, and the Palenque sarcophagus must be recognized not simply as pious celebrations of the Maize God epic but as purposeful expressions of personal redemption. The lords so commemorated emulate the corn deity on his triumphal journey through the purgatorial Underworld and beyond to an ultimate, deeply desired, union with the cosmos.

Acknowledgments

This chapter developed from collaborative work with Mary Miller while on a fellowship at History of Art Department, Yale University, in 2002, and was first presented at the 22nd University of Pennsylvania Museum Maya Weekend, 2004. I want to express my gratitude for the assistance and suggestions of Oswaldo Chinchilla, Allen Christenson, Michael Coe, Barbara Fash, Judith Strupp Green, Sharon Edgar Greenhill, Stephen Houston, Justin Kerr, Bruce Love, Barbara MacLeod, Cameron McNeil, Frauke Sachse, Peter Schmidt, Joel Skidmore, David Stuart, Andrew Weeks, and Marc Zender.

Notes

1. For some of the practical and symbolic uses of cacao see S. D. Coe and M. D. Coe 1996; McAnany 1995; L. A. Parsons 1969; Reents-Budet 1994a; D. Stuart 1988, 1989; Taube 1994a; and J. E. S. Thompson 1956.

2. Glyphic conflations often appear to be whimsical fusions or strategies to save space in the inscriptions. In many cases, however, there is a semantic purpose, especially where they form compound nouns.

3. Today we find *iximte'* and its cognate *iximche'* as plant names in Yukatek, Ch'orti', Tzeltal, K'iche', Q'anjob'al, and Jakalteco. Yet none are varieties of maize or cacao, referring instead to a range of unrelated trees and shrubs (the best known of which is the *ramón*, or breadnut, tree, *Brosimum alicastrum* Sw.).

4. The caption to the prone figure (E1-3) begins **pa-ka-la-ja** to make *paklaj iximte'* '(the) Maize Tree is face-down,' an explicit reference to the position he adopts (for *paklaj* see Stuart, Houston, and Robertson 1999:32). That to the seated figure (A1-3) begins **u-BAAH-?**, where the final sign is a scroll representing speech, poetry, or song (Stephen Houston and Marc Zender, personal communication 2004). This is a rare compound, with other examples on Quirigua Monument 26 at C8 (C. Jones 1983: Figure 13.2), Naranjo Panel 1 at B2 (I. Graham 1978:105), and in a Maya text painted on a Teotihuacan mural (see Taube 2003c:Figure 11.8b).

5. The protagonist is named **[CH'OK]CHAN** *ch'ok chan(al)* 'Young Snake' in one caption (A3) and a fuller **UH-CHAN-na IXIM[TE'] AJ-CH'OK CHAN-la** *uh chan iximte' aj ch'ok chanal* 'Jeweled? Sky, Maize Tree, He of Young Snake' in one of the longer columns (F1-4) (my thanks to Marc Zender for *uh chan* as '(be)jewel(ed) sky,' personal communication 2004). Parenthetically, the name *ch'ok chanal* also appears as a name or title on Calakmul Stela 114, created in or around A.D. 431.

6. The Maya Maize God was first examined in detail by Eduard Seler (for example, 1902–23:3:595) and Herbert Spinden (for example, 1913:89–90) and is treated in the ethnographic writings such as those of Raphael Girard (1962), among others. In unpublished work, Nicholas Hellmuth also contributed a number of important observations (cited in Taube 1985:172).

7. Although not ever-present, T504 **AK'AB** 'darkness' glyphs (one seen beneath the bier here in Figure 8.2a) are distinctive features of Sustenance Mountain in Maya art. The reference to darkness could locate the mountain within the Underworld, although, since the same sign marks the vessel of Chaak, containing rainwater, it more likely refers to dark thunderclouds inside. Page 65a of the Dresden Codex (1975) makes reference to this *ak'ab ha'al* 'dark rain,' and according to the Chilam Balam of Chumayel water was created on the day 11 Ak'bal, the day name of *ak'ab* (Roys 1933:117).

8. The sense behind the **ha-li** spelling is uncertain. The *–l* ending can be adjectival, and the use of disharmonic *–li* could suggest *haal, ha'al,* or possibly *ha'il*. *Ha'il* can mean 'watery' and *ha'al* is 'rain' in a number of Mayan languages, but compounds like these are usually formed with logographic **HA'** 'water' (Lacadena 2000).

9. At the time of writing, this sign (numbered T533 in J. E. S. Thompson 1962) is an active topic of debate among epigraphers, with contributions from Luís Lopes, Barbara MacLeod, David Mora-Marin, and David Stuart, among others.

10. The "psychoduct" that emerges from the sarcophagus of Pakal of Palenque and ascends to the temple sanctuary far above (see Ruz 1973:232) was designed to carry the

deceased's departing breath-essence. For the ordering of T533 prior to T58 **SAK** in this spelling of the death phrase see Zender (1999).

11. Pakal's transformation into a tree is hard to appreciate at first since his body lies over the tree, which thus seems to grow from the plate below. The same overlapping convention, however, is applied to the ancestor portraits on the sarcophagus sides, which are plainly fusions or embodiments; it is seen again in the Codex Borgia versions.

12. The opening phrase of a text encircling the outside rim of the sarcophagus lid mentions the Maize God and must refer to the scene in some way. David Stuart (personal communication 2004) has recently suggested that it reads 'The Maize God's burden(?) forms thusly,' in reference to the ancestral fruit trees (see also Schele and Mathews 1998:341–342).

13. This translation is courtesy of Joel Skidmore.

14. The damaged glyph within the blossom can be recognized from other examples as the gopher head **BAAH** or **ba**. Its role here is unknown. If in some way a phonetic cue, it could allude to the frangipani, whose full name seems to have been *baak nikte'* 'bone flower.' One Early Classic incised vessel depicts the plant as an anthropomorphic tree with bone-petaled flowers (Hellmuth 1988:Figure 4.2).

15. For discussions of Mesoamerican World Trees see Freidel, Schele, and Parker 1993; Furst 1977; Heyden 1993, 1994; León Portilla 1973; Roys 1933; Schele 1992, 1996; Seler 1902–23; Taube 1994a, 2005; and Tozzer 1907, 1941.

16. The crocodilian World Tree has been identified in Olmec art of the first millennium B.C. (Reilly 1995:38) (Figure 8.4b). The humanoid heads appended to the "trunk" probably represent individual fruits. Mexican World Trees in later periods were also considered to be fruitful. One in the Postclassic Codex Fejérváry-Mayer (1971:1), representing the south, is a cacao tree; in the Codex Borgia (page 53) the fifth, central place, is occupied by a maize plant—in close accord with Maya thought (Figure 8.5b).

17. Directional World Trees in the Dresden Codex show axe-wielding storm gods, Chaaks, seated in their boughs (pages 30–31, 69). There is some parallel here with the royal title *kaloomte'* '? Tree,' which has versions aligned to the four cardinal directions and uses a glyph for the root *kal* that depicts a Chaak brandishing an axe. Ethnographic sources also tie storm gods to World Trees, telling of the eastern "trunk of heaven" in which the Chaaks live during the dry season (Redfield and Villa Rojas 1934:116).

18. The spelling *ahiin* is a revision from *ayiin* (letter from David Stuart to Luís Lopes 2003).

19. David Stuart (personal communication 2003) first told me about these sculptures, and both Barbara Fash and Cameron McNeil (personal communications 2004) generously sent me materials about them.

20. A fine plate excavated at Uaxactun, Guatemala, depicts the inverted Maize God/Tree in the lowest, Underworld register of the scene—his eyes closed in death as he awaits resurrection (R. E. Smith 1955:Figure 72f).

21. The same ritual specialist who described Christ's walk as the sun along a road in the sky also tells of his return: "diving here upon the earth" (Sosa 1985:429–430).

22. The cacao pods serve only as a generic reference to fruit here, since the texts mention not *kakaw* but what may be *tzen(?)* 'food, sustenance' (Bricker 1986:148). This point is reiterated in an analogous section on page 46 of the Madrid Codex, where the text supplies the same *pak'* and *tzen(?)* terms, while the scene again shows the patron gods embodied as trees, this time as upright trunks without cacao pods.

23. The initial recognition of God L outside the codices was by Michael Coe (1973:91, 107), with more recent analyses by Taube (1992a:79–88) and M. E. Miller and S. Martin (2004: 58–63, 281). On one painted ceramic (K5359) God L is captioned with glyphs reading **13-? yu-CHAN**, whereas in the Dresden Codex (pages 7 and 10) his owl avatar is named **13-CHAN-NAL[?] ku-yu** *oxlajuun chanal ? kuy* '13 Sky ? Owl.' The latter, although with different numbers at times, usually appears in the headdress of God L. In the Dresden Codex (for example, page 14), God L is named with an iconic depiction of rain followed by a blackened portrait head.

24. This enigmatic character is conceivably the Classic period version of the *Popol Vuh*'s Seven Hunahpu, brother of One Hunahpu. He may also appear on the vessels K8540 and K8736.

25. Schellhas (1904:35–36) linked Ek Chuah to God M in the codices, and Taube (1992a:90–92) has discussed the characteristics Ek Chuah shares with God L. Ek Chuah is doubtless equivalent to Ik Chaua, a Chontal Maya deity (J. E. S. Thompson 1970:306). As first noted by J. E. S. Thompson (1962:282), the name glyph of God M in the codices is identical to one used for the Jaguar God of the Underworld—a god of fire and warfare—in Classic period inscriptions. There is good reason to view God M as an aspect or derivation of the Jaguar God of the Underworld (Grube 2000:98–99; M. E. Miller and S. Martin 2004:281), who had been conflated with a Mexican merchant god, probably Yacatecutli (Kelley 1976:72; Martin 2005).

26. Compare, for example, El Peru (Guatemala) Stelae 33 and 34 (J. Miller 1974: Figure 2, 6) to K1398 and K1560 (Kerr 1989:81, 98).

27. My thanks to Barbara MacLeod who reassessed the translations of Roys and of Barrera Vásquez and Rendón and made this version for me (personal communication 2004). Oxlahun-ti-ku means 'Thirteen God/s' and, as mentioned above, this number appears in one glyphic name for God L. The reference to 'insignia' comes from *cangel(kanhel)*, which seems to have been a staff of some sort (Roys 1933:67). The reference to 'smut' comes from *zabac(sabak)*, a black dye that could refer to body paint or possibly a magical powder (J. E. S. Thompson 1970:265, 281–82). Interestingly, in the sixteenth-century *Relaciones de Yucatan* (1:51), Spanish chroniclers tell us that the Yukatek Maya already "knew of the flood and the fall of Lucifer." J. E. S. Thompson posited a connection to the world destruction and Oxlahun-ti-ku episodes (1970:340), and we might now extend that to God L.

28. J. E. S. Thompson made the first speculative connection between Schellhas's God K and K'awiil (1970:226)—subsequently proven by David Stuart (1987:15–16)—

interpreting the name as a union of *k'aa* 'surplus, abundance' and *wi'il* 'sustenance' (Barrera Vasquez 1980:359, 922; J. E. S. Thompson 1970:289).

29. Complex aspects to K'awiil's character remain to be understood, especially where his name seems to function more like a general term for embodiment or image (see Freidel, Schele, and Parker 1993:193–199; Houston, Stuart, and Taube in press), or his body hand-crafted by other gods in several scenes on vessels.

30. The two vases in question are K2068 and K2772 (Kerr 1990:211, 285). The earth is represented as a house, with corn kernels inside seemingly symbolized by piled stones (Taube 1986).

31. There is greater complexity to their relationship, since on other occasions God L holds a severed head or effigy of K'awiil, while on page 46 of the Dresden Codex he spears K'awiil with an *atlatl* dart.

32. The identification of jade earspools here was by Karl Taube (1994a:227), who also noted their appearance on page 52 of the Madrid Codex, in a scene where cacao is an offering. The same motif seems to be represented in the hieroglyph T66 (J. E. S. Thompson 1962), which represents a positive augury in the codices.

33. This translation draws elements from the three published versions listed. Bolon Tz'akab can be translated as 'nine/many generations' and, although this could be a name for the seeds that will found humankind, Landa (1941[1566]:140, 142) makes clear that it represents a distinct deity.

34. Compare the blunt-nosed serpent on this vessel with those representing flowers on Figure 8.5a and, especially, Figure 8.4b.

35. For deeper discussions of embodiment in Mesoamerica see López Austin (1988) for Central Mexico and, especially, Houston, Stuart, and Taube (2006) for the Maya.

9

The Language of Chocolate

References to Cacao on Classic Maya Drinking Vessels

David Stuart

The importance of cacao in Classic Maya society was not widely appreciated until the decipherment of glyphic texts on ceramics in the 1980s, when it became clear that seemingly countless ceramic vessels were inscribed with a dedicatory formula identifying them as drinking vessels for chocolate (D. Stuart 1986, 1988, 1989). Now scholars readily see chocolate as a key element of courtly life, having a profound role in political economics and display, feasting events, and ritual. Chocolate even permeates many examples of Maya religious iconography, as Martin (this volume) so cogently reveals. My own chapter is grounded in the work of decipherment and offers a comparative but far from exhaustive look at what the ancient written record tells us about cacao beverages in Maya elite society. In the pages to follow I focus mostly on the decipherment of inscribed tags on drinking vessels that often contain descriptions about the varieties of cacao or the "recipes" for which they were intended.

It comes as little surprise that the ancient Maya, like other Mesoamericans, were keenly aware of a variety of chocolate beverages and that they took pains to label their cacao vessels accordingly. For example, the ethnohistorical sources from Central Mexico make clear that many types of chocolate drinks were enjoyed by elites of the Highlands. The Florentine Codex describes the rich variety of chocolate offered to Mexica Aztec rulers, including "green cacao-pods, honeyed chocolate, flowered chocolate, flavored with green vanilla, bright red chocolate, *huitztecolli*-flavored chocolate, flower-colored chocolate, black chocolate, white chocolate" (Sahagún 1950–82, Book 8, 1954:40). As we will see, the language of chocolate as expressed on Classic Maya ceramics seems to mirror some of these descriptive categories among the Nahua. There are also a variety of descriptions of chocolate that are distinct to the earlier Maya material, and, it is important to stress, much remains to be done on the decipherment and interpretation of chocolate-related terms in the ancient sources.

To trace the history of the decipherments surrounding cacao and its uses in Classic times, we should first turn to Coe's seminal publication on Maya ceramics, *The Maya Scribe in His World* (M. D. Coe 1973). In the early 1970s, Maya writing was very far from being deciphered, as revealed by the simple fact that not one glyph on a vessel illustrated by Coe was truly readable. The importance of Coe's work was to lay the ground for future analysis by pointing out the repetitive nature of the glyphs found on pottery, thus forming what he dubbed a "Primary Standard Sequence" (PSS). Although none of the glyphs could be read at the time, Coe labeled many of the constituent elements with labels that remain familiar to students of Maya glyphs to this day, including the "initial sign," the "wing quincunx," and the "fish."

Around the same time of Coe's publication, Lounsbury (1974) first deciphered the *kakaw* glyph but, ironically, long before its presence was identified on Maya ceramics. Lounsbury noted the likely spelling **ka-ka-wa** in the pages of the Dresden and Madrid codices, in direct association with scenes of gods holding bowls of cacao pods and beans (Figure 9.1)(1974:138). The form of the glyph is fairly simple: two **ka** 'comb' signs above a **wa** syllable, producing *kakaw*. There was little to question in Lounsbury's initial decipherment, and it came to be widely accepted in the epigraphic community. Well over a decade would pass before the common and earlier Classic form of the cacao glyph was identified on a great many inscribed ceramic vessels (D. Stuart 1988). This is the variant based on the ubiquitous fish sign (Figure 9.2), so used because it

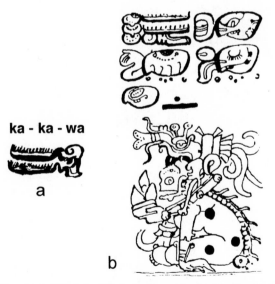

ka - ka - wa

a

b

Figure 9.1. The *kakaw* glyph (ka-ka-wa) in the Dresden Codex. a. The syllables **ka-ka-wa**. b. Representation of the Death God holding an offering bowl of cacao pods. Drawing by Carlos Villacorta from the Dresden Codex (Villacorta C. and Villacorta 1976:130a, 19).

Figure 9.2. A typical Late Classic period cacao glyph with the fish **ka** sign before **wa**. The two small dots in front of the fish's mouth serve as a "doubler" for the **ka**. From Kerr 1810. Drawing by David Stuart.

Figure 9.3. An Early Classic period chocolate vessel with a large cacao glyph label. Provenience unknown. Private collection. Photograph by David Stuart.

was the original, archaic form of the syllable **ka** (from *kay* 'fish'). As one would expect, the **ka** is often doubled, and there are two ways of doing this in Maya orthographic practice: either with two small dots near the top front of the fish's head, indicating a repetition of the sign, or by another **ka** in front of the fish, usually in the form of the common fin abbreviation of the fish. A -**wa** suffix necessarily follows these groupings of elements, producing **ka-ka-wa**. Note, however, that even at a very early date a single **ka** 'fish' with **wa** sufficed to spell the word *kakaw*. One imposing example comes from an Early Classic ceramic vessel simply and directly labeled with the glyph *kakaw* (Figure 9.3). As we will see, there is a considerable amount of textual material on ceramics that describes various concoctions and chocolate drinks.

At about this same time, Stephen Houston, Karl Taube, and the author made the important observation that other glyphs on ceramics refer to the vessels themselves (Houston, Stuart, and Taube 1989). The key breakthrough in this was the identification of the simple possessed noun **U-la-ka**, *u-lak* 'his/her plate' on wide-rimmed dishes (Houston and Taube 1987). These, of course, were not containers for drinks, but the rigid structure of Coe's PSS showed that *u-lak* on plates alternated with the so-called "wing-quincunx" found exclusively on bowls and cylindrical vessels. Logically, it seemed that the wing-quincunx glyph must also refer to its own category of vessel by means of a possessed noun. Based on the work of several scholars (Houston, Stuart, and Taube 1989; B. MacLeod 1990) we now know that the glyph reads *y-uk'ib'* 'his/her drinking cup.' By 1990, then, the basic components of the PSS of glyphs were deciphered, revealing that hieroglyphic tags on pottery were dedicatory in nature and served to specify the "owner" of a given vessel that could be described in various ways.

The 'cup' noun can certainly appear by itself in many examples, serving as a straightforward name tag for the object (*y-uk'ib'* NAME). But these are of little interest for our present analysis of cacao references. Far more common are various sorts of prepositional phrases that specify the beverage intended for the vessel. For example, a handful of vessels show the sign sequence **TA-SAK-HA'** after *y-uk'ib'* spelling the fuller phrase *y-uk'ib' ta sakha'* 'his/her cup for clear (or white) water.' This is too literal a translation, however, because *sakha'* (or its various truncated forms *saka'* or simply *sa*) usually refers to *atole*, a common corn-based drink of Mesoamerica. Interestingly, in seventeenth-century Ch'olti' Mayan *zaca* (as it is written in Moran's lexicon) means "bebida buena, chocolate de cacao, maiz y achiote" (Morán 1935). This list of ingredients suggests that ancient references to *sakha'* may well have been to drinks that at least in part consisted of chocolate, though I suspect that *sakha'* in ancient texts (such as in K4995) could have referred to one of several different concoctions.[1]

The *sakha'* example illustrates the basic structure of the written labels on Maya drinking vessels, but *kakaw* is far more common. In fact, it is nearly ubiquitous, appearing on hundreds upon hundreds of ceramics. The two glyphs for *y-uk'ib'* and *kakaw* together form the basic elements of the great majority of texts inscribed on Maya drinking vessels. A simple text might read *y-uk'ib' kakaw* '(it is) his drinking cup (for) cacao' (Figure 9.4), as in the case of a remarkable Early Classic cup made not of ceramic but of a cut "tun" shell (*Tonnea galea*) (G. E. Stuart 2001).

Figure 9.4. Hieroglyphic text on a shell drinking cup. Early Classic. Provenience unknown. Private collection. Note the cacao glyph in the second block. Drawing by George Stuart.

This mode of tagging vessels was popular in the center of the Maya area, in what is today the Peten region of northern Guatemala and adjacent areas of Mexico and Belize. In this core region we find that the earliest glyphs on Maya ceramics seem to be labels for vessels and their cacao contents. These appear in the central area near the very beginnings of the Early Classic period, probably no later than 250 A.D. Perhaps the very earliest example of an inscribed vessel is a sherd excavated at Tikal, Guatemala, dating to the "proto-Classic" Cimi phase (Figure 9.5), and bearing the two signs **yu-ta** (Coggins 1975:Figure 31b). This can only be a part of the common **TA-yu-ta-la** grouping that often precedes *kakaw* in later examples and which remains only vaguely understood. The initial **TA**-{#}is the all important preposition, preceding what may be a possessed noun or adjective probably based on *yut*. Some have likened this to *(w)ut* 'eye, face, seed or fruit,' as a reference to the beans of the cacao fruit (B. Macleod 1990). I have entertained the possibility that *yutal* could be an adjective simply meaning 'fruity,' but I see this as unlikely, given the appearance of the *yut* as a possessed noun in the spelling **U-yu-ta-la?** on one carved vase (see Dütting 1992:Figure 17). It is difficult to analyze *yut* as a nominal root, however, and for now the semantics of the term remain cloudy.

During the Early Classic period, inscribed vessels were common in the central Peten at large and politically important centers such as Uaxactun and Tikal in Guatemala. Based on the sample of unprovenienced ceramics now available,

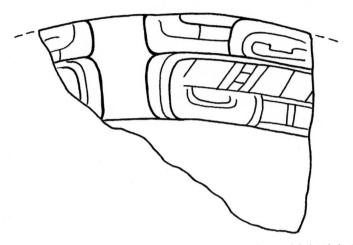

Figure 9.5. A very early inscribed sherd bearing a partial cacao label. Tikal, Guatemala. Drawing by David Stuart after Coggins (1975:Figure 31b).

it is doubtful that this can be attributed simply to the preponderance of vessels recovered from the extensive excavations at these central sites. Large-scale excavations at other major centers even within the Peten, such as Altar de Sacrificios and Seibal, failed to recover much in the way of early ceramic wares bearing hieroglyphs (R. E. W. Adams 1971; Sabloff 1975). Nor has much inscribed early pottery been found in more recent excavations at, for example, Calakmul, Mexico, or Caracol, Belize. The evidence suggests that the tradition of inscribing certain elite ceramics with cacao labels began in the area of Uaxactun and Tikal, probably no later than 300 A.D.

What would have led to the early advent of written labels on ceramics within such a fairly restricted area? This, to me, is part of a larger and still somewhat mysterious set of issues surrounding the social and political changes that occurred during the Preclassic to Classic transition, when the role of literacy in elite society seems to have expanded and shifted. Writing had long been established in the central Peten region before this time (as revealed most recently by the discovery of the painted texts of the San Bartolo murals [Saturno, Taube, and Stuart 2005]), but it was in the years between 100 A.D. and 300 A.D. that the rapid development and spread of inscribed stelae occurred in the Lowlands. Thus, at the beginning of the Classic period there was a major shift toward a more public display and consumption of the written word on monuments, as well as on more portable media. The marking of ownership and specific contents on cacao vessels must be viewed as part of this larger trend that began in the central Peten sites around 250 A.D.

Whereas the historical origin of inscribed cacao vessels can be traced to the center of the Maya area, many regions developed their own subtraditions of this practice throughout the Classic period, sometimes in seeming isolation. A good example is western Yucatan, Mexico, where, for a time during the eighth century, a great many carved and incised vessels bearing cacao labels appeared (Grube 1990; Tate 1985). Most fall under the archaeological designation Chocholá, and historically this style seems to have been concentrated at the elite community of Oxkintok, and it may not have lasted for a very long time. Similarly, at the other end of the Maya region, Copan, Honduras, exhibits its own idiosyncratic style of inscribing elite chocolate vessels. These, too, are often carved and modeled (unusual for the Late Classic period Peten sites), and their inscriptions are extremely fine in detail. But they seem to be quite rare in the overall body of Copan ceramics (Bill 1997). Significantly, some prominent sites of the Maya region played little part in the practice of inscribing ceramics; Palenque, Mexico, is an obvious example, probably because its ceramic tradition was fairly well isolated from the developments in pottery of the central Peten kingdoms (Rands 1974).

As noted, the *kakaw* glyph is extremely common on inscribed ceramics, but some important examples appear in a very different setting. In the mural paintings of Bonampak, Mexico, a large round cloth bundle bears the glyphic label **5-PIK ka-(ka)-wa**, or *jo' pik kakaw* (Figure 9.6) This is clearly a numerical statement based on the numeral classifier *pik*, meaning units of eight thousand. In this instance, then, the label simply states 'forty thousand cacao beans,' no doubt indicating the contents of the bundle. As it happens, eight thousand was a pan-Mesoamerican unit for the counting of cacao beans; the Aztec used the Nahuatl word *xiquipilli* for this unit, which also had the more

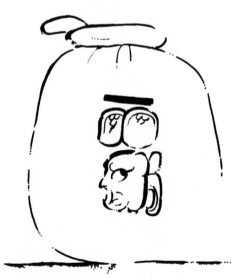

Figure 9.6. Cacao bundle. Mural detail. Late Classic period. Room 3, Bonampak, Mexico. Drawing by David Stuart, after infrared photographs by Gene Ware, courtesy of Mary Miller and Stephen Houston.

general meaning of 'bag' or 'sack' (J. R. Andrews 1975:484). According to Diego de Landa's *Relación*, the Maya of Yucatan used the same unit as well: "Their count is by fives up to twenty, and by twenties up to 100, and by hundreds up to four hundred, and by four hundreds up to eight thousand; and they used this method of counting very often in the cacao trading" (Landa 1941 [1566]:98).

Bundles of cacao beans are often depicted in other court scenes on Maya pottery, always with slightly smaller numbers. Probably the most common are **2-PIK** (2 x 8,000 beans) or **3-PIK** (3 x 8,000) beans. The bundles often rest on the floor or on a platform before an enthroned lord with visitors, no doubt to specify the gift or tribute payment brought by the guest. I suspect that these court scenes representing the transfer of wealth may help to explain the social and political setting for cacao drinks in Classic Maya palaces. Chocolate beverages were certainly enjoyed by Maya elites on a routine basis, but they were also important in the interactions and social negotiations among elites. The inscriptions on vessels that were given as gifts and exchanged among kings and court members would have served as testaments to these all-important relationships and interactions.

Inscribed pottery from the Late Classic period reveals that cylindrical vessels were nearly exclusively marked as containers for cacao, whereas lower bowls, sometime globular in shape, bore *ul*, or *atole* maize gruel. But there are some interesting exceptions to this pattern. One large tripod plate excavated at Holmul, Guatemala, bears a text indicating that it is a *lak* 'dish' for *iximte'el kakaw*, a specific named "type" of liquid cacao that is nearly ubiquitous on cylinder vessels (see Reents-Budet 1994c:Figure 3.8c). It may seem odd that a plate would be used as a cacao vessel, but surely the deep sides of the dish make it a very usable container for a liquid, probably a "punch bowl" of sorts shared among several drinkers who would dip small cups into it.

The Varieties of Cacao

Cacao was not the only drink mentioned on Maya ceramics, although it was the most common by a large measure. On low-rimmed bowls we sometimes find the phrase **yu-k'i-b'i TA-u-lu**, *y-uk'ib' ta ul*, '(it is) his drinking cup for *atole*,' referring to the ubiquitous corn beverage of Mesoamerica. One vessel (K2227) displays an interesting combination of references to cacao and *atole* (Figure 9.7), two drinks that otherwise were kept very separate in their usage patterns. This bowl was owned by a royal woman perhaps from the northern Peten region south of Calakmul. The inscription marks it as a drinking cup 'for chocolatey atole' (*ti kakawal ul*), with chocolate an additive to another liquid base. Just this sort of adjectival construction ('his her cup for x drink') is the

Figure 9.7. Partial label of a vessel (K2777) for 'chocolatey *atole*' (*kakawal ul*). Drawing by David Stuart.

Figure 9.8. Label from a tripod vessel. Early Classic period. Possibly from the Ucanal region of northeastern Guatemala. Drawing by David Stuart after Hellmuth (1988).

basic format for ceramic inscriptions, but in nearly all cases cacao is the basic drink described by means of various types and descriptions.

Indeed, only very occasionally do we find Maya vessels bearing the simple label 'his drinking cup for cacao.' Instead, scribes usually preferred to mark vessels as containers intended for specific types of cacao liquids (Table 9.1). The patterns strongly indicate that the distinctions involve descriptive terms of the flavor or condition of the cacao as well as possible additives to a chocolate base. To cite a simple example, we find on an Early Classic period incised vessel the insertion of modifying terms before *kakaw* (Figure 9.8). In its entirety, the opening phrase is **yu-k'i-b'i TA-? na-la ka(-ka)-wa** *y-uk'ib' ta ? nal kakaw* '(it is) his cup for ? cacao.' The main component of the modifier—a sign representing a snake passing through a flower blossom (Figure 9.8, upper right)—remains undeciphered, but *nal* is perhaps telling as the widespread Mayan word for young maize.

One of the most well known of all cacao vessels is the "lock top" pot (see Hurst, Figure 5.7, this volume) recovered from Tomb 19 at Río Azul, Guatemala (R. E. W. Adams 1999; Hall et. al. 1990; D. Stuart 1986). The lid can be fastened to the body of the vessel with a slight rotation, allowing the entire pot to be lifted and carried in suspended fashion. The elegant text of fifteen glyphs presents two examples of the **ka-ka-wa** glyph, both appearing on the lid in different prepositional phrases (Figure 9.9). The structure is highly unusual and would seem to indicate two different intended contents for the vessel ('for x cacao, for y cacao'). The glyphs can be easily read, even though their significance is at times murky:

yu-k'i-b'i TA-wi-ti-ki ka-ka-wa TA-ko-xo-ma mu-lu ka-ka-wa
y-uk'-ib' ta witik kakaw ta koxom mul(?) kakaw
'(It is) his cup for *witik* cacao, (and) for *koxom mul(?)* cacao'

The cacao-related terms *witik* and *koxom mul* are unique to this vessel, and partially for this reason they are difficult to translate. The first appears as part of the place name of Copan *Ux witik*, ('Three *Witiks*'), and for some time I have considered this to be a plant name of some type. *Wi'* is a widespread Mayan term for 'root,' but I am not sure how to analyze the *-tik* ending. Because I have found no attestations of *witik* in the dictionaries of historical or modern Mayan languages, I prefer to leave it untranslated. Similarly, *koxom* is an odd word, perhaps based on the widely attested root *kox* 'pheasant.' *Mul* is 'pile, mound' throughout Lowland Mayan languages and, interestingly, in Ch'orti' is the base for the derived noun *muluk* or *muruk*, meaning "any mound growing plant, potato, any tuber" (Wisdom 1950). These are hardly very strong associations, however.

Table 9.1. A selection of labels on Maya ceramics (omitting the varied dedicatory verbs and other phraseology that precede the possessed noun *y-uk'ib*, "his.her cup")

Y-uk'ib' ta kakaw	His/her cup for cacao
Y-uk'ib' ta tzih	His/her cup for pure (cacao)
Y-uk'ib' ta tzih kakaw	His/her cup for pure cacao
Yuk'ib' ta yutal kakaw	His cup for ? kakaw
y-uk'ib' ta ach' kakaw	His/her her cup for new cacao
Y-uk'ib' ta yutal k'an kakaw	His her cup for ? ripe cacao
Y-uk'ib' ta yutal chab'il kakaw	His/her cup for ? sweet cacao
Y-uk'ib' ta iximte'el kakaw	His/her cup for iximte' cacao
Yuk'ib' ta yutal iximte'el kakaw	His/her cup for ? iximte' cacao

Figure 9.9. Cacao labels from the Río Azul "lock-top" vessel (see also Figure 5.7, this volume). Drawing by David Stuart.

The modifiers *witik* and *koxom mul* might be better analyzed as very localized terms, such as place names. As Stephen Houston (personal communication 2005) points out, the *mul* ending is suggestive of a number of historical and modern toponyms, where it basically refers to a 'mound,' either natural or artificial. I believe that this analysis has some merit, given that other modifiers on cacao seem to be well established as place references. For example, on K7529 we find that the glyph for cacao is prefixed by what seems to be a clear emblem glyph of Naranjo, Guatemala (Figure 9.10a). The sense here seems to be that the vessel was a container for 'Naranjo cacao,' and, indeed, from its style and its inscriptions it appears to have been produced in what is today the eastern Peten region, perhaps near Naranjo. Other, later vessels sometimes take the modifier **5-KAB'** before cacao, which similarly appears to be a place reference (Figure 9.10b). The same combination serves as the emblem glyph of the site of Ixtutz, again located in the eastern Peten region.

I suspect that a geographical pattern underlies these scattered examples of cacao varieties tied to place names. Río Azul, Naranjo, and Ixtutz all are in the eastern area of the central Lowlands, near present-day Belize and adjacent to areas that we know were significant cacao-producing regions in early Colonial times. If their importance in cacao production extended back into the Classic period, perhaps some scribes took the opportunity to specify special regional varieties of chocolate on drinking vessels.

Another simple modifier on a Late Classic vessel (K625) mentions **K'AN-na ka(-ka)-wa**, *k'an kakaw*, probably meaning 'ripe cacao' (Figure 9.11). It follows

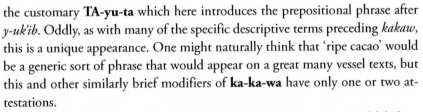

Figure 9.10. Cacao labels incorporating place names. (*Top*) a. "Naranjo" cacao (K7529). (*Bottom*) b. "Ixtutz" cacao (mentioned in the final two blocks) (K4681). Drawings by David Stuart.

the customary **TA-yu-ta** which here introduces the prepositional phrase after *y-uk'ib*. Oddly, as with many of the specific descriptive terms preceding *kakaw*, this is a unique appearance. One might naturally think that 'ripe cacao' would be a generic sort of phrase that would appear on a great many vessel texts, but this and other similarly brief modifiers of **ka-ka-wa** have only one or two attestations.

In a few instances we find the phrase *chab'il kakaw* as the special label on drinking vessels, no doubt with the adjective derived from *chab'* 'honey.' One example is K681, a pot said to have been owned by the noted Naranjo ruler Aj Wosaj (Figure 9.12). The addition of honey to chocolate beverages no doubt would have added a savory sweet taste to what would otherwise have been bitter concoctions. Sahagún (1950–82, Book 8, 1979:40) mentions the use of honey as an additive to cacao drinks enjoyed by rulers of the Aztec. There is also the possibility that *chab'* literally 'honey' or 'honeybee,' held the wider adjectival meaning of 'sweet-tasting.' In modern Ch'orti,' for example, the adjective *chab'al* is "sweet food or object, candy, sweet part of anything" (Wisdom

Figure 9.11. Vessel (K625) label for 'ripe cacao' (*k'an kakaw*). Drawing by David Stuart.

Figure 9.12. Mention of 'sweet cacao' (*chab'il kakaw*) on a vessel from the Naranjo area (K681). Drawing by David Stuart.

1950). Similarly, in Chontal the cognate form *chap'* is glossed as 'sugar, sweet' (Knowles 1984). The Naranjo vessel may therefore be labeled simply the cup for 'sweet cacao.'

A very important modifier on cacao is spelled **tzi-hi,** and at times this can serve alone to indicate the contents of a vessel. We find in a great many examples on both Early and Late Classic ceramics the sequence **TA-tzi-hi(-li) ka-ka-wa**, apparently for *ta tzih(il) kakaw* 'for *tzih* cacao' (Figure 9.13a). *Tzih* can be spelled either with the syllable sequence **tzi-hi** or at times with the probable logogram **TZIH** depicting three volutes. All epigraphers who have studied glyphs on ceramics have wrestled with the cloudy semantics of *tzih*, although the best translation of it at present is probably 'pure' or 'new,' as first suggested by Grube (cited in B. MacLeod 1990:399). In Ch'orti,' *tzih* is glossed as "rawness, crudeness, newness" (Wisdom 1950), and, interestingly, its cognate in Colonial Tzotzil appears in the extended term *tzeel kokov* 'pure chocolate' (Laughlin and Haviland 1988). The sense in this and related entries in Tzotzil is 'unadulterated' (*sin mezcla* in the original Spanish), perhaps suggesting that the *tzihil kakaw* of ancient ceramics was anything but a mixed concoction. When the *tzih* term appears alone (*y-uk'ib ta tzih*), as seems especially common

Figure 9.13. The word *tzih* on chocolate vessels. a. Label marking the contents as *tzihil kakaw* 'fresh(?) cacao.' The entire text reads *u jaay y-uk,ib, ti tzihil kakaw* 'his vessel, his drinking cup, for fresh(?) cacao' (translation after M. D. Coe 1973:115). b. The use of *tzih* alone as a term for drink. From the text of vessel K8728. Drawings by David Stuart.

on Late Classic pots from the area of Xultun (K5646, K4572, K7459) (Figure 9.13b), I suspect that it was enough to mark the vessel as being 'for the pure stuff,' as it were.

It is very easy to confuse spellings of *tzih* with another important but different modifying term I read as the noun *ixim* 'maize,' or, more fully, *iximte'* (Figure 9.14a, b). The confusion stems from the visual similarity of the head variant of the "spotted kan" (**tzi** or **TZIH**) and another profile glyph depicting the well-known tonsured Maize God, first identified by Taube (1985). (Some evidence suggests that even Maya scribes were at times not careful in making the necessary distinctions among signs they wrote so routinely in the ceramic labels.) Many examples of the maize deity's head can be seen before *kakaw* spellings, nearly always with an intervening **TE'** or **TE'-le**. I suggest that the maize head hieroglyph is the logogram **IXIM**, corresponding to the widespread general word for 'maize' in Mayan languages (proto-Mayan *ixim*). This reading is based on the presence of an **i**-{#}sign prefix in two examples (K3120, the "Altar vase," and K791), in addition to its obvious visual connection to corn. The reading is not yet confirmed, and here I entertain it as a working hypothesis pointing to the fuller phrase *ta iximte'el kakaw* 'for *iximte'* cacao.' *Iximte'el kakaw* is probably the most frequent "type" of chocolate mentioned on Classic

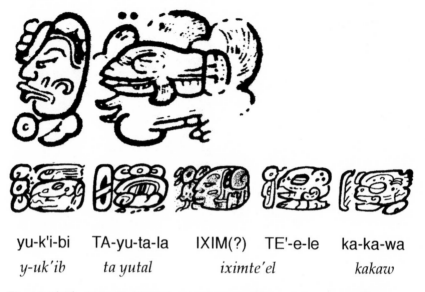

yu-k'i-bi	TA-yu-ta-la	IXIM(?)	TE'-e-le	ka-ka-wa
y-uk'ib	*ta yutal*		*iximte'el*	*kakaw*

Figure 9.14. The Maize God (**IXIM**) and **TE'** as a modifier on *kakaw.* a. Miscellaneous Text 9, glyphs D and E. Tikal, Guatemala. b. Burial 196 vessel. Tikal, Guatemala. Drawing by David Stuart after Culbert (1993:Figure 84).

Figure 9.15. A possible reference to *ach' kakaw,* "fresh cacao," on vessel K8713. Note the rare use of two fish **Ka** elements for the full spelling **ka ka-wa**.

Maya ceramics, often following the enigmatic *ta yutal.* Typically, early examples are stripped of all but the essential components, so that we have, as in one example, **yu-k'i-bi IXIM-TE' ka-ka-wa**. In at least one case (on K6642), the contents are simply given as **IXIM ka-ka-wa.**

Iximte' is not a word for 'maize,' but it is an attested plant name in many Mayan languages. Oddly, cognate forms of *iximte'* or *iximche'* can refer to several seemingly unrelated plant species. Among the Ch'orti,' *iximte'* refers to a wild Lowland tree known as *fruta de cabro* or *guiliguiste.* Johanna Kufer (personal communication 2005) informs me that this is *Karwinskia calderoni,* which bears poisonous seeds and has leaves used medicinally for some skin ailments. An identical plant name exists in Yukatek, *iximche,* which is a fruiting tree, *Casearia nitida,* or smooth casearia (Bolles 2001). This plant plays an important role in the ceremonial life of the Yukatek Maya, especially in the construction of the altars and cosmological images at the center of the Ch'a Chaak rain ceremony. Interestingly, its leaves are still used as cups from which to drink the ritual beverage *b'aalche'*. I have no data on the use of this plant or its fruits as an additive to drinks, however.

In my early research on inscribed vessels I considered whether the glyphic labels citing *tzih* or *iximte'* before *kakaw* were related to an important medicinal plant called *itzimte'* in Yukatek. In Yukatek, *itzimte'* or *itzinte'* refers to a "planta con que dan sabor y buen olor al pozole, cocimiento de camotes y otras cosas de las indias" (plant with which they give flavor and aroma to posole, cooked with *camotes* and other things of the Indies)(Perez 1877). Roys (1931) identified this as *Clerodendrum ligustrinum*, an aromatic flowering tree found throughout the Maya area. Although tempting at one time, I now doubt that the *tzih* and *iximte'* terms that modify *kakaw* can be related to this Yukatek term.

The problem in identifying a botanical species associated with the glyphic *iximte'* reference may lie in its very wrong-headedness: it may not be a plant name at all. Simon Martin (this volume) makes the important observation that *iximte'* and *kakaw* may have a more intimate association with one another, forming a collective term that unites the symbolism of maize with chocolate. In one telling image, the Maize God himself is called the *iximte'* and bears cacao fruit over his body (see Martin, Figure 8.1, this volume). The very presence of the two words together is indicative of an intimate connection, perhaps where cacao was seen as a conceptual offshoot of the principal and universal foodstuff, maize.

Other modifiers on cacao clearly emphasize its "fresh" qualities. Marc Zender (personal communication 2002) has recently pointed out another interesting and apparently unique description of cacao from a Classic polychrome vessel (K8713) (Figure 9.15). Here the prepositional phrase reads **TI-a-ch'a ka ka-wa**, *ti ach' kakaw*, 'for fresh cacao.' Semantically this closely approximates the sense of the adjective *tzih* as described earlier, and the choice of the word *ach*,' restricted historically to Tzeltalan languages, may reflect some interesting difference in local dialect.

The Tikal Jade Vessel: Insights into the Mythology of Cacao

Turning away from the specific terms associated with chocolate on Classic period pottery, let us look at some of the larger religious meanings of cacao in Maya mythology, expanding on some of the observations offered by Martin (this volume). We begin with an extraordinary jade mosaic vessel excavated in Burial 116 at Tikal, which bears an incised text on its lid (Figure 9.16). The inscription cites Jasaw Chan K'awil, the tomb's occupant, near its end, but before

Figure 9.16. Miscellaneous Text 56. Tikal, Guatemala. Drawing by David Stuart.

this we find an intriguing text quite unlike the dedicatory formula we might normally expect, even on a container so lavish and ornate.

The inscription begins with the oddly truncated date "9 Imix," followed by a verb expression consisting of the logogram representing a sprouting shoot followed by cacao. It seems natural to conclude that the meaning is 'the cacao sprouts,' even if the linguistic value of the verb logogram remains elusive. After this, we find a mythical place name ('first' followed by an inverted earth sign) familiar from the text on the famous canoe bones, also from Burial 116, depicting the Maize God floating and sinking into a primordial sea (Harrison 1999: Figure 82). The watery setting for the "sprout" event is even more explicitly mentioned in the fifth glyph of this difficult text, where we read of **K'AN-NAHB**,' possibly 'the precious sea.' The next two glyphs are familiar as *iximte'el kakaw*, probably serving here to specify the special quality of cacao tree that sprouted on 9 Imix.

I take this opening portion of the text on the jade vessel to be a record of the mythological origin of cacao. The aquatic setting is hardly historical, and the opening 9 Imix is also very suggestive, given the basic aquatic symbolism of the day sign (J. E. S. Thompson 1950). Imix is equivalent to the Central Mexican day Cipactli, which has a close visual and cosmological correspondence to the mythical alligator-like creature whose tail transforms into the cacao tree in several Maya representations, including on several remarkable stone vessels from Copan (see this volume: Martin, Figure 8.8a; McNeil, Hurst, and Sharer, Figure 11.12). The jade vessel from Tikal makes the explicit statement that the king of Tikal consumes the purest, elemental form of chocolate—cacao as it was first created.

Conclusion

After more than two decades of work devoted to the decipherment of *kakaw* and related glyphs on Maya vessels, we can say that many hieroglyphic labels refer to chocolate drinks in combination with other substances and flavorings, whereas others simply seem to highlight the flavors and "freshness" of the cacao beverage. One fascinating pattern to consider further focuses on the temporal differences in the nature of cacao descriptions on vessels. In the Early Classic period there is far more variety in the terminology, as shown, for example, by the Río Azul "lock top" jar, with its mention of two different cacao types that make no other appearance among hundreds of other inscribed vessels. By Late Classic times one clearly discerns a standardization in the types of cacao featured with written labels, with *tzih kakaw* or *iximte' kakaw* appearing in seemingly endless numbers.

Certainly there remain significant questions of epigraphic analysis and interpretation in dealing with these highly repetitive texts, and a more refined understanding of them will no doubt emerge in coming years. Given the steady number of new vessels that emerge from scientific excavation and, sadly, from looting, there will also be more written labels to study and compare with the patterns I have described here. What probably will not change, however, is the sense that the Classic Maya took their chocolate very seriously and that it was a drink of pleasure as well as political and social importance.

Acknowledgments

I would like to thank Cameron McNeil for her invitation to contribute to this volume and for her good humor and patience as I completed the manuscript. Writing this chapter presented an opportunity to revisit several old questions regarding inscriptions on vessels, and in the process I learned a good deal from conversations with Stephen Houston, John Justeson, Barbara MacLeod, and Simon Martin. The exchange of ideas at the 2005 Maya Meetings at Texas, devoted to "Glyphs on Pots," was especially helpful. I am also grateful to Johanna Kufer for answering my questions about Ch'orti' plant terminology.

Note

1. Vessels referenced in this chapter with "K numbers" (for example, K791) refer to Justin Kerr's immensely useful photographic database of decorated and inscribed Maya ceramics. Many of these vessels were published in six volumes of *The Maya Vase Book* (Kerr 1989–2000); they are also available on the internet at *www.mayavase.com*. Any student of Maya art and epigraphy relies heavily on Kerr's treasure trove of images.

10

The Social Context of *Kakaw* Drinking among the Ancient Maya

Dorie Reents-Budet

The ancient Maya developed a complex society renowned for its monumental architecture, colossal sculptures, and portable carvings that adorned their towns and the bodies of the elite; for scientific and intellectual achievements in mathematics, astronomy, philosophy; and for the only true writing system (that is, the graphic representation of spoken language) in the ancient Americas. During the Classic period apogee (A.D. 250–900) of the Maya culture, artisans created copious objects in a variety of media that were essential components of the sociopolitical and economic systems of the ruling elite (M. D. Coe and J. Kerr 1998). Among these artifacts were decorated pottery vessels for serving food, especially vessels for *kakaw* (chocolate) beverages (Figures 10.1a, 10.1b) (Reents-Budet 1994a). Unlike their ceramic predecessors of earlier centuries (1200 B.C.–A.D. 150) (Figure 10.2), which were characterized by elegantly simple forms and monochrome or occasionally bichrome slip-painted surfaces, Classic period elite service wares were elaborately embellished with painted, incised, or modeled imagery or various combinations of these. Skilled painters adorned the service wares with renderings of elite life and portraits of powerful rulers. They also portrayed the supernatural beings and religious myths that explained the universe and the place of the Mayas therein, and they sanctioned Maya rulership by way of their special association with deities and supernatural forces (Figure 10.3) (Fields 1989; Fields and Reents-Budet 2005; Freidel and Schele 1988a, 1988b; Freidel, Schele, and Parker 1993; Houston and Stuart 1996). The accompanying hieroglyphic texts are simultaneously explanatory captions and historical documents pertaining to these formidable individuals as well as commentaries on the function of the vessels and visual poetry of the highest creative order (Reents-Budet 1998).

Figure 10.1. (*Top*) a. Late Classic period Maya polychrome vase for serving chocolate beverages and giving as gifts during elite feasts. (*Bottom*) b. Rollout. The scene portrays a feast inside a palacelike structure with a noble figure seated on a low throne. A large polychrome vase with a conical lid is in front of the noble, and a second person seated on the floor in front of the throne hands another polychrome vase to the seated lord. Collections of the New Orleans Museum of Art. Photographs copyright Justin Kerr (K2800).

Figure 10.2. Late Preclassic Maya jar with a simple geometric motif rendered in bichrome slip paint. The jar was found in the tomb of a noblewoman. Burial 167, North Acropolis, Structure 5D-sub-10-1st. Tikal, Guatemala. Instituto de Antropología e Etnología, Guatemala City (reg. no. 17.1.1.089).

Why did food-service wares develop from quotidian containers into an extraordinary ceramic tradition characterized by effusive painted decoration featuring elite life and the mytho-religious foundations of social stratification and rulership? The answer lies in the social context in which the vessels were used and the foodstuffs they contained. Representations of foods and vessels from Classic Maya painted art depict plates containing piles of tamales; jars filled with special drinks, including those made from fermented honey and maguey; and cylindrical vases in which *kakaw* beverages were prepared and served (B. MacLeod 1990; Reents-Budet 1994c:75–83). Although these comprise commonly consumed foods, it is the special context of banquets held in the residences of the elite and the palaces of rulers that caused the transformation of everyday containers into specialized vessels of enhanced social affect and political meaning (Reents-Budet 2000a; also see Reents-Budet 1994b:Figure 2.20 for a portrayal of feasting). The banquets, in turn, were the cornerstone and focal point of an elite economic system based on feasting with its concomitant gift-giving that included both basic commodities and luxury goods (Reents-Budet 2000b). Although feasting events likely were held at all levels of ancient Maya

Figure 10.3. Late Classic period Maya polychrome vase depicting the deity Its'amnaj (God D), one of the principal ancient gods who created the cosmos. Here the deity gestures toward a large basket on which sits the decapitated head of the Maize God, which is being retrieved by his sons the Hero Twins, Yax Balam and Hun Ajaw (depicted on the other side of the vase). Collections of the Museum of Fine Arts Boston (acc. no. 1988.1169, gift of Landon T. Clay) (also Smithsonian Institution Maya Ceramics Project sample number MS1126, Kerr no. 504). Photograph by D. Reents-Budet.

society, those hosted by the socioeconomic and political elite would have been notable for their opulence, a hypothesis based on sixteenth-century ethnohistoric accounts of aristocratic feasts (for example, Landa 1941 [1566]) and the Classic period archaeological and pictorial records (Reents-Budet 1998).

The Classic Maya were not unique New World consumers of *kakaw* beverages nor is it certain that they were the first Mesoamericans to devise an elite economic system with feasting as a primary component. The consumption of *kakaw* in Mesoamerica dates to as early as the Preclassic period (1200–400 B.C.) among the Olmec (S. D. Coe and M. D. Coe 1996; Millon 1955a), who developed the first complex society of Mesoamerica (M. D. Coe and R. D. Diehl 1980; Reilly 1994a, 1995). Primary evidence for an Olmec origin of *kakaw* consumption is that the Mayan word "*kakaw*" is a loan from Mije-Soque, the purported language spoken by the Preclassic Olmec (Justeson et al. 1985;

Kaufman and Justeson, this volume; Kelley 1976; for an alternate perspective see Dakin and Wichmann 2000). The drinking of *kakaw*-based beverages may have comparable ancient origins among the Maya and their neighbors in northern Honduras (Henderson 2002), although today the earliest Lowland Maya evidence comes from Colha, Belize, where *kakaw* residues have been discovered inside spouted vessels (Hurst et al. 2002), a specialized form that first appears in the site's ceramic record ca. 400 B.C. (Powis et al. 2002).

From 1000 B.C. to the sixteenth century, *kakaw* drinks remained a primary component of social and political events among the indigenous peoples of Mexico, Belize, Guatemala, Honduras, El Salvador, and as far south as Nicaragua and Costa Rica, its consumption crossing nearly all socioeconomic and political boundaries. Archaeological and inferential evidence from early sites in Mexico intimate that feasting rites, with their economic overtones and political connotations, were an ancient Mesoamerican tradition with origins during the Preclassic period as early as 1100 B.C. (Pope et al. 2001; von Nagy, Pohl, and Pope 2001). Similar evidence for feasting among the Classic period Maya has been found during excavations of palaces and other elite buildings at a number of sites (Reents-Budet 2000b), including, but not restricted to, Aguateca (Inomata 1995); Dos Pilas (Demarest, Morgan, and Wolley 2002); Motul de San José (Foias 1998, 1999); Nakbe (Hansen 1997), and Tikal (Harrison 1970, 2000)—all in Guatemala—and Altun Ha in Belize (D. Pendergast 1979). Extensive middens have been found at the base of the platforms that support palaces and other high status buildings of seemingly socio-administrative function, the earliest of which may date to ca. 600 B.C. (Clark and Blake 1994; Hansen 1997). Unlike the typical trash deposits at Maya sites, these middens are notable for their high concentrations of figurines and other special-function objects, edible-animal bones, and dense deposits of finely painted ceramic serving vessels, especially plates and cylindrical vases. These deposits presumably are the remains of feasting events (Foias 1999; D. Pendergast 1979), although why the Maya allowed such trash to accumulate around elite buildings remains a curious and unexplored behavioral pattern.

The best documentation of feasting rites among the ruling elite comes from elsewhere in Mesoamerica during Terminal Classic (A.D. 800–1250) and especially Postclassic times (A.D. 1250–1521) among the Zapotecs and Mixtecs of Oaxaca in southern Mexico (Byland and Pohl 1994; Monaghan 1990), the Mexica (Aztecs) of Central Mexico (Brumfiel 1987; Charlton and Nichols 1992; Elson 1999; Garraty 2000; Michael E. Smith 1986; Spores 1974), and the Maya of Yucatan (Landa 1941 [1566]). Descriptions of sumptuous feasts among the nobility with the requisite gift-giving extravaganzas are featured in the writings of such sixteenth-century Spanish chroniclers as Francisco de Burgoa (Burgoa 1989 [1674]:123–125), Diego Durán (1971:434–435), and Bernardino de Sahagún (1950–82, Books 1–12) in Highland Mexico, and Diego de Landa (1941 [1566]) in Yucatan.

Among modern descendants today in Mexico, feasts remain a key component of pivotal life events such as baptism, betrothal, and marriage among Zapotec, Mixtec, and Mije-Soque peoples in Oaxaca, in southern Veracruz and Tabasco (Monaghan 1990), and among the Maya in Yucatan and Chiapas, Mexico, and Highland Guatemala (D. Tedlock 2002; J. E. S. Thompson 1938:602; Vogt 1969, 1993). As in modern times, the ancient feasting rites provided the official environment for securing and maintaining social and political alliances, for acquiring wealth through gift exchange, for garnering prestige through conspicuous consumption, and for the validation of social or political hierarchy, or both, via religious doctrine and supernatural sanction (Brumfiel 1987; Clark and Blake 1994; J. Pohl 1999). Ancient and modern Mesoamerican feasting patterns, then, are congruous with those of other world cultures that employ feasting as a fundamental component of economics, politics, and community relations (Junker 2001; Rathje 2002).

Mesoamerican elite feasting rites usually began with a member of the nobility hosting a banquet on the occasion of such events as a ruler's accession to the throne, a war victory, a marriage, a religious celebration, or a similarly important sociocultural event. The host would amass many foods and high-quality craft goods, especially cloth, feathers, and adornments of jadeite and other precious materials. As described by Bishop Landa (1941 [1566]:92) in the sixteenth century and portrayed on pictorial vases of the seventh century, the gathered guests ate and drank prodigious amounts, feasting on tamales, meat stews, and sumptuous fruits (Figure 10.4a) and consuming many vases of frothy *kakaw* drinks and fermented beverages (Figure 10.4b; compare with Maya vase feasting scene on K1599 [in Reents-Budet 1994b:51–53, Figure 2.20]).[1] The participants enjoyed speeches and the performance of historical and religious stories, sometimes even playing roles in these pageants (Burgoa 1989 [1674]; Landa 1941 [1566]:Chapter XLII; Sahagún 1950–82:Books II and VIII). The featured stories exalted the host's personal history and his connections to supernatural forces and mytho-religious events.

At the conclusion of the banquet, the guests would receive as gifts precious materials (for example, quetzal feathers, spondylus shell), crafted items (for example, cotton mantles), and such prized foodstuffs as turkeys, baskets of maize and other important grains, and especially bundles of valuable *kakaw* beans (Figure 10.5; compare with Maya vase feasting and tribute/gift giving scene

Figure 10.4. Illustrations of an Aztec feast. Sixteenth-century. (*Top*) a. Eating *tamales* and meats. (*Bottom*) b. Drinking *kakaw*. From the Florentine Codex (Sahagún 1950–82:Book 2, Chapter 27, folio 26).

on K5505 [in Reents-Budet, Bishop, and MacLeod 1994:213, Figure 5.52]). These items would be used by the recipients in their own households and for distribution to select members of their local constituency as gifts and payment for service and support in a variety of social and political affairs. Especially well-documented among the Mixtecs and Zapotecs, the participation in a feast obliged the attendees to reciprocate in the form of unspecified future support of the host as well as to sponsor their own feasting events with the concomitant gift-giving (Monaghan 1990:764). In sum, the social, political, and economic interaction engendered by the feasting system created strong ties among the parties, reifying their sense of community by way of a fabric of overlapping rights and obligations developed between sponsors and participants.

The feasting system not only created a forum for sociopolitical alliance formation but it also was an essential economic mechanism wielded by Mesoamerica's ruling elites, a process particularly well-documented among Highland Mexican cultures (Aguirre Beltrán 1979; Dow 1973; Hayden and Gargett 1990; Monaghan 1990; J. Pohl 1994; Spores 1974; Wolf 1959), and which likely was a primary factor underlying the Late Preclassic development of Classic Maya society (Clark and Blake 1994; Freidel, Reese-Taylor, and Mora Marín 2002). As an economic catalyst, the system propagated a circular movement of goods from the center to the periphery and from the periphery to the center. This two-way system contributed to the development of social relationships among the aristocratic participants and between the elite class and those in lower socio-

Figure 10.5. An Aztec feast illustrating the presentation of gifts, including pottery vessels, bags of *kakaw* beans, live turkeys, finely decorated cotton mantles, and baskets filled with an unknown commodity. Sixteenth-century. From the Florentine Codex (Sahagún 1950–82: Book 9, Chapter 7, folio 27).

political and economic tiers of Mixtec, Zapotec, and Mexica society; members of the lower tiers participated as suppliers and producers of goods and as recipients of a portion of the system's economic largesse in compensation for their support and participation (Brumfiel 1987; Monaghan 1990:759, 762–764; J. Pohl 1999). The system also prompted the development of elite patronage of specialized craft production and the growth of trade networks to acquire from nonlocal sources exotic materials to be used in crafted products, which, in turn, had greater social value as gifts because of their exotic materials (Blanton el al. 1996; Earle 1977; Halperin 1988; Helms 1993; Polanyi 1957; Renfrew 1985). These processes had social and economic ramifications throughout the society, binding together producers and consumers across socioeconomic boundaries and prompting the development of specialized craft production. The result was the extension of relations far beyond the local community via the creation of a cross-polity network of supply and alliance and a cross-cultural system of luxury-goods procurement (Blanton et al. 1996:2–6; Freidel, Reese-Taylor, and Mora Marín 2002).

The ancient Mesoamerican inventory of feasting gifts includes a prodigious amount of specially crafted items, some of which were produced by specialists under the patronage of the aristocratic class. These items usually were not exchanged through the common market system by which mundane commodities circulated (Zantwijk 1985) but were distributed through the competitive gift-giving accompanying aristocratic feasts (Berdan 1988; Blanton 1996:83; Burgoa 1989, v. 25:352; Elson 1999:163). Of the specialized craft items, polychrome pottery was a prominent gift, especially among the Postclassic Mixtecs (Lind 1987; J. Pohl 1999). Elsewhere in Highland Mexico, finely painted vessels and, in particular, Cholula Polychrome pottery were the favored feasting ware among the nobility and in the royal Aztec court at Tenochtitlan (Charlton and Nichols 1992; Garraty 2000; Noguera 1954; Sahagún 1950–82, Book 9, 1959:Plate 24; Book 10, 1961:78; Michael E. Smith et al. 2000). These expertly crafted and painted food service vessels were decorated with renderings of the ruling elite, their deified ancestors, and, especially, representations of the supporting mytho-religious ideologies. The vessels functioned as containers for edibles and also as portable props whose mytho-political imagery lent power and prestige to their owners and the event during which they were used. As gifts for the assembled guests, the ceramics were highly prized not only for their visual messages but also because of their direct connection to exclusive craft workshops staffed by accomplished artists and to the noble patron who mandated their production.

Paralleling John Pohl's discussion of elite feasting among the Postclassic Mixtecs (J. Pohl 1999), I propose that this same type of socioeconomic system underlies the development of technically sophisticated polychrome pottery by the Maya during the Early Classic period (A.D. 250–550), in particular the cylindrical drinking vessels painted with intricate scenes and hieroglyphic imagery (see Figure 10.1). That these cylindrical vases were used to hold *kakaw* is confirmed by portrayals on the vessels of palace feasts wherein cylinder vases brimming with frothy *kakaw* are offered by attendant women or sit next to the host and close at hand to the gathered guests (Figure 10.6). Further substantiation of function is provided by the hieroglyphic text painted around the rims of many vases that records their function as drinking vessels for *kakaw* beverages (Figures 10.7a, 10.7b) (Houston, Stuart, and Taube 1992; B. MacLeod 1990; B. MacLeod and D. Reents-Budet 1994:106–153; Stuart 1988; Taschek and Ball 1992).

Figure 10.6. Late Classic period Maya painted vase whose palace scene depicts an aristocratic meeting and feasting event during which *tamales* are served in a large plate, and a painted ceramic vessel is brimming with foamy *kakaw* beverage. Collections of Duke University Museum of Art (acc. no. 1980.116) (also Maya Ceramics Project sample number MS0607, Kerr no. 5353). Photograph by D. Reents-Budet.

Figure 10.7 a. The Buenavista Vase was found in a regal burial at Buenavista del Cayo, Belize. b. Rollout. Its hieroglyphic text states that this is the *kakaw* drinking vase of K'ak' Tiliw, who was a powerful ruler of the nearby site of Naranjo, Guatemala, during the eighth century A.D. National Collections of the Institute of Archaeology, Belize (registration #27/189–9). Photographs copyright Justin Kerr (K4464).

Preclassic (800 B.C.–A.D. 250) Maya painted pottery is dominated by monochrome slip-painted vessels (see, for example, Culbert 1993; Gifford 1976; Lowe 1975; R. E. Smith 1955; Valdez 1987), typically red or orange in color (see Figure 10.2). These early wares represent a technically and aesthetically sophisticated ceramic tradition in both the forming of the vessel and the decoration of its surface. Whether of simple or composite form, Preclassic vessels are elegantly proportioned, their angles and curved surfaces coalescing into a harmonious ensemble of shape. The fired slip paints produce a hard surface characterized by a smooth, waxy finish, visually rich in coloration and resistant to wear damage. The surface clarity and durability, expert firing, and formal aesthetic refinement of Preclassic wares imply production by accomplished craftspeople who must have been at least part-time, if not full-time, specialists.

This sophisticated yet modest decorative tradition gave way to one of the most elaborate low-fired pottery painting traditions created anywhere in the world, making its first appearance during the initial centuries (ca. A.D. 100–300) of the Classic period (A.D. 250–900) in the Peten Lowlands of Guatemala. Preclassic composite vessel forms yielded to more simple shapes; the Classic period repertoire was dominated by the open-faced plate, the round-sided bowl, and especially the parallel-sided cylindrical vase. Foremost among the reasons underlying this dramatic change in vessel shape was the desire for an unencumbered and relatively flat pictorial surface on which to paint imagery. In short, the aesthetic changed from a Preclassic period emphasis on vessel shape to the Classic period dominance of imagery.

But why was pictorial and hieroglyphic imagery so desirable on food service vessels? The primary reason was because the vessels had become a key component of feasting events that were directly connected to elite sociopolitics and economics. These *kakaw* serving vessels transcended their primary function as food service wares and were transformed into indispensable status markers and essential gifts; that is, they became social currency (Price 1989). This development was an extension of Late Preclassic and Protoclassic ceramic innovations wherein specific pottery forms, some of which were tagged with idiosyncratic symbols pertaining to place and person, were linked to particular rituals of rulership and even to individual members of the political elite (Reese-Taylor and Walker 2002:101–102, 107). It is but a small socio-artistic step from these Protoclassic wares to those of the Classic period whose exterior surfaces are enveloped in iconic tableaux featuring social, political, and divine power.

Maya artists devised a number of features to augment the value of the feasting vessels as social currency (Reents-Budet 1998), foremost of which was scarcity attributable to the high degree of artistry needed to produce these special objects, which thereby precluded wide-scale production and access (Reents-Budet 1994b:36–71). Second, vessels were the products of specialized workshops supported, in part, by elite patronage and staffed by highly trained artisans and renowned painters, some of whom were members of the ruling elite (Reents 1987; Reents-Budet 1994a, 1998; D. Stuart 1987). And third, their painted imagery embodied political and supernatural power, thereby promoting the social, political, economic, and mytho-religious power of the host (Reents-Budet, Bishop, and MacLeod 1994:164–233). The scenes may feature a ruler's personal history such as accession to the throne, victories on the battlefield and in the ceremonial ballcourt, visits by foreign dignitaries from powerful polities, and the prodigious amounts of tribute paid to him. Other tableaux portray the mythological and religious ideologies underlying Classic period social hierarchy that reinforced, through supernatural sanction, a lord's right to rule. These three features are among the prime characteristics that imbued Classic period pictorial pottery with sufficient prestige to be effective carriers of elite affect within a feasting sociopolitical system.

The scenes decorating Maya elite pottery served much the same function as the wall murals and pictorial lintels of the Mixtec royal palace at Mitla, Oaxaca, and the display of historical codices during royal feasts sponsored by the ruling elite (J. Pohl 1999). The Maya ceramic versions were more portable proclaimers of elite power than are lintels and, to a certain extent, precious codices. As high-status gifts, they were tools for sociopolitical propaganda that reified a feast host's social and political power. Such gifts were later used by the recipients during their own banquets, thereby continuing the multifaceted food and sociopolitical service roles of the vessels among the subsequent users and their local constituencies.

The remains of polychrome ceramic vessels are found in myriad domestic and administrative contexts that crosscut socioeconomic tiers of ancient Maya society especially among the upper and middle level elites (see, for example, LeCount 2001). This archaeological pattern indicates that *kakaw* consumption and feasting activities were not restricted to the topmost ruling elite. The painted ceramics found in aristocratic contexts, however, generally represent higher quality ceramic production, are more elaborately decorated, and more frequently include in their hieroglyphic texts the personal names and titles of members of the nobility. This contrasts with pottery found in lower tier socioeconomic contexts whose hieroglyphic texts often are pseudo-glyphic passages that replicate the concept of writing but do not record spoken language or the names of historical individuals (B. MacLeod in D. Reents-Budet 1994:140–142). Therefore, the quality of the vessel and the degree of elaboration of surface decoration are positively correlated with the sociopolitical or economic position, or both, of the patron/user and, generally, the recipient of the *kakaw* drinking vase. The presence of highly decorated and personalized vessels (or fragments thereof) in mid-level socioeconomic contexts, however, implies that secondary elites and perhaps, too, nonelites of established hinterland families took part in the feasting system as primary recipients, down-the-line participants, and/or sponsors of their own events (LeCount 1999).

Many cylinder vases are painted with palace scenes chronicling the array of courtly events during which feasts were held (Reents-Budet 2000a). The scenes often depict representations of food-filled vessels, including plates, bowls, and, especially, cylinder vases (Figures 10.1, 10.6). The hieroglyphic text painted around their rims, termed the Primary Standard Sequence (PSS) (M. D. Coe 1973), also makes reference to food in its "contents" section (Figure 10.8) (Houston, Stuart, and Taube 1989; B. MacLeod 1990; B. MacLeod and D. Reents-Budet 1994:106–163). The PSS on plates states that they were used to serve tamales, and the texts on bowls record their contents as *atole*, a kind of gruel made from maize. The most detailed contents section is found on cylinder vases, which records their function as *kakaw* drinking vessels. The text often describes the vase's particular kind or "recipe" of *kakaw* beverage such as "tree-fresh *kakaw*," "bitter *kakaw*," or the especially valued "foamy *kakaw*" (Figure 10.8) (B. MacLeod and D. Reents-Budet 1994:115–119, 146–147). Foam on the top of the beverage was the most highly prized attribute of the drink because the consumer experiences enhanced taste and aroma when the bubbles burst in the mouth, sending forth the encapsulated gustatory and olfactory sensations. When describing Aztec *kakaw* drinks, the sixteenth-century Spanish chronicler Bernardino de Sahagún notes that the good *kakaw* preparer "aerates it, filters it, strains it, pours it back and forth; she makes it form a head, makes foam" (Sahagún 1950–82, Book 10, 1961:93) (Figure 10.9). The aesthetic qualities of *kakaw* drinks, then, are not restricted to taste but also include aroma and the

Figure 10.8. Detail of the Primary Standard Sequence hieroglyphic text from a polychrome bowl that notes its intended contents as "foamy *kakaw*." Collections of the Los Angeles County Museum of Art (acc. no. AC1992.129.1, General Acquisition Fund). Photograph copyright Justin Kerr (K4976).

Figure 10.10. The scene on this vase implies a palace feasting event that includes a painted cylinder vase filled with dark brown foamy *kakaw* to be consumed by the participants. Collections of the Princeton Art Museum (acc. no. 86–91) (also Smithsonian Institution Maya Ceramics Project sample number MS1406). Photograph copyright Justin Kerr (K767). (Also see Figure 10.14).

Figure 10.9. Detail of a Classic period Maya vase depicting the aerating of a *kakaw* beverage by pouring the liquid from one jar into another placed on the floor. Collections of the Princeton Art Museum (acc. no. 75–17, the Hans and Dorothy Widenmann Foundation). Photograph copyright Justin Kerr (K511).

color of the bubbles, a darker brown head promising better flavor and essence (Figure 10.10) (S. D. Coe and M. D. Coe 1996:86–93).

The Classic Maya seemingly also valued the geographic origin of the *kakaw* and its container. This is indicated by the elaborated contents section painted on some vases, which lists more than the type of drink. These texts mention the place of origin of the drinking vessel, for example a "Waxaktun *kakaw*

Figure 10.11 a. Late Classic period Maya vase. Photograph by D. Reents-Budet. b. Rollout. The "contents section" of the Primary Standard Sequence text painted around the rim of this vase qualifies it as a "Waxaktun *kakaw* drinking vessel." Photograph copyright Justin Kerr (K1743). Collections of the Mint Museum of Art (acc. no. 84.217.15) (also Maya Ceramics Project sample number MS1444, Kerr no. 1743).

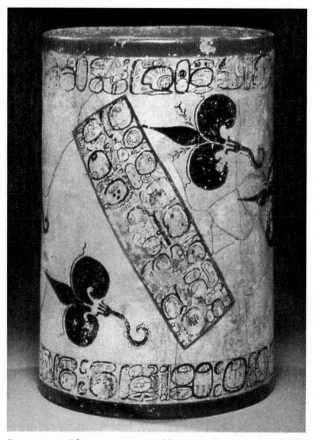

Figure 10.12. This vase was painted by a member of the ruling family of Naranjo, in eastern Guatemala. The Primary Standard Sequence text ends with a detailed "signature phrase" in which the artist records his personal name, family appellation, and the names of his parents, who were Naranjo's queen and king from A.D. 755 to 780. Collections of the Art Institute of Chicago (acc. no. 1986.1080, Ethel T. Scarborough Fund). Photograph copyright Justin Kerr (K635).

drinking vessel"; that is, a vessel and contents originating at the important site of Waxaktun, Guatemala (Figure 10.11a, b) (B. MacLeod and D. Reents-Budet 1994:115; also see S. D. Coe and M. D. Coe 1996:59–68).

It should be stressed that these vases are unlike the mundane, relatively thick-walled pottery dishes oftentimes made from a coarse ceramic paste. Instead, they frequently have very thin walls, are made from well-processed clays with volcanic ash temper, and have parallel sides with no visible deviation in form. This focus on craftsmanship may be emphasized in the texts on some that qualify them as 'thin-walled, gourd-like drinking vessels' (*u-tsimal hay y'uk'ib*; see B. MacLeod and D. Reents-Budet 1994:127, K530; but see D.

Stuart 2005:128 for 'clay vessel' as an alternative reading). This phrase harks back to the thin-walled tree calabash or gourd that was and continues to be the traditional drinking vessel throughout Mesoamerica (D. Tedlock 2002). When qualifying a ceramic vase, then, the elaborated contents section highlights not only the *kakaw* beverage and origin of the *kakaw* beans but also the technical expertise of the potter whose skill allowed him or her to replicate the thin wall of a calabash in the challenging medium of limestone-based clays for hand-built vessels of low-fired earthenware (B. MacLeod and D. Reents-Budet 1994:127; Reents-Budet 1998).

Following the contents section, the final part of the PSS is a name phrase that typically records the regal titles and sometimes even the personal name of the owner or patron of the vessel (B. MacLeod 1990). Not surprisingly, named patrons frequently are members of the ruling elite, including paramount rulers of dominant Classic period polities (see, for example, Taschek and Ball 1992) (see Figure 10.7). In a few instances, the final phrase ends with the titles or personal name of the artist who painted the vase, some of whom are recorded as members of the ruling family who seemingly were not in direct line to inherit the throne (Figures 10.12, 10.13). These signatures are found only on the highest quality vases whose painting represents the pinnacle of Classic period artistry. This pattern of vessels painted by artists who were members of the nobility and representing the highest technical and aesthetic expressions strongly implies the existence of "palace schools" (Reents-Budet et al. 2000); that is, pottery workshops or artists' studios that were closely connected to the elite strata and ruling families of Classic Maya society (M. D. Coe and J. Kerr 1998; Reents-Budet 1998; D. Stuart 1987). The "name-tagging" of vessels (Houston and Taube 1987) with the names of both the owner/patron and the painter imbued them with added prestige because of their association with powerful and creative individuals (Houston, Stuart, and Taube 1992; Reents-Budet 1998). The increased prestige augmented the value of the drinking vessel and, by direct association, its *kakaw* contents. A typical PSS from a finely painted pictorial cylinder vase (see Figures 10.12 and 10.13) establishes it as the tree-fresh *kakaw*-food drinking vase that belonged to K'ak' Ukalaw Chan Chaak (here named with his alternative nominal "he of flint"), the divine ruler of Naranjo. The vase was painted by the noble Naranjo artist Ah Maxam whose mother was Lady Shell Star of Yaxhá and whose father was K'ak' Ukalaw Chan Chaak, the king (and patron/owner of the vase). This royal son and artist, however, was not in direct line for the throne because the next king of Naranjo was K'e?-ji ?-le? K'awil (Martin and Grube 2000:80).

Kakaw played a second major role in the Classic period feasting system as one of the most valuable gifts given to the participants, reflecting its treasured

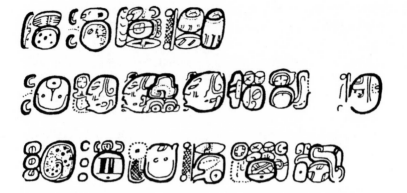

Figure 10.13. The Primary Standard Sequence from the vase in Figure 10.12. The "contents section" notes that this is a vase for drinking tree-fresh *kakaw*-food that belonged to K'ak' Ukalaw Chan Chaak (here named with his alternative nominal "He of Flint"), the divine ruler of Naranjo, the vase having been painted by the noble Naranjo artist (line 1) whose mother was Lady Shell-Star of Yaxhá (line 2) and whose father was the king (and the patron/owner of the vase) K'ak' Ukalaw Chan Chaak (line 3). Collections of the Art Institute of Chicago (acc. no. 1986.1080, Ethel T. Scarborough Fund). Drawing by Diane G. Peck and Diane McC. Holsenbeck after M. D. Coe (1973).

status. The economic value of *kakaw* in Mesoamerica, from pre-Columbian to Colonial and extending to modern times, is firmly established by sixteenth- century ethnohistoric accounts from Highland Mexico and the Yucatan Peninsula (for example, Landa 1941 [1566]; Oviedo y Valdés [in Landa 1941 [1566]:95, n. 417]; Sahagún 1950–82) and by the modern survival of *kakaw* as a prized commodity (D. Tedlock 2002; Vogt 1969, 1993; also see S. D. Coe and M. D. Coe 1996:97–99; Millon 1955a). During Late Postclassic times and continuing into the Colonial period, *kakaw* beans functioned as an abstract representation of value; that is, as money. For example, in the markets of Tenochtitlan, the capital of the Aztec empire, the beans could be exchanged for any number of commodities. They also served as payment for work service and to buy one's way out of forced labor (slavery) (S. D. Coe and M. D. Coe 1996:98–99). *Kakaw* beans were the preferred payment for tax or service obligations because they were a readily convertible capital medium in most of the prevailing economic systems of the myriad cultures of Mesoamerica and also of those to the south in Central America (McAnany et al. 2002:129).

Similarities of use, which thereby imply a similar economic and social worth of *kakaw* among the Classic Maya, are suggested by representations of aristocratic activities painted on the pictorial ceramics. Many scenes portray the presentation of tribute resulting from alliance obligations, victories on the battlefield, betrothal rites and marriages, and diplomatic endeavors as well as gift exchange

Figure 10.14. This vase documents the presentation of war tribute to a high official, likely a ruler, who sits on a movable bench throne placed on the uppermost step of a palace building. The tribute sits on the steps below him and includes bundles that likely contain *kakaw* beans; stacks of cloth; spondylus shells; and prisoners of war. A feast is indicated by the plate of tamales and the cylinder vase filled with frothy *kakaw* placed in front of the seated lord at the upper left of the scene. Collections of the Princeton Art Museum (acc. no. 86–91) (also Smithsonian Institution Maya Ceramics Project sample number MS1406). Photographs copyright Justin Kerr (K767).

during accompanying feasting events (Figure 10.14) (Reents-Budet 2000a; also see Schele and Mathews 1991, 1998). The four predominant tribute and gift items, based on their frequency of depiction on the pictorial pottery, are feathers, spondylus shell, textiles and bundles of *kakaw* beans (Reents-Budet in press). That the cloth bundles contain *kakaw* beans is confirmed by hieroglyphs painted on the wrapped parcels naming their contents as *b'ul* 'beans' (S. Houston, quoted in M. E. Miller 1997).

Conclusion

In summary, *kakaw*, as both a delicious food and a repository of financial strength, was among the seminal commodities of Classic Maya society. Among the ruling elite, *kakaw* and *kakaw*-drinking were tightly bound together with the fundamental political processes of alliance formation and socioeconomic enrichment. This intertwining of *kakaw* and social process is discerned particularly in the pictorial representations of palace feasts painted on Classic Maya pottery, by the hieroglyphic texts accompanying these scenes, and by the actual vessels that were used during feasting events. By the Early Classic period, feasting rites, under the control of the ruling elite of Maya society, had become an essential social, economic, and political mechanism, which maintained its importance to Maya culture well into the Colonial period.

Kakaw was one of the most prominent and crucial commodities of the feast, serving as the preferred drink and essential gift of prestige and privilege. The importance of *kakaw* in the Classic period is underscored by the rapid development of polychrome pottery, especially the pictorial cylindrical drinking vases painted with scenes of elite Maya life and religious mythology. These vases often were created by renowned artists, some of whom were members of the ruling elite and whose distinguished social status and creativity elevated the prestige of the object. The elaborate drinking vessels were used to serve the esteemed *kakaw* beverages to the feasting guests and were, as well, gifts for the participants. Later, during feasts sponsored by the new owner, the vase would again signal social prestige and political connection. Among the Classic Maya, then, *kakaw* was intimately connected to contemporary politics and economics, the three being intertwined in the never-ending pursuit of social prestige, political influence, and economic power.

Acknowledgments

I wish to thank John Pohl and John Monaghan for sharing their research on feasting in Oaxaca and for insightful discussions about similarities among the ancient Maya. I thank also Joseph Ball, Elizabeth Graham, and David Pendergast for lively discussions about palace middens and Classic Maya courtly life, especially those at Buenavista del Cayo, Belize (Joseph Ball), Lamanai (Elizabeth Graham and David Pendergast), and Altun Ha (David Pendergast). Conversations with Dennis Tedlock and John Henderson have been seminal in honing my thoughts on the roles of *kakaw* in Maya society, and I thank Dennis for mentioning the noble positions in the sixteenth-century K'iché court. Thanks also are extended to Nikolai Grube, Stanley Guentar, and Barbara MacLeod for years of hieroglyphic collaboration and assistance. The Maya Ceramics Project (Department of Anthropology, National Museum of Natural History, Smithsonian Institution) has provided exceptional access and intellectual environment to conduct years of research on Maya pottery, with special thanks to project scientists Ronald L. Bishop and James Blackman. Thanks also are extended to Justin and Barbara Kerr whose archive of photographs and years of discussions have advanced my research.

Note

1. "K + number" (e.g. K5400) refers to the archival number of Classic period Maya pottery vessels in the Maya Vase Database created and compiled by Justin Kerr. The database is available online at www.famsi.org.

11

The Use and Representation of Cacao During the Classic Period at Copan, Honduras

Cameron L. McNeil, W. Jeffrey Hurst, and Robert J. Sharer

Cacao had a significant place in ritual at Copan, Honduras, from at least the Early Classic period (ca. A.D. 250–600), but probably long before. Within the human-produced mountains of the Copan Acropolis, Early Classic queens and kings were entombed with a diversity of comestibles containing cacao.[1] Although cacao iconography has not been found in the Early Classic material culture record at Copan, by Late Classic times (ca. A.D. 600–900) sculptured cacao pods appear on ceramic cache vessels and stone censers, vessels bearing cacao glyphs are first produced in the area, and one temple displays open sculpted cacao pods on its façade. Its representation at Copan designates cacao as a sacred tree linked to the rebirth of ancestors and their journey from the Underworld; to maize; and to feminine attributes of fertility.

Documentation of cacao and cacao iconography at Copan demonstrates a unique tradition in the Maya world. Although the Copan Maya, particularly during the Late Classic period, employed symbolism linked to cacao that is also found at other Classic period sites, the degree to which they used this symbolism and that they did not employ other Maya traditions linked to cacao until the Late Classic, sets this polity apart from other Maya centers. Copan's position on the southeastern periphery of the Maya region meant that it was at a crossroads between Maya traditions and those of other ethnic groups to the east and south (Bill 1997; W. L. Fash 2005; Longyear 1952; Viel 1993). Not surprisingly, then, Copan's use of cacao symbolism reflects the hybrid culture of the valley, combining traits common to the Maya with those related to non-Maya neighbors in the Ulua River Valley and sites such as Naco along the Chameleon river (see Figure 11.1).

In this chapter we discuss the importance of cacao in Early Classic tomb and cache offerings at Copan, focusing on the results of vessel residue analysis conducted on thirty-seven samples from these contexts. We then explore the

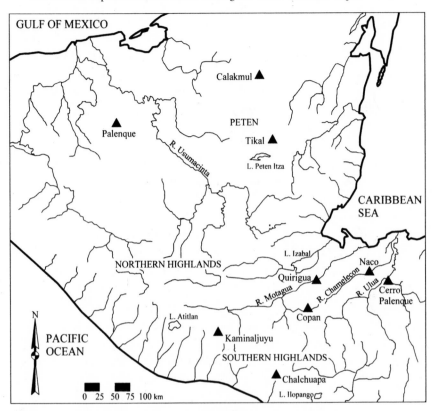

Figure 11.1. Map of Copan, Honduras and neighboring areas. Copan is located in the southeastern Maya periphery. Redrawn after Sharer 1994:Figure 1.1.

cultivation of cacao at Copan and its religious significance for the people of the polity. We conclude with evidence for the continuity of these traditions between the Early and Late Classic periods at Copan and between the Copan Maya and neighboring groups—both Maya and non-Maya.

Early Classic Cacao Use at Copan

Cacao in Early Classic Archaeological Residues at Copan

In the 1990s, the Early Copan Acropolis Program (ECAP) of the University of Pennsylvania Museum, under the direction of Robert J. Sharer, began a tunneling project into select areas of the Acropolis to investigate its development. The central architecture of most ancient Maya cities comprises solid pyramidal platforms supporting vaulted buildings. To mark a change in rulership or other important event, such as a calendrical period ending (for example, 9.0.0.0.0 8 Ajaw 13 Keh, or December 11, A.D. 435), the Maya ritually killed and then buried buildings by fashioning new structures atop them. The ECAP excavators dug into the earliest levels of these human-made mountains, discovering more than fifty Early Classic buildings and their construction history. A second objective of ECAP was to determine whether these early levels substantiated the lineage history depicted on stelae and altars at the site—particularly on Altar Q, a monument of the sixteenth ruler, Yax Pahsaj Chan Yopat. Altar Q records the sixteen kings of the Copan dynasty beginning with K'inich Yax K'uk' Mo', who was made Copan's king in A.D. 426 but did not arrive in Copan until A.D. 427 (Fash 2001; D. Stuart 2000).

The ECAP excavations discovered three royal tombs, referred to as the Hunal (Burial 95-2), Margarita (Burial 93-2), and Sub-Jaguar (Burial 92-2) tombs, as well as two additional elite interments, Burials 92-3 and 95-1. Evidence from the tomb in the Hunal structure indicates it held the remains of K'inich Yax K'uk' Mo,' Copan's dynastic founder, who reigned from A.D. 426 to 437 (Sharer et al. 1999; Sharer 2004). The tomb in the Margarita structure, the most sumptuous burial of the three, is presumed to hold the spouse of the founder, the first queen of the Classic period Copan dynasty (Bell 2002; Sharer et al. 1999). The individual in the Sub-Jaguar tomb is likely Ruler 8, Wil Ohl K'inich, who reigned from A.D. 532 to 551 (Sharer and Traxler 2003).

As a sacred mountain, with ancestors entombed in its deepest recesses, the Copan Acropolis was imbued with tremendous power. The royal tombs containing the revered dead were filled with precious offerings, including cacao,

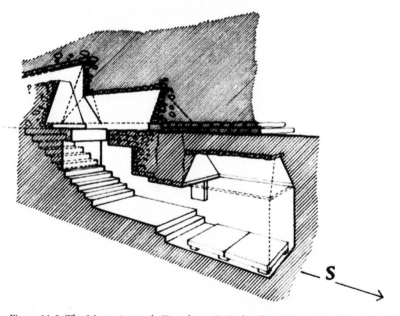

Figure 11.2. The Margarita tomb (Burial 93–2). Early Classic period. Copan, Honduras. The tomb contains both a lower and upper chamber. A corridor was added to the tomb to allow re-entry after a structure was built over it. Drawing by Rudy Larios.

and both the Hunal and Margarita burial chambers were likely reentered for the purpose of conducting rites of veneration for some period after the death of the rulers. The queen's tomb (the Margarita tomb) has a vaulted corridor that was constructed specifically to allow re-entry after a later building was placed on top of the Margarita structure (see Figure 11.2) (Bell et al. 2004). These tombs may have functioned, both symbolically and materially, as sacred caves in the heart of the Acropolis, which held the individuals who came to signify the mother/father deities of the Classic period Copan Maya.

Sixty-three ceramic vessels representing a diversity of forms were recovered from the three royal tombs and two elite burials. The vessels were lifted from their contexts, placed in stable plastic containers, wrapped in foil, and transported to the Centro Regional de Investigaciones Arqueológicas (CRIA) laboratory adjacent to the site. The contents of each vessel were then excavated in a closed laboratory to protect this material from pollen and phytolith contamination. The vessels from the Margarita and Hunal tombs were excavated layer by layer by Cameron McNeil in a closed room of the laboratory, with special care taken to isolate the thinnest layer resting on the bottom for pollen, phytolith, and chemical residue analysis. The material in the Sub-Jaguar tomb vessels was excavated in the laboratory by Loa Traxler (1994), who carefully removed tomb wall fall and other contaminants in the vessels before sampling. The vessel residue from Burial 92-3 was sampled by Christina Carrelli (personal communication 2002) while the vessel was *in situ* because it was found broken into pieces. The vessels with the best preserved contents came from the upper offering platform of the Margarita tomb and from an offering cache just outside the tomb.

Under permits issued by the Instituto Hondureño de Antropología e Historia the residue samples from these vessels were exported to W. Jeffrey Hurst of Hershey Technical Laboratories for extraction and reverse-phase High Performance Liquid Chromatography analysis (see Hurst, this volume). Thirty-one of the samples have been analyzed. Hurst's analysis involves the identification of theobromine and caffeine in residues. His results identified *Theobroma* (cacao) in eleven of these vessels (Table 11.1). These include two cylinder tripod vessels, two small cylinder vessels, one platter, one deer effigy vessel, three ring-based bowls, one vertical-walled cache bowl, and one large bowl with mammiform supports (Figures 11.3, 11.4, 11.5, 11.6). Theobromine and caffeine were found in nine vessels, theobromine alone in two vessels, and caffeine alone in another. The chemical signature in the pulp and seeds of the cacao pod is virtually identical, so although this analysis can tell us that cacao was present in a vessel, it cannot identify whether this signature is a product of the seeds or the pulp.

Caffeine is found in a variety of genera, but in Mesoamerica theobromine is found in only two members of the genus *Theobroma* (*Theobroma cacao* L.

Table 11.1. Results of the analysis of vessel residues for the presence of cacao

	Context	Vessel and Sample Numbers	Vessel Description	Theobromine Present	Caffeine Present
1.	Hunal Tomb, Burial 95-2	Vessel 1, 1/6/381–138 2000M-138	Effigy vessel in the form of a deer	Positive	Positive
2.	Hunal Tomb, Burial 95-2	Vessel 9, 1/6/381–1 Residue sample:1999M-198	Cylinder tripod with decorative pattern referred to as "cacao beans"	Negative	Positive
3.	Hunal Tomb, Burial 95-2	Vessel 10, 1/6/381–13 2000M-258	Fine-lined painted vase	Negative	Negative
4.	Hunal Tomb, Burial 95-2	Vessel 16, 1/6/381–38 Residue sample: 1999M-208	Cylinder tripod with decorative pattern referred to as "cacao beans"	Negative	Negative
5.	Hunal Tomb, Burial 95-2	Vessel 19, 1/6/381–42 Residue sample: 2001M-031	Cylinder tripod with lid	Negative	Negative
6.	Margarita Tomb, Burial 93-2, Chamber 1	Vessel 2, 1/6/423–1 Residue sample: 2001M-204	Wide bowl	Negative	Negative
7.	Margarita Tomb, Burial 93-2, Chamber 1	Vessel 10, 1/6/420–7 Residue sample: 2000M-411	Ring-based bowl	Negative	Negative
8.	Margarita Tomb, Burial 93-2, Chamber 1	Vessel 11, 1/6/420–9 Residue sample: 2001M-308	Ring-based bowl	Negative	Negative
9.	Margarita Tomb, Burial 93-2, Chamber 1	Vessel 12, 1/6/420–5 Residue sample: 2000M-234	Ring-based bowl	Negative	Negative
10.	Margarita Tomb, Burial 93-2, Chamber 1	Vessel 14, 1/6/420–2 Residue sample: 2001M-263	Cylinder tripod	Negative	Negative
11.	Margarita Tomb, Burial 93-2, Chamber 1	Vessel 15, 1/6/420–6 Residue sample: 2001M-281	Ring-based bowl	Negative	Negative
12.	Margarita Tomb, Burial 93-2, Chamber 1	Vessel 18, 1/6/481–1 Residue sample: 2001M-223	Ring-based bowl	Positive	Negative
13.	Margarita Tomb, Burial 93-2, Chamber 2	Vessel 1, 1/6/208–1 Residue sample: 1994M-75	Cylinder tripod	Positive	Positive
14.	Margarita Tomb, Burial 93-2, Chamber 2	Vessel 5, 1/6/208–6 Residue sample: 2001M-214	Cylinder tripod	Positive	Positive
15.	Margarita Tomb, Burial 93-2, Chamber 2	Vessel 8, 1/6/215–2 Residue sample: 2001M-295	Ring-based bowl	Positive	Positive
16.	Margarita Tomb, Burial 93-2, Chamber 2	Vessel 9, 1/6/215–1 Residue sample: 2001M-254	Cylinder tripod	Negative	Negative

continued

	Context	Vessel and Sample Numbers	Vessel Description	Theobromine Present	Caffeine Present
7.	Offering 93-16, outside the Margarita Tomb	Vessel 2, 1/6/206–2 Residue sample: 2004M-058	Large open bowl with mamiform feet	Positive	Negative
8.	Sub Jaguar Tomb, Burial 92-2	Vessel 1, 1/7/290–16 Residue sample: 1993M-193	Small cylinder	Positive	Positive
9.	Sub Jaguar Tomb, Burial 92-2	Vessel 2, 1/7/290–19 Residue sample: 1992M-111	Small cylinder with lid	Negative	Negative
0.	Sub Jaguar Tomb, Burial 92-2	Vessel 3, 1/7/290–99 Residue sample: 1998M-104	Small cylinder	Positive	Positive
1.	Sub Jaguar Tomb, Burial 92-2	Vessel 4, 1/7/290–15 Residue sample: 1993M-198	Cylinder tripod	Negative	Negative
2.	Sub Jaguar Tomb, Burial 92-2	Vessel 6, 1/7/290–9 Residue sample: 1992M-109	Small cylinder tripod with lid	Negative	Negative
3.	Sub Jaguar Tomb, Burial 92-2	Vessel 13, 1/7/290–11 Residue sample: 1992M-105	Large cache vessel	Positive	Positive
4.	Sub Jaguar Tomb, Burial 92-2	Vessel 16, 1/7/290–21 Residue sample: 1993M-200	Large cylinder tripod	Negative	Negative
5.	Sub Jaguar Tomb, Burial 92-2	Vessel 17, 1/7/290–23 Residue sample: 2001M-323	Platter	Positive	Positive
6.	Sub Jaguar Tomb, Burial 92-2	Vessel 20, 1/7/290–29 Residue sample: 1993M-188	Platter	Negative	Negative
7.	Sub Jaguar Tomb, Burial 92-2	Vessel 21, 1/7/400–7 Residue sample: 1994M-088	Ring-based bowl	Negative	Negative
8.	Sub Jaguar Tomb, Burial 92-2	Vessel 23, 1/7/290–12 Residue sample: 1992M-084	Ring-based bowl	Negative	Negative
9.	Sub Jaguar Tomb, Burial 92-2	Vessel 28, 1/7/290–29 Residue sample: 1992M-100	Platter beneath cylinder tripod	Negative	Negative
0.	Sub Jaguar Offering	Vessel 1, 1/7/402–1 Residue sample: 1997M-200	Cylinder	Negative	Negative
1.	Burial 92-3	Vessel 2, 1/5/15–3 Residue sample: 1993-129	Ring-based bowl	Positive	Positive

and *Theobroma bicolor* Bonpl.), both of which were considered types of "cacao" in pre-Columbian times. Theobromine and caffeine occur together in significant amounts only in *T. cacao*, with theobromine occurring in a much higher concentration than caffeine. Therefore the presence in one vessel of caffeine, without theobromine, makes it unlikely that cacao was in this vessel. *T. cacao* may, however, have been present in the two vessels that contain theobromine but not caffeine. Alternatively, these vessels could have contained *T. bicolor*, which contains theobromine but only tiny amounts of caffeine in its seeds (see Kufer and McNeil, this volume; Sotelo and Alvarez 1991). One seed of *T. bicolor* was found sealed in a vessel in an Early Classic offering at Tikal,

Figure 11.3. Vessel 1 (1/6/381-138), a ceramic deer effigy vessel from the Hunal tomb. Early Classic period. Copan, Honduras. Excavated by the Early Copan Acropolis Program of the University of Pennsylvania Museum. Collection of the Instituto Hondureño de Antropología e Historia. Photograph by Cameron L. McNeil.

Figure 11.4. Vessels containing cacao. Margarita tomb. Early Classic period. Copan, Honduras. a. Front row left to right: Vessel 8 (1/6/215-2) is a ring-based bowl that contained the bones of small fish; Vessel 18 (1/6/481-1) is a thin-walled, orange-paste, ring-based bowl. Back row left to right: Vessel 1 (1/6/208) is a stuccoed tripod vase; Vessel 5 (1/6/208-6) is a black tripod vessel with a red band. Vessel 18 came from the lower chamber where the queen's body rested. The other three vessels were found in an offering chamber above her (see Figure 11.2 for tomb plan). b. Vessel 1 (1/6/208) with lid. This vessel features a goggle-eyed figure peering out of a building. David Stuart has proposed that the drawing on the vessel depicts the spirit of "K'inich Yax K'uk' Mo' inside Hunal temple" (in Fash 2001:95). Excavated by the Early Copan Acropolis Program of the University of Pennsylvania Museum. Collection of the Instituto Hondureño de Antropología e Historia. Photographs by Cameron L. McNeil.

Figure 11.5. Vessel 2 (1/6/206-2). Offering 93-16. Early Classic period. Copan, Honduras. This vessel with mammiform supports has a small figure with crossed legs on the front. Excavated by the Early Copan Acropolis Program of the University of Pennsylvania Museum. Collection of the Instituto Hondureño de Antropología e Historia. Photograph by Cameron L. McNeil.

Figure 11.6. Vessels containing cacao. Sub-Jaguar tomb. Early Classic period. Copan, Honduras. Front row, left to right: Vessel 17 (1/7/290-23) is a large platter; Vessel 1 (1/7/290) and Vessel 3 (1/7/290-99) are small cylinders. Back row: Vessel 13 (1/7/290-11) is a large cache vessel. Excavated by the Early Copan Acropolis Program of the University of Pennsylvania Museum. Collection of the Instituto Hondureño de Antropología e Historia. Photograph by Cameron L. McNeil.

Guatemala (Moholy-Nagy, Haviland, and Jones 2003:95). Seeds of this plant are also used to make beverages (see this volume: Kufer and McNeil; McNeil, Chapter 17).

Each tomb had a significantly different microenvironment, which should be taken into account when considering these results. The Hunal tomb vessels, with the exception of the deer effigy vessel, contained little debris from wall collapse and other taphonomic processes but also retained little or no discernible residue. Flooding in the tomb, observed during Hurricane Mitch in 1998, may have been a periodic occurrence and could have affected the survival of chemical signatures in the vessels. The vessels in the Margarita tomb chamber, which may also have been subject to flooding, were generally full to their lip with wall collapse and artifacts, particularly shell and jade beads. Some of these vessels retained faunal material. Vessels that rested above the tomb in the upper offering chamber appear to have been more protected than those in the lower chamber, with nearly all containing defined residues. The Sub-Jaguar tomb also suffered from water infiltration; some vessels contained pools of water when the tomb was first opened (McNeil et al. 2002). The deposition of fallen stucco and rock was variable within the tomb chamber with some vessels filled with debris whereas others contained only small amounts. The Sub-Jaguar tomb had the most cacao vessels in a single tomb chamber. One of the cacao-containing vessels, a ring-based bowl, came from an elite male burial (92-3) that contained only two vessels. A vessel containing *T. cacao* or *T. bicolor* was also recovered from an offering (Offering 93-16) placed outside of the Margarita tomb.

Cacao in the Hunal Tomb

Cacao was found in at least one vessel in each of the four royal or elite burials from which residues were analyzed. In the purported tomb of K'inich Yax K'uk' Mo', built within the Hunal structure, only one vessel tested positive for cacao, an effigy vessel in the form of a deer, Hunal tomb Vessel 1 (see Figure 11.3). Most of the tomb's vessels were found on the floor tucked underneath the stone burial slab which held the corpse and adornments of jade, shell, and worked bone (Bell et al. 2004). Vessel 1 was placed in the southeastern corner of the tomb and was one of only a few vessels that did not appear to have been displaced by flooding and earthquakes during the last fifteen hundred years. Vessel 1 contained a spondylus shell scoop carved in the shape of a human hand (Figure 11.7). The palm of the scoop was stained reddish-brown by a mixture of cacao residue and cinnabar. The presence of the delicate shallow scoop may indicate that the contents of the deer effigy vessel were in a powdered and unprepared form as the scoop's shape and material would not allow it to be an effective serving utensil for either cacao beverages or seeds. In modern Maya markets, powdered mixtures of maize and cacao, called *panecita* or *pinole*, are

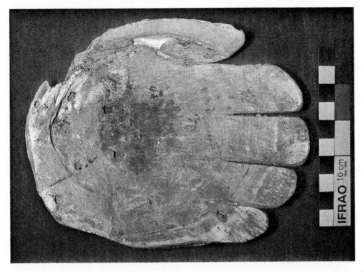

Figure 11.7. Hand (1/6/466-1) carved from a spondylus shell. Hunal tomb. Early Classic period. Copan, Honduras. This hand was embedded in the residue of the deer effigy vessel in Figure 11.3. The cacao and cinnabar in the vessel stained the palm a rich reddish-brown. Excavated by the Early Copan Acropolis Program of the University of Pennsylvania Museum. Collection of the Instituto Hondureño de Antropología e Historia. Photograph by Cameron L. McNeil.

still sold (see McNeil, Chapter 17, this volume). The deer effigy vessel may have held a supply of such a mixture to sustain the king on his long journey to the afterworld.

The Hunal tomb also contained one vessel that tested positive for caffeine but not theobromine. The presence of the caffeine alone is somewhat puzzling as no caffeinated substance other than cacao is known to have been consumed in pre-Columbian Mesoamerica (see Bletter and Daly, this volume).

Cacao in the Margarita Tomb

The Margarita tomb is assumed to be that of the spouse of K'inich Yax K'uk' Mo', the ancestral mother of the Classic period Copan dynasty. Her tomb is composed of an upper chamber for the placement of offerings and a lower chamber that contained the body of the royal lady and a large array of vessels, carved jade artifacts, stingray spines, and hematite mirrors (Bell 2002). The Margarita tomb chamber contained only one vessel that tested positive for cacao, Vessel 18 (see Figure 11.4a), a thin walled, orange-paste, ring-based bowl. Flooding of the chamber may have washed away residues in some of the tomb vessels.

Three vessels from the unflooded offering chamber, above the queen's burial, contained cacao, and more vessels wait to be tested (see Figure 11.4a). One is a ring-based bowl and two are cylinder tripods. One of these, Vessel 1 (Figure 11.4a, 11.4b) was imported from Central Mexico and then decorated in

Copan. Found on the south side of the upper offering chamber platform, this vessel features a fine-line painting of a talud-and-tablero-style building that resembles the Hunal structure with a goggle-eyed figure in its doorway (Figure 11.4b). David Stuart has suggested that this vessel depicts the spirit of K'inich Yax K'uk' Mo' inside Hunal, his final resting place (in Fash 2001:95). It seems particularly significant that this vessel, the most ornate on the upper offering platform which recalls the power of K'inich Yax K'uk' Mo', contains cacao. The cacao residue comprised a 3 mm layer across the bottom of the vessel and was surprisingly well-preserved, retaining the hue of dark chocolate. This residue is likely the remains of a ritual beverage.

Palynological analysis conducted on the residue from this vessel revealed that it contained a small amount of pollen when compared with the other cacao-containing vessels found on the upper offering platform. Its lid afforded some degree of protection from contamination through wall collapse and from decaying ritual plants that likely adorned the platform. Pollen in this sample came from pine (*Pinus*), cattail (*Typha*), and grass (Poaceae). Other research suggests that these plants were used to decorate important ritual areas in the Copan Acropolis, and their pollen may have entered the vessel when the drink was being prepared (McNeil 2002). This pollen also could have been present in the water used to concoct the cacao drink, or it may have floated into the drink on the wind.

It seems unlikely that the beverage in this vessel was sweetened. Honey, a pollen laden substance, was the most common sweetener available to the ancient Maya. Had the vessel contained honey, one would expect to find more pollen in the residue. Charles Wisdom (1940:91) notes in his book on the modern Ch'orti', a group widely believed to be the descendants of the Copan Maya, that *chilate*, a drink consisting of cacao and maize, is not sweetened when produced for ceremonial occasions.

A small ring-based bowl (see Figure 11.4a) from the upper offering chamber contained an abundance of tiny fish bones and scales mixed with a powdery brown material that has been identified as cacao. Zooarchaeologist Colin Amundsen identified the bones as those of a small fish comparable in size to a sardine. The modern Lenca, an ethnic group whose ancestors may also have been present at ancient Copan, offer small river fish, cacao, and maize *chicha* as part of rituals to the lightning god and for success with agricultural animals (Chapman 1985:130–139). These rites may be a modern version of ancient rituals relating to wild animals and hunting of the type offered to the Mountain and Earth Lord (Chapman 1985). It is possible that the offerings placed over time in the platform above the tombs of the queen and king were made to ensure the aid of these ancestors in bringing rain and agricultural fertility.

Offering 93-16

An elaborate stone-lined cache of offerings (Offering 93-16) was found beneath the floor of the Margarita structure on the same level as the upper offering platform. It contained, among other offerings, a large bowl (Vessel 2) holding charred turkey bones and covered by an inverted vessel (Figure 11.5) (Davis-Salazar and Bell 2000:1115). Residue from the bowl tested positive for theobromine but not caffeine, indicating that the vessel held either *T. cacao* or *T. bicolor.*

Cacao in the Sub-Jaguar Tomb

Four vessels from the Sub-Jaguar tomb tested positive for the presence of cacao. Two of these are small fine-lined stucco-decorated cylinder vessels, one is an unslipped basin of a ceramic type often used in caches, and the fourth is a platter (see Figure 11.6). Painted ceramics frequently picture this last vessel type holding tamales, which are sometimes covered in a reddish sauce (Reents-Budet 1994a:Figure 2.20, 3.2). Possibly this unidentified sauce was made of cacao like a *mole* sauce, or the tamales may have contained cacao. In Guatemala today, tamales containing cacao are called "tamales *negros*" or "tamales *dulces*" and are consumed during festivals (see McNeil, Chapter 17, this volume).

Cacao in Burial 92-3

The identity and status of the individual in Burial 92-3 remain unknown. The interment probably dates to the mid-sixth century (Bell et al. 2004:149). Only two vessels were buried with the individual. One of them, a ring-based bowl, contained cacao. Artifacts in this burial, particularly an ornate shell collar, may indicate that it is a redeposited royal burial (Sharer 2004:310).

Observations on Cacao Vessels at Copan

The results of the residue analysis of the Early Classic period vessels provide new information on pre-Columbian cacao use, demonstrating that some widely held conceptions are incorrect. First, cacao was found in a diversity of vessel forms, not only those designed to hold beverages. In addition, the presence of elaborate cylinder vessels, which were negative for cacao contents (see Table 11.1), implies that this vessel form may have held a range of other elite beverages such as ritual maize *atoles*, maize *chicha*, drinks of fermented fruit, palm wines, or *balché* (see Pugh, this volume).

Second, the discovery of two vessels at Copan with faunal material and the chemical signature for *T. cacao* or *T. bicolor* suggests that cacao was used in sauces during the Early Classic period. The small vessel of fish bones and cacao (Vessel 8, Burial 93-2) and the vessel with turkey bones and *T. cacao* or *T. bicolor* (Vessel 2, Offering 93-16) may have contained cacao sauces, possibly *moles*. W. Jeffrey Hurst is in the process of analyzing the Vessel 2 residue to determine whether it contains ground chile peppers—a primary component in all *moles*. The idea that *moles* (sauces of ground seeds) are of pre-Columbian origin runs contrary to Colonial Mexican folk history (S. D. Coe and M. D. Coe 1996:216–218).

Third, the absence in the tombs of vessels bearing cacao glyphs demonstrates that the custom of marking vessels for cacao (and the common practice of burying such vessels with members of the nobility) was not commonly practiced during Early Classic times at Copan (see this volume: Reents-Budet; Stuart).[2]

Although the foods inside the Copan vessels likely represent the diversity of comestibles available to elite Maya, the offerings in the tombs and caches were not meant as food for mortals; they were gifts for revered ancestors who likely held the status of gods. The offering platform above the Margarita tomb, in particular, may have functioned as an important location within the Acropolis where later rulers could commune with their ancestors and call on their ever-present power. All of the vessels in ritual contexts in these Early Classic tombs contained some amount of cinnabar and occasionally hematite. This was particularly apparent when the senior author extracted pollen from the samples. Without the use of heavy metal flotation methods, it was not possible to separate the pollen from the minerals. Initially, it was assumed that the mineral component in the vessels entered them through depositional forces, and this could be the case with some of the vessels. In addition, as Sedat and Sharer (1994) have noted, cinnabar was sprinkled over the queen's corpse, located in the lower chamber of the Margarita tomb, some time after her death. The practice of placing cinnabar on the body of the ruler after the flesh had decayed may have been extended to sprinkling this mineral over offerings left in ritual contexts. However, at least in the case of the two vessels which contain cacao and have lids (Vessel 1 from the Margarita upper offering platform and Vessel 2 from Offering 93-16), it is clear that the minerals were intentionally mixed with the comestible offering when it was first prepared, because the mineral component was only apparent after mixing the residue with various chemicals and putting it through a centrifuge, at which point the minerals separated from the lighter organic components. These vessels likely contained the best of what could be offered to the rulers, the finest foods made even more sacred through the addition of precious minerals. Each ceramic container may have functioned as a small cache, possibly with symbolic value attached to the combination of the specific foods and minerals in it.

The Cultivation of Cacao at Copan

The identification of cacao in vessel residues at Copan is particularly important because cacao macroremains are rare at the site. Charles Miksicek (in B. L. Turner et al. 1983:110) reported fragments of cacao seeds recovered from excavations directed by Claude Baudez, but these seeds cannot now be located for analysis. Although some scholars have argued that the elevation of Copan is too high to support large-scale growth of the trees (B. L. Turner et al. 1983), *T. cacao* does grow well today in the lower elevations of the valley and it is likely that it was grown at Copan during the Classic period. In nineteenth-century maps of the valley the area of the Sesesmil *quebrada* to the north of the Acropolis is designated as *cacahuatal* (cacao orchard) supposedly because of the large cacao plantations along its course at that time (René Viel, personal communication 2005). Given the relatively high altitude and restricted amount of arable land in the valley, however, it is unlikely that Copan produced large surpluses of cacao for trade outside the area.

The Valley of Copan is situated near some of the best areas in Mesoamerica for the cultivation of *T. cacao*, including the lower Motagua Valley to the west and the lower Ulua Valley to the northeast (Millon 1955a:76). Both Diego de Landa and Gonzalo Fernández de Oviedo y Valdés, Spanish chroniclers of the sixteenth century, mention that the people of Yucatan traded goods and slaves for cacao from Honduras (Landa 1941 [1566]:94–95). Landa notes that, "the occupations to which they had the greatest inclination was trade, carrying salt and cloth and slaves to the lands of Ulua and Tabasco, exchanging all they had for cacao and stone beads which were their money" (Landa 1941 [1566]:94–95). Vasquez de Espinosa recorded in the sixteenth century that "The Río Ulua has over 20 leagues of [beautiful banks] lined on both sides with many farms, gardens and cacao plantations" (Millon 1955a:77) (see Figure 11.1).[3] As will be discussed below, Copan shared one form of cacao iconography with these areas.

Cacao During the Late Classic at Copan

Cacao Iconography at Copan

Between the Early and Late Classic periods a change occurred in the role of cacao in elite practice at Copan. Although the analysis of vessel residues has clearly demonstrated that cacao was an important elite offering during the Early Classic period, it is not represented on Copan-produced vessels or in sculpture. However, the Late Classic period witnessed a dramatic increase in cacao's visibility in the Acropolis. Cacao first appears in the artistic canon in the form of simple ceramic cache/censers with cacao pod adornments. At some stage more elaborate versions of these cache vessels were produced with modeled faces likely representing ancestors (David Stuart, personal communication March 2004) and a variety of ornamentations. By the second half of the Late Classic period, large stone censers (*saklaktuns*) with sculpted cacao pods were created and placed in front of temples. All of these artifacts represent trees bearing cacao pods. Many of the artifacts with cacao iconography are without secure provenience because they were found by archaeologists during the end of the nineteenth century and early part of the twentieth century when the recording of artifact location was not as detailed as it is today. The earliest documented cacao iconography is found in a cruciform offering chamber beneath Stela P, which was erected in A.D. 623 by the eleventh ruler, Butz' Chan. This chamber contained, among other offerings, four round censer/cache vessels with cacao pod adornments (see Figure 11.8). From at least this time until the end of the Classic period at Copan (ca. A.D. 822–900), cacao appears on ceramic vessels and stone sculpture.[4] Also, during the Late Classic (the Coner ceramic phase), locally crafted blackware vessels were first produced, some of which bear carved inscriptions that include the cacao glyph (Bill 1997). Although these vessels have not been found in royal tombs, they have been recovered from elite burials (Longyear 1952; Nakamura and Fuentes 1999), and one was excavated from a refuse deposit

Figure 11.8. Ceramic cache vessel adorned with a cacao pod. Found in an offering chamber under Stela P. A.D. 623. Copan, Honduras. Courtesy of the Instituto Hondureño de Antropología e Historia. Photograph by Cameron L. McNeil.

in the Late Classic royal complex Group 10L-2 (Cassandra Bill, personal communication 2002).

Depictions of cacao during the Late Classic demonstrate that the meaning of this tree at Copan extended beyond its value as a desired component of beverages and foods. Cacao trees are associated clearly with the power of the ruling Copan elite, and at the site cacao is most frequently represented by a tree-like form with cacao pods growing from it.

In Classic Maya cosmology, trees are often associated with the death and rebirth of humans (Schele and Mathews 1998). Among the mid-twentieth-century Yucatek Maya it was believed that the world had seven heavens and that a great ceiba tree (or World Tree) grew up through the center of the earth, acting as a bridge or road via which the dead could reach the highest level of heaven (Landa 1941 [1566]:132). The roots of the tree reach into the Underworld. World Trees are often depicted in Classic period iconography as verdant *sacbes* (roads or formal pathways) for the dead to follow into the underworld (Schele and Mathews 1998:115). At Copan, a World Tree is carved into the surface of the altar at the foot of the Hieroglyphic Stairway (Structure 26), the tree rises out of the "jaws of a saurian deity which symbolize(s) the earth" (Fash 1988:165). Four human figures perch in the tree's branches, each one named by a now-eroded hieroglyph. William Fash interprets these individuals as ancestors of K'ak Yipyaj Chan K'awiil, the fifteenth ruler of the Classic period Copan dynasty, who ruled from approximately A.D. 749–763, expanding the stairway and dedicating its accompanying altar (Fash 1988:165).

On Pakal's sarcophagus at Palenque, Mexico, the World Tree takes a cruciform shape. In Maya iconography, the branches of the World Tree frequently appear in this form, which is an idealization of the way ceiba branches grow naturally. A cross-like form also divides space into four sections that meet in the center, thereby creating a quincunx form, another sacred Maya symbol (see Kufer and Heinrich, this volume).

World Trees may provide the path for ancestors to reach the heavens, but in Maya iconography ancestors also may be reborn as trees. On a Maya vase in the Ethnologisches Museum, Berlin, a cacao tree springs from the bones of a dead lord, symbolizing his rebirth as this tree (Schele and Mathews 1998:122–123; see this volume: Barrera and Aliphat F., Figure 14.1a; Martin, Figure 8.2b). The reborn tree-lord is flanked by two other tree-people, although neither of them is a cacao tree. At Palenque, Pakal's ancestors are similarly depicted as tree-lords or -ladies on the sides of his sarcophagus. Two images of his mother, Lady Sak-K'uk', render her upper torso with a tree growing from it, which bears large cacao fruits (Schele and Mathews 1998:121) (Figure 11.9). Similar themes of individuals reborn as plants or trees can be found in modern Maya

Figure 11.9. Representation of Lady Sak' K'uk', the mother of Pakal, on his sarcophagus. Late Classic period. Palenque, Mexico. Drawing by Eliud Guerra after Schele and Mathews (1998:121).

communities. In Santiago Atitlan, Guatemala, an area inhabited by Tz'utujiil-speaking Maya, Allen Christenson has noted that "each grave is planted with a tree, representing the rebirth of the individual to a new life" (Christenson 2001: Figure 6.37). Maude Oakes (1951a:212) wrote of a similar practice among the people of Todos Santos, Guatemala, where maize was planted on new burials.

In the 1930s, ethnographer Ruth Bunzel (1967:46) documented the association between cacao and the "Resuscitation of Christ (a Post-Colonial representative of the Maize god)" in the community of Chichicastenango, Guatemala. In a passage that brings to mind the World Tree, Christ promised the cacao tree that "it shall be that you shall ascend into heaven, and the clouds and the mists of the sky will descend upon you in this world" (Bunzel 1967:240). In this myth, cacao is responsible for the continued life of Christ (see also McNeil, Chapter 17, this volume). It is not possible to know the antiquity of this myth, but it may preserve pre-Columbian associations between rebirth and cacao.

At Copan, World Trees are portrayed on stelae, altars, and ceramic censers. These trees are often abstracted images similar to that of the foliated cross on Pakal's sarcophagus lid at Palenque (Schele and Mathews 1998). Many of the Copan representations, however, clearly designate them as cacao trees, demonstrating that at this site the sacred World or Cosmic Tree often took the form of a cacao tree. This contrasts with the more common rendering in most Classic period Maya art of the sacred World Tree as a maize plant or ceiba tree—although these representations are also found at Copan (McNeil et al. 2002; see also Martin, this volume). This choice on the part of Copan's people implies that cacao's importance increased during the Late Classic period.

Cacao and Copan Ceramics

Cacao-tree-like cache and censer vessels first appear at Copan ca. A.D. 620 and continue to be produced throughout the Coner ceramic phase (ca. A.D. 600–900) (Willey et al. 1994:84–91). They constitute the most common form of cacao imagery throughout the Late Classic period at Copan. These vessels typically are cylindrical, although a few are rectangular. Generally, three to four single cacao pods adorn the upper section of the cache vessel, and sometimes their lids are decorated with three to four cacao pods spaced evenly along the edge and occasionally with a flower form at their apex (Figure 11.8). Most of these containers have been recovered from caches underneath stelae and altars (Fash 1988; Stromsvik 1941:Figure 20c). They also have been found in elite burials (Longyear 1952) and in caches within important ceremonial structures, where they sometimes contain offerings of shell, jade, and obsidian (E.W. Andrews et al. 2003; Fash 1988; Maca 2002). The distribution of these cacao pod vessels is restricted to the southeastern Maya area and non-Maya lands of Honduras. One similar example was found at Quirigua, Guatemala, but most are from Copan and the nearby Naco and Ulua valleys (Henderson and Joyce, this volume; Patricia Urban, personal communication February 2004), which were inhabited by non-Maya-speaking peoples. Distinctly different censers adorned with cacao pods and cacao-associated figures have been recovered at other Mesoamerican sites, such as Río Bec, Mexico (provenience not secure) (Pérez-Romero and Cobos 1990; see Martin, Figure 8.9a, this volume), Tulum (see Martin, Figure 8.9b, this volume), Escuintla and Lago Amatitlan (Chinchilla Mazariegos 2005:13, 18; Mata Amado and Rubio 1994), and at other sites on the Pacific Slopes of southern Guatemala (Schmidt, de la Garza, and Nalda 1998:562).

The cacao cache vessels recovered since the 1980s in primary contexts contain various offerings (Andrews 2003:75; Fash 1988:165–166; Maca 2002:240, 415). The most elaborate assortment of artifacts was found in a cacao-pod cache vessel interred underneath the altar set into the base of Copan's Hieroglyphic Stairway, which bears a carving of ancestors in the branches of the World Tree as discussed above (Fash 1988; Gordon 1902). David Stuart excavated this cache in the mid-1980s. The vessel contained:

> a lanceolate flint knife, two jades, several stingray and sea anemone spines, and a spiny oyster shell. . . The two jades which he selected for burial were

immediately recognized by Stuart as being Early Classic . . . These objects were buried by Smoke Shell not simply for their 'monetary value,' but because they actually embodied the ruler portrayed in the stairway and temple. (Fash 1988:165–166)

A more modest cacao-pod cache vessel was found in an offering above an elite tomb in Group 9J-5. This vessel contained stones covered with cinnabar (Maca 2002:240).

Ceramic Cache vessels with modeled faces

Four ceramic cache vessels with cacao-pod adornments on the rims and a modeled face on the front have been found in elite Late Classic contexts at Copan (Figure 11.10). Two others of the same form and style with modeled faces but with damaged upper sections, also have been found; one of these bears a diadem of a cross-sectioned cacao pod on its forehead (see Longyear 1952:Figure 88f). Unfortunately, the original contexts of all but one of these vessels could not be determined by the senior author. The faces modeled on these cylindrical (four vessels) and rectangular (one) cache containers may represent ancestors (David Stuart, personal communication March 2004). The sixth vessel bears a representation of the Jaguar God of the Underworld in what appears to be a diving god position; unfortunately, the lid is missing (Figure 11.10). The rectangular container is the only one whose lid has survived; the lid rises to an apex with a flower form on top (see Figure 11.10). This vessel was excavated from Structure 10L-41A in Group 10L-2, the palace complex of the sixteenth ruler, Yax Pahsaj Chan Yopat. It has been theorized that Structure 10L-41A was built as a residence for a member of Yax Pahsaj's family or for the ruler himself (E. W. Andrews and C. Bill 2005; E. W. Andrews et al. 2003:94). The cache vessel was found beneath the floor of the central room. It contained the remains of shell, jade, and burned chert and had a speleothem (cave formation) lying alongside it (E. W. Andrews et al. 2003:75, 79).

These vessels may have been manufactured and offerings placed inside them to channel the spirit of a specific ancestor or of ancestors in general. The face floating on the surface of each tree-like cache container clearly symbolizes the concept of individuals reborn as trees. The rich offerings inside the vessels may have been considered a means of "animating" them so that the living could commune with and call on the powers of the deceased.

In addition to recalling cacao trees, as is clearly the case with the cylindrical examples, the vessels can be viewed as small houses. Possibly each rectangular cache vessel (whether with or without a modeled face) was constructed as a miniature "Origin Tree House," as described by Schele and Mathews (1998:79).

Figure 11.10. Late Classic ceramic cache vessels with cacao pod adornments around their rims. Copan, Honduras. Rectangular vessel with a modeled face (left). Found in a cache under the floor of Structure 10L-41A, Courtyard B of Group 10L-2. Excavated by the Middle American Research Institute, Tulane University, New Orleans, under the direction of E. Wyllys Andrews V as part of Proyecto Arqueologico Acropolis Copan directed by William L. Fash. Lidded cylindrical vessel with a modeled face, framed by forms which may represent spondylus shells (Middle). A cacao tree limb with pods arches directly above the face and over this is a diadem representing a cross section of a stylized cacao pod. Information on the vessel's context was not available. Rounded vessel with the Jaguar God of the Underworld or an ancestor in his guise (right). This vessel was recovered in the 1930s during the Carnegie Institution of Washington Excavations. Courtesy of the Instituto Hondureño de Antropología e Historia. Photograph by Cameron L. McNeil.

The physical appearance of the vessels with modeled faces also recalls images of ancestors resting in the branches of the World Tree on the altar at the foot of the Copan Hieroglyphic Stairway (Gordon 1902) and representations of Lady Sak-K'uk', the mother of Pakal, at Palenque (see Figure 11.9) (Schele and Mathews 1998:121). The hollow, dark space inside the container in which the offerings were placed, like the Early Classic tombs, may have been perceived as symbolic caves and places to commune with those in the Underworld—the offering of speleothems and stalactites in some of these subterranean caches and occasionally within the vessels themselves (E. W. Andrews et al. 2003:75; Strömsvik 1940:69, 72, 73, 75) emphasizes this association.

The cache vessel decorated with the image of the Jaguar God of the Underworld and cacao is unique at Copan (see Figure 11.10). Censers, cache vessels, and urns adorned with this Underworld deity are found throughout the Classic Maya world (Stuart 1998). While this vessel appears to represent the Jaguar God of the Underworld as a cacao tree, the figure on the front may actually be an ancestor in the guise of the god. The juxtaposition of the Jaguar God of the Underworld and cacao emphasizes associations between this tree and the land of the dead (for more information on links between cacao and the Underworld see this volume: Kufer and Heinrich; Martin).

An elaborate deposit found outside the tomb of Ruler 12, K'ak-u-? Ha'?-K'awiil, contained smashed censers and lids representing the past kings of the Classic period dynasty. These censers were likely intentionally broken as part of a cancellation ritual in honor of the deceased Ruler 12 (Fash 2001:106). The censer lid that represents K'inich Yax K'uk' Mo' wears a belt with cacao-pod-like forms hanging from it (Figure 11.11). Normally, such belts bear shells, much like those on many of the Copan stelae; however, these adornments appear more cacao pod-like and could have been used to signify K'inich Yax K'uk' Mo's position as the most important ancestor of the Copan dynasty. Another censer lid from the same deposit is decorated with an acrobat figure bearing a cacao pod on his head (see Schmidt, de la Garza, and Nalda 1998:Figure 339).

Figure 11.11. Ceramic censer lid found outside the tomb of Ruler 12. Copan, Honduras. Excavated by the Copan Mosaics Project as part of Proyecto Arqueologico Acropolis Copan directed by William L. Fash. Instituto Hondureño de Antropología e Historia. Drawing by Eliud Guerra after a photograph in W. L. Fash (2001).

Cacao on Stone Censers at Copan

Fragments from at least seven Late Classic period stone censers (*saklaktuns*) with cacao iconography have been found at Copan. Thematically they reflect associations between cacao and the earth (here depicted in the form of crocodiles), the feminine/fertility, and maize. Two lids and one base from three stone censers in the form of inverted crocodiles, with their bases the crocodile's head and their lids the upside-down body, have been found in Copan's Acropolis (Figure 11.12).[5] None of these censers is identical, and two are more finely carved than the other (David Stuart, personal communication March 2005). Each of the lids renders the World Tree as a crocodile with cacao pods sprouting from the sides of its tail. The tail bears thin leaf-like lines, which may represent young maize plants. This depiction of the World Tree as a crocodile is also found on a stela at Izapa, Mexico, and on a Late Classic ceramic vessel in the Dumbarton Oaks collection (Taube 2001:218); a more abstracted form is on

Figure 11.12. Front and side view of two sections of separate stone censers in the form of crocodiles. There are the remains of at least three such censers at Copan, Honduras. Restoration of the censers was conducted by the Copan Mosaics Project as part of Proyecto Arqueologico Acropolis Copan directed by William L. Fash. Instituto Hondureño de Antropología e Historia. Photograph by Edgardo Sanabria.

Copan's Stela C (Schele and Mathews 1998:142–143) (see Martin, Figure 8.4a, b, this volume). Such saurian creatures can represent the World Tree as well as the earth (Taube 2001).

One *saklaktun* lid features a diving figure with a *pax* god on its rear; the deity bears the characteristic jaguar paws above his face on either side of his forehead and three dots beneath each eye (Lara 1996) (Figure 11.13). Four cacao pods, two on each side, grow from the body of the diving figure. Taube (2003a) has noted that acrobat figures in Maya art represent trees or plants. Although the *pax* symbol can represent the Underworld and is clearly associated with jaguars, in this context it is a hieroglyph for "*te* (tree)" (Montgomery 2002:230), designating the acrobat figure as a tree.[6] Unfortunately, the base of the lid has not been found, and the raised feet and head have not survived.

There were at least three Late Classic *saklaktun* bases covered in cacao pods

0   5   10   15   20   cms.

Figure 11.13. Stone censer lid of a diving god with cacao pods growing from his body. The *Pax* God face on the back of the figure designates the diving god as a "tree." Copan, Honduras. Instituto Hondureño de Antropología e Historia. Drawing Edgar Zelaya.

at Copan. Only one of these remains complete and is on display in the *Museo de Esculturas* of the Copan archaeology park. None of these bases is identical, each varying in style and size. A well-tended cacao tree in its prime can bear many cacao pods on its trunk and branches. Yet all three of these bases depict a tree beyond a cacao grower's dreams, perhaps underscoring the importance of cacao tree production to the people of Late Classic Copan. The censer bases have lost their original associations with lids, with only one possible pairing among the group. Its lid is in the form of a cross, signifying that it is a World Tree or *axis mundi*, with pendant cacao pods growing from it (Figure 11.14). Although this cross never had a human head, its form is highly evocative of a woman pregnant with cacao. Two pods hang from the lid in the place of female breasts, and one large cacao pod rests where an abdomen would be. When placed on top of the base fragment, the lower section becomes the figure's cacao-laden skirt: Stone cacao pods once hung from the cross form where a person's arms would be. At the back of the *saklaktun* is a cross-hatched circle, possibly representing either a jaguar spot or a mirror.

This fecund *saklaktun* explicitly ties cacao to fertility and the female sex. The form of the censer is similar to other Classic period artworks of women (or goddesses) with cacao pods sprouting from their bodies or covered in cacao seeds such as those from Palenque (see Figure 11.9) and in sites along the Gua-

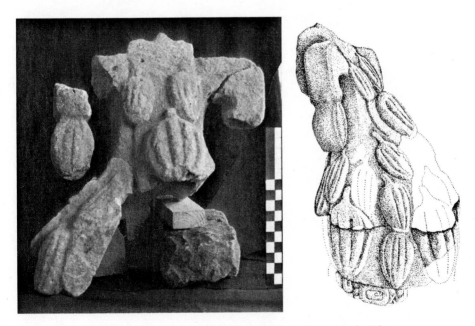

Figure 11.14. Censer in a form evocative of the female body. a. Front view. b. Side view. Late Classic period. Copan, Honduras. Collection of the Instituto Hondureño de Antropología e Historia. Drawing by Edgar Zelaya.

temalan Pacific coastal region—all areas where cacao can be grown. Curiously, the mother of Yax Pasaj, in whose reign this censer (see Figure 11.14) was likely created, was from Palenque, and associations between women and cacao could have come to Copan through her, but pre-Columbian associations between women and cacao are more common in the Highland and Pacific coastal zones of Guatemala. Figurines from the Pacific Coast of Guatemala feature deities with cacao pods growing from their bodies, and most of these are female (Figure 11.15a). Some bear water vessels on their heads or back, recalling images of Chac Chel from the Dresden Codex, and at least one has children as well as cacao pods sprouting from her (Chinchilla Mazariegos 2005:14–15). A Classic period censer lid, also from the Pacific Coast, is modeled in the form of a woman offering a container with two cacao pods inside (Figure 11.15b). She is covered in naturalistically rendered life-sized cacao seeds, some of which have a transverse line down the middle resembling a reptilian or serpent eye.[7] Another sculpture linking a female image and cacao is found on an Early Classic censer lid from the Pacific slopes of southern Guatemala; here the woman is attired as a Teotihuacan-style war goddess who rises out of a pile of cacao

Figure 11.15. a. Figurine in the form of a woman with cacao pods growing from her body. Late Classic. Pacific Coast, Guatemala. Collection of the Museo Popol Vuh, Universidad Francisco Marroquín, Guatemala City. b. Censer lid. A female figure adorned with life-sized cacao seeds holds a container with two cacao pods inside. Classic period. Pacific Coast, Guatemala. Collection of the Museo Nacional de Arqueología y Etnología, Guatemala City. Drawings by Eliud Guerra.

pods (Chinchilla Mazariegos 2005:14, Figure 10). This ideological association between women and cacao has survived into modern times, where it remains central to social and ritual practices among some Maya ethnic groups (see this volume: Faust and Hirose; McNeil, Chapter 17). While the Copan censer is clearly not a woman—it does not have a head—its form may draw on Classic period associations between women, fertility, and cacao.

Cacao and Maize

Cacao and maize are an important pair in the preparation of ritual offerings and were also paired in Late Classic iconography (see Martin, this volume). Both cacao and maize are represented as cosmic trees in the art of Late Classic Copan. A censer lid found in the same sculpture pile (Number 17) as the censer in Figure 11.14 also is in the form of a cross with its upper back portion ending in a maize ear (Lara 1996). Another large *saklaktun* lid in the form of an upside-down bird bears a maize ear in its tail feathers, making an interesting contrast with the depictions of inverted crocodiles growing cacao pods from their bodies (Lara 1996). It is possible that cacao at Copan was associated with

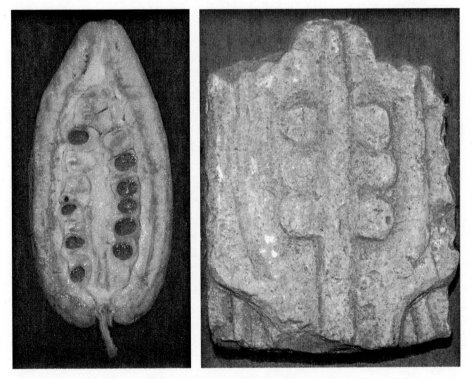

Figure 11.16. a. Cacao pod cut in half lengthwise. b. Stone mosaic sculpture block which may represent an open cacao pod. Temple 22, Copan, Honduras. Collection of the Instituto Hondureño de Antropología e Historia. Photographs by Cameron L. McNeil.

the earth and had feminine attributes and that mature maize was associated with the sky and had male attributes.

Associations of male rulers and gods with maize are abundant at Copan. Temple 22, a Late Classic monument to agricultural fertility, displays elegantly carved young maize gods on its façade. Art historian Jennifer Ahlfeldt (personal communication 2004) has recently suggested that iconographic elements on this temple may represent open cacao pods (Figure 11.16 a, b). Ahlfeldt also has pointed out that these elements resemble diadems worn by Chaak figures (rain gods) depicted on the corners of Temple 22.

Discussion

The combined archaeological, art historical, and microbotanical data from Early and Late Classic Copan confirm the importance of cacao in the ritual life of the polity's elites. The identification of cacao in eleven vessels from Early Classic royal and aristocratic burials, comprising a third of all vessel residues analyzed, attests to its significance as a mortuary offering. Analysis of the vessel residues has demonstrated that cacao was not solely an ingredient for beverages but was also used in a variety of solid foodstuffs.

During the Early Classic period, cacao was an important offering placed in the tombs of the deceased, as in the Teotihuacan-style lidded vessel from the Margarita tomb (see Figure 11.4). This vase is painted with a representation of the lineage founder, K'inich Yax K'uk' Mo', inside the doorway of a temple, and may be a precursor of the Late Classic cache vessels decorated with cacao pods and modeled human faces of deified ancestors. That some of these Late Classic censers are in the form of a house or temple underscores this possible continuity of iconography. By the Late Classic, the resurrection of the honored dead had become intimately associated with cacao, and the deceased were now represented on cache vessels adorned with cacao pods.

The dramatic increase in cacao iconography during the Late Classic period at Copan, particularly the depiction of cacao trees and the representation of ancestors as cacao trees, may be a result of increased cacao production in the polity during this period. Rosemary Joyce (2005) has pointed out that tree crops represent a long-term investment in the land and may tie kin groups to a specific area in ways that maize produced through slash-and-burn agriculture does not. In addition, tree crops organized into a productive and diverse forest like the Yucatek Maya *pet-kot* (Gomez-Pampa, Flores and Sosa 1987) can aid in conserving resources while still supplying valuable foods.

The prevalence of ceramic censer/cache vessels in the form of cacao and ceiba trees may indicate that they were ritually paired in much the same way as the prevalence of the large stone censers carved in the form of maize or cacao cosmic trees similarly suggests their ideological pairing.

Representations of cacao at Copan share similarities with other Maya sites, but Copan is unusual in the frequency and range of associations of cacao imagery, here being linked simultaneously to the earth, the female sex, rebirth, and the Underworld. The absence of locally made vessels with the Primary Standard Sequence (PSS) dedicatory hieroglyphic texts containing cacao glyphs during the Early Classic period and the paucity of PSS pottery inscriptions during Late Classic times may be a reflection of the accessibility of cacao in the Copan region. In addition, intensified warfare in the Guatemalan Peten, where many vessels with cacao glyphs have been found (see Stuart, this volume), may also have made cacao drinking vessels and their associated feasting rites with social and political overtones more significant for the rulers of that region as compared to their counterparts at Copan. Instead, the Copanec rulers on the southeastern Maya periphery may not have been as entangled in the social politics of the tightly spaced competitive kingdoms of the Peten Lowlands.

The representation of cacao as a World Tree, embodied by all of the cacao-bearing *saklaktuns* at Copan, is less common at most other Maya sites and reveals an association or perception of cacao that may have been particularly significant in the cosmology of the Copan Maya. This connection with cacao could have been a product of cultural diffusion from the non-Maya peoples of eastern Honduras who inhabited one of the major cacao-growing zones of Central America. The connection between these areas, as evidenced by their ritual representations of cacao, can be seen in the similar artistic use of ceramic cacao pod adornments for censers and cache vessels in the Copan, Quirigua, Ulua, and Naco valleys, a practice that survived into the subsequent Postclassic period in the Ulua Valley east of Copan (Rosemary Joyce, personal communication February 2004).

Although this chapter focuses on cacao and its roles among Copan's elites, additional research is needed to investigate the role of cacao among the lower socioeconomic and political tiers of the polity. Did these people, too, place cacao in the burials of their deceased, or were other comestibles the preferred foods for the afterlife of the nonelite? Further, when did these mortuary practices featuring cacao first develop at Copan?

Acknowledgments

We are grateful to the Instituto Hondureño de Antropología e Historia, in particular Gerente Margarita Durón de Galvez, Lic. Carmen Julia Fajardo, and Prof. Oscar Cruz M. This chapter benefitted from advice provided by Barbara

Fash and David Stuart and from editorial comments made by E. Wyllys Andrews V, Eric Hilt, Rosemary Joyce, Johanna Kufer, Simon Martin, and Dorie Reents-Budet. We appreciate the beautiful artwork which Edgar Zelaya and Eliud Guerra contributed to this chapter. We would like to thank the IIE Fulbright and the Foundation for the Advancement of Mesoamerican Studies for their support of this research. The ECAP excavations were directed by Robert J. Sharer and conducted under the auspices of the Instituto Hondureño de Antropología e Historia, with support from the University of Pennsylvania Museum (Francis Boyer and Shoemaker Research Funds), the Asociación Copan, the United States Agency for International Development mission in Honduras, the National Geographic Society Committee for Research and Exploration, the National Science Foundation, the Selz Foundation, the Foundation for the Advancement of Mesoamerican Studies, the Maya Workshop Foundation, the Holt Family Foundation, the Kislak Foundation, the University of Pennsylvania Foundation, and a number of private donors. In addition, we appreciate the help and advice of Jennifer Ahlfeldt, Ellen Bell, Cassandra Bill, David Burney, Lida Piggot Burney, Oswaldo Chinchilla Mazariegos, Lynn Grant, Fernando Lopez, Allan Maca, Seiichi Nakamura, William Parry, Timothy Pugh, Jorge H. Ramos, Fredy Rodriguez, Carolina Sandoval, Loa Traxler, Patricia Urban, and René Viel.

Notes

1. Human-produced mountains are composed of pyramidal structures capped by temples or palaces.

2. An imported vessel from the late Early Classic bearing what may be a cacao glyph was found in a modest elite tomb by John Longyear (1952:45, Figure 111f).

3. A slight change in translation was made per the advice of Rosemary Joyce (personal communication May 2005).

4. The last date on an altar at the site is A.D. 822 on Altar L (Fash 2001:81). It is unlikely that any of the sculptures depicting cacao were produced after this date.

5. The authors are grateful to David Stuart for sharing his notes on the crocodile sculptures.

6. The authors appreciate Simon Martin's comments on this sculpture.

7. Some oval sculptured elements with transverse lines have been described as cacao elements, but from what McNeil can determine through examining cacao seeds and experimenting with processing and cooking them, cacao seeds do not split in this manner. This confusion may have arisen because of the similarity between the shape of these forms and cacao beans.

12

Cacao in Greater Nicoya

Ethnohistory and a Unique Tradition

Larry Steinbrenner

In the first decades following the Spanish Conquest, *Theobroma cacao* L.—also known in ancient times as *cacao, coco, cacaguat, cacaguate,* and *cacavate* (Benzoni 1857:148; Oviedo 1851–55 v. 1:315, 318)—was one of the most valued commodities produced by lower Central American colonies located in Greater Nicoya, an archaeological subarea comprising modern Pacific Nicaragua and northwestern Costa Rica (Figure 12.1) (Bergmann 1969; W. R. Fowler 1987; M. MacLeod 1973; P. MacLeod 1996; Rosés Alvarado 1982). Greater Nicoya was distinguished from surrounding areas by the presence of migrant Mesoamerican populations from Central Mexico, and, as in Mesoamerica proper, the post-Conquest importance of cacao here had pre-Conquest antecedents.[1] In fact, much of what we know about pre-Columbian cacao production in the Americas derives from ethnohistoric accounts of Greater Nicoya.

Traditionally, it has been assumed that cacao was introduced into Greater Nicoya (and Lower Central America in general) during the Mesoamerican Postclassic period (A.D. 900–1521) by the Nicarao, one of the aforementioned migrant Central Mexican groups (see, for example, W. R. Fowler 1989a, 1989b). This argument has been based explicitly on similarities between Mesoamerican and Greater Nicoyan usage and cultivation practices and upon the presumed Nicarao monopoly of the crop. The implicit basis for the argument has been the venerable but outdated Mesoamericanist tradition of assuming *ad hoc* that much of Greater Nicoyan culture is explainable as the result of diffusion from Mesoamerica (see, for example, Lothrop 1926; M. D. Coe 1962; L. A. Parsons and B. J. Price 1971). This argument also appeared to draw support from Cuatrecasas's (1964) hypothesis (widely accepted by archaeologists, but cf. Motamayor and Lanaud 2002; Motamayor et al. 2002) that cacao originated in the Yucatan. However, although cacao use in Greater Nicoya does demonstrate

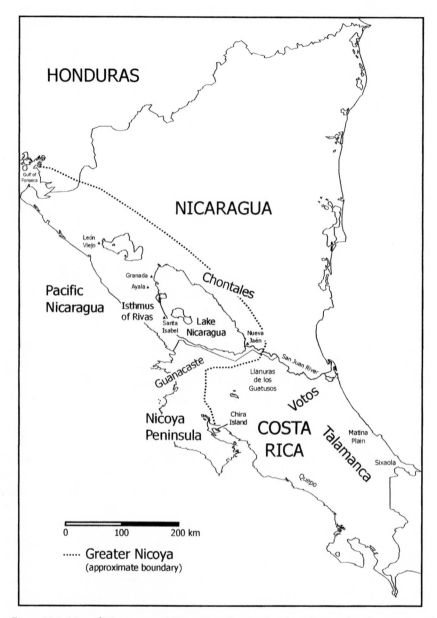

Figure 12.1. Map of Nicaragua and Costa Rica, showing locations discussed in the text. Map by Larry Steinbrenner.

some strong parallels to cacao use in Mesoamerica, a close reading of ethnohistoric accounts hints that there were also significant differences in cacao-related practices which potentially suggest a greater antiquity for the crop in Lower Central America and possibly South American influences as well.

In this chapter I will first identify and summarize the major ethnohistoric accounts of Nicaragua and Costa Rica pertaining to cacao production and use. Then I will discuss similarities and differences between Greater Nicoyan and Mesoamerican practices and their implications. This discussion will also incorporate archaeological evidence of cacao use in Greater Nicoya (and, more generally, in Nicaragua and Costa Rica), examine the problem of why there is currently little of this kind of evidence available, and address how future research might be more successful in providing archaeological evidence of cacao use by the pre-Columbian peoples of Greater Nicoya.

Ethnohistoric Sources

The most important account of cacao production and use in pre-Columbian Greater Nicoya is provided by Gonzalo Fernández de Oviedo y Valdés, the official chronicler of the Indies, who visited Greater Nicoya between 1527 and 1529 and included an account as part of his massive *Historia general y natural de las Indias, islas y tierra-firme del mar oceáno* (1851–55), originally published in 1535. It is Oviedo's account "which establishes the fact that cacao was an aboriginal cultivated plant in Nicaragua" (Millon 1955a:73). Oviedo provides information about cacao use in Nicaragua in two key sections of his *Historia*: Volume 1, Book 8, Chapter 30, which deals specifically with the cultivation of the cacao plant, and Volume 4, Book 42, which deals more generally with Nicaragua as a whole. Oviedo provides detailed information on such diverse topics as production, orchard layout and ownership, harvesting practices, curing and preparation of seeds, recipes for cacao products, ritual and commercial use, and the presumed Nicarao monopoly (see below).

The only Conquest-era chronicler who rivals Oviedo in terms of detail about cacao in Greater Nicoya is Girolamo Benzoni, an Italian traveler who provided a short description of the cultivation and use of the crop in his *Historia del Mondo Nuovo* (1857), first published in 1565. Additional Conquest-era sources are most valuable for the information they provide about areas in which cacao may have been cultivated prehistorically. Primary among these are Juan López de Velasco's *Geografía y descripción universal de las Indias* (1894), based on a series of Colonial questionnaires completed in the 1570s, and the *Tasación de tributos* 1548–51, an unpublished tribute assessment list (cited in Bergmann 1969). The letters of Juan Vázquez de Coronado, the conquistador of Costa Rica, provide the earliest comments on cacao cultivation in that country (Bergmann 1969:95–96; P. MacLeod 1996:84). Although written in the seventeenth century, a traveler's account by Antonio Vázquez de Espinosa (who first visited Nicaragua in 1613), also provides possible insights into areas of prehistoric cacao cultivation, as do contemporary writings to the King of Spain by the Costa Rican cleric Agustín de Ceballos (Bergmann 1969:96; Rosés Alvarado 1982:253–254). Although cacao is also discussed by other chroniclers whose work was based on second-hand accounts of Lower Central America (like Peter Martyr D'Anghera), these secondary sources add little new information about cacao-related practices.

Ancient areas of production

The ubiquity of cacao in Nicaragua and Costa Rica is taken for granted in the various ethnohistoric sources, but these same sources tend to be vague with regard to the exact communities where the crop was grown before the arrival of the Spanish. In Nicaragua, only one place is specifically noted to be a center of cacao production: the pre-Columbian town of Tecoatega, where Oviedo visited a cacao harvest festival (1851–55 v. 4:93–94), and which was located somewhere north of the modern city of Chinandega (W. R. Fowler 1989a:67). Later accounts provide more detail: the *Tasación de tributos* 1548–51 (Bergmann 1969:95) indicates cultivation in the districts of the important Colonial Nicaraguan towns of León and Granada relatively soon after the Conquest (the Spanish arrived in Greater Nicoya in 1522), and López de Velasco (1975:177, 181) confirms that the fields surrounding these towns were fertile in cacao about twenty years later. Around the same time, López de Velasco (1894:312) also reports the gathering of cacao near Nueva Jaén (modern San Carlos) at the head of the San Juan River on the eastern Chontales side of Lake Nicaragua. By the early 1600s, Vázquez de Espinosa could confirm that the cacao plantations of León were a "great source of wealth" (1942:248) and that the slopes of Mombacho Volcano (near Granada) provided "the best and largest variety [of cacao] in all those provinces" (1942:261).

Information from Costa Rica is even rarer. Most of the good sources for Nicaragua do not discuss cacao cultivation in Costa Rica at all. Oviedo, however, mentions a particular method for preparing cacao used in "la provincia de Nicoya" (modern Guanacaste, including the Nicoya Peninsula) and on Chira Island in the Gulf of Nicoya (1851–55, v. 1:318), inferring the presence of cultivation at least this far south. Beyond Greater Nicoya, Vázquez de Coronado reported cacao use in 1563 in the Indian province of Quepo on the Pacific slope of the Central Cordillera (an area not under Spanish control at the time of his visit) as well as cultivation by the indigenous people of Talamanca and by the Votos in northern Costa Rica (P. MacLeod 1996:84). Agustín de Ceballos's 1610 report of abundant cacao in the Matina Plain and/or the Sixaola Valley on the Atlantic Coast that was the "best of the realm in quantity and quality" (Rosés Alvarado 1982:253–254; cf. Bergmann 1969:96) seemingly confirms Vázquez de Coronado's earlier report of indigenous cacao cultivation in Talamanca, since the exploitation of Costa Rica's Atlantic Coast did not expand until the mid-seventeenth century (cf. Rosés Alvarado 1982).[2] A much later account from 1783 reports that the Guatusos cultivated cacao in Llanuras de los Guatusos, a Highland area south of Lake Nicaragua and adjacent to the headwaters of the San Juan River that was never conquered by the Spanish (Bergmann 1969:96). Although the reported use of cacao by the Guatusos may, however, suggest a great antiquity predating the Conquest (for example, beverage chocolate was offered to their sun god, a practice reminiscent of South American Cuica traditions; cf. Bergmann 1969:88), we must obviously be doubly cautious about inferring pre-Columbian cultivation in this area based on reports made more than 250 years after the first arrival of the Spanish in Costa Rica.

If the ethnohistoric record is somewhat vague about the exact loci of pre-Columbian cacao cultivation throughout Nicaragua and Costa Rica, it none-theless seems clear that the distribution of the plant was widespread. Yet a myth persists that cacao was grown only in areas under Nicarao control, which is generally taken to mean primarily in Greater Nicoya on the Pacific Coast (cf. Bergmann 1969; W. R. Fowler 1987:159, 160; Millon 1955a:74, 235). The basis for this myth is an important passage in Oviedo:

> The Indians of the Chorotega tongue are the ancient lords and native people of those parts . . . and those of Nicaragua and its language are new-comers, they . . . are those who brought to the land the cacao or almonds that run as money in those parts; and in the power of those are the estates (*heredamientos*) of the trees that bear that fruit; and not in the power of the Chorotegas is a single tree of these. (Oviedo 1851–55, v. 4:60–61)

Oviedo uses the word "Nicaragua" here to name both the Nicarao and their language, Nahuat, a Nahua language closely related to the Nahuatl of Central Mexico's Aztecs. The "Chorotega" mentioned in this passage represent another migrant Mesoamerican group, Oto-Manguean speakers who arrived in Greater Nicoya centuries earlier (ca. A.D. 800 or 900) than the Nicarao, who may have arrived as late as A.D. 1350 (Salgado 1996). At the time of the Conquest, Greater Nicoya appears to have been largely under Chorotega control, whereas the Nicarao controlled the Isthmus of Rivas and possibly the eastern shore of Lake Nicaragua. Neighboring pockets of Nahua speakers on the Pacific Coast around the Gulf of Fonseca (also known as the Nahuatlato) and in central Gua-nacaste (the Bagaces) are also generally grouped with the Nicarao. The Nicarao have also been associated with the Pipil, a larger and more complex Nahua group involved with large-scale cacao production in Guatemala and El Salvador (W. R. Fowler 1987, 1989a, 1989b, and this volume), and may also have been affiliated with poorly documented Nahua trading colonies established on the Atlantic Coast at the mouth of the San Juan River (the Desguadero) and in the Sixaola area (the Sigua) (Lothrop 1926).

The ubiquity of Nahua groups in Central America and Oviedo's account have tempted scholars (for example, Bergmann 1969; W. R. Fowler 1989a, 1989b; Millon 1955a) to knit them into a sort of implicit "cacao cartel" and draw speculative connections between the colonies and accounts of cacao production, even in areas far from the apparent center of Nicarao power in Rivas. Bergmann (1969:96), for example, suggests that it was the Bagaces and Sigua colonies that introduced cacao into, respectively, Nicoya and the Sixaola Valley, and by the same model we might easily attribute the cacao cultivated at the mouth of the San Juan to the presence of the Nicarao colony on the eastern shore of Lake Nicaragua. Everywhere there is cacao, it seems, one finds Nahua speakers.

Yet the co-occurrence of Nahua colonies and cacao cultivation does not necessarily imply that the latter was introduced by the former. It is equally plausible that the presence of indigenous cacao in these areas is what first attracted the Nahua colonists in the first place. As well, models suggesting Nahua control of cacao production cannot explain the documentary accounts of widespread cacao cultivation in Costa Rican areas beyond Nahua control, such as Quepo, Chira Island, and the Talamanca, Voto, and Guatuso territories. Clearly, cacao trees were "in the power" of more groups than the Nicarao. The Nahua-control model does not even account particularly well for reports of cacao production closer to the Nicarao heartland shortly after the Conquest. León and Granada, the two towns where cacao cultivation was already underway during the time of the *Tasación de tributos* 1548–51, were both founded in 1524 in areas formerly under Chorotega control rather than in Nicarao territory. Is it likely that in only twenty-odd years an indigenous Chorotegan population under new Spanish masters could have become proficient at the cultivation of a notoriously finicky tree crop with which they were presumably unfamiliar—assuming they possessed "not a single tree" of cacao? It would seem there is some basis for arguing that Oviedo overstates the case for a Nicarao cacao monopoly.

Cultivation

Oviedo and Benzoni both provide detailed accounts of cacao cultivation— probably the most extensive sixteenth-century accounts that are available on this subject. The relevant passage from Oviedo on this subject is worth quoting at length:

I first want to describe how they grow and cultivate these trees as precious things. They plant in the lands that seem fertile and good and they choose a site with water close by for irrigation during dry periods. They plant them in straight lines and separated ten to fifteen feet in between to allow enough space because they grow and crown out in such a manner that below them all is shaded and the sun cannot reach the earth except for a few parts between some branches. Because some years the sun scalds them in such a way that it fruits in vain and doesn't form correctly and is lost. To remedy this they put other trees in between; the Indians call these other trees *Yaquaquyt* and the Christians call them blackwood. They grow almost twice the size of the cacao and they protect them from the sun, and make shade with their branches and leaves. (Oviedo 1851–55, v. 1:317)[3]

Benzoni's (1857:149) account, which deals with the cultivation of individual cacao trees rather than orchards, confirms the tree's need for shade and adds the unusual detail that it was common to plant a larger shade tree nearby which was

Figure 12.2. Reproduction of Benzoni's original illustration of the practices of doubling the cacao shade tree and drying cacao on large mats. (The figure on the left is demonstrating the use of a fire drill and is unrelated to the topic of cacao production.) Drawing by Larry Steinbrenner after Benzoni (1857:149).

bent double over the cacao tree to protect it from the sun (Figure 12.2). This practice appears to have been unique to Nicaragua (Millon 1955a:118).

Extremely useful information about cacao cultivation is contained in these accounts. For example, Oviedo confirms the presence of a system of irrigation, a necessity for growing cacao in a region with a pronounced dry season (cf. López de Velasco 1894:318) and a technique of cultivation that was widespread throughout regions of Mesoamerica where rainfall could not be depended upon throughout the year (Millon 1955a:76, 110). This system probably involved the use of canals (A. M. Young 1994:26) and in this respect may have resembled irrigation systems inferred for Pipil cacao orchards in Guatemala and El Salvador (W. R. Fowler 1989b:231). Both accounts make it clear that indigenous cultivators recognized the necessity of shade trees to protect the cacao crop, and Oviedo's account is specific enough for us to identify a precise species, *Gliricidia sepium* (Jacq.) Steud. This tree is most widely known as *madre de cacao* ('mother of cacao') and still serves to shade cacao in modern Guatemalan and Nicaraguan orchards (Millon 1955a:21, 36, 38), although it appears to be more commonly known in Nicaragua by the name that Oviedo provides: *madero negro*, or blackwood (Incer 2000:207). In Nicaragua, it appears that *madre de cacao* is more commonly applied to a species of coral tree (*Erythrina umbrosa* Kunth) (Millon 1955a:21; Squier 1852, v. 1:159–160).

Oviedo is also quite precise regarding the layout of the cacao orchard, which followed a plan that endured until at least the nineteenth century, when the American diplomat Ephraim Squier (1852, v. 1:159–160) visited a Nicaraguan orchard that differed from Oviedo's only in the substitution of plantains (a Colonial introduction) and coral trees as shade trees. The enduring nature of this particular system of cultivation suggests that it was extremely well developed by the time of European contact.

Unfortunately, although both Oviedo (cf. 1851–55, v. 1:316) and Benzoni provide basic descriptions of the cacao fruit—for example, Benzoni (1857:149) referred to it as being "like almonds, lying in a shell resembling a pumpkin in size"—they do not provide enough detail to definitively associate ancient Nicaraguan cacao with a specific modern variety, such as *criollo* (*T. Cacao* ssp. *cacao*) or *forastero* (*T. cacao* ssp. *sphaerocarpum*). It is probably safe to infer, however, that the ancient cacao was most closely related to *criollo*, the milder and tastier variety (S. D. Coe and M. D. Coe 1996:28). Nicaragua was once renowned for producing an exceptional variety of *criollo* cacao that contained beans twice the size of other varieties, until a devastating plague wiped out the entire crop in the early twentieth century (Millon 1955a:37).

Harvesting and curing

Benzoni provides a short account of the process of harvesting and curing cacao. After cacao pods have been harvested, the cultivators "pick out the kernels and lay them on mats to dry; then when they wish for the beverage, they roast them in an earthen pan over the fire, and grind them with the stones which they use for preparing bread" (Benzoni 1857:149–150). The result was a paste that provided the foundation for beverage cacao. The "stones" referred to here are likely the *manos* and *metates* that are common in the Greater Nicoyan archaeological record, but, curiously, the "earthen pans" do not appear to correlate with any type of vessel in Nicaraguan archaeological assemblages (see, for example, Healy 1980; Salgado 1996; Steinbrenner 2002), although we might expect to find *comals* (a ubiquitous pan-shaped ceramic form in Central Mexico) in large numbers in an area colonized by Mesoamerican immigrants. Oviedo (1851–55, v. 1:318) reiterates the essential details provided by Benzoni, adding only that the Nicaragua cacao harvest typically lasted from February to April and that harvested seeds were laid out to cure several times during the day rather than simply being left in the sun all day.

Oviedo provides a firsthand account of how the Nicarao celebrated the completion of the cacao harvest (1851–55, v. 4:93–94). On a visit to Tecoategа, Oviedo observed about sixty men painted to appear clothed (some of them made up as women) and dancing around a large pole, at the top of which was a seated, painted "idol" representing *"el dios del cacaguat o cacao"* (the god of cacao). Four posts formed a platform framework near the top of the pole, and wrapped around these was a thick cord, to the two ends of which were tied two boys of seven or eight years; these *voladores* threw themselves off the platform and "flew" repeatedly around the pole, propelled by the action of the unwinding cord. At the end of the ceremony, the idol was removed and stored in a temple until the following year. Oviedo's description and accompanying illustration make it clear that this is a variation of the *volador* ceremony, which is still practiced in modern Nicaragua as well as in many other parts of Mesoamerica, and which is often associated with fertility and harvest rituals (for example, Larsen 1937; Leal 1977–78). The specific identity of Oviedo's "cacao god" is unknown: it may have been the Greater Nicoyan counterpart of various Mesoamerican gods associated with cacao and trade, such as the Central Mexican god Yacatecuhtli (Millon 1955a:119–120; J. E. S. Thompson 1956:103), his Maya counterpart Ek Chuah (God M), or Ch'ok Kakaw (Young Maize), who is depicted with cacao pods sprouting from his body in Classic Maya scenes (Marc Zender, personal communication 2002).

Preparation

Oviedo (1851–55, v. 1:318–319) notes that the thick paste that resulted from grinding cacao was formed into small cakes which were left to stand before being used to make drinks (see McNeil, Figure 17.5, this volume). The longer the cake was let stand, the higher the quality of the beverage product, with five or six days being ideal. A red dye made from the seeds of *Bixa orellana* L. (*annatto, achiote*) was added to the paste to give it the color of blood, a practice that Oviedo found appalling but in keeping with what he describes as the locals' taste for human blood. Oviedo also discusses a specific method of extracting cacao fat in Nicoya province (1851–55, v. 1:318–319). As in Mesoamerica, the cacao paste was mixed with water and sometimes spices and was served most commonly in calabashes (Benzoni 1857:148–150; Bergmann 1969:85; S. D. Coe and M. D. Coe 1996:64–66; Millon 1955a:165). Ground, toasted maize was another common additive in indigenous Mesoamerican cacao preparations and remains an ingredient in the modern Nicaraguan beverages *pinolillo* (which is traditionally made of *Theobroma bicolor* Bonpl. pulp rather than *T. cacao* seeds [A. M. Young 1994:15]) and *tiste*, though it is not mentioned by Benzoni or Oviedo.

Uses

Oviedo, who did not like the look of cacao, was happy to proclaim its virtues and versatility, observing that drinking cacao satisfied thirst and hunger and that the natives used it to protect their complexions from the sun and air, although Christians would find this usage to be dirty (1851–55, v. 1:318). He also reports that cacao had medicinal value: he notes a native belief that one who has consumed cacao in the morning will not die if bitten by a poisonous snake during the day, and he relates how cacao butter provided an effective balm when he himself suffered a severe injury traveling from León to Nicoya province (1851–55, v. 1:318–320). As well, Oviedo reports that some natives consumed the pulp and uncooked seeds (1851–55, v. 1:321). Benzoni (1857:148–150) was also a grudging admirer of cacao beverages, noting that although he initially avoided drinking cacao, he eventually tried it and found that "it satisfies and refreshes the body without intoxicating."

In Mesoamerica, cacao was extensively used in ritual and was often associated with major life events such as birth, marriage, and death (J. E. S. Thompson 1956:104). The ritual use of cacao is not well documented for Greater Nicoya, but it can perhaps be inferred, especially given the aforementioned analogous association of cacao with human blood. Oviedo does specifically note that cacao was prepared for use in marriage ceremonies (1851–55, v. 4:49), though whether the bride and groom exchanged foaming cups of the beverage as is often depicted in Mixtec codices is unknown. Benzoni (1857:152) also notes that cacao was consumed frequently during dance festivals. It is likely that cacao's ritual importance partially explains why the tree was prized above all others among the natives of Greater Nicoya (Oviedo 1851–55, v.1:315; cf. Benzoni 1857:150). It seems unlikely that this value derived solely from the perceived nutritional and restorative value of cacao.

In Greater Nicoya cacao was used as money, just as it was across Mesoamerica (cf. Andagoya 1865:33; Benzoni 1857:149; Oviedo 1851–55, v. 4:36). Oviedo notes that the natives of Greater Nicoya could buy all things with cacao beans, and he even provides some sample prices: a *munonzapote* fruit (likely *níspero*, *Pouteria sapota* L.) was worth a half bean; a rabbit, ten beans; a slave, one hundred; the services of a prostitute, eight to ten beans (Oviedo 1851–55, v. 1:316).[4] These appear to have been "ballpark" prices for these commodities rather than fixed rates; an interview conducted by Francisco de Bobadilla and reported in Oviedo indicates that bargaining was the norm in the Nicaraguan marketplace (Oviedo 1851–55, v. 4:54). Oviedo also indicates that prostitutes were not the only ones in Greater Nicoya who accepted cacao for services rendered; officials serving in public offices could be remunerated with cacao, among other things such as maize or cotton mantles (1851–55, v. 4:54).

Cacao was valuable enough in Greater Nicoya to encourage counterfeiting. Oviedo notes that unscrupulous traders were known to "fake" beans through the seemingly laborious process of removing the bark or shell of a true cacao bean and stuffing it with earth (1851–55, v. 1:316). The fake beans were then mixed with true beans, in the hopes that unwary consumers would not notice them. Sahagún reports similar devious practices from the Valley of Mexico (1950–82, Book 10, Chapter 18, 1961:65). The use of cacao as a medium of exchange appears to have endured in Nicaragua until at least the nineteenth century, when Squier observed cacao being used for this purpose in markets in Granada and León (1852, v. 1:160).

Ownership and access

In some areas of the New World, particularly Mesoamerica, the use of cacao and ownership of cacao plants and/or orchards appears to have been restricted to members of elites (Millon 1955a:131, 167; J. E. S. Thompson 1956:106). Peter Martyr, for example, called cacao "the drink of the noble and rich classes" in Mesoamerica (cited in Millon 1955a:167). Certainly, the ownership of cacao plots may have been subject to some type of restriction in Greater Nicoya, as evidenced by Oviedo's previously noted observation that the Nicarao "controlled" cacao production in Nicaragua . . . or at least, gave Oviedo reason to think that they did. Oviedo reports that cacao fields were *heredamientos* controlled by caciques and lords, who owed their possession of these plots to greater princes called *calachuni* or *teyte*, although the word *heredamiento* suggests that inheritance must also have played some role in the transmission of these properties (Oviedo 1851–55, v. 1:316; see W. R. Fowler, this volume, for a discussion of inheritance of cacao trees in neighboring El Salvador). Oviedo claims that only lords and principal men made cacao beverages, because, for the common people, drinking cacao was tantamount to impoverishing oneself or eating or throwing one's money away (1851–55, v. 1:317).

Oviedo's account does not specify that common people were not allowed to drink cacao, only that they probably could not afford to do so. Benzoni's account (1857:150) suggests that consumption of cacao was perhaps somewhat more casual and widespread than Oviedo's account does; he notes that he was frequently offered the beverage as he traveled throughout Nicaragua and eventually came to drink it quite regularly, apparently as others did. Millon suggests this indicates a lack of sumptuary regulations regarding the use of cacao in Nicaragua akin to those that appear to have been in place in Pipil-controlled El Salvador, where only lords and great warriors were allowed to drink cacao (Millon 1955a:168).

Cacao production in Nicaragua and Costa Rica appears to have been geared towards meeting the local demand rather than to producing an export luxury good intended only for elite use and/or trade (Bergmann 1969:95; P. MacLeod 1996:84). As Bergmann (1969:95) observes, it is significant that only in Nicaragua in the 1548–1551 *Tasación de tributos* was post-Conquest cacao tribute measured in Spanish units rather than in the indigenous units (*xiquipiles* and *zontles*) used everywhere else in Mesoamerica—including neighboring El Salvador (W. R. Fowler 1987:161). Bergmann (1969:95) notes that Oviedo's extensive discussion of cacao makes no mention of these indigenous units, and suggests that before the Conquest, Nicaragua had no use for these units because it did not participate in the broad commercial movement of cacao across Mesoamerica. This argues against the common assumption that cacao was introduced into Greater Nicoya as a focal crop by Nahua-speaking trader-migrants (see, for example, Abel-Vidor 1980; Bergmann 1969; W. R. Fowler 1987, 1989a; A. M. Young 1994), since, presumably, traders with an overriding interest in cacao would not have forgotten how to measure it.

Mesoamerican Origins, or Autochthonous Traditions?

The preceding summary of ethnohistoric information concerning the distribution, cultivation, preparation, use, and ownership of cacao in Greater Nicoya clearly draws a number of parallels with cacao cultivation and use in Mesoamerica. The peoples of Greater Nicoya grew cacao in irrigated orchards as did groups in other Pacific coastal regions (such as El Salvador and Guatemala) and often used a common Mesoamerican shade tree, *Gliricidia sepium*, to protect their crop. They employed the same *mano* and *metate* technology that was in common use throughout Mesoamerica to grind their cacao seeds into paste. The Nicarao celebrated the cacao harvest with a *volador* ritual based on a Central Mexican harvest festival prototype, made the same symbolic equation between cacao and blood that Mesoamerican groups did, and seem to have used cacao as an important element in various types of rituals (including marriage), just as their northern counterparts did. And, finally, the ancient peoples of Greater Nicoya used cacao as a currency as did Mesoamericans, and there is evidence that elite groups attempted to place the crop under their restricted control.

All this evidence seemingly supports Oviedo's statement and the prevailing but untested assumption that cacao was introduced into Greater Nicoya by Mesoamerican colonists, most likely the Nicarao. Yet these are very broad similarities, and there are enough unique practices associated with cacao cultivation and use in Nicaragua and Costa Rica to give us reason to suspect that the crop may have a longer history in the area, one that predates the arrival of Mesoamerican groups. As already noted, the doubling of shade trees observed by Benzoni was unique to this area and is more easily explained as a practice appropriate to individual tree cultivation. This practice alone might infer an older—or at least, distinct—tradition of "cacao culture" based on the exploitation of naturally occurring trees. The use of more than one kind of shade tree (that is, the use of the coral tree as well as the blackwood) might also be meaningful if we make the reasonable assumption that the longer a plant is grown in an area, the greater innovation we might expect to see in how it is managed and/or exploited by groups in the same area. Based on this same principle, we might also expect to see methods of preparing and using cacao in Greater Nicoya that are unlike those documented for Mesoamerica. Although the diversity of cacao beverage "recipes" reported by chroniclers across Mesoamerica (compare Millon 1955a:163–167) makes it difficult to claim that most of the beverages consumed in Nicaragua are the products of an independent local tradition rather than just another variation on a widespread Mesoamerican theme, that Greater Nicoyans used cacao for more than beverages is worth considering. For example, Oviedo's account explicitly notes that cacao was used medicinally—specifically, as an antivenin, as a medicinal salve, and as "sunscreen" face paint (1851–55, v. 1:318–320). There is no reason to assume that these innovative uses were introduced from Mesoamerica as opposed to being products of a potentially long, independent tradition of experimentation.

The generally higher degree of availability and lack of prohibitions regarding the use of cacao in Greater Nicoya tends to support the argument that the crop was not introduced by an elite group bent on controlling and exploiting it. After all, if an elite Nicarao group did introduce the crop, this group does not appear to have done a very effective job in maintaining its intended monopoly, judging by the documented distribution of cacao in areas of Central America and Nicaragua well beyond the sphere of Nicarao control (or even influence). Even if the Chorotega in particular did not have any cacao trees of their own, as Oviedo claimed, it seems certain that the same cannot be said for diverse other Central American groups beyond the Nicarao. A more likely possibility is that the Nicarao, rather than introducing cacao per se, introduced a new approach to growing cacao in Nicaragua; that is, a "Mesoamerican-style" approach focusing on orchard cultivation, and it is not impossible that they chose to colonize Greater Nicoya precisely because they saw the potential to more systematically exploit a crop that was already present in the area. Alternatively, the Nicarao may have focused on intensive cacao cultivation to economically compete more effectively with the Chorotega, who had the (presumably considerable) advantages of a longer history in the area as well as a documented monopoly on another luxury crop, the highly prized *níspero* fruit (Oviedo 1851–55, v. 4:61).

Either way, the apparent lack of use of *xiquipiles* and *zontles* does seem to argue against the idea that the Nicarao were growing cacao to participate in a widespread trade network, as already noted. The idea that cacao production was geared to meet local needs rather than to produce a luxury trade good seems to better fit the available evidence.

The argument for a greater antiquity of cacao use in Greater Nicoya (as well as in Nicaragua and Costa Rica in general) is supported by the documentation of some of the unique practices from this area which suggest South American rather than Mesoamerican influence, and might therefore date to a time (that is, before A.D. 800 or 900) when groups speaking a Chibchan-related language still dominated the lands that would later be colonized by Mesoamericans. Speakers of Chibchan and Misumalpan (a closely related family) once dominated lower Central America as well as northwestern South America and at the time of the Conquest appear to have remained preeminent in areas of Nicaragua and Costa Rica beyond the bounds of Greater Nicoya where cacao use was recorded (Constenla Umaña 1991, 1994). Bearing this in mind, it is intriguing that the medicinal qualities of cacao (including its beans, butter, and even its bark) were apparently appreciated in parts of northwestern South America (D. Stone 1984:70; see also Bletter and Daly, this volume), as they were in Greater Nicoya. Equally interesting is that the aforementioned pulp-based *pinolillo* beverage and Oviedo's account of the occasional consumption of cacao pulp are reminiscent of South American practices pertaining to cacao consumption. A.

M. Young (1994:15) observes that the eastern boundary of Colombia's Choco Province forms a sort of boundary with regard to the way cacao is used in the Americas: above the line, beans are used to make beverages, whereas below the line, the pulp is used to make a "frothy beverage with a citrus-like flavor." It is possible that the line could once have been drawn further north (see also this volume: Henderson and Joyce; McNeil, Chapter 17). Unfortunately, however, the general dearth of ethnohistoric and/or archaeological data regarding the use and potential cultivation of cacao in pre-Columbian South America and lower Central America (cf. Bergmann 1969:87; Bletter and Daly, this volume; S. D. Coe and M. D. Coe 1996:26; Millon 1955a:267; Motamayor and Lanaud 2002:85; D. Stone 1984:69; A. M. Young 1994:15), makes it difficult to determine whether cacao cultivation and use in Nicaragua and Costa Rica were similar in other ways to practices from further south.

Although ethnohistoric accounts of cacao use in Greater Nicoya are certainly not absent, the lack of archaeological data that might support these accounts certainly rivals the lack of archaeological data in South and Central America. If cacao use and cultivation were to be inferred solely on the basis of the archaeological record, it would be difficult for even the most creative archaeologist to argue that cacao was as significant a commodity in Greater Nicoya as ethnohistory suggests, or even to argue that it was grown in this area in pre-Columbian times at all. Notably, this is as true for areas where ethnohistorians indicate that cacao was cultivated (that is, areas formerly under Nicarao control) as it is for areas where cacao was supposedly not cultivated, such as León and Granada (formerly under Chorotega control).

The lack of archaeological data is perhaps not surprising given that the archaeology of Nicaragua, in particular, is far less well known than that of any other country of Central America and also given that so many of the potential definitive material indicators of cacao use—especially, the tree, its pods and seeds, calabash drinking vessels, and wooden *molinillo* stirring sticks (the latter curiously undocumented for Greater Nicoya, though they are used modernly)—are perishable articles that usually decay rapidly in tropical environments. The relatively good preservation of organic artifacts (including possible cacao seeds) recently recovered from fieldwork at the Santa Isabel site in Rivas, Nicaragua (McCafferty and Steinbrenner 2003; McCafferty et al. n.d.; Steinbrenner 2002) seems to be an exception to this general rule. On the other hand, well-preserved items of material culture that have been ethnohistorically associated with cacao preparation, like *manos* and *metates*, have not been subjected to the kind of residue or use-wear analyses that might connect them to cacao cultivation archaeologically and have, therefore, instead been associated almost exclusively with maize cultivation. The same situation applies for ceramic vessels, at least some of which likely contained cacao at some point in their use-histories, like pots recovered from various Mesoamerican contexts (for example, Hall et al. 1990; Henderson and Joyce, this volume; Hurst, this volume; Hurst et al. 1989; McNeil, Hurst, and Sharer, this volume; D. Stuart 1988).

Greater Nicoya also appears to lack representations of cacao plants or use comparable to the artistic depictions in various media (for example, murals, codices, ceramics, sculpture) from El Salvador, the Maya area, or Central Mexico. For example, out of tens of thousands of ceramic, lithic, and bone artifacts recovered from the Santa Isabel site, the only artifact that might be symbolically associated with cacao was a ceramic object (a pendant or possible penis sheath, cf. Enslow 1990:92) that may represent a cacao pod (Figure 12.3) (McCafferty and Steinbrenner 2003; Steinbrenner 2002).

Yet if the archaeological record has to date remained silent about the subject of cacao use in Greater Nicoya, it has occasionally hinted that cacao's distribution extended beyond the reach of the Nicarao. Macrobotanical remains from the Ayala site in the Department of Granada included cacao, from an area that was beyond Nicarao territory and from a Bagaces period (A.D. 300–800) context which long predated the arrival of any Mesoamerican group in the area (Salgado 1996:179). A possible cacao-shaped rattle found in Las Huacas in the center of the Nicoya peninsula (D. Stone 1984:74: provenience unreported) also suggests a ritual significance for the plant outside Nicarao territory. If the aforementioned Santa Isabel cacao artifact is a penis sheath, this would also suggest southern rather than northern connections, since penis sheaths are more typical of South America than Mesoamerica (for example, Chapman 1974:30–31).

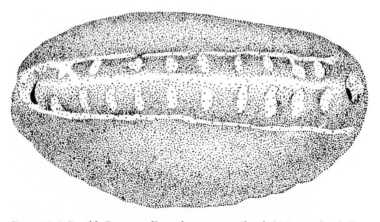

Figure 12.3. Possible "cacao pod" pendant or penis sheath (7.5 cm x 4 cm). Excavated at Santa Isabel, Nicaragua. Drawing by Eliud Guerra.

Conclusion

The preceding survey and discussion of the ethnohistoric evidence for *Theobroma cacao* cultivation and use in Greater Nicoya suggests that although cacao use in Nicaragua and Costa Rica was considerably influenced by the presence of various groups of Mesoamerican colonists that arrived after A.D. 800 or 900, it is unlikely that the presence of the crop can be explained through an outdated model that suggests that one of these groups introduced cacao into the area and then proceeded to monopolize its cultivation. A more parsimonious explanation is that cacao was known and used (though not necessarily systematically cultivated) in Lower Central America before the arrival of the Mesoamericans and that the late-arriving Nicarao introduced a new orchard-based system for cultivating and exploiting it when they arrived upon the scene. The presence of cacao may have been one of the motivating factors leading to the Nicarao colonization of Greater Nicoya, or the Nicarao may have focused on this crop in response to the economic challenge posed by the well-established Chorotega. These two hypotheses are not necessarily incompatible: it may have been a little of both.

Although the scant archaeological data that are currently available are not incompatible with the new model proposed here, in truth, they are also insufficient to corroborate most of what ethnohistory tells us and therefore cannot provide any kind of definitive answer to this question. Future research in Greater Nicoya focusing on macro- and microbotanical remains is desperately needed to correct this problem. Ethnohistory has pointed the way for future research; it is hoped archaeology will now step forward and decisively demonstrate whether the power of the Nicarao over cacao was as absolute as Oviedo claimed or as limited as other ethnohistoric sources seem to imply.

Acknowledgments

Thanks to Dr. Geoffrey G. McCafferty, whose ongoing research at Santa Isabel has been supported by the University of Calgary and by the Social Sciences and Humanities Research Council of Canada (SSHRC). Thanks also to Dr. J. Scott Raymond, who encouraged me to continue studying cacao production in Greater Nicoya. And finally, thanks to Cameron McNeil for her insightful feedback and editing. My own research has been supported by a University of Calgary Thesis Research Grant and by a SSHRC Doctoral Fellowship.

Notes

1. The boundaries of Mesoamerica are widely acknowledged to have shifted over time (cf. Evans 2004:19). For the purposes of this chapter, "Mesoamerica" generally re-

fers to those regions of this culture area whose enduring "Mesoamerican-ness" is beyond question (such as Central Mexico and the Maya area) and excludes peripheral areas (like Greater Nicoya) that can only be properly included in Mesoamerica at certain periods in their prehistory.

2. Rosés Alvarado (1982) and Bergmann (1969) cite different archival sources with regard to Agustín de Ceballos's letter to the king about cacao cultivation on the Atlantic coast; the former claims the letter discusses the Matina Plain, whereas the latter suggests that it discusses Sixaola. Because the archival sources cited for the letter are different, it is conceivable that both interpretations are correct and that the authors are citing two distinct letters dealing with virtually identical subject matter. Unfortunately, neither primary source was accessible to me at the time of this writing to provide clarification. However, since Sixaola and the Matina Plain are both within the Talamanca area, the Ceballos accounts confirms Vázquez de Coronado's report in either case.

3. This translation is based on A. M. Young (1994:28).

4. The ten-bean rate for a prostitute's service is repeated by Oviedo in a later volume (1851–55, v. 4:37) and was confirmed by López de Gómara (1975:121) in 1552.

PART III

Cacao in the Colonial Period

13

The Good and Evil of Chocolate in Colonial Mexico

Manuel Aguilar-Moreno

The *cacahuaquahuitl* (cacao tree) was highly valued among the Aztecs; its seeds were used as currency and also were made into *cacahuaatl* (chocolate), a prestigious beverage available mainly to the nobility, which served as a stimulant and in some forms as an aphrodisiac (Hernández 1959; Motolinia 1971). Cacao also had an important place in pre-Columbian religion. Its roles as an elite celebratory beverage and an offering for the gods are apparent in both Contact period accounts and in its representation in pre-Columbian art (see this volume: Henderson and Joyce; McNeil, Hurst, and Sharer; Martin; Reents-Budet; Stuart). Although the Spanish prohibited the use of some sacred Aztec plants (such as amaranth and psychotropic mushrooms), the flavor of cacao appealed to these newcomers and they recognized that it was a profitable commodity. Spanish attempts to gain from cacao involved using it in much the same way as the Aztecs had: it was demanded as tribute (see this volume: Fowler; Gasco), depicted in gardens in religious spaces, and offered to saints. The adoption of cacao by the Spanish meant not only incorporating it into their commercial network but also into their religion—a religion that struggled to define a beverage which also seemed to be a food.

In this chapter I explore examples of the way cacao, or chocolate, was incorporated into the Catholic Colonial society of Mexico and some of the problems that cacao presented for its new devotees. First, a Catholic cacao "god" was placed in the Cathedral of Mexico City, no doubt as a way to collect valuable tribute that was formerly offered to Emperor Motecuhzoma and to pre-Columbian deities. Second, cacao appears in an early Colonial mural of the Garden of Paradise. Last, I examine the controversies raised by the use of cacao as a comestible in Catholic culture, which had carefully defined prohibitions regarding the consumption of food and drink during fast periods, prohibitions which were confounded by the difficulty of defining whether chocolate was a food or a beverage. These cases will illustrate the continuities of some of the attributions and meanings of this important commodity, which Latin America, and particularly Mesoamerica, gave to the world as part of a complex process of transculturation.

Cacao in pre-Columbian Mexico

Among the Mexica (Aztecs) in pre-Columbian times cacao was an important item of tribute to the ruler and an offering to the gods (Berdan and Anawalt 1992; Sahagún 1950–82, Book 2, 1981:152). Sahagún and numerous Colonial sources state that the drinking of chocolate was exclusive to the Aztec elite: the royal house, the lords and nobility, the long-distance traders (*pochteca*), and the warriors. Apparently, the only commoners who were privileged to consume this luxurious commodity were soldiers in battle, because cacao was considered to be a stimulant (S. D. Coe and M. D. Coe 1996:93).

As an eyewitness to the Conquest, Bernal Díaz del Castillo, described a banquet given by the Emperor Motecuhzoma II, where:

> they brought him some cups of fine gold, with a certain drink made of cacao, which they said was for success with women; but I saw that they brought more than 50 great jars of good cacao with its foam, and he drank of that; and the women served him drink very respectfully. (Díaz del Castillo 2002 [1568]:167)

In this passage, Díaz makes a statement about the aphrodisiacal property of cacao, an idea that would be reinforced by the studies of Francisco Hernández, the royal physician and naturalist to Philip II of Spain. Hernández was in Mexico from 1572 to 1577 in search of medicinal plants to add to the European pharmacopoeia. He created an enormous book about the plants of New Spain that describes more than three thousand species. In that volume, Hernández provides a chocolate recipe, which he affirms excites the venereal appetite (Hernández 1959, v. 2:246, 305). This recipe contains three plant products traditionally used to flavor Aztec chocolate beverages: the *hueinacaztli* flower (*Cymbopetalum penduliflorum* [Dunal] Baill.), which tastes spicy like black pepper; the *tlilxochitl* bean (*Vanilla planifolia* Andrews), which is the famous vanilla; and the *mecaxochitl* flower (*Piper* ssp.), a relative of black pepper. According to Hernández, when cacao is mixed with these flavorings, "it gives an agreeable taste, is tonic, warms the stomach, perfumes the breath, combats poisons, and alleviates intestinal pains and colics" (S. D. Coe and M. D, Coe 1996:91). There is no direct evidence that the consumption of chocolate produces aphrodisiacal effects. I am not aware, however, of people today who have tried chocolate with the large variety of Aztec flavorings mentioned by Hernández and Sahagún. The insistence that "the excess of the beverage can intoxicate, derange and disturb" is intriguing (Sahagún 1950–82, Book 11, 1975: Section 7). It is very probable that the Aztecs were mixing cacao with alcoholic substances (see this volume: Henderson and Joyce; McNeil, Chapter 17). The popular idea that chocolate has aphrodisiac qualities has been revived from time to time. Today, some modern researchers believe that phenylethylamine, one of the many chemical compounds in chocolate, is the same mood-altering chemical that the body releases into the brain when an individual is in love (S. D. Coe and M. D. Coe 1996:270).

Cacao in Early Colonial Mexico

The first discussions of cacao by representatives of the Catholic Church in Mexico record its appealing flavor and qualities. Motolinia (1971, Chapter 8:218–219) wrote that cacao "when ground and mixed with corn and other seeds, which are also ground . . . serves well as a beverage and is consumed in this form. . . It is good and they consider it a nutritious beverage." Sahagún (1950–82, Book 11, 1975:119–120) wrote:

> This cacao, when much is drunk, when much is consumed, especially that which is green, which is tender, makes one drunk, takes effect on one, makes one dizzy, confuses one, makes one sick, deranges one. When an ordinary amount is drunk, it gladdens one, refreshes one, consoles one, invigorates one. Thus it is said: I take cacao. I wet my lips. I refresh myself.

Also, Bartolomé de las Casas (1909:552) expresses: "The drink (chocolate) is water mixed with a certain flour made of some nuts called cacao. It is very substantial, very cooling, tasty, and agreeable, and does not intoxicate."

That cacao beans were used as money among the Aztecs is documented in the early Colonial times by Motolinia, who tells us that the daily wage of a porter in Central Mexico was 100 cacao beans (S. D. Coe and M. D. Coe 1996:98). Anderson, Berdan, and Lockhart (1976:213) mention a Nahuatl document from Tlaxcala in 1545 that shows that a turkey cock was worth two hundred cacao beans, a small rabbit was thirty beans, one turkey egg was three, a newly picked avocado was three, a fish wrapped in maize husks was three, one large tomato was one, and a tamale was one cacao bean. If these data are accurate, they provide an insight into the purchasing power of Aztec workers, indicating that they were somewhat better off economically than Mexican workers of today.

The use of cacao beans as money and offerings by the Mexica in the Valley of

Mexico continued through at least the sixteenth century. An interesting illustration of this is the veneration of the so called "Christ of the Cacao," a dramatic and beautiful sixteenth-century image of Christ that is still displayed in a side chapel of the cathedral of Mexico City (Figure 13.1). The cathedral is adjacent to the great ancient temple of the Aztecs, the Templo Mayor. When the Indians went to worship in the cathedral, they left offerings of cacao beans as alms at the feet of the Christ, much as they might have once paid tribute to gods at the Templo Mayor. The true beneficiaries of these offerings would have been the priests at the cathedral. Thomas Gage, a friar who worked in both Mexico and Guatemala in the early seventeenth century, noted the wealth of many monks in Mexico and the frequency with which they consumed chocolate (Gage 1946 [1648]:33, 39, 145–147). He was himself the perfect example of how a religious official could grow rich by encouraging the offering of cacao and other prestige

Figure 13.1. Christ of the Cacao. Sixteenth century. The Cathedral of Mexico City. Photograph by Fernando Gonzalez y Gonzalez.

items to saints and Christ images in churches. When he finally left his position as a religious official in Colonial America, he went heavy with pearls and precious stones which he deemed the lightest way to transfer his wealth back to Europe (unfortunately for him he was robbed by pirates before he ever reached the shores of his homeland) (Gage 1946 [1648]:332, 349–350).

The Christ of the Cacao statue is not the only representation of cacao in a Colonial Catholic religious context. A cacao tree is depicted in the sixteenth-century murals of Malinalco, Mexico. These murals may reveal something about how cacao was perceived in the early Colonial period. Between 1543 and 1575, Augustinian friars built the Monastery of La Purificación y San Simón in Malinalco. On one wall of the cloister, the *tlacuilos* (indigenous artists), directed by the monks, painted an image of monkeys hanging from a cacao tree in a paradisiacal garden (Figure 13.2). In the next few pages I will provide

Figure 13.2. Monkeys in a cacao tree. Mural detail. Sixteenth century. Augustinian Monastery, Malinalco, Mexico. Photograph by Fernando Gonzalez y Gonzalez.

an interpretation of the role of the cacao tree in the religious context of the sixteenth-century Indian-Christian transculturation in Mexico.

The Christian cloister embodied a sacred center, or microcosm, in the same manner as did pre-Hispanic pyramids. These cloisters represented the Celestial Jerusalem, the "pure world" described in the Apocalypse, which has at its center an *omphalos* (a cosmic navel) indicated by a well, tree, fountain, or column; this is where the *axis mundi* (axis of the world) passes as a kind of celestial stairway that connects the cosmic levels of the divine upper- and underworlds, with the surface of the earth, where humans dwell. The Romanesque and Gothic cloisters of Europe, with religious narratives carved in the capitals or painted on the walls, were the inspiration for the Mexican monasteries which practically functioned as illustrated books, creating for the monks an atmosphere conducive to meditation and prayer (Sebastián, Monterrosa, and Terán 1995).

The frescoes of the lower cloister of Malinalco depict a botanical and zoological garden intended as a description and interpretation of life after death. They present the idea of the Christian paradise where the souls of the faithful will enjoy the glory of God (Figure 13.3). For the Aztecs there were four possible places to go in the afterlife. Three were heavens, or paradises: *Tonatiuh Ilhuicatl* (house of the sun), *Tlalocan* (paradise of Tlaloc, the rain god), and *Chichihuacu-*

Figure 13.3. View of the Paradise Gardens. Sixteenth century. Corridor of the cloister of the Augustinian Monastery, Malinalco, Mexico. Photograph by Fernando Gonzalez y Gonzalez.

auhco (paradise of children). The other place was *Mictlan*, the Underworld, the region of the dead and nothingness. In contrast to Christian thought, the type of death and social class of the deceased, not his or her morality, determined the destiny of a soul. The Aztec heavens were described by Sahagún (1950–82, Book 3, 1978 and Book 6, 1969) as places of fertility and abundance, full of flowers, fruit, and trees. The Aztecs believed that the souls of the dead who entered into the "house of the sun" were converted into *chalchihuites* (precious green stones) and after four years would be transformed into flying creatures (birds, butterflies, and bees) to return to earth (Sahagún 1950–82, Book 3, 1978:47–48). In Augustinian thought the birds symbolized the liberated souls of wholly spiritual individuals (St. Augustine 1950, v. 9:527).

The implications of a botanical and zoological garden within a sacred setting were rich and diverse for both Spanish and Indian cultures. These traditions converged and were fused in the theme of the Malinalco frescoes, combining the concepts of earthly dominance (terrestrial paradise) with the promises inherent in a pleasant afterlife (celestial paradise). The type of garden depicted in the murals was also adequate for a sixteenth-century monastery in Mexico, a place so central to many aspects of community life. The intention of the Augustinian friars was to paint a garden scene that portrayed not only their concepts of a celestial paradise but also their intense desire to establish a terrestrial paradise in the "New World" (Peterson 1993:137). In the same way that Vasco de Quiroga in Michoacán and the Franciscan Order elsewhere were trying to incarnate the utopia of Thomas Moore in the American continent, the Augustinians wanted to create a harmonious world of Indians and friars living in "Perfect Christianity." This concept has been called the *Jerusalén Indiana* (Indian Jerusalem) (Aguilar 1999:26).

Most of the floral and faunal imagery depicted in the "paradise garden" of this cloister is native; it comes from the living experience and natural world of the indigenous artists (Peterson 1993:85–117). The cacao tree appears in a section of the murals as a central feature of the plants that constitute the garden of the Indian-Christian Heaven, reflecting its status as a precious and sacred element in Aztec culture (Figure 13.4). Spider monkeys hang from its branches, just out of reach of the snake, who twines around an adjoining tree.

In the Mesoamerican cosmogonies, monkeys were ancestral to humankind and endowed with vitalizing, creative powers (Braakhuis 1987:31–33). With their nimble grace, song-like hoots, and manual dexterity, they were perceived as the originators of the performing and visual arts, including the elite professions of scribes and painters (*Popol Vuh* 1993; Benson 1994:137–139).

The Christian connotations of monkeys and apes were negative. The animals symbolized low human passions and sinners, and since apes appeared to parody human actions, they represented the lustful nature of humans or people in a state of degeneration (Peterson 1993:104–105).

Thus, the images preserved in these murals compel us to wonder what this animal is doing in a natural paradise depicted on the walls of a Christian monastery. Associations between monkeys and cacao are common in Mesoamerican iconography (Figure 13.5). Since cacao was native to Mesoamerica, indigenous people knew that the plant does not have a mechanism for opening its pods and dispersing its seeds to reproduce. This is the role of the monkeys, who steal the pods to enjoy the delicious white pulp enveloping the seeds. Monkeys either consume the pulp with the seeds intact and distribute them through defecation, or they chew off the pulp and discard the seeds. Thus, monkeys act as seed disseminators, keeping the natural cycle of the cacao tree viable. In this sense

Figure 13.4. Spider monkeys hang from a cacao tree to right of the tree that holds the snake of the Garden of Paradise. Mural detail. Sixteenth century. Augustinian Monastery, Malinalco, Mexico. Photograph by Fernando Gonzalez y Gonzalez.

the monkeys are embodiments of creation and fertility (Braakhuis 1987:29–31). The sweet, tasty pulp is probably what also attracted humans to the cacao plant in ancient times (S. D. Coe and M. D. Coe 1996:22). On the other hand, the reputation of cacao as an aphrodisiac and inductor of drunkenness, probably led the Catholic friars to view the cacao tree as one of the sinful trees of paradise, associated with animals symbolizing the baser human passions. Thus, in the nascent syncretic Indian-Christian view of the world, there was a dual interpretation of the reality that satisfied the needs and motivations of the two cultural groups engaged in the post-Conquest dialogue.

Set within the vegetation on the mural and to the right of the cacao tree, there is a medallion that encloses the monogram of the Virgin Mary as Mother of Christ and Queen of Heaven (M interlaced with A and a royal crown) (Figure 13.6). Although the connotations of a symbol representing the Virgin Mary in the context of monastery walls could be understood easily by the European monks, the symbolic power of this image to indigenous members of the community may have been more complicated. In the Indian mind, the Virgin Mary would likely have been a substitute for Coatlicue, the mother goddess of earth, a symbol of fertility in that sacred paradise. Conversely, the friars could have interpreted the Virgin's monogram, as well as the monograms of Jesus Christ (IHS) and the Augustinian Order, as a symbol of the presence of Christianity in the earthly and heavenly paradises.

The amazing mural program of Malinalco is a living testimony to the efforts of the sixteenth-century Augustinians to create the "City of God" among the Indians of the New World. The emotions of the actors in that marvelous utopian experience truly are imprinted in the murals of the cloister.

As we can see, the Colonial exchange created a process of transculturation in which a new *mestizo-criollo* culture was taking form in Latin America. This new culture took elements from both original cultures but was different from each. In this atmosphere, corn, chilies, and chocolate were absorbed into the Colonial cuisine of Mexico and eventually transplanted to Spain and the rest of Europe (Aguilar 1999:86–87; S. D. Coe and M. D. Coe 1996:110–111).

Figure 13.5. Monkeys and cacao pods. Carving on a Classic period Maya vase. Denver Art Museum. Photograph courtesy of Justin Kerr (K5185).

Figure 13.6. Cacao tree and the monogram of the Virgin Mary as Mother of Christ and Queen of Heaven. Sixteenth century. Augustinian Monastery, Malinalco, Mexico. Photograph by Fernando Gonzalez y Gonzalez.

Because of its bitter, astringent flavor, it took time for the Spanish and other Europeans to develop a taste for chocolate. The addition of milk and sugar to natural cacao was probably influenced by this quality. The Jesuit José de Acosta, writing in 1590, had a very interesting comment in this respect:

> The main benefit of this cacao is a beverage which they make called Chocolate, which is a strange thing valued in that country. It disgusts those who are not used to it, for it has a foam on top, or a scum-like bubbling. . . It is a valued drink, which the Indians offer to the lords who come or pass through their land. And the Spanish men, and even more the Spanish women, are addicted to the black chocolate. (Acosta 1940 [1590]:251)

As chocolate consumption increased and its flavorings were altered to reflect regional preferences, people all around the world became "chocoholics." But in Colonial Mesoamerica, as in the Catholic countries of Europe, there were ecclesiastical prohibitions, in particular regarding the use of chocolate during fasts. Some religious orders debated whether to prohibit their members from drinking chocolate, but it proved impossible to enforce that extreme position.

The main issue concerning whether chocolate broke the ecclesiastical fast was to define whether it was a drink or a food. If it was a food, not just a drink, then it could not be taken by practicing Catholics during the fasting hours, which ran from midnight until Holy Communion (in 1962, Vatican Council II shortened this period to one hour). Nor could it be taken on the fast days of Lent. A fast was a penance intended to mortify the flesh by denying it any kind of food.

The issue was argued among ecclesiastics (including popes) and laymen for about four hundred years. Some religious orders (the Jesuits, for example) supported the drinking of chocolate on the grounds that it did not break the fast because it was just a beverage. The Dominicans took the opposite view. The dispute became more acidic when, in 1629, the Spaniard Juan de Solórzano y Pereyra made the usual claim that chocolate excited the venereal appetite, arguing that in order to protect the flesh from sin (which was the reason for the fast), the beverage should be prohibited (S. D. Coe and M. D. Coe 1996:151–152).

It is in this context that I introduce our third case of study. I will analyze a manuscript entitled *Acerca del chocolate*, which is a treatise that discusses whether chocolate breaks the ecclesiastical fast. It is attributed to an anonymous Spanish Carmelite theologian friar writing in Rome, Italy, in response to an inquiry about the issue from an also anonymous monsignor or bishop living in Mexico in approximately 1730. The manuscript was formerly owned by Mexican historian Federico Gómez de Orozco and is kept as Manuscript 426 (MSS 426) in the Library of the University of California, San Diego. I assume that the writer is a Carmelite because Gómez de Orozco states that the document was found in a pile of old papers in the Carmelite School of Santa Ana in Mexico City (MSS 426:1). That the friar wrote the treatise in Italy is clearly implied in its text (MSS 426:20). The impeccable and cultured style of writing, which seems proper of the peninsulars, led me to assume that he is Spanish. The recipient of the manuscript is referred to as *Ilustrisimo y Reverendisimo Señor* (Very Illustrious and Reverend Sir), which is normally a title of high respect to prelates of honorary rank, like a monsignor, or of jurisdictional and hierarchical rank, like a bishop. What is not clear is whether the recipient was settled in Spain or Mexico City. I assume he lived in Mexico City, only because the document was found there, but it could have been brought from Spain.

The Carmelite theologian starts by addressing a question that the monsignor or bishop had asked him, concerning a rumor that an Italian preacher in Rome in a sermon during Lent condemned the use of chocolate during the fast period, and that later in another sermon he retracted this position (MSS 426:5). The Carmelite says that he was present at the two sermons and that the situation was very delicate because there had been for many years an animated controversy between social and religious groups regarding the use of the tasty beverage in fasting periods and that he will answer the question from a historical point of view, not taking any side. As a consequence, he named his document "Memories of the Theological History of Chocolate in Times of Fast."

The Italian preacher said that until the thirteenth-century, fast consisted of only one meal a day about noon. After that time a light meal (collation) was introduced to be taken at night. In more recent years another collation was added for the morning that included the "drugs" of the New World (chocolate and coffee). His argument was that people already eat generously, so the fast was a necessary penance to offer a sacrifice to God. The problem was that some individuals deliberately interpreted his words with a certain maliciousness and spread the rumor that he said that to drink a cup of chocolate during fast time would be a mortal sin (MSS 426:7). Based on such a statement, some liberal theologians counterattacked, saying that it was licit to drink as many cups of chocolate as desired because, like wine, chocolate was a beverage not a food.

In a second sermon the preacher refuted the gossips, talking about the real spirit of the fast. He said:

> Whoever preaches the Christian Morality with too much rigor, sins, because it makes it detestable to the people. In the same way, whoever teaches with excessive laxity, also sins, because such a person is teaching a falsehood. He says that the misinterpretation of his words regarding the use of chocolate manifests a very loose understanding of the Christian doctrine to accommodate it to serve the human appetites. In this sense, chocolate is repugnant to the spirit of the fast, and it is a serious error in teaching that says, that in times of fast, it can be drunk licitly whatever the amount of chocolate. That position is heretical, it goes against the teaching of our Holy Roman Church, and should be punished. If a foreigner would arrive suddenly and listen to our disputes, he would get the idea that the Catholics are an inhuman sect of flagellants and misanthropes, exhausted by bloody disciplines and severe fasts. But if he sees at the same time the lavish banquets, sumptuous feasts and the rich style of life, he would realize that the Catholics live a strong contradiction. (Mss 426:8–11)

Immediately the Carmelite continues, saying that what the preacher really told the faithful was to live a life of moderation. But the individuals that practice a loose morality and a comfortable life pretended to discredit him, spreading the rumors so that he was obliged to retract his condemnation of the drink because of orders he received from higher ecclesiastic authorities. The great danger of the falseness of the liberal ideas about the fast is that they pretend to subordinate the fast to the needs of the sin of gluttony (MSS 426:12–13).

With the purpose of presenting the causes of the dispute between theological parties in regard to the role of chocolate during fasting, in the next few pages of the document the Carmelite reviews the history of chocolate, mentioning that it originated in the province of Chiapas, Mexico. He refers to Luis López's book *Instructorium*, printed in Salamanca in 1585, which states in Chapter 112 that chocolate was used in America but provides no information regarding its use in Europe at this time. This leads the Carmelite to think that chocolate arrived in Spain around 1600 and later spread to other parts of Europe. Our theologian continues, saying that father Thomás Tamburino, a great canonist, mentioned in his book *Decálogo*, that chocolate was introduced "recently" to Italy. Tamburino died in 1675, which indicates that the beverage arrived around 1650 to 1660 (MSS 426:19–20).

Next, the Carmelite mentions that among the first theologians to discuss the famous debate about chocolate and fast was Antonio de León Pinelo in 1636, who, in his erudite analysis, did not support the compatibility of chocolate with fasting. What our Carmelite does not say is that León Pinelo concludes with the reasonable statement that if the cacao is mixed only with water, then it is licit, because it is simply a beverage.

Until this point in his study, the Carmelite had maintained a relatively balanced opinion, but suddenly he reveals his deep conservatism by strongly criticizing a treatise about the subject, written in 1645 by Father Thomás Hurtado, a professor of theology in the University of Seville, calling him a Probabilistic Theologian.[1]

Hurtado, expressing a moderate middle-ground perspective, said that it is licit to take chocolate during the fast if it is only mixed with water, not with milk or eggs.

Our belligerent Carmelite bitterly attacks Hurtado's stance:

The good Christians guided by the light of God know about the repugnance between the Fast and this tasty drink; but motivated in part by the stinging stimulus of gluttony, to moisturize deliciously the mouth, and castigated by the light of God, which makes clear the violation of the fast, they experience serious remorse of conscience, and with this disturbed and shattered consciousness, they drink the sweet liquor and commit sin. But in the same way, the thirsty and anxious sick person wants to drink and looks for a doctor, who allows it; likewise also these Christians go in search of theologians that advise and imprint in them a laxity of consciousness. Escorted by these brave theologians, being dulled already the remorse caused by the natural, and divine light, those Christians drink joyfully, and united with their theologians condemn as rigorists and overly-scrupulous those who manifest a different opinion and practice opposite customs. (MSS 426:21)[2]

Our Carmelite considers Hurtado's arguments to be tricky and totally erroneous. Father Hurtado says, based on St. Thomas Aquinas, that if you drink chocolate in times of fast with the purpose of quenching the thirst or for medicinal help, then it is licit. On the other hand, if you drink chocolate with the intention of nurturing the body, then you commit a sin (MSS 426:23).

The Carmelite strikes again, saying that of course everybody will declare that they need chocolate as medicine and will appease their consciences, thinking it is valid. He judges Father Hurtado's Probabilistic Theology as a dangerous enemy of the ecclesiastic and civil laws, because Hurtado says that if ordinary people find it impossible to practice the human law, that law should be changed or adjusted.

The Carmelite states with passion: "Father Hurtado does not acknowledge the fact that chocolate, exciting the sensuality, goes against the mortification and affliction of the flesh, which is the intrinsic purpose of the fast" (MSS 426:24–25). He strongly criticizes Probabilistic Theology as a prejudicial doctrine that pretends the use of geometric and scientific methodologies to create new ideas that only distort the traditional values. He adds with drama: "According to that lax theologian, it does not matter that chocolate provokes lust, it can be drunk because the objective of the law does not fall under the law itself." The Carmelite disagrees with Hurtado that chocolate is a drink per se, like wine. He thinks that chocolate is a paste dissolved in water, that it contains nutrients, and, therefore, it is a food. Hurtado supports his arguments with the opinions of several popes, including Gregory XIII, Paulus V, and Pius V, who declared that chocolate does not break the fast. The papal point of view provided a great deal of power to his arguments (MSS 426:26–28).

Our stubborn Carmelite still opposes the position of the popes, because at stake in this historical dispute is the outcome of the rivalry between the conservative traditional theology and the more liberal probabilistic theology. If the Carmelite theologian would accept Hurtado's forceful arguments, that would mean the acceptance of the triumph of the liberal probabilistic theology (MSS 426:29). This situation illustrates that religious disputes are never exempt from the influence of human passions.

Hurtado went on to explain that chocolate, like wine and beer, was formulated by pagan people but that this does not make it bad and that it should not be forbidden to Christians based on its origin. He adds that even if sugar and honey have been dissolved in chocolate there is no break of the fast, because they become integrated into the beverage. Leandro de Murcia, a Capuchin priest, wrote that the ideas of Father Hurtado were falsehoods and opposed to Christian piety and doctrine (MSS 426:30).

Father Hurtado concludes his interesting dissertation by writing that chocolate is definitely a beverage and not a food; therefore it does not break the Christian fast. Moreover, he adds that chocolate is highly medicinal, and he quotes a certain physician Ramírez: "Anyone can have a healthy life and good nutrition drinking everyday a cup of chocolate" (MSS 426:31–32). Our Carmelite bitterly opposes such conclusions and ends his document saying that if the imprudent recommendation of the physician Ramírez would be considered true, all cacao produced in Spanish America would not be sufficient to sustain the craving of the world's population.

This dispute about chocolate as a violation of the ecclesiastic fast went on for more than four hundred years. Today there are still people who believe that chocolate breaks the Christian fast, which now only consists of one hour before receiving Holy Communion.

One dispute over drinking chocolate in seventeenth-century Chiapas may have led to the murder of a bishop. Friar Thomas Gage (1946 [1648]) worked briefly in Chiapas when a dispute arose over ladies of the upper classes being served chocolate by their servants during mass. The bishop ordered that this custom be stopped, but the women refused to cease the practice insisting that they were delicate and that the chocolate was required to settle their stomachs during the religious service. When the women refused to obey his command, the bishop ordered that anyone consuming chocolate during mass would be excommunicated. The women then chose to attend mass at smaller churches where they could drink their chocolate; they gave their donations to those religious houses, causing a large loss of revenue to the cathedral and the bishop. The bishop then threatened to excommunicate priests and friars that were allowing the drinking of chocolate during mass. Shortly thereafter, the bishop was struck sick and died, allegedly from a cup of poisoned chocolate slipped into his house by one of the angered ladies (Gage 1946 [1648]:160–163).

Conclusion

Although the Spaniards attempted to halt many ritual practices of Mexico's indigenous people, cacao consumption was not one of them. Lured by the flavor of the bean, the Spaniards became cacao consumers and profited from its trade. The murals at Malinalco display the beginnings of this adoption. However, when chocolate conquered the Spaniards and later other Europeans, it was not without conflict. The stimulating, some might say "sinful," pleasure of consuming cacao created an animated theological controversy and in at least one case may have led to murder.

Acknowledgments

I want to thank Cameron McNeil for her insightful editing suggestions and Michelle Dupont for bringing my attention to some important documentary sources.

Notes

1. The Probabilistic Theology, or Probabilism, establishes a moral system in which the lawfulness of a doubtful action is interpreted by maintaining that one is free to act against the law if the reasons for his opinion are more probable than those that favor the law (Broderick 1976:494).

2. Text translated by Manuel Aguilar-Moreno.

14

The Itza Maya Control over Cacao

Politics, Commerce, and War in the Sixteenth and Seventeenth
Centuries

Laura Caso Barrera and Mario Aliphat F.

The Itza, the last independent Maya kingdom, carried out a dynamic and active
political and economic resistance to Spanish encroachment into their territory.
For more than a hundred and fifty years, after Cortés's first *entrada* into the
Peten region in 1525, the Itza reconstructed an ancient central Peten exchange
system, occupying the vacuum left by the collapse of the maritime trade network of the Chontal (Acalan). Cacao (*Theobroma cacao* L.), achiote (*Bixa
orellana* L.), and vanilla (*Vanilla planifolia* G. Jackson), a triad integrated as
the chocolate cultural complex; as well as salt, feathers, cotton, textiles, slaves,
sacrificial victims, and Spanish iron tools, were subject to brisk and intensive
inter-regional exchange.[1] The sociopolitical response of the Itza, in the face of
the Spanish menace, was to concentrate on incorporating and diminishing the
internal conflict and division created by the different competing Itza *parcialidades*.[2] Thus, cacao, *achiote*, and vanilla, as integrated elements of ritual and
elite conspicuous consumption, became strategic commodities for the Itza.

Cacao grows as an intensive crop in *cacaotales* (see below), known in Maya
as *pakal* or *pakal che*, in only a few places of the Maya area.[3] The Itza were able
to integrate and control the production of some of these regions and even to
compete directly with the Spanish commercial network. In this chapter we
attempt to establish the most important parameters of the political and social
economy of cacao in the period between the first Spanish contact and the final
conquest of the Itza.

The Nature of *Theobroma cacao* as a Traditional Crop

The cultivation of *Theobroma cacao* demands a high degree of care and labor as
well as agricultural knowledge and skills. A small broad-leafed understory tree,

it needs shade and minimal fluctuations in climate (see McNeil, Chapter 1, this volume). Cacao's sensitivity to environmental conditions limited its production and ensured its place as a precious commodity in Maya culture.

Cacaotales or pakaloob

Orchard-gardens (*solares* or the Maya *pak che col*) are small-scale agrosylvicultural systems with highly diverse floral and faunal composition (Barrera Marín 1980; Torquebiau 1992). In them, we find numerous trees, shrubs, and herbaceous plants with multiple uses, which are integrated in close interaction with other plants and animals. The orchard-gardens are located near or around the homes of traditional Maya farmers (Barrera Marín 1980). Among the more interesting characteristics of this agroecosystem are its resilience and basic structure: the productivity of the *solar* can be intensified or reduced without changing the basic structural composition provided by the tree species, ensuring agricultural flexibility and lowering risks for the traditional Maya farmer.

In the Manche Ch'ol region in the sixteenth and seventeenth centuries, there were tree orchards known in Choltí as *pakab* and in Yukatek as *pakal*.[4] These were extensive orchards where the Manche Ch'ol tended *cacaotales*, annatto trees, and vanilla orchids. The basic differences between the actual *pak che col* and the historic *pakab* were the extent of the groves, and the specialization of their production, transforming them into true plantations.

In the Chontalpa region of Tabasco, Mexico, traditional farmers (Chontal Maya and *mestizo*) have planted and tended *cacaotales* since pre-Hispanic times. The traditional *pakaloob* or *cacaotales* were originally established on high grounds, beginning with the felling of the forest. The *cacaotal* is, in the Chontalpa, a multicropping agroecological system (Gliessman 1998) which produces many staples and natural resources; nevertheless, *cacaotales* are intensified tree-gardens, with a high density of individual trees (625 cacao trees per hectare). The cacao harvest begins three or four years after the *cacaotal* is established, and it lasts for about thirty to forty years. The average production of cacao in the Chontalpa today is 410 kg/ha. (Córdoba-Avalos et al. 2001). The variation in productivity is high, both at the level of the *cacaotales* and at the level of individual trees.

Today the Itza recognize and manage complex agroforestry systems, including the *pakal*. In their southern settlements, the Itza plant various types of cacao (*cacau*), which are described by fruit color: *Ix kan* 'yellow,' *ix sac* 'white,' *ix chak* 'red,' *ix box* 'black,' and *ix morado* 'purple' (Atran 1993:670). Its natural fragility and the need for deep fertile soils make the cacao tree a difficult and demanding crop, especially in the conditions of the central Peten area; intensification of production in the form of plantations combined with fluctuating agricultural conditions increases the possibilities of failure.

In the Maya area, higher levels of cacao production are circumscribed to the fertile alluvial soils of the river systems. Such conditions are found northwest of the Peten in the district of Chontalpa, province of Tabasco. This area was formerly the most important cacao-producing region in the Gulf of Mexico, and it maintained its importance well after the Conquest (West, Psuty, and Thom 1969).

The Central Peten Region

William Rathje (1972) has proposed that the central Peten ancient Maya sites formed a dynamic core which played a key role in the development of long-distance exchange networks. The synergy produced by this exchange established the conditions for the flourishing of the Classic Maya polities. Tribute and trade as well as raiding, looting, and direct capture (of places, goods, and people) are among the possible exchange mechanisms now being addressed to explain the political economy of the ancient Maya polities. Exchange and procurement of prestige goods relied on the circulation of scarce or difficult to obtain products which are conspicuously consumed, paraded, and utilized only by the elite to demonstrate social status and power (Friedman and Rowlands 1978; Blanton et al. 1996). The production, exchange, circulation, and transfer of prestige goods, given the power status disparity between the core and the periphery, generate high competition, as well as conflict, between polities and thus foster a differential degree of participation in the luxury goods exchange networks (McAnany et al. 2002:126–128).

Cacao does not grow well in the Peten central district, although it can be found in some home gardens or as an unusual tree in the *pakal*, or tree orchards, of the present-day Itza. Cacao and *cacaotales* can, however, be established in the deep and fertile soils of the neighboring rivers that radiate from the lake district, such as the Usumacinta and Pasión-Salinas, the Belize river systems, the Polochic-Lake Izabal, and the not too distant Sula River in Honduras.

Vases, Chocolate, and Political Power Among the Itza

The Itza are a Maya group whose place of origin seems to have been in the Peten, Guatemala (Boot 1997a:165–187). Stuart (this volume) proposes that the earliest vessels bearing cacao glyphs come from this area. Glyph-bearing vessels appear in the central Peten region near the very beginnings of the Early Classic period, probably no later than 250 A.D. (Coggins 1975; Stuart, this volume). There are inscribed and painted glyphic texts on Peten monuments and ceram-

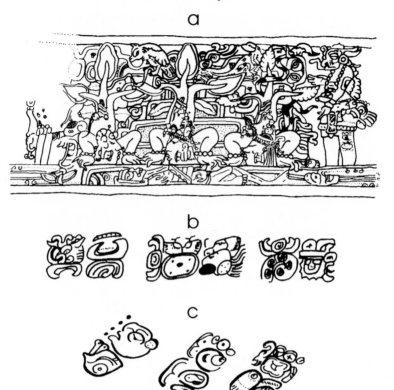

Figure 14.1. Maya tripod vessel (K6547). Early Classic period. a. Lord "Son of Itza" reborn as a cacao tree sprouting at the base of a tomb in a temple-pyramid. b. Glyphic phrase on K6547, 'His vase to drink cacao, name ?, son of Ahau-Itza.' c. Nominal phrase, vase K4787, 'Can Ek, his art his station (Atelier?) Sacred Ahau of Ucanal, Bacab.' Drawings by Mario Aliphat F.

ics from the Classic period with the nominal phrase of Canek and the title Itza Ahau (Figure 14.1).

These texts come from different sites in the Peten, including Seibal, Ucanal, and Motul de San José, and we find them later in the inscriptions at Chichen Itza, Yucatan, Mexico (Boot 1997b:5–21; Schele and Mathews 1998:187). The name Canek belongs to the last noble lineage that ruled the Itza Maya until the Spanish conquest of Tah Itza in 1697. Apparently, the Itza fled the Peten region during the Late Classic period (700–900 A.D.), when wars were escalating among the principal Maya polities (Tikal, Caracol, and Calakmul) and took refuge in the northeastern part of the Yucatan, where they founded Chichen Itza (Boot 1997a:178–179; Schele and Mathews 1998:201–204). Evidence indicates that the Canek dynasty had ruled the Itza since Katun 8 Ahau

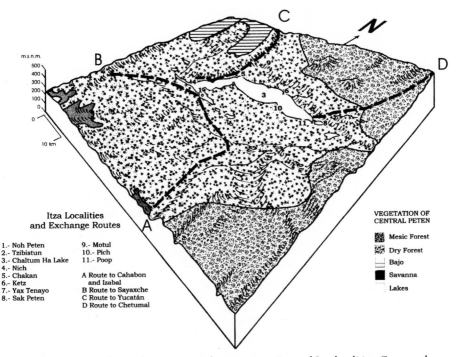

Figure 14.2. Map of central Itza territory showing vegetation and Itza localities. Cartography by Mario Aliphat F. based on Caso Barrera (2002) and G. E. Jones (1998).

(1204–1224), when they left Chichen Itza (1250 A.D.), establishing themselves at Lake Peten and founding the city of Noh Peten (AGI, Guatemala 151 bis, f. 539 v) (Figure 14.2).[5] In glyphic texts we find the nominal phrase Canek in nine registers in vases and monuments, showing the long and deep history of this governing lineage (see Figure 14.1c).

The political structure and the territory of the Itza were tightly bound to their religion and cosmogony. The center of their political organization was Ahau Canek, who acted as *primus inter pares* (first among equals). At his side in the government was the principal priest, Ah Kin Canek, who also played an important political role. These two men represent the apex of political power; below them were four kings (*ahauoob*); below these, there were four other principals (*halach uinicoob*); and below all of them were numerous other chiefs and captains that ruled the towns (AGI, Escribanía 339 A, f. 39v).[6]

The Itza territory, or Tah Itza, appears to adapt to the same cosmogonic quadripartite pattern shown in its political organization. The central point was the principal island of Noh Peten (Figure 14.2) which was considered sacred. Then the territory was divided into four *parcialidades* which corresponded to the four principal lineages: Canek, Pana, Couoh, and Tut. Noh Peten was the political and religious capital, where Canek, Ah Kin Canek, and the four *ahauoob* resided and where rituals and sacrifices took place. The island, too, was divided into four quarters. The residence of Canek represented the center point and was where the image of Yax Chel Cab, or the *axis mundi*, which marks the center of the universe, was venerated. There were twenty-two Itza subdivisions, each one ruled by a principal (Caso Barrera 2002:217–218).

The Itza Maya capital of Noh Peten was governed by Canek Ahau and a council formed by the twenty-two principals of the city districts. Among the members of this council were the *Halach Uinic* and *Batab*, political and military offices. Documents record fourteen principals bearing the title *Ach Cat*, one with the double title *Ach Cat-Halach Uinic*, two received the title *Noh Dzocan*, another two had the title *Noh*, and one had the title *Dzocan*. Only one individual received the title *Ah Ch'atan* (Caso Barrera and Aliphat 2002). The title *Ach Cat* stands out among the others because it has not been reported in the pre-Hispanic political organization of the Yukatek Maya and thus appears unique to the Peten Itza. According to Grant Jones (1998:87–88, 100–103), this title comes from the Nahuatl title *achcauhtli*, which means 'elder brothers,' a term that was used for individuals in political and military office among the Mexica (Aztecs). We analyzed the word *Ach* from cognate terms in other Maya languages: in Quiche and Cakchiquel, *Ach* can be translated as 'company,' 'likeness,' and 'kinship' (Ximénez 1985:57). For example, the words *Ach popochi* mean 'captain of war' or 'principal.'[7] When we analyze the meaning of the components of this term, we find that it refers to those who were companions of the mat (*pop*), or those who shared the mat. *Hach* in Yukatek Maya means 'something truthful,' and it is also used as a superlative (Barrera Vásquez 1980:166–167). There is another important example of a word that has been analyzed using Cakchiquel and Yukatek Maya: the word *itza*, that Barrera Vásquez divided into *itz*, translating it from the Cakchiquel as *brujo* or *uay* and *ha* that in Yukatek means 'water,' obtaining the final meaning for *itza* as 'the sorcerer of water' (Barrera Vásquez 1980:271). This translation has proven to be accurate, since from ethnohistorical sources we know that the Itzas considered themselves sorcerers or *uayoob* (Caso Barrera 2002:234). Returning to the title *Ach Cat*, we know that Avendaño wrote *Cat* but it should have been *K'at*.[8] We translated this word from the Yukatek, meaning "a vase or drinking vessel made of clay" (Barrera Vásquez 1980:383). *Ach K'at* could then mean 'Those who shared the vase' or 'Companions of vase.' This would mean that holders of this title were 'Principals of the Vase' or 'Nobility of the Vase.' Perhaps *Ach Kat* was an honorary title or office given to certain individuals who had achieved a high rank in the political organization. The importance of this title can be attested to by the great importance of drinking vessels in the Maya area since the Classic period and the ritual significance of the act of drinking chocolate for the Maya (S. D. Coe and M. D. Coe 1999; Reents-Budet, this volume; J. E. S. Thompson 1956).

Houston, Stuart, and Taube (1992) state that these drinking vessels for cacao were part of the gifts that the elite exchanged during important celebrations in the Classic period. Gifts sealed alliances and corroborated agreements among the rulers of the principal polities and those subordinate to them (Houston, Stuart, and Taube 1992:499–512). These vessels depict palace scenes of lords meeting other lords and noblemen and being served chocolate and food in richly painted pottery (Reents-Budet 1994d:253–264; D. Tedlock 2002:168). Dennis Tedlock (2002:168–169), has proposed that some palace scenes could represent betrothal arrangements, established with feasting and the drinking of cacao.

For the Mexica, the consumption of cacao was also restricted to the principals and nobility. They gave great banquets where they exchanged gifts, especially of cacao pods or beverages. Some of the most spectacular Mexica banquets, were those celebrating the installation of a new king (*tlatoani*). During such feasts the members of the high-ranking nobility exchanged gifts such as jewelry, feather adornments, pipes full of tobacco, and *cargas* of cacao. They also served different kinds of food and cacao in finely carved calabashes (Durand-Forest 1967:167–168). The Mexica *tlatoani* received his allies with banquets and cacao beverages, and he offered them cacao, flowers, and perfumes. Mexica weddings were celebrated with food and drinks like *cacaupinolli*, a beverage made from ground cacao and maize (Durand-Forest 1967:168–169).

Landa states that among the Yukatek Maya there were festivities where the principals would drink cacao and give each other vases of great beauty:

> And they have two ways of celebrating these feasts, the first, which is that of the nobles and of the principal people, obliges each one of the invited guests to give another similar feast. And to each guest they give a roasted fowl, bread and drink of cacao in abundance, and at the end of the repast, they were accustomed to give a *manta* to each to wear and a little stand and vessel, as beautiful as possible. (Landa 1941 [1566]:92)

In 1557, fifteen years after the conquest of Yucatan by the Spaniards, a meeting was held which brought together the *Halach Uinic* of the Xiu, don Francisco de Montejo, as well as the governors and principals of the provinces of Ah Canul, Hocaba, Chakan, and Sotuta with whom they had constant disputes over territorial limits. This meeting was to establish and ratify the boundaries of the Xiu towns with those of the other provinces. The *Halach Uinic* and the other principals met at the town of Mani to testify to the demarcation of the limits in dispute. Francisco de Montejo Xiu, as a host, gave the lords from the visiting provinces gifts such as five four-hundred *cargas* of cacao, five cotton mantles, a string of precious red stones as long as one's arm, and five strings of precious green stones. These gifts were presented by the *Ah Kulels*, officers at the command of the *Halach Uinic* (Morley and Roys 1941:623–625). The precious red and green stones as well as cacao, were gifts that only members of the nobility and ruling classes could exchange in a strict protocol. Apart from the gifts, the lords consumed three *arrobas* of *ci´* while they conferred and deliberated.[9] López de Cogolludo (1971, v. 1:236) also states that when members of the Yukatek nobility sold slaves or cacao groves, the deal was sealed by drinking in front of witnesses. These two testimonies confirm that the act of drinking and eating among the Maya nobility was a way of sealing social and political agreements and business transactions.

We can conclude then, that drinking vessels were important symbols of power and status among the Maya and particularly among the Itza, and that ritual drinking was a way to conduct negotiations and seal alliances among principals. In this context the *Ach K'at* title embodies the relationship between a ritual object (drinking vessel) and the participation of an elite individual in a government council. This ruling body was formed by a *Halach Uinic* and a *Batab*, probably acting as government and military advisors to Canek, the *Ah Ch'atan* or principal advisor, who likely conducted negotiations, and the *Noh Dzocan*, who would have enforced agreements.

In 1696, Fray Andres de Avendaño arrived in Noh Peten to try to convince Ahau Canek and his subjects that the time had arrived in which their prophecies stated "that the Itza and the Spaniard should drink from the same calabash and eat from the same plate, as a sign that they were brothers" (Avendaño 1696:35v). Avendaño's statement demonstrates his familiarity with the Maya metaphor of negotiation. The friar tried to accomplish the surrender of the Itza by using the symbolism of drinking and eating together. In reply, one of their leaders told Avendaño that it was a much better idea that the Itza should leave the Peten to go back to Yucatan with the Spaniards, so that they could lay claim to the government and territory of Yucatan that belonged originally to their ancestors.

Cacao: Trade and War

Cacao was an extremely important commodity for the Itza Maya. They not only consumed it as chocolate, or *zaca*, a ritual beverage, during meetings of the governing elite, but they also used it as a means of exchange to obtain important products such as salt and metal tools.[10] Peten lands are not good for the cultivation of cacao. When Hernán Cortés passed through Itza territory in

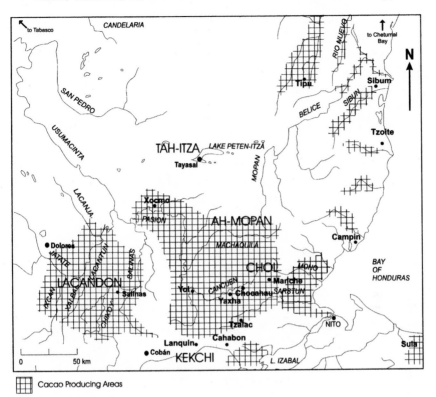

Figure 14.3. Map of cacao-producing areas in the Southern Maya Lowlands. Cartography by Mario Aliphat F. based on AGI, Guatemala 67,179, 181; Bergmann (1969); Caso Barrera (2002); and G. E. Jones (1989).

1525, Ahau Canek told him that he had some cacao orchards near Nito (Figure 14.3), because those lands were very good for cacao cultivation, which reinforces the idea that Peten lands were poor for *cacaotales* development (Cortés 1981:242–244).[11]

Before the arrival of the Spaniards there was a commercial route under the control of the Itza, who had established commercial posts and resting places running southeast through their territory to Nito, an important trading center. The Maya Chontal from Acalan also had economic interests in Nito and made part of their journey toward this city by sea and land. Cortés mentions Tenciz, a port controlled by the Itza, where river traders disembarked to continue their journey by land (Cortés 1981:242–244). Nito was an important port of trade where merchants from different areas came to exchange goods. In this settlement there were *barrios* with people from distant provinces such as Acalan. The Chontal *barrio* was controlled by the brother of Paxbolon, the ruler of the Acalan. The Chontal from Acalan produced cacao, which they traded along with other products such as feathers, jaguar pelts, slaves, and tortoiseshell spoons used to sip the froth from chocolate (Scholes and Roys 1968:29–30).

The important maritime trading activity conducted by the Chontal Acalans ceased with the Spanish conquest. When the Chontal commercial activities declined, the Itza became the rulers of a new trading network among the *encomienda* towns of Yucatan, the fugitive towns, the Manche Ch'ol, the Lacandons, and the Mopans as well as with the *encomienda* towns of Verapaz (Caso Barrera 2002:231; G. D. Jones 1989:104) (see Figures 14.2 and 14.3).[12] The products over which the Itza most wanted to exert control were cacao, vanilla, and achiote. These last two were used as flavorings for cacao beverages. The Maya commercial activities were undertaken by merchants called *ah yikales*, which in Yukatek means 'rich man,' 'powerful,' and 'principal' (Ciudad Real 2001:296). The word *ikal* means 'to sort the raging sea and wind' (Ciudad Real 2001:306), which suggests that the *ah yikaloob* must have been long-distance traders using maritime routes. After the Conquest these merchants must have found it very difficult to conduct their commercial activities. It is obvious that the merchants belonged to the nobility; one of the first *ah yikal* to be known by the Spaniards was a principal named Yum Be, whose canoe and belongings, including cacao seeds, were taken by Columbus (Colón 2003:285).[13] In Yukatek, the word *ah p'olom* means 'trader, the person who buys and sells' (Ciudad Real 2001:512). We suppose that this appellation refers to merchants who were commoners. The Manche Ch'ol have the same terms for these two different kinds of dealers; *aical* is translated as 'rich man,' and *ah polon* or *ah chon* are the words for 'traders' (Morán 1695). Among the Itza, the lineage and *parcialidad* of the Pana held the title *ah yikal*. It seems that the members of this *parcialidad* were in control of the commercial network of the Itza kingdom (AGI, Guatemala 151 bis, f. 125).

The Mopan Maya were part of the Itza polity and were closely related to the Pana. They had some degree of autonomy and even moved to a territory near the Manche Ch'ol (see Figure 14.3), with whom they had close relations and commerce, becoming middlemen between that group and the Manche Ch'ol. The Mopan lands were good for cacao and achiote cultivation, and the Mopan were able to supply the Itza with these products (Caso Barrera 2002:303). Another *parcialidad* Itza was that of the Xocmoes, who also strived for more autonomy from the Itza kingdom as well as for fertile lands where they could grow cacao, but unlike the Mopan/Itza relationship, in time the Xocmoes became bitter enemies to the Itza (Villagutierre y Sotomayor 1933:380). Fray Gabriel de Salazar stated in 1620 that the Xocmo speak the *ah itza achi*, or Itza language (AGI, Guatemala 181). The same friar wrote that the Xocmoes had towns and cacao orchards near the Manche Ch'ol town of Yol. This town was established at the margins of the Cancuen River but had to be abandoned because of constant attacks from the Lacandon Maya.[14] The Xocmoes then moved to a new location near the Xocmo River, or Icbolay River (see Figure 14.3). At their new town, they continued to trade with the Manche Ch'ol and even with the *encomienda* towns of Verapaz, exchanging cacao and achiote for axes and machetes (AGI, Guatemala 67, f.27) (see Figure 14.3). Factionalism inside the Itza kingdom developed over the need to obtain cacao and achiote, demonstrating the importance of these valuable resources.

The Itza were attracted to the sphere of power and trade of the newly established towns of runaway Indians who had fled the northern *encomienda* towns of Yucatan and settled close to Itza territory. These towns provided the Itza with important products such as metal tools, and salt, which were exchanged for cotton mantles, honey, wax, and dyes (Caso Barrera 2002; Farriss 1984; G. D. Jones 1989). The *encomienda* town of Tipu became an attractive place for Maya nobles fleeing the Colonial authorities, as in the case of a *maestro de capilla*, 'choirmaster,' who left the town of Hecelchakan accused of idolatry and took refuge in Tipu, where he became rich and successful by planting eight thousand cacao trees. Tipu had been a cacao-, achiote-, and vanilla-producing town since pre-Hispanic times, becoming a strategic economic and political center for the Itza. Friar Fuensalida stated in 1618 that the people of Tipu were wealthy because they raised great quantities of cacao (López de Cogolludo 1971, v. 2:219–220). Twelve leagues from Tipu was the town of Lucu, where the friars Orbita and Fuensalida found that they "have the best achiote of all New Spain as well as thick cacao, that was red and of very good taste as well as vanillas called *cizbiques* that were very good and fragrant for chocolate" (López de Cogolludo 1971, v. 2:215). Lucu was also considered very wealthy because of its many cacao groves at the margins of the Belize River. This suggests that the indigenous populations of the riverine settlements of the province of Bacalar supplied cacao and the principal products for chocolate-making to the Itza as well as to the principals and nobility of northern Yucatan. Apart from its economic importance, the Itza considered Tipu a key location because the Spaniards tried to enter their territory several times through this town. The Itza exerted constant pressure on the rulers of Tipu, and even threatened them, until the rulers rebelled against Spanish domination in 1638 (Caso Barrera 2002; G. D. Jones 1989, 1998). After this, the Itza finally secured political and economic control over this important town and cacao-producing region.

Another important area which supplied the Itza with cacao and achiote was the Pasíon-Machaquila River Basin in the southern part of the Peten. This region was inhabited by the Manche Ch'ol, the Mopan, the Lacandon (see Figure 14.3), the Xocmo, and the Ah Xoy; the last were Indian fugitives from the town of Coban. The only source of salt in northern Guatemala is Salinas de Los Nueve Cerros (*Bolon Uitz*). The Itza fought the Lacandon constantly to control this natural resource, until finally they exerted effective domination over it (Caso Barrera 2002:231). Being in charge of this vital resource gave the Itza the means to exert pressure on the Manche Ch'ol and Lacandon populations, imposing on them the exchange of salt for cacao, achiote, and vanilla. The cacao groves of the Manche Ch'ol were situated in the fertile lands of the river valleys, with the waterways used as means of communication and bulk transportation. The Manche Ch'ol towns were in the southern arch that links the Pasíon-Machaquila River to southern Belize, and to the lower part of the Polochic River, to the region surrounding Lake Izabal. Their territory was adjacent to that of the Mopan, Lacandon, and Xocmo.

Apparently, the Manche Ch'ol had small *milpas* and concentrated on the production of their cacao, achiote, and vanilla plantations, which each required intensive specialized work and care (AGI, Guatemala 67, 181). The Manche Ch'ol had two achiote (*quivi* in Choltí) crops a year; the summer crop was called *yaxkinil quivi*, and the winter crop was called *zutzil quivi*. They also cultivated vanilla, which they called *chisibic*, and a kind of "big cacao" called *uaal cab* (Morán 1695). The documentary sources do not provide information about the type of tenure arrangement of these plantations, but like Millon (1955b:698–712) we suppose that they were private holdings belonging to the nobility or elite. As we have mentioned, among the Yukateks and the Itza the cacao orchards belonged to the principals and the nobility, and it is highly probable that this was the case for the Manche Ch'ol. The Choltí words *haatz hitzimbil* seem to confirm that certain trees were private property, since they mean 'forbidden tree.' The word *haatz* in Yukatek means 'property, something that can be divided as an inheritance' (Barrera Vásquez 1980:182). In Choltí the word *haatz* means 'tree,' and *hitzil* and *hitzimbil* signify 'forbidden' (Morán 1695).

Production in these *cacaotales* seems to have been of high quality and of great quantity, as the Manche Ch'ol had to provide cacao and achiote not only to the Itza, but also to the *encomienda* towns of Coban and Cahabon. The Spaniards required these two towns to pay their tributes and *repartimientos* in cacao and achiote, which they obtained by trading metal tools such as axes and machetes with the Manche Ch'ol (AGI Guatemala 67. 181). The friar Francisco Gallegos stated in 1676:

> The neighboring catholic Indians [to the Manche Ch'ol] considered these mountains as their Indies (colonies), where they obtain great profit by means of cacao and of thirty six thousand pounds in achiote that come

from Verapaz and Castillo, and having the Indians of Verapaz very few or none achiote trees. (Gallegos 1676:3)[15]

The Manche Ch'ol also traded cacao, achiote, and metal tools, with the Itza, receiving in exchange salt, dyes, cotton textiles, and clothing (AGI, Guatemala 181). In the beginning of the seventeenth century the Itza had commercial relationships with the Manche Ch'ol, who had important traders, or *ah yikaloob*. These merchants transported their goods in canoes until they reached the Itza-controlled port of Tzibistun, where they disembarked (AGI, Guatemala 67, f. 19) (see Figure 14.1):

> All the Manche Indians, particularly the elderly know the language of Ah Itza and to this town [of the Itza] and that of Xocolo which is near Santo Domingo [Yol] going down the river, is where they sent all their merchandise. In the town of Santa Cruz Yaxcoc, there is a powerful Indian trader, relative of the *cacique* named Coatzum and he transports all the cargoes which he trades not with the Christians, because he has already bartered with them when they arrive at this point, but with five infidel towns [Itza towns]. (AGI Guatemala 67, f. 16)

In 1630 the Spaniards were trying to reduce the threat that the Manche Ch'ol and the Lacandon represented to the already Christianized Maya towns in Chiapas, Mexico, and in Guatemala. To attain this goal the Dominican Order sent friars to evangelize them. They intended to establish a Spanish town in the heart of Manche Ch'ol territory. The Itza reacted violently to this action, which was perceived as an imminent threat to their territory. They conducted a surprise attack on the Manche Ch'ol town of San Miguel Manche, killing its rulers and taking three hundred prisoners. The principal governor, Martin Cuc, was sacrificed and his flesh was consumed. As a result of the Itza attack, the Manche Ch'ol towns rebelled against Spanish domination and Christianity, abandoning their new settlements (Tovilla 1960:265). Tovilla wrote:

> The Indians of Manche have continuous wars with those of Ah Itza, but they've always been defeated because they are so few and the Ah Itza so many. Most of the years the Itza come in the month of *yaxkin*, which is summer, to take prey, as they did last 1630 when they took more than a hundred people and we expect them to come again this year. After the Ch'ol became Christians they persecuted them even more, because they border their territory and the Itza do not want the Ch'ol to show the Spaniards the way, fearing they will be punished for all their wrongdoing and wickedness. (Tovilla 1960:185)

Other Colonial Guatemalan documents echo the same story:

> The Ch'ol Indians are docile and easy to reduce, but deep into the forests
> there is another nation called Ah Itza. They are rebellious and go hunt-
> ing for human flesh to eat. They are opposed to receiving Holy baptism
> and they don't want the neighboring Ch'ol to receive it either. (AGI,
> Guatemala 179)

The Itza managed by decisive actions to secure their borders for a few more
years. By means of war and violence, they took control of the cacao and achiote
production and forced compulsive trade on their neighbors. The Itza raided
Manche Ch'ol and Lacandon towns, taking slaves and victims for human sacrifice, actions showing a strong correlation between the quest for controlling
cacao-producing towns and the acts of war and sacrifice (Caso Barrera 2002).

In 1695 when the Spaniards conquered the Lacandon town of Sac Balam,
the Lacandon denied having any commercial ties or communication with the
Itza to avoid taking the Spaniards into the Itza territory (AGI, Guatemala 152,
f. 898v). The Spaniards soon realized this was a lie, because there was a road
from the Itza town of Saclemacal to Manche territory, used by Lacandon and
Manche Ch'ol traders, Kekchí people from Coban and San Agustin Lanquín,
and people from Sacapulas (AGI, Guatemala 151 bis, f. 128v). All these peoples
gathered at a meeting place, which seems to be what Fray Francisco Gallegos
called in 1676 "*feria del achiote*" (Gallegos 1676:7).[16] This trading took place
near the town of the Ah Xoy, a town of Kekchí fugitives from Coban, who
traded with both the Manche Ch'ol and the people from the *encomienda* towns.
Gallegos also stated that the Indians of Coban sold young men and women
to the Ah Xoy in exchange for achiote (Gallegos 1676). After cacao, achiote
was the second most important product; this was also true for the Itza and
the *encomienda* towns. Friar Francisco Morán wrote that in 1626 one Manche
Ch'ol town produced two thousand pounds of achiote worth $1700 pesos. This
provides some idea of the importance of this product, which was used as a dye
and a flavoring for cacao and other foods (AGI, Guatemala 181).

Despite all their efforts, bravery, and acts of war, the Itza were unable to stop
the advance of the Spaniards. As early as 1630, the Spanish had been attempting
to pacify and reduce the Manche Ch'ol, finally achieving their goal in 1689.[17]
With the aid of Cahabon Indians, they rounded up and resettled the Manche
Ch'ol near Rabinal in the Urran Valley (Ximénez 1973, v. 5:281, 462–465).
The Spaniards knew that if the Manche Ch'ol stayed in their territory, they
would flee their towns once again. It was decided to remove them all to the
Guatemalan Highlands, an act which caused the annihilation of the Manche
Ch'ol (Ximénez 1971, v. 7:220). In 1695 the Lacandon were also finally con-

quered and removed from their place of origin (Ximénez 1973, v. 5:446–447; de Vos 1980:190–211). As a result of these actions the entire Manche Ch'ol and Lacandon populations disappeared and with them the prosperous production of cacao, achiote, and vanilla of their fertile valleys. From this moment on, the brisk cacao trade ceased to exist, and the trading network controlled by the Itza collapsed. In 1697, Martín de Ursúa took possession of the Itza capital city of Noh Peten, marking the end of the last Maya kingdom.

Discussion

Theobroma cacao is a difficult and unpredictable crop which grows only in favored places. The ecological adaptations of *T. cacao* to the tropical rainforest ecosystem fill a special ecological niche, which has ensured natural limitations to the potential distribution of this tree. Cacao does not grow well in the Peten central region. The genetic flexibility of cacao varieties at the local level provides the potential for cacao production in some ideal and localized habitats. Nevertheless, cacao production from an agricultural point of view is low and dispersed. In pre-Columbian and Colonial Mesoamerica, cacao production regions were established where the local conditions were optimal, including La Chontalpa, Chetumal, the Belize River valleys, the Pasíon-Salinas river system, the Izabal region, and the Sula Valley.

The Itza territory had specific natural resources such as fertile lands that produced maize, cotton, dyes, and some *pataxte* (*T. bicolor*), achiote, vanilla, and cacao. These last three products were of extreme importance for the Itza, but Itza lands were not well suited for large-scale production of these crops. Local demands for these commodities were greater than the limited local production. The need to have access to these valuable resources made the Itza resort to trade, raiding, and control of the cacao-producing areas. Itza political hierarchy consumed and demanded vast quantities of ritual beverages made with cacao and flavored with achiote and vanilla. The *Ach K'at* (lords of the vessel), together with Ahau Canek and Ah Kin Canek, celebrated their assemblies and accords by drinking flavored cacao.

In the late Postclassic period, just before the arrival of the Spaniards, the Itza traded cotton textiles and dyes with the Chontal of Acalan for cacao and other sumptuous commodities. After the Spanish conquest of Yucatan and Guatemala, the Itza became the leaders of a new trading network between the *encomienda* towns of Yucatan, the fugitive towns, the Manche Ch'ol, Lacandon, and Mopan, and the *encomienda* towns of Verapaz. In the *encomienda* towns from the Bacalar district, such as Tipu, the Itza acquired access to cacao, achiote, and vanilla as well as metal tools, which these towns obtained through exchange with the *encomienda* towns of northern Yucatan. To the south, the Itza also traded with the Manche Ch'ol and the Mopan, this last group becoming their middlemen with the Manche Ch'ol. The principal products of this commerce were cacao and achiote, but the Manche Ch'ol also supplied the Itza with metal tools, which were obtained by trading with the *encomienda* towns of Verapaz. In the meantime the Itza were constantly fighting with the Lacandon for the control of another valuable resource: salt. The only source of this mineral in the greater Peten region is Salinas de los Nueve Cerros. This was an extremely important product, and it was used by the Itza as an exchange good for cacao and achiote.

Conclusion

The Spaniards tried throughout the seventeenth century to stop the threat that the Itza polity represented by efforts to control the borders of their dominions and by relocating and Christianizing the "infidel" Indian populations, especially the Manche Ch'ol. Facing the imminent risk of the Spaniard advance toward their territory, the Itza decided to promote rebellions against the Spaniards among the *encomienda* towns of Bacalar. In 1630 they also attacked the Manche Ch'ol towns that had been reduced and Christianized, forcing them to abandon their towns and to rise up against the Spaniards. From this moment, the Itza imposed a compulsive form of trade with the towns in Bacalar as well as among the settlements of the Manche Ch'ol and the Lacandon. The archival sources do not supply information on the possible tribute paid by these populations to the Itza king—it seems that the Itza compelled only these towns to trade with them. The Itza control over valuable resources was highly correlated with the traffic of slaves, victims for human sacrifices, and war. Finally, this complex network of production, social relations, and commerce under the control of the Itza polity came to an end with the Conquest. The Spaniards were unable to reestablish the production of cacao, achiote, cotton, salt, and natural dyes because they removed the Manche Ch'ol and the Lacandon populations from their places of origin causing their annihilation. The extinction of these Maya populations marked the total destruction of the specialized cacao production endemic to this region.

Acknowledgments

We would like to thank the National Council of Science and Technology-Mexico for providing major financial support through the Project "Relaciones entre Mayas de Yucatan, El Peten y La Verapaz siglos 17–19" (Relationships among the Maya of Yucatan, Peten and Verapaz, 17–19 c.). Laura Caso Barrera had the support of the American Philosophical Society, through the Mellon Resident Research Fellowship, to carry out basic research for this chapter at their collections in Philadelphia. We would also like to thank Cameron McNeil for inviting us to participate in this book and for her careful editorial work. Finally, we want to express our thanks to the reviewers of this chapter. Their comments are graciously acknowledged.

Notes

1. For the Manche Ch'ol, cacao, achiote, and vanilla form a triad of cultivated plants such as the maize-beans-squash complex common to all Mesoamerican peoples.

2. *Parcialidades* are wards, political and territorial subdivisions of a district, town, or province.

3. *Pakal* is property where things are planted (Barrera Vásquez 1980:625).

4. We use the term Manche Ch'ol to refer to the Choltí-speaking people (according to Morán 1695) that occupied the southern crescent of the Peten. This population is not related to the Ch'oles living in Chiapas and Tabasco today.

5. When the Spaniards asked Canek if his kingdom had been inherited by his ancestors, he said yes, since his ancestors left Chichen Itza they and their descendants had been granted this kingdom.

6. The original document states in Spanish: "Debajo de ellos se encontraban cuatro reyes y otros cuatro principales. Por debajo de los reyezuelos y caciques habían capataces, capitanes y cabezas."

7. The definition of *Ach popochi* in the Tesoro states: "significa el capitán y todo junto, el hombre que es compañero en asiento o trono, para que cuando empezarán y nombrarán capitanes para la guerra les dieran preeminencia a tener entre los demás señores" (Ximénez 1985:58).

8. Probably Avendaño misspelled the term *Cat*, or he simply didn't glottalize the C'.

9. *Ci'* is the Yukatek Maya word that appears in the original document; it is translated as *balché*, or wine.

10. *Zaca* was considered a "good beverage" or chocolate made of cacao, maize, and achiote. It is also defined as froth (Morán 1695:89–91).

11. Nito was a Manche Ch'ol town on Amatique Bay, near Lake Izabal (Golfo Dulce).

12. Fugitive towns were new settlements established by runaway Yukatek or Kekchí Mayas from *encomienda* towns who fled from Spanish domination to unconquered regions.

13. Yum Be, is the first Maya name or title known in Spanish. Its translation could be 'lord of the road.'

14. The Lacandon were a Choltí-speaking population, who, before the Conquest lived near Lago Miramar (Chiapas) on an island called Lacam Tun. At the end of the sixteenth century they were forced by the Spaniards to flee this town, and they estab-

lished their new capital at Sac Balam near the Lacatun River (Guatemala). This Maya group resisted Spanish domination until 1695, when they were finally subjugated. Some years later the entire Lacandon population disappeared because of diseases and forced removal from their homeland. For more information on the Lacandon see Jan de Vos (1980).

15. The Spanish documents were translated into English by Laura Caso Barrera.

16. By the term *feria del achiote*, Gallegos refers to a marketplace where achiote was traded by the Itza, Manche Ch'ol, Lacandon, and even people from the *encomienda* towns mentioned above.

17. To reduce the Indian population was to congregate them in a new settlement under Spanish control.

Cacao Production, Tribute, and Wealth in Sixteenth-Century Izalcos, El Salvador

William R. Fowler

The role of cacao as a luxury item and as money in the pre-Columbian Me-soamerican world is widely recognized (Bergmann 1969; Millon 1955a). As a luxury item, its use probably can be traced to the time of Initial and Early Formative village agricultural societies, dating to as early as 2000 B.C. (Evans 2004:107, 112). Consumption of cacao beverages is thought to be attested to archaeologically in the Maya Lowlands by the widespread distribution of a distinctive form of spouted vessel that occurs in Middle Formative (1000–400 B.C.) and Late Formative (400 B.C.–A.D. 250) ceramic assemblages and by the presence of cacao residue in some of these vessels (Hurst et al. 2002; Powis et al. 2002). This same vessel form also occurs in Chalchuapa, western El Sal-vador, in Middle Formative contexts (Sharer 1978:19, 23, 145, 151). Dating to several centuries later, the macrobotanical remains of a cacao tree, pods, fruit, and seeds have been recovered in excavations at Joya de Ceren; entombed by a massive volcanic eruption at around A.D. 600, these remains demonstrate cacao cultivation in the Zapotitán Valley of west-central El Salvador (Gerstle and Sheets 2002:79; Lentz 1996; Lentz and Ramírez-Sosa 2002; Sheets and Woodward 2002:191). Spanish tribute assessments dating to 1532 and 1548–51 indicate that cacao was still produced in this region in the early to mid-six-teenth century, and the same documents indicate a prodigious level of produc-tion in the Izalcos region of western El Salvador, some 25 km west-southwest of Joya de Ceren (W. R. Fowler 1989a:159–169) (Figure 15.1).

The origin of the use of cacao as money in Mesoamerica is connected with long-distance trade, marketplace exchange, and the need for formalized media of exchange. These phenomena are associated, in turn, with the emergence of the state, urbanism, and stratified society, which were in place by the Middle to Late Formative (Evans 2004:194). By the time of the Conquest, the use of

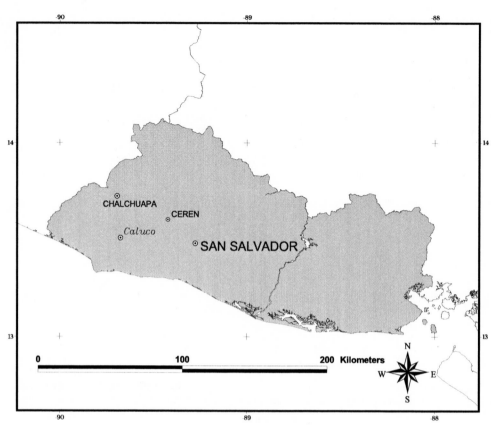

Figure 15.1. Map of El Salvador. Map by Francisco Estrada-Belli based on data distributed by the National Aeronautics and Space Administration (http://servir.nsstc.nasa.gov, 2004).

cacao as money was widespread in Mesoamerica, from Central Mexico to Yucatan, and south as far as Nicaragua (Berdan et al. 2003:102). The Nahua Pipils of the Izalcos region were clearly full participants in these patterns.

Izalcos and Cacao

One of the richest and most renowned areas of the Spanish Colonial empire in the sixteenth century was the Izalcos region, in the valley of the Río Ceniza of western El Salvador. Its famed wealth was based on its exceptional production of cacao, the most important cash crop of early Colonial Central America (W. R. Fowler 1987, 1995; M. J. MacLeod 1973:Chapter 5). In his classic dissertation, René Millon (1955a:72) cautiously suggested that the Izalcos had been an important region of pre-Columbian cacao production. And more than three decades ago, John Bergmann (1969:91) pointed out that early tribute records from the sixteenth century provide reliable indications of the distribution of pre-Conquest cacao production in Mesoamerica. Bergmann noted that in the 1548–51 tribute assessment conducted by President Alonso López de Cerrato (AGI AG 128; see Kramer 1994:17, 18, 21; Rodríguez Becerra 1977:94–96, 118–121), Izalcos was second in cacao tribute only to the much more extensive Suchitepequez region of southwestern Guatemala. Thirteen of the fifteen towns of the Izalcos region paid tribute in cacao (W. R. Fowler 1995:21). The most heavily assessed were the four towns known as "los Yçalcos": Izalco, Caluco, Naolingo, and Tacuscalco (Tasaciones de los naturales de las provincias de goathemala . . ., AGI AG 128, ff. 82, 82v., 86, 111v., 1548–51). Both Izalco and Caluco paid 1,000 *xiquipiles* (about 18,000 lb.), Naolingo paid 685 *xiquipiles* (about 12,330 lbs.), and Tacuscalco paid 400 *xiquipiles* (about 7,200 lb.) in cacao tribute each year. (A *xiquipil* was eight thousand cacao "beans"; three *xiquipiles* comprised a *carga*—the amount one man could carry with a tumpline—which weighed about 50 lb.) It is virtually impossible, Bergmann (1969:92–93) reasoned, that such high tribute demands could have been met had these towns not produced cacao before the Conquest (cf. Millon 1955a:72, 117).

Today, as a result of extensive archival research, there is no need to argue or to speculate on the existence of pre-Conquest cacao production in the Izalcos region (W. R. Fowler 1989a:162, 165). Current research has shifted to the use of documentary data for more complete analysis of social and economic issues related to cacao production in sixteenth-century Izalcos. We have also begun to pay more attention to the structure of the local economy in which cacao circulated as money. Cacao was important in sixteenth-century Mexico and Central America not only because it was a highly valued agricultural commodity, the production and exchange of which generated wealth, but also because cacao beans served as coin (Borah and Cook 1958). And although it is widely known that cacao was used in the early Colonial period as a medium of exchange, especially for small transactions (Feldman 1985:86; M. J. MacLeod 1973:68; Rodríguez Becerra 1977:105–106), much research remains to be done on how and why cacao remained an integral part of the early Colonial economy. The principal factors to be considered are the use of cacao as a commodity for paying tribute, the scarcity of coin in small denominations in New Spain, demand for the crop in Mexico, increasing Spanish demand, the passage of the New Laws in 1542 which required that Indian labor be remunerated, and the employment of Indian labor in a wide range of agricultural and mining activities (Rojas 1998). All these factors stimulated supply and demand, and the production of cacao in places like Caluco responded accordingly in the sixteenth century.

The native inhabitants of the region at the time of the Conquest (1524) were

Nahua-speaking Pipils whose ancestors had migrated from Mexico to Central America during the Postclassic period (W. R. Fowler 1989a:32–49). Current archaeological evidence indicates that Nahua speakers arrived in the Izalcos region in the early part of the Late Postclassic, around A.D. 1200 (Sampeck 2005).

The importance of cacao as a source of wealth in Mesoamerica attracted numerous Spanish *encomenderos*, royal officials, and priests as well as Spanish and Ladino merchants, traders, and adventurers to the region in the sixteenth century (W. R. Fowler 1989a:165). The activities and interactions of these individuals have been chronicled in detail by Escalante Arce (1992), W. R. Fowler (1991, 1993, 1995), and M. J. MacLeod (1973). They were drawn to the area by widely circulated reports that hailed the Izalcos as one of the jewels of the Spanish crown. The dynamic cacao industry based in the Izalcos towns soon led to the establishment, in 1553, of the Spanish merchant town of La Trinidad de Sonsonate, which became a magnet, drawing outsiders to the region (Escalante Arce 1992:1:28, 34, 55–60, 109; W. R. Fowler 1995:52–53; Lardé y Larín 2000:301–307; M. J. MacLeod 1973:82; Rubio Sánchez 1977:20; Sherman 1979:242–243).

Visible reminders of the former wealth of the region are the ruins of the once sumptuous churches of La Asunción in Izalco and San Pedro y San Pablo in Caluco (Escalante Arce 1992:1:229–233; Lardé y Larín 2000:431, 434). Construction of both, financed by their *encomenderos* with lavish funds from the cacao boom, began around 1567–68 and was completed in the early seventeenth century. The two churches were destroyed by the powerful Santa Marta earthquake of 1773, which also destroyed many religious and civic buildings in southeastern Guatemala and devastated Antigua Guatemala (Feldman 1993: 66–71). The Caluco church was an exquisite example of Spanish American *mudéjar* (Muslim influenced) architecture (Markman 1968), and it is well documented archaeologically (W. R. Fowler 1995; Verhagen 1995a, 1997:147–175). What remained of it in the late twentieth century was further destroyed by the powerful earthquakes that struck El Salvador in early 2001.

The economic importance to the crown of the Izalcos cacao towns ensured that their demographic, social, and economic history would be well represented in documents; these are now preserved in Spanish Colonial archives, especially the Archivo General de Indias. Contemporary observers extolled the opportunities that the Izalcos cacao boom offered (W. R. Fowler 1989a:165). An elegant paean to the wealth of Izalcos was Fray Thomas de la Torre's 1552 claim that "within six years there would be six Medinas del Campo there, because it is the richest land for cacao that exists in the Indies" (Fray Thomas de la Torre to

Crown, AGI AG 8, 22 May 1552). This wealth was produced primarily at the household level of production.

Documentary evidence discussed in this chapter indicates that cacao production in the Izalcos region remained largely in the hands of indigenous Pipil peasants. They worked the cacao orchards at the household level of production organized at the kin-ordered mode (Wolf 1982:92) of production to raise enough of the crop to pay their tribute and to produce a surplus for labor payment and marketplace trade.

The documents also indicate the impending collapse of the Izalcos cacao industry (W. R. Fowler 1987, 1991, 1993, 1995:44–48; M. J. MacLeod 1973:91–95). The native Pipil population had been decimated by at least four major epidemics. The cacao orchards suffered from poor maintenance of trees and irrigation canals, cattle damage, soil exhaustion, wind damage, insect damage, and climatic change. The crown, clergy, audiencia officials, and *encomenderos* became increasingly alarmed over the possible loss of tribute revenue, and their concern led to a number of *visitas*, or official inspections (M. J. MacLeod 1973:90). For their part, the Indians often resorted to the Spanish legal machinery to attempt to secure relief from tribute obligations that they could no longer meet.

Social and Political Organization

Before going into further detail on the matters of cacao production, tribute, and wealth, I should like to summarize briefly some pertinent data and interpretations on pre-Conquest social and political organization of the Izalcos Pipil. Here I rely heavily on interpretations of Nahua social and political organization from Central Mexico, especially those of Lockhart (1992), as an analogue. First I want to establish the existence of the *altepetl*, or "ethnic state," among the Izalcos Pipil. As Lockhart (1992:14) states, "at the heart of the organization of the Nahua world, both before the Spaniards came and long after, lay the *altepetl* or ethnic state." Lockhart (1992:15) characterizes the *altepetl* as "the principal container of Nahua life." As the most durable and the most fundamental of all Nahua political units, one should expect to find the *altepetl* present wherever Nahuas lived.

An important point in considering the Pipil case is that the *altepetl* is fundamentally a territorial unit, as revealed by the linguistic root of the word. Lockhart (1992:14) explains that the word *altepetl* derives from a metaphorical doublet *in atl, in tepetl*, meaning 'the water(s), the mountain(s)' (compare Ouweneel 1990:5). Lockhart (1992:14) notes that this "refers in the first instance to territory, but what is meant is primarily an organization of people holding sway over a given territory." According to Lockhart (1992:14), the minimum requirements of an *altepetl* in pre-Conquest times were: (1) a territory; (2) a set of named constituent parts; and (3) a dynastic ruler, or *tlatoani*. Documentary and archaeological evidence from the Izalcos region suggest that it conforms to these minimum requirements.

Izalco was very often referred to in sixteenth-century documents as "Tecpan Izalco." The Nahua term *tecpan* may be glossed as "'where the lord is': palace, establishment of a ruler or lord" (Lockhart 1992:610). As in Central Mexico, the term *tecpan* referred to the territory and dependents of a native lord; in other words, it was the seat of a noble lineage (P. Carrasco 1976a:21–24; Lockhart 1992:104–105) which held a territory. Indeed, the very name "Pipil" (from Nahua *pipiltin*, plural of *pilli* 'noble') should probably be understood as a reference to noble lineages. The lineage was internally stratified among its titular head, nobles, and commoners subject to the noble house. The noble lineages had important political and economic functions which played an essential role in social stratification.

The constituent units of the Nahua *altepetl* were known as *calpolli* 'big house' (Lockhart 1992:16). Pipil commoners were members of *calpolli* (referred to as *calpulli* in sixteenth-century Spanish documents), politico-territorial divisions that were, also as in Central Mexico, residential wards that served as units of tribute collection and constituted the basic production units above the level of the household (P. Carrasco 2000:180; Castillo 1984:72–74; Hicks 1982; Kellogg 1986b:103–104; Lockhart 1992:16; Offner 1983:163; Ouweneel 1990:5–6).

Caluco in the late sixteenth century was divided into five *calpolli*, known as Caluco, Comalapa, San Martín, Miahuatlan, and Apaneca. Table 15.1 presents demographic data by *calpolli* derived from a 1582 census discussed below.

Izalco and Caluco were considered twin settlements by observers in the late sixteenth century (Escalante Arce 1992:1:226–227), and in pre-Conquest times they almost certainly formed an *altepetl* divided into complementary moieties

Table 15.1. Demographic data by *calpolli* derived from a 1582 census

Calpulli	Households	Male	Female	Persons	Ratio
Caluco	147	265	248	513	3.49
Comalapa	26	43	42	85	3.27
San Martín	83	131	128	259	3.12
Miahuatlan	56	96	83	179	3.20
Apaneca	44	75	71	146	3.31
TOTAL	356	610	572	1182	3.32

(W. R. Fowler 1995:40). Nahulingo and Tacuscalco stood in the same complementary relationship to each other. The four settlements together and their territory may have constituted a complex *altepetl* (*sensu* Lockhart 1992:20).

Contemporary observers of the sixteenth century often referred to these four principal Izalcos settlements as "dos pueblos hechos quatro," a clear reference to *reducción*, or forced resettlement into Spanish-style nucleated settlements after the Conquest (Escalante Arce 1992, v. 1:22). Beginning in 1529, following general custom for the Spanish Indies (Solano 1990), a continuous stream of royal decrees mandated that Indian settlements be "reduced" and brought into Spanish-style nucleated towns or villages with streets running east-west and north-south from a central plaza in which was located the church and the *cabildo* (town hall) with a jail. House lots were parceled out to indigenous families by priests and *caciques*, and common lands were assigned for cultivation.

To judge from the repetition of royal decrees to resettle the Indians (Escalante Arce 1992, v. 1:22–26), we may infer that implementation of the policy of *reducción* in the Izalcos towns was not realized or perhaps not even attempted until some time between 1540 and 1553 (Escalante Arce 1992, v. 1:27; W. R. Fowler 1995:40). Escalante Arce (1992, v. 1:26) suggests that the new formalized settlements were probably in place by about 1553 in Izalco, Caluco, Nahulingo, and Tacuscalco, since by this time the towns had their own priests and Spanish-style indigenous governments.

The archaeological evidence indicates an even later date for full, practical implementation of forced nucleation of the Izalcos Pipil population. Sampeck's (2005) regional archaeological survey of the Río Ceniza Valley shows a population decline in the region and concentration in the main centers during the Marroquín phase (1580–1640), recognized by the appearance of distinctive ceramic markers such as Ming porcelain and imported majolicas of Guatemalan, Mexican, and Panamanian origin (see Lister and Lister 1987). During the preceding Lopez phase (A.D. 1524–1580), settlement in the entire region does not show primate centers of occupation or any significant nucleation (Sampeck 2005). Household remains are evenly distributed across the landscape, forming a nearly continuous scatter in the immediate zone of Caluco, Izalco, Nahulingo, and Tacuscalco (Sampeck 2005). Similarly, in her survey and excavations in the central zone of Caluco, Verhagen (1997:235–238) found that the earliest remains date to the 1580s with the exception of one locus which may be slightly earlier. Therefore, with regard to changes in settlement and forced nucleation, or *reducción*, we may conclude on the basis of the historical data that the process may have begun by 1540 or 1550, but the archaeological data reveal unequivocally that the process was not complete until the 1580s. Before the implementation of forced nucleation, the Izalco and Caluco *altepetl* formed a dispersed rural settlement evenly distributed across the local landscape.

It was common practice in the Conquest period to subdivide an *altepetl* to assign *encomiendas*. Izalco/Caluco was divided in 1532 for the purpose of assigning *encomiendas* to two Spaniards (Escalante Arce 1992, v. 1:218). At that time, Tecpan Izalco (the northern sector) became known simply as Izalco, and Caluco Izalco (the southern sector) became known as Caluco. The latter town was listed as one of the two "Yçalcos" in the 1549 Cerrato *tasación*, and it is frequently referred to as "Caluco Yçalco" or "Izalco de Girón" (a reference to its *encomendero*) in sixteenth-century documents (Feldman 1992:49,56).

The head of the Caluco *calpolli* proper, don Gregorio de Valencia, was the *gobernador indígena* of the town; that is, the preeminent officer in the native *cabildo*. Other *cabildo* officers included two *alcaldes ordinarios*, don Miguel Gómez and don Gaspar Arias; two *regidores*, don Toribio Ruiz and don Alonso López; and three *principales*, don Juan Vázquez, don Diego López, and don Benigno Vázquez (Escalante Arce 1992, v. 2:15). Although bearing Spanish names, all of these individuals were indigenous.

Land Tenure and Household Production of Cacao

The cacao orchards surrounding the Izalcos towns were divided into hundreds of small holdings, owned predominantly by Pipil families. But this was by no means the only pattern. Some indigenous producers with moderate-sized holdings (more than two thousand cacao trees) imported wage labor (*alquilones*) from the Highlands, especially the Alta Verapaz region of Guatemala, until this source of labor dried up in the 1570s (Escalante Arce 1992, v. 1:55; W. R. Fowler 1995:42; M. J. MacLeod 1973:92). Spaniards, Ladinos, and Mulattoes also acquired small- to moderate-size holdings, and, M. J. MacLeod (1973:97, 126–127) to the contrary, even some Spanish *encomenderos*, especially those whose grants were relatively small, acquired land and planted cacao and other crops (W. R. Fowler 1995:45). Gaspar de Cepeda, for example, the *encomendero* of Nahuizalco, bought land that was already planted in cacao, and proceeded to plant more. Upon his death in 1567, assessors counted more than twenty thousand cacao trees in three orchards (Cuenta y tasación de los pies de cacao que tenía Gaspar de Cepeda, AGCA A1.43-365-4171, f. 1023, 9 May 1567). The trees were planted so densely that they did not yield very much cacao. Witnesses reported that the trees were spaced only seven or eight feet apart instead of the customary twelve feet (Cuenta y tasación de los pies de cacao que tenía Gaspar de Cepeda, AGCA A1.43-365-4171, f. 1024v., 9 May 1567). Interestingly, a modern cacao cultivation manual recommends a spacing of fifteen feet between trees (Van Hall 1932:100).

Thus, the situation with regard to Izalcos land tenure and cacao production in the late sixteenth century was fluid and complex. To begin to understand the development of this situation better, in this chapter I focus on a salient aspect of Izalcos cacao production that can be observed in the documentary data: social and economic inequalities among peasant households, which, in turn, can be correlated with differential ownership of cacao lands and control of or access to labor. I argue that the origins of these inequalities may be traced to trends in pre-Conquest land tenure and production. In the early Colonial period, tribute demands were scaled to these inequalities in ownership and control of factors of production; the more cacao trees one owned, the more tribute he or she paid (W. R. Fowler 1987:145–146). Widows and orphans paid full tribute on inherited cacao lands. Extraordinarily, the ownership of the means of production brought poverty rather than wealth or even self-sufficiency. In many cases Indian cacao cultivators paid more in annual tribute than they could have gained from the sale of their lands (Diego Garcia de Valverde to Crown, AGI AG 10, f. 7, 8 Apr. 1584). In other words, ownership of cacao orchards became a liability rather than an asset. By the 1580s the tribute system had "levelled" pre-Conquest differences in stratification, evident in the documents, that arose from differential ownership of cacao lands and unequal production.

A rare glimpse of pre-Conquest Pipil land tenure is provided by the proceedings of a 1580–81 dispute over land and water rights between the towns of Tacuscalco and Naolingo (Pleyto entre los yndios de Tacuscalco y los de Naolingo, AGCA A1.12-674-6178, 1580–81). Indian and Spanish witnesses testified that land between these two towns had been communal in ancient times. For example: "las haziendas, como son millpas de cacao, las tienen entretegidas y rrebueltas los unos con los otros, porque antiguamente es cosa notoria que no tenian tierras partidas ni conocidas" ["their property, being cacao orchards, they have interwoven and mixed up, ones with the others, because it is well known that anciently they did not have lands divided up nor distinguished"]. This being the case, it seems certain that land-use rights, at least during some period in the pre-Conquest history of these towns, were assigned by corporate leaders. The lands that were once under corporate control had gradually been transformed into private holdings which were held by individual families and could be inherited, bought, and sold. This pattern is similar to the situation of land ownership among central Mexican Nahua populations in late pre-Conquest times as it is understood by modern scholarship (P. Carrasco 2000:180; Castillo 1984:79–84; S. L. Cline 1984, 1986:125–159; Gibson 1964:263–268; Harvey 1984; Hoekstra 1990; Kellogg 1986a; Lockhart 1992:142, 154; Prem 1988:50–52; Michael E. Smith 1996:145–146). Although land was allocated by *calpolli* and *altepetl* authorities, "in actual practice, individuals and households worked it, held it on a long-term basis, and inherited it" (Lockhart 1992:142).

An historical trend towards private ownership of cacao orchards can be suggested for the pre-Columbian Izalcos Pipils. In the only explicit early historical reference that I have found to pre-Hispanic Pipil cacao production, a witness stated that the native lord of Izalco, who was known as Tehuehue, "por ser señor natural que hera en tiempo de su gentilidad siempre tubo grandisima suma de millpas de cacao el d[ic]ho pueblo mas que otro ninguno de aquella comarca" ["being the natural lord that he was, in the time of his heathendom he always had a very great number of cacao orchards, the said town more than any other of that region"] (Pleitos seguidos por el senor fiscal de la audiencia contra don Diego de Guzmán, AGI EC 331A, f. 1772, 11 Mar. 1583). I infer from this statement that in pre-Conquest times the native lords of Izalcos probably controlled cacao production in the sense that their holdings were more extensive than those of commoners, and they exercised prebendal domain (see Wolf 1966:51) in the region at the time of the Conquest. Nevertheless, while Tehuehue's holdings were undoubtedly vast, ownership of cacao orchards was not solely a prerogative of the nobility.

A Portrait from the Documents

The observation that ownership of cacao orchards was not exclusive to the elite takes us back to a consideration of the household level of production, and it is supported by data from two very lengthy and extremely detailed legal documents concerning cacao tribute and production in Izalco and Caluco in the 1570s and 1580s (Pleitos seguidos por el señor fiscal de la audiencia contra don Diego de Guzmán, AGI EC 331A and EC 331B, 1583–84; Vissita y tasación de tributos de los Yndios del pueblo de Caluco, AGI JU 334, 1582–83). These documents, one of which (AGI EC 331) is more than four thousand folios long, include house-by-house surveys with census and economic data. The number of orchards and even the exact number of cacao trees owned by each family are reported. The amount of cacao tribute levied and the amount of back-tribute owed are noted in each case. Sequences of inheritance of the cacao orchards are recorded. Additional information is included on maize cultivation, the raising of chickens and turkeys, and ownership of houses, lots, and horses. A most interesting feature is that most individuals have good Nahuat surnames such as Cuat, Panti, Suchit, Tamagaz, Tezcat, Mixcuat, Mazat, and Ocelochimal, to mention just a few.

For the past several years, I have worked on a compilation and analysis of the data in the Caluco document, and I can now offer a preliminary report of the results. This document was compiled in 1582 and 1583 under the supervision of Lic. Antonio de Collazos, who was appointed *juez de comisión* to conduct a new "quenta y padrón" of the town. The Indians of Caluco initiated the action, seeking redress for a faulty *tasación* that was conducted by Lic. Diego García de Palacio in 1575 (M. J. MacLeod 1973:90). The earlier *tasación* recorded 547 tributaries, whereas the Indians counted no more than about 360 in 1582—a difference of 34 percent in their tributary population.

Collazos arrived in Caluco on July 17, 1582. He spent the next two months organizing and preparing to conduct the census, which he began on September 17 and concluded on October 22. While preparing, Collazos was assigned one "yndio principal" from each of the five *calpolli*. They were said to be "personas pláticos y entendidos" in the affairs of the town. The house-by-house census record includes the 1575 count of cacao trees owned by each tributary recorded by García de Palacio, which was widely regarded as exaggerated. On January 3, 1583, Collazos commenced an inspection of the cacao orchards, counting the number of plots and trees owned by each individual. He completed this task on January 28 and, indeed, found far fewer trees than García de Palacio had reported. After the field survey, Collazos inspected irrigation canals, many of which he reported as poorly maintained, damaged, or dried up. At the behest of Diego de Herrera, one of the town *encomenderos*, the judge visited the town *tianguis*, or marketplace, to observe *negras* and *mulatas* selling cheese, dried fish, molasses candy, *turrones*, soap, and other items to the Indians at inflated prices.

Beginning on February 4, Collazos presided over a hearing in which fifty-four witnesses—residents of the town and region—were called to testify on past and current conditions, population levels, and cacao production. The hearing proceeded according to prepared questionnaires. The witnesses included Indians, Spaniards, and *mulatos*, all of whom knew the town well. Their trenchant testimony is an open window on daily life in Caluco in the 1580s and a revealing view of culture change in the region since the mid-sixteenth century.

The Collazos visita concluded on June 8, 1583, almost eleven months after it began. His final tributary count was 449 (AGI JU 334, f. 689v., 8 June 1583). Despite this finding, however, the audiencia did not lower cacao tribute. The tribute assessment remained at 1,000 *xiquipiles* (eight million cacao beans, or approximately seventeen thousand pounds), the same amount levied against Caluco since the Cerrato *tasación* of 1549.

Statistical analysis of these data is still in progress, but I can provide an overview of the patterns. The total population of the town was 1,182 persons residing in 356 households, an average of 3.3 people per household (see Table

15.1). Almost all of these were nuclear-family households, many of which included adopted orphans. Only fourteen joint consanguineal households, with two or more married, coresident couples occur in the census. In other words, nuclear-family households account for 96 percent of all known households in Caluco in 1582. This pattern is very different from household composition in sixteenth-century Central Mexico studied by Pedro Carrasco (1964, 1976b), S. L. Cline (1993), Harvey (1986), Kellogg (1986b, 1993), Offner (1984), and Prem (1974). Forty-four widows and widowers lived alone, and seventy-eight couples were childless. This is probably related to the impact of epidemic disease which resulted in a continuous population collapse in the Izalcos region during the sixteenth century (W. R. Fowler 1995:41–44). Certainly related to disease is the relatively large number of second marriages and the number of couples (forty-seven) in which the female is considerably older than the male. It is not unusual to find a 50- or 60-year-old woman married to a 30-year-old man. Most or all of these cases were actually forced marriages arranged by the *encomenderos* and local secular clergy to increase tributary counts (M. J. MacLeod 1973:88).

It seems that almost everyone in Caluco, including poor widows and orphans, owned cacao trees. That is a slight exaggeration, but there were 343 owners of cacao trees among the 449 tributary entities in the census (76 percent). Caluco's cacao orchards were packed with almost 800,000 trees in 1,668 orchards of varying size and density. The average number of orchards owned by individuals was 4.8; the mean number of trees per individual was 2,327. Most people (272, to be precise) owned fewer than 5,000 trees. Sixty-two individuals owned between 5,000 and 10,000 trees, and only nine people owned 10,000 trees or more. The maximum number of trees owned by a single individual was 23,800, and he had inherited them from two different deceased relatives.

A series of entries typically begins with the native *gobernador* of the town or the *cacique* of the *calpolli*, who, predictably, owns more cacao orchards, plants more maize, and has more animals than the majority of his subjects. In Caluco the *gobernador*, don Gregorio de Valencia, and his wife, doña Francisca, both 30 years old, owned a total of ten orchards, seven of which she had inherited from her first husband. The ten orchards contained a total of 15,370 cacao trees. Don Gregorio's daughter, doña Maria, who was married to don Francisco Cortés, the *cacique* of Tecpa, a Pipil town of central El Salvador located some 65 km to the east, owned four orchards, three of which they had put in the possession of her father. Don Gregorio's adopted daughter, doña Ysabel Ximénez, 18 years old, married to don Pedro de Alvarado, owned a total of thirteen orchards, five of which she had inherited from her mother, and seven from her grandmother, Ysabel Tezca, who had once owned thirteen orchards all together. Pedro Sanchez, 20, and María Suchil, 16 or 17, lived in don Gregorio's house; she had inherited three orchards with a total of 2,800 trees from her father. If my calculations are correct, don Gregorio's household owned or controlled a total of twenty-nine orchards containing some 33,570 cacao trees.

According to production estimates in the same document on Caluco (AGI JU 334), these trees in their prime might have produced as many as 17 *cargas* or about 50 *xiquipiles* (400,000 cacao "beans," or roughly 850 lb.) of cacao annually. The total tribute levied against this household was 20 *xiquipiles*. In theory, therefore, a surplus could have been produced for payment of labor and trade in the marketplace. This was not the case, however, since the cacao industry of Izalco was in decline in the 1580s; the trees were old, and the annual harvest had fallen to about 25 percent of what it had been in the past. Informants in the Collazos inquiry stated that young cacao trees begin to yield fruit within four to six years after planting (cf. Van Hall 1932:175–176). The productive life span of a cacao tree was said to be about thirty to forty years; thus, from about 1540 until 1575 or so surplus production presumably would have been a reality. The differential surplus-producing capacity of individual households was reflected in local differences in social stratification.

Another important factor with regard to production was the necessity of irrigation for cacao production in the Izalcos region (Feldman 1985:84). References to Izalco's irrigation canals and the need for them abound in the documents (for example, AGI EC 331A, f. 47, 30 June 1581). Disputes over water rights were not uncommon in the sixteenth century. Collazos found that many irrigation canals in the Caluco zone were damaged or in bad repair (AGI JU 334, 28 Feb. 1583). Thus, it was necessary to invest a significant amount of labor in the construction, maintenance, and repair of hydraulic infrastructure.

Conclusion

The nature and character of cacao trees are crucial in regard to the question of the origin of the differences in ownership and productive capacity among households. Since a new cacao tree could not be expected to yield fruit for four to seven years after being planted, each tree represented a capital investment that would not yield immediate or short-term returns. Constant tending and frequent replacement of exhausted trees were required to keep orchards producing at their peak. The intensification of production that occurred in the mid-sixteenth century made such care even more necessary. Ultimately, this level of intensification could not be maintained due in large part to the catastrophic impact of at least three major waves of epidemic disease that struck El Salvador from 1520 to 1577 (W. R. Fowler 1995:41–44). These facts were underscored by a witness from Izalco who stated that "los dichos naturales muertos tenian mucho cuydado como cosa heredada de sus antecesores y ansi munchas casas se an acabado y muchas millpas se an perdido por no aver avido quien las aya beneficiado" ["the said dead natives took great care [in tending the trees] as [they were] something inherited from their ancestors, and thus many houses have been wiped out, and many orchards have been lost since there has been no one to tend them"] (AGI JU 334, f. 449, 5 Feb. 1583).

Clearly, the phenomena of private ownership and inheritance of cacao trees and orchards can be traced to developments that occurred before the Conquest. My main reason for thinking this is that although the archives, especially the AGCA, contain numerous records of land transfers from Indians to Spaniards and Ladinos, I am aware of none that record transfers between Indians, with the significant exception, of course, of the inheritance records. The patterns of inheritance evident in the documents were undoubtedly in place when the Spaniards conquered the region in 1524.

This raises a very obvious dual question: when did private ownership of productive resources (cacao orchards) begin in Izalcos, and what caused it? This seems to be a case similar to Antonio Gilman's (1976, 1981) explanation of the origins of social stratification in Bronze Age Mediterranean Spain. In this argument, capital-intensive agriculture (in this case, the cultivation of olive trees and grape vines) and small-scale hydraulic systems, because they represent considerable investments in productive forces and imply the transformation of property relations, are critical factors in the development of social stratification. The same kind of transformation must have taken place among the Izalcos Pipils after they settled in the region during the Late Postclassic.

Acknowledgments

This chapter would not have been written without Cameron McNeil's encouragement. I thank John Byram, Jeb Card, René Millon, Cameron McNeil, and an anonymous reviewer for their helpful comments. I am grateful to the directors and the staffs of the Archivo General de Indias in Seville, Spain, and the Archivo General de Centroamérica in Guatemala City, Guatemala, for their kind assistance. My research in the archives was supported by the American Philosophical Society, the National Endowment for the Humanities, the U.S.-Spanish Joint Committee for Cultural and Educational Cooperation, and the Wenner-Gren Foundation for Anthropological Research. While working in the AGI, I enjoyed the advice and friendship of many colleagues, especially Wendy

Kramer, George Lovell, Fritz Schwaller, and Elías Zamora. I thank Chris Lutz of the Centro de Investigaciones Regionales de Mesoamérica for supplying me with a beautifully clear typescript paleography of the entire *legajo* of AGI JU 334. I am very grateful to Evelin Guadalupe Sánchez for invaluable advice and assistance on the compilation and statistical analysis of the data in AGI JU 334 and especially for debating their meaning with me.

16

Soconusco Cacao Farmers Past and Present

Continuity and Change in an Ancient Way of Life

Janine Gasco

The Soconusco region of Chiapas, Mexico (Figure 16.1), is ideally suited for cacao cultivation, and in prehistoric and historic times the area was one of the principal cacao-producing zones of Mesoamerica (see Bergmann 1969; S. D. Coe and M. D. Coe 1996; Gasco 1989a; Gasco and Voorhies 1989; Lowe, Lee, and Espinosa 1982; Millon 1955a). Although cacao cultivation was once the predominant economic activity of the region, since the nineteenth century other agricultural products (particularly coffee but also cotton, bananas, and, more recently, mangos) have surpassed cacao as primary export crops, and cattle ranching also has become an increasingly important part of the Soconusco economy (Báez Landa 1985; Villafuerte, Carmen, and Meza 1997). Nevertheless, many Soconusco residents continue to cultivate cacao on small farms and in kitchen gardens, and almost 13,000 hectares of cacao trees were reportedly under cultivation in the Soconusco in 2000, which represents 57 percent of the total area under cacao cultivation in the state of Chiapas (INEGI 2002). Recent data, however, suggest that cacao cultivation is declining in the region, and the great majority of cacao trees are old and are not being replaced (Jaime Cueto, personal communication July 2002).[1]

During the past several years, I have conducted research on Postclassic and Colonial period Soconusco, focusing extensively on the role of cacao in the regional economy. In the Late Postclassic period, a growing demand for cacao across Mesoamerica almost certainly led to both increased cacao production in the Soconusco and an expanded role for the entire region within the Mesoamerican economic system. A desire to gain easier access to Soconusco cacao presumably was a factor leading to the Aztec conquest of the region in the late 1400s; as a tributary province, Soconusco was required to pay the equivalent of more than 10,000 pounds of cacao beans as well as other products annually to

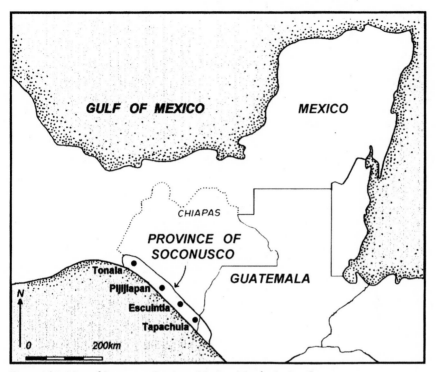

Figure 16.1. Map of Soconusco Province, Mexico. Map by Janine Gasco.

the Aztec empire (Gasco 2003; Gasco and Voorhies 1989; Voorhies and Gasco 2004).

For the Colonial period, I have analyzed socioeconomic patterns within the indigenous communities of Soconusco as they relate to the cacao industry (Gasco 1989b, 1993, 1996, 1997). Based on an analysis of patterns of ownership of cacao trees and access to imported goods, I determined that a socioeconomic leveling process took place during the course of most of the Colonial period within indigenous Soconusco towns. By the late eighteenth and early nineteenth centuries, however, growing economic disparities had emerged in and around the provincial capital of Tapachula.

In this chapter I approach the Soconusco cacao industry from the perspective of ethnoecology. I recently began an ethnoecological study of the Soconusco region that is designed to contribute to the growing body of literature on ethnoecology, a multidisciplinary field of study that explores relationships between humans and the natural world (for example, C. S. Fowler 2000; Gragson and Blount 1999; Muchena and Vanek 1999; Nazarea 1999; Toledo 1992). In other parts of Mesoamerica ethnoecological research has demonstrated that indigenous, or traditional, farming and agroforestry practices are often environmentally sound and protect forest habitats (for example, Alcorn 1990; Gó-mez-Pompa and Kaus 1990). Traditional ecological knowledge is increasingly being incorporated into development projects that are designed to promote sustainability (see Alcorn 1999; Bellon 1995; Brokensha, Warren, and Werner 1980; Warren, Slikkerveer, and Brokensha 1999).

The general goal of the Soconusco ethnoecology project is to document indigenous, or traditional, ecological knowledge in the Soconusco region by exploring how rural residents perceive and learn about their environment, how these perceptions are reflected in day-to-day activities that impact the environment, and the extent to which perceptions, knowledge, and activities are being transformed in the face of dramatic economic, environmental, and demographic changes in the early twenty-first century. Wherever possible, I use historical evidence in an effort to document change over time. A more long-term goal of the project is to determine if traditional ecological knowledge might be used effectively in the design of sustainable agriculture or agroforestry projects in the region.

One component of this ethnoecological research concerns historical and contemporary relationships between the environment and cacao cultivation in the Soconusco. The evidence indicates that historically, the economic viability of the Soconusco region depended upon a heavily forested environment. Most of the area is classified as Tropical Deciduous Forest, but the southeastern portion is classified as Evergreen or Semi-evergreen Seasonal Forest (Breedlove 1981).

In this study I propose that the current decline in the Soconusco cacao industry represents more than just a simple change in economic production; instead it is a symptom of more fundamental changes that are having dramatic effects on the Soconusco environment and ultimately on the lives of people across the region. Moreover, I will suggest that a better understanding of the ecological history of the Soconusco can provide us with tools to improve environmental and economic conditions in the area.

I begin by briefly reviewing what we know about cacao cultivation and the environment in the pre-Columbian period in the Soconusco. I then discuss evidence from the Colonial period and the nineteenth century, and I conclude by looking at contemporary trends and issues that cacao farmers in Soconusco face today.

Cacao in Pre-Columbian Soconusco

The precise origins of cacao cultivation in the Soconusco region remain unknown, but local soil and climatic conditions are ideal for growing cacao, and linguistic evidence suggests that cacao was cultivated there early, perhaps by the Middle Formative period (ca. 900–400 B.C.) or before. Linguists have argued that the term for cacao originated within the Mije-Soquean language family—presumably because cacao was first cultivated by Mije-Soquean farmers—and subsequently was borrowed into other Mesoamerican languages (Campbell and Kaufman 1976; Justeson et al. 1985; Kaufman and Justeson, this volume; but see Dakin and Wichmann 2000 for an alternative view). A Mije-Soquean language was native to the Soconusco region, probably extending back into the Formative period (ca. 1800 B.C.–A.D. 200) (Campbell 1988). The Olmecs, who also spoke a Mije-Soquean language, are sometimes credited with domesticating cacao (S. D. Coe and M. D. Coe 1996:36–39), but it is also possible that farmers in the Soconusco region might have been among the first Mesoamericans to cultivate cacao (see Motamayor et al. 2002; Ogata 2002b; and Ogata, Gómez-Pompa, and Taube, this volume, for further information regarding the origins of cacao cultivation in Mesoamerica). The florescence of the Late Formative period (ca. 400 B.C.–A.D. 200) Soconusco site of Izapa may have been linked in some way to the cacao industry (Lowe, Lee, and Espinosa 1982:43ff.), and it is likely that cacao production played an important role in the Soconusco economy for most of the pre-Columbian era.

By the Late Postclassic period (ca. A.D. 1200–1520), an expanding commercial system and the demand for luxury goods like cacao, fine salt, obsidian, metal goods, and decorated textiles had increased dramatically (Michael E. Smith and F. Berdan 2003). Cacao production almost certainly increased in Postclassic Soconusco. Archaeological data from sites in the Soconusco indicate that in the Late Postclassic period, local residents had unprecedented access to long-distance trade goods, a situation that presumably is linked to expanding cacao production and increased trade in which long-distance merchants traded imported goods for Soconusco cacao (Gasco 2003; Voorhies and Gasco 2004).

In the last decades of the Late Postclassic period, the Soconusco region was conquered by the expanding Triple Alliance/Aztec Empire, and subsequent tribute assessments recorded in the *Matrícula de tributos* (Castillo Farreras 1974) and the Codex Mendoza (Berdan and Anawalt 1992) list the goods that were paid annually by Soconusco towns to the Aztecs. These tribute assessments make it clear that a major—if not main—reason for this conquest was to provide the Aztecs with greater or more reliable access to Soconusco cacao. As noted above, Soconusco towns paid more than ten thousand pounds of cacao beans annually in tribute. In terms of labor investment and value, cacao was clearly the most important tribute item paid by the region. Cacao, however, was not the only product paid in tribute, and the other tribute items also provide clues about what the Soconusco environment must have been like.

There are three categories of Soconusco tribute goods: cultigens (cacao beans and gourd containers [*tecomates*] for drinking chocolate; game (jaguar pelts) and wildfowl (bird skins and feathers); and jewelry/precious stones (amber, gold, and jade) (Gasco and Voorhies 1989). It is likely that the amber, gold, and jade were not local products but instead were acquired through trade. However, the cultigens as well as the game and wildfowl undoubtedly came from the Soconusco. These products suggest what the Soconusco landscape must have looked like in the Late Postclassic period; there would have been cacao orchards and the higher canopy trees necessary to provide shade for the cacao, as well as farm plots, and large stands of primary forests that provided the habitat for wild game and birds.

We know from demographic data that population density in Late Postclassic Soconusco was relatively low, somewhere between 6.5–8.5 people per km^2 (Gasco 1987a:98, 121–122; Gasco 1989c:384). A low population density may have contributed to the maintenance of a heavily forested environment. In summary, the available data indicate that throughout much of the pre-Columbian period, perhaps as far back as the Early to Middle Formative period (1800–400 B.C.), cacao was a key economic product in the Soconusco region. For the Late Postclassic period we have more information about other products of the region and its population density, both of which help us to better understand the local environment and to recognize that a forested landscape would have not only been necessary to provide shade for the valuable cacao but also to provide the conditions and habitat necessary for virtually all of the area's other economic products. In pre-Columbian Soconusco, maintenance of the forest was critical for the continued viability of the region's economy.

Colonial Period and Nineteenth-Century Cacao Industry

A wide range of evidence for the Colonial period allows for a much more detailed look at general environmental conditions and cacao cultivation in the province of Soconusco. Numerous Colonial documents provide general descriptions of the region. Common themes include the agricultural potential of the area because of its fertility; the unhealthy conditions in the region because of the heat, insects, and wild animals; and the difficulty of moving across the region because of the broken terrain, the dense vegetation, and the impossibility of crossing the torrential rivers, particularly during the rainy season (Gasco 1987a:75, 1989a, 1989–90; Ponce de León 1961 [1574]). Another common theme in documents from Colonial officials in the Soconusco is that the low population of the province was preventing the area from realizing its full potential. Numerous pleas to higher level authorities request that policies be enacted to encourage immigration to the Soconusco because the cacao groves were languishing (Gasco 1989–90; Ponce de León 1961 [1574]).

Demographic data confirm that throughout most of the Colonial period, population density across the province was even lower than it had been at the time of the Spanish conquest. Mortality rates in the Soconusco region in the early decades of the Colonial period were extremely high; the depopulation figure may have been as high as 95 percent or more (Gasco 1987a:79–86, 1989c:374–376). Moreover, population recovery was slow; throughout the Colonial period, population density across the Soconusco never exceeded 1.5 persons per km^2 (Gasco 1987a:98, 121–122, 1989c:384).

The continued importance of cacao for the Soconusco economy is emphasized in numerous Colonial documents. The earliest efforts by Spaniards to extract resources from the Soconusco focused on gold, but with the local gold supply presumably depleted, tribute payments from 1548 to the mid-eighteenth century consisted largely of cacao (Gasco 1989a). The earliest Colonial tribute payments in cacao indicate that the Spaniards took their cue from Aztec tribute documents, such as the Codex Mendoza noted above; Soconusco tribute in 1548 was 200 *cargas* (loads) of cacao, exactly what the province had paid to the Aztecs (Gasco and Voorhies 1989). During the next two hundred years, the indigenous residents of Soconusco paid cacao as part of their annual tribute assessment, although the amounts changed from year to year.

Other Colonial records provide additional information about cacao production. In 1582, sixty years after the imposition of Spanish Colonial rule, in the

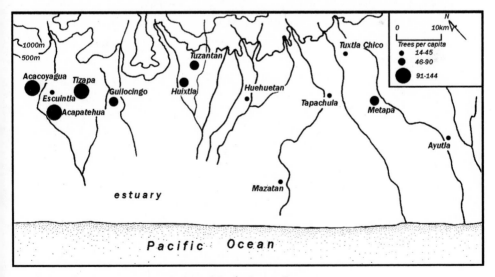

Figure 16.2. Soconusco towns in 1820. Map by Janine Gasco.

small Soconusco town of Guilocingo (see Figure 16.2) cacao orchards were privately owned, and fifteen of the town's eighteen Indian *tributarios* (tribute-paying heads of household) owned an orchard (AGI, Escribanía de Cámara 331-A, "Provisión a Francisco de Santiago. . ." f. 1527–1545v). The size of individual cacao holdings ranged from 200 to 3,200 trees, and the average number of cacao trees per person was 343 (see Gasco 1990 for a more complete analysis of this document). Cacao farmers in Soconusco reportedly plant cacao trees at intervals of between 2.5 m and 4 m, producing between 625 and 1,600 cacao trees per hectare.[2] If we use a figure of 1,100 trees per hectare—roughly the middle of the range—the cacao orchards in Guilocingo in 1582 would have required approximately 14 hectares of land.

Using a formula derived from this 1582 document, I have estimated previously that approximately 1,500,000 cacao trees were under cultivation across the entire province of Soconusco in the late sixteenth century (see Gasco 1987b:116–117, 132). Applying the figure of 1,100 trees per hectare as discussed above, we can see that there may have been almost 1,400 hectares of cacao trees in late sixteenth-century Soconusco. This represents 0.24 percent of the area of the Soconusco region.[3] Although cacao was the most important product of the region, only a very small part of the province was devoted to cacao cultivation in the late sixteenth century, and the number of cacao trees declined even further in the later Colonial period.

The combined evidence from general environmental descriptions, from demographic data, and from what we can reconstruct about total area of land devoted to cacao cultivation suggests that during the Colonial period the Soconusco landscape was even less populated, and that an even greater proportion of land may have been covered by forest than had been the case in the pre-Columbian period.

In the eighteenth and nineteenth centuries we get additional glimpses of some of the dynamics of the Colonial cacao industry in Soconusco. Between 1718 and 1735, *padrones* (census documents) for thirteen Soconusco towns note whether each Indian tributary family had a cacao orchard (unfortunately, the number of trees in these orchards is not provided) (AGCA A3.16 358 4613; A3.16 358 4625; A3.16 358 4626; A3.16 359 4627; A3.16 359 4628; A3.16 359 4629; A3.16 359 4631; A3.16 359 4632; A3.16 359 4648; A3.16 359 4643; A3.16 359 4647; A3.16 367 4758). Of the almost 300 households recorded, 83 percent had a cacao orchard. Although it would be informative to know more about how large these orchards were, these data suggest that cacao cultivation remained a primary economic activity for the indigenous population of the region. Tributaries continued to pay tribute in cacao, although annual payments fell to 56 *cargas* in 1728 (AGCA A3.16 296 3996), the lowest figure for the entire Colonial period. This figure is almost 75 percent lower than the tribute rates of the late sixteenth century (Gasco 1987b:126). Similarly, Colonial period population figures were at their lowest levels early in the eighteenth century (Gasco 1989c).

The most detailed documents, providing evidence regarding cacao cultivation and more general environmental conditions, date to the end of the Colonial period. In 1819–20, the Subdelegado of the province of Soconusco, don Antonio García Girón, conducted an agricultural survey of the entire province in which he recorded the number of cacao trees, achiote trees (*Bixa orellana* L.), vanilla vines (*Vanilla planifolia* Andrews), and coffee (*Coffea arabica* L.) bushes owned by Soconusco residents (AGCA A1.17 313 2188). García Girón also noted that agricultural production was almost exclusively in the hands of the region's indigenous population.[4] In 1821, census records for each Soconusco town provide names of all household heads, and for some towns all household members are named (AGCA A1.44 47 550; A1.44 46 549; A1.44 46 548; A1.44 46 547; A1.44 46 542). Thus, by comparing the names in these two contemporary sets of documents, it is possible to determine how cacao orchards and other agricultural resources were distributed within communities and across the entire province. I have used these documents previously to explore socioeconomic relations within and among communities (Gasco 1996), but here I want to use these same data to examine environmental conditions.

Table 16.1 is a summary of the total number of cacao trees under cultivation for thirteen Soconusco towns as reported in the agricultural survey.[5] In Table 16.1, I have also calculated the estimated number of hectares under cultivation (using the figure mentioned above of 1,100 trees per hectare), and, based on population counts, I have calculated the average number of trees per person in each town.

To put the numbers in Table 16.1 into perspective, remember that the 1582 report from the town of Guilocingo showed that at that time there was an average of 343 trees per person. We know that by 1582 the Soconusco cacao industry was already in decline (see M. J. MacLeod 1973:68–79), but note here that per capita tree counts had become much lower by the early nineteenth century, ranging from 14 to 144 trees per person. Similarly, the late sixteenth-century estimate for total trees under cultivation was approximately 1,500,000, whereas the figure for the early nineteenth century is fewer than 500,000. This decline presumably is linked to the overall population decline noted above and reflects that, on average, individual cacao orchards were much smaller in the early nineteenth century than they had been previously. Perhaps most cacao farmers had reduced the size of their holdings to a level that could be sustained

Table 16.1. Number of cacao trees, estimates of hectares under cultivation, population counts, and average number of cacao trees per person, Soconusco, 1820

Town	Number of cacao trees	Number of hectares	Pop.	Avg. number of trees per person
Ayutla Parish				
Ayutla	3,308	3	119	28
Tapachula Parish				
Tapachula	124,520	113	3,199	39
Tuxtla Chico	147,534	134	3,298	45
Metapa	22,910	21	302	76
Mazatan	5,491	5	395	14
Huehuetan Parish				
Huehuetan	5,480	5	340	16
Huixtla	15,385	14	192	80
Tuzantan	31,235	28	505	62
Guilocingo Parish				
Guilocingo	14,754	13	293	50
Tizapa	7,629	7	84	91
Escuintla Parish				
Escuintla	23,057	21	609	38
Acapetahua	7,937	7	84	94
Acacoyagua	15,579	14	108	144
Totals	424,819	386	9,528	45

with family labor. Nevertheless, despite the low numbers, cacao remained the dominant agricultural product in the province.

I have discussed elsewhere the important socioeconomic differences that were emerging in certain communities within the province by the end of the Colonial period (Gasco 1996). In and around Tapachula (see Figure 16.2), fewer indigenous families owned cacao orchards, and, among those who did, there were large differences between families with very small orchards and those with very large orchards; the smallest orchard had 20 trees and the largest had 5,272 trees. In contrast, in communities more distant from Tapachula, most Indian families owned a cacao orchard, and there were fewer differences among families in terms of the size of their orchards.

Figure 16.2 illustrates the spatial variability among Soconusco towns in terms of number of cacao trees per capita in the nineteenth century and shows again the general differences between Tapachula and its neighbors on the one hand and towns more distant on the other (with the exception of Metapa and Escuintla). Although Tapachula and Tuxtla Chico had the largest total number of trees, proportionally fewer people in these communities were involved in the cacao industry as owners of trees, foreshadowing even more dramatic economic changes in the late nineteenth and twentieth centuries.

Table 16.2. Numbers of old trees, young trees, and seedlings in Soconusco towns, 1820

Town	Old trees		Young trees		Seedlings		Total trees
	#	%	#	%	#	%	
Ayutla	1,438	43	1,870	57	0	0	3,308
Tapachula	70,768	57	35,780	29	17,972	14	124,520
Tuxtla Chico	98,514	67	42,847	29	6,173	4	147,534
Metapa	18,350	80	4,460	19	100	<1	22,910
Mazatan	1,193	22	806	15	3,492	63	5,491
Huehuetan	1,222	22	2,254	41	2,004	37	5,480
Huixtla	7,841	51	4,059	26	3,485	23	15,385
Tuzantan	12,535	40	9,032	29	9,668	31	31,235
Guilocingo	8,598	58	2,019	14	4,137	28	14,754
Tizapa	3,365	44	1,536	20	2,728	36	7,629
Escuintla	9,224	40	5,943	26	7,870	34	23,057
Acapetahua	1,329	17	2,135	27	4,473	56	7,937
Acacoyagua	10,481	67	1,494	10	3,604	23	15,579
Totals	24,4878	58	114,235	27	65,706	15	424,819

Table 16.2 is a summary of the data in the agricultural survey for another aspect of the cacao industry in 1820. The agricultural survey recorded not only the total number of cacao trees owned by individuals in each town, but it also noted how many trees were old, young, or seedlings (*almacigos*, or very young plants not yet transplanted in the orchards). The percentage of trees in these three categories in each town provides an indication of the relative health of a community's cacao holdings taken as a whole. If we compare these figures from town to town, a few towns stand out as having what would seem to be excessively high percentages of old trees and/or excessively low percentages of seedlings. Again, it is primarily the towns around Tapachula that show particularly low percentages of seedlings, figures that might predict a future decline in the cacao industry for these towns.

The 1820 agricultural survey also provides information about other agricultural products in the Soconusco. It records the number of achiote trees, vanilla vines, and coffee bushes each individual owns (Table 16.3). This is one of the earliest records of coffee cultivation in Mexico that I am aware of, and it is interesting that coffee was first planted in Huixtla and neighboring Tuzantan, and in Escuintla, not around Tapachula, where it would come to dominate the economy later in the nineteenth century. Vanilla is a vine of the orchid family that grows around tree trunks and limbs, so it requires a shaded forest habitat. As far as I know, it has virtually disappeared as a cultivated plant in Soconusco. Achiote is the fourth agricultural product listed in the survey. It is a small tree that grows in tropical regions of Mesoamerica, and its seeds are used in the red coloring added to cacao beverages and other foods.

Table 16.3. Number of cacao trees, achiote trees, vanilla vines, and coffee bushes in Soconusco towns, 1820

Town	Population	Number of Cacao Trees	Achiote	Vanilla	Coffee
Ayulta	119	3,308	0	0	0
Tapachula	3,199	124,520	0	0	0
Tuxtla Chico	3,298	147,534	1,057	0	0
Metapa	302	22,910	12	0	0
Mazatan	395	5,491	55	697	0
Huehuetan	340	5,480	532	0	0
Huixtla	192	15,385	1,184	164	381
Tuzantan	505	31,235	2,247	730	668
Guilocingo	293	14,754	218	156	8
Tizapa	84	7,629	0	209	0
Escuintla	609	23,057	110	367	130
Acapetahua	84	7,937	563	263	0
Acacoyagua	108	15,579	120	171	0
Totals	9,528	424,819	6,098	2,757	1,187

Across much of the Soconusco region at the end of the Colonial period, the indigenous farmers, who still made up the majority of the population, cultivated plants that thrived in a forested environment. With the exception of the recently introduced coffee bushes, these plants were native to the area and had been successfully cultivated there since pre-Columbian times. In and around Tapachula, however, we get the first hints of impending changes. Although the cacao industry there was still important, compared to other towns the number of trees per capita was low and seedlings were not being planted to replace old trees.

Other data indicate that the late eighteenth and early nineteenth centuries were times of important changes that grew out of the Bourbon Reforms—policies that were designed to increase Spain's control over and profits from her colonies (Brading 1984). In Soconusco, one of the policies implemented in the late eighteenth century required individuals and communities to provide written proof of title for their lands. Many indigenous communities were unable to do this, and as a result Spaniards and other non-Indians who were migrating to the Soconusco region were able to acquire lands that formerly had been claimed by *pueblos de indios*. The number of Spanish-owned haciendas increased rapidly at this time, particularly in Tapachula (Gasco 1996).

By the end of the Colonial period, new economic activities began to replace traditional ones in and around Tapachula. These activities did not rely as much on the presence of a forest habitat. That many of the new Spanish haciendas were cattle ranches meant that not only was the forest cut to make way for pasture, but cattle also roamed freely, destroying crops and cacao orchards. In 1811 a number of complaints were filed by indigenous farmers living in Tapachula and surrounding towns. These farmers claimed that their fields and cacao orchards had been damaged by cattle from Spanish haciendas, a charge they were able to prove, and they eventually received monetary compensation for the damage (AGCA A1 324 2393). This trend away from forest resources continued into the later part of the nineteenth century. The destruction of the forest habitat around Tapachula was brought about in part by the introduction of cattle and other crops, such as cotton and bananas, which require full sun.

The development of the Soconusco coffee industry deserves more than the sentence or two I am going to give it here. But generally, successful coffee grows at higher elevations than cacao, and my concern in this study is with cacao and the other forest products that were cultivated at lower elevations. More-over, coffee, like cacao, is usually shade-grown in the Soconusco, so the coffee industry has tended to promote a forested environment (Cortina Villar 1993; Helbig 1964). Finally, population density, which remained low throughout the Colonial period, began to increase in the nineteenth century. By 1900 it had reached 4.7 persons per km^2. This figure, however, is still well below estimated pre-Columbian population densities.[6]

In summary, for most of the Colonial period, land-use patterns across the Soconusco did not change dramatically. Because of a sharp population decline early in the Colonial period and slow recovery, population densities remained low. Cacao production also fell, although cacao continued to be the primary product of the region; the indigenous population continued to pay its tribute in cacao until well into the eighteenth century, and the region continued to attract merchants who traded with local farmers for their cacao. The first glimmers of impending changes begin to appear in the late eighteenth and early nineteenth centuries primarily in and around Tapachula, a growing urban center.

The period between Independence from Spain (1821) and the Revolutionary era of the early twentieth century is very poorly researched for the Soconusco region. There were certain changes in land-use patterns and labor relations linked to the growth of the coffee industry. Also, during this period there was an increase in foreign immigration to the area (largely associated with the coffee industry, see Helbig 1964). But the evidence suggests that the most dramatic changes did not take place until the twentieth century.

Contemporary Trends in the Soconusco Cacao Industry and Prospects for the Future

Several of the changes described above that began in the early nineteenth cen-tury in and around Tapachula can now be seen throughout the Soconusco region. One factor that has contributed to these changes is population growth. Population in the Soconusco increased exponentially in the twentieth century. From the 4.7 persons per km^2 recorded for 1900, population density had climbed to 32 persons per km^2 in 1950, and, by 2000, population density had reached 122 persons per km^2.[7] During the course of the twentieth century, several trends—the introduction of new crops, expanded cattle ranching, and tremendous population growth—created conditions that now threaten not only the cacao industry but the forest itself.

Part of the initial phase of my ethnoecological research has focused on talking to rural families about the decisions they are making, including the decision to abandon cacao cultivation.[8] We also asked people if the continued existence of the forest is important to them. Virtually everyone we spoke to sees a link between the continued existence of the forest and their own livelihoods and identities as *campesinos* (rural farmers). They see the current trend toward decreased rainfall to be linked with cutting the forest, a link with some scientific validity (for example, O'Brien 1998). Older residents (people over 50) speak nostalgically about how much of their diet used to consist of wild game and fowl. Many also continue to use household implements (for example, brooms, gourd containers) made from plant resources rather than purchase the same items, which typically are made of plastic or other synthetic material. With respect to cacao cultivation, we discussed a number of issues with the people we interviewed. We found widespread recognition that the Soconusco region is ideally suited for cacao cultivation, and people generally knew that Soconusco cacao is considered to be of high quality. Although people value cacao for their own consumption, they complain that they are unable to sell their cacao, that middlemen do not pay them decent prices, and that there is little help from the government. We also asked people about what they knew about the varieties of cacao currently under cultivation in the Soconusco. I knew that government programs in the 1970s-80s had promoted the replacement of the native *criollo* cacao variety with *forastero* varieties (for example, *calabacillo*, *amelonado*, Costa Rica) and hybrid varieties (*trinitarios*, *mejorados*) (López Báez 1985; López Báez and Sandoval Gallardo 1983; Jaime Cueto, personal communication July 2002). *Forasteros* and hybrids are heartier and provide greater yields per tree whereas *criollos* have higher quantities of fat and superior flavor (Prescilla 2001:21–26; A. M. Young 1994:42–47). It is estimated that *criollos* make up less than 5 percent of cacao trees around the world, yet producers of the world's finest chocolates are increasingly utilizing the *criollo* variety (Gadsby 2002).

In the Soconusco, it is difficult to find *criollos* today, although many people say they have kept a few *criollo* trees for personal use because the flavor and overall quality of *criollo* cacao is perceived to be so much better than *forastero*. During the summer of 2002, we were able to confirm that a tree identified by its owner as a *criollo* was a *criollo*.[9] In other cases, however, trees identified as *criollo* by their owners were not actually *criollo*s.

The dilemmas faced by Soconusco cacao farmers and the possibilities for a revival of the cultivation of *criollo* cacao in the region are illustrated by the following discussion that is based on interviews with don Gregorio Antonio of Acacoyagua in 2002 and 2003. Many of don Gregorio's comments were echoed by others I interviewed, and the issues he raised reflect some of the fundamental problems facing the Soconusco region today. I have known don Gregorio for twenty years, during which time he has always grown cacao. During the summer of 2000, however, I was surprised to discover that he had sold his cacao orchard (and the new owner had pulled out all of the cacao trees and planted mangos). Don Gregorio had purchased property farther from town, where, he told me, it is more peaceful. When we talked in the summer of 2002, he had not planted cacao at his new property. His decision to abandon cacao cultivation was based on his inability to find buyers who would pay enough for his cacao to make it worth his while.

Don Gregorio is luckier than many other local farmers because he has been able to buy not only a parcel where he grows food for his family, but he has also purchased an adjoining piece of property, that he called his "*pedacito de bosque*" (a little piece of forest) of about 5 hectares of forest that he initially decided not to cut or use at all except to enjoy. He told me that he considered the forest to be the basis for the continued well-being of the people of Soconusco. Yet he told me that he could not keep this pedacito of forest unproductive forever. He lamented that no one seems to be able to help him find some way that he could maintain the forest yet still earn money from the land. He believed that the variety of cacao that the state agronomists were promoting did not grow well there. He said they developed it somewhere else, so it is not well adapted to conditions in Soconusco. As I talked to him and others I could not help but think about the agricultural survey from 1820 discussed above in which we saw that in places like Acacoyagua, almost everyone relied on cacao, vanilla, and achiote as their cash crops, and that these would be perfectly suited to don Gregorio's *pedacito* of forest.

We had several conversations about the different varieties of cacao, and I explained what I knew about the *criollo* variety— that it had been largely replaced by *forasteros* and hybrids, a process he remembered well. He knew that we had confirmed that his relative and neighbor, don Rafael Antonio, had a tree of the *criollo* variety (see note 9), and in the winter and spring of 2003, don Gregorio planted seeds from this tree on 1 hectare of his forest plot. When we visited him during the summer of 2003, the seedlings had been planted, but it is too early to know whether they will become productive *criollo* trees. If they are successful, will he be able to find a buyer who will pay a higher price for a superior product? Is there any future for *criollo* cacao in Soconusco, and how can don Gregorio and others find a better way to market their cacao?

The decline of the cacao industry in Soconusco has broader implications for the region's inhabitants and environment. The evidence presented here has shown that historically the most valuable products of the Soconusco region were those that thrived in a forested environment. My concern about rapidly changing land-use patterns in the early twenty-first century is based on more than nostalgia for an earlier way of life. With burgeoning population growth and rapidly changing economic conditions, Soconusco farmers are now cutting the forest at unprecedented rates to feed their families and to shift to agricultural products that are easier to market and that do not grow in a forested environment. What are the likely outcomes of these changes? Around the world there is growing evidence that deforestation is contributing to climate change; in the Soconusco, declining rainfall, one possible outcome of deforestation, would clearly create a disaster for the region and its people. The short-term benefits of cutting the forest may create devastation in the long-term.

Conclusion

Research that explores historical land-use patterns and the ways that humans interacted with their environments in the past can play an important role in the discussions of contemporary land-use policy. The choices about land-use that people—farmers, agronomists, and policy makers—make in the next few years will have profound and long-term consequences, and a better understanding of historical trends might contribute to a better decision-making process. In the case of Soconusco—and many other tropical forest regions—there is a great deal to be learned from land-use practices that both preserved the environment and sustained a way of life for three thousand years.

Acknowledgments

The research upon which this chapter is based was conducted over many years with the help of a number of institutions and individuals. Archival research was supported by grants from the National Science Foundation, the Wenner-Gren Foundation for Anthropological Research, and the National Endowment for the Humanities. Ethnoecological research was supported by a Sally Casanova

RSCAAP Fellowship from California State University, Dominguez Hills. Finally, the kind people of Soconusco have helped me at every stage of my work, and I am grateful for their support.

Notes

1. Ing. Jaime Cueto, Instituto Nacional de Investigaciones Forestales, Agrícolas, y Pecuarias (hereafter INIFAP), Campo Experimental, Rosario Izapa.

2. Ing. Jaime Cueto (see note 1) reported (July 15, 2002) that local growers use 4 m spacing, Gregorio Antonio, cacao grower in Acacoyagua, told me that in that area, growers use 3 m intervals (July 2, 2002); and a document (AGCA, A1 324 2393) reports that in 1811 growers planted trees at 2.5 m intervals.

3. I use here a figure of 5,800 km^2 for the area including all of the municipios from Mapastepec to the Guatemalan border (Rodriguez 1974).

4. The exceptions were Ayutla, which was populated by mulattoes, and Escuintla, where a large portion of the agricultural products were in the hands of people who were classified as laboríos, a category that included Indians who had left their towns of origin (so were not *indios de pueblo*) and non-Indians.

5. Data for a fourteenth town, Cacaohuatan, is not provided in the document.

6. Censo General de la Población, Tomo 2, 1900, Dirección General de Estadistica, México. D.F.

7. Censo General de la Población, Tomo 7, 1950, Dirección General de Estadistica, México, D.F., and for 2000, Instituto Nacional de Estadistica, Geografía e Informatica.

8. The Soconusco Ethnoecological Project began in 2002 and was supported with funds from the Sally Casanova Research, Scholarship, and Creative Activities Awards Program, California State University, Dominguez Hills. Please note that I am still at an early stage of this research, and the evidence presented here is anecdotal. Nevertheless, it reflects the views of twelve adult residents of the town of Acacoyagua who were interviewed in 2002 or 2003. Future research will expand this sample and allow for more conclusive interpretations.

9. In July, 2002, I took a cacao pod from a tree identified by its owner as *criollo* to Ing. Jaime Cueto of INIFAP, Rosario Izapa. Ing. Cueto confirmed that this cacao was *criollo*.

PART IV

Mesoamerican Cacao Use in the Twentieth and Twenty-First Centuries

Traditional Cacao Use in Modern Mesoamerica

Cameron L. McNeil

Many individuals in Mesoamerican communities continue to cultivate or purchase cacao, using it in beverages and foods and in rituals. The consumption of cacao is tied to many life passage events, particularly marriage and childbirth. It is an important ritual offering and has a range of associations (water, fertility, rebirth), most of which appear to have originated in the pre-Columbian era. Although traditional cacao uses across Mesoamerica clearly have some commonalities, there are also customs unique to specific communities. The documentation of these practices is particularly important as many are dying out.

In this chapter, I will first discuss some of the beverages and foods produced from cacao in Mesoamerica. Then I will examine the importance of cacao in ritual and secular events of Mesoamerica and explore the meaning of these uses. My research in Guatemala and Honduras provides the basis for this work, the focus of which is on the Maya. Information on modern cacao use is augmented with data from ethnographies written during the last hundred years.[1] Seven publications, all of which are heavily drawn on for this chapter, provide the most extensive primary documentation of modern Mesoamerican cacao use: Bunzel (1967), Chapman (1985, 1986), V. D. Davis (1978), Girard (1995), E. C. Parsons (1936), and W. Popenoe (1919a).

For our purposes, the word "cacao" refers to *Theobroma cacao* L., and the term *pataxte* refers to *Theobroma bicolor* Bonpl. Some, perhaps all, Maya groups recognize *T. bicolor* as a form of cacao, and it is, therefore, integral to a discussion of cacao in modern communities.

Methodology

Fieldwork was conducted for this chapter. Permission for this research was approved through the Institutional Review Board of the Graduate School and University Center, City University of New York. Primary research was carried out in Guatemala in Solola; Santiago Atitlan; towns along the western coast, including Mazatenango and San Antonio Suchitepequez; Coban; and Antigua. Research was also pursued in Copan, Honduras. The structure of the research was centered on informal interviews and participant observation. Photographs were taken and are used with permission of the individuals in the photos. In endeavoring to learn more about modern cacao practice, the author focused on areas where cacao use is known to continue, seeking out owners of cacao orchards, vendors of cacao products, producers of cacao beverages and foods, and practitioners of rituals involving cacao.

The Role of Cacao in the Production of Comestibles

Today intensive use of cacao is most common close to areas where *T. cacao* and *T. bicolor* can be grown easily, although it does not follow that cacao use remains intensive in all areas where it can be grown. In many modern communities of Guatemala and Honduras today's cacao market is restricted to trade within the Maya and Ladino communities in which it is produced or between closely associated areas. For example, along the west coast of Guatemala many Maya and Ladino families grow cacao, when possible, in their backyards and

Figure 17.1. A cacao and *pataxte* seed broker in the market. Mazatenango, Guatemala. Photograph by Cameron L. McNeil.

gardens and sell the seeds or cacao tablets to market vendors who sell it to other members of the community (Figure 17.1). Some of these tablets and seeds are then traded to the communities in the Highlands where cacao trees will not grow, or they are sold in the large markets in Guatemala City; little of this product reaches the international market.

Preparation of cacao seeds

Today, in Guatemala and Honduras, much of the cacao consumed locally comes from small orchards (*cacaotales*) (Figure 17.2), where one can find a diverse mixture of *criollo* and *forastero* types and hybrids (see McNeil, Chapter 1, this volume). The fruit and seeds of these varieties are not equal, with some having a much sweeter and tastier pulp and some with less bitter seeds (see McNeil, Chapter 1). In addition, the flavor and quality of both the fruit and the seeds is affected by the stage at which the pods are harvested and the manner in which they are processed.

There is a loose protocol for harvesting and processing cacao seeds: pods are

Figure 17.2. Woman with a cacao pod from her garden. She said that this pod, which contained both lavender and white seeds, was a hybrid of local *criollo* and "Panama Red" cacao. Mazatenango, Guatemala. Photograph by Leslie H. Sheehan.

Figure 17.3. Fresh cacao seeds, the remains of a sweet beverage of the pulp, are fermenting in a plastic basket in the background. Fermented seeds from the day before are drying on the patio in the foreground. Photograph by Cameron L. McNeil.

taken off the tree; seeds are generally fermented in the pulp; the pulp is cleaned off; the seeds are dried in the sun (Figure 17.3). However, within this protocol there is a tremendous amount of variation in each stage. On the Pacific Coast of Guatemala, where beverages of the pulp are commonly made before the seeds are used, the pod may be harvested just before it is fully ripe—when it is "green"—to obtain the best pulp.[2] For this reason, market vendors of tablets of cacao sometimes sell varieties of these tablets produced from cacao seeds in various stages of ripeness—some from green pods—when the fruit is better for *refrescos* (drinks produced from the pulp) and those made from the fully ripe pod, when the pulp is reduced. The author believes that the cacao from the fully ripened pod has the most fragrant smell and best flavor.

The flavor and quality of the seeds are also influenced by the fermentation process. Seeds may be fermented in their pulp for one day or for several days. Archaeologist David Sedat (personal communication 2004) noted that when he was growing up in Coban, families closely guarded their process of fermenting cacao seeds in competition to produce the best cacao for market. Although all seeds are dried in the sun, not all are toasted before being ground up for a beverage. The ultimate flavor of the comestible produced from cacao is also likely affected by the age of the seeds, as old seeds can be stale and dry.

Cacao Beverages

In Mesoamerica, beverages made from the pulp of *T. cacao* or *T. bicolor* are largely undocumented. Recent investigations in the Highlands and west coast of Guatemala, however, revealed that such beverages were common in areas where the pods were accessible and were once common even in areas where the pods arrived through trade. Cacao pulp is sweet and appealing, and it seems likely that in areas where cacao was abundant, people would have found a way to use it. A fruit beverage of the cacao pulp is commonly made along the Pacific Coast of Guatemala. Called *refresco de pocha* (*pocha* apparently is the word for the cacao pod), this beverage is produced by placing the contents of the pod (pulp and seeds) in a container with a little water, beating the mixture with a wooden stick, and, when the pulp has been loosened, adding more water and some sugar (Figure 17.4). Some informants said that they drank the beverage immediately, although one woman said that she placed it in a cool place for three days to let it ferment before consuming it; she also said that it did not

Figure 17.4. *Refresco de pocha*. The cacao seeds are clearly visible through the glass of the pitcher. Mazatenango, Guatemala. Photograph by Cameron L. McNeil.

reach the stage of becoming alcoholic. This fermentation process may infuse the beverage with appealing bubbles. *Refrescos* of *T. bicolor* are rarer than *refrescos* of *T. cacao* in Mesoamerica, although they are commonly produced in Nicaragua (A. M. Young 1994:15).

Some people interviewed on the Pacific Coast of Guatemala said that alcoholic beverages of cacao pulp were sometimes made, although producing them is illegal and people were not comfortable with providing much information regarding their creation. Two men said that the *refresco de pocha* was allowed to sit for twenty to thirty days to produce a *guaro* (alcoholic beverage made from fermented fruit), although this period of time seems overly long and more conducive to producing vinegar than alcohol. In Santiago Atitlan, a town largely inhabited by Tz'utijiil Maya, one informant said that formerly *guaro* was made of whatever fruit was in season, including cacao and *pataxte*. This informant also said that a *fábrica* (small factory) which produced a special *guaro* of cacao and *pataxte* once operated in the town but was closed after the military moved in during the early 1970s. The *guaro* was made by placing the contents of the *T. cacao* and *T. bicolor* pods into a container with *cal* (powdered lime), *sebo* (animal fat), *panela* (unrefined cane sugar), and *jocote de leche* (a variety of Spanish plum, *Spondias* sp.). This was then mixed with water. Sometimes rice liquid also was added. The mixture was cooked, strained through a colander or a cloth, and left to sit for three days, at which time it had turned to alcohol and could be consumed. The informant noted that a fermented beverage of cacao was produced particularly for when a man went to ask permission to marry a woman. This informant thought that alcoholic ritual beverages of cacao and *pataxte* might still be produced, but said that this was not something people would speak openly of because it was *guaro clandestino*. Cacao seeds may also be ground and placed into alcoholic substances produced from plants other than cacao. Among the Lenca of Honduras, cacao seeds are ground and added to *chicha* (an alcoholic beverage produced from maize) and offered to the earth (Chapman 1985:197).

The most common form in which cacao is consumed in communities of Mesoamerica is as a beverage made from its seeds (cacao is also used in *moles* and in *tamales*). The range of cacao beverages produced today in indigenous communities is similar to that found at the Contact period (see Landa 1941 [1566]; McNeil, Chapter 1, this volume). Although certain ethnic groups may mix a special cacao drink for a given ritual occasion and apply a name to it not used in other contexts, the general names for drinks which contain either *T. cacao* or *T. bicolor* seeds are *atole* (also used for plain maize drinks), *atole de cacao*, *atole de puzunque*, *atole de zúchile*, *saká'*, *chilate*, *batido*, *pinole* (*pnul*, *pinol*, *pinolli*), *pozol*, *panecita*, *bebida*, *arroz con cacao*, *chocolate*, and *tiste* (*batido*, *pinole* and *pozol* do not always contain cacao) (Table 17.1) (Girard 1995; Oakes 1951a; W. Popenoe 1919a; Wisdom 1940; field notes February 2005).

The ingredients and the process for making these beverages are somewhat fluid among different communities of Mesoamerica, making it difficult to attach a specific recipe to a given term. Also, several of these terms may be used for a beverage with the same contents. Even within one town, the ingredients in a specifically named beverage may not be the same in every household or mean the same thing to every market vendor. For example, in the area of San Antonio Suchitepequez, some producers of *panecita* said that it was made of

Table 17.1. Some beverages made from *T. Cacao* and *T. Bicolor*

Name	Contents	Ethnic Group/Area	Source
Atole de cacao	Maize, water mixed together with the addition of ground cacao seeds and various spices and/or unrefined sugar	Widespread	Field notes 2005
Atole de puzunque	50% toasted ground cacao seeds, 50% green cacao (sun-dried-not toasted), cinnamon, water, vanilla, toasted tortillas, no sugar	K'iche' and Ladino	Field notes 2005
Atole de sapuyul	Sapuyul (see Table 17.2), cacao seeds, *pataxte* seeds, maize, water, no sugar	K'iche' and Ladino	Field notes 2005
Atole de zúchile	Ground cacao and pataxte seeds, sapuyul, water and maize (rice may also be added), no sugar	K'iche' and Ladino	Field notes 2005
Batido	50% roughly ground cacao seeds, 50% finely ground cacao seeds, beaten with tepid water. *Achiote*, sugar, sapuyul and a range of spices may be added.	Highland Guatemala	Popenoe 1919a:405
Chilate	Made of ripe toasted maize and water—boiled with sugar for secular use. Cacao is sometimes added. This drink is unsweetened when produced for ritual.	Eastern Guatemala—Ch'orti' Honduras—Lenca	Wisdom 1940; Chapman 1986; Kufer 2005
Chocolate	In indigenous communities this name is applied to beverages containing ground cacao and a range of other ingredients. In Ladino communities it is most commonly used for beverages produced from tablets of cacao, unrefined sugar and cinnamon.	Widespread	Kufer 2005 Popenoe 1919a:307–408 Field notes 2005
Guaro (of cacao and pataxte)	Cacao pulp and seeds, pataxte pulp and seeds, *cal* (powdered lime), sebo (animal fat), unrefined sugar, *jocote de leche* (*Spondias* sp.) and rice liquid (sometimes)	Tz'utijiil Maya	Field notes 2005
Panecita	Mix of toasted ground maize, cinnamon and cacao seeds *or* possibly once a mix of ground cacao and *pataxte* seeds	K'iche' and Ladino	Field notes 2005

continued

Continued—Table 17.1. Some beverages made from *T. Cacao* and *T. Bicolor*

Name	Contents	Ethnic Group/Area	Source
Pinole, pinolli, pinol, pnul, kah, ch'aj	Mix of toasted ground maize and cinnamon *or* Mix of toasted ground maize, pataxte seeds and cinnamon *or* Mix of toasted ground maize and ground cacao seeds	Widespread	Field notes 2005
Pozol, pozole	Tortilla dough mixed with ground cacao, hot water and unrefined sugar—three pounds of dough to "four ounces of cacao"	Widespread	Popenoe 1919a:408–9
Refresco de cacao, refresco de pocha	Cacao pulp (still attached to seeds), water and sugar (can be consumed fresh or fermented)	K'iche' and Ladinos along the Pacific Coast of Guatemala	Field notes 2005
Saka'	Maize gruel produced from cooked ground kernels, which retain their epicarp— mixed with ground cacao and sometimes sweetened. In some areas botanical foaming agents are added to this beverage.	Widespread	Faust and Hirose López, this volume
Tiste	Sugar, cacao, and rice (or maize) in a 4:1:0.5 mixed with water. Vanilla, cinnamon and *achiote* may also be added.	Widespread in southern Mesoamerica	Popenoe 1919a; Kufer 2005

Note: Recipes attached to a specific name are highly variable not only regionally but also within a given community. The preparation of maize for beverages also varies between communities: sometimes it is soaked in lime to remove the epicarp (nixtamalization); sometimes this process is skipped; most commonly it is ground, but not always. In cases where the author was unaware of the specific preparation of maize for a given beverage, no information is provided in the chart.

ground maize, cinnamon, and *T. cacao*, whereas others said that *panecita* also included *T. bicolor* and may formerly not have included maize.

Preparation of modern beverages frequently begins with purchased chocolate tablets (or, more rarely, factory-made cocoa powder). These tablets may be made locally and sold in the market or produced in a factory. In the western section of Guatemala, Mazatenango and Mixco are the two most important areas for cacao tablet production. Mazatenango tablets are generally small and thick (ca. 5.5 x 1.9 cm), whereas Mixco tablets are wider and thin (ca. 11 x 0.6 cm), resembling pancakes. Popenoe, describing the preparation of such tablets in 1919, wrote that they were made of two pounds of sugar to one pound of ground cacao, with vanilla and/or cinnamon added for flavoring (W. Popenoe 1919a:407). In 2005, informants detailed the same ratio of sugar to cacao for tablet production. Various spices may be added to the cacao and sugar mixture such as cinnamon, vanilla, *achiote* (also known as *annatto*) (*Bixa orellana* L.), ground chile peppers (*Capsicum* sp.), *sapuyul* (*Pouteria sapota* [Jacq.] H. E. Moore and Stearn), or pepper, as well as fragrant or flavorful flowers (see Table 17.2). The sugar used in the cacao tablets is generally *panela*, an unrefined form,

Table 17.2. Ingredients in cacao beverages discussed in the text

Common name(s)[a]	Scientific name	Section of plant used in comestible	Present in Pre-Columbian Mesoamerica
Achiote	Bixa orellana L.	Seed	yes
Black pepper	Piper nigrum L.	Fruit	no
Cacahuaxochitl, molinillo	Quararibea funebris (La Llave) Vischer	Flower	yes
Cacao	Theobroma cacao L.	Seed or pulp	yes
Canela, cinnamon	Cinnamomum sp.	Bark	no
Chile peppers	Capsicum sp.	Fruit	yes
Jocote de leche, Spanish plum	Spondias sp.	Fruit	yes
Maize	Zea mays L.	Kernel	yes
Panela, unrefined cane sugar	Saccharum sp.	Sap	no
Orejuela (ear flower), muk	Cymbopetalum penduliflorum (Dunal) Baill.	Flower	yes
Pataxte	Theobroma bicolor Bonpl.	Seed or pulp	yes
Sapuyul	Pouteria sapota (Jacq.) H.E. Moore & Stearn	Seed	yes
Vanilla	Vanilla planifolia Andrews	Seed pod	yes

Source: Information in this table comes from Coe and Coe (1996), McNeil (field notes 2005), and Popenoe (1919a).

a. When possible, the English common names are presented. The most frequently used terms in modern Mesoamerica are listed when they differ significantly from the English terms.

rather than white granulated sugar. While it is being ground, the mixture may be heated by a fire beneath the *metate*. The tablets are made either by hand or in a mold (W. Popenoe 1919a:407). Today, most tablets appear to be mold-made, although one woman in the San Antonio Suchitepequez market was seen molding tablets with her hands (Figure 17.5). The tablets are generally a solid circle, but some artful producers on the coast make them in the form of flowers.

Maize *atole* is the most common drink in traditional Mesoamerican communities and is treated as a food rather than something to wash down food. In Chichicastenango, Guatemala, it is called *bebida* (the drink) (Bunzel 1967:41).[3] *Atoles* with cacao (*atole de cacao*) may be made either of ground maize or from tortillas (which have been toasted and ground), mixed with water, cacao, and possibly other additives. *Atole* is sometimes sweetened with honey (Wisdom 1940). In some areas the maize was toasted (Bunzel 1967:41). In regions where cacao use is common, its addition to *atole* on a daily basis is likely related to its accessibility, to tradition, and to economic status. Redfield and Villa noted in 1934 when talking of Chan Kom, a village in the Yucatan Peninsula, where cacao was not easy to grow, that cacao may be added to *atole* for consumption on nonfestival days by members of better off families (Redfield and Villa 1934:57).

Figure 17.5. A woman making tablets containing cacao, *panela*, and *sapuyul* in the market. San Antonio Suchitepequez, Guatemala. Photograph by Cameron L. McNeil.

In the area of San Antonio Suchitepequez, in the heart of a prime cacao-growing zone, unsweetened *atole* with cacao is the mainstay of daily meals in some households (Figure 17.6). Various cacao beverages are produced by K'iche' (and some Ladino) families that live in this area. Two of these drinks are *atoles* with cacao: *atole de puzunque* and *atole de zúchile*. *Atole de puzunque*, an un-sweetened *atole*, is made with cacao composed of 50 percent sun-dried toasted cacao seeds and 50 percent untoasted cacao seeds (described as *verde* [green] by the informant) mixed with cinnamon, vanilla, and toasted ground tortillas. The K'iche' woman who described this beverage said that the untoasted seeds were crucial for achieving the best foam on the beverage. *Atole de zúchile*, is also unsweetened and is made with ground *sapuyul*, cacao, *pataxte* and maize (rice may also be added). The word *zúchile* is derived from the Nahuatl word *xochitl* 'flower,' and hence translates as 'flower *atole*.'

Figure 17.6. A K'iche'an family's supply of *atole de puzunque* in Mazatenango, Guatemala. Photograph by Cameron L. McNeil.

Chilate, a beverage described by Wisdom in eastern Guatemala, is made from "ripe maize which is toasted, ground, and boiled with sugar. If consumed ceremonially, it is not sweetened, ground cacao seeds are added to it and it is beaten until it froths" (Wisdom 1940:91). *Batido* (beaten) is made by grinding cacao seeds on a *metate* for a short period and then putting aside half of the roughly ground seeds. The remaining half is ground to a fine powder. These two sections are mixed, put into a *guacal* (calabash bowl) with tepid water, and beaten until the cacao fat rises to the surface (W. Popenoe 1919a:405). *Batido* is sometimes colored red by adding *achiote* (*Bixa orellana*). Various seasonings are added to this beverage such as vanilla, cinnamon, black pepper, ear-flower (*Cymbopetalum penduliflorum* [Dunal] Baill.), and occasionally the ground seeds of *Pouteria sapota* (sugar is also sometimes used) (W. Popenoe 1919a:405–407).

Another form of maize gruel, *saka'*, may contain cacao. According to Faust and Hirose López (this volume), *saka'* is made from maize kernels cooked without first being soaked in quicklime to remove the epicarp. The cooked maize is ground and mixed with water, honey, and sometimes cacao.

Pinole (from the Nahuatl *pinolli* and also written *pinol*, *pnul*, and, in Maya, *kah*, *ch'aj*), and *panecita* are similar beverage mixes (Redfield and Villa 1934:40; Field notes February 2005). The term "pinole" may be used to refer to a powdered mixture (and the subsequent beverage) which consists of toasted, finely ground maize and cinnamon, but in some areas, such as along the Guatemalan Pacific Coast, this term is applied to beverages that contain maize, *pataxte*, and cinnamon. In other areas of Guatemala, where *pataxte* is unknown or uncommon, *pinole* may contain maize, cinnamon, and cacao (Figure 17.7). In Mazatenango and San Antonio Suchitepequez the term *panecita* is generally used for mixtures of ground maize, *canela*, and cacao. However, an elderly K'iche' woman told the author that formerly *panecita* contained both *pataxte* and cacao and that in times past the term *pinole* was only used for a mixture of maize and cinnamon. These powdered mixtures are stirred into hot water, where they absorb the liquid and develop a thick, hearty consistency. Writing in the early twentieth century, Wilson Popenoe (1919a) noted that *pinole* was

Figure 17.7. A man selling *pinole* containing maize, cacao, and cinnamon in the market. Solola, Guatemala. Photograph by Cameron L. McNeil.

not used ceremonially and was only included as a part of meals, like coffee. The *pinole* he described was sweetened with more additives than were documented by the author in modern communities, such as anise and, occasionally, ear-flower (W. Popenoe 1919a:408).

Another beverage containing cacao, and similar to *pinole*, is *pozol*. *Pozol* is made by mixing tortilla dough (*masa*) with ground cacao (three pounds of dough to "four ounces of cacao"), hot water, and *panela* (W. Popenoe 1919a:408–409). *Tiste*, the last beverage mentioned above, is referred to by Popenoe (1919a:409) as a Ladino creation but was particularly common in Greater Nicoya (see Steinbrenner, this volume). A cold drink, *tiste* was made in the twentieth century by mixing sugar, cacao, and rice in a 4:1:0.5 ratio, respectively (Popenoe 1919a:409). Cinnamon and *achiote* were also added to *tiste* to flavor it and color it red, and vanilla was sometimes used (W. Popenoe 1919a:409). Today, *tiste* is the most commonly consumed cacao-containing beverage in Copan, Honduras, and is even sold in some restaurants.

In some areas, such as certain communities in Copan, where cacao has been re-introduced after people had turned to coffee production, cacao beverages are made in ways similar to coffee. Seeds are soaked in water but only to soften the hulls and not specifically to ferment them, and cacao is frequently mixed with coffee to produce a hybrid beverage.

Various ingredients common to cacao beverages at Contact period, and certainly during pre-Columbian times, have been replaced by more accessible imported goods. Wilson Popenoe noted in 1919 that the use of ear-flower (*Cymbopetalum penduliflorum*), a flower with "a resinous bitterness," once traditional in some types of cacao beverage, was being displaced as an additive by imported pepper and cinnamon although vanilla was still used (1919a:405). *Panela* also has largely replaced honey as an additive, and cinnamon has replaced the spicy flowers of *Quararibea funebris* (see Table 17.2). According to archaeologist David Sedat (personal communication 2005), ear-flower continues to be sold in Alta Verapaz, Guatemala.

Other ingredients that are added to cacao beverages have received little attention until the twentieth century but were likely used long before. The most important of these is the toasted ground seeds of *Pouteria sapota*, which are called *sapuyul* (western Guatemala, K'iche'), *saltul* (eastern Guatemala, Pokonchi), *saltulul* (central/eastern Guatemala, Q'eqchi'), and *pisle* (Oaxaca Valley, Mexico) (Bunzel 1967; E. C. Parsons 1936; W. Popenoe 1919a:405–406). W. Popenoe (1919a:405–406) wrote that some Maya told him that this was added for flavor, although others stated that it was a filler. Both statements may be correct. Although too much of this oily substance can cause stomach problems, the addition of a small amount into a cacao beverage adds a pleasant and interesting flavor. Untoasted, the soft beige cotyledon tastes similar to almonds, but with a bitter edge. The toasted seeds have an oily, slightly burned, nutty flavor. *Sapuyul* is sold in markets in Highland Guatemala and along the Pacific Coast in tablets made from the same molds as cacao or formed by hand. *Sapuyul* is softer and oilier than cacao, however, and does not hold the tablet form after it is purchased. In the market *sapuyul* can be bought in tablets which only contain ground *Pouteria sapota* seeds or in tablets with maize, *canela*, and cacao, which are called *zúchile* and can be used to make the *atole de zúchile* discussed above.

Cacao was highly prized for its foam, and early Colonial writers described how it was produced by pouring the beverage from one container to another to agitate it or by mixing it with a specially constructed stick (MacNutt 1912, v. 2:355; Sahagún 1950–82, Book 4, 1957:117). These early authors may have been missing a key ingredient of the frothy beverage. Twentieth-century ethnographers and botanists have documented the addition of small amounts of various ingredients that aid in creating a froth (Baer and Merrifield 1971; Bunzel 1967; Ogata 2002b; W. Popenoe 1919a). Among the Lacandon, a vine referred to as *suguir* (called *ajsukir* in V. D. Davis [1978]) is added to cacao beverages to produce the froth (Baer and Merrifield 1971:210; V. D. Davis 1978:213), and in Oaxaca, Mexico, a vine called *Popozocamecatl* (Ogata 2002b) is added. Without a description of either of these plants, it is not possible to know whether they are the same species. Conceivably, these additives contain saponins. Plant extracts containing saponins easily produce a foam and are frequently used to create natural soaps. Along the west coast of Guatemala, where foamed drinks are still prepared, the foam is called the *flor de cacao*. In some modern communities, foamy cacao drinks are no longer made; possibly the techniques used to produce the foam have been lost (J. E. S. Thompson 1956).

Beverages are not the only comestible produced from cacao. Ground cacao seeds are sometimes used in *tamales* and *moles*. In Guatemala, *tamales* containing cacao are a festival food and are called either *tamales dulces* or *tamales negros*. *Tamales dulces* may have cacao mixed into the corn *masa* and a sweet filling, whereas *tamales negros* contain a cacao *mole* and chicken inside of plain maize *masa*. *Tamales* containing cacao are also made in Mexico. *Moles* with various ground seeds as a base (squash seeds, peanuts and/or *T. cacao* seeds) as well as chile peppers are made in Guatemala and Mexico. *Moles* containing *T. bicolor* seeds were not documented, but the discovery of turkey bones in a Classic period vessel at Copan which may have contained *T. bicolor* suggests that *moles* may formerly have been made of these seeds (see McNeil, Hurst, and Sharer, this volume). The use of the term *cacahuate*, which means 'cacao of the ground,' for peanuts in Mesoamerica implies a similarity in the way peanuts and cacao were perceived. Although the flavor of the peanut is not similar to that of *T. cacao* seeds, it is similar to the flavor of roasted *T. bicolor* seeds, and it is possible that peanuts, which can be grown more easily and abundantly, have replaced *T. bicolor* in some of its former uses. Today, the principal form of festival *mole* sauce in Copan is made of peanuts; perhaps formerly *pataxte* seeds were used.

The Role of Cacao in Traditional Mesoamerican Communities

In this section I discuss the context in which cacao beverages and foods are consumed, in an attempt to ascertain cacao's meanings and associations in modern Mesoamerica. In many regions of Mesoamerica, cacao use has significantly diminished since the Colonial period. In those areas where cacao is still used, there is sometimes a continuity with pre-Columbian and early Colonial practices. Ethnographers document the role of cacao in ritual life as an offering not only to ancestors but also to the Chacs (rain gods), the gods of the mountains (sometimes ancestor deities), and the Earth Goddess, as well as to the saints and to Christ, who are often barely disguised representatives of pre-Conquest deities (see this volume: Kufer and Heinrich; Martin; Pugh). In addition, cacao continues to be an important gift for significant life passage events. When the author asked people in various regions of Guatemala when they used cacao, the most common answers were: for holidays, for childbirth and for breast-feeding mothers, as a gift that men offer to the family of a woman whose hand they wish to request in marriage, and for Easter.

Cacao seeds were formerly an important item of exchange, akin to, but not the same as a currency (Millon 1955a). This use, as well as the importance of cacao in elite rituals, has connected it to concepts of wealth and power. At times cacao appears to be a token gift, recalling this past importance, such as when small amounts of seeds are exchanged or offered (Bunzel 1967:44; Chapman 1985; Wagley 1949:90); seeds may also symbolize rebirth (Bunzel 1967). At other times cacao is described as a special comestible, whose consumption unites those attending a ceremony (Oakes 1951a:330).

Cacao can be a gift or can be used ritually in a variety of forms—whole seeds, ground seeds, complete pods, tablets, seeds in virgin water, or beverages.[4] Bunzel (1967) recorded that cacao seeds were used in all *cofradia* (religious brotherhood) rituals in Chichicastenango. Cacao pods and *pataxte* pods are frequently used in Highland Maya rituals around the area of Lake Atitlan (Santiago Atitlan, Solola, and Palopa) and in adjacent sections of the Pacific Coast of Guatemala, as well as in the *aldeas* around Coban (Christenson 2001; McDougall 1955; Prechtel 1999; field notes 2005). Maud Oakes wrote that the Maya of Todos Santos, Guatemala, placed ground maize and cacao on leaves as offerings to the saints in the church along with candles (Oakes 1951a:168).

Oakes may be describing a gift of *pinole*, although this is not commonly a ritual offering.

A number of ethnographers describe the gift of cacao in social and religious situations in groups of seeds—generally in numbers one, five (or numbers divisible by five), seven, or nine (Bunzel 1967; Chapman 1985; Faust and Hirose López, this volume; Girard 1995; Kufer and Heinrich, this volume; Pugh, this volume; Wagley 1949). Anne Chapman notes that cacao seeds are one of the items (along with animal blood and fermented beverages) with which the earth god and angels (frequently a term for the Chacs) are "paid" (1985:12). Seeds have also been reported as a gift when seeking a woman's hand in marriage, possibly as a token dowry (see below). I could find no twentieth-century ethnographer who documented the continued use of cacao as money, although several wrote in the early part of the century that informants could recall this use in the recent past—clearly a social memory of this practice existed at that time (Chapman 1985; Wisdom 1940:34).

Cacao and the Ancestors

Ceremonies involving cacao frequently acknowledge and recall the power of ancestors. In this context, the use of cacao appears to be an affirmation of ancestor worship and the mother/father deity concepts common in Mesoamerica (see Gustafson 2002). The use of cacao in ritual is perceived as necessary to observe the traditions of the ancient lineage ancestors, much as cacao at ancient Copan was linked to reborn ancestors (McNeil, Hurst, and Sharer, this volume). Bunzel notes that in Chichicastenango:

> the symbolism of cacao seems to be somewhat as follows: All ceremonies were instituted by Christ for the benefit of the first ancestors; on the cacao He placed His special blessing, therefore its presence on the table is evidence of the authenticity of the ritual, and guarantee that one is following in the ways of the ancestors. (Bunzel 1967:44)

The first ancestors "sowed the first seeds" in the world, and their descendants carry on their traditions (Bunzel 1967:240). The Lenca of Honduras profess a similar belief. Chapman, discussing Lenca religion, writes that the use of cacao and copal in ritual was dictated by God to Adam and Eve. God said:

> While returning, that way by where you are going to go, you will find some pods, cut them from the tree right there. In the pods you are going to see some grains or beans, these are the cacao. And there is a tree nearby, you are going to cut a piece of it, and it is going to provide some sort of resin, this resin is the copal. (Chapman 1986:17)

Chapman also notes that "copal and cacao come from the four corners of the world. They are a testament of the ancient ones" and "are what it is offered for everything: for goods, products and work" (1985:98–99). Both cacao and copal are deemed to have supernatural origins (Chapman 1985:103).

Ethnographer Maud Oakes participated in an important *cofradia* ritual, in which *batido* was consumed.[5] She writes:

> The ceremony that accompanies the passing of the gourd cups of *batido* is most impressive. They are passed by one man who holds the cup high in his right hand and says to the receiver the equivalent of "God bless you." The receiver accepts it, holds it high, and says to all: "Greetings to the ancient ones," sometimes repeating it for each person, and they answer with the same phrase. (Oakes 1951a:331)

Earlier in her ethnography, Oakes notes that the communal consumption of *batido* "signifies the union of all the participants, that all are one" (1951a:122).

In Santiago Atitlan, the fruits of *T. cacao* and *T. bicolor* are part of a group of plants that are brought from the coast for religious rituals (particularly Easter) and are said to be important because they mark the outside entrance to a cave where the gods and ancestors live (Christenson 2001; Prechtel 1999):

> All of the great saints and nuwal ancestors live in Paq'alib'al. Their spirits live there in the center of the mountain. This is also where the south wind is born. . . . The entrance is guarded by two pumas and two jaguars and is adorned with abundant fruits such as *corozos*, bananas, *melacotones*, plantains, *zapotes*, cacao, and *pataxtes* to show that the heart of the nuwals are present inside and that they have the power to give abundance and fertility. Inside is a gigantic snake one meter thick and fifty meters long that watches over the saints. (Christenson 2001:84)

Cacao in Easter Ceremonies

Cacao is particularly attached to Easter ceremonies, perhaps because of its pre-Columbian associations with "reborn" ancestors and "reborn" maize, which have been transferred to the rebirth of Christ (see this volume: Martin; McNeil, Hurst, and Sharer). In Santiago Atitlan, an informant told the author that during the month leading up to Semana Santa (Holy Week preceding Easter), cacao rather than coffee must be consumed or the heart will turn black. Bunzel writes something similar regarding the Thursday before Easter in Chichicastenango: "today they drink no coffee, just sweetened water or chocolate" (1967:217). In Chichicastenango the blessing of the cacao, conducted at all *cofradia* rituals is called the "Resuscitation of Christ" (Bunzel 1967:46). In San Antonio Suchitepequez people said that the month before Easter is the time

when cacao is used most. Arches (*arcos*) decorated with cacao, *pataxte*, *meloco-
ton* (*Sicana odorifera* [Vell.] Naudin), and plantains (*Musa* spp.) are put up in
the communities of Chicacao, Mazatenango, and San Antonio Suchitepequez
on the Pacific Coast of Guatemala on the Tuesday before Easter and remain
up until that sacred day (Figure 17.8). Altars are decorated with *pataxte* and
cacao in churches and *cofradias* in the area of Lake Atitlan and in adjacent areas
along the coast. A K'iche' Maya woman in the area of Mazatenango said that
cacao beverages were most widely produced at Easter. She added that on good
Thursday and good Friday of Semana Santa, *atoles* with cacao are taken to the
churches and given to everyone there, particularly the people who are putting

Figure 17.8. A figure of Christ being carried under an arch decorated with cacao and
pataxte, among other important coastal fruits. A figure of Judas hangs from the top beam.
Chicacao, Guatemala. Photograph courtesy of Rony Romeo Reyes Rosales.

up the holiday decorations. An informant in San Antonio Suchitepequez said that the offering of fruits on arches over the street in the week leading up to Semana Santa "is a benediction to god to make more good fruit for the coming year." *Pataxte* was frequently cited as an important adornment during holy week because of its strong fragrance (see Kufer and McNeil, this volume). In San Antonio Suchitepequez the black and white painted arches have fueled religious debates between Catholics and their Evangelical neighbors, who believe that the arches are the work of the devil. Catholics participating in erecting the arches said that it was important for them to continue this tradition because it belonged to their ancestors. The color of the arches recalls pre-Columbian iconography where black and white checks symbolized mountains (Furst 1978; Reents-Budet 1998). The arches hung with fruit may have antecedents in the religious traditions of the nearby Highlands, where, as explained above, the cave opening to the world of the earth lords is marked with the same fruits (Christenson 2001).

Offerings to the Chacs, the Earth Lord, and the Goddess to ensure fertility

Easter celebrations fall within a month of traditional rain ceremonies that mark preparations to begin the new agricultural season. Since these ceremonies are conducted to ensure the "rebirth" of maize it is not surprising that cacao is commonly used in rituals attached to both events (Chapman 1985, 1986; Girard 1995; Kufer and Heinrich, this volume). Cacao use in rain and fertility ceremonies was documented in the early Colonial period; among the Aztec, small amaranth idols, embodiments of the Tlalocs (gods of rain and the mountains) had their own small vessels of cacao (Sahagún 1950–82, Book 2, Chapter 35, 1951:152). Water and cacao appear to have particularly strong associations with one another. Kufer and Heinrich (this volume) suggest that this association may have been fostered by cacao's preference for growing in river valley bottoms. Among the Lenca, individuals who have consumed cacao as part of rain-making and fertility rituals at the start of the maize season must be careful near water holes as the creatures that live inside them (generally animistic embodiments of water—frequently a giant serpent) can sense the cacao in their bodies, and, desiring it, may pull them in by causing a tree branch to drop on their heads (Chapman 1985:122). A story told in Santiago Atitlan describes "tall girl," who is conceived under a cacao tree and is the personification of water (Prechtel 2001:91–92). In that area, the great Lake is believed to be the grandmother of all people (field notes 2005).

A number of scholars have documented practices in Guatemala, Honduras, and Mexico that involve pouring offerings of cacao into *cenotes*, holes, caves, springs, and ponds (Brown 2002:28–29; Bunzel 1967; Chapman 1985; Christenson 2001; Girard 1995; Kufer and Heinrich, this volume; E. C. Parsons

1936). Both Vogt (1981), writing about Chiapas, Mexico, and Brown (2002) writing about Highland Guatemala, record that offerings poured into bodies of water are made to the Earth Lord who dwells below ground and in caves. Among the Ch'orti' of eastern Guatemala, offerings made at springs and ponds are to the Chacs and the Lunar/Water/Earth Goddess (Girard 1995:25, 113, 164). The Ch'orti' believe that Chacs carry water from sacred ponds and springs to the skies so that it can then rain onto the fields—the sacred water is "where the rain gods drink"; fields are also watered by the tears of the earth goddess (Girard 1995:25, 33). Kufer and Heinrich (this volume) document a rain ceremony conducted by the Ch'orti'. Two turkeys and *chilate* (a drink combining maize, cacao, and sacred water) are poured into the spring to feed the gods so that "they can work in the production of rains and food" (Girard 1995:113; see also Kufer and Heinrich, this volume). Girard writes that the spring functions as "the navel of the world" (Girard 1995:113). The gods must be fed well so that they will produce rain and food for the people (Girard 1995:113). The Lenca have a ceremony to lift lightning back up to the sky and to "pay" the lightning for bringing the rain. In this ceremony two of the offerings are nine small fish from the river and nine grains of cacao (Chapman 1985:132).

Mythic associations of cacao

Cacao clearly had important mythic associations during the Classic period (S. D. Coe and M. D. Coe 1996; J. E. S. Thompson 1956), and it is not surprising that some of these—links with Christ, rebirth, rain ceremonies, and ancestors—have extended into modern times. Other mythic associations are more localized or may represent variations on ancient connections with cacao. In the *Book of the Chilam Balam of Chumayel*, a beverage of cacao with *achiote* "is what first glues together the mouth"—a first food (Roys 1967:96). Among the K'iche' of Chichicastenango, cacao is the taboo tree, which must be protected, mentioned, and used in every ceremony, because this tree protected Christ when he was fleeing those tormenting and persecuting him. When Christ first asked for help, the cacao tree initially responded, with some trepidation, that it was not capable of the task and that "our lord Manuel Lorenzo [the whirlwind]" will shake the tree. Christ, in response, told the tree that if it helped him, it would be remembered forever, but that if it did not he would destroy it at judgment day. Christ also offered to bless the tree in heaven, but the tree replied that it could not go to heaven because its roots were stuck down into the ground. Christ told the tree that he would put it "into the clouds and mists of heaven," bringing these to the tree if he could not bring the tree to them and said that the tree would thrive along the coasts (Bunzel 1967:239–241). Thereupon the cacao tree covered Christ in white blossoms, sheltering him from the sun and his enemies (Bunzel 1967:44, 240).[6] In the traditional recounting of this story the K'iche' say that their ancestors sometimes traveled two days to get cacao for their rituals, but today the K'iche' only purchase it in the market (Bunzel 1967:241). In Santiago Atitlan a similar story is told about cacao, although in this tale the sun takes refuge under a cacao tree at the "umbilicus of the sky" at mid-day while the moon brings him his food (Prechtel 2001:12). In Mitla, Mexico, there are stories of phantasms on the road who sometimes appear in the form of Motecuhzoma, who tells them to take chocolate, a turkey, candles, bread, and copal to the church, and in exchange he will give them a sack full of gold (E. C. Parsons 1936:289). In Mitla, people continued to visit the archaeological ruins with offerings of chocolate, turkey, and bread for Motecuhzoma in the 1930s (E. C. Parsons 1936:301).

Cacao Use in Secular and Religious Events Relating to Life Passage Markers

As noted earlier, cacao use is attached to many life passage events (J. E. S. Thompson 1956), such as birth, the request for godparents, marriage arrangements, marriage ceremonies, and death. In some communities, cacao is used in only certain of the life passage markers, such as an offering at birth, but not at marriage. See J. E. S. Thompson (1956) for the most thorough discussion of cacao's attachment to specific life markers.

Midwives play an important role in many traditional Maya communities. When a woman learns that she is pregnant, she arranges for a midwife to help with the pregnancy and birth. Midwives are frequently paid in food and money. Among the Poqomam of Chinaulta, Guatemala, a basket of chocolate, bread, and *guaro* is given to the chosen midwife. In accepting the food, the midwife accepts responsibility for helping the mother to bring her child into the world successfully (Reina 1966:238–239).

Cacao remains an important component of the postpartum diet among many Mesoamerican peoples (Kufer 2005; Nash 1970; Oakes 1951a; W. Popenoe 1919a; Reina 1966; Fieldnotes 2005). Popenoe writes that *pinole* (containing maize and cacao) is considered particularly good for promoting the production of a large supply of breast milk (W. Popenoe 1919a:408), implying that cacao is a galactagogue (an inducer of milk production). Reina records that "following a birth, the mother is expected to have a more specialized diet than during pregnancy. She takes *atole* of lima beans (*habas*), chicken soup, chocolate, and a small amount of guaro in the morning in order to regain her strength" (Reina 1966:243). Many informants in the areas of Santiago Atitlan, Guatemala City, and along the Pacific Coast said that various types of cacao beverages were important to bring down the milk of the mother and to ensure a large supply of milk. An individual in Santiago Atitlan also said that a beverage of chocolate consumed just before the baby is born can make the birth process proceed more rapidly.

Cacao is sometimes mentioned as a required gift for one or both of the godparents (most frequently for the *padrino* [godfather]) (Bunzel 1967; E. C. Parsons 1936; Wisdom 1940). Among the Ch'orti', mothers gave gifts of cacao seeds to the *padrino* (Wisdom 1940:34). In Chichicastenango, when the *padrino* arrived to "instruct" the baby concerning his or her duties in life, he was first given an *atole* of maize and cacao (Bunzel 1967:156). Then the *padrino* and parents took the child to be baptized at the church, after which the *padrino* was given tamales and some cacao seeds at the child's home. The cacao seeds are said to be "the sign that our [child] has received the blessing, and that you, *compadre* [*padrino*], have been charged with this rite and custom of our ancestors" (Bunzel 1967:160).

Pre-Columbian and early Colonial baptism rituals have been described by Spanish chroniclers (Landa 1941 [1566]:105; Marjilde Jesus, Mazariegos, and Guillen 1984 [1695]:19; Sahagún 1950–82, Book 4, Chapter 35, 1979:113–114), and some similar rituals survive today. The Tzeltal in Chiapas, Mexico, practice a rite called *ki'n ha'* 'water ceremony,' which is held a Maya month (twenty days) after the birth of a child to ensure the entry of the soul into the body (Nash 1970:116). The mother, grandmother, child, and midwife enter a sweatbath and rinse the mother and child with hot water and then cold water; excessive crying is taken as a sign the child's soul is not firmly set in its body, and a soul-calling ceremony must then be performed (Nash 1970:116). Three days after the child's ritual bathing the mother invites a gathering of female relatives for a ritual "called *st' mut'* (eat the chicken)." For this ceremony the women each bring "a peso's worth of bread, some chocolate, and ten tortillas. Two hens are cooked in boiling water, and the food is eaten by the women" (Nash 1970:1970). Oakes documents a similar tradition among the Mam of Todos Santos in Highland Guatemala, where twenty days after the birth of a child the mother shares a gourd of *batido* (ground corn and cacao) with her friends and family (Oakes 1951a:131).

Marriage arrangements and ceremony

Cacao continues to have strong associations with marriage in many indigenous communities (E. C. Parsons 1936; Steggerda 1941) as it did in Early Colonial and pre-Columbian times (Boone 2000; Mary E. Smith 1973; D. Tedlock 2002; Tozzer 1913). The rituals of arranging a marriage in modern Maya communities remain remarkably similar to those observed by Thomas Gage in the first half of the 1600s (see Gage 1946 [1648]:237). In the twentieth century the *padrino* or *casamentero* takes the place of negotiator in the marriage, which was formerly held by the *cacique* (head of the group). The *padrino* and *madrina* of marriage ceremonies are also frequently given cacao as thanks for their services. Cacao is more commonly documented, however, as a gift to the family of the prospective bride by the family of the groom (Bunzel 1967; E. C. Parsons 1936; Redfield and Villa 1934; Wagley 1949; field notes 2005). Redfield and Villa note that among the Yukatek Maya of Chan Kom, "A drink known as *x-taan chucua* used to be made as a part of the gifts offered to a girl's parents when the agreement for marriage was solemnized. Powdered cacao was beaten into water with a little corn meal, strained and mixed with Tabasco pepper and cinnamon" (Redfield and Villa 1934:40). In Chichicastenango, among the K'iche,' "the seeds of cacao are the first gift offered in the opening negotiations for marriage" (Bunzel 1967:44). This practice also formerly occurred in Santiago Chimaltenango, among the Mam, where marriage requests were made with "a spray of wildflowers, four *reales*, and four cacao seeds. These articles were rolled up in a large kerchief which was given to the girl's parents" (Wagley 1949:129).[7] Individuals in Guatemala City, Mazatenango, and Santiago Atitlan all noted that cacao beverages of various types were important gifts when a man went to ask for a woman's hand in marriage; as noted earlier, a special *chicha* of cacao was formerly produced in Santiago Atitlan for such an occasion. In lists of goods required for wedding feasts in the Yucatan during the late 1930s, Steggerda includes "chocolate" along with various forms of alcoholic beverages and bread, as well as the items of clothing purchased for the bride (1941:48).

Death

Although the use of cacao as an elite mortuary offering in pre-Columbian times has been established by several finds (Hall et al. 1990; McNeil, Hurst, and Sharer, this volume; Powis et al. 2002), cacao consumption at modern funerals has been less commonly noted than at other life passage events. The offering of alcoholic substances or maize *atoles* is more common (Wisdom 1940). In Mitla, Mexico, Elsie Clews Parsons described a woman who was buried with "holy water, a very small gourd cup, thirteen little tortillas, no larger than a copper quinto, and two broken up cacao beans which represent money"—all to aid her in her journey (E. C. Parsons 1936:146–147).

The Mexica offered chocolate to dead souls on the celebrations of Todos Santos in the early Colonial period (Durán 1971:442). In Mitla during the 1930s chocolate was poured on the graves of the dead on Todos Santos, and in Tehuantepec a cup of chocolate was placed on the family altar (L. A. Parsons 1970:281). In Coban, *pataxte* is an important adornment of Q'eqchi' altars for Day of the Dead rituals (field notes 2005). Like cacao's associations with Easter and Christ, this may relate to concepts linking cacao and reborn ancestors, or it may simply reflect a belief that cacao is a food that is appealing to the dead ancestors.

Associations between women and cacao

In the pre-Columbian period there is evidence of associations between women and cacao (see McNeil, Hurst, and Sharer, this volume). In modern communities, it was difficult to find direct evidence of this linkage. The story of the "tall girl" who is conceived under a cacao tree may be a remnant of this. Also, the widespread belief that cacao is vital to the production of breast milk sufficient to feed a child may derive from such an association or may be an ancient tradition which encouraged this connection. In Santiago Atitlan, one informant told the author that the breasts of the goddess of the midwives are *pataxte*

Figure 17.9. A chest containing a sacred bundle. The image of a pregnant woman is carved on the front of the chest; cattails are carved on the sides. This box hangs from the ceiling because of the female association with the moon. Inside are sacred cacao and *pataxte* seeds. Confraternity of San Juan. Santiago Atitlan, Guatemala. Photograph by Cameron L. McNeil.

pods. Also in Santiago Atitlan, sacred seeds used by midwives are stored at the *cofradia* San Juan in a box with carvings of a pregnant woman on the front and cattails on the sides; both images are linked to the great goddess (Figure 17.9). Midwives can use the seeds stored in the box to remedy the umbilicus of a baby when it does not heal correctly, as well as for other curing rites.

Miscellaneous uses for cacao

Among the Lenca of Honduras, fortune tellers sometimes use cacao beans to determine a person's future. Nine hands (a hand equals five seeds) are cast upon a table and read (Chapman 1985:209). Although this style of fortune telling is common across Mesoamerica, normally the bright red poisonous seeds of *Erythrina* sp., a tree belonging to the Fabaceae family and sometimes used as a shade tree in cacao plantations, are used for this purpose.

Conclusion

Some unifying themes are found in Mesoamerican cacao use practices. A number of the surviving religious traditions and customs involving cacao imply that it has an important role in ensuring the success of the milpa, because cacao "protected" maize (Chichicastenango) or because the water necessary for growing plants was born under a cacao tree (Lake Atitlan), or because cacao is one of the most important foods to offer gods and ancestors so that they will ensure a successful harvest (eastern and western Guatemala, western Honduras, Highland Mexico, Belize). Cacao consumption also inaugurates births, whether it is the rebirth of Christ, the birth of a new maize field, or the birth of a child. Its use is tied to celebrations marking the continuance of lineages: it is frequently offered by prospective bridegrooms and consumed at weddings, during childbirth, and at baptisms. Lastly, its consumption is often used to recall and honor the ancestors.

Traditional forms of cacao use continue to decrease in Mesoamerica, as cacao is replaced in daily life by more accessible goods such as coffee (McNeil, field notes 2005; McBryde 1945), and in ritual practices with factory-produced carbonated and alcoholic beverages (McNeil, field notes, 2005; Reina 1966). Scholars should work to document traditional Mesoamerican cacao use before this knowledge is lost.

Acknowledgments

I am indebted to Leslie H. Sheehan, Juan Carlos Rodriguez, and Renee Walker for their fieldwork assistance. I appreciate the support and encouragement that I received from Hugh C. Henderson, Margaret D. Henderson, and Michael F. Sheehan. I would like to thank Betty Faust, Eric Hilt, and Johanna Kufer for their insightful comments on this chapter. Many people helped me with this research in the Guatemalan communities of Lago Atitlan, Mazatenango, and San Antonio Suchitepequez. I would like to thank the staff at the Hotel Alba in Mazatenango who introduced me to people knowledgeable about cacao in the community. I also appreciate the help of Armando Cáceres, Lidia Girón, Fernando Lopez, Julia Sandoval, David Sedat, and Miguel Torres.

Notes

1. Although Mesoamerican communities of a hundred years ago were not "modern" in comparison to those of today, there is a continuity of tradition with those communities of the recent past.

2. Much of the cacao encountered in Mesoamerica is green when unripe, but some varieties may be purple or greenish-red. In using the term "green" I am repeating the description given by an informant in the Mazatenango market.

3. In Todos Santos, Guatemala, the word *bebida* refers to *pinole* (Oakes 1951b:39).

4. The definition of "virgin water" varies among Maya groups. In modern communities, it may be water blessed by a Catholic priest that is brought from a church, or it may be water collected from a sacred body of water.

5. Oakes's explanation of *batido* is somewhat confusing. In one place she describes it as containing cacao, whereas in another she lists its contents without listing cacao (Oakes 1951a:122, 131). *Batido* is generally a beverage with cacao since its name means "beaten" (W. Popenoe 1919a:405) and beating a drink consisting only of maize would seem to have little purpose.

6. In Chichicastenango, the word "flowers" refers to offspring (Bunzel 1967:229). Possibly, this story refers to the descendants of the first ancestors who care for and raise maize. If so, then cacao would act as an ancestor to all.

7. These practices recall a Ch'ol marriage recounted in an Early Colonial Spanish document where a young man and woman each exchanged five cacao seeds as a sign that they accept each other (Tozzer 1913:507).

18

Cacao, Gender, and the Northern Lacandon God House

Timothy W. Pugh

The Northern Lacandon of Chiapas, Mexico, once performed their most critical rituals in the *yatoch k'uj* 'god house.' Women were excluded from most god house rites with a few exceptions, including a cacao-frothing ritual. Cacao, which was associated with females, was not the most important offering for the Lacandon—that role was relegated to an alcoholic drink called *balché*, which was associated with males. In this chapter I examine the nature of gender in everyday life, the sacred context of the god house, and how cacao fits into the social and ritual milieu of the Lacandon. It is argued that cacao and *balché* represented and helped perpetuate unequal gender relations within Northern Lacandon communities.

The Northern Lacandon formed from migrant groups displaced by the Conquest (Boremanse 1998:9–13; De Vos 1980:244–257; Palka 1998:457–458). Before the late sixteenth century, speakers of Ch'ol Maya occupied the current location of the Lacandon in Chiapas (Figure 18.1). The Spanish forcibly removed the Ch'ol in A.D. 1586 (see Caso Barrera and Aliphat F., this volume). Refugees from Guatemala and Yucatan who spoke various dialects of Yukatekan Maya filled the relatively vacant region and combined to eventually form the Northern Lacandon and the Southern Lacandon (De Vos 1980:223–231). The Northern Lacandon dialect is linguistically closer to Itzaj Maya (spoken in central Peten) than it is to Southern Lacandon or Yukatek proper (Hofling 2001). The first recorded encounter with the Northern Lacandon occurred at the beginning of the eighteenth century, when they began trading with settlements near Palenque, Mexico. In the mid-nineteenth century, they exchanged honey, beeswax, tree gums, tobacco, and cacao with central Peten (Schwartz 1990: Table 3:12). The Northern and Southern Lacandon of the twentieth century both call themselves *Hach Winik* 'true people' but considered each other to be different ethnic groups (Boremanse 1998:3–8).

This chapter, which focuses upon the Northern Lacandon, is based upon

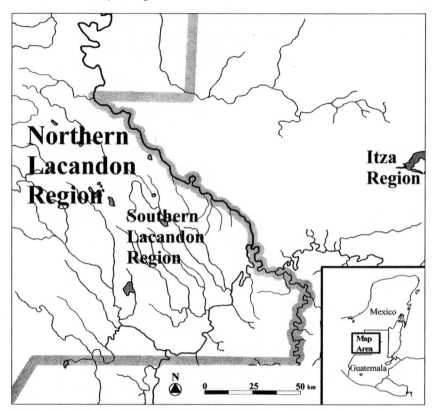

Figure 18.1. Yukatekan-speaking regions in Chiapas, Mexico, and Peten, Guatemala.
Map drawn by Timothy Pugh.

data collected by ethnographers from the beginning to the end of the twentieth
century. Errors and oversights in those studies may be repeated here. Most of
this work was conducted by men, and Lacandon females avoid contact with
males; therefore, there is an inherent bias in favor of the male perspective (Boremanse 1998; Bruce 1979; McGee 1990; Soustelle 1935; Tozzer 1907). In addition, many of the researchers focused upon male-oriented religious activities,
inadvertently ignoring those of females (McGee 2002:18–21). One notable exception was Virginia Davis (1978), who described female ritual activities. This
paper shines its analytical spotlight on brief discussions of cacao extracted from
the ethnographic research, but it cannot explicate the myriad details lacking
from these works, as none of the earlier studies of the Lacandon focused upon
cacao.

Ritual Exclusion

Ritual performances are orchestras of metaphors designed to affect participants (Fernandez 1972:56–58). During such performances groups communicate about themselves to themselves and others (Leach 1976:45); Thus, rituals help to both structure and reflect everyday life (V. Turner 1982:61–87). Ritual actions and spaces often provide participants with a condensed image of society, its principal categories, and the sacred landscape—a microcosm (Geertz 1980:13; Wheatley 1971:436–451). Elements excluded from this image are silenced and disempowered.

The efficacy of ritual activities is a source of social power (Kertzer 1988). Successful ritual practitioners often have high status in their communities. Of specific interest here is how certain members of communities are excluded from participating in such events. Restriction of access is a powerful source of social asymmetry (Devereaux 1987:102–106). Women are very often excluded (Holden 1983:2–3). They are sometimes considered polluting and potentially dangerous because they menstruate and can give birth. Alternatively, some groups exclude women to protect them from the dangers of contact with sacred states (Douglas 1966:159–179); to prevent supernatural beings from becoming sexually attracted to their fertility (Aguilera 2004: 90–92); or to obscure the contributions that women make to the social reality (Strathern 1988:133). Nevertheless, in some communities, their fertility or polluting potential qualifies women as key ritual participants (Bloch 1986:42–45; C. Thompson 1983:122–124). However, even when women become central to ritual activities, they may remain subordinate to male practitioners (C. Thompson 1983:124–126). There are no cross-cultural constants regarding the inclusion and exclusion of women in rites, as these factors are tied into the larger social reality. In some cases, such as that described below, women may play a limited role in otherwise exclusively male performances.

One must also distinguish between sex and gender, as the two are neither synonymous nor inseparable (Butler 1993). Women may physically be excluded, while the female gender in the form of masks or representations of gendered body parts or functions may be the central focus of the rites (Strathern 1988:103–107; Tonkin 1983:167–172). Here I consider gendered symbolism and ritual exclusion and inclusion among the Northern Lacandon and how these ideologies relate to everyday life outside the god house.

Gender Relations among the Northern Lacandon

The complexities of Northern Lacandon gender relationships have been documented by Boremanse (1998) and McGee and Gonzalez (1999). At the time of Boremanse's study, Lacandon men claimed that the primary reason they married was to be fed, with some men practicing polygamy as a sort of sub-sistence security. In certain contexts, spouses were called "the one I eat with" (Boremanse 1998:36–40). Men also depended on their wives to prepare edible offerings for deities (Boremanse 1998:40). The latter task was once so demand-ing that women in some communities asked their husbands to abandon the religion, which they also believed was ineffective, in favor of Christianity (V. D. Davis 1978:60). The husbands' roles included working in the fields, hunting, and interacting with deities on behalf of their families. Women worked several hours more per day than men. Men might request that their wives help in the fields, but men rarely did "women's work" (Boremanse 1998:40–48; McGee 2002:51). McGee (2002:67) indicates that Lacandon women felt uncomfort-able teaching him "women's work" and drew the line when he asked to learn how to make tortillas.

Northern Lacandon believed that anger was sinful and rarely expressed anger or made accusations in public (Boremanse 1998:57–75). Vengeance and envy were generally ameliorated by convincing the deities that one's adversary de-served punishment in the form of sickness, death, or poor harvests. Gossiping and moving to new locations were also options for relieving anger (Boremanse 1998:17, 59–75). The social constraints against anger and accusation do not appear to have applied to male interactions with their wives. Men were clearly dominant in the household and might reprimand or even strike their wives. Parents might also become angry at and strike children. However, physical violence is not common as wives generally obey their husbands and children obey adults (Boremanse 1998:39–46). Despite the belief that anger was wrong, one of the characteristics defining Lacandon deities was their quick fury. Many rites were conducted to appease or avoid the anger of the gods (Boremanse 1998:60–66).

Lacandon Symbols and Rituals

In Chiapas, the Lacandon lived in a "forest of symbols" (following V. Turner 1967). For example, the ceiba tree represented the *axis mundi*; the yearly foliage cycles of cork and mahogany trees marked four of the seven seasons; the plume-ria and other flowers were the wombs that gave birth to gods; mahogany, cedar, *balché*, and guano were sacred woods; copal, rubber, annatto, cacao, *balché*, and honey provided offerings; various animals signified social groups; and plants and animals provided the basis for many toponyms (Boremanse 1993:326–332; V. D. Davis 1978:21, 72–215; 1998:17; McGee 1990:31–33; 2002:Table 4.1; Tozzer 1907:40–43). In this chapter, cacao will be considered in relation to other vegetal symbols, especially the sacred *balché* drink, a milky white alcoholic beverage made from water, honey or sugarcane, and the bark of the *balché* tree (*Lonchocarpus* spp.) (Litzinger 1984:115–131; McGee 1991:442–443).

At creation, the deity Hachakyum formed the ancestors of the Northern Lacandon Maya. The *tzul* (white foreigners) and *kaj* (non-Lacandon Maya) were created by Hachakyum's elder brother, Akyantho'. Akyantho' gave his creations money and the seeds of many domesticated plants, including cacao. The *tzul* originally possessed the cacao and the *kaj* had the money, but the former conquered the latter, enslaved them, and took their money. In return, the *tzul* gave the *kaj* cacao (H. F. Cline 1944:112). The myth illustrates that the Lacandon did not utilize cacao as a foundation of social identity; they tied it to "others," the *kaj* and *tzul*. As demonstrated in many of the other chapters of this volume (see Faust and Hirose López; Kufer and Heinrich; McNeil), cacao was important to many *kaj* (and *tzul* certainly have had a long association with money and conquest). In addition, as suggested below, cacao is associated with Lacandon women, who, although insiders, are marginalized from core aspects of social identity.

The cacao plant served as a polysemic symbol among the Lacandon. Although the precise significance of the plant was not recorded, the Lacandon, like the Maya of Yucatan, likely parallel the pod and its beans with female

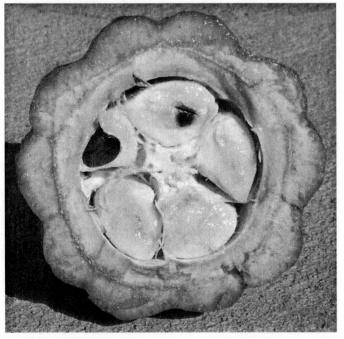

Figure 18.2. The quinquepartite structure of the cacao pod. Photograph by Juan Carlos Rodriguez.

genitalia (Faust 1998a:616). In addition to female genitalia, cacao is associated with life, death, sustenance, and economic value. Cacao beans frequently
occurred in counts of five in Lacandon ritual events (see below). "Five" was a
critical number for most Maya groups, many of whom imagined the world as
a quincunx, or four parts and a center. A cacao pod contains twenty to fifty
cacao beans (Millon 1955a:10), but when it is bisected across the width (Figure
18.2), five seeds usually appear on the surface in a flower-like pattern, because
the seeds are most commonly arranged in five rows in the pod (Cuatrecasas
1964:427). Other offerings, such as tamales, occurred in *tzaplik* (counts of five)
(V. D. Davis 1978:205). Nevertheless, cacao beans were found in counts of five
in various contexts. The quinquepartite structure of the pod likely lent to its
association with the number five.

Cacao served as a sort of currency among the Contact and Colonial period
Maya, and the merchant god Ek Chuaj is one of the deities associated with the
plant (Landa 1941 [1566]:95, 164). The Lacandon may have recognized that
among certain *kaj* (non-Lacandon Maya), cacao once functioned as a currency.
As mentioned, in a creation myth, the *kaj* were originally given money and the
tzul (non-Maya foreigners) were given cacao but later forced the former to trade
commodities. Similar stories describe how *tzul* obtained domesticated animals,
but those of the Lacandon escaped to become wild animals analogous to the
domesticated animals of the former. For example, the goats of the *tzul* were
paralleled with deer, dogs with jaguars, and pigs with peccaries (H. F. Cline
1944:112). The juxtaposition of cacao and money also seems to parallel these
two substances. Nevertheless, it is somewhat ironic that it was the Lacandon
who traded cacao with the *kaj* of nineteenth century Peten.

The significance of many Lacandon symbols is not easily discerned, because
in sacred contexts their meaning reverses. When an object moved from one cosmic plane to another, it was transformed. For example, when copal was burned
as an offering, it became corn dough or tortillas for the deities (V. D. Davis
1978:24). In addition, when the deities visited this world, they saw things in
reverse form; for example, caves and stone ruins appeared to them as thatched
houses, and weak substances appeared strong (V. D. Davis 1978:25). Cacao
lacked a symbolic reverse; hence, an offering of cacao remained cacao when
received by the gods (V. D. Davis 1978:26–27). In fact, no edible offerings
were reversed, which clearly differentiates them from inedible offerings, many
of which transformed into edible items when offered to the deities (V. D. Davis
1978:191).

The Lacandon were very concerned with dreams, and the significance of
a substance in a dream was also changed but not always in the same way as
reversals. If one dreamed of frothy cacao, it foreboded death through "foaming

at the mouth" (Bruce 1979:292). Thus, the significance of cacao was altered, though its foaming quality remained constant and was, therefore, highlighted. Dreaming of drinking *balché* or other alcoholic beverages predicted "fever and vomiting" (Bruce 1979:132).

The Northern Lacandon did not consume cacao and *balché* in everyday contexts, which distinguished the substances from other edible ritual offerings (V. D. Davis 1978:191, 214). Because *balché* and cacao were only consumed during ritual events, these substances helped compose the frame that differentiated the rites from everyday life. Furthermore, they were critical metaphors of the performances.

The primary ritual space and consumption location for cacao and *balché*, at least for men, was the god house. Each household group ideally had a god house. God houses were intentionally built in the "traditional" style (a dirt floor, wooden frame, no interior walls, and a thatched roof) rather than with the modern construction materials that the Lacandon used to build their own homes. These structures were believed to resemble the homes of the deities (McGee 1990:55–57). They vary in size from 2.5 x 3 m to 4.5 x 9.8 m with the long axis extending north to south (V. D. Davis 1978:55). Most of the recorded god houses have very similar orientations resulting from the practice of pointing the long axis toward the relatively immobile star Polaris (the North Star). The Lacandon oriented the rest of the domestic group with the god house; thus, it was the grounding point (McGee 2002:137–138).

God houses were sacred locations, as they were associated with supernatural beings, intersections between the earth and sky (McGee 1990:55), and points where members of distinct social groups (families) interacted (Boremanse 1998: 23–24; V. D. Davis 1978:55–59). The Lacandon rarely socialized outside the context of the god house, and visits to the homes of other Lacandon were highly ritualized (Boremanse 1998:18–23). Behaviors within the god house were subject to taboos. Women and creatures, with the exception of honey-producing bees, were technically excluded (V. D. Davis 1978:55–59; Tozzer 1907:63). God house rites are "the most gender-segregated of all Lacandon activities" (McGee and Gonzalez 1999:177–180).

Northern Lacandon god houses (Figure 18.3) had similar layouts from at least 1902 (Tozzer 1907:Figure 33) to 1985 (McGee 1990:Figure 5.3). Their central foci were *lakij k'uj* 'god pots,' which were ceramic incense burners with images of particular deities modeled and painted on one side. The Lacandon interacted with their deities through these god pots. The vessels were placed on the western edge of a bed of palm leaf matting extended north to south bisecting the god house. Male participants sat on wooden benches in the east side of the structure (V. D. Davis 1978:Figure 6; McGee 1990:Figure 5.3).

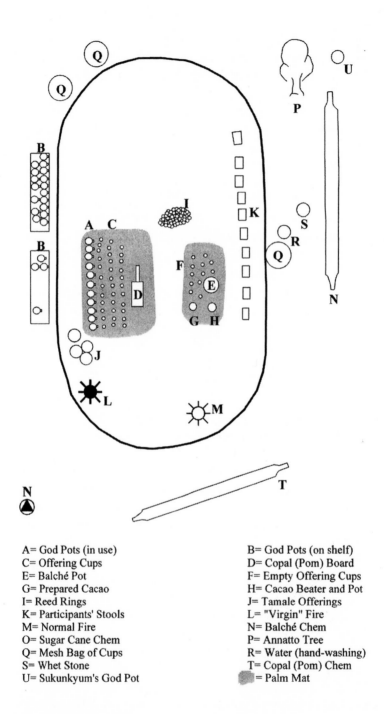

Figure 18.3. Northern Lacandon god house plan. Drawing by Timothy Pugh after Virginia D. Davis (1978:Figure 8).

A= God Pots (in use)
C= Offering Cups
E= Balché Pot
G= Prepared Cacao
I= Reed Rings
K= Participants' Stools
L= "Virgin" Fire
M= Normal Fire
O= Sugar Cane Chem
Q= Mesh Bag of Cups
S= Whet Stone
U= Sukunkyum's God Pot

B= God Pots (on shelf)
D= Copal (Pom) Board
F= Empty Offering Cups
H= Cacao Beater and Pot
J= Tamale Offerings
L= "Virgin" Fire
N= Balché Chem
P= Annatto Tree
R= Water (hand-washing)
T= Copal (Pom) Chem
= Palm Mat

The Lacandon placed edible and inedible offerings on the east side of the long north to south mat. A smaller palm leaf mat rested on the east side of the house. Upon this mat the Lacandon placed a jar filled with the *balché* to be offered to the deities and consumed by participants, several cups (McGee 1990:Figure 5.3; Tozzer 1907:Figure 33), and, in some cases, a bowl containing prepared cacao, a vessel for foaming the cacao, and the cacao beater (V. D. Davis 1978:Figure 6).

The various parts of the cacao pod played critical roles in the "births," "lives," and "deaths" of Lacandon god pots. The deity Hachakyum formed humans from clay (H. F. Cline 1944:108). Lacandon men likewise formed god pots, but simply forming clay into a vessel did not create a line of communication with the deities. It was also necessary for the vessels to be ensouled, which involved retrieving a stone from the cave or ruins occupied by the deity represented by the god pot. This stone was placed inside the bowl of the censer, which also represented a cave. The stone was the mechanism that allowed the Lacandon to communicate with the deity (V. D. Davis 1978:74). The Lacandon also placed five cacao beans and some copal ash into the censer bowl. The beans represented the diaphragm, heart, liver, lungs, and stomach of the god pot (V. D. Davis 1978:73). In addition, the Lacandon sang an awakening song and struck the vessel with colored beads (V. D. Davis 1978:77–85). Once ensouled, the vessel allowed the Lacandon to communicate and make offerings to a particular deity. While "alive," god pots were positioned with their faces to the east (Tozzer 1907:Figure 33). As discussed below, cacao flavored the primary offerings; hence, it helped sustain the deities.

Cacao also played a role in the "deaths" of god pots, which previously occurred yearly. During the termination rite, the paint, which formed part of the deity's image, was burned off, and the stone and cacao beans inside the vessel were removed (McGee 2002:136). The stone along with some copal residue was then placed in the new replacement god pot (V. D. Davis 1978:73). Hence, the killing of one god pot entailed the birth of another. The removal of the organs (cacao beans) and animating stone of the old god pot was reminiscent of a sacrificial event (McGee 1998:46). The "dying god" pots were given a final offering of *posol*, a corn drink, in a cup made from half a cacao husk. This was the only time that a cacao husk was used for this purpose, as offering cups were typically made from squash gourds. After its final offering, each god pot was then faced toward the west, and the cacao husk cup was placed over its head (Tozzer 1907:140). The vessel's death was also symbolized by burning the paint, which represented the deity's "clothes and skin," from the exterior of the vessel (McGee 1998:45; 2002:136). Dead vessels were placed in caves and covered by palm leaves, which replicated a thatch roof placed over human burials (V. D. Davis 1978:76; McGee 1998:45; Tozzer 1907:147).

The purposes of communicating with the deities through god pots were to make offerings for good harvests and health and to mediate with angry deities. Copal and rubber were burned in the bowl of the incense burner; food and cigars were placed in the mouths of the deity images; but the offering of *balché* was the core rite involved in human interactions with god pots. It was also a critical vehicle through which Northern Lacandon identity was externalized (McGee 1990:82; 1991:450–456). Offerings were also made in the caves and ruins occupied by particular deities (McGee 1990:57–58; 2002:129–136). Since the bowls of god pots represented caves, they were analogues of the caves of deities. A collection of god pots evoked the sacred landscape.

God pots and god houses were owned by male heads of household (Boremanse 1998:29; V. D. Davis 1978:55). Sometimes men of different households shared a god house (V. D. Davis 1978:55–57). In addition to housing ritual events, god houses were places where men interacted and made many communal decisions. Some men, known as *t'o'oj-il*, were recognized as having a greater ability to interact with deities, which added to their political power (Boremanse 1998:66–69). Women were denied access to the god house and were not part of its social network and relations with deities; hence, they were marginalized and disempowered (Boremanse 1998:53).

T'o'oj-il once wore ceremonial tunics painted with various designs. One such tunic recorded by Tozzer (1907:71–72, Plate 15) included various red and black dots and lines and two crude images of young goats, one female and one male. Of interest here is a pair of parallel concentric rings painted on each side of the garment. These images were found on other ceremonial tunics, including one displayed in the Na Bolom Museum in San Cristobal de las Casas, Chiapas, Mexico. *T'o'oj-il* occasionally painted them on their everyday tunics (Tozzer 1907:72). These were the *uyim* 'breasts' of the robe (Tozzer 1907:71). *Uyim* refers only to breasts of female mammals, including women (Hofling, personal communication 2003). Male ritual specialists in some non-Lacandon Maya groups dressed as females for particular rites (G. D. Jones 1998:334–335; J. E. S. Thompson 1930:110–112), and supernumerary genders among shaman are not uncommon (Angelino and Shedd 1955:121–125). The *t'o'oj-il* were not dressed in women's clothing; nevertheless, female breasts were painted on some of their ritual tunics. Breasts are the most basic means of sustenance and their appearance on the tunics likely related to the sustaining of the god pots.

Despite the feminine anatomical imagery, women's access to the god house and its activities was very limited (V. D. Davis 1978:56; McGee 1990:49; Tozzer 1907:107). However, women entered the structure for several reasons, sometimes as performers. If men were not available and an emergency arose, women could enter the god house to make offerings (Boremanse 1998:40;

V. D. Davis 1978:56). In addition, during a young girl's first initiation rite, her mother entered to help with her training (V. D. Davis 1978:56). When Tozzer (1907:111) visited the Lacandon, an elderly widow made the sacred robe of the ritual sponsor inside the god house. A wife of the sponsor also entered to help prepare the "virgin" fire (Figure 18.3) to ignite the incense in god pots (Tozzer 1907:130–134). Women also went into the sacred house to obtain a ration of *balché* (Tozzer 1907:130), but this practice disappeared by the late twentieth century. Of interest here is still another exception which continued until recently, in which the first wife of the god house owner entered to foam the cacao (V. D. Davis 1978:214; Tozzer 1907:128). Tozzer (1907:105) suggested that women never took an active part in god house rituals, but I argue that the cacao frothing was a significant performance.

Ritual Offerings

Lacandon women were excluded from most supernatural interactions but were responsible for preparing most edible offerings, including cacao, tamales, *posol*, and corn pudding. They prepared these in ceremonial cooking houses, where they also produced one inedible offering: red paint made from annatto. Symbolizing blood, annatto was used to paint objects and people involved in ceremonial activities (V. D. Davis 1978:169–191; McGee 1998:45). Annatto was eaten in other contexts, but here it was mixed with a white clay base (V. D. Davis 1978:169). The foods produced in the ceremonial cooking house were special and were called by names different from the same foods prepared in the secular kitchen (V. D. Davis 1978:191). Preparation was directed by the sponsor's senior wife, and most offerings were produced with indigenous tools rather than with the "western" tools available in the secular kitchen (V. D. Davis 1978:60–61; McGee 1990:48). The ceremonial kitchen house was about 2.5 x 6 meters and included various items such as a large table, a *mano* and *metate*, and clay cooking pots. Some ceremonial kitchens broke the "traditional" rule and incorporated a metal grinder for processing corn (V. D. Davis 1978:60–61).

Although women were excluded from most activities of the god house, they conducted rituals in the ceremonial kitchen (V. D. Davis 1978:60–64; see Bruce 1979:Figure 7). These rites focused upon the preparation of edible offerings and were led by the ritual sponsor's first wife. This arrangement found its way into religious beliefs, as Naihachakyum, the wife of Hachakyum, instructed the women in her ceremonial kitchen how to prepare cacao for the deities' deity, K'akoch (V. D. Davis 1978:214). These and other activities of women were not documented as well as those of men (McGee 2002:20–21). Nevertheless, some rites conducted in the ceremonial cooking house resembled those of the god house. For example, the ritualized sharing of corn pudding in both the god house and the cooking house followed a social hierarchy (V. D. Davis 1978:207–211).

The production of the cacao offering was highly ritualized and, like many activities of Lacandon women, was described by Virginia Davis (1978:213–214), and is paraphrased here. Before preparing the raw cacao beans, the ritual sponsor presented them to the deities. In this rite, the sponsor placed five cacao beans in four gourd cups on the palm mat altar in front of the god pots in the god house and allowed the deities to "see" them by pouring the beans from cup to cup. The cacao beans were then roasted and ground by the sponsor's senior wife. The ground beans were then combined with *ajsukir*, a plant which facilitated the foaming of the mixture (V. D. Davis 1978:213).

Lacandon men were in charge of interacting with deities and producing inedible offerings such as bark headbands, rubber figures, and copal incense and one edible offering, *balché* (V. D. Davis 1978:131). *Balché* was prepared solely by men during a long ritual event. It was fermented in a *chem* 'canoe' made from a dugout mahogany tree. Paradoxically, this "canoe" held liquid inside rather than outside. The *balché chem* lay to the east of the god house with its long axis extending north to south (Figure 18.3) (V. D. Davis 1978:Figure 8; McGee 1990:Figure 5.3; Tozzer 1907:Figure 33). When not in use, the canoe was turned upside-down and covered with palm leaves; in this position the *chem* symbolized a god house (McGee 1990:84–85; 1991:442).

The Lacandon watched the natural foaming of *balché*, produced by carbon dioxide released by microbial growth during fermentation, to discern when it was ready for consumption (Litzinger 1984:124–126). The foaming quality was also emphasized in a song chanted during the production and consecration of the drink (V. D. Davis 1978:90–105). The chant describes the foamy *balché* as floodwater, venom, and spittle and refers to the *balché* canoe as *Itza* (V. D. Davis 1978:90–104). Much of the foam was scooped from the surface of the *balché* into a plantain leaf, which also contained maize kernels, tobacco, and chili peppers. The leaf was then folded and cached in the forest along with the god pot of an Underworld deity (Litzinger 1984:124–128).

Annatto paint and *balché* seem to have been contrasted through their anomalous gender associations. All ritual objects, places, and participants were painted with annatto before important rites (V. D. Davis 1978:169–178; Tozzer 1907:72–73). Annatto paint and *balché* may have been allomorphs. Only the initiated could be painted with annatto and drink *balché*. Furthermore, *balché* prepared participants for interactions with deities just as annatto paint prepared the entire earthly setting for interactions with deities. Aside from these exceptions, the preparatory roles of females and males paralleled them with food and nonfood, respectively.

In sum, Lacandon men and women had distinct roles in the preparations for ritual events. Men produced most inedible offerings in the god house. They also made the *balché* in the *chem*, which is also a god house. Women produced edible offerings and annatto paint in the ceremonial cooking house. One's labor can help define one's social identity (Fajans 1997:7–8), and among the Lacandon the labor involved in feeding the deities was the most socially important. The ability to correctly perform the *balché* rite was a foundation of Northern Lacandon identity (McGee 1990:129). Because Lacandon men and women contributed differently to sustaining the gods and because the labor involved was carried out in different locations, these activities were important aspects of gender differentiation. However, while women made edible offerings, men carried the offerings to the god house and fed the deities. Hence, the men acted as "brokers" with the god pots, thereby restricting females from most ritual activities. The only offering that was carried to the god house by a woman was the cacao mixture.

The senior wife of the ritual sponsor generally carried the prepared cacao from the kitchen house to god house and placed it on a palm leaf altar adjacent to the vessel containing *balché*. The cacao cup and cacao beater were also placed on the altar (Figure 18.3). The cacao beater was "a smoothly whittled wooden stick with a corrugated ball on the end" (V. D. Davis 1978:213). The female sponsor foamed the cacao mixture by whirling the beater between her palms. Tozzer (1907:128) noted that a small amount of the corn drink *posol* is added to the mixture before foaming, but Virginia Davis (1978:213) did not mention this practice. The importance of the cacao preparation rite is apparent in Lacandon mythology which described that female deities foamed cacao before it was offered to K'akoch (V. D. Davis 1978:214). The women sometimes chanted a song while preparing and/or foaming of the cacao (V. D. Davis 1978:217–218). Among the Maya of Yucatan, the cacao beater connotes a penis and the foaming process is analogous to sexual intercourse (Faust 1998a:616).

The principal offering of some performances was *balché*; in others it was *posol*. Cacao could be mixed with either of these (V. D. Davis 1978:213). Cacao mixed with *balché* produced *uyonin* and cacao mixed with *posol* resulted in *ominuka* (Tozzer 1907:102–103). After the cacao was foamed, it was added to the principal offering. Virginia Davis (1978:214) noted that the female sometimes left the god house immediately after the foaming. In Tozzer's (1907:128) description of a New God Pot Ceremony, however, the male sponsor poured *balché*, and the female sponsor added cacao foam into each small gourd offering bowl. When the female sponsor poured the cacao she had foamed into a cup containing the *balché* dispensed by her husband, the performance combined female and male substances, perhaps signifying fertility and procreation.

One offering bowl filled with the cacao/*balché* mixture was placed in front of each god pot participating in the event. The foaming, pouring, and placing of cups was repeated two more times so that each god pot had three offering cups. Later in the ritual the god pots were "fed" by male participants who spooned small amounts of the substance into the mouths of the pots. Cacao was also later added to the *balché* consumed by the human participants. Although female participation in this rite was extremely limited, it was undoubtedly a performance.

Discussion

In a recent review of his research among the Northern Lacandon, McGee (2002: Table 4.2, 144) indicates that cacao was a condiment and a secondary offering because it was always added to another offering. He also mentions, however, that the role of women in Lacandon society is not adequately represented in the ethnographic record (McGee 2002:18–21). Lacandon females avoided social interaction with males; hence, their perspectives were not strongly represented in data collected by male anthropologists (Boremanse 1998:41). Interestingly, of the thorough descriptions of the Northern Lacandon, the greatest detail concerning the significance of cacao was provided by a female researcher. In fact, Virginia Davis (1978:Figure 8) was the only anthropologist to include the prepared cacao, beater, and cup in her floor plan of the god house. Given the amount of time invested in the preparation of cacao, one wonders whether the importance of this comestible was underestimated along with female activities and beliefs.

Another problem concerning knowledge of cacao is that its significance changed dramatically over the past thirty years. Virginia Davis (1978:191, 214) described that cacao was a sacred substance and that the Lacandon did not purchase commercially produced chocolate or consume cacao outside of a sacred context. McGee (2002:113), on the other hand, lists "Nestlé's Quik" among items purchased by Northern Lacandon families. He further links this and similar purchases to an overall shift from food to craft production among the Lacandon. As Lacandon men spent more time producing crafts and selling them to tourists, they spent less time growing their own food, including cacao (McGee 2002:112–114). Furthermore, god house rituals have become commoditized and now are performed for tourists instead of deities (McGee 2002:150–152). Virginia Davis's (1978:214) description of the substance as sacred and McGee's (2002:144) later indication that it was a "secondary offering" indicate a transformation in the significance of the substance.

The Lacandon observed the foaming of *balché* to discern when it was ready for consumption. In other words, the foam indicated when the beverage had become sufficiently alcoholic and sacred. Hence, they associated foaming with transformation. This foam was also equated with flooding (V. D. Davis 1978:95). The Maya in Colonial period Yucatan paralleled flooding with the transformative cycles of destruction and creation (Freidel, Schele, and Parker 1993:106–107). Frothing transformed the consistency of cacao and metamorphosed it into a fertile liquid. Like the foam of *balché*, the liquid cacao beverage was intermingled with air to produce an anomalous intermediate state. Similar intermingling of air and water has been tied to liminality, transformation, and death (Chase and Chase 2004) perhaps explaining the juxtaposition of *balché* foam and the god pot of the Underworld deity. The process of frothing the cacao was likely associated with sex. Interestingly, the venomous foam of the *balché* was removed and the frothy and fertile cacao foam was added.

The god house and ceremonial kitchen house manifest a gendered dichotomy exemplifying complementary male and female labor obligations (Boremanse 1998:40). *Balché* and cacao ritual paraphernalia were placed together on a palm leaf mat in the east side of the god house. These items corresponded respectively with the male sponsor who poured the *balché* and his senior wife who briefly entered to foam and pour the cacao. The female sponsor oversaw its processing in the sacred context of the ceremonial kitchen, carried the mixture to the god house, and then frothed the mixture. Her participation in the rite did not begin when she entered the god house; it began when she initiated the preparation of ceremonial foods. Her movement from the ceremonial kitchen carrying prepared cacao was anomalous and bridged the two separate but codependent domains. The last stage of cacao preparation, its frothing, occurred inside the god house in front of the god pots and epitomized female labor and women's contributions to the event. When the male and female sponsors mixed the *balché* and cacao, they effectively combined the labor of males and females, once again bridging the divide between the ceremonial kitchen and the god house. The combination of usually separate male- and female-authored objects or practices in the context of ritual performance can evoke the collective (Thomas 1991:55). Thus, these performances may have affected solidarity among participants. Such complementary practices can obscure inequalities, however (Devereaux 1987:110).

The task of feeding, which is a feminine role outside the god house, was accomplished by males inside the god house. In domestic contexts, it was the senior male who was feared, but in the god house that role fell to the deities. The role of the adult males shifted from dominance to submission in the god house. Some ritual sponsors once wore tunics painted with representations of women's breasts. In the god house, males seem to have assumed some of the nurturing roles that females took outside the god house to similarly sustain and create reciprocal relationships with deities. As in Tonkin's (1983:171) discussion of female masks, the use of female body symbolism in central rites emphasizes the power of women; however, a representation "shares in or takes power from the represented" (Taussig 1993:2). Painting women's breasts on tunics might have been a symbolic appropriation of women's most basic means of sustenance and part of their social power.

Ritual spaces are typically liminal or ambiguous (Leach 1976:34–35; Van Gennep 1960:26–40). Ambiguity does not correspond with chaos as distinct categories can be juxtaposed to emphasize the shared whole as well as complementary oppositions within the whole. In the case of the androgynous tunic and the nurturing behaviors of the males, the cross-sex symbolism may result in a "completed state"; hence, the *t'o'oj-il* may have objectified themselves as "mediatory objects" (following Strathern 1988:205). The Maya of Yucatan believed that children and the elderly were relatively androgynous and balanced, but that "persons in their reproductive years . . . need a partner to balance a more strongly one-sided sexual essence" (Faust 1998a:624). The tunic and nurturing behaviors may have allowed males to transcend their singular gender identities to temporarily become a complete person in the absence of their spouses.

The cacao/*balché* mixture offered to the deities was similarly complete, as it bridged the same-sex domains of the god house and kitchen house. However, this mixture did more than simply mediate between male and female domains, because the *balché* and cacao were juxtaposed with the male and female sponsors or husband and wife, respectively. It is critical that this is the point at which the "rule" of ritual exclusion was set aside, as this "deviation" emphasizes "co-authorship" (following Strathern 1988:140–143). The labor of the sponsors was combined, thereby evoking marital codependence. As mentioned, children may have been considered androgynous; hence, the production of the drink may represent procreation. Strathern (1988:201) described that, among the Hagen of New Guinea, androgynous "wealth items" involved in ritual exchanges between males represented domestic relationships. She further suggested that the objects helped male exchange partners to conceptualize their relationship in marital terms. A similar process may have been at work among the Lacandon. The marriage of the sponsors embodied in the cacao/*balché* may have served as a metaphor for the relationship between the males and the deities, with the former taking on the nurturing role.

Although women were largely excluded from the god house, the female gender was included. It is unlikely that the use of female bodily symbolism on male ritual tunics would have had a dramatic impact on sexual inequality. The exclusion of women, however, certainly silenced their voices from this space of social power. In addition, it may have obscured their co-authorship of ritual offerings (Strathern 1988:163). This is not to say that the contributions of females were totally masked, as the Lacandon ceremonial kitchen house stood only a few meters away and was clearly visible from within the god house. Furthermore, the foaming of the cacao by the female sponsor and its mixing with the *balché* was certainly iconic of co-authorship. However, the female processing of the various ritual foods and the red pigment was certainly "eclipsed" (following Strathern 1988:155–158) by the males serving these items to the deities. In the process, males monopolized the prestige of presenting the offerings to and acting as brokers with the deities.

Conclusion

The *balché* rite helped to unify communities (McGee 1991:452). Nevertheless, it also identified disparate gender roles and reinforced gender inequality within the community. In the context of the god house, the cacao foaming rite represented women's labor performed in the kitchen house. The restriction of female participation to this performance and the eclipsing of female roles by males metaphorically evoked the subordinate position of females in Northern Lacandon society while adding to the prestige of males. When the cacao mixture was combined with men's labor in the form of *balché*, the complementary labor relations and obligations of Lacandon men and women were melded into one. The ritual participants, audience, and deities consumed this androgynous microcosmic cocktail just as they internalized the unequal social roles and relationships that it conveyed.

Acknowledgments

I would like to thank Cameron McNeil for organizing this volume and for her comments. I also thank Tomomi Emoto for helping to edit this chapter.

19

Food for the Rain Gods

Cacao in Ch'orti' Ritual

Johanna Kufer and Michael Heinrich

The worship of rain gods is one of the oldest and most continuous religious traditions in Mesoamerica. This is not surprising, as the cultivation of maize, the main staple, depends on seasonal rainfall. Since the advent of agriculture, drought has been a serious threat to the subsistence economy of people in Mesoamerica (Haug et al. 2003; Hodell et al. 2001). The destructive effects of drought are dramatically exemplified by the Ch'orti' Maya who live in eastern Guatemala near the Classic period Maya site of Copan in western Honduras. Their ancestors may have lived in this area and adjacent parts of Guatemala and El Salvador for more than a thousand years. This land was once fertile and rich in natural resources (Metz 1995:27–28), fertile enough even for the cultivation of cacao, which requires a rich soil and continuous humidity. From Colonial times, however, droughts and subsequent famines have been recurrent problems, reported for the years of 1653, 1709, 1720, 1746–1751 and 1801–1809 (Metz 1995:37–38). During the twentieth century, deforestation and erosion have caused severe environmental degradation, leading to the disappearance of commercial cacao cultivation and to frequent famines. In 2001, the people in the Ch'orti' area experienced a major famine which was reported even in European newspapers. Parallel to the increasing threats to their natural environment, the Ch'orti' have experienced strong pressure to give up their cultural traditions. Unlike Maya groups in Highland Guatemala, the Ch'orti' have been geographically isolated from other indigenous groups for a long time, with Ladinos (culturally nonindigenous Spanish-speaking Guatemalans) as their closest neighbors. Ladinos often call themselves *civilizados*, implying that the *indios* or *inditos*, as they call the Ch'orti',' lack civilization. On the one hand, victims of discrimination because of their indigenous identity, the Ch'orti' are, on the other hand, often regarded as no longer Maya by some Western leaders of the Maya movement, which is dominated by young, educated Highland Maya (Brent Metz, personal communication 2003; for a discussion of the effects of the Maya movement in the Ch'orti' area, see Metz 1998). Despite this difficult situation, the Ch'orti' continue to keep alive traditions which are rooted in Classic Maya culture. Their language has been proposed as the only still-viable descendant of the prestige language spoken by the Classic Maya elite and written in Maya hieroglyphs (Houston, Robertson, and Stuart 2000), and some of their religious practices show interesting parallels with the Classic Maya (Looper 2003).

Methodology

The research presented here was primarily conducted during five weeks in 2003, but it also draws on sixteen months of earlier fieldwork, starting in March 2000. Initially, the focus of our research in the Ch'orti' area was on medicinal plant uses (Kufer et al. 2005). Investigation of local cacao uses was included following a suggestion by Cameron McNeil. Data for this chapter were mainly obtained using unstructured interviews and participant observation. Informed consent was obtained from research participants for publication of the collected information, including photographs.

Contemporary Cacao Uses in Eastern Guatemala

Whereas cacao is today an important cash crop for other Maya groups (Emch 2003; M. K. Steinberg 2002), commercial cacao cultivation in the Ch'orti' area was given up about one generation ago because of environmental degradation. Nevertheless, cacao beans are sold in the markets and are used by Ch'orti' and Ladinos for preparing traditional beverages and foods, particularly for festive occasions (Kufer 2005). Sometimes it is not easy to distinguish between indigenous and nonindigenous traditions, especially when the same name is used for preparations of different origin, as in the case of "hot chocolate," which Ladinos prepare with sugar and cinnamon, whereas the Ch'orti' add toasted maize and unrefined cane sugar (*dulce de panela*). Ladinos also prepare *tiste*, a cold drink containing *achiote* (*Bixa orellana* L.), sugar, cinnamon, and ground cacao. Although local people, including at least one *tiste* maker, assume that both the name and the recipe are of Ch'orti' origin, the word *tiste* is derived from the Nahuatl *tiztli* and was possibly brought to eastern Guatemala by the Pipiles.

Rain Ceremonies in the Ch'orti' area

In the Ch'orti' area, the principal rain-calling ceremonies are commonly termed *traída del invierno* (fetching of the rainy season) and conducted between the last week of April and May 3, the Day of the Cross. A ritual specialist for these ceremonies is called *Padrino de Invierno* (Godfather of the Rain). Until the mid-twentieth century, rain ceremonies were carried out by *padrinos* in several hamlets of the *municipios* of Jocotán and Olopa, and a very elaborate agrarian cult was performed by the confraternities of the towns of Chiquimula and Quetzaltepeque (Girard 1962). In the latter, *padrinos* are elected or nominated for a limited period, whereas in all other places this role was inherited and life-long. There is a notable difference in ceremonial organization between Quetzaltepeque and the rest of the Ch'orti' area. In the former, the strong position of the confraternities resembles the situation in Highland Guatemala, whereas in the latter there is more emphasis on individual sacred specialists, in a way similar to the Yukatek Maya (Fought 1969). Individual sacred specialists are more vulnerable than a confraternity, which incorporates most of the adult members of a community at some time in their lives. This may explain why elaborate public rain ceremonies have survived only within the confraternity of St. Francis the Conqueror in Quetzaltepeque, whereas the rest of the Ch'orti' area suffered a dramatic decline in ritual life during a time of increasingly frequent droughts following deforestation and violent quarrels over land. Today, in the hamlets of Jocotán, rain ceremonies are only conducted secretly within some families, because rain-making *padrinos* have been killed in the past and people are aware of the dangers of this role (Hull 2003:53–54). The Ch'orti' in Honduras still perform rain ceremonies, which remain largely hidden from outsiders (Martínez Perdomo 1997). There is little communication between Quetzaltepeque and Jocotán, the administrative center of the Ch'orti' area, where regional offices of Guatemalan Maya organizations are located. Even Ch'orti' with an active interest in the Maya movement had never witnessed a ceremony in Quetzaltepeque and thought the activities of the Confraternity of St. Francis the Conqueror were purely of Catholic-Christian origin. However, they clearly are an example of a syncretistic development of an originally indigenous cult.

Rain Ceremonies at the Confraternity of St. Francis the Conqueror, Quetzaltepeque

The ceremonies at the confraternity of Quetzaltepeque are described and discussed in detail below. Major parts (ritual offering to the spring and preparation of ritual foods) were witnessed by Kufer in April 2003; other parts (setting of the *mesa*, watering of the *oratorio*) are reported according to interview data provided by the confraternity members who conducted them. Additional information from historical ritual practices described by Raphael Girard is cited where relevant. In this account, the focus is on the central role of cacao, together with maize, in Ch'orti' rain ceremonies. Some other ritual plants important in this context are summarized briefly in Table 19.1.

Table 19.1. Some plants important in Ch'orti' rain ceremonies

Copal, Ch'orti': ujtzub'

Locally produced copal is the resin of *Bursera bipinnata* (DC.) Engl. (Burseraceae). In Ch'orti' and other Maya rain ceremonies, copal smoke symbolizes rain clouds (e.g., Christenson 2001:95). The close association between copal and rain is particularly evident in the rain cult described from Chiquimula, where a bowl made of copal resin, called *sas tun*, was used for the "fetching of the rain," instead of water collected from a sacred spring (Girard 1962:164). *Sas tun* is also the name for crystals used for divination by Ch'orti' and Yucatec Maya healers (Wisdom 1940:345, Ankli et al. 1999).

Amate, Ch'orti': jun (*Ficus* sp., a wild relative of the fig tree)

The *amate* tree is strongly associated with magical powers, probably because of its apparent lack of flowers: the tiny flowers are enclosed in a structure appearing to be a "fruit that grows by itself." Local people believe it produces a red flower, lasting only for a single night, on extremely rare occasions. Its finder will be lucky and successful for the rest of his life. In pre-contact Mesoamerica, strangler figs were the source of bark paper (*amatl*), an important utensil for ritual blood offerings. The sacred amate tree has been demonized rather than allocated to a Catholic Saint: In local stories, the power of the amate tree is often associated with the devil (see for example, Dary 1986:390–394)

Conte, Ch'orti': k'om (*Philodendron anisotomum* Schott, probably also the similar species *P. tripartitum* [Jacq.] Schott, Araceae)

The leaves of the *conte* vine are cross-shaped and bright green. Cross-shaped or trifoliate leaves are of general importance in Maya ritual. The *conte* vine itself seems to be used in other parts of the Mayan area as well, for example by the Mam (Hostnig, Hostnig, and Vásquez V. 1998:163, 165, 186). According to Girard (1962:108), the three leaflets symbolize the Father, the Mother and the Son, i.e., the couple of Gods of the Center of the Earth and their offspring, the young Maize God. It is important to note the difference between this concept and Trinity in the Christian-Catholic sense (the Holy Spirit has been "replaced" by the Virgin Mary).

Crosses of *madre cacao* (Ch'orti': *kan te'*), *Gliricidia sepium* (Jacq.) Stevd. (Fabaceae)

G. sepium is called "*madre cacao*" because it is used, probably since pre-contact times, to provide shade and improve soil quality in cacao plantations. In sixteenth century Yucatec year ending ceremonies, a statue of the god Bolon Dzacab was placed upon a standard made from a tree called *kanté* in years under the sign of Kan (Landa 1941:141). The Bacab of Kan years, Hobnil, was one of the gods worshipped by cacao growers in a ceremony in the month of Muan (Landa 1941:164). *Kan te'* means "yellow tree" in Ch'orti', a name probably referring to its role as world tree at one of the four corners of the world, which are associated with specific colors. In Ch'orti' cosmology, the yellow corner is located in the Southeast and associated with St Anthony of the Wilds, the patron of woods and wild animals (Girard 1962:131, footnote 36). *Kan te'* is also the tree which helps the Hero Twins to defeat their abusive older brothers by magically growing very tall so that the latter cannot get down and are transformed into monkeys (Tedlock 1996:105–106).

Greenery (*verdío*)

Consists of: banana or plantain leaves (*Musa* spp.), *carrizo* (a local bamboo, possibly *Chusquea* sp.) and *canutillo* (a Commelinaceae). Girard mentions the use of the Ch'orti' word for water, *ja*, in referring to the "greenery," but this may be a confusion with *ja's*, Ch'orti' for "plantain." A small aquatic plant called *parpar* (*Heteranthera reniformis* Ruiz and Pav. [Pontederiaceae], is used to adorn the canoe under the altar. Girard (1962:111) reports that a plant called *paj-paj* was used to feed the frogs in the canoe and interprets the name as an imitation of frog sounds.

Of the four confraternities in Quetzaltepeque, St. Francis the Conqueror's is the most important and is in charge of the agrarian cult. Its members are usually peasants from the surrounding hamlets. The ritual specialists, a married couple called *Padrino* and *Madrina* Titular (Godfather and Godmother in Office), take on their service for a period of two years, during which they live on the permanent premises of the confraternity in town. They get support and advice from ritual specialists who have formerly carried out this office, called *Padrino* and *Madrina* Guiante (Guiding *Padrino* and *Madrina*). Five mostly young men are in charge of the ritual adornment and are referred to as *adornantes*, loosely translatable as (ritual) 'decorators.' Ethnicity is a complex issue in Quetzaltepeque (Little-Siebold 2001). At the time of this study, the *padrino* (Don Beto) and *madrina* (Doña Andrea) in office were peasants from a nearby hamlet who explicitly identified themselves as nonindigenous. Don Beto pointed out, however, that in his function as *padrino*, he temporarily adopted cultural traits like the indigenous typical dress, because St. Francis the Conqueror was "an indigenous man."

The Rain Ceremony: An Overview

The rain ceremony consists of two major parts. The first, an offering to the sacred spring of the River Conquista, is conducted only once on April 23 and inaugurates the rainy season. According to Girard, local people regard the spring as the navel of the universe, the place where Jesus Christ died on the cross and spilled his blood, which transformed into the first rain (Girard 1962:225). The second part is the setting of the *mesa* for the rain gods, which is repeated every ninth night during the rainy half of the year in St. Francis the Conqueror's *oratorio* in town. The *oratorio* is a simple large windowless building with an altar containing the image of St. Francis. Next to the *oratorio* is a sheltered area for cooking, hereafter called the "confraternity kitchen." The ceremonies are conducted every year on the same date, starting shortly before the beginning of the rainy season and the sowing, regardless of the current weather conditions. This differs from rain ceremonies carried out in case of insufficient rainfall after the maize has been sown but before the plants have completed their life cycle (for example, Faust 1998b; Freidel, Schele, and Parker 1993:29–33). We first give a chronological overview of the days of ritual and then explain them in detail.

April 22

- At the sacred spring: Adorning crosses with *conte* leaves (*Philodendron anisotomum*, Araceae; see Table 19.1)

- Confraternity kitchen: Preparing maize *tamalitos*
- *Oratorio* of St. Francis: Replacing dry altar adornment with basic green adornment (*conte* leaves and green coconuts)

April 23

- Confraternity kitchen: Preparing hot *chilate* with cacao, black *chilate*, *tamales*, bean *empanadas*, maize tortillas
- Ritual offering to the sacred spring (midnight)

April 24

- Adorning St. Francis the Conqueror's altar with full greenery
- Placing aquatic animals in a canoe under the altar
- Setting the *mesa* (midnight)

May 2, and from then on every ninth night

- Repetitions of the setting of the *mesa*
- "Watering" the *oratorio* interior. (The Spanish expression *regar* is used in the context of watering plants in a garden. It is also used locally to refer to the action of the rain gods who water the fields.)

Ritual food preparation

All foodstuffs for the festival are prepared by women in the confraternity kitchen, including food destined for participants in the ceremonies and ritual food offerings. Although this contrasts with contemporary ceremonies in Yucatan, where ritual food offerings are mostly prepared by men (for example, Faust 1998b:94, 96), it presumably reflects the pre-Contact situation, as indicated by Diego de Landa, who mentions women preparing ritual foodstuffs in sixteenth-century Yucatan (Landa 1941 [1566]:128). Ch'orti' men do not participate in the preparation of ritual foods, with the exception of the mixing of black *chilate* at the sacred spring (see below). Even in this case, the ingredients (cacao and maize) are first ground by the *madrina* (Figure 19.1). As among other Maya groups (Pugh, this volume), the area where ritual food is prepared is a sacred female-dominated space which complements the male-dominated sacred space where the ritual offerings are presented. On April 22, *tamalitos* are prepared from ground maize, while on April 23, *tamales* (Ch'orti': *b'ak'atpa*), which also contain meat and seasonings, are prepared, as well as other festival foods such as *empanadas de frijol* (maize tortillas filled with black beans) and a maize drink called *chilate*.[1]

Figure 19.1. A *madrina* grinding maize for *chilate*. Quetzaltepeque, Guatemala. Photograph by Johanna Kufer.

Chilate, a Ch'orti' Ritual Maize Drink

The Ch'orti' prepare a variety of different maize drinks. For profane use, the most important beverages are *atol agrio* (Ch'orti': *pajbursa*), a sour fermented maize drink, and *pinol* (Ch'orti': *ch'aj*), or 'maize coffee,' a hot drink prepared from heavily toasted maize which is typically consumed with meals. Maize drinks for ritual occasions are called *chilate* (from the Nahuatl *chilatl*) in local Spanish. This is the Ch'orti' equivalent of the ritual maize drink called *sakha'* or *saka'* by other Maya groups (for example, Faust and Hirose, this volume). An unsweetened variety used mainly for ritual offerings is called *sak sa'* 'white corn drink' in Ch'orti',' an expression also known from Classic period vessels presumably used for serving a similar drink. Other, usually sweetened, *chilate* varieties are consumed as festival drinks and are called *u yara sa'* 'thin corn drink' and *pan sa'* 'corn drink with bread.' The latter contains small pieces of wheat bread which are sometimes referred to as "flowers" (López García 2003); these may replace either real flowers or the froth which forms on beaten chocolate drinks and is sometimes called "flower" (see McNeil, Chapter 17, this volume). *Chilate* is sometimes simply referred to as *sa,'* the general Ch'orti' term for maize drinks. It is made from parched maize without soaking with lime or ashes, a process called "nixtamalization" which is routinely carried out when preparing tortillas and many other maize-based foods and drinks. For serving to the participants in ceremonies at Quetzaltepeque, the *chilate* is boiled with water and poured hot into *jícaras* (Ch'orti': *simaj*), cup-shaped vessels made from the relatively small, elongated fruit of a species of calabash tree (*Crescentia alata* Kunth) by cutting off the upper part of the fruit horizontally. A small amount of chocolate is poured into the *chilate* in each *jícara* (Figure 19.2). This bitter chocolate is made from parched ground cacao beans with ground maize and water. As both *chilate* and chocolate are rather thick, the chocolate forms a distinct dark "blob" in the light-colored *chilate* (Figure 19.3). Hot *chilate* with cacao is also served at festivities during the "dry half of the year" (see below), especially at the festival

Figure 19.2. Chocolate is poured from a *guacal* into a *jícara* containing hot *chilate*. Quetzaltepeque, Guatemala. Photograph by Johanna Kufer.

Figure 19.3. Chocolate forms a distinct dark "blob" in the hot *chilate*. Quetzaltepeque, Guatemala. Photograph by Johanna Kufer.

of St. Francis the Conqueror on December 19 at midnight. Black *chilate* for ritual offerings is different: The cacao beans are not parched, and it is prepared with cold water without boiling or heating. Ideally, black *chilate* is made with "virgin water" from a sacred mountain spring whose water is not used for profane purposes.[2] The maize flour is ground very fine with water on the grinding stone. Ground maize and ground cacao are mixed with water to make a dark, homogeneous drink, which is served in *guacals* (Ch'orti': *ruch*), bowls made from the larger, round fruits of another species of calabash tree *Crescentia cujete* L.; the fruit is parted into two halves with a vertical cut (see Figure 19.2).[3]

Preparations at the sacred spring

The ritual offering takes place on April 23. The spring is in a woody area at the foot of an *amate* tree (*Ficus* sp.; see Table 19.1) with a *conte* vine climbing up its trunk. There is a small clearing next to it which is lined on one side with a long row of crosses, one for each *padrino* who took on the two-year service, including the one currently in office. The crosses are made from the *madre cacao* tree (*Gliricidia sepium*) (Girard 1962:81), called *kan te'* 'yellow tree' in Ch'orti', which has been used, probably since pre-Contact times, to provide shade and enrich the soil in cacao plantations, as indicated by its Spanish name. In 2003, there were forty-nine crosses; however, records in the confraternity books indicate that sixteen years earlier, there were eighty-six. Some crosses were destroyed

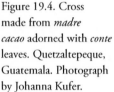

Figure 19.4. Cross made from *madre cacao* adorned with *conte* leaves. Quetzaltepeque, Guatemala. Photograph by Johanna Kufer.

in a fire, and there are plans to replace the missing crosses, which would make this visual representation of the antiquity of the ceremony even more impressive. All crosses are adorned with the cross-shaped, bright green leaves of the *conte* vine on April 22 during the daytime (Figure 19.4).

Preparations and ritual adornment at the *oratorio* of St. Francis

On the night of April 22, the adornment of St. Francis the Conqueror's altar is changed. Old adornments are removed, and the altar and three candle holders in front of it are covered with an elaborate coat of shiny green *conte* leaves. In addition, in 2003, green coconuts (*Cocos nucifera*) containing coconut milk (*agua de coco*), were suspended from the altar ceiling. Confraternity members explained that the year is divided into a dry and a wet half, reflected in the adornment of the altar. This may include red, yellow, and purple flowers (that is, "warm colors"), and dry, artificial adornments in the dry half of the year, but only "greenery" and white objects (including flowers) during the wet half.[4] The wet half of the year is characterized by a continuous layer of heavy dark clouds; in the dry half, the sky is either completely clear and bright or dotted with small white clouds, but not completely covered. As Girard (1962:79–80) pointed out the ceremonies of the agrarian worship of the wet season are carried out in the dark of the night in enclosed spaces, whereas the solar worship of the dry season takes place in the bright light of the day. Although the full "greenery" adornment is not put in place yet, white maize ears are tied to the altar (compare Girard 1962:109). These will be donated later in the year to farmers, who will sow grains taken from these ears at the four corners of their *milpas* (maize fields). Allegedly, the grains become impregnated with the sacred power at the altar, enabling them to keep away strong winds which might threaten to destroy the maize plants within the field.

During the festivities, the altar and the whole *oratorio* must be kept cool to "call" the rainfall. Because the ceremonies take place in the hottest part of the year, coolness and dampness must be induced by watering the whole building (see below); by using plants from humid areas as adornment; and by excluding the "warm" colors, red, and yellow, from adornment and ritual dress. The ritual specialists also must avoid overheating their bodies, which would jeopardize the attraction of the "angels" (rain gods), but they cannot achieve this by taking showers because abstention from bathing or showering is part of the behavior restrictions, called *dieta*, which apply for the ritual specialists during all days of ritual. An important measure for "keeping cool" is to drink *fresco de cacao*, a cold, unsweetened preparation made from ground cacao beans and water which must not be boiled, locally called *agua viva* 'living water,' because "water that has been boiled is already dead."[5] On April 24, the altar receives its full adornment of *verdío* 'greenery' (see Table 19.1). According to Girard (1962:109), the fully adorned altar represents the World Tree, or *axis mundi*. Similar concepts have been described from other Maya groups (for example, Christenson 2001:105).

Aquatic animals

Confraternity members provided the following description of the arrangement under the altar: A dugout canoe, referred to as the "Candle of Pearl, the Center," and said to represent the sacred spring, is placed under the altar and filled with water collected from the sacred spring on April 23. Aquatic animals such as frogs or toads, fish, and freshwater prawns are placed into it, together with a small aquatic plant called *parpar* (*Heteranthera reniformis*, Pontederiaceae).[6] In the recent past (not more than thirty years ago), sea animals were brought in from the coast, including at least once, a crocodile. Additionally, frogs and toads may make their own way into the *oratorio* during the wet season because St. Francis "calls them," just as he summons pilgrims to bring him offerings.

Ritual Offering to the Sacred Spring

On April 23, around nightfall, the decorators start to gather and pack the ritual objects needed for the ceremony. At about 9:30 P.M., the procession leaves Quetzaltepeque and walks up to the spring, the *padrinos* wearing the traditional white clothes and blue kerchiefs under their hats.[7] The *madrina* does not attend the ceremony at the sacred spring, neither during her time in office nor afterwards. The reason given for this tradition by Doña Andrea, the *madrina* in office at the time of this study, was that she had to look after the confraternity building and kitchen while everybody else was away. In former times, only selected male representatives of the hamlets of Quetzaltepeque participated in the ritual at the spring (Girard 1962:85). About halfway to the spring, the *padrino* in office lights a candle, burns incense, and prays at a spot a few steps downhill to the left of the road (Figure 19.5). This place was described as 'like a door to the mountain lakes' (*como puerta de las lagunas que hay en el cerro*) 'opposite the Enchanted Waterhole' (*Poza Encantada*). Girard (1962:86) reports the belief that the road is closed for the night by two mountains which join at nightfall, forming an entrance to the underworld which can only be passed safely if one knows the prayer to open it. After passing this "door," the procession continues on, leaves the major road, and follows a narrow path through a wood until arriving at the spring at 10:30 P.M. The *padrinos* light one by one the candles in front of each of the crosses representing earlier generations of *padrinos*, while praying and burning incense. A rectangular space on the ground is cleared and laid with banana leaves for arranging the *mesa* (table, or altar). The decorators mix ground cacao and maize with water from the spring in five *guacals* to obtain black *chilate*. Five white candles are fixed on the *mesa*, one in each corner and one in the center (see Figure 19.6). This so called quincunx pattern—a central element surrounded by four elements marking the periphery—is used by Maya ritual specialists to "sanctify space and open a portal to the Otherworld" (Freidel, Schele, and Parker 1993:128–131; see also Faust and Hirose, this volume). Food is placed next to each candle, including, in 2003, five *tamalitos*, a large *tamal*, a stack of maize tortillas, a chicken (wrapped in maize husks), a *jícara* with hot *chilate* and chocolate, a *guacal* with cold black *chilate* (to be offered to the spring), a stack of *empanadas* filled with black beans, sweet bread wrapped in white cloth, and a mug of coffee. A bottle of liquor and a pack of cigarettes are placed in the center. One by one, the five ritual specialists seated at the *mesa* begin their meal, starting with the *guiding padrino* and continuing in counterclockwise order. Coffee and sweet bread were given to everyone attending the ceremony. Until at least 1957, coffee was apparently not used in this ceremony (Girard 1962:89). In 2003, the ritual specialists had both coffee and hot chilate with chocolate on their table, whereas the visiting pilgrims received a *jícara* of hot *chilate* with chocolate earlier at the confraternity, but were only served coffee at the spring.[8] After the meal, the ritual specialists smoke cigarettes, drink a small amount of liquor, and finish with a prayer.[9] The food remaining on the mesa is collected in baskets, returned to the Confraternity, and offered to visiting pilgrims the next day. "Leftovers" from the ritual meal are highly appreciated because they have been saturated with sacred power during the ritual.

Next, the *padrinos* pray and burn incense at the sacred spring. The spring has an undercurrent leading into the ground, which is normally almost completely obstructed by a stone. The *padrino* in office removes the stone and

Figure 19.5. *Padrino* praying at the "door to the mountain lakes." Quetzaltepeque, Guatemala. Photograph by Johanna Kufer.

Figure 19.6. The *mesa* at the sacred spring with ritual foods and drinks laid out in a quincunx pattern. Quetzaltepeque, Guatemala. Photograph by Johanna Kufer.

sacrifices a young (not fully grown) turkey hen by drowning her in the spring. She is sucked into the ground by the water current; that is, "swallowed by the serpent" (compare Girard 1962:95). Next, the black *chilate* from the five *guacals* is splashed into the water (Figure 19.7). Finally, a large (adult) male turkey is sacrificed by cutting his throat and the blood let to drip into the water. Before leaving, people attending the ceremony fill bottles brought for this purpose with 'blessed water' (*agua bendita*); that is, water from the sacred spring. On the way back into town in the early morning hours, a prayer is offered at the "entrance to the mountain lakes," and two *guacals* with black *chilate* are splashed out at this spot.

Figure 19.7. Splashing black *chilate* into the sacred spring. Quetzaltepeque, Guatemala. Photograph by Johanna Kufer.

Setting of the *Mesa*

The next night, on April 24 at midnight, 'The Setting of the *Mesa*' (*se pone la mesa*) is carried out. The table in front of the altar of St. Francis is covered with green banana leaves and set with five *guacals* containing black *chilate*, again in a quincunx pattern (Figure 19.8). A swizzle-stick is laid on the table, and the *guacals* are covered with a piece of banana leaf and a new white cloth, literally a 'cloth without sin' (*paño sin pecar*, compare Faust and Hirose, this volume). The rain gods, called *angeles* 'angels' or *hombres trabajadores* 'working men' (Ch'orti': *ajpatnar winik'ob*), are riding cloud horses, according to Girard a "modernized" version of the original mount in the form of water-filled serpents (Girard 1962:125). This concept is beautifully illustrated in the Story of the Maize Earners, still alive as an oral tradition in the hamlets of Jocotán: During a time of famine, three men go looking for work and arrive at God's *milpa*. The work they are assigned to is to make rain with a sword while riding a white horse. God also has some permanent *milpa* workers riding black horses which

Figure 19.8. The *mesa* at the temple of St. Francis the Conqueror set in a quincunx pattern with *guacals* containing black *chilate*. Quetzaltepeque, Guatemala. Photograph by Johanna Kufer.

are considered too wild for the protagonists (Dary 1986). It is often emphasized that the clouds which bring copious "blessings" of rain are black; thus, the dark chocolate blob in the hot *chilate* may be associated with the color of the rain clouds.

Watering of the *Oratorio* Interior

On April 25 at midnight, the *oratorio* interior is watered all over. This is the most obvious use of sympathetic magic during the rain ceremonies. In 2003, there was some controversy over whether this should take place on April 24 or 25, and whose duty it was. According to Girard (1962:112), the watering was carried out daily, starting on April 25, to "call the rains," and would cease after the regular rainfall started because then its purpose had been fulfilled.

Repetitions of the Setting of the Mesa

During the wet half of the year, the setting of the *mesa* is repeated every nine nights, starting on May 2. Every time, the full greenery adornment is renewed, the *madrina* whisks the old black *chilate* with the swizzle-stick (in a manner similar to that of Northern Lacandon women; see Pugh, this volume), and the *padrino* splashes the contents of the four *guacals* from the corners of the table into the four corners of the confraternity patio, whereas the central *guacal* is emptied under the altar. The *madrina* prepares fresh black *chilate*, and the *padrino* places the newly filled *guacals* on the *mesa*. On the morning of May 3, when the Day of the Cross is celebrated, the greenery adornment is fresh, and black *chilate* has just been splashed out for the first time. These repetitions must be carried out as a routine in any kind of weather. They are seen as a feeding of the rain-bringing 'angels' or 'working men.' Like human men working their *milpa*, the 'angels' have to eat well to be able to do the hard but noble work of maize cultivation. Girard (1962:252) reports that *padrinos* may even, as a last resort, attempt to starve the rain gods to enforce the temporary suspension of their work (that is, the rainfall), during the time of the *canicula* (pause in the rainy season) in July and August. Another ritual is performed only if the rains are late: white candles are placed into the candleholders (*cirias*) standing at the altar, and they are "bathed" in the river.

The Turning of the Mesa

On October 25, the rainy half of the year ends, and the 'Turning of the *Mesa*' (*se voltea la mesa*) is carried out. This act closes the cycle of agricultural labor and inaugurates the dry season, which is a time of leisure and rest for men and gods (Girard 1962:279). After the *guacals* are emptied for the last time, they are washed and turned upside down (*embrocado*). The greenery adornment of the rainy season is replaced by the dry, multicolored decorations of the dry season.

Capturing and Imprisoning the Winds

Girard reported another agrarian ritual involving cacao. In February, the winds were locked in a gourd filled with cacao beans for the 260 days of the Tzolkin (ritual calendar), to be released only on October 24, after the maize had been harvested and the agricultural cycle had been closed (Girard 1962:33). This ritual was not mentioned by anybody during the current study. Since questions were asked about cacao uses in general rather than about this particular ritual, the possibility that it is still performed cannot be ruled out completely. Apart from the lack of rain, wind is the greatest threat to the *milpa*. Two ritual practices to protect the *milpa* from damaging winds were mentioned during the course of this study. One is the above-mentioned sowing of maize from St. Francis's altar in the corners of the *milpa*; the other is to deposit the solid remains of the maize used for making *chilate* in the *milpa*.

What makes cacao sacred?

Reviewing the ritual uses of cacao among the Maya makes one think that the scientific name of cacao, *Theobroma*—'food of the gods'—could not be better chosen. Of all plants used as ritual food offerings, cacao is second in importance only to maize. It is not hard to explain why maize is sacred for the peoples of Mesoamerica, who depend on it as a staple to an extreme degree. But why is cacao sacred? Since ritual uses of psychotropic plants have received a lot of attention in the popular press, "plant of the gods" has almost become a synonym for "hallucinogenic plant." However, though aphrodisiac and inebriating properties have been ascribed to chocolate since early Colonial times (S. D. Coe and M. D. Coe 1996:101), with the exception of stimulating caffeine the psychoactive compounds so far identified in cacao are present in amounts too small to produce an effect. For example, to obtain a *Cannabis*-like response from the anandamide contained in cacao would require 25 kg of chocolate (Smit and Rogers 2001). The quantity of caffeine in a typical serving of hot chocolate is smaller than in coffee or tea but sufficient to produce a stimulating effect and a general feeling of well-being (Smit and Rogers 2002). This may provide one explanation for some ritual uses of cacao, especially as a ceremonial drink during long nocturnal rituals and for important social occasions, similar to the way other caffeine-containing drinks such as tea and coffee are consumed ceremonially. As described for the Ch'orti' ritual at the sacred spring, coffee has partly or completely replaced cacao as a ritual drink in many Maya ceremonies (W. R. Adams 1987), but it is seldom, if ever, used as a ritual offering. In the latter context, the symbolism of cacao is more important than its phytochemistry. Similarly, *T. bicolor*, a relative of cacao, plays a prominent role in Highland Maya ritual, although its mature seeds do not contain more than traces of caffeine (see Kufer and McNeil, this volume).

The symbolism of cacao

The cacao tree exhibits an important prerequisite for being a symbolically meaningful plant in Mesoamerica. It can be interpreted as a transformed human body, with its trunk representing the body and legs, its branches the arms and the large fruit, directly born on the trunk and larger branches, representing the head. The idea of humans being reborn as plants, especially fruit trees, is common among Classic period and contemporary Maya (Christenson 2001:206–207; Schele and Mathews 1998:122–123). This theme is also found in a contemporary Ch'orti' legend about *guerrillero* hero Valentin Ramos, who escapes death and torture by turning into a tree (Brent Metz, personal communication 2003). Most plants important in Maya ritual are in some way anthropomorphic: They either have a large head-like fruit like the squash, or the shape of the whole plant resembles the human body, as in the case of palms, banana plants and many trees. Plants which have both an upright "body" and bear large fruits (or ears) directly on or near the main axis are particularly anthropomorphic. These include maize; the cacao tree; the *zapote* tree (*Pouteria sapota*), whose ground seeds are often added to ritual maize and chocolate drinks (Hostnig, Hostnig, and Vásquez V. 1998:164, Prechtel 1999:287); and the calabash trees (*Crescentia cujete* and *C. alata*), which produce the vessels used for ritual drinks.[10] Cacao, however, is more important than other trees with edible head-like fruits. Only maize is more ubiquitous than cacao in ritual food offerings, and, in most cases, both are offered together. A possible explanation is that cacao and maize show a surprising number of opposing characteristics, while sharing an anthropomorphic appearance. Since structuring the universe in paired opposites is a central principle underlying Mesoamerican cosmology (M. E. Miller and K. Taube 1987), a conceptual pairing of cacao with the all-important maize adds significantly to the symbolic importance of cacao. The oppositions between maize and cacao are manifold:

- Maize can be different colors, but white maize is the most important variety in certain Maya rituals, such as Ch'orti' rain ceremonies, and was the material for the mythical creation of the first humans; the fermented cacao seeds used in eastern Guatemala are dark, almost black, when peeled and/or ground.[11]
- Maize thrives in full sunshine; cacao is so dependent on shade that it is mostly cultivated under special shade trees called *madre cacao*.
- Maize has an annual life-cycle and survives the dry season as a seed only; cacao bears fruit many times in its life and lives for more than twenty years.
- Maize needs humidity only during a few months of the year; cacao needs continuous humidity.
- Maize ears grow upwards; cacao pods hang down. Both are referred to as *mazorcas* in Spanish.
- Maize grows in most kinds of soil, including on poor, stony slopes; cacao needs rich, deep soil.
- Traditional maize cultivation requires hard work; traditional (extensive) cacao cultivation is not regarded as serious work, in the way fishing and hunting are not regarded as serious work by the Ch'orti.'

- Maize grains are on the outside of the cob (after removal of the husks); cacao beans are embedded in the pulp.

A number of tropical fruit trees share most of these characteristics with cacao, but none of them has black edible parts. The only plant with black edible grains is the black bean (*Phaseolus vulgaris*), but it is an annual plant and does not produce a head-like fruit. Thus, the black bean is the "companion" of maize in profane contexts (in everyday meals and on the *milpas*), whereas cacao is its complementary partner in ritual. The conceptual pairing with maize has important implications for the symbolism of cacao: Whereas some symbolic meanings of cacao can be directly derived from characteristics of the tree itself, other associations seem to be derived from the role of cacao as the complementary principle to maize within a dualistic universe. Moreover, the pairing of opposites often implies a mutual dependence, as between husband and wife, and the idea that balance between the two opposites is required for the functioning of the whole.

Cacao and darkness, caves, night

Its need for shade and the dark color of its fermented seeds are central to the association of cacao with caves, darkness, the night, and the dark, wet half of the year. This meaning is at the heart of cacao's symbolism and is linked to many secondary symbolic meanings. As caves are places of transformation and rebirth, cacao is also associated with these processes. The color black has further symbolic meanings: Many ancient Maya deities and modern images of saints and virgins worshipped in the Maya area are black (Orellana 1981). An example from eastern Guatemala is the Black Christ of Esquipulas, a very important pilgrimage center for people from all parts of Guatemala and from neighboring countries as well (Hunter and DeKleine 1984). Last, black is the color of the thick clouds of the rainy season, which form a continuous cover in the sky.

Cacao, a "cool" plant

The cacao tree needs shade and humidity to grow and is thus associated with cool, humid places as are the plant species used for "greenery" adornment. Additional criteria indicating a "cool" nature according to the local hot/cold classification system are the fatty consistency of its seeds and their diuretic action, due to theobromine. In Don Beto's words, "there is hardly a cooler thing than cacao." Heat is regarded as damaging for most kinds of ritual activities, but it is particularly feared in the context of rain ceremonies. The cool nature of cacao makes it an ideal plant for controlling dangerous heat during rituals, as the use of *fresco de cacao* shows.

Cacao and merchants

The Maya merchant gods are closely associated with cacao because the seeds were used as a kind of money. Cacao growers in sixteenth-century Yucatan worshipped the merchant god Ek Chuah during the month of Muan (Landa 1941 [1566]:164). In comparison to a subsistence farmer, a merchant could make "easy" money, just like somebody lucky enough to have a cacao grove. In the Highland Maya drama of Rabinal Achi, tending an orchard of cacao and *pataxte* (*T. bicolor*) is described as an easy, affluent way of life (D. Tedlock 2003:49). In contrast, maize cultivation is considered hard but sacred work. Like other Maya, the Ch'orti' have a strong work ethic, illustrated by the expression "working men," which they use in referring to the rain gods.

Cacao and the Female Gender

Maize is associated with the male gender because it is also associated with the day, the sky, the sun, and the male rain gods. Cacao is associated with the female gender because it is associated with the night, the earth, the moon, caves, and the female deities of springs and waterholes. Whereas the association between cacao and the female gender is rather subtle and implicit in the Ch'orti' rain ceremony of Quetzaltepeque, it is overt and explicit in Tzutujil youth initiations at Santiago Atitlan (Prechtel 1999).[12] Other examples of associations between women and cacao include the "orchard of ancestors" on King Pakal's sarcophagus at Palenque, Mexico, where his mother is represented as a cacao tree (Schele and Mathews 1998); contemporary Yukatek curing ceremonies (Faust and Hirose, this volume); and Northern Lacandon ritual (Pugh, this volume). Nevertheless, it is important to bear in mind that these gender associations are neither rigid nor absolute. There are some notable exceptions among contemporary and historical Maya. In Classic Maya iconography, there is evidence for an association of maize with the female gender in certain contexts, especially for the mature grain of maize as opposed to the green maize plant (Bassie-Sweet 2001). Similarly, cacao seeds as money are often associated with male merchant gods, whereas the majority of gender-specific associations of cacao are with the female gender. These exceptions also occur for other gender-specific associations in Maya culture, such as the interpretation of the full moon as male, while all other moon phases are female, and the transformation of the (male) Hero Twin Xbalanke into the moon (B. Tedlock 1992 [1982]:183).

Conclusion

The role of cacao in Ch'orti' rain ceremonies illustrates the complex and inextricable relationship between subsistence farmers and their natural environment, which encompasses traditional knowledge in many areas such as ecology, agronomy, physiology, and nutrition. It may at first be surprising to find Maya religious traditions with Classic period roots underlying the supposedly Catholic worship of St. Francis the Conqueror in the twenty-first century, but for someone brought up in the Western tradition of seeing the natural and the supernatural as mutually exclusive categories, it is perhaps no less surprising to find traditional ecological knowledge at the heart of a religious cult. As a plant which needs continuous humidity and rich soil, the cacao tree is an indicator for the fertility of the land, and its disappearance from an area, as happened in eastern Guatemala, is a severe warning that the natural resources are being exploited in an unsustainable way. For the Ch'orti' and other Mayan groups, cacao is a culturally meaningful plant not only because of its effects on the human body when it is consumed, but also as a symbol of the precious resources of water and plant growth. The regeneration of these resources must not be taken for granted. It requires yearly ritual activities as well as continuous protection of the neuralgic points of a fragile ecosystem, such as springs or waterholes and the woodland surrounding them; in other words, the kind of environment the cacao tree needs to thrive. Other plant species representing this kind of environment are used for the "greenery" adornment in St. Francis's *oratorio*, and several tree species producing large head-like fruits play a prominent role in Maya rituals. In Ch'orti' rain ceremonies, however, and likely in other Maya rituals as well, cacao exceeds them all in importance because it is the only plant which unites the characteristics of preference for shade and humidity and an anthropomorphic structure with the rare quality of having dark seeds, which reflect the darkness of caves, the night, the shade under a canopy and the rainy season when the sun is hidden by a heavy layer of rain clouds. The dark seeds, along with a number of other biological and ecological characteristics, also make cacao a complementary opposite for maize. This pairing with the sacred maize plant, the basis of Maya subsistence economy, within the conceptual framework of a universe structured into complementary and mutually dependent opposites, makes cacao unique among other culturally meaningful plants.

Acknowledgments

The authors would like to thank all research participants in eastern Guatemala, especially the members of the confraternity of San Francisco Conquistador at Quetzaltepeque, for their patient explanations and the kind invitation to witness the rain ceremony. Kufer would like to thank the School of Pharmacy, University of London, for a Ph.D. studentship, as well as the Richard Cannell

Travel Fund and the German Academic Exchange Service for travel grants. Special thanks to Cameron McNeil for the initial suggestion to study cacao uses in eastern Guatemala and for continuous discussions, encouragement, and being a most helpful editor ever since. Many thanks also to Kerry Hull and Brent Metz for very helpful discussions, to Nikolai Grube for valuable comments on the manuscript, to Harald Förther for providing many useful contacts and botanical support, and to Elfriede Pöll, Universidad del Valle de Guatemala, for botanical and institutional support.

Notes

1. Ch'orti' words, as provided in the text, are no longer used in Quetzaltepeque but only in some hamlets of Jocotán.

2. The concept of virgin water is also known from the Yucatan (Faust and Hirose, this volume).

3. Girard (1962:113, 312) reports the indigenous name *boronté* for black *chilate*; he translates *boron* as 'nine' and identifies it with the "nine drinks" Ixmucané prepares in the *Popol Vuh* for the creation of the first humans. The number nine is associated with the night, which is ruled by the Nine Lords of the Night, and the Underworld, which has nine levels according to Maya notions (for a more detailed discussion of numerical symbolism, see Faust and Hirose López, this volume). No Ch'orti' dictionary reports *boron* as "nine"; however, *bolon* means 'nine' in other modern Maya languages and Classic period Maya.

4. This color symbolism does not seem to be universal within the Ch'orti' area. In rain ceremonies at Chiquimula, green, white, red and dark-colored adornments were used (Girard 1962:168). On the other hand, red elements are excluded from the ritual *mesas* on the Day of the Dead in November; that is, in the dry half of the year (López García 2000).

5. *Fresco de cacao* may originally have been *chicha*, an alcoholic maize beverage, with cacao. *Chicha* is locally called *fresco*, and alcoholic beverages with ground cacao are widely used in rituals by many Maya groups and their indigenous neighbors. The ban on home production of *chicha* in Guatemala and Honduras had devastating consequences on indigenous rituals in many areas (for example, Chapman 1985).

6. Frogs and toads play an important role in Ch'orti' rain ceremonies, either in the form of the actual animals or represented by four old men who crouch under the altar table and imitate frog sounds (Girard 1962:110). In contemporary Yukatek rain ceremonies, small boys imitate the sounds of frogs (Faust 1998b:105, Freidel, Schele, and Parker 1993:32). Frog sounds mark the beginning of the rainy season in an impressive way, and the dramatic change of the "soundscape" from the shrill sounds of cicadas that dominate the dry season to the multiple voices of different frog and toad species can even be observed in towns such as Quetzaltepeque. Other important aquatic animals are fish. Girard (1962:96) reports that a tiny metal fish hanging over the altar of St. Francis was considered his son; that is, the young Maize God. The Lenca, the Ch'orti's

indigenous neighbors in Honduras, place nine little living fish on an altar in some of their ceremonies (Chapman 1985:135, 174). Fish also seem to have played an important role in Classic Maya rituals (McNeil, Hurst, and Sharer, this volume).

7. In Ch'orti,' there is only one color term for blue and green, *yaxax*. Hence the *padrinos'* kerchiefs are conceptually the same color as the greenery adornment.

8. This is one of many examples where coffee has replaced a cacao beverage on ritual occasions, probably because of coffee's superior alerting effect, which is the result of higher caffeine content.

9. According to the confraternity president, cigarettes and liquor are necessary as stimulants for the ritual specialists, who must stay awake during several days and nights of ritual and can take only very brief rests. He pointed out that cigarettes and liquor (both classified as "hot") are never placed on St. Francis's altar during the wet half of the year and did not form part of the offerings. According to Girard (1962:91), however, cigarette smoke represents rain clouds in a way similar to copal smoke.

10. To us, cacao pods, especially the elongated, pointed fruits of *criollo* cacao, may not look very much like a human head. However, the shape of these fruits resembles maize ears, which are often depicted as heads in Mesoamerican iconography. A head shaped like a maize ear (or a cacao pod) seems to have been regarded as desirable, as indicated by the practice of cranial deformation, which was widespread, particularly among elite individuals.

11. The dark color of the cacao variety used in eastern Guatemala develops during the fermentation process at the same time as the typical aroma. Even if the seeds are put to dry immediately after being removed from the fruit, fermentation and formation of dark brown oligomeric procyanidins occurs to some degree; roasting is not required for these processes to take place. This has important symbolic implications, as any kind of treatment with heat such as roasting would reverse the cool nature of the cacao beans. The color symbolism may differ in areas where other cacao varieties are used, since some forms contain at least some white seeds, especially *criollo* cacao, which was the only variety of *T. cacao* used in pre-Contact Mesoamerica.

12. "The Female Earth and Male Earth needed each other. The lowland dominion of *chocolate*, honey, salt, parrots, bananas, and cotton had all the *rain clouds* that the highland realm of lake fish, tomatoes, avocados, *hard jewelled corn*, rope and reed mats needed *to water their pine mountains and fields*. (. . .) If the people of the Male Earth stopped their elaborate courting of the Female Earth, the two Earths would fight, with the human inhabitants as their warriors" (Prechtel 1999:272, emphasis by authors).

20

Cacao in the Yukatek Maya Healing Ceremonies of Don Pedro Ucán Itzá

Betty Bernice Faust and Javier Hirose López

Maya use of chocolate in ceremonial contexts is increasingly well documented by epigraphers, iconographers, archaeologists, historians, and ethnographers. This wealth of information has made possible comparative analysis of a symbol system underlying variations across time and space. To this collaborative effort we offer some observations and interpretations of the symbolic uses of cacao (*Theobroma cacao* L.) in contemporary Yukatek Maya healing ceremonies (*k'ex*), including its use in a ritual beverage as well as in an uncooked, uneaten offering associated with ritual numbers and placements. The pairing of cacao beans with chile peppers, the positions in which they are placed, and their associations with other symbols suggest sexuality, fertility, and generational cycles. They form part of a partially implicit symbol system used by the healer in referring to the circumstances of the patient as part of a family extended through time and related to space through the path of the sun.

Research History and Setting

Faust first met Don Pedro Ucán Itzá in 1986, when doing research on rural development, agricultural techniques, and traditional practices in Pich, Campeche.[1] He invited her to observe, photograph, and record his ceremonies because he has no apprentice and wished to preserve the information for future generations. In 2001, Faust introduced him to her student Javier Hirose, asking permission for Hirose to do his Master's thesis on the way land is used symbolically in this healer's ceremonies. Hirose made clear to Don Pedro his wishes to learn some Maya techniques and plant uses to incorporate into his own healing practices but decided not to explain his prior commitment to traditional Chinese medicine until the end of his thesis research.

In 1986, Faust (1988a, 1998a) observed the first ceremony; it is compared with four others conducted in patients' homes observed in 2001–2002 by Hirose (2003). All of these were performed in patients' homes. In addition, both authors have observed other healing rituals of less duration and complexity performed in the healer's home with instructions for later placement of cacao beans and chile peppers in the house yard of the patient. Ritual prayers are in Mayan, but Don Pedro's conversations with these patients and the two researchers have been in Spanish. Faust has taken two courses in Yukatek Mayan but is far from fluent; Hirose has not studied Mayan. Don Pedro and his adult children are bilingual; the grandchildren speak only Spanish, although they understand Mayan.

The healer's specialized knowledge was passed on to him through an oral family tradition in the predominantly Maya community of Mayapan, in the center of the state of Yucatan, Mexico, near the famed archeological site of the same name. The pre-Columbian city was the Late Postclassic administrative center of a long-distance inland trade route replaced in the fifteenth century by a coastal network of merchant-sailors, the Putún Acalán. During Colonial times, remaining elite Maya families in interior and southern communities of the peninsula continued to trade cacao from Tabasco, Belize, Guatemala, and Chiapas to both Maya and Spanish populations (Farriss 1984; G. D. Jones 1982).

Don Pedro is a *h'men*, a Yukatek Maya priest-healer who can conduct community-wide ceremonies to call the rains, as well as petition the Maya Spirit Beings to assist with various problems, including curing serious illnesses of persons, cattle, and crops. His knowledge of rituals and related astronomy, geography, and medicinal plant lore is part of an oral tradition taught to him by his father, Viviano Ucán Rosel, and by another healer in Mayapan, Felipe Tamay, who initiated him at the age of eighteen (in approximately 1950), after his father's death. Don Pedro recalls that in those days there were many *h'meno'ob* (Mayan plural for *h'men*) in Mayapan and neighboring communities, and all of them used cacao and chiles in their curing ceremonies.

The traditional knowledge of Don Pedro's lineage, their use of cacao, and his mother's maiden name "Itzá," may be indications of family ancestry associated with the dispersion of an elite Itza lineage out of Chichen Itza to Mayapan, some of whom apparently migrated to the Guatemalan Peten during early Colonial times. Others who stayed in interior towns of Mexico's Yucatan Peninsula were involved both in long-distance cacao trade and in small-scale cattle ranching (Farriss 1984; G. D. Jones 1982). Thus, Don Pedro's personal and family history of small-scale cattle ranching, organizing bullfights during community fiestas, and administering a large cattle ranch for an absentee owner are further possible indications of the inheritance of elite traditions.

In journeys by bus to heal patients in various rural communities, Don Pedro carries both cacao beans and copal incense with him since these are not easily obtained. Village stores generally carry chocolate in commercially prepared tablets for making hot drinks, but cacao beans and copal are found only in the central farmers' markets of the major cities of the peninsula. Merchant networks bring cacao beans from the growers in Tabasco and copal from Guatemala.

From many conversations with Don Pedro, we have concluded that he understands health as a multifaceted state dependent on proper orientation to the cosmos, the family, and the community. The maintenance of this state depends on correct behavior in relation to others, both human and nonhuman (with the latter including plants, animals, houses, land, tools, churches/temples, and celestial bodies, all of which have guardian spirits, or souls). Before a new house can be occupied or land cleared for farming, a ceremony to "cure" it must be performed, even though it is not "sick." It must be "seated," according to Don Pedro, in order that it be properly disposed to its work and to the people who use it. The seating appears to be similar to the ensouling of places described by Vogt (1998). It is done with ritual prayers and the placement of crosses and cacao beans around the periphery of a square and in its central point. This quincunx pattern is referred to by Don Pedro as *kantis* in Yukatek Mayan.

Previous interpretations of the symbolism in Don Pedro's use of cacao beans with chile peppers was earlier reported by Faust (1988a, 1998a), who analyzed the sexual symbolism related to parenting and the cycle of generations. These human cycles are isomorphic with the daily and yearly cycles of the sun, which, in turn, are related to the life cycle of plants affected by seasons. In all these cases, "birth" (including dawning of the sun and sprouting of plants) is followed by increasing strength, fertility, aging, death, descent into the earth (burial), decomposition, regeneration in the dark, and a new birth. Adding to this conceptual pattern is the idea of the center of rectangular agricultural fields and house yards as umbilici, with their corners as hands and feet, which echoes the square world with the center established by the noon sun (Faust 2002; Hirose 2003). Thus, Creation constructed a spatial and temporal order of cycles (including the life cycle of human beings), within a *kantis*.

The variations in these ceremonies and the comparison between those of 1986 and those of 2001–2002 provide an indication of underlying basic values and concepts that guide adaptations to new circumstances. Victoria Bricker (1981); David Freidel, Linda Schele, and Joy Parker (1993); Gary Gossen (1994); Eva Hunt (1977); Shirley Mock (1998); June Nash (2001); Andrea Stone (2002); and Evon Vogt (1976, 1998) are some of the scholars who have presented evidence for these underlying continuities in Mesoamerican processes of cultural change.

Methodology

The methodology used in this research is long-term participant observation, including informal conversations and formal interviews focused by specific questions. It has included recording audio and video cassettes, writing field notes, and taking photographs, with the consent of Don Pedro.

Faust, as a grandmother, has had access to all-female gatherings of Don Pedro's family and others in the community; Hirose, as a father, has been included in all-male groups. The different gender of the two researchers has resulted in greater access to areas of local discourse and joking than any one researcher could easily have obtained. This access has contributed to the interpretation of cacao as a symbol associated not only with wealth but also with female sexuality and good fortune in relation to the reproduction of the family. Symbols have been interpreted with reference to joking, everyday talk, their placement in various rituals, their relationship to each other, and explicit exegesis by the healer and other participants in healing rituals.

Cacao in Contemporary Yukatek-Maya Healing Ceremonies

In the contemporary Yukatek Maya healing ceremonies that we have observed, cacao is included in offerings on altars to the Wind Lords and to other spirits

Figure 20.1. A female patient holds cacao beans in her hands while the healer turns her in a circle around the burning incense (case 3). Pich, Campeche, Mexico. Photograph by Javier Hirose.

associated with life as well as burial offerings to the Earth Lord. The Wind
Lords and other spirits are called to partake of ritual foods and drinks, including one that is flavored with roasted and ground cacao. They are also offered a
sacrificed chicken with cacao beans and chile peppers arranged first on a floor
altar and later in a burial pit.

In the floor altar, the sacrificed rooster faces east, with copal incense burning
close to its head (Figure 20.1). In a counterclockwise ritual motion cacao beans
and chile peppers are carefully placed next to burning candles in each of the
cardinal directions and in the center near a candle at the head of the dead bird.
During ritual prayers, the burning copal is carried in a frying pan or cooking
pot in a counterclockwise circuit.

Cacao in Ritual Beverages

The hot beverage made from the toasted cacao beans ground with sugar and
cinnamon is traditionally placed in a gourd shell (*luch* in Maya, *jícara* in Spanish) made by women from the fruit that in mythological symbolism was the
potent skull of the father of the Hero Twins, who engendered them by spitting
his essence into the hand of their mother, Blood Woman (D. Tedlock 1985).
Connections of cacao with both death and birth continue in the use of the
same chocolate beverage served in the traditional *luch* for what are considered to be "traditional" celebrations of marriage, baptism, and *bix* (ceremonies
on the anniversary of the death of a family member)(Faust 1998a:636; Sosa
1985:269–280). In more explicitly Maya rituals connected with agriculture and
healing, cacao is an ingredient in the ritual corn beverage, *saka,'* which is similar
to the local everyday corn gruel (*pozole*) but is prepared without quicklime.[2]
Saka' is made by simply cooking and grinding dried corn with its epicarp and
preferably flavoring it with honey and cacao beans that have been roasted and
then ground. The essential ingredient is the whole grain corn. In an emergency,
however, a corn gruel can even be made of tortillas broken up in water, but this
requires apologies to the Spirit Beings.

The *saka'* is consumed by humans only after being placed on the altar and
left there for twenty to thirty minutes so that the Spirit Beings can drink its
spiritual essence. It is also necessary that small portions of the beverage be
carried in a counterclockwise circuit (east, north, west, south) and thrown to
the cardinal directions and up and down in the center of the ritual space. Sosa
(1985), in his work with another *h'men*, identified this center (*u hol gloriyah*) as a
spiritual conduit between the three levels: sky world, this world where we walk,
and the Underworld. Hanks has also documented this ritual circuit and the
space delimited where "the corners are connected, not by perpendicular lines
intersecting in the middle, but by the perimeter running point by point E, N,
W, S, and C, or E, S, W, N, and C" (Hanks 1990:300). The counterclockwise

movement establishes ritual space, and the clockwise movement terminates it, returning the space to everyday use (Hanks 1990:299). In our experience with Don Pedro, the participants may all be present for this offering of *saka'* to the spirit beings, or the *h'men* may do this alone. After the offering, the remaining *saka'* is distributed to the patient and other participants, including the *h'men*. In contrast, the final closing clockwise circuit is done quietly and unobtrusively by the *h'men* after the midnight burial of the sacrificial chicken, when other participants have returned to the house.

With the exception of cacao beans and copal incense, all ingredients used in rituals are commonly available in rural communities throughout the Yucatan Peninsula. To the best of the authors' knowledge, neither of these is produced today anywhere in the peninsula. Nevertheless, ritually placed cacao beans, *saka'* (flavored with freshly ground cacao), and copal incense smoke continue to be essential sustenance for Yukatek Maya spirit beings, who are expected to heal the sick, to bring the rains, and to assist the crops (Faust 1998a, 1998b).

Ritual Numbers of Raw Cacao Beans Paired with Chile Peppers as Symbols in Healing Ceremonies

In contrast to the use of toasted cacao as flavoring in *saka',* the use of raw cacao beans in healing ceremonies is entirely symbolic. Not only the patient but also the family, the household, and the work place (orchard, cornfield, or cattle pasture) are to be protected against future attacks by malevolent winds. In these ceremonies, cacao beans accompany a sacrificed virgin rooster. This "innocent" rooster is considered an exchange for the patient, a gift to the Spirit of the Earth (also known as the Earth Lord) as compensation to that spirit, who will not be able to "eat" the dead body of the patient.

Don Pedro says that the preferred chiles are the dried red ones, ca. 3 cm in length, referred to locally as *chile parado* in Spanish (*Capsicum annuum* L., scientific identification by agronomist Jorge Mendoza González). Don Pedro gave the Maya term as *mal ha'*, although Mendoza found that it is referred to as *yax ik* in Yaxcabá, Yucatan, a community farther east. These particular chiles have the distinctive characteristics of being bright red at maturity and growing in an erect position on the plant. In local humor they are likened to the erect human penis. In a healing ritual for a pubescent girl, the pairing of cacao beans and chiles was done with specific references both to the pairing of husband and wife and to that of the parent and child of the same sex (see Faust 1998a for a detailed analysis of this symbolism).

Each curing ceremony that Don Pedro does is slightly different, depending on the available items and the family situation. Both authors have observed that the numbers and placements of the cacao beans and their partnered chile peppers can vary, but the variations indicate an underlying cultural logic. Cacao is absolutely necessary, and there must be some reference to the four-sided square with its center. Beyond this minimum, it is best to have chiles as well and best of all to have 13 of each, in most cases. However, in the first case observed (case 1, see Table 20.1), involving ritual assistance for passage to adulthood combined with healing, 20 cacao beans and 20 chile peppers were used in the burial. The reason given for this exception was that 20 refers to the 20 digits of the four human extremities, indicating a female "complete person," who will marry a male "complete person" to produce the next generation. The connection of this reasoning to the aspects that suggested a rite of passage is not clear, although it may be that the girl was in the process of becoming a female "complete person," an adult woman.

We have observed that Don Pedro sometimes forgets to specify chiles when he instructs the patient's family concerning the ingredients that they must buy and have ready for him to use in the ceremony. He normally carries both cacao beans and dried *chile parado* (as well as copal incense) with him when he goes to remote villages where people cannot easily obtain special ingredients, but he does not always take the chiles. The chiles are important, but there are other kinds of chiles available, and they tend to be in people's homes. Hirose has seen

Table 20.1. Ritual numbers of cacao beans used in phases of ceremony

Phases of the ceremony	Numbers of cacao beans	Totals	Placements	Combination with chilies	Totals
Cleansing	5+4+4 (case 3)	13	Father(5), mother(4), daughter(4)	0	0
Floor Altar	2+2+2+2+2 + more in gourd (case 1)	10	Four corners and center Gourd of cacao beans south Gourd of chili peppers north	2+2+2+2+2 + more in gourd	10
	2+2+2+2+5 (case 3)	13	Four corners and center	0	0
	2+2+2+2+5 (case 4)	13	Four corners and center	0	0
Burial Altar (with sacrificed rooster)	4+4+4+4+4 (case 1)	20	Head, tail, sides (wings/feet) and center	4+4+4+4+4=20	20
	2+2+2+2+5 (case 2)	13	Head, tail, sides (wings/feet) and center	1+1 (head and tail only)	2
	5 (case 3)	5	Center	1 (center)	1
	2+2+2+2+5 (case 4)	13	Head, tail, sides (wings/feet) and center	0	
House yard	2+2+2+2+5 (case 2)	13	Four corners and center	1+1+1+1+1 (Four corners and center)	5

chile peppers used alone once, in a ceremony to expel a "bad wind" out of a house yard. This wind had repeatedly made one of Don Pedro's granddaughters ill. She would get well with his medicines and rituals and then fall ill again a week or so later. Finally, the burial of chiles in the center of their home's dirt floor stopped the illness from returning. This ceremony could only be performed by the father of the sick child and with no women or children present, emphasizing the congruence between the protective aspect of chiles and that of the father of the family.

Orientation of Cacao Beans and Chiles in the Ceremony

Unless there is a scarcity of cacao beans or chiles, they are placed in pairs in each of the five Maya directions, 2 cacao beans and 2 chiles for each cardinal direction, with the remaining 5 of each placed in the center.[3] The first are placed in the east, followed by north, west, south, and center, in a counterclockwise ritual motion. Don Pedro refers to the center of this design as the *tuch luum* 'the navel of the earth.' In times of scarcity, the design can be indicated with just five cacao beans placed in the center with 1 chile. In one case observed by Hirose (case 3, Table 20.1), the single chile was a chile habanero (*Capsicum chinese* Jacq.), the most common type in daily use in the peninsula. Its placement in the center, together with the 5 cacao beans adds to our other impressions of the primary significance of this center as an indication of a vertical dimension, discussed by a number of authors (Faust 1998a; Gossen 1974; Hirose 2003; Sosa 1985; Villa-Rojas 1987 [1945]; Vogt 1976). In another case observed by Hirose (case 4, Table 20.1), no chiles were present in any phase of the ceremony. The cacao beans were placed in the position and number most commonly used to form the quincunx, but in the burial pit they were topped with tortillas and the sacred corn beverage *saka'* instead of chiles.

The distribution of cacao beans and chile peppers on the ritual altar corresponds to the center of a ritual circuit made by Don Pedro previously in the healing ritual, when he offers the cacao-flavored *saka'* to the Wind Lords of the Maya sacred directions. In this ritual action, he throws some of the beverage to each of the 4 cardinal directions in turn, ending by throwing it straight up in the center of the ritual space created by his previous actions and ducking out of the way so that it can fall straight down. This vertical motion is re-emphasized by a final pouring of some *saka'* from the gourd, to fall directly on the same spot.

Multivalency is a common property of cultural symbols (see discussions in Gossen 1974, B. Tedlock 1982, D. Tedlock 1985, and Vogt 1976). Don Pedro's exegesis of the symbols of his own ceremonies is no exception. When asked by Faust (interview on November 10, 2002), he had two explanations for the use of the number 5 in ritual. When offering *saka'* 5 times to the spirit beings, the number 5 refers to the Wind Lords of the 4 cardinal directions plus the Chief Wind Lord, who resides in the center, but it also refers to the quincunx symbol. Don Pedro places cacao on the floor altar and in the burial altar of the sacrificed chicken in 5 locations. These correspond to the cardinal directions (or sides) of the world, the cornfield, and the house yard, and their respective centers, or navels. This is the horizontal pattern of the world, established by the path of the sun, which rises from the eastern horizon and sets on the western one, thereby marking these as the east and west sides of the primeval square. The sun's movement from east to west also implies a right side facing north and a left side facing south (for discussion of parallel symbolism in ethnographic accounts from the Maya Highlands, see Gossen 1974 and Vogt 1976). The movement of sunrise and sunset points, north and south from equinox, throughout the solar year establish eastern and western sides of the square, and the northernmost sunrise and sunset points of summer solstice form the northeastern and northwestern corners. The southernmost sunrise and sunset points of winter solstice form the southeastern and southwestern corners. In healing ceremonies, the cacao beans and chiles are placed at the cardinal points and not at the intercardinal corners (Faust 1998a:615); this contrasts with agricultural rituals, in which the corners are salient (Faust 1998b:129–133).

Numerical References to Celestial and Underground Worlds

On another occasion (Faust field notes, August 14, 1986), Don Pedro described the meaning of the number 13 with reference to the sky, as a vertical pattern. The sky has levels, like a pyramid, that the sun climbs up and then comes down; there are 6 steps up, with 7 as the highest platform and then 6 down, making 13 positions that the sun transverses every day. The base of the pyramid is square with one side facing each direction and the highest level corresponding to the zenith and to a central point in a quincunx. However, Don Pedro has also mentioned to both authors some of the 13 Maya constellations (see Milbrath 1999) that transverse the sky levels, which are, in turn, associated with specific saints and with the moon, winds, clouds, and certain planets, with the sun the lord of the highest level (for similar ethnographic findings, see Sosa 1985; B. Tedlock 1992).

In the Underworld there is a corresponding but inverse pyramid with 9 levels, that begins with the 4 sides facing cardinal directions and ends with a central point at the nadir. This inverse pyramid has 4 steps down to the bottom level which count as 5 and then 4 steps up, summing to 9 (Faust 1988a:165). In the interview about cacao and related numbers (November 10, 2002), however, Don Pedro gave another interpretation of the meaning of 9, stating that 9 results from a count of the 8 critical points on the periphery of the square established by the sun's path plus the central point of that square. He used a stick to draw a square in the dirt, oriented so that each side faced a cardinal direction, with intercardinal corners. Beginning in the east, he traced a counterclockwise circuit indicating the 4 cardinal directions (the midpoint on each side) and the 4 intercardinal corners (sequentially counting to 8), and then to the center point, named 9.

The way numbers are used in the placement of cacao beans in the *k'ex*, corresponds to key points in Don Pedro's quincunx of nine points and his paired pyramids which are three-dimensional versions of the same quincunx. The cacao beans are usually placed in the midpoints of each side of the quincunx (the cardinal directions) and in the center, which refers to the vertical direction. In its reference to the path of the sun, this design refers to time as well as to space. The center point refers to noon and midnight and also to the Celestial World and the Underworld, where invisible Beings "affect this world where we walk."

Variations in Numbers and Placement of Cacao Beans and Chile Peppers

We have found that the same healer varies his ritual presentation of cacao beans with chile peppers according to the situation. Although the differences appear to depend to some extent on the relative scarcity or abundance of cacao beans and chile peppers, the alternatives follow a pattern of use. The numbers include 1, 2, 5, 13, and 20, and the placements are related to the quincunx.

In the first healing ceremony observed by Faust in 1986 (case 1), Don Pedro placed 2 cacao beans and 2 chile peppers in each cardinal direction and in the center of the floor altar, at the head of a sacrificed chicken, a total of 20. During the burial of the inedible parts of the chicken as a gift to the Lord of the Earth, these numbers were doubled: 4 (or 2 pairs) cacao beans and 4 chile peppers in each cardinal direction and also in the center, 20 of each. Neither Faust nor Hirose has seen this arrangement repeated, and it appears to be related to other special aspects of that ceremony performed for a pubescent girl who was suffering from delayed menarche. This was a rather unusual case of the *k'ex* ceremony since the whole extended family participated. Gender roles and generational cycles were highlighted in symbolic placements, with exegesis by the healer. The future marriage and motherhood of the patient were subjects of reference, and this may account for the pairings, since other ceremonies tended to use odd numbers.

This first case is also the only ceremony observed that included a small, polished stone axe head, similar to those found in a quincunx design in caches as early as the Olmec site of La Venta (Freidel, Schule, and Parker 1993:133–137; Joralemon 1976; Kent Reilly 1994b). In the Maya area, such celts, or ritual axes, are still associated ethnographically with lightning, and they are represented in pre-Columbian contexts as piercing the forehead of the god K'awiil, whose multiple symbolism refers to lightning, spiritual essence, the vision serpent, blood, and inheritance of royal lineage (Freidel, Schele, and Parker 1993:444–445; Milbrath 2002:119–142; Taube 1992a:69–79). There appears to be some continuity in meaning since Don Pedro used this ritual axe only with a patient whose future production of offspring was endangered by delayed menarche. In Table 20.1 we present the variations in the ritual use of the cacao beans and their combination with chiles in the different stages of the four observed *k'ex* ceremonies.

In the floor altar (on the level where human beings walk) we find some interesting variations. The initial ritual placement with candles and incense is an offering to the spirits that consume the smell and essences of all the ritual items, including a sacrificed "virgin" rooster, cacao beans, and chile peppers. In case 1, there was 1 candle, 2 cacao beans, and 2 chile peppers in each corner and again in the center, next to the chicken. In case 2, where there were not 5 candles available, 2 were placed east and west, with the incense and the sacrificed chicken in the middle. These 2 are the principal directions in Maya cosmology and are referred to explicitly as the places of the rising and setting of the sun (B. Tedlock 1992:18–21). In case 1, when the spiritual offerings on the indoor floor altar were being consumed, the *h'men* presented another altar on a table outdoors, approximately in the center of the yard, where *saka'* was offered along with 5 candles and incense. Again the candles were placed in the cardinal directions with 1 in the center, under the table. Finally the *saka'* that was presented to the Wind Lords with prayer was taken on a counterclockwise ritual circuit and then thrown to the 4 directions plus up and down in the center.

In another situation, Hirose observed that a patient, who had traveled a distance to be cured in the home of the *h'men*, was sent home with the entire dead bird together with its ritual accompaniments of cacao beans and chiles to be buried in the corners and center of his house yard. We have not listed this case in the table as we do not have the numbers of cacao and chiles included in the package. In case 3, the *h'men* explained the symbolism explicitly to the participants, stating that the square tabletop represented the family's house yard. After placing a tortilla on each side of the square, he placed 2 cacao beans on each of the 4 exterior tortillas, while in the center he placed 5 (Figure 20.2).

In case 1, for the prepubescent girl, there was an additional ritual associated with the burial. Don Pedro had diagnosed the cause of her illness as a bad wind that was preventing "her blood from coming down" (delayed menarche). In this very special case, a cloth was used to cover her head during the burial ceremony. It had been bought in advance according to the directions of the *h'men* that it be white, all cotton, new, never washed, and spotless. There was no explicit connection made between this cloth and the cacao beans, but in the sixteenth century Landa (1978 [1566?]:44–45) described an initiation ritual for

Figure 20.2. The healer represents the family's house yard with cacao beans and tortillas in a discussion with the patient and her family (case 3). Pich, Campeche, Mexico. Photograph by Javier Hirose.

pre-adolescents that included placing on their heads white cloths—with cacao seeds attached to them. In a Poqomam community of the Guatemala Highlands, Ruben Reina (1966:137) observed that female authorities (*capitanas*) in traditional religious rituals, "wear folded white cloths on top of their heads, and in their hands they have small baskets of flowers wrapped with white cloth."

In the 1986 ceremony observed by Faust (case 1), the cacao beans were not attached to a white cloth but were placed together with an equal number of *chiles parados* in the pit with the dead chicken. These orientations duplicated those of earlier placements on the floor altar in the house; however, the number of each was doubled. In the pit there were 4 beans and 4 chiles in each direction as well as in the center. These were specifically and repeatedly described by Don Pedro as 2 pairs, parents and grandparents.

In case 2, Hirose (2003) found that only 2 *chiles habaneros* were placed on the sacrificed chicken in the burial pit, on its head and tail, respectively, corresponding to east and west. In addition to the chiles, the *h'men* placed in the pit 13 cacao beans, 2 in each cardinal direction and 5 in the center (Figure 20.3). In case 3 (Hirose 2003), the number of cacao beans was reduced to only 5, and these were all placed on top of the body of the chicken, covered with

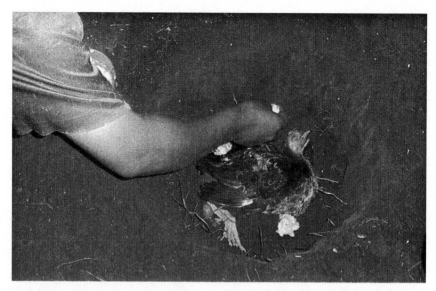

Figure 20.3. The cacao beans are placed in a burial pit, two in each cardinal direction and five in the center. Note the two *chiles habaneros* placed on the head and tail of the sacrificed chicken, corresponding to east and west, respectively (case 2). Pich, Campeche, Mexico. Photograph by Javier Hirose.

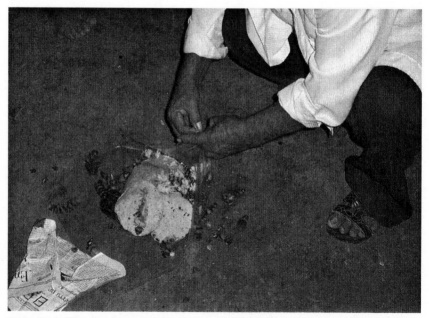

Figure 20.4. Five cacao beans are placed on the sacrificed chicken, covered with *saka'*, and topped with a single *chile habanero* (case 3). Pich, Campeche, Mexico. Photograph by Javier Hirose.

saka, and then topped with a single *chile habanero* (Figure 20.4). In case 2, for an unknown reason, no cacao beans or chile peppers were placed on the floor altar, although they were later used in the burial of the sacrificed chicken. In addition, the *h'men* indicated that that same night 2 cacao beans together with 1 chile pepper should be buried in each corner of the patient's house yard and 5 more cacao beans and 1 chile pepper in its center (Hirose 2003). This is of interest as the total for cacao again is 13 while that for chiles is 5, indicating possibly a celestial reference for the cacao (to the 13 levels or steps in Don Pedro's sky pyramid) and a protective function of the chile pepper, as 5 is the number of points in the quincunx. In this case, the quincunx enclosed the house yard and may function as a protection against the Earth Lord's desires to carry victims to their graves.

Upside-down Placements of Cacao and Other Ritual Symbols and Actors

Hirose has observed that the sacrificed chicken always appears to be placed stomach down (*embrocado*). This he has interpreted in relation to other observations of such placements, including the placement of ritual breads *embrocados* in the earth oven to be cooked for the Day of the Dead and for other rituals. He has also found that the *h'men* himself sleeps *embrocado*, and that one of the *h'men's* grandsons sleeps in this position is an indication that he may have the "gift," the ability to become a *h'men*. In an interview, Hirose explicitly asked about this observed placement, and Don Pedro confirmed its importance but without explaining its significance. Barrera Vásquez (1991:576) gives *nok* as the Mayan translation of *embrocado*, with references that include turning a vessel upside down to pour liquid out and falling forward over the table from exhaustion. The Maya-Quiché ritual expert whom Dennis Tedlock consulted concerning the translation of the *Popol Vuh* found very amusing the reference to a female crab being *embrocado* and Zipacna (a mythical crocodile) having to turn stomach up to try to capture and eat (a metaphor for sexual intercourse) the crab. This was explained as the inverse of the normal positions of male and female during sexual intercourse and resulted in the Hero Twins being able to take advantage of the vulnerable position of Zipacna to crush him (D. Tedlock 1985:87–93, n. 244–245).

Faust, informed by Hirose of the importance of the *embrocado* position for contemporary rituals, later discovered a related ritual placement of cacao in an *embrocado* position. Don Pedro told her that when the gourd tree (*luch* or *guiro*) does not produce fruits, it can be cured by filling a gourd with cacao beans, covering it with a white cloth, and placing it upside down (*embrocado*), in a pit beside the tree. This is only done for this one type of tree which is the proper "spouse" for cacao, since hot chocolate traditionally is served in these gourds

(Faust field notes: November 10, 2002). The qualities of the white cloth to be used in this ritual act are exactly the same as those for the white cloth used in the curing ceremony for the pubescent girl: unused, spotless, never-washed—a cloth in the state that it left the loom. In both cases there is a connection of this state with desired future fertility.

Zuhuy is the Mayan word that describes this quality of original purity, and it is used to describe not only this cloth but a variety of other pure or virgin or natural things: the young sacrificial rooster that has never covered a hen, water taken from a natural source distant from human settlement, high forest that shows no evidence of having been cut and burned for *milpa* agriculture, a young woman who stays home helping her mother (Redfield and Villa Rojas 1962:130–131). In all these cases the state of separate purity is to be "sacrificed" through interaction in order to produce continuity of life. Through sex the virgin becomes a parent, through human cutting and burning of forest corn is produced for food, through ritual sacrifice a *zuhuy* rooster returns health to those near death. Thus, the quality of *zuhuy* is part of a cycle of regeneration which requires the breaking of boundaries and thus of order, and includes death and destruction, which in turn must be controlled in a cycle of renewed order. The old Mayan name for *milpa* maker is killer of the forest, *kimsah k'ax* (Barrera Vásquez 1991:319), and when high forest was still being felled it was necessary to perform a ceremony apologizing to and asking permission of the Lord of the Forest, Yum Balam (Terán and Rasmussen 1994:160). As *milpa* fires should be constrained by firebreaks, so too sexuality should be restricted to one's household mate. Redfield and Villa Rojas (1962:167) reported the belief in Chan Kom that an adulterous couple escaping from community observation by a surreptitious trip to the *milpa* or woods can bring forth the *kazap-ik*, a wind that causes epidemics in human communities and their cattle herds. Faust (1998b:91) reports a belief among the old people that adultery can cause drought or epidemics.

Interpretation of Cacao Use in *K'ex*

In the various *k'ex* ceremonies that we have observed Don Pedro performing, the placement of cacaos and chiles is always in relation to the center and often includes placement in the cardinal directions as well. The preferred number is 13 of each; in case of scarcity, this can be reduced to 5 of each, or even in the extreme to 5 of cacao and 1 chile pepper, all placed in the center. We observed no instance of the ritual use of fewer than 5 cacao beans, suggesting a strong tie to the 5 points of the quincunx. In the case of floor altars in the house, sometimes only cacao beans were included; however, in the ritual burial pit the cacao was always accompanied by at least 1 chile pepper, apparently indicating protection from the earth lord who "wishes to eat the dead."

Gender Roles and the Genital Symbols

The pairing of numbers of cacao beans and chiles appears to express a sexual connotation embedded in a generational context, although when asked about the meaning of cacao beans and chiles, Don Pedro replied that the purpose of the cacao is to "attract the good," while that of the chiles is to "repel the bad." The latter is particularly important to include in the ritual burial, associated with the dangers of death. Maya men are generally expected to protect their homes, wives, and children from harm; women are expected to pray to the Virgin for the health of their families, thus attracting good. Faust's (1988a; 1998a, b) earlier interpretation of male sexual symbolism for chile peppers and female for cacao beans is not made explicit by Don Pedro, although it appears to be part of the partially out-of-awareness system of associations that he uses in symbolic healing activities. Faust's exegesis relied on her year of fieldwork that included observations of many Maya ceremonies and participation in three pilgrimages. She was also privileged to hear the everyday talk of various friends, including that of the large extended family with whom she lived. There were all-female conversations in the kitchens and men's talk overheard in various holiday gatherings that included jokes about double meanings concerning sexuality, intercourse, and pregnancy.

Both authors observed later ceremonies in which everyday references and joking concerning sexuality and reproduction confirm these connotations in the broader context. The *chile parado* preferred by Don Pedro for use in curing ceremonies is the one whose association with the erect penis is particularly evident from its shape and habit of growing straight up from the branch rather than hanging down like other fruits. Since chiles were domesticated in the New World by 2000 B.C. (Walsh and Sugiura 1991:23), it seems probable that these cultural associations are pre-Columbian and were spread throughout the Spanish Empire during Colonial times, along with chiles, cacao, and corn.

In the case of cacao, although the symbolic association with sexuality is not as evident, it is possible to decipher from the following: (1) the manner in which the cacao beans are paired with chile peppers, (2) the appearance of the seeds and the fruit, and (3) the jokes about sexuality made by women preparing the hot beverage made from the beans. The beans used by Don Pedro are a reddish brown, oval, and frequently have a slight longitudinal crease, thus reminding some people of the female vulva.[4] The fruit is also oval with longitudinal creases; when ripe it has a reddish purple color. Alternatively, the fruits may be understood to represent breasts full of mother's milk, due to their shape and how they hang from the tree. In order to prepare the hot chocolate beverage, the cacao beans are toasted and ground with sugar and cinnamon, dissolved with boiling water, and beaten with a wooden pestle inside an oval vessel. Maya women jokingly compared these movements to those of the penis in the vagina during sexual intercourse (Faust 1998a:616).

Gender in Generations

Such symbolism of explicitly sexual genitalia is presented in a context that includes not only the pairing of opposite sexes but the generational pairing of same sex individuals of different generations: mother with daughter (a pair of cacao beans), father with son (a pair of chiles) within the quincunx altar setting (Faust 1998a:639–640). Such pairings of generations by gender is substantiated by numerous comments concerning the importance of having at least one "pair" of children, representing both genders. It is explicitly said of a woman who finally has a daughter, that she finally has her replacement (*relevo*). Those couples who have only girls or only boys are equally pitied, especially the parent who has no *relevo*. The strong cooperation and interdependency between husband and wife, each within their own role, corresponds with the teaching of this role to sons and daughters by the parent of the same gender (Elmendorf 1976, Faust 1988a).

Ritual Humor/Ancient Murals

The conjunction of symbolism concerning parenting with that referring explicitly to sexual intercourse and genitalia and both in the context of a religious ceremony is very similar to the ritual humor described by Bricker (1973) for more public rituals associated with saints' days in the Maya Highlands of Chiapas, Mexico, where sexual acts are mimicked and satirized in public performances. In Yukatekan celebrations of Carnival, there is similar ribald public joking about a mythical being known as "Juan Carnival." Juan is essentially the spirit of both life and sexuality, a disruptive character that disturbs public order, disrespects household boundaries, and whose sexual exploits are loudly denounced. The role of his woman is played by a man in a dress and wig, with a huge fake abdomen of pillows to indicate pregnancy. From under her dress, she gives birth to a gourd in the middle of the town plaza, writhing and groaning with labor pains and shrieking about having been abandoned by Juan (Faust 1988a:201–202).

Interestingly, this gourd "baby" is of the type used to carry water to the fields, with a slight indentation in the middle producing a shape resembling a female torso. It is the same gourd represented in the mural on the north wall of the Preclassic (50 B.C.) site of San Bartolo, Guatemala, from which emerge five babies with symbols for blood. Close to this image is another that represents the emergence of the Maize God from Flower Mountain, according to preliminary iconographic analysis based on similarities to the Maya creation myth in the *Popol Vuh* and to previous analyses of Mesoamerican epigraphy and iconography (see Saturno, Taube, and Stuart 2005, and its supplemental drawing by Heather Hurst).

During contemporary festivities for Carnival, after the birth of the gourd baby, an effigy of Juan Carnival is burned in front of the Catholic Church at midnight, the Tuesday before Ash Wednesday, thereby beginning the solemn Lenten season of Christian tradition. However, with a mixture of mock shame and barely disguised glee, people widely and repeatedly comment that none of us would be here without Juan. Sexuality is here represented as tightly connected with having sons and daughters, and having children is clear evidence of having sex. Both are aspects of the continuity of community life, embodied in male and female co-workers who participate in the adaptation of inherited social institutions to new situations.

In this same manner cacao beans and chile peppers connect the patient with the quincunx structure of the cosmos and the flow of energy through its "center," carrying life into the future, while tricking the Earth Lord with a chicken sacrifice.

Ethnohistorical and Archaeological Support for Gender Symbolism in the Ritual Use of Cacao

In the sixteenth century, Díaz del Castillo (1970 [1500s]:167, cited by Pérez-Romero and Cobos 1990:39) described indigenous associations of cacao with sexual pleasure, including the use of cacao beverages to obtain "access" to women. A sixteenth-century Colonial official, García de Palacio (1983:74–75, also cited by Pérez-Romero and Cobos 1990:39) mentioned that in Guatemala the indigenous men, "got together with their women in filthy ceremonies," before planting cacao trees.

The pre-Columbian iconography also gives evidence of sexual connotations for cacao, associated with women and the Underworld, seen as a place for re-birth and regeneration of life (Barthel 1978:81–90). In Palenque, Mexico, during the Classic period, the cacao tree was a symbol of royal lineage (McAnany, 1995:75). Cacao is also strongly associated with the founders of the Copan dynasty (McNeil, Hurst, and Sharer, this volume).

In pre-Columbian times, temples and their associated sculptures were "terminated" through symbolic destruction. Caches included broken ceramics and blood-letting implements. Sometimes termination symbolism was combined with that for renewal and dedication, indicating a form of rebirth (S. B. Mock 1998). Similarly to building terminations and renewals, elite human burials often contain both bloodletting tools and evidence of rituals, as well as ceramic vessels to provision the spirit in its journey to the realm of benevolent ancestors (Freidel 1998). Biochemical analysis of residues in vessels from Río Azul, Guatemala, and Copan, Honduras, has revealed the presence of cacao as food and beverage.

Other symbolic uses of cacao in ceremonies have been documented in the Colonial *Popol Vuh* (D. Tedlock 2002) and in the hieroglyphic texts found on some ceramic vessels in Classic period burial contexts (S. D. Coe and M. D. Coe 1996). Contemporary Lacandon (Pugh, this volume) and Ch'orti' (Kufer and Heinrich, this volume) ceremonies still include offerings of cacao, with female associations, paired with male symbols. In these cases, as in our Yukatek Maya case, cacao is presented in association with male symbols and related to an underlying concept of fertility, lineage, and the regeneration of cycles.

Conclusion

We acknowledge Maya adoption of medical concepts and treatment from various sources but propose that the strong association of cacao with the archaeologically salient "quincunx" pattern is an indication of conceptual continuity. Girard (1966:33) noted the same ritual pattern among twentieth-century Ch'orti' Maya.

These modern ritual practices may be modified versions of a pre-Columbian symbol system involving cacao, the *kantis*, and gender in transformations associated with termination and rebirth. Comparison of rituals across time may help elucidate continuities that underlie responses to changing technologies, identities, orientations, and aspirations. The *kantis*, ritually outlined with cacao beans, connects the patient to house, yard, agricultural field, this world, the Underworld, and the Celestial World through their isomorphic perimeters and the energizing/nurturing umbilici of all these orienting squares. The perimeter, including sides and corners, is created by the path of the sun through time and space, day and year signaling cardinal directions. The sun's power at noon forms the *u hol gloriyah*, a vertical channel for the transmission of energy, represented by the central point of the *kantis*.

Perhaps it is those who become detached from the organizing structures of space/time/energy that lose internal strength and thus become vulnerable to the winds, which cause some illnesses and complicate others. Ritual placement of cacao beans and chile peppers in the center and cardinal directions of the *kantis* forms a connection to the Whole and all its parts, a binding to place and time that securely "seats" the soul of the patient and other family members participating in the ritual. Returning to that secure base, with its protective perimeter, appears to be a prerequisite for healing from illnesses brought by the winds, which can be controlled by their Lords. An etic explanation could be that this ritual symbolism assists the patient's immune system as a type of placebo (through emotions that affect endocrine levels, see Hahn 1995:89–96). An emic explanation of the ceremony could be that the symbolic actions involving cacao and chile pepper placements in the quincunx "re-dedicate" the patient to participation in the energized and ordered cosmos, while the illness itself is transferred to the sacrificed chicken and "terminated" with ritual offerings in a burial cache.

Acknowledgments

The authors thank their research consultant, Don Pedro Ucán Itzá, for his teachings and invitations to photograph and participate in Maya ceremonies. We also thank his family for their assistance and hospitality and Mexico's Centro de Investigación y de Estudios Avanzados del Instituto Politécnico Nacional for financial and logistic support. We are grateful to Cameron McNeil for her invitation and assistance in making it possible for us to present a previous version in the 2002 meetings of the American Anthropological Association where participants and audience provided helpful suggestions. And finally we thank our respective families who have helped each of us understand other families and each other.

Notes

1. Campeche is one of three states within the Mexican portion of the Yucatan Peninsula. Don Pedro was born and grew up in another, the state of Yucatan, but has lived in Campeche since his twenties.

2. The everyday beverage is referred to as *posol* by some authors, to distinguish it from the *pozole* known in other areas of Mexico. In Yucatan, however, this ordinary beverage is called *pozole*. A wife traditionally puts dried kernels of maize in water with quicklime, boiling the mixture and then letting it set until the epicarp is loose and can be washed off the kernels. She then grinds the maize into a dough, wraps it in a cloth, and gives it to her farmer husband, who carries it to the fields before dawn with salt and a gourd of water. Around ten in the morning the dough is dissolved in the water to make a gruel that is drunk out of a gourd or a plastic bowl. Salt is often simply licked off the back of the hand as an accompaniment, although sometimes it is added directly to the gruel. This *pozole* sustains a traditional farmer until he returns home for the main meal of the day around one or two in the afternoon. The ritual beverage *saka'* looks similar but is prepared differently, without quicklime.

3. For Maya ritual numbers, we are adopting a convention of using the Arabic numerals to emphasize the symbolic importance of specific numbers in Maya thought. For example, the numeral 5, in the placement of 5 cacao beans in the center of the ritual

altar, refers to the four sides of a square and their central point, which make up the quincunx, an important concept in Maya cosmology.

4. The authors have been informed by Cameron McNeil that the seeds she has seen do not have this crease. It is unknown if the crease appears in beans that have been dried and stored for a period of time or if we are seeing different varieties. Two other associations of creased ovals with vulva are found with *empanadas* and papayas. In the first ceremony observed by Faust, *empanadas* were included as part of the ritual foods. These were stuffed with brownish red, ground squash seeds. As this reddish substance oozed out between the sealed lips of the puffed up empanadas cooking on the grill, the women began to giggle and make comments among themselves concerning the resemblance of the *empanadas* to menstrual discharge. In that case the patient was suffering from delayed menarche, and the association was specifically relevant to the desired change in the patient. Association of the papaya fruit with the vulva also is related to its oval shape with a longitudinal crease. Cutting along the crease with a knife results in oozing white sap, jokingly referred to as vaginal discharge associated with sexual arousal.

21

From Chocolate Pots to Maya Gold

Belizean Cacao Farmers Through the Ages

Patricia A. McAnany and Satoru Murata

Belizean chocolate—the moniker does not carry the same cachet as Swiss or Belgian chocolate, does it? Although the heavily marketed European brands have gained global prestige and name recognition, the nations of reference are far away from the tropical climes in which cacao is grown today and was grown in the past. Contemporary name-tagging of chocolate is linked to processing techniques and packaging locales rather than to centers of cultivation—one of the many injustices of a temperate-focused, global economy. Nevertheless, Belizean chocolate, sold under the sobriquet of *Maya Gold*, is enjoying modest recognition today under a fair trade agreement negotiated between a British candy company and Maya cacao-growers of southern Belize. This resurgence of chocolate production in the Belize zone of the Maya lowlands follows a period of lower-level production during the preceding two hundred years. Contemporary production levels recapitulate the established position that the Belize zone once held as a cacao producer, notwithstanding key distinctions introduced by the structure of global capitalism. In this chapter, evidence of the former prominence of Belizean cacao is adduced from historical accounts, relict stands of *Theobroma cacao* L. trees, and archaeobotanical, chemical, and archaeological remains. In one of the great circularities of history, a crop that once provided pre-Columbian and Colonial Mesoamerica with its most universally acknowledged standard of value and closest approximation to a medium of currency, now fills a cash crop niche among subsistence farmers of southern Belize.

The central theme of this study is the deep history of cacao cultivation in the Belize zone, which is demonstrated by the continuity of cacao farming from Middle Preclassic to contemporary times (800 B.C. to present). A Caribbean watershed landscape that is conducive to chocolate farming, the Belize zone provides the frame for this longitudinal perspective on cultivation and consumption of a premier cultigen of Mesoamerica. This chapter is divided into three sections. First we turn to the contemporary situation in which cacao is produced for a world market. This commodity-based cultivation is shown to differ significantly from ethnographically documented, lower levels of production for ritual practice and localized exchange. These arrangements characterize the last two centuries. In the Caribbean valleys that today comprise Belize, precious little is known about cacao production during the late seventeenth, the eighteenth, and the early part of the nineteenth centuries. Demographic collapse, insect blights, poor maintenance of orchards, and competition from South American producers conspired to depress drastically cacao production throughout Mesoamerica during the late Colonial period (Feldman 1985:87; M. J. MacLeod 1973:239–240). For the sixteenth and first half of the seventeenth century, however, Colonial documents indicate that cacao production thrived throughout Belize; these accounts are summarized in the following section on the ethnohistory of Belizean cacao. The deeper history of cacao cultivation during pre-Columbian times is interpreted from remains of cacao beans, charred wood, chemical traces, artifacts, and relict stands of cacao orchards. Macrobotanical remains, likely of burned cacao wood, that date to the Middle Preclassic period (800–400 B.C.) suggest that some of the earliest farmers of Belize cultivated cacao along with maize and other key subsistence items.

How Maya Gold entered the World Market

Traditional cultivation of cacao among southern Belize Maya farmers

Only in recent decades has Belizean cacao become a player in the global market and hence acquired a considerable boost in importance among its producers; nevertheless, cacao seems always to have retained its ritual and economic significance among Maya cultures of the Belize zone. Some of the best ethnographic accounts of the traditional cultivation of cacao are provided by J. Eric S. Thompson, who, in the 1920s conducted multiple studies in the Toledo district of southern Belize (Figure 21.1). Cacao played vital roles in rituals concerning marriage, birth, and baptism; that is, in significant rites of passage (J. E. S. Thompson 1956:104). For example, a soon-to-be-groom of the Mopan Maya village of San Antonio in the Toledo district, upon acceptance of his proposal by the bride's parents, would pay all the costs of a feast held to celebrate the betrothal, which included "a hog, a gallon of rum, tortillas, and cocoa" (J. E. S. Thompson 1930:80).

Cacao was symbolically intertwined with the most important subsistence crop in Mesoamerica—maize (J. E. S. Thompson 1956:105). Mopan Maya of

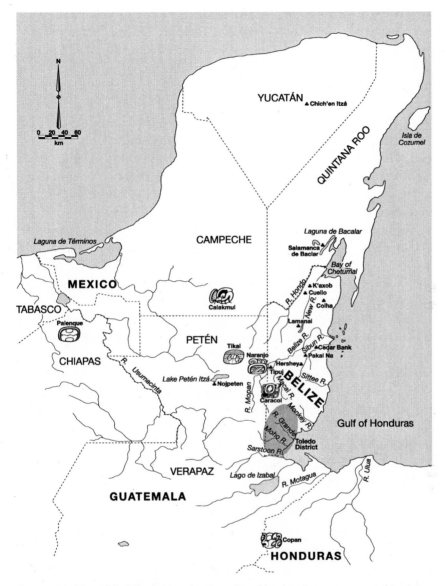

Figure 21.1. Map of the Maya region showing selected locales relevant to cacao cultivation in the Belize zone. Illustration by Satoru Murata.

San Antonio traditionally held an all-night vigil on the night before the *milpa* was to be sown. During the vigil "the seed to be sown is placed on the table before the cross and one or two candles are lighted and placed in front of it . . . then a calabash containing a little cacao and ground maize is placed before it between the candles" (J. E. S. Thompson 1930:48–49).

Cacao also played a role in other aspects of Maya subsistence, for example in a ritual to enhance the success of fishing (J. E. S. Thompson 1956:104). One of the most popular methods utilized by San Antonio Maya fishermen entailed introducing poison into the waters to be fished. Up to twenty San Antonio men who took part in fish-poisoning would pass the night in a vigil at one of the men's huts, lighting copal and candles and setting aside an offering of cacao during the course of the night (J. E. S. Thompson 1930:90). In view of these associations between cacao and crucial events of everyday life, it is not surprising to learn of the pronounced significance of the cacao tree itself, which was considered the "directional tree" of two of the 20 Maya days: Manik and Cauac (J. E. S. Thompson 1956:103). Cacao continued to occupy an essential role in ritual practices of Toledo district Maya peoples, at least until very recently (M. K. Steinberg 2002:60–61; Wilk 1991:119–120).

Cacao held economic significance, albeit on a smaller scale than today, within traditional cultivation as well. Q'eqchi' Maya of southern Belize bartered cacao for *huipiles* (traditional embroidered dresses) and mats with traders from Alta Verapaz (*cobaneros*), until at least the early twentieth century (J. E. S. Thompson 1964:21). According to Thompson (1930:185–186; 1956:100), the practice of using cacao beans as a form of "currency" survived in this region throughout the Colonial period and well into the nineteenth century. Overall, however, ethnographically documented locales of traditional cacao cultivation before Belizean chocolate entered the global market are geographically circumscribed compared to both the present and the early Colonial period. Locales are restricted to the Mopan and Q'eqchi' villages of southern Belize as reported by J. E. S. Thompson (1930; 1956; 1964).

Long after European cacao processing—including the addition of sugar and the production of "solid" chocolate—had become the norm, the traditional mode of cacao consumption among Toledo Maya maintained a strong degree of pre-Columbian continuity in the form of liquid cacao drinks. Preparation of the drink by the Mopan Maya as documented by J. E. S. Thompson (1930) entailed shelling, fermentation, and then drying the cacao beans on a piece of bark. The beans were then roasted on a pottery *comal* (or *sok*) and ground on a stone *metate*. The ground cacao was next mixed with maize flour and soaked in water, after which the mixture was reground on the *metate*. Finally, the mixture was placed on the fire, boiled, and served after the addition of "a con-

Figure 21.2. Mrs. Chun prepares cacao drink on a stone *metate* during a March 2003 visit by the authors. San Antonio, Toledo district, Belize. Photograph by Patricia A. McAnany.

siderable quantity of black pepper" (J. E. S. Thompson 1930:186). Thompson considered black pepper to be a modern substitute for chile (1956:107). During 2003, the authors had the opportunity to visit the Mopan Maya village of San Antonio and observe the traditional preparation of cacao drink by an elder Maya woman, Mrs. Chun, who was assisted by her daughter (Figure 21.2). The method of preparation from roasting to serving followed closely the steps described by Thompson with only one new introduction—sugar. Nearly eight decades after Thompson's visits to the Toledo district, there remains an impressive degree of cultural stability in the preparation of the chocolate drink, which "differs but slightly from that described by the early Spanish chroniclers" (J. E. S. Thompson 1930:186). Mrs. Chun commented, however, that many younger females were not interested in learning to use a *metate* or prepare chocolate in the customary fashion, so the stability of traditional cacao preparation may be in jeopardy in southern Belize.

Belize enters the global chocolate market

During the twentieth century, Maya farmers in southern Belize have produced a series of cash crops with emphasis on bananas during the early 1900s and rice after 1930 (Emch 2003:112). Cacao continued to be grown for domestic purposes, but, beginning in the late 1970s, new "improved" varieties of cacao were introduced from Costa Rica and elsewhere (M. K. Steinberg 2002:63). This hybrid stock required only three years for maturation to fruit-bearing trees (traditional varieties required five) and produced, on average, more than five times the yield of old varieties (Wilk 1991:121). In 1977, Hershey Foods Corporation established a 500-acre cacao farm called Hummingbird-Hershey Ltd. (see location of "Hershey" in Figure 21.1) and signed an agreement with the government of Belize to buy all cacao produced in the country at a world-market price of $0.85USD/lb (Emch 2003:124). With an assured market and attractive price, Toledo Maya began to invest more energy in cultivating this culturally important crop (M. K. Steinberg 2002:63; Wilk 1991:119). In the mid-1980s, farmers from ten villages in the Toledo district organized groups to pool money and labor and purchase hybrid seeds (Wilk 1991:119). The Toledo Cacao Growers Association (TCGA) emerged from these groups. The main goals of the TCGA were to coordinate marketing, provide credit, purchase agrochemicals in bulk (Wilk 1991:119), and establish cacao on leasehold land, to which they hope eventually to gain title (Emch 2003:124). With the help of multiple international development projects funded by the United States Agency for International Development (Emch 2003:124–125; Wilk 1991:119), cacao production in the Toledo district grew exponentially during the 1980s: from 70 farmers selling 1,086 pounds to Hershey in 1983 to 365 farmers selling 31,738 pounds in 1990 (Emch 2003:126, Table 7).

In addition to generating income, the enhanced economic significance of ca-cao has affected Maya life in several fundamental ways. One involves changes in how this crop is culturally perceived. Once a ritually and ceremonially charged plant, cacao is increasingly perceived by Toledo Maya as a commodity rather than a cultural component of their ritual practice (M. K. Steinberg 2002:59). Although it is still common for a cacao drink to be served on special occasions, M. K. Steinberg (2002:61) notes that the commodification of cacao had secu-larized its role among many southern Belize Maya.

The economic importance of cacao also is straining the communal land-use system of the Toledo district. One of only a few locales of cacao production within Belize (others include Tiger Sandy Bay Farm in central Belize and Hum-mingbird Citrus Limited [formerly owned by Hershey Foods Corporation] in the Cayo district; see Figure 21.1), the Toledo district groves are composed of dispersed trees on Mopan and Q'eqchi' Maya Reservation lands. Traditionally, land used for crop production was communally owned and could not be sold or rented. Cacao trees, however, can be sold, lent, or rented (Wilk 1991:120), rendering the planting of cacao trees an effective means of obtaining *de facto* ownership of land, which thenceforth could be passed down from generation to generation (M. K. Steinberg 2002:63). Wilk (1991:120) observes that this mode of privatizing land through cacao planting did not cause serious impact on the common-pool swidden lands in the past, as only small amounts of cacao were planted. With the entrance of Belizean cacao into the world market and the alluring price-tag placed on sacks of beans, the number of trees—and hence the acreage of land on which they are planted—has increased significantly, generating unease and resistance among some members of the community (M. K. Steinberg 2002:63; Wilk 1991:120). Villagers were antipathetic to this trend not only because conversion of land to cacao orchards removed land from the communal system (M. K. Steinberg 2002:63; Wilk 1991:120) but also because this transformation in land use engendered greater economic inequalities. A few individuals with the resources to plant and harvest sizable groves of cacao made large profits at the expense of communal land (Wilk 1991:121). In both Q'eqchi' and Mopan villages, angry farmers have destroyed new cacao orchards to protest this trend (M. K. Steinberg 2002:63; Wilk 1991:120). Allegedly, some farmers who wanted to establish a claim to communal lands planted cacao groves in expectation of the day when reservation lands would be privatized and parceled out by the government (M. K. Steinberg 2002:63; Wilk 1991:120). Because only farmers who are relatively well off possess the capital to invest in new cacao orchards, they are in the advantageous position of potentially gaining control of both the money-producing cacao trees and the land on which they are planted. Cacao cultivation, under the influence of the global economy, constitutes a challenge to the traditional land tenure system (Wilk 1991:120) and also may be pushing Maya society into one that is increasingly class-based (M. K. Steinberg 2002:63).

In 1992, after a relatively rapid drop in the world-market price of cacao (down to $0.55USD/lb), Hummingbird-Hershey Ltd. ceased buying cacao from Maya farmers (Emch 2003:128). This sudden disruption of the market—by the sole purchaser of the produce—left thousands of pounds of cacao to rot on trees and almost caused a complete abandonment of the industry (M. K. Steinberg 2002:63). Then, in 1993, the TCGA struck a deal with Green & Black's, a British candy-producing company. Under a five-year rolling contract, the Toledo district would become the sole provider of organically grown cacao to be processed into a new Green & Black's product called *Maya Gold* (Figure 21.3; Emch 2003:128; M. K. Steinberg 2002:64). Green & Black's also wanted the arrangement between them and the Maya farmers to be certified by the Fairtrade Foundation, a private firm in Britain that investigates whether a trade relationship between a first world company and third world producers is sufficiently advantageous to the latter. Following the recommendation of Fairtrade, Green & Black's agreed to buy all the cacao that the Toledo Maya can produce for $1.45USD/lb—nearly three times the world-market price (Worldaware 1994). The *Maya Gold* chocolate bar became the first product to bear the international Fairtrade sticker (Figure 21.4; Green & Black's 2004).

Toledo district Maya grew cacao organically not so much out of ecological sensitivity but because they could not afford expensive pesticides (M. K. Steinberg 2002:62). As noted above, one of the original aims of the TCGA was to purchase agrochemicals in bulk. Fortunately for the Toledo Maya, their inability to apply toxic chemicals to their cacao has allowed them to tap into a niche market that prizes purity and is willing to pay a premium for it. M. K. Steinberg (2002:62–63) reports that, in an effort to fight pests, some farmers have abandoned the "improved" hybrid varieties of cacao (the cultivation of which was recommended by Hummingbird-Hershey Ltd. because of higher yields) because they are prone to infestation. Instead, they have returned to

Figure 21.3. Mrs. Chun sitting next to a bag of organic cacao. The sack is labeled "Product of Belize" and is destined for a United Kingdom market. San Antonio, Toledo district, Belize. Photograph by Patricia A. McAnany.

Figure 21.4. Green and Black's chocolate bars, featuring *Maya Gold*, that bear the Fairtrade seal of approval. Photograph by Satoru Murata.

cultivating traditional varieties of cacao that are hardier, even if the yield is lower.

Thus, the commercial relationship between Toledo district Maya and Green & Black's is advantageous to the environment, because it strongly discourages the use of harmful pesticides, as well as to the cacao producers, as it ensures a profitable market for a sustained period of time. It is also advantageous to Green & Black's, because the establishment of conditions favorable to the producers earned them the Fairtrade endorsement (Emch 2003:129). The amount of cacao bought by Green & Black's increased from $10,000USD in 1993 to more than $100,000USD in 1997 (Emch 2003:128). Green & Black's claims that the demand for *Maya Gold* far surpasses the current production level (M. K. Steinberg 2002:64), attesting to the profitability of the enterprise. Unfortunately, on October 8, 2001, the Toledo district sustained a direct hit from Hurricane Iris that destroyed an estimated 85 percent of the cacao trees (Emch 2003:128). The deleterious effect of Hurricane Iris brought into question the future of the cacao industry of southern Belize (Emch 2003:129); however, Green & Black's was determined to continue with its relationship with the

Maya of Belize. In October 2003, Green & Black's was awarded a grant of £225,000 by the United Kingdom Department for International Development to redevelop the cacao market in Belize (Green & Black's 2003). With this funding, Green & Black's aims to increase the number of farmers—from the current 180 to a projected 600—as well as to assist farmers in achieving a geometric increase in total yield (from 30 tons/year to 200 tons/year within three years). If successful, this increase will generate a net income of $400,000USD for the Toledo economy (Green & Black's 2003).

As long as a productive relationship continues between the Toledo Cacao Grower's Association and Green & Black's and the popularity of Maya Gold holds strong, the economic importance of the cacao crop in southern Belize will be maintained. Certainly the current situation is more favorable both for the producers and the environment than past arrangements; however, social and economic aspects, such as communal land holding, seem destined for significant alteration as a result of intensified orchard production. As cacao becomes an increasingly valuable commodity, its ritual significance also appears to be diminished. Cacao cultivation under the banner of global fair trade, therefore, differs in fundamental ways from cacao production of pre-Columbian times.

Ethnohistory of Belizean Cacao

Cacao production upon the advent of Spaniards

Scholes and Roys (1968:3) note the early Colonial presence of two zones of cacao cultivation proximate to the Maya Lowlands. To the west, the well-known cacao orchards of Gulf Coast Tabasco constitute a region that is still producing cacao for domestic consumption within Mexico. The second zone encompasses the Caribbean watershed orchards from Belize to the Ulua River Valley of Honduras to the east. Maya of Yucatan are said to have imported cacao from both of these zones (Scholes and Roys 1968:316). In describing cacao production in the region of concern in this chapter, Bergmann (1969:86; Figure 1) characterizes southern Belize as a "secondary cacao district," whereas the Tabasco and Honduran orchards are each considered a "major cacao district" in pre-Columbian America. This assessment conflicts with that of J. E. S. Thompson (1964:41), who argues for the presence of large cacao orchards along the Belize River and around the Bay of Chetumal and suggests that these production areas must have exported cacao "both to Yucatan, too dry, and the highlands, too high, for these money-producing orchards." As we shall see, ethnohistorical research conducted by Grant Jones (1989, 1998) provides considerable support for Thompson's assertion and further expands the extent of cacao orchards in the Belize zone.

During early Colonial times, Spaniards appropriated locales of cacao production by means of the *encomienda* system. Colonial chapels (*visitas*) were generally built by *encomenderos* to Christianize indigenous populations in return for having been granted use of their land and labor by imperial decree (G. D. Jones 1989:41–42). Many, but not all, of the *encomiendas* established in the river valleys of Belize were composed of small settlements of Maya farmers who cultivated cacao, among other crops. In this respect, *visita* location and cacao production were closely linked.

Melchor and Alonso Pacheco established a series of small cacao-producing *encomiendas* soon after 1544 along the rivers of northern Belize and up the Belize River as far inland as Tipuj (G. D. Jones 1998:40). These were part of the notorious Spanish province of Bacalar that included southern Quintana Roo and the northern half of Belize. Apparently, by the early seventeenth century most of the *encomenderos* were absent and had ceded control to a "ruthless band of local cutthroats who roamed the countryside extorting cacao and other goods from the Mayas" (G. D. Jones 1989:84). This vivid description indicates that cacao was readily available in Maya villages within the Bacalar province. During the late sixteenth century, the population around the Bay of Chetumal appears to have been about two thousand; houses were spread along the shoreline and surrounded by fields of maize and orchards that included cacao and *mamey* trees (G. D. Jones 1989:97).

Farther inland, cacao groves also flourished during the early Colonial period as attested by Spaniards who often traveled to the interior by way of the New River. In this regard, the Colonial site of Indian Church (Lamanai) continued to function as an important trans-shipment point or node separating Peten overland trade from Caribbean water-borne trade (D. M. Pendergast 1993). Most historically documented *entradas* into the Peten (as well as pilgrimages by friars attempting to convert the Itza of Nojpeten) stopped at Indian Church before continuing south to the head of the New River Lagoon. After reaching the south shore of the lagoon, travelers faced an overland portage that included a creek crossing. Finally, the entourage would arrive at the north shore of the Belize River near the Colonial Maya communities of Lucu and Chantome (G. D. Jones 1989:xvi–xvii). In 1618, while waiting at Lucu for Maya canoes and paddlers to carry him upstream towards Tipuj, Fray Bartolomé de Fuensalida noted that cacao trees lined the river banks of the town and that the trees bore a reddish-brown pod, the fruit of which was very tasty without any additives (López de Cogolludo cited in G. D. Jones 1989:103–104).

The Belize and Xib'um (Sibun) valleys have been characterized as a zone of dispersed small-scale cacao farmers not subjected to *reduccion* by Spaniards because of the productivity of their orchards (G. D. Jones 1989:103). As noted above, J. E. S. Thompson (1964:41) suggests that some of the sixteenth-century orchards in this zone were quite large. Grant Jones (1989:119–121, 140) suspects that cacao production within Belize expanded during the early part of the seventeenth century as Yukatek Maya populations from the north fled south to areas not well controlled by Spanish Colonial authorities and sought means of livelihood. The overall demand for cacao rendered as tribute to Colonial authorities or traded within the underground Maya economy increased through the early part of the Colonial period. Evidence of this trend is provided by Fray Bartolomé de Fuensalida who noted during his 1618 visit to Tipuj that eight thousand new cacao trees had been planted by the *maestro de capilla*, a refugee from the northern Campeche town of Hecelchakan (G. D. Jones 1989:104, 140). The Colonial *visita* of Tipuj in the upper Belize River valley appears to have been a highly successful producer of high-quality cacao, a factor that contributed greatly to the wealth and importance of the Colonial settlement (Graham, Jones, and Pendergast 1989; G. D. Jones 1989:140; Muhs, Kautz, and MacKinnon 1985).

In the next drainage to the south of the Belize Valley—the contemporary Sibun or Colonial Xib'um Valley—cacao cultivation also thrived during the early Colonial period, and archival records contain anecdotal accounts of native insurgencies and flight from a *visita* called Xib'um (G. D. Jones 1989:200–202, 234–236). J. E. S. Thompson (1974:30) opined that the name Xib'um meant 'male bird,' and he placed a Colonial Maya village called Hopan or Zaui in the mid-reaches of the drainage near the archaeological site of Pakal Na (Scholes and Thompson 1977:Map 2-1; J. E. S. Thompson 1974: foldout map, 1977: Map 1-1; Figure 1). A 1677 account by Fray Joseph Delgado (J. E. S. Thompson 1977:67; Ximénez 1971–1975:Book 5, Chapter 33) indicates the town of Zaui was a day and a half's journey overland by foot from Tipuj. Unfortunately, this village cannot securely be placed in the Sibun drainage and likely was not the Xib'um mission. Direct references to the small population living at a Xib'um *visita* refer to the early part (rather than the later part) of the seventeenth century. Extensive archaeological survey within the Sibun Valley indicates that a likely location for the *visita* is farther downriver near Gracy Rock, where early Colonial material has been documented at a site called Cedar Bank (see Figure 21.1; McAnany, Harrison-Buck, and Morandi 2004).

Ever the itinerant missionary, the Dominican Fray Joseph Delgado also provided an account of travel during the same year from the Moho River of southern Belize to the Belize River. In this journey, he was accompanied by three Spaniards who left their cacao and annatto (achiote) plantations on the Moho River of southern Belize (G. D. Jones 1998:433). In 1620, half a century previous, Friar Gabriel Salazar traveled the lands of the Manche and Ch'ol Maya of northeastern Guatemala and southern Belize. During this trip, he was informed of a large town called Yaxal (Río Yaxal is the present-day Moho River), which "was in the channels of the coast of Bacalar and had 400 Indians and beautiful cacao orchards near the lands of Tzoite, where there is much cacao" (Salazar 2000:29). These accounts provide evidence of the continuous existence of cacao orchards in southern Belize through the seventeenth century, although they also hint at increasingly direct control of groves by Spaniards by the late seventeenth century. For the Pacific-Coast Guatemalan orchards, M. J. MacLeod (1973:239) notes that during this same time (seventeenth century) the *encomienda* system (in which Spaniards "owned" the labor and resources of a granted area but not necessarily the land) had largely given way to outright ownership of cacao orchards by "non-Indians."

The political economy of cacao during the early Colonial period is complex. In the Belize zone, cacao farmers appear to have been growing the crop in response to the tribute demands of two masters (Spanish and indigenous Itza) as well as for a brisk trade conducted under the noses of Spanish Colonial authorities. Spanish *encomenderos* demanded cacao as well as the labor involved in its cultivation and harvesting in order to supply the Yukatek and Mexican cacao markets in addition to a growing overseas demand. Of the cacao-acquisition strategies employed by the powerful and independent Itza, Grant Jones (1989:102) simply states that "cacao did not grow well in the central Peten . . . and the Itzas and their neighbors had to depend on importation of the product or control over subject populations who could supply them with it" (see also Caso Barrera and Aliphat F., this volume). "Presenting" cacao to Itza rulers, such as Ajaw Kan Ek', no doubt was a frequent *raison d'être* for a trek from Tipuj. The received translation (G. D. Jones 1998:35) of a 1524 conversation between the conquistador Hernán Cortés and Kan Ek' suggests that the Itza exercised considerable political muscle in southern Belize during the sixteenth century. Before the arrival of Cortés, Ajaw Kan Ek' already knew of the presence of a group of Spaniards in the area of Lago de Izabal; he had received news from "vassals working in cacao orchards located near where they [Spaniards] were said to be and from merchants who traveled daily between Nojpeten and the [Caribbean] coast." This extension of Itza power into the Belize zone not only ensured the flow of cacao beans into the Peten but also freed the Itza ruler from dealing with Chontal Maya traders who controlled production in the Tabasco area and had earlier established a measure of influence in the Bay of Honduras (Scholes and Roys 1968:316). Epigraphic evidence from the Classic period suggests that competition over these two fertile cacao-producing zones—Tabasco and Belize—is deeply rooted in the geopolitics of earlier times.

Deeper History of Cacao Cultivation and Ritual Use

In 1956, J. Eric S. Thompson noted that "archaeological material bearing on cacao is rare" (1956:101) and restricted primarily to iconographic imagery of cacao beans, pods, or fruit-bearing trees. Fifty years later, the corpus of evidence relating to cacao has expanded significantly and includes hieroglyphic, chemical, and macrobotanical materials. An enhanced understanding of the larger cosmological underpinning of cacao use during the Classic period has served to deepen temporally Thompson's emphasis on the "ritualistic importance of cacao" (1956:102). Here, direct evidence of cacao cultivation and use in the Belize zone during pre-Columbian times is complemented by relevant information on Classic Maya royal courts. Finally, Preclassic evidence of cacao cultivation and use is synthesized.

Cacao and Classic Maya royal courts

The substantial appetite for cacao at royal courts of the Peten and northern Yucatan likely was satisfied through a combination of trade and tribute in a manner analogous to the ethnohistorically known Aztec and Itza strategies of procurement. A vivid example of the presentation of cacao to a royal court comes from Bonampak, Mexico, where the cleaning of murals in Room 1 revealed that the white cloth bags stacked against the throne scene painted on the end wall were marked hieroglyphically as containing a tabulated amount of cacao (M. E. Miller 1997). In this scene, the now familiar glyph for cacao (*ka-ka-w[a]*) is surmounted by paired glyphs that are topped with a bar. Houston (1997:40) reads the glyph compound as "5 *pi kakaw*" (also spelled *pih*) and notes that David Stuart considers "pi" to represent a count of eight thousand. The Nahuatl term for the same count is *xiquipil*. The mural shows the bundles placed at the foot of a large throne on which a royal family is seated; the total count of presented cacao beans would have been forty thousand. The standard cacao *carga* (load) carried by a porter is reported to have been three *xiquipil* (or three *pih*) which means that the cacao beans presented in this scene could have been transported with relative ease by two porters. "Five *pih kakaw*" could represent the standard tribute amount offered to a Classic Maya royal court during a single presentation event, or it could simply be an amount chosen by a mural artist to fill a composition. Given the prolonged harvesting season for cacao (six to eight months) and the dearth of storage features within palace complexes, it is possible that royal courts were supplied constantly with small amounts of cacao such as the five *pih kakaw* of the Bonampak mural. In this respect, the royal demand for cacao—at any one point in time—would not have been onerous, but the constancy of the demand could have taxed production levels and transport capabilities in the long run.

Classic period painted polychrome vessels that bear the *kakaw* glyph as part of a Primary Standard Sequence and often include a name and title as part of a dedication text are renown (Houston, Stuart, and Taube 1989; Reents-Budet 1994a; Reents-Budet, this volume; D. Stuart 1989; Stuart, this volume). A rare polychrome cylindrical vessel (see Reents-Budet, Figure 10.7, this volume) that has been systematically excavated and recorded is particularly relevant to Belizean chocolate because it was found in the tomb of a young male at the upper Belize River Valley site of Buenavista (Tascheck and Ball 1992). The hieroglyphic band identifies the vessel as used for cacao by the *k'uhul ajaw* 'divine lord' of Naranjo, K'ak' Tiliw Chan Chaak (Houston, Stuart, and Taube 1992; B. MacLeod and D. Reents-Budet 1994:129). Naranjo, a major seat of much-contested power during the Late Classic period, is only 25 km northwest of Buenavista and immediately west of the international boundary between Guatemala and Belize. Another link between Belizean cacao and the gateway center of Naranjo surfaced in 2003 in the upper Sibun Valley. Excavation of the front façade of a Late Classic pyramid at a site called Hershey yielded an incised pottery sherd on which a portion of the Naranjo emblem glyph can be discerned (Figure 21.5; Morandi 2004). The political implications of the presence of the

Figure 21.5. The Naranjo emblem glyph incised on a sherd. Late Classic period. Excavated at the Hershey site, Sibun Valley, Belize. Photograph by Patricia A. McAnany.

Naranjo glyph at a site in a cacao-producing valley is bolstered by the construction style at the Hershey site (today still surrounded by a cacao orchard), which emulates Peten architecture. Circular shrine structures (a prominent characteristic of lower valley Sibun sites) are conspicuously lacking from the Hershey site. This pattern allows us to consider the idea that the sphere of influence exerted by Naranjo during the Late Classic period extended south of the Belize Valley and wrapped around the eastern side of the Maya Mountains.

More support for the strategic importance of Belize as a Classic period chocolate producer (as well as a source of innumerable highly desired marine products) is provided by glyphic evidence of Classic period martial conflicts. Although there is a lively literature regarding the motivations and goals of Maya warfare, texts and imagery of tributary offerings rendered by vanquished powers provide evidence that the maintenance of a steady flow of goods necessary to the materialization of the values and hierarchy that underscored the Classic period ritual economy was of critical importance. Given this perspective, the Gulf and Caribbean supply zones were key areas in which to exert political influence. The wealth of centers such as Palenque and Naranjo—gateways to these respective supply zones—must have been considerable. Hieroglyphic texts indicate that such strategic positioning came at a great price, however; both sites were involved in an unusually high number of martial conflicts as power shifted between the supraregional capitals located at Tikal and Calakmul (Martin and Grube 2000:21).

In short, hieroglyphic and geopolitical evidence supports an important role for the Belize zone in sustaining Classic period Maya royal courts. Given the cultural significance of the "cacao-drinking" ceremony, as indicated by the ubiquity of polychrome vessels painted with the *kakaw* glyph, it is highly likely that vintage-quality chocolate beans from fermentation vats in Belize often graced the cacao-grinding *metates* of Classic period Maya royal courts.

Belizean chocolate production during the Classic period

What of the direct lines of evidence regarding Classic period cacao cultivation in the Belize zone? Four categories of evidence are reviewed below: relict stands of cacao, site centers located on what today is prime land for growing cacao, a dispersed residential pattern as required by small-scale cacao cultivation, and preserved cacao beans.

Relict stands of cacao

For many years, botanists have noted that the Amazonian rain forest contains the greatest genetic diversity of the genus *Theobroma*, yet scant evidence of traditional bean processing has been documented in that area (A. M. Young

1994:15; see Bletter and Daly, this volume). A tropical understory tree species, *Theobroma cacao* can survive and spread with minimal human interaction; therefore its distribution within Mesoamerica could be the result of human transport of a desired cultigen or just the biological expansion of a successful species. Based on a comprehensive study of the distribution and molecular variation of *T. cacao* in Mesoamerica, Ogata (2002a; see Ogata, Gómez-Pompa, and Taube, this volume) concludes that most trees found in Mesoamerica in areas in which there has not been commercial cultivation during historical times likely are remnants of ancient cacao groves rather than wild species. If correct, this means that modern distributions of *T. cacao* can be used to infer the locations of cacao groves from early Colonial and possibly more distant times. In the Bladen Reserve of southern Belize, for instance, Brokaw et al. (1997) have documented a band of rain forest with high species diversity that is paralleled at lower elevations with a forest community that includes *T. cacao* in association with ancient Maya house platforms (K. Tripplett, personal communication January 6, 2004). Further research in this area by Dunham (1996:324) has resulted in documentation of cacao trees in high valleys along the eastern flank of the Maya Mountains, an area of no known Colonial period orchards. Similarly, in the middle reaches of the Sibun Valley, on a farm owned by Victor and Edith Quan, a relict stand of cacao has been found on the east side of the river (McAnany, personal observation 2003), an area with no evidence of nearby Colonial period occupation. Conversations with elder residents of Belize who have worked in the lumber and *chicle* industries and traveled extensively through the backwoods of Belize have yielded innumerable descriptions of uninhabited tracts of forest that contain cacao trees. Further genetic studies of these relict stands are needed to confirm that they represent pre-Hispanic species of cacao and to document this rich part of Belize's botanical heritage.

Site centers on prime cacao-growing land

Contemporary Q'eqchi' and Mopan cacao farmers of southern Belize inhabit a landscape containing not only relict stands of cacao but also architectural ruins of ancient settlements. Nearby Late Classic centers at Lubaantun, Nim Li Punit, Pusilha, and Uxbenka are located immediately proximate to the best agricultural soils available in the region (Dunham, Jamison, and Leventhal 1989:289; Hammond 1975), indicating that they were not disembedded from the production potential of their surrounding landscape. To the north, in the upper part of the Sibun Valley, a site called Hershey is so named for the cacao orchard formerly owned by Hershey Foods Corporation within which it is located (McAnany and Thomas 2003; McAnany et al. 2002). Although the recent history of this coincidence precludes extrapolation into the past, the suitability of the site location for cacao cultivation is beyond dispute. In the northern half of Belize, land use has changed dramatically, and prime cacao-growing lands have been converted to pastures, citrus orchards, and sugarcane fields. Nonetheless, the distribution of centers in the upper Belize River valley—Xunantunich, Buenavista, and Cahal Pech—are proximate to lands that are highly suitable for cacao cultivation (Healy and Awe 1995, 1996; LeCount 2001; LeCount et al. 2002; Tascheck and Ball 1992). The pattern continues into northern Belize, where, despite the ubiquity of sugarcane fields, the limestone-derived soils are reputed to have supported sizable cacao groves during the early Colonial period.

Dispersed residential compounds

A prominent feature of household archaeology within the Belize zone is the presence of residential compounds—often of substantial size and duration—that are configured in a dispersed pattern. The upper Belize Valley, for instance, once was populated in this fashion as is evident from settlement maps such as Barton Ramie (Willey et al. 1965). This dispersed pattern is consonant with the pattern noted in archival sources by Grant Jones (1989:103) as that typical of cacao growers. Because pre-Hispanic cacao was not grown as a monocrop but rather as an understory species within a diverse, high-canopy forest, harvested trees were dispersed as was the residential pattern of the harvesters. Given this, successful cacao cultivation could not be practiced in areas in which populations were tightly packed and demands for food and firewood diminished the rain forest. Although a dispersed settlement pattern, in and of itself, cannot be used as an indicator of cacao cultivation, it is symptomatic of lower population densities and a known land-use pattern practiced by cacao farmers.

Finally, direct evidence of chocolate beans has emerged from a dry cave on the eastern flank of the Maya Mountains of southern Belize. While documenting caves used for ancient Maya rituals, Keith Prufer (personal communication, January 5, 2004) discovered preserved cacao beans that had been placed beneath an inverted Early Classic bowl, one of several accoutrements associated with the interment of an individual who had been placed inside a chamber that was later sealed. This fortuitous discovery indicates that, contrary to statements regarding the impossibility of cacao-bean preservation, fifteen-hundred-year-old cacao can be retrieved from archaeological contexts.

Preclassic cacao in the Belize zone

The cylindrical polychrome vessel that is so commonly associated with ancient cacao drinking represents a Classic period addition to the Maya assemblage of earthenware forms. Likely introduced from elsewhere, this shape appears in the Maya region during the Early Classic when the prestige and influence of the Highland city of Teotihuacan, Mexico, was in ascendance. The Preclassic precursor took a radically different form, namely, a spouted jar that sometimes included a handle or stirrup strap. Dubbed a "chocolate pot" for reasons that have yet to be understood completely, this monochromatic form has never been found with a painted hieroglyphic text. A case could be made for considering the famous Río Azul chocolate pot (see Hurst, Figure 5.7, this volume)—with its stirrup-strap handle, painted hieroglyphic text that includes the *ka-ka-w[a]* glyph, and chemical residue of theobromine (Hall et al. 1990)—as a transitional form (that is, an Early Classic [A.D. 250–600] jar without a spout). Preclassic spouted vessels were produced as singular customized items that often display appliqués, gadrooning, or distinctive surface finishes that distinguish them from other more mundane Preclassic pottery vessels (McAnany, Storey, and Lockard 1999:138; Powis et al. 2002). This form, so radically different from the simple cylinder of later times, is found well to the south of the southern boundary of Mesoamerica with a distribution that extends north to Belize during the Middle Preclassic period. During Late Preclassic times (400 B.C.–A.D. 250), the range expands to the Mexican Highlands as far as Tlatilco (Powis et al. 2002:87–88). Just as the Classic period polychrome cylindrical form is commonly found within mortuary contexts, so the monochromatic spouted vessel also is retrieved principally from burials, often of males. Although tomb burials are rare during the Preclassic period, the interments with which spouted vessels were placed generally include distinctive items of personal adornment; moreover, such burials are likely to have been covered with a layer of red hematite powder such as in the Preclassic burials of K'axob in northern Belize (McAnany 2004; McAnany, Storey, and Lockard 1999:138).

The use of the spouted vessel in a Preclassic and antecedent variant of the cacao-drinking ceremony has been confirmed by W. Jeffrey Hurst and his team of chemists from Hershey Foods Corporation. Traces of the chemical compound theobromine were identified in three of fourteen samples extracted from spouted vessels (Hurst et al. 2002; Powis et al. 2002:97–98; see also Hurst, this volume). The pottery vessels, each bearing customized decorative elements, had been excavated from Middle and Late Preclassic burials at Colha, a Belizean site well known as a center of stone tool production from the Late Preclassic through Postclassic periods (400 B.C.–A.D. 1200).

Evidence that personalized pottery vessels containing chocolate residue were deposited in burials of important men and women in Preclassic Maya settlements, while extraordinary, does not demonstrate that cacao was grown in the Belize zone during this time. Macrobotanical or pollen evidence must be sought in order to demonstrate production as well as consumption. Burned wood samples from Middle and Late Preclassic deposits at three sites, Cuello, Kokeal, and K'axob, have yielded specimens that Charles Miksicek has identified as *Theobroma cacao* (Hammond and Miksicek 1981:260–269; Miksicek 1983:97,103; B. L. Turner and C. H. Miksicek 1984:Table 1). Charred fragments resembling cacao beans and pods also have been reported from Preclassic Cerros (Crane 1996:271). Although it is possible that these macrobotanical remains are of "wild" cacao, that chemical residue of the cacao drink has been identified from a coeval time period strengthens the interpretation of these remains as that of a closely cultivated species, possibly from the seasonal pruning of highly prized trees. Middle Preclassic villages—particularly those of Belize—are remarkable in the sophistication of their architecture, pottery, and suite of cultigens. To that impressive roster, it appears that the planting and management of cacao trees should be added.

Viewing the Preclassic period from the ancient Belizean entrepôt of Cerros, Freidel (1979) suggested that the archaeological concept of an interaction sphere is highly relevant to understanding the processes at work during the Preclassic period. Cerros was a gateway community through which Caribbean marine products were moved into the interior. Given the small but tantalizing amount of evidence of cacao production in northern Belize during the Preclassic period, it is possible that chocolate was moved out of the region via this port on the Chetumal Bay. Two thousand years later, Spaniards established Bacalar on the northern side of the bay for the purpose of exporting cacao thus appearing to have echoed a very ancient pattern.

Conclusion

Cultivation and consumption of cacao—the latter employing distinctive customized pottery vessels—enjoy a deep history within the Belize zone. In most of its Caribbean-watershed valleys, the small country possesses a climate and edaphic conditions that are suitable for cacao cultivation. Archaeological research in Belize has yielded evidence suggesting that cacao was integrated into the repertoire of orchard species cultivated by Maya farmers by the Middle Preclassic period. Through the Classic period, cacao production appears to have expanded and to have become entangled in the competitive ritual economies of Peten royal courts. Hieroglyphic texts indicate that sites on the western edge of the Belizean cacao zone—specifically Naranjo and Caracol—were involved in a large number of martial conflicts, possibly because of their strategic position relative to the movement of cacao. The dispersed pattern of much Classic period settlement within Belize and the contemporary presence of relict stands of cacao allude to the importance of cacao production during the Classic period. During the Late Postclassic and early Colonial periods, cacao orchards assumed continued importance in Belize, within indigenous Maya political economies and the Spanish-controlled Colonial economy. With a foot in both worlds, Maya cacao farmers apparently traded with and presented tribute to the Itza royal court at Nojpeten while simultaneously providing cacao to Spanish *encomenderos*. From the Colonial period collapse of the cacao industry in Mesoamerica until late in the twentieth century, production within Belize (particularly southern Belize) appears to have been focused on small-scale intraregional exchange. Ethnographic accounts document the continued ritual importance of cacao among Mopan and Q'eqchi' Maya farmers during the early twentieth century. The expansion of Hershey Foods Corporation into Belize in 1977 started another cycle of intensified cacao production, particularly among Toledo Maya farmers who organized into a cooperative called the Toledo Cacao Growers Association that is composed largely of Q'eqchi' and Mopan Maya farmers. This latest cycle of cacao production has strained the communal land system and effected greater economic inequalities among Maya families, but it also has provided the Toledo district of Belize—chronically depressed economically—with a cash crop in high demand. The addition of a United Kingdom market by way of a British candy company called Green and Black's—complete with the negotiation of a Fairtrade agreement with Toledo organic cacao farmers—has provided farmers with a better profit margin than is often the case when "developing" nations produce for faraway consumers in "developed" nations.

Overall, ethnographic, ethnohistorical, and archaeological evidence support the notion that the Belize zone has always been a key area of cacao production. Through the ages, cacao farmers have harvested the pods of this tropical understory tree to satisfy the desire for chocolate among Preclassic emergent elites, Classic period royal courtiers, Colonial *encomenderos*, and contemporary "chocoholics" with a social conscience.

Acknowledgments

The authors wish to acknowledge the generous hospitality of the Q'eqchi' and Mopan Maya people of the Toledo Ecotourism Association (TEA) for hosting members of the Xibun Archaeological Research Project (XARP) in 2001 and 2003. Special thanks go to Pablo Ak and Reyes Chun, TEA coordinators. Mrs. Chun, of San Antonio, generously demonstrated the traditional technique of preparing the cacao drink. Bert Faux, manager of Hummingbird Citrus Ltd., kindly gave of his time to chronicle the history of that chocolate grove. Steve Downard, owner of the Tiger Sandy Bay cacao grove, also assisted this project in innumerable ways. Many thanks to the Quan family, Victor and Edith, as well as their assistant, Juan Sho, for showing us the relict stand of cacao in the middle Sibun Valley. We also express our appreciation to Mario Peres who showed Kirsten Tripplett, XARP project botanist, a cacao tree in the upper Indian Creek Valley, a tributary of the Sibun River.

Permission to study the archaeological remains of the Sibun Valley was granted by the Department of Archaeology (now Institute of Archaeology) in Belmopan, Belize. We express our gratitude to the staff and commissioners who have graciously facilitated this research, particularly Jaime Awe, Theresa Batty, Allan Moore, John Morris, George Thompson, and Brian Woodye. Financial support for XARP was provided by a four-year grant from the National Science Foundation (BCS-0096603), a grant from the Ahau Foundation (Dr. Peter D. and Ms. Alexandra Harrison), and the Division of International Programs at Boston University. The authors wish to thank the many staff members, students, specialists, and volunteers, who over the course of four field seasons, helped to bring the deep history of a hitherto little-known archaeological district into focus.

Bibliography

Archives and Libraries

American Philosophical Society Library, Philadelphia, Pennsylvania
AGCA   Archivo General de Centroamerica, Guatemala
AGI   Archivo General de Indias, Seville, Spain
AG   Audiencia de Guatemala
EC   Escribania de Camara
JU   Justicia
AHDSCLC   Archivo Histórico Diocesano de San Cristóbal de las Casas
BL   Bancroft Library, Latin Americana: Mexican and Central
          American Collections, University of California, Berkeley
TL   Tozzer Library, Special Collections, Harvard University

Documents and Anonymous Manuscripts

Manuscript 426 (MSS 426)
1730 Acerca del Chocolate. Attributed to an anonymous Carmelite monk. Formerly owned
      by Mexican historian Federico Gómez de Orozco. Repository: Mandeville Special Col-
      lections Library of University of California, San Diego (UCSD). Accessible through
      internet at <http://orpheus.ucsd.edu/speccoll/DigitalArchives/mss0426>, accessed May
      1, 2004.
1898–1900 *Relaciones de Yucatán. Coleccion de Documentos Inéditos Relativos al Descubrimiento
      Conquista y Organización de las Antiguas Posesiones Españolas de Ultamar.* 2nd Series.
      Madrid.
1900 *Descubrimiento Conquista y Organización de las Antiguas Posesiones Españolas de Ultamar.*
      2nd Series. Madrid.

General References

Abel-Vidor, Suzanne
1980 The Historical Sources for the Greater Nicoya Archaeological Subarea. *Vínculos* 6(1–
      2):155–186.
Acosta, José de
1590 *Historia natural y moral de las Indias.* Casa de Juan de Leon, Seville.
1940 [1590] *Historia natural y moral de las Indias.* Fondo de Cultura Económica, Mexico City.

2002 [1590]   *Natural and Moral History of the Indies*, edited by J. E. Mangan and translated by F. López-Morillas. Duke University Press, Durham, North Carolina, and London.

Adams, Richard E. W.

1971   *The Ceramics of Altar de Sacrificios*. Papers of the Peabody Museum of Archaeology and Ethnology Vol. 63 No. 1. Harvard University, Cambridge.

1999   *Rio Azul: An Ancient Maya City*. University of Oklahoma Press, Norman.

Adams, Walter R.

1987   Una sugestión respecto del papel del café y el cacao en el ritual Maya. *Anales de la academia de geografía e historia de Guatemala* 61:141–149.

Adamson, G. E., S. A. Lazarus, A. E. Mitchell, R. L. Prior, G. Cao, P. H. Jacobs, B. G. Kremers, J. F. Hammerstone, R. B. Rucker, K. A. Ritter, and H. H. Schmitz

1999   HPLC Method for the Quantification of Procyanidins in Cocoa and Chocolate Samples and Correlation to Total Antioxidant Capacity. *Journal of Agricultural and Food Chemistry* 47(10):4184–4188.

Addison, G. O., and R. M. Tavares

1951   Observações sobre as espécies do gênero *Theobroma* que ocorrem na Amazônia. *Boletim Técnico do Instituto Agronômico do Norte* 25(3):1–20.

Adomako, Daniel

1972   Cocoa Pod Husk Pectin. *Phytochemistry* 11(3):1145–1148.

Aguilar, Manuel

1999   Tequitqui Art of Sixteenth-Century Mexico: An Expression of Transculturation. Unpublished Ph.D. dissertation, Latin American Studies, University of Texas, Austin.

Aguilera, Miguel

2004   Unshrouding the Communicating Cross: The Iconology of a Maya Quadripartite Symbol. Unpublished Ph.D. dissertation, Anthropology Department, State University of New York, Albany.

Aguirre Beltrán, Gonzalo

1979   *Regions of Refuge*. Monograph series no. 12. Society for Applied Anthropology, Washington, D.C.

1982   *Advertencia, a la historia de la medicina en México, desde la época de los indios hasta la presente, de Francisco de Asís Flores y Troncoso*. Edición facsimilar a la edición original de 1886. Vol. 2. Instituto Mexicano del Seguro Social, Mexico City.

Akkeren, Ruud W. van

1999   Sacrifice at the Maize Tree: Rab'inal Achí in Its Historical and Symbolic Context. *Ancient Mesoamerica* 10(2):281–295.

Alcorn, Janis B.

1984   *Huastec Mayan Ethnobotany*. University of Texas Press, Austin.

1990   Indigenous Agroforestry Strategies Meeting Farmers' Needs. In *Alternatives to Deforestation: Steps Toward Sustainable Use of the Amazon Rainforest*, edited by A. B. Anderson, pp. 141–151. Columbia University Press, New York.

1995   Ethnobotanical Knowledge Systems—A Resource for Meeting Rural Development Goals. In *The Cultural Dimension of Development*, edited by D. M. Warren, L. J. Slikkerveer, and D. Brokensha, pp. 1–12. Intermediate Technology Publications, London.

Allen, J. B.

1988   Geographical Variation and Population Biology in Wild *Theobroma cacao*. Unpublished Ph.D. dissertation, University of Edinburgh.

Allen, Paul H.

1956   *The Rain Forests of Golfo Dulce.* Stanford University Press, Stanford, California.

Alva, Walter

1986   *Frühe Keramik aus dem Jequetepeque-Tal, Nordperu Cerámica Temprana en el valle de Jequetepeque, Norte del Perú.* Verlag C. H. Beck, Munich.

Alvarado, Pedro de

1924 [1525]   An account of the conquest of Guatemala in 1524, edited by S. J. Mackie. Cortes Society, New York.

Alvarez, Carlos, and Luis Casasola

1985   *Las Figurillas de Jonuta, Tabasco.* Universidad Nacional Autónoma de México, Mexico City.

Amorozo, M. C. M., and A. Gély

1988   Uso de plantas medicinais por cabloclos do baixo Amazonas, Barcarena, PA, Brasil. *Boletim do Museu Paraense Emílio Goeldi. Série botânica* 4(1):47–131.

Andagoya, Pascual de

1865   *Narrative of the Proceedings of Pedrarias Davila in the Provinces of Tierra Firme or Castilla del Oro, and of the Discovery of the South Sea and the Coasts of Peru and Nicaragua.* Translated and edited by C. R. Markham. Hakluyt Society, London.

Anderson, Arthur, Frances Berdan, and James Lockhart

1976   *Beyond the Codices: The Nahua View of Colonial Mexico.* University of California Press, Berkeley and Los Angeles.

Andrews V, E. Wyllys, and Cassandra R. Bill

2005   A Late Classic Royal Residence at Copán. In *Copán: The History of an Ancient Maya Kingdom*, edited by E. W. Andrews V and W. L. Fash, pp. 239–314. School of American Research Press, Santa Fe, New Mexico.

Andrews V, E. Wyllys, Jodi L. Johnson, William F. Doonan, Gloria E. Everson, Kathryn E. Sampeck, and Harold E. Starratt

2003   A Multipurpose Structure in the Late Classic Palace at Copan. In *Maya Palaces and Elite Residences*, edited by J. J. Christie, pp. 69–97. University of Texas Press, Austin.

Andrews, J. Richard

1975   *An Introduction to Classical Nahuatl.* University of Texas Press, Austin.

Andrews, J. Richard, and Ross Hassig (translators and editors)

1984   *Treatise on the Heathen Superstitions that Today Live among the Indians Native to this New Spain, 1629 by Hernando Ruíz de Alarcón.* University of Oklahoma Press, Norman.

Angelino, Henry, and Charles L. Shedd

1955   A Note on Berdache. *American Anthropologist* 57:121–126.

Ankli, Anita

2000   Yucatec Mayan Medicinal Plants: Ethnobotany, Biological Evaluation and Phytochemical Study of *Crossopetalum gaumeri*. Unpublished Ph.D. dissertation, Swiss Federal Institute of Technology, Zurich.

Ankli, A., O. Sticher, and M. Heinrich

1999   Medical Ethnobotany of the Yucatec Maya: Healers' Consensus as a Quantitative Criterion. *Economic Botany* 53:144–160.

Armella, Edgardo C., and Silvio A. Giraldo

1980   Lista de plantas utilizadas por los indigenas Chami de Risaralda. *Cespedesia* 9(33–34):5–114.

454   Bibliography

Arrellano Hernández, Alfonso

2002   Textos y contextos: Epigrafía y pintura mural. In *La pintura mural Prehispánica en México, Volume 2 Book 4*, edited by B. de la Fuente, pp. 331–357. Instituto de Investigaciones Estéticas, Universidad Nacional Autónoma de México, México, D.F.

Asahi Foods Co., Limited

2003   CUPUACU Trademark, Goods and Services IC 030. US 046. G & S: CHOCOLATE CANDIES. FIRST USE: 20011118. FIRST USE IN COMMERCE: 20011118. In http://tess2.uspto.gov/bin/gate.exe?f=searchss&state=fspsd2.1.1, May 1, 2004. (REGISTRANT) Asahi Foods Co., Ltd. CORPORATION JAPAN Shimotsuya-Kitaino 1 Kumiyama-cho, Kuse-gun, Kyoto JAPAN 613-0035, U.S.

Ashmore, Wendy

1989   Construction and Cosmology: Politics and Ideology in Lowland Maya Settlement Patterns. In *Word and Image in Maya Culture: Explorations in Language, Writing and Representation*, edited by W. F. Hanks and D. S. Rice, pp. 272–286. University of Utah Press, Salt Lake City.

Athyade, M. L., G. C. Coelho, and E. P. Schenkel

2000   Caffeine and Theobromine in Epicuticular Wax of *Ilex paraguariensis* A. St.-Hil. *Phytochemistry* 55(7):853–857.

Atran, Scott

1993   Itza Maya Tropical Agro-forestry. *Current Anthropology* 34(5):633–670.

Augusto, F., A. L. Valente, E. dos Santos Tada, and S. R. Rivellino

2000   Screening of Brazilian Fruit Aromas Using Solid-Phase Microextraction-Gas Chromatography-Mass Spectrometry. *Journal of Chromatography A* 873(1):117–127.

Aulie, Wilbur H., and Evelyn W. de Aulie

1978   *Diccionario Ch'ol-Español Español-Ch'ol*. Serie de Vocabularios y Diccionarios Indígenas "Mariano Silva y Aveces", Núm. 21. Instituto Lingüístico de Verano, Mexico City.

Avendaño y Loyola, Andrés de

1696   *Relazion de las dos entradas que hize a la conversion de los gentiles Ytzaex y Cehaches. Ms. 1040*. Edward E. Ayer Collection, Newberry Library, Chicago, Illinois.

Baer, Phillip, and William R. Merrifield

1971   *Two Studies on the Lacandones of Mexico*. Publications in Linguistics and Related Fields, No. 33. Summer Institute of Linguistics, University of Oklahoma, Norman.

Baez Landa, Mariano

1985   Soconusco: region, plantaciones y soberania. In *La formacion historica de la frontera sur*. Cuadernos de la Casa Chata 124. Centro de Investigaciones y Estudios Superiores en Antropologia Social y Secretario de Educacion Publica, Mexico City.

Bainbridge, J. S., and S. H. Davies

1912   Essential Oil of Cocoa. *Journal of the Chemical Society* (101):2209.

Baker, G. B., J. F. T. Wong, R. T. Coutts, and F. M. Pasutto

1987   Simultaneous Extraction and Quantitation of Several Bioactive Amines in Cheese and Chocolate. *Journal of Chromatography* 392:317–331.

Balée, William

2003   Historical-Ecological Influences on the Word for Cacao in Ka'apor. *Anthropological Linguistics* 45(3):259–280.

Balick, Michael J. and Paul Alan Cox

1996   *Plants, People and Culture: The Science of Ethnobotany*. Scientific American Library, New York.

Barrera Marín, Alfredo
1980   Sobre la unidad habitación tradicional campesina y el manejo de los recursos bióticos en el área Maya Yucatanense. Árboles y arbustos de los huertos familiares. *Biotica* 2(2):47–61.

Barrera Vásquez, Alfredo (editor)
1980   *Diccionario Maya Cordemex, Maya-Español, Español-Maya.* Ediciones Cordemex, Mérida, Yucatán, Mexico.
1991   *Diccionario Maya: Maya-Español, Español-Maya.* 2nd ed. Editorial Porrúa, Mexico City.

Barrera Vásquez, Alfredo, and Silvia Rendón
1948   *El libro de los libros de Chilam Balam.* Fondo de Cultura Económica, Mexico City.

Barthel, Thomas S.
1978   Mourning and Consolation: Themes of the Palenque Sarcophagus. In *Third Palenque Round Table (Part 2)*, edited by M. G. Robertson, pp. 81–90. University of Texas Press, Austin.

Bassie-Sweet, Karen
2002   Corn Deities and the Male/Female Principle. In *Ancient Maya Gender Identity and Relations*, edited by L. S. Gustafson and A. M. Trevelyan, pp. 169–190. Bergin and Garvey, Westport, Connecticut.

Bassols Batalla, Angel
1967   *Recursos naturales: climas, agua, suelos, teoría y usos.* Nuestro Tiempo, Mexico City.

Beck, H. T.
1991   The Taxonomy and Economic Botany of the Cultivated Guaraná and Its Wild Relatives and the Generic Limits within the Paullinieae (Sapindaceae). Unpublished Ph.D. dissertation, Department of Biology, The Graduate School, City University of New York.

Bekele, F., and I. Bekele
1996   A Sampling of the Phenetic Diversity of Cacao in the International Cocoa Gene Bank of Trinidad. *Crop Science* 36:57–64.

Bell, Ellen E.
2002   Engendering a Dynasty: A Royal Woman in the Margarita Tomb, Copan. In *Ancient Maya Women*, edited by T. Arden, pp. 89–104. Altamira Press, Walnut Creek, California.

Bell, Ellen E., Robert J. Sharer, Loa P. Traxler, David W. Sedat, Christine Carrelli, and Lynn Grant
2004   Tombs and Burials in the Early Classic Acropolis at Copan. In *Understanding Early Classic Copan*, edited by E. E. Bell, M. A. Canuto, and R. J. Sharer, pp. 131–157. University of Pennsylvania Museum of Archaeology and Anthropology, Philadelphia.

Bellon, Mauricio R.
1995   Farmers' Knowledge and Sustainable Agroecosystem Management: An Operational Definition and an Example from Chiapas, Mexico. *Human Organization* 54(3):264–272.

Beltramo, Massimiliano, and Daniele Piomelli
1998   Reply: Trick or Treat from Food Endocannabinoids? *Nature* 396:636–637.

Bennett, Bradley C., Marc A. Baker, and Patricia G. Andrade
2002   *Ethnobotany of the Shuar of Eastern Ecuador.* The New York Botanical Garden Press, Bronx, New York.

Ben-Shabat, S., E. Russo, E. Fride K., and R. Mechoulam
2002   *Salvia divinorum* with Cannabinoids-like Activity: In Search of Plants, Other than *Cannabis sativa*, with Cannabinoid Receptor Activity. Paper presented at the 43rd Annual Meeting of the Society for Economic Botany, Bronx, New York.

Benson, Elizabeth P.
1994   Multimedia Monkey, or, the Failed Man: The Monkey as Artist. In *Seventh Palenque Round Table, 1989*, edited by V. M. Fields, pp. 137–144. Pre-Columbian Art Research Institute, San Francisco.

Benzoni, Girolamo
1857 [1565]   *History of the New World.* Translated and edited by W. H. Smyth. Hakluyt Society, London.

Berdan, Frances F.
1988   Principles of Regional and Long-Distance Trade in the Aztec Empire. In *Smoke and Mist: Mesoamerican Studies in Memory of Thelma D. Sullivan*, edited by K. Josserand and K. Dakin, pp. 639–656. British Archaeological Reports, International Series, no. 402. BAR, Oxford, England.

Berdan, Frances F., and Patricia R. Anawalt (editors)
1992   *The Codex Mendoza.* University of California Press, Berkeley.
1997a   *The Essential Codex Mendoza.* University of California Press, Berkeley.
1997b   Pictorial Parallel Image Replicas of Codex Mendoza. In *The Essential Codex Mendoza.* University of California Press, Berkeley.

Berdan, Frances F., Marilyn A. Masson, Janine Gasco, and Michael E. Smith
2003   An International Economy. In *The Postclassic Mesoamerican World*, edited by M. E. Smith and F. F. Berdan, pp. 96–108. University of Utah Press, Salt Lake City.

Bergmann, John F.
1969   The Distribution of Cacao Cultivation in Pre-Columbian America. *Annals of the Association of American Geographers* 59(1):85–96.

Berlin, Brent, Dennis E. Breedlove, and Peter H. Raven
1974   *Principles of Tzeltal Plant Classification: An Introduction to the Botanical Ethnography of a Mayan-Speaking People of Highland Chiapas.* Academic Press, New York.

Berrin, Kathleen
1988   Catalogue of the Wagner Murals Collection. In *Feathered Serpents and Flowering Trees: Reconstructing the Murals of Teotihuacan*, edited by K. Berrin, pp. 137–161. The Fine Arts Museum, San Francisco.

Betendorf, J. F.
1910   Chronica da Missão dos Padres da Companhia de Jesus no Estado do Maranhão. *Revista do Instituto Histórico e Geográfico Brasileiro* 72:1–697.

Bierhorst, John
1985   *A Nahuatl-English Dictionary and Concordance to the CANTARES MEXICANOS with an Analytic Transcription and Grammatical Notes.* Stanford University Press, Stanford, California.
1990   *The Mythology of Mexico and Central America.* William Morrow and Company, New York.
1992   *History and Mythology of the Aztecs: The Codex Chimalpopoca.* University of Arizona Press, Tucson.

Bill, Cassandra
1997   Patterns of Variation and Change in Dynastic Period Ceramics and Ceramic Production at Copan, Honduras. Unpublished Ph.D. dissertation, Department of Anthropology, Tulane University, New Orleans.

Bispo, Marcia S., Marcia Cristina C. Veloso, Heloísa Lúcia C. Pinheiro, Rodolfo F. S. De Oliveira, José Oscar N. Reis, and Jailson B. De Andrade
2002   Simultaneous Determination of Caffeine, Theobromine and Theophylline by High Per-
       formance Liquid Chromatography. *Journal of Chromatographic Science* 40(1):45–48.

Blake, Michael, and J. E. Clark
1999   The Emergence of Hereditary Inequality: The Case of Pacific Coastal Chiapas, Mexico.
       In *Pacific Latin America in Prehistory: The Evolution of Archaic and Formative Cultures*,
       edited by M. Blake, pp. 55–74. Washington State University Press, Pullman.

Blanton, Richard E.
1996   The Basin of Mexico Market System and the Growth of Empire. In *Aztec Imperial Strate-
       gies*, edited by F. Berdan, R. Blanton, E. Boone, M. Hodge, M. E. Smith, and E. Umberger,
       pp. 47–84. Dumbarton Oaks Research Library and Collection, Washington, D.C.

Blanton, Richard E., Gary M. Feinman, Stephen A. Kowaleski, and Peter N. Peregrine
1996   A Dual-Processual Theory for the Evolution of Mesoamerican Civilization. *Current An-
       thropology* 37(1):1–86.

Bloch, Maurice
1986   *From Blessing to Violence: History and Ideology in the Circumcision Ritual of the Marina of
       Madagascar.* Cambridge University Press, Cambridge.

Bolles, David
2001   *Combined Dictionary-Concordance of the Yucatecan Maya Language.* Reports submitted to
       FAMSI, <http://www.famsi.org/reports/96072/>, accessed May 1, 2005.

Bonavia, Duccio
1994   *Arte e historia del Perú antiguo.* Colección Enrico Poli Bianchi/Duccio Bonavia; dirección
       y organización, Luis Enrique Tord; [fotografías, Daniel Gianonni, Carlos Rojas]. Banco
       del Sur, Arequipa, Perú.

Boom, Brian M.
1987   Ethnobotany of the Chácobo Indians, Beni, Bolivia. *Advances in Economic Botany* 4:1–
       68.

Boone, Elizabeth Hill
2000   *Stories in Red and Black: Pictorial Histories of the Aztecs and Mixtecs.* University of Texas
       Press, Austin.

Boot, Erik
1997a Kan Ek', Last Ruler of the Itsá. *Yumtzilob* 9(1):5–21.
1997b No Place Like Home: Maya Exodus. Itsá Maya Migrations Between ca. A.D. 650 and
       A.D. 1450. In *Veertig jaren onderweg*, edited by H. J. M. Claessen and H. F. Vermulen,
       pp. 165–187. DSWO Press, Leiden, Netherlands.

Borah, Woodrow, and Sherbourne F. Cook
1958   *Price Trends of Some Basic Commodities in Central Mexico, 1531–1570.* Ibero-Americana
       40. University of California Press, Berkeley.

Boremanse, Didier
1993   The Faith of the Real People: The Lacandon of the Chiapas Rain Forest. In *South and
       Meso-American Native Spirituality: From the Cult of the Feathered Serpent to the Theology
       of Liberation*, edited by G. Gossen, pp. 324–351. Crossroad, New York.
1998   *Hach Winik: The Lacandon Maya of Chiapas, Southern Mexico.* Monograph 11. Institute
       for Mesoamerican Studies, State University of New York at Albany.

Bove, Frederick J., Sonia Medrano B., Brenda Lou P., and Barbara Arroyo L.

1993   *The Balberta Project: the Terminal Formative-Early Classic Transition on the Pacific Coast of Guatemala*. University of Pittsburgh, Department of Anthropology, Pennsylvania, and *Asociación Tikal*, Guatemala.

Braakhuis, H. E. M.

1987   Artificers of the Days: Functions of the Howler Monkey Gods among the Mayas. *Bijdragen Tot de Taal-, Land-, en Völkerkunde* 143:25–53.

Brading, David

1984   Bourbon Spain and its American Empire. In *Cambridge History of Latin America*, edited by L. Bethell. Vol. 2. Cambridge University Press, Cambridge.

Breedlove, Dennis E.

1981   *Introduction to the Flora of Chiapas, Part I*. California Academy of Sciences, San Francisco.

Breedlove, Dennis E., and Robert Laughlin

1993   *The Flowering of Man: a Tzotzil Botany of Zinazantán*. Smithsonian Contributions to Anthropology, No. 35. Smithsonian Institution Press, Washington, D.C.

Bricker, Victoria R.

1973   *Ritual Humor in Highland Chiapas*. University of Texas Press, Austin.

1981   *The Indian Christ, the Indian King: The Historical Substrate of Maya Myth and Ritual*. University of Texas Press, Austin.

1986   *A Grammar of Mayan Hieroglyphs*. Middle American Research Institute, Publication 56, Tulane University, New Orleans.

Bright, Chris

2001   Chocolate Could Bring the Forest Back. *World Watch* 14(6):17–28.

Broderick, Robert

1976   *The Catholic Encyclopedia*. OSV, Huntington, Indiana.

Brokaw, N. V. L., J. S. Grear, K. J. Tripplett, A. A. Whitman, and E. P. Mallory

1997   The Quebrada de Oro Forest of Belize: Exceptional Structure and High Species Richness. *Tropical Ecology* 38(2):247–258.

Brokensha, David, David M. Warren, and Oswald Werner (editors)

1980   *Indigenous Knowledge Systems and Development*. University Press of America, Lanham, Maryland.

Brown, Linda A.

2002   The Structure of Ritual Practice: An Ethnoarchaeological Exploration of Acitivity Areas at Rural Community Shrines in the Maya Highlands. Unpublished Ph.D. dissertation, Department of Anthropology, University of Colorado, Boulder.

Bruce, Robert D.

1979   *Lacandon Dream Symbolism: Dream Symbolism and Interpretation among the Lacandon Maya of Chiapas, Mexico*. Ediciones Euroamericanas, Mexico City.

Bruinsma, K., and D. L. Taren

1999   Chocolate: Food or Drug? *Journal of the American Dietetic Association* 99:1249–1256.

Brumfiel, Elizabeth

1987   Elite and Utilitarian Crafts in the Aztec State. In *Specialization, Exchange and Complex Societies*, edited by E. Brumfiel and T. Earle, pp. 102–118. Cambridge University Press, Cambridge.

Bruni, R., A. Medici, A. Guerrini, S. Scalia, F. Poli, C. Romagnoli, M. Muzzoli, and G. Sacchetti

2002   Tocopherol, Fatty Acids and Sterol Distributions in Wild Ecuadorian *Theobroma subincanum* (Sterculiaceae) Seeds. *Food Chemistry* 77(3):337–341.

Brutus, Timoleon. C., and Arsene V. Pierce-Noel

1960   *Les Plantes et les Legumes d'Haiti qui Guerissent*. Imprimerie De L'Etat, Port-Au-Prince, Haiti.

Bunzel, Ruth L.

1952   *Chichicastenango: A Guatemalan Village*. Ethnological Society Publications, Vol. 22. J. J. Augustin, Locust Valley, New York.

1967 [1952]   *Chichicastenango*. University of Washington Press, Seattle.

Burger, Richard L.

1992   *Chavín and the Origins of Andean Civilization*. Thames and Hudson, London and New York.

Burgoa, Francisco de

1989 [1674]   *Geográfica Descripción* 1. Editorial Porrúa, Mexico City.

Butler, Judith

1993   *Bodies that Matter: On the Discursive Limits of "Sex."* Routledge, New York.

Byland, Bruce E., and John M. D. Pohl

1994   *In the Realm of 8 Deer: The Archaeology of the Mixtec Codices*. University of Oklahoma Press, Norman.

Cáceres, Armando

1999   *Plantas de uso medicinal en Guatemala*. Editorial Universitaria, Universidad de San Carlos de Guatemala.

Campbell, Lyle

1985   *The Pipil Language of El Salvador*. Mouton, Berlin.

1988   The Linguistics of Southeastern Chiapas, Mexico. In *Papers of the New World Archaeological Foundation*. Vol. 50. Salt Lake City, Utah.

Campbell, Lyle, and Terrence Kaufman

1976   A Linguistic Look at the Olmecs. *American Antiquity* 41(1):80–89.

Campbell, Lyle, and Ronald W. Langacker

1978a Proto-Aztecan vowels, 1. *International Journal of American Linguistics* 44(2):85–102.

1978b Proto-Aztecan vowels, 2. *International Journal of American Linguistics* 44(3):197–210.

1978c Proto-Aztecan vowels, 3. *International Journal of American Linguistics* 44(4):262–279.

Cárdenas, Dairon, and Gustavo G. Politis

2000   *Territorio, movilidad, etnobotánica manejo del bosque de los Nukak Orientales: Amazonía Colombiana*. Estudio Antropológicos 3. Ediciones Uniandes, Bogotá, Colombia.

Carlsen, Robert S., and Martin Prechtel

1991   Flowering of the Dead: An Interpretation of Highland Maya Culture. *Man* 26(1):23–42.

Carrasco, Michael D., and Kerry Hull

2002   Cosmogonic Symbolism of the Corbeled Vault in Maya Architecture. *Mexicon* 24(2): 26–32.

Carrasco, Pedro

1964   Family Structure of 16th-Century Tepoztlan. In *Process and Pattern in Culture*, edited by R. A. Manners, pp. 185–210. Aldine, Chicago, Illinois.

1976a Los linajes nobles del México antiguo. In *Estratificación social en la Mesoamérica prehis-pánica*, edited by P. Carrasco and J. Broda, pp. 9–76. Instituto Nacional de Antropología e Historia, Mexico City.

1976b The Joint Family in Ancient Mexico: The Case of Molotla. In *Essays on Mexican Kinship*, edited by H. Nutini, P. Carrasco, and J. Taggart, pp. 45–64. University of Pittsburgh Press, Pittsburgh, Pennsylvania.

2000 Cultura y sociedad en el México antiguo. In *Historia General de México*, edited by I. Bernal, pp. 153–233. El Colegio de México, Mexico City.

Casas, Bartolomé de las

1909 *Apologética historia de las Indias*. Nueva Biblioteca de Autores Españoles, Madrid.

Caso Barrera, Laura

2002 *Caminos en la selva. Migración, comercio y resistencia: Mayas yucatecos e itzaes siglos XVII–XIX*. El Colegio de México-FCE, Mexico City.

Caso Barrera, Laura, and Mario Aliphat F.

2002 Organización política de los itzaes desde el posclásico hasta 1702. *Historia Mexicana* 51(4):713–748.

Castillo Farreras, Victor M.

1974 Matricula de tributos, comentarios, paleografia y version. *Historia del México*, Codices 27–30.

1984 *Estructura económica de la sociedad mexica*. Universidad Nacional Autónoma de México, Mexico City.

Chabran, Rafael, Cynthia L. Chamberlin, and Simon Varey

2000 Five Special Texts: Cacao, Chili, Corn, Tobacco, and Tomato. In *The Mexican Treasury: The Writings of Francisco Hernández*, edited by S. Varey, pp. 107–116. Stanford University Press, Stanford, California.

Champion, Thomas C.

1989 Introduction. In *Centre and Periphery: Comparative Studies in Archaeology*, edited by T. C. Champion, pp. 1–21. Unwin Hyman, London.

Chapman, Anne

1974 *Los Nicarao y los Chorotega según a fuentes históricas*. Ciudad Universitaria, Costa Rica.

1985 *Los hijos del cópal y la candela: Ritos agrarios y tradicion oral de los lencas, Vol. I*. Centre d'Estudes Mexicaines et Centramericaines, Universidad Nacional Autónoma de México, Mexico City.

1986 *Los hijos del cópal y la candela: Tradición Católica de los Lencas de Honduras, Vol. 2*. Centre d'Estudes Mexicaines et Centramericaines, Universidad Nacional Autónoma de México, Mexico City.

Charlton, Thomas H., and Deborah L. Nichols

1992 Late Postclassic and Colonial Period Elites at Otumba, Mexico: the Archaeological Dimensions. In *Mesoamerican Elites: An Archaeological Assessment*, edited by D. Chase and A. Chase, pp. 242–258. University of Oklahoma Press, Norman.

Chase, Diane Z., and Arlen F. Chase

2004 The Ever-Changing Maya: Ritual Adaptations and the Archaeological Record. Paper presented at the 69th Annual Society for American Archaeology Meetings, Montreal.

Chatt, Eileen M.

1953 *Cocoa: Cultivation, Processing, Analysis*. Interscience, New York.

Chattaway, M. Margaret

1937 The Wood Anatomy of the Family Sterculiaceae. *Philosophical Transactions of the Royal Society of London, series B-Biological Sciences* 228:313–366.

Cheesman, E. E.

1944 Notes on the Nomenclature, Classification and Possible Relationships of Cacao Populations. *Tropical Agriculture* 21(8):144–159.

Chevaux, K., L. Jackson, M. E. Villar, J. Mundt, J. Commisso, G. Adamson, M. M. McCullough, H. Schmitz, and N. Hollenberg

2001 Proximate, Mineral and Procyanidin Content of Certain Foods and Beverages Consumed by the Kuna Amerinds of Panama. *Journal of Food Composition and Analysis* 14:553–563.

Chinchilla Mazariegos, Oswaldo

2005 Cacao Gods and Goddesses. In *Kakaw: El chocolate en la cultura de Guatemala*, edited by O. Chinchilla Mazariegos, pp. 13–19. Museo Popol Vuh, Universidad Francisco Marroquín, Guatemala City, Guatemala.

Christenson, Allen J.

1998 *Scaling the Mountain of the Ancients: The Altarpiece of Santiago Atitlán*. University of Texas Press, Austin.

2001 *Art and Society in a Highland Maya Community: The Altarpiece of Santiago Atitlán*. University of Texas Press, Austin.

2003 *Popol Vuh: The Sacred Book of the Maya*. O Books, Winchester, England.

Ciudad Real, Antonio de

2001 *Calepino maya de Motul*. Critical and annotated edition by René Acuña. Plaza y Valdes, México.

Clark, John E., and Michael Blake

1993 The Power of Prestige: Competitive Generosity and the Emergence of Rank Societies in Lowland Mesoamerica. In *Factional Competition and Political Development in the New World*, edited by E. M. Brumfiel and J. W. Fox, pp. 17–30. Cambridge University Press, Cambridge.

Clark, John E., and Dennis Gosser

1995 Reinventing Mesoamerica's First Pottery. In *The Emergence of Pottery: Technology and Innovation in Ancient Societies*, edited by W. Barnett and J. Hoopes, pp. 209–222. Smithsonian Institution Press, Washington, D.C.

Clavijero, Francisco Xavier

1780 *Storia antica del Messico*, Cesena, Mexico City.

Clement, Charles R.

1990 Origin, Domestication and Genetic Conservation of Amazonian Fruit Tree Species. In *Ethnobiology in Theory and Practice*, edited by D. A. Posey and W. L. Overal, pp. 249–263. Museu Paraence Emílio Goeldi, Belém, Brazil.

1991 Amazonian Fruits: A Neglected, Threatened and Potentially Rich Resource Requires Urgent Attention. *Diversity* 7(1, 2):56–59.

1999 Fourteen Ninety-Two and the Loss of Amazonian Crop Genetic Resources. 1. The Relation between Domestication and Human Population Decline. *Economic Botany* 53:188–202.

Clendinnen, Inga

1987 *Ambivalent Conquests: Maya and Spaniard in Yucatan, 1517–1570*. Cambridge Latin American Studies, 61. Cambridge University Press, Cambridge.

Cline, Howard F.

1944   The Lore and Deities of the Lacandon Indians, Chiapas, Mexico. *Journal of American Folklore* 57(224):107–115.

Cline, Sarah L.

1984   Land Tenure and Land Inheritance in Late Sixteenth-Century Culhuacan. In *Explorations in Ethnohistory: Indians of Central Mexico in the Sixteenth Century*, edited by H. R. Harvey and H. J. Prem, pp. 277–309. University of New Mexico Press, Albuquerque.

1986   *Colonial Culhuacan, 1580–1600: A Social History of an Aztec Town.* University of New Mexico Press, Albuquerque.

1993   *The Book of Tributes: Early Sixteenth-Century Nahuatl Censuses from Morelos.* Latin American Studies Series, 81. UCLA Latin American Center Publications, Los Angeles.

Codex Borgia

1993   Akademische Druck- und Verlagsanstalt, Graz.

Codex Fejérváry-Mayer

1971   Akademische Druck- und Verlagsanstalt, Graz.

Codex Nuttal: a Picture Manuscript from Ancient Mexico

1975 [1902]The Peabody Museum Facsimile, edited by Z. Nuttal, with new introductory text by A. G. Miller. Dover Publications, Inc., New York.

Codex Vaticanus 3773 (Codex Vaticanus B)

1972   Akademische Druck- und Verlagsanstalt, Graz.

Codex Dresdensis (Dresden Codex)

1975   Akademische Druck- und Verlagsanstalt, Graz.

Coe, Michael D.

1962   Costa Rican Archaeology and Mesoamerica. *Southwestern Journal of Anthropology* 18(2):170–183.

1973   *The Maya Scribe and His World.* The Grolier Club, New York.

1975   *Classic Maya Pottery at Dumbarton Oaks.* Dumbarton Oaks, Washington, D.C.

1982   *Old Gods and Young Heroes: the Pearlman Collection of Maya Ceramics.* The Israel Museum, Jerusalem.

1989   The Hero Twins: Myth and Image. In *The Maya Vase Book: A Corpus of Rollout Photographs of Maya Vases, Volume 1*, edited by J. Kerr, pp. 161–184. Kerr Associates, New York.

Coe, Michael D., and Richard Diehl

1980   *In the Land of the Olmec: The River People.* University of Texas Press, Austin and London.

Coe, Michael D., and Justin Kerr

1998   *Art of the Maya Scribe.* Thames and Hudson, London and New York.

Coe, Michael D., and Mark Van Stone

2001   *Reading the Maya Glyphs.* Thames and Hudson, New York.

Coe, Michael D., and Gordon Whittaker

1982   *Aztec Sorcerors in Seventeenth Century Mexico: The Treatise on Superstitions by Hernando Ruiz de Alarcón.* Institute for Mesoamerican Studies, Publication No. 7, State University of New York, Albany.

Coe, Sophie D.

1994   *America's First Cuisine.* University of Texas Press, Austin.

Coe, Sophie D., and Michael D. Coe
1996   *The True History of Chocolate*. Thames and Hudson, London.
1999   *La verdadera historia del chocolate*. FCE, Mexico City.
Coggins, Clemency Chase
1975   Painting and Drawing Styles at Tikal: An Historical and Iconographic Reconstruction.
        Unpublished Ph.D. dissertation, Department of Art, Harvard University, Cambridge.
1988   The Manikin Scepter: Emblem of Lineage. *Estudios de Cultura Maya* 17:123–158.
Colón, Hernando
2003   *Historia del Almirante*. Edited by Luis Arranz Márquez. Dastin, Madrid.
Conqueror, Anonymous
1917   *Narrative of Some Things of New Spain and of the Great City of Temestitan Mexico*. The
        Cortes Society, New York.
Constenla, Adolfo
1981   Comparative Chibchan Phonology. Unpublished Ph.D. dissertation, Department of
        Linguistics, University of Pennsylvania, Philadelphia.
Constenla Umaña, A.
1991   *Las lenguas del Area Intermedia: Introducción a su estudio areal*. Editorial de la Universidad
        de Costa Rica, San José.
1994   Las lenguas de la Gran Nicoya. *Vínculos* 18–19:209–227.
Cook, O. F.
1915   *Tribroma*, a New Genus Related to *Theobroma*. *Journal of the Washington Academy of Sci-
        ences* 5:287–289.
1916   Branching and Flowering Habits of Cacao and Patashte. *Contributions from the U.S.
        National Herbarium* 17:609–625.
Córdoba-Avalos, Victor, Miguel Sánchez Hernández, Nestor Estrella Chulim, Alfonso Macías
        Láylle, Engleberto Sandoval-Castro, Tomas Martínez-Saldaña, and Carlos Fredy Ortiz-
        García
2001   Factores que afectan la producción de cacao (*Theobroma cacao* L.) en el ejido Francisco 1.
        Madero del Plan Chontalpa, Tabasco, México. Universidad Juárez Autónoma de Tabas-
        co. *Universidad y Ciencia* 17(34):93–100.
Corominas, Joan
1980–1983   *Diccionario crítico etimológico Castellano e Hispánico*. Con la colaboración de José
        A. Pascual. Gredos, Madrid.
Cortés, Hernán
1981   *Cartas de relación*. Editorial Porrúa, Mexico City.
Cortina Villar, Sergio
1993   Sistemas de cultivo de café en el Soconusco: Notas para su estudio. In *El café en la fron-
        tera sur: La produccion y los productores del Soconusco, Chiapas*, edited by D. V. Solis, pp.
        52–65. Instituto Chiapaneco de Cultura, Tuxtla Gutierrez, Chiapas, México.
Cosgrove, Denis
1989   Geography Is Everywhere: Culture and Symbolism in Human Landscapes. In *Horizons
        in Human Geography*, edited by D. Gregory and R. Walford, pp. 118–135. MacMillan,
        London.
Crane, Cathy J.
1996   Archaeobotanical and Palynological Research at a Late Preclassic Maya Community,

Cerros, Belize. In *The Managed Mosaic: Ancient Maya Agriculture and Resource Use*, edited by S. Fedick, pp. 262–277. University of Utah Press, Salt Lake City.

Cuatrecasas, José

1964   Cacao and Its Allies: A Taxonomic Revision of the Genus *Theobroma*. *Contributions from the U.S. National Herbarium* 35(6):379–614.

Culbert, T. Patrick

1993   *The Ceramics of Tikal: Vessels from the Burials, Caches and Problematical Deposits*. Tikal Report No. 25 Part A. The University Museum of the University of Pennsylvania, Philadelphia.

Cyphers Guillén, Ann

1984   Possible Role of a Woman in Formative Exchange. In *Trade and Exchange in Early Mesoamerica*, edited by K. G. Hirth, pp. 115–123. University of New Mexico Press, Albuquerque.

1993   Women, Rituals, and Social Dynamics at Ancient Chalcatzingo. *Latin American Antiquity* 4(3):209–224.

Dahlin, Bruce H.

1979   Cropping Cash in the Proto-Classic: A Cultural Impact Statement. In *Maya Archaeology and Ethnohistory*, edited by N. Hammond and G. Willey, pp. 21–37. University of Texas Press, Austin.

Dakin, Karen, and Søren Wichmann

2000   Cacao and Chocolate: A Uto-Aztecan Perspective. *Ancient Mesoamerica* 11(1):55–75.

Daly, Douglas C.

1993   Notes on *Bursera* in South America, Including a New Species. Studies in Neotropical Burseraceae 7. *Brittonia* 45:240–246.

Dary, Claudia

1986   *Estudio antropológico de la literatura oral en prosa del oriente de Guatemala*. Editorial Universitaria, Guatemala.

Davis, E. Wade, and James A. Yost

1983   The Ethnobotany of the Waorani of Eastern Ecuador. *Botanical Museum Leaflets, Harvard University* 29:159–217.

Davis, Virginia D.

1978   Ritual of the Northern Lacandon Maya. Unpublished Ph.D. dissertation, Department of Anthropology, Tulane University, New Orleans.

Davis-Salazar, Karla L., and Ellen E. Bell

2000   Una comparación de los depósitos funerarios de dos mujeres elites en la acrópolis de Copan, Honduras. In *13th Simposio de investigaciones arqueológicas en Guatemala*, edited by J. P. Laporte, H. P. Escobedo, A. C. de Suasnávar, and B. Arroyo, pp. 1113–1128. Ministerio de Cultura y Deportes, Instituto de Antropología e Historia y Asociación Tikal, Ciudad de Guatemala.

De la Cruz, M., R. Whitkus, A. Gómez-Pompa, and L. Mota-Bravo

1995   Origins of Cacao Cultivation. *Nature* 375:542–543.

De Vos, Jan

1980   *La paz de Dios y del Rey: La conquista de la selva Lacandona (1525–1821)*. Fondo de Cultura Económica, Mexico City.

DeFilipps, Robert A., Shirley L. Maina, and Juliette Crepin

2004   *Medicinal Plants of the Guianas (Guyana, Surinam, French Guiana)*. Department of Botany, National Museum of Natural History, Smithsonian Institution, Washington, D.C.

Demarest, Arthur, Kim Morgan, Claudia Wolley, and Héctor Escobedo

2003   The Political Acquisition of Sacred Geography: The Murcielagos Complex at Dos Pilas. In *Maya Palaces and Elite Residences: An Interdisciplinary Approach*, edited by J. J. Christie, pp. 120–153. University of Texas Press, Austin.

Denevan, William M., and John M. Treacy

1987   Young Managed Fallows at Brillo Nuevo. *Advances in Economic Botany* 5:8–47.

Devereaux, Leslie

1987   Gender Differences and the Relations of Inequality in Zinacantan. In *Dealing with Inequality: Analyzing Gender Relations in Melanesia and Beyond*, edited by M. Strathern, pp. 89–111. Cambridge University Press, Cambridge.

Diamond, Jared

2001   Anatomy of a Ritual (Ingestion of Hallucinogens via Enema). *Natural History* 110(6):16–20.

Díaz del Castillo, Bernal

1963 [1568] *The Conquest of New Spain*. Penguin Classics, London.

1970 [1568] *Historia verdadera de la conquista de la Nueva España*. Colleccion Sepan Cuántos 5, Mexico City.

1999 [1568] *Historia verdadera de la conquista de la Nueva España*. Edited by Felipe Castro Gutierrez. Editores Mexicanos Unidos, Mexico City.

2000 [1568] *La verdadera historia de la conquista de México*. Editorial Porrúa, Mexico City.

Diego Antonio, Diego de, Francisco Pascual, Nicolas de Nicolas Pedro, Carmelino Fernando Gonzales, and Santiago Juan Matias

1996   *Diccionario del idioma Q'anjob'al*. Proyecto Lingüístico Francisco Marroquín, Antigua, Guatemala.

Douglas, Mary

1966   *Purity and Danger: An Analysis of the Concepts of Pollution and Taboo*. ARK Paperbacks, London.

Dow, James

1973   Saints and Survival: The Functions of Religion in a Central Mexican Indian Society. Ph.D. dissertation, Brandeis University. University Microfilms, Ann Arbor.

Duke, James A.

1968   *Darien Ethnobotanical Dictionary [and Appended Editorial Comments on D. E. D.]*. . Battelle Memorial Institute, Columbus, Ohio.

1972   *Isthmian Ethnobotanical Dictionary*. Published by the author, Fulton, Maryland.

1975   Ethnobotanical Observations on the Cuna Indians. *Economic Botany* 29:278–293.

1992   *Handbook of Phytochemical Constituents of GRAS Herbs and Other Economic Plants*. CRC Press, Boca Raton, Florida.

2004   Phytochemical and Ethnobotanical Databases. National Germplasm Resources Laboratory, Beltsville, Maryland. <http://www.ars-grin.gov/duke>, accessed December 30, 2005.

Duke, James A., and Rodolfo Vasquez

1994   *Amazonian Ethnobotanical Dictionary*. CRC Press, Boca Raton, Florida.

Dull, Robert A., John R. Southon, and Payson Sheets

2001   Volcanism, Ecology and Culture: A Reassessment of the Volcan Ilopango TBJ Eruption in the Southern Maya Realm. *Latin American Antiquity* 12(1):25–44.

Dunham, Peter S.

1996   Resource Exploitation and Exchange among the Classic Maya: Some Initial Findings of the Maya Mountains Archaeological Project. In *The Managed Mosaic: Ancient Maya Agriculture and Resource Use*, edited by S. L. Fedick, pp. 315–334. University of Utah Press, Salt Lake City.

Dunham, Peter S., Thomas R. Jamison, and Richard M. Leventhal

1989   Secondary Development and Settlement Economics: The Classic Maya of Southern Belize. In *Prehistoric Maya Economies of Belize*, edited by P. A. McAnany and B. L. Isaac, pp. 255–292. Research in Economic Anthropology Supplement 4. JAI Press, Greenwich, Connecticut.

Durán, Diego

1967   *Historia de las Indias de Nueva España, e islas de la tierra firme.* 2 vols. Edited by Angel Maria Garibay K. Editorial Porrúa, Mexico City.

1971   *Book of the Gods and Rites and the Ancient Calendar.* Translated by F. Horcasitas and D. Heyden. University of Oklahoma Press, Norman.

Durand-Forest, Jacqueline

1967   El cacao entre los aztecas. *Estudios de Cultura Náhuatl* 7:155–182.

Dutting, Dieter

1992   The Hieroglyphic Texts of Chichen Itzá. *Baessler Archiv* 41(1):167–205.

Earle, Timothy

1977   A Reappraisal of Redistribution: Complex Hawaiian Chiefdoms. In *Exchange Systems in Prehistory*, edited by T. Earle, pp. 213–229. Academic Press, New York.

Earnest, Howard Hoyle

1999   A Reappraisal of the Ilopango Volcanic Eruption in Central El Salvador. Ph.D. dissertation, Department of Anthropology, Harvard University, Cambridge. University Microfilms, Ann Arbor.

Easby, Elizabeth K., and John F. Scott

1970   *Before Cortés: Sculpture of Middle America.* The Metropolitan Museum of Art, New York.

Eberl, Marcus

2001   Death and Conceptions of the Soul. In *Maya: Divine Kings of the Rainforest*, edited by N. Grube, pp. 310–319. Könemann, Cologne.

Edmonson, Munro S.

1965   Quiche-English Dictionary. Publication 30. Middle American Research Institute, Tulane University, New Orleans.

Elmendorf, Mary L.

1976   *Nine Mayan Women: A Village Faces Change.* Shenkman Publishing, New York.

Elson, Christina

1999   An Aztec Palace at Chiconautla, Mexico. *Latin American Antiquity* 10(2):151–167.

Emch, Michael

2003   The Human Ecology of Mayan Cacao Farming in Belize. *Human Ecology* 31(1):111–131.

Emmart, Emily Walcott

1940   *Badianus Manuscript*, with a foreword by Henry E. Sigerist. The Johns Hopkins Press, Baltimore.

Enslow, Sam

1990   *The Art of Prehispanic Colombia: An Illustrated Cultural and Historical Survey*. McFarland, Jefferson, North Carolina, and London.

Erickson, B. J., A. M. Young, M. A. Strand, and E. H. Erickson, Jr.

1987   Pollination Biology of *Theobroma* and *Herrania* (Sterculiaceae) 2. Analyses of Floral Oils. *Insect Science and Its Application* 8(3):301–310.

Erneholm, Ivar

1948   *Cacao Production of South America: Historical Development and Present Geographical Distribution* 34. Meddeland fran Gotteborgs Hogskolas Geogrfiska Institution, Gothenburg, Sweden.

Escalante Arce, Pedro Antonio

1992   *Códice Sonsonate: Crónicas Hispánicas, 2 vols*. Consejo Nacional para la Cultura y el Arte, San Salvador.

Evans, Susan Toby

2004   *Ancient Mexico and Central America: Archaeology and Culture History*. Thames and Hudson, New York.

Eynden, Veerle Van den, Eduardo Cueva, and Omar Cabrera

2003   Wild Foods from Southern Ecuador. *Economic Botany* 57(4):576–603.

Fajans, Jane

1997   *They Make Themselves: Work and Play among the Baining of Papua New Guinea*. University of Chicago Press, Chicago, Illinois.

Farris, James S.

1983   The Logical Basis of Phylogenetic Analysis. In *Advances in Cladistics*, Vol. 2, edited by N. Platnick and V. Funk, pp. 7–36. Columbia University Press, New York.

Farriss, Nancy M.

1984   *Maya Society Under Colonial Rule: The Collective Enterprise of Survival*. Princeton University Press, Princeton, New Jersey.

Fash, William L.

1988   A New Look at Maya Statecraft from Copán, Honduras. *Antiquity* 62(234):157–169.

2001   *Scribes, Warriors and Kings*. Thames and Hudson, London.

2005   Toward a Social History of the Copan Valley. In *Copan: The History of an Ancient Maya Kingdom*, edited by E. W. Andrews and W. L. Fash, pp. 73–101. School of American Research Press and James Currey, Santa Fe and Oxford.

Faust, Betty B.

1988a   Cosmology and Changing Technologies of the Campeche Maya. Unpublished Ph.D. dissertation, Department of Anthropology, Syracuse University, Syracuse, New York.

1988b   When Is a Midwife a Witch? A Case Study from a Modernizing Maya Village. In *Women and Health: Cross-Cultural Perspectives*, edited by P. Whelehan, pp. 21–36. Bergin and Garvey Press, Granby, Massachusetts.

1998a   Cacao Beans and Chili Peppers: Gender Socialization in the Cosmology of a Yucatec Maya Curing Ceremony. *Sex Roles* 39(7/8):603–642.

1998b   *Mexican Rural Development and the Plumed Serpent: Technology and Maya Cosmology in the Tropical Forest of Campeche, Mexico*. Bergin and Garvey Press (Greenwood Publishing Group), Westport, Connecticut.

Feldman, Lawrence H.

1985   *A Tumpline Economy: Production and Distribution Systems in Sixteenth-Century Eastern Guatemala.* Labyrinthos, Culver City, California.

1992   *Indian Payment in Kind: The Sixteenth-Century Encomiendas of Guatemala.* Labyrinthos, Culver City, California.

1993   *Mountains of Fire, Lands That Shake: Earthquakes and Volcanic Eruptions in the Historic Past of Central America.* Labyrinthos, Culver City, California.

2000   *Lost Shores, Forgotten Peoples: Spanish Explorations of the South East Maya Lowlands.* Duke University Press, Durham and London.

Fernandez, James W.

1972   Persuasions and Performances: Of the Beast in Every Body . . . And the Metaphors of Everyman. *Daedalus* Winter:39–60.

Fernández, Pedro L., Fernando Pablos, María J. Martín, and A. Gustavo González

2002   Study of Catechin and Xanthine Tea Profiles as Geographical Tracers. *Journal of Agriculture and Food Chemistry* 50(7):1833–1839.

Fields, Virginia M.

1989   The Origins of Divine Kingship among the Lowland Classic Maya. Unpublished Ph.D. dissertation, Department of Anthropology, University of Texas, Austin.

Fields, Virginia and Dorie Reents-Budet (editors)

2005   *Lords of Creation: The Origins of Sacred Maya Kingship.* Los Angeles County Museum of Art and Scala Publishers Ltd., Los Angeles.

Figueira, A., J. Janick, M. Levy, and P. Goldsbrough

1994   Reexamining the Classification of *Theobroma cacao* L. Using Molecular Markers. *Journal of the American Society for Horticultural Science* 119:1073–1082.

Fischer, Edward F.

1999   Cultural Logic and Maya Identity: Rethinking Constructivism and Essentialism. *Current Anthropology* 40(4):473–499.

Fish, D., and S. J. Soria

1978   Water-Holding Plants (Phytotelmata) as Larval Habitats for Ceratopogonid Pollinators of Cacao in Bahia, Brazil. *Revista Theobroma* 8:133–146.

Fisher, N. D., M. Hughes, M. Gerhard-Herman, and N. K. Hollenberg

2003   Flavanol-rich Cocoa Induces Nitric-Oxide-Dependent Vasodilation in Healthy Humans. *Journal of Hypertension* 21(12):2281–2286.

Flament, I.

1989   Coffee, Cacao and Tea. *Food Reviews International* 5:317.

Foias, Antonia

1998   *Proyecto Arqueológico de Motul de San José: Informe No. 1, Temporada de Campo 1998.* IDAEH. Ministry of Tourism, and Asociación Tikal, Guatemala.

2000   Entre la política y economia: Resultos preliminares de las primeras temporadas del Proyecto Arqueológico Motul de San José. In *XIII Simposio de investigaciones arqueológicas en Guatemala, 1999,* edited by J. P. LaPorte, H. Escobedo, A. C. Suasnávar, and B. Arroyo, pp. 945–973. IDAEH, Ministry of Tourism, and Asociación Tikal, Guatemala.

Foster, George M.

1953   Relationships between Spanish and Spanish-American Folk Medicine. *Journal of American Folklore* 66:201–217.

1988   The Validating Role of Humoral Theory in Traditional Spanish-American Therapeutics. *American Ethnologist* 15:120–135.

1994   *Hippocrates Latin American Legacy. Humoral Medicine in the New World.* Gordon and Breach, London.

Fought, John

1969   Ch'orti' Mayan Ceremonial Organization. *American Anthropologist* 71:472–476.

Fowler, Catherine S.

2000   Ethnoecology: An Introduction. In *Ethnobotany: A Reader*, edited by P. E. Minnis, pp. 13–16. University of Oklahoma Press, Norman.

Fowler, Jr., William R.

1987   Cacao, Indigo, and Coffee: Cash Crops in the History of El Salvador. *Research in Economic Anthropology* 8:139–167.

1989a   *The Cultural Evolution of Ancient Nahua Civilizations: The Pipil-Nicarao of Central America.* University of Oklahoma Press, Norman.

1989b   The Pipil of Pacific Guatemala and El Salvador. In *New Frontiers in the Archaeology of the Pacific Coast of Southern Mesoamerica*, edited by F. Bove and L. Heller, pp. 229–242. Anthropological Research Papers No. 39. Arizona State University, Tempe.

1991   The Political Economy of Indian Survival in Sixteenth-Century Izalco, El Salvador. In *Columbian Consequences, Vol. 3: The Spanish Borderlands in Pan-American Perspective*, edited by D. H. Thomas, pp. 187–204. Smithsonian Institution Press, Washington, D.C.

1993   'The Living Pay for the Dead': Trade, Exploitation, and Social Change in Early Colonial Izalco, El Salvador. In *Ethnohistory and Archaeology: Approaches to Postcontact Change in the Americas*, edited by J. D. Rogers and S. M. Wilson, pp. 181–199. Plenum Press, New York.

1995   *Caluco: Historia y arqueología de un pueblo Pipil en el siglo XVI.* Patronato Pro-Patrimonio Cultural, San Salvador.

Franco, M. R., and T. Shibamoto

2000   Volatile Composition of Some Brazilian Fruits: Umbu-caja (*Spondias citherea*), Camu-camu (*Myrciaria dubia*), Araca-boi (*Eugenia stipitata*), and Cupuacu (*Theobroma grandiflorum*). *Journal of Agricultural and Food Chemistry* 48(4):1263–1265.

Freidel, David A.

1979   Culture Areas and Interaction Spheres: Contrasting Approaches to the Emergence of Civilization in the Maya Lowlands. *American Antiquity* (44):36–54.

1992   Children of the First Father's Skull: Terminal Classic Warfare in the Northern Maya Lowlands and the Transformation of Kingship and Elite Hierarchies. In *Mesoamerican Elites. An Archaeological Assessment*, edited by D. Z. Chase and A. F. Chase, pp. 99–117. University of Oklahoma Press, Norman.

1998   Sacred Work: Dedication and Termination in Mesoamerica. In *The Sowing and the Dawning: Termination, Dedication and Transformation in the Archaeological and Ethnographic Record of Mesoamerica*, edited by S. B. Mock, pp. 189–193. University of New Mexico Press, Albuquerque.

Freidel, David A., and Linda Schele

1988a   Kingship in the Late Preclassic Maya Lowlands: The Instruments and Places of Ritual Power. *American Anthropologist* 90(3):547–567.

1988b   Symbol and Power: A History of the Lowland Maya Cosmogram. In *Maya Iconography*, edited by E. Benson and G. Griffin, pp. 44–93. Princeton University Press, Princeton, New Jersey.

Freidel, David A., Kathryn Reese-Taylor, and David Mora Marín

2002   The Origins of Maya Civilization: The Old Shell Game, Commodity, Treasure, and Kingship. In *Ancient Maya Political Economies*, edited by M. Masson and D. Freidel, pp. 41–86. Altamira Press, Walnut Creek, California.

Freidel, David A., Linda Schele, and Joy Parker

1993   *Maya Cosmos. Three Thousand Years on the Shaman's Path*. William Morrow, New York.

Friede, Juan

1953   *Los Andakí, 1538–1947: Historia de la aculturación de una tribu selvática*. Fondo de Cultura Económica, Mexico City.

Friedman, J., D. Bolotin, M. Rios, P. Mendosa, Y. Cohen, and M. J. Balick

1993   A Novel Method for Identification and Domestication of Indigenous Useful Plants in Amazonian Ecuador. In *New Crops*, edited by J. Janick and J. E. Simon, pp. 167–174. Wiley, New York.

Friedman, Jonathan, and Michael J. Rowlands

1978   Notes Towards an Epigenetic Model of the Evolution of 'Civilization.' In *The Evolution of Social Systems*, edited by J. Friedman and M. J. Rowlands, pp. 201–276. University of Pittsburgh Press, Pittsburgh, Pennsylvania.

Fuente, Beatríz de la (editor)

1999   *Pre-Columbian Painting: Murals of Mesoamerica*. Jaca Book and Antique Collector's Club, Milan.

Fuentes y Guzmán, Francisco

1932   *Recordación florida*. Sociedad de Geografía e Historia, Guatemala.

Furlan, Andrea L., and Ricardo Bressani

1999   Recursos Vegetales con Potencial Agroindustrial de Guatemala. Caracterizacion Química de la Pulpa y las Semillas de *Theobroma bicolor*. *Archivos Latinoamericanos de Nutricion* 49(4):373–378.

Furst, Jill Leslie

1977   The Tree Birth Tradition in the Mixteca, Mexico. *Journal of Latin American Lore* 3(2):183–226.

1978   *Codex Vindobonensis Mexicanus 1: A Commentary*. Publication No. 4. Institute for Mesoamerican Studies, State University of New York, Albany.

Gadsby, Patricia

2002   Endangered Chocolate. *Discover* 23(8):64–71.

Gage, Thomas

1946 [1648] *The English American: A New Survey of the West Indies*. Routledge, London.

Galeano, Gloria

2000   Forest Use at the Pacific coast of Chocó, Colombia: A Quantitative Approach. *Economic Botany* 54(3):358–376.

Gallegos, Francisco

1676   *Memorial que contiene las materias y progresos del Chol y Manche, presentado a su señoría don Francisco de Escobedo [...]*. Joseph de Pineda Ibarra, Guatemala.

Garber, James F., W. David Driver, Lauren A. Sullivan, and David M. Glassman

1998   Bloody Bowls and Broken Pots: The Life, Death, and Rebirth of a Maya House. In *The*

Sowing and the Dawning: Termination, Dedication and Transformation in the Archaeological and Ethnographic Record of Mesoamerica, edited by S. B. Mock, pp. 125–133. University of New Mexico Press, Albuquerque.

García de Palacio, Diego

1983 [1575] *Carta-Relación y forma de Diego García de Palacio, oidor de la real audiencia de Guatemala*. Fuentes para el Estudio de la Cultura Maya, No. 2. Universidad Nacional Autónoma de México, Mexico City.

1985 [1576] *Letter to the King of Spain*, edited and translated by E. G. Squier, with additional notes by A. von Frantzius and F. E. Comparato. Labyrinthos, Culver City, California.

García, Hernán, Antonio Sierra, and Gilberto Balam

1996 *Medicina Maya tradicional: Confrontación con el sistema conceptual Chino.* Educación Cultura y Ecología, A.C., Mexico City.

García-Barriga, Hernando

1974 *Flora medicinal de Colombia.* Instituto de Ciéncias Naturales, Bogotá, Colombia.

1992 *Flora medicinal de Colombia: Botánica médica.* 2 ed. 3 vols. Tercer Mundo, Santafé de Bogotá, Colombia.

Garí, Josep A.

2001 Biodiversity and Indigenous Agroecology in Amazonia: The Indigenous Peoples of Pastaza. *Etnoecológica* 5(7):21–37.

Garibay K., Ángel María

1993 *Poesía Náhuatl I: Romances de los señores de la Nueva España; Manuscrito de Juan Bautista de Pomar, Tezcoco 1582.* Universidad Nacional Autónoma de México, Mexico City.

Garraty, Christopher

2000 Ceramic Indices of Aztec Eliteness. *Ancient Mesoamerica* 11:323–340.

Gasco, Janine

1987a Cacao and the Economic Integration of Native Society in Colonial Soconusco, New Spain. Unpublished Ph.D. dissertation, Department of Anthropology, University of California, Santa Barbara.

1987b Economic Organization in Colonial Soconusco, New Spain: Local and External Influences. *Research in Economic Anthropology* 8:105–137.

1989–90 Un plan de desarrollo del siglo XIX: El reconocimiento de los canales y esteros de la provincia de Soconusco en 1820. *Anuario Centro de Estudios Indígenas* 3:127–138.

1989a The Colonial Economy in the Province of Soconusco. In *Ancient Trade and Tribute: Economies of the Soconusco Region of Mesoamerica*, edited by B. Voorhies, pp. 287–303. University of Utah Press, Salt Lake City.

1989b Economic History of Ocelocalco, a Colonial Soconusco Town. In *Ancient Trade and Tribute: Economies of the Soconusco Region of Mesoamerica*, edited by B. Voorhies, pp. 304–325. University of Utah Press, Salt Lake City.

1989c Una vision de conjunto de la historia demografica y economica del Soconusco colonial. *Mesoamerica* 10(18):371–399.

1990 Población y economía en Soconusco durante el siglo 16: El ejemplo del pueblo de Guilocingo, 1582. *Mesoamerica* 20:249–265.

1993 Socioeconomic Change within Native Society in Colonial Soconusco, New Spain. In *Ethnohistory and Archaeology: Approaches to Postcontact Change in the Americas*, edited by D. Rogers and S. Wilson, pp. 163–180. Plenum Press, New York.

1996   Cacao and Economic Inequality in Colonial Soconusco, Chiapas, Mexico. *Journal of Anthropological Research* 52(4):385–409.

1997   The Social and Economic History of Cacao Cultivation in Colonial Soconusco, New Spain. In *Chocolate, Food of the Gods*, edited by A. Szogyi, pp, 155–164. Greenwood Press, Westport, Connecticut.

2003   Soconusco. In *Postclassic Mesoamerican World*, edited by M. E. Smith and F. F. Berdan, pp. 282–296. University of Utah Press, Salt Lake City.

Gasco, Janine, and Barbara Voorhies

1989   The Ultimate Tribute: The Role of the Soconusco as an Aztec Tributary. In *Ancient Trade and Tribute: Economies of the Soconusco Region of Mesoamerica*, edited by B. Voorhies, pp. 48–94. University of Utah Press, Salt Lake City.

Geertz, Clifford

1980   *Negara: The Theatre State in Nineteenth-Century Bali*. Princeton University Press, Princeton, New Jersey.

Gentry, Alwyn H.

1982   Neotropical Floristic Diversity: Phytogeographical Connections between Central and South America, Pleistocene Climatic Fluctuations, or an Accident of the Andean Orogeny? *Annals of the Missouri Botanical Garden* 69:557–593.

Germosén-Robineau, Lionel

1995   *Hacia una farmacopea Caribeña: edición Tramil 7*. Enda-caribe, Santo Domingo, Dominican Republic.

Gerstle, Andrea I., and Payson Sheets

2002   Structure 4: A Storehouse-Workshop for Household 4. In *Before the Volcano Erupted: The Ancient Cerén Village in Central America*, edited by P. Sheets, pp. 74–80. University of Texas Press, Austin.

Gibson, Charles

1964   *The Aztecs Under Spanish Rule: A History of the Indians of the Valley of Mexico, 1519–1810*. Stanford University Press, Stanford, California.

Gifford, James C.

1976   *Prehistoric Pottery Analysis and the Ceramics of Barton Ramie in the Belize Valley*. Memoirs No. 18. Peabody Museum of Archaeology and Ethnology. Harvard University, Cambridge.

Gilabert-Escriva, M. V., L. A. G. Goncalves, C. R. S. Silva, and A. Figueira

2002   Fatty Acid and Triacylglycerol Composition and Thermal Behaviour of Fats from Seeds of Brazilian Amazonian *Theobroma* Species. *Journal of the Science of Food and Agriculture* 82(13):1425–1431.

Gillespie, Susan D., and Rosemary A. Joyce

1997   Gendered Goods: The Symbolism of Maya Hierarchical Exchange Relations. In *Women in Prehistory: North America and Mesoamerica*, edited by C. Claassen and R. A. Joyce, pp. 189–207. University of Pennsylvania Press, Philadelphia.

Gillespie, Susan D., and Ana Lucrecia E. de MacVean

2002   The Flowers in the Popol Vuh. *Revista Universidad del Valle de Guatemala* 12:10–17.

Gilman, Antonio

1976   Bronze Age Dynamics in Southeast Spain. *Dialectical Anthropology* 1:307–319.

1981   The Development of Stratification in Bronze Age Europe. *Current Anthropology* 22:1–23.

Girard, Raphael

1962   *Los Mayas Eternos.* Libro Mex Editores, Mexico City.

1966   *Los mayas: Su civilización, su historia, sus vinculaciones continentales.* Libro Mexicano, Mexico City.

1995   *People of the Chan.* Translated by B. Preble. Continuum Foundation, Chino Valley, Arizona.

Glenboski, Linda Leigh

1983   *The Ethnobotany of the Tukuna Indians, Amazonas, Colombia.* Universidad Nacional de Colombia, Bogotá, Colombia.

Gliessman, Stephen R.

1998   *Agroecology: Ecological Processes in Sustainable Agriculture.* Sleeping Bear Press, Chelsea, Michigan.

Gómez-Pompa, Arturo, and Andrea Kaus

1990   Traditional Management of Tropical Forests in Mexico. In *Alternatives to Deforestation: Steps Toward Sustainable Use of the Amazon Rain Forest,* edited by A. B. Anderson, pp. 45–64. Columbia University Press, New York.

Gómez-Pompa, Arturo, José Salvador Flores, and Mario Aliphat Fernandez

1990   The Sacred Cacao Groves of the Maya. *Latin American Antiquity* 1(3):247–257.

Gómez-Pompa, Arturo, José Salvador Flores, and Victoria Sosa

1987   The "Pet-Kot": a Man Made Tropical Forest of the Maya. *Interciencia* 12(1):10–15.

Gordon, George B.

1902   The Hieroglyphic Stairway, Ruins of Copan. In *Memoirs of the Peabody Museum of American Archaeology and Ethnology,* vol. 1, no. 6, pp. 151–186. Peabody Museum Press, Cambridge, Massachusetts.

Gossen, Gary

1974   *Chamulas in the World of the Sun: Time and Space in Maya Oral Tradition.* Harvard University Press, Cambridge.

1986   Preface. In *Symbol and Meaning Beyond the Closed Community: Essays in Mesoamerican Ideas,* edited by G. Gossen, pp. ix–x. Institute for Mesoamerican Studies of the State University of New York, Albany.

1994   From Olmecs to Zapatistas: A Once and Future History of Souls. *American Anthropologist* 96(3):553–570.

Gragson, Ted L., and Ben G. Blount (editors)

1999   *Ethnoecology: Knowledge, Resources, and Rights.* University of Georgia Press, Athens.

Graham, Elizabeth A., Grant D. Jones, and David M. Pendergast

1989   On the Fringes of Conquest: Maya-Spanish Contact in Colonial Belize. *Science* 246: 1254–1259.

Graham, Ian

1978   *Corpus of Maya Hieroglyphic Inscriptions, Vol. 2, Part 2: Naranjo, Chunhuitz, Xunantunich.* Peabody Museum of Archaeology and Ethnology, Harvard University, Cambridge.

Green & Black's

2003   Green & Black's Maya Gold Development Project. *Green & Black's Organic Chocolate.* <http://www.greenandblacks.co.uk/html/media_release.php>, accessed February 3, 2003.

2004   "Our Story." *Green & Black's Organic Chocolate.* <http://www.greenandblacks.co.uk/html/our_story.php>, accessed February 3, 2004.

Grenand, Pierre, Christine Moretti, and Henri Jacquemin

1987   *Pharmacopées Traditionnelles en Guyane: Créoles, Palikur, Wayãpi*. ORSTOM, Paris.

Grube, Nikolai

1990   The Primary Standard Sequence on Chocholá Style Ceramics. In T*he Maya Vase Book: A Corpus of Rollout Photographs of Maya Vases, Volume 2*, edited by J. Kerr, pp. 320–330. Kerr Associates, New York.

1991   An Investigation of the Primary Standard Sequence on Classic Maya Ceramics. In *Sixth Palenque Round Table, 1986*, edited by V. M. Fields, pp. 223–232. University of Oklahoma Press, Norman.

2000   Fire Rituals in the Context of Classic Maya Initial Series. In *The Sacred and the Profane: Architecture and Identity in the Southern Maya Lowlands*, edited by P. R. Colas, K. Delvendahl, M. Kuhnert, and A. Pieler, pp. 93–109. Acta Mesoamericana 10. Markt Schwaben, Hamburg.

Grube, Nikolai, and Werner Nahm

1994   A Census of Xibalba: A Complete Inventory of Way Characters on Maya Ceramics. In *The Maya Vase Book: A Corpus of Rollout Photographs of Maya Vases, Vol. 4*, edited by J. Kerr, pp. 686–715. Kerr Associates, New York.

Gubler, Ruth

1991   Concepts of Illness and the Tradition of Herbal Curing in the Book of Chilam Balam of Nah. *Latin American Indian Literatures Journal* 7(2):192–214.

Gustafson, Lowell S.

2002   Mother/Father Kings. In *Ancient Maya Gender Identity and Relations*, edited by L. S. Gustafson and A. M. Trevelyan, pp. 141–168. Bergin and Garvey, Westport, Connecticut, and London.

Hahn, Robert A.

1995   *Sickness and Healing: An Anthropological Perspective*. Yale University Press, New Haven.

Hall, Grant D., Stanley M. Tarka, Jr., W. Jeffrey Hurst, David Stuart, and Richard E. W. Adams

1990   Cacao Residues in Ancient Maya Vessels from Rio Azul, Guatemala. *American Antiquity* 55(1):138–143.

Halperin, Rhoda

1988   *Economics Across Cultures: Toward a Comparative Science of Economy*. St. Martin's Press, New York.

Hammerstone, J. F., L. J. J. Romanczyk, and W. M. Aitken

1994   Purine Alkaloid Distribution within *Herrania* and *Theobroma*. *Phytochemistry* 35:1237–1240.

Hammerstone, J. F., S. A. Lazarus, A. E. Mitchell, R. Rucker, and H. H. Schmitz

1999   Identification of Procyanidins in Cocoa (*Theobroma cacao*) and Chocolate Using High-Performance Liquid Chromatography/Mass Spectrometry. *Journal of Agricultural and Food Chemistry* 47:490–496.

Hammond, Norman

1975   *Lubaantun: A Classic Maya Realm*. Peabody Museum of Archaeology and Ethnology, Harvard University, Cambridge.

Hammond, Norman, and Charles Miksicek
1981   Ecology and Economy of a Formative Maya site at Cuello, Belize. *Journal of Field Archaeology* 8(3):259–269.

Hanks, William F.
1990   *Referential Practice, Language, and Lived Space among the Maya.* University of Chicago Press, Chicago, Illinois.

Hansen, Richard
1997   Ideología y arquitectura: poder y dinámicas culturals de los Mayas Preclásicos de las Tierras Bajas. Paper presented at the Segunda Mesa Redonda de Palenque. Palenque, Mexico.

Harborne, Jeffrey B., and Billie L. Turner
1984   *Plant Chemosystematics.* Academic Press, London.

Harrison, Peter
1970   The Central Acropolis, Tikal, Guatemala: A Preliminary Study of the Functions of Its Structural Components During the Late Classic Period. Unpublished Ph.D. dissertation, Department of Anthropology, University of Pennsylvania, Philadelphia.
1999   *The Lords of Tikal.* Thames and Hudson, London.

Hart, John Hinchley
1911   *Cacao, a Manual on the Cultivation and Curing of Cacao.* Duckworth, London.

Harvey, Herbert R.
1984   Aspects of Land Tenure in Ancient Mexico. In *Explorations in Ethnohistory: Indians of Central Mexico in the Sixteenth Century,* edited by H. R. Harvey and H. J. Prem, pp. 83–102. University of New Mexico Press, Albuquerque.
1986   Household and Family Structure in Early Colonial Tepetlaoztoc: An Analysis of the Códice Santa María Asunción. *Estudios de Cultura Náhuatl* 18:275–294.

Haug, G. H., D. Günther, L. C. Peterson, D. M. Sigman, K. A. Hughen, and B. Aeschlimann
2003   Climate and the Collapse of Maya Civilization. *Science* 299:1731–1735.

Hayden, Brian, and Rob Gargett
1990   Big Man, Big Heart? A Mesoamerican View of the Emergence of Complex Society. *Ancient Mesoamerica* 1(1):3–20.

Healy, Paul
1974   The Cuyamel Caves: Preclassic Sites in Northeast Honduras. *American Antiquity* 39:435–447.
1980   *Archaeology of the Rivas Region, Nicaragua.* 2nd ed. Wilfred Laurier University Press, Waterloo, Ontario.

Healy, Paul, and J. J. Awe (editors)
1995   *Belize Valley Preclassic Maya Project: Report on the 1994 Field Season.* Occasional Papers in Anthropology No. 10. Department of Anthropology, Trent University, Peterborough, Ontario.
1996   *Belize Valley Preclassic Maya Project: Report on the 1995 Field Season.* Occasional Papers in Anthropology No. 12. Department of Anthropology, Trent University, Peterborough, Ontario.

Helbig, Carlos
1964   *El Soconusco y su zona cafetalera en Chiapas.* Instituto de Ciencias y Artes de Chiapas, Tuxtla Gutierrez, Chiapas, México.

Hellmuth, Nicholas M.

1988   Early Maya Iconography on an Incised Cylindrical Tripod. In *Maya Iconography*, edited by E. P. Benson and G. G. Griffin, pp. 152–174. Princeton University Press, Princeton, New Jersey.

Helms, Mary

1993   *Craft and the Kingly Ideal: Art, Trade, and Power.* University of Texas Press, Austin.

Henderson, John S.

1979   The Valle de Naco: Ethnohistory and Archaeology in Northwestern Honduras. *Ethnohistory* 24(4):363–377.

2002   Brewing Kakaw in the Formative Period. Paper presented at the 2002 Annual Meetings of the American Anthropological Association, New Orleans.

Henderson, John S., and Rosemary A. Joyce

2001   What Does it Mean to Interact? An Agent-Centered Perspective on the Mesoamerican Formative. Paper presented at the 66th Annual Meeting of the Society for American Archaeology, New Orleans.

Hendon, Julia A., and Rosemary A. Joyce

1993   Questioning 'Complexity' and 'Periphery': Archaeology in Yoro, Honduras. Paper presented at the 59th Annual Meeting of the Society for American Archaeology, St. Louis.

Hernández, Francisco

1959   *Historia natural de la Nueva España (1572–1577).* Universidad Nacional Autónoma de México, Mexico City.

2000   *The Mexican Treasury: The Writings of Dr. Francisco Hernández,* edited by S. Varey. Translated by R. Chabran, C. L. Chamberlin and S. Varey. Stanford University Press, Stanford, California.

Herraiz, T.

2000   Tetrahydro-ß-Carbolines, Potential Neuroactive Alkaloids, in Chocolate and Cocoa. *Journal of Agricultural and Food Chemistry* 48(10):4900–4904.

Herrera, Antonio de

1945   *Historia general de los hechos de los castellanos en, las Islas, y tierra firme de el Mar Oceano* 4. Editorial Guarania, Buenos Aires.

Heyden, Doris

1993   El árbol en el mito y el símbolo. *Estudios de Cultura Náhuatl* 23:201–220.

1994   Trees and Wood in Life and Death. In *Chipping Away on Earth,* edited by E. Q. Keber, pp. 143–152. Labyrinthos Press, Lancaster, California.

Hicks, Frederic

1982   Tetzcoco in the Early Sixteenth Century: The State, the City, and the Calpolli. *American Ethnologist* 9:230–249.

Hill, Warren D., and John E. Clark

2001   Sports, Gambling, and Government: America's First Social Compact? *American Anthropologist* 103(2):331–345.

Hirose López, Javier

2003   La salud de la tierra: el orden natural en el ceremonial y las prácticas de sanación de un médico tradicional Maya. Unpublished Master's thesis, Departamento de Ecología Humana, CINVESTAV-Unidad Mérida.

Hodell, David A., Mark Brenner, Jason H. Curtis, and T. Guilderson

2001   Solar Forcing of Drought Frequency in the Maya lowlands. *Science* 292:1367–1370.

Hoekstra, Rik

1990   A Different Way of Thinking: Contrasting Spanish and Indian Social and Economic Views in Central Mexico (1550–1600). In *The Indian Community of Colonial Mexico: Fifteen Essays on Land Tenure, Corporate Organizations, Ideology and Village Politics*, edited by A. Ouweneel and S. Miller, pp. 60–85. CEDLA, Amsterdam.

Hofling, Charles A.

2001   Archaeological and Linguistic Correlations in Yukateko Mayaland. Paper presented at the Congreso International de Cultura Maya, Mérida, Mexico.

Holden, Pat

1983   Introduction. In *Women's Religious Experience: Cross Cultural Perspectives*, edited by P. Holden, pp 1–15. Croon Helm, London.

Hoopes, John

1995   Interaction in Hunting and Gathering Societies as a Context for the Emergence of Pottery in the Central American Isthmus. In *The Emergence of Pottery: Technology and Innovation in Ancient Societies*, edited by W. Barnett and J. Hoopes, pp. 185–198. Smithsonian Institution Press, Washington, D.C.

Hostnig, Rainer, Rosanna Hostnig, and Luis Vásquez V.

1998   *Ethnobotánica Mam*. GTZ/ BMfaA/ DK-GRAZ/ IIZ, Guatemala.

Houston, Stephen D.

1997   A King Worth a Hill of Beans. *Archaeology* 50(3):40.

Houston, Stephen D., and David Stuart

1996   Of Gods, Glyphs, and Kings: Divinity and Rulership among the Classic Maya. *Antiquity* 70:289–312.

1998   The Ancient Maya Self: Personhood and Portraiture in the Classic Period. *RES* 33:73–101.

Houston, Stephen D., and Karl Taube

1987   "Name Tagging" in Classic Mayan Script: Implications for Native Classifications of Ceramics and Jade Ornaments. *Mexicon* 9(2):38–41.

2000   An Archaeology of the Senses: Perception and Cultural Expression in Ancient Mesoamerica. *Cambridge Archaeological Journal* 10(2):261–294.

Houston, Stephen D., John Robertson, and David Stuart

2000   The Language of Classic Maya Inscriptions. *Current Anthropology* 41:321–356.

Houston, Stephen D., David Stuart, and Karl A. Taube

1989   Folk Classification of Classic Maya Pottery. *American Anthropologist* 91(3):720–726.

1992   Image and Text on the "Jauncy Vase." In *The Maya Vase Book: A Corpus of Rollout Photographs of Maya Vases, Volume 3*, edited by J. Kerr, pp. 499–512. Kerr Associates, New York.

2006   *The Memory of Bones: Body, Being, and Experience among the Classic Maya*. University of Texas Press, Austin.

Hull, Kerry M.

2003   Verbal Art and Performance in Ch'orti' and Maya Hieroglyphic Writing. Unpublished Ph.D. dissertation, Department of Anthropology, University of Texas, Austin.

Hunt, Eva

1977   *The Transformation of the Hummingbird: Cultural Roots of a Zinacantecan Mythical Poem.*
Cornell University Press, Ithaca, New York.

Hunter, John M., and Renate DeKleine

1984   Geophagy in Central America. *Geographical Review* 74:157–169.

Hurst, W. Jeffrey, Robert A. Martin, and Stanley M. Tarka, Jr.

1998   Analytical Methods for the Quantitation of Methylxanthines in Caffeine. In *Caffeine*,
edited by G. Spiller, pp. 13–34. CRC Press, Boca Raton, Florida.

Hurst, W. Jeffrey, Stanley M. Tarka, Jr., and Keith L. Prufer

1998   The CE Determination of Caffeine and Theobromine in Samples of Archeological Interest. Paper presented at the PittCon, New Orleans, March 5, 1998.

Hurst, W. Jeffrey, Robert A. Martin, and Barry L. Zoumas

1982   Biogenic Amines in Chocolate: A Review. *Nutritional Reports International.* 26:1081–
1086.

Hurst, W. Jeffrey, Robert A. Martin, Stanley M. Tarka, Jr., and Grant D. Hall

1989   Authentication of Cocoa in Maya Vessels Using High Performance Liquid Chromatography. *Journal of Chromatography* (466):279–289.

Hurst, W. Jeffrey, Stanley M. Tarka, Jr., Terry G. Powis, Fred Valdez, and Thomas R. Hester

2002   Cacao Usage by the Earliest Maya Civilization. *Nature* 418:289–290.

Hurtado, Tomas

1645   *Chocolate y tabaco. Ayuno eclesiástico y natural.* Francisco García, Impresor del Reyno,
Madrid.

Iglesias, Genny

1985   *Hierbas medicinales de los Quichuas del Napo.* Ed. Abya-Yala, Quito, Ecuador.

Incer, Jaime

2000   *Geografía dinámica de Nicaragua.* Hispamer, Managua, Nicaragua.

INEGI (Instituto Nacional de Estadistica, Geografia e Informatica)

2002   *Anuario estadistico.* 2002 ed. INEGI, Aguascalientes, Mexico.

Ingold, Tim

1987   *The Appropriation of Nature.* University of Iowa Press, Iowa City.

Inomata, Takeshi

1995   Archaeological Investigations at the Fortified Center of Aguateca, El Petén, Guatemala:
Implications for the Study of the Classic Maya Collapse. Unpublished Ph.D. dissertation, Department of Anthropology, Vanderbilt University, Nashville, Tennessee.

Jackson, Peter

1989   *Maps of Meaning.* Unwin Hyman, London.

Johnson, Jean Bassett

1939   The Elements of Mazatec Witchcraft. *Etnologiska Studier* 9:119–149.

Jones, Christopher

1983   Monument 26, Quirigua, Guatemala. In *Quirigua Reports, Vol. 2*, edited by R. J. Sharer,
pp. 118–128. Paper No. 13. University Museum, University of Pennsylvania, Philadelphia.

Jones, Grant D.

1982   Agriculture and Trade in the Colonial Period Southern Maya Lowlands. In *Maya Subsistence Studies in Memory of Dennis E. Puleston*, edited by K. V. Flannery, pp. 275–293.
Academic Press, New York.

1983   The Last Maya Frontiers of Colonial Yucatan. In *Spaniards and Indians in Southeastern Mesoamerica*, edited by M. J. MacLeod and R. Wasserstom, pp. 64–91. University of Nebraska Press, Lincoln.

1984   Maya-Spanish Relations in Sixteenth Century Belize. *Belcast Journal of Belizean Affairs* 1(1):28–40.

1986   The Southern Maya Lowlands During Spanish Colonial Times. In *Supplement to the Handbook of Middle American Indians*, edited by R. Spores, pp. 88–102. Vol. 4. University of Texas Press, Austin.

1989   *Maya Resistance to Spanish Rule: Time and History on a Colonial Frontier.* University of New Mexico Press, Albuquerque.

1998   *The Conquest of the Last Maya Kingdom.* Stanford University Press, Stanford, California.

Jonghe, Edouard de

1905   Histoyre du Mechique; manuscrit français inédit du xvie siècle. *Journal de la Société des Américanistes de Paris* 2:1–41.

Joralemon, Peter D.

1976   The Olmec Dragon: A Study in Pre-Columbian Iconography. In *Origins of Religious Art and Iconography in Preclassic Mesoamerica*, edited by H. B. Nicholson, pp. 27–72. UCLA Latin American Center Publications and Ethnic Arts Council of Los Angeles, Los Angeles, California.

Joyce, Rosemary A.

1992   Innovation, Communication and the Archaeological Record: A Reassessment of Middle Formative Honduras. *Journal of the Steward Anthropological Society* 20(1–2):235–256.

1996a   The Construction of Gender in Classic Maya Monuments. In *Gender and Archaeology*, edited by R. P. Wright, pp. 167–195. University of Pennsylvania Press, Philadelphia.

1996b   Meals that Matter: What Decorated Pots Are Doing in Formative Period Contexts. 66th Annual Meeting of the Society for American Archaeology, New Orleans.

1999   Social Dimensions of Pre-Classic Burials. In *Social Patterns in Pre-Classic Mesoamerica*, edited by D. C. Grove and R. A. Joyce, pp. 15–47. Dumbarton Oaks, Washington, D.C.

2001   *Gender and Power in Prehispanic Mesoamerica.* University of Texas Press, Austin.

2004   Mesoamerica: A Working Model for Archaeology. In *Mesoamerican Archaeology*, edited by J. A. Hendon and R. A. Joyce. Blackwell Publishing Ltd., Oxford.

2005   Building Houses: The Materialization of Lasting Identity in Formative Mesoamerica. Paper presented at the Center for Archaeological Investigations Visiting Scholar Conference, "The Durable House: Architecture, Ancestors, and Origins," Southern Illinois University, Carbondale. March 18–19, 2005.

Joyce, Rosemary A., and John S. Henderson

2001   Beginnings of Village Life in Eastern Mesoamerica. *Latin American Antiquity* 12(1):5–23.

Junker, Laura Lee

2001   The Evolution of Ritual Feasting Systems in Prehispanic Philippine Chiefdoms. In *Feasts: Archaeological and Ethnographic Perspectives on Food, Politics, and Power*, edited by M. Dietler, and B. Hayden, pp. 267–310. Smithsonian Institution Press, Washington, D.C.

Justeson, John, William Norman, Lyle Campbell, and Terrence Kaufman

1985   *The Foreign Impact on Lowland Mayan Language and Script.* Publication 53. Middle American Research Institute, Tulane University, New Orleans.

Kaufman, Terrence

1963   Mixe-Zoque Diachronic Studies. Manuscript in possession of the author.

1994   The Native Languages of Meso-America. In *Atlas of World's Languages*, edited by C. Moseley and R. E. Asher, pp. 34–41. Routledge, London.

2000–2004   Olmecs, Teotihuacaners, and Toltecs: Language History and Language Contact in Meso-America. Unpublished manuscript in possession of the author.

2001   Language Contact in Preclassic Meso-America and the Languages of Teotihuacán. Paper presented at the Annual Meeting of the Society for American Archaeology, New Orleans, April 19, 2001.

Kawanishi, K., Y. Uhara, and Y. Hashimoto

1985   Alkaloids from the Hallucinogenic Plant *Virola sebifera. Phytochemistry* 24(6):1373–1375.

Kelley, David H.

1976   *Deciphering the Maya Script*. University of Texas Press, Austin.

Kellogg, Susan M.

1986a   Aztec Inheritance in Sixteenth-Century Mexico City: Colonial Patterns, Prehispanic Influences. *Ethnohistory* 33:313–330.

1986b   Kinship and Social Organization in Early Colonial Tenochtitlan. In *Supplement to the Handbook of Middle American Indians*, Vol. 4: Ethnohistory, edited by V. Bricker, pp. 103–121. Editor, R. Spores. University of Texas Press, Austin.

1993   The Social Organization of Households among the Tenochca Mexica Before and After the Conquest. In *Prehispanic Domestic Units in Western Mesoamerica: Studies of the Household, Compound, and Residence*, edited by R. S. Santley and K. G. Hirth, pp. 207–224. CRC Press, Boca Raton, Florida.

Kennedy, Nedenia C.

1981   The Formative Period Ceramic Sequence from Playa de los Muertos, Honduras. Unpublished Ph.D. dissertation, Department of Anthropology, University of Illinois.

Kenyhercz, Thomas M., and Peter T. Kissinger

1977   Tyramine from *Theobroma cacao. Phytochemistry* 16(10):1602–1603.

Kerr, Justin

1989   *The Maya Vase Book: A Corpus of Rollout Photographs of Maya Vases, Volume 1*. Kerr Associates, New York.

1990   *The Maya Vase Book: A Corpus of Rollout Photographs of Maya Vases, Volume 2*. Kerr Associates, New York.

1992   *The Maya Vase Book: A Corpus of Rollout Photographs of Maya Vases, Volume 3*. Kerr Associates, New York.

1994   *The Maya Vase Book: A Corpus of Rollout Photographs of Maya Vases, Volume 4*. Kerr Associates, New York.

1997   *The Maya Vase Book: A Corpus of Rollout Photographs of Maya Vases, Volume 5*. Kerr Associates, New York.

2000   *The Maya Vase Book: A Corpus of Rollout Photographs of Maya Vases, Volume 6*. Kerr Associates, New York.

Kertzer, David I.

1988   *Ritual, Politics, and Power*. Yale University Press, New Haven, Connecticut.

Kidder, Alfred V.

1947   *The Artifacts of Uaxactun, Guatemala*. Carnegie Institution, Washington, D.C.

Kim, H., and P. G. Keeney
1984   Epicatechin Content in Fermented and Unfermented Cocoa Beans. *Journal of Food Science* 49:1090–1092.

Kirchoff, Paul
1952   Meso-America. In *Heritage of Conquest: The Ethnology of Middle America*, edited by S. Tax, pp. 17–30. Macmillan, New York.

Knapp, A.
1937   *Cacao Fermentation*. Bale, Sons and Curnow, London.

Knowles, Susan
1984   Dictionary of Chontal. Unpublished manuscript in possession of the author.

Koehler, P. E., and R. R. Eitenmiller
1978   High Pressure Liquid Chromatographic Analysis of Tyramine, Phenylethylamine and Tryptamine in Sausage, Cheese and Chocolate. *Journal of Food Science* 43:1245–1247.

Kondo, K., R. Hirano, A. Matsumoto, O. Igarashi, and H. Itakura
1996   Inhibition of LDL Oxidation by Cocoa. *Lancet* 348:1514.

Kramer, Wendy
1994   *Encomienda Politics in Early Colonial Guatemala, 1524–1544: Dividing the Spoils*. Westview Press, Boulder, Colorado.

Kreiser, W. R., and R. A. Martin
2000   Cocoa and Its Products. In *Official Methods of Analysis*, edited by W. Horwitz, pp. 16–17. 17th ed. Association of Official Analytical Chemists, Gaithersburg, Maryland.

Kris-Etherton, P. M., and C. L. Keen
2002   Evidence that the Antioxidant Flavonoids in Tea and Cocoa are Beneficial for Cardiovascular Health. *Current Opinion in Lipidology* 13(1):41–49.

Kufer, Johanna
2005   Plants Used as Medicine and Food by the Ch'orti' Maya: Ethnobotanical Studies in Eastern Guatemala. Unpublished Ph.D. dissertation, School of Pharmacy, University of London.

Kufer, Johanna, Harald Förther, Elfriede Pöll, and Michael Heinrich
2005   Historical and Modern Medicinal Plant Uses: the Example of the Ch'orti' Maya and Ladinos in Eastern Guatemala. *Journal of Pharmacy and Pharmacology* 57(9):1127–1152.

Kufer, Johanna K., Nikolai Grube, and Michael Heinrich
in press   The Cultural Significance of Cacao in Eastern Guatemala: A Multidisciplinary Perspective. Accepted by *Environment, Development and Sustainability*.

Lacadena, Alfonso
2000   On the Reading of Two Appellatives of the Rain God. Paper presented at the 5th European Maya Conference: "Maya Religious Practices: Processes of Change and Adaptation," University of Bonn, December 9–10, 2000.

Landa, Diego de
1941 [1566]   *Landa's relación de las cosas de Yucatán*. Translated and edited by A. M. Tozzer. Papers of the Peabody Museum of American Archaeology and Ethnology Vol. 18. Harvard University, Cambridge.
1978 [1566]   *Yucatan Before and After the Conquest*. Dover, New York.
1986 [1566]   *Relación de las cosas de Yucatán*. Editorial Porrúa, S. A., Mexico City.

Lara, Ankarino Sibbing
1996   The Sculpted Stone Vessels of Copán, Honduras: A Stylistic, Iconographic, and Textual

Analysis of Saklaktuns. Senior thesis, Department of Anthropology, Harvard University, Cambridge.

Lardé y Larín, Jorge

2000   *El Salvador: Descubrimiento, conquista y colonización*. 2nd ed. Consejo Nacional para la Cultura y el Arte, San Salvador.

Larsen, Helga

1937   Notes on the Volador and Its Associated Ceremonies and Superstitions. *Ethnos* 4:179–192.

Las Casas, Fray Bartolomé de

1877   *Historia de las Indias*, México.

Lau, George F.

2002   Feasting and Ancestor Veneration at Chinchawas, North Highlands of Ancash, Peru. *Latin American Antiquity* 13(3):279–304.

Laughlin, Robert M.

1975   *The Great Tzotzil Dictionary of San Lorenzo Zinacantán*. Smithsonian Contributions to Anthropology No. 19. Smithsonian Institution Press, Washington, D.C.

Laughlin, Robert M. and John B. Haviland

1988   *The Great Tzotzil Dictionary of Santo Domingo Zinacantan*. Smithsonian Contributions to Anthropology, Number 21. 3 vols. Smithsonian Institution Press, Washington, D.C.

Laurent, V., A. M. Risterucci and C. Lanaud

1994   Genetic diversity in cacao revealed by cDNA probes. *Theoretical and Applied Genetics* 88:193–198.

Lavalle, José Antonio de and Werner Lang (editors)

1978   *Arte precolombino, segunda parte: escultura y diseño*. Banco de Credito del Peru en la Cultura Lima, Lima, Peru.

Leach, Edmund

1976   *Culture and Communication*. Cambridge University Press, Cambridge.

Leal, Luis

1977–1978   Los Voladores from Ritual to Game. *New Scholar* 8:129–142.

LeCount, Lisa J.

1999   Polychrome Pottery and Political Strategies among the Late and Terminal Classic Lowland Maya. *Latin American Antiquity* 10(3):239–258.

2001   Like Water for Chocolate: Feasting and Political Ritual among the Late Classic Maya at Xunantunich, Belize. *American Anthropologist* 103(4):935–953.

LeCount, Lisa J., Jason Yaeger, Richard M. Leventhal, and Wendy Ashmore

2002   Dating the Rise and Fall of Xunantunich, Belize: a Late and Terminal Classic Lowland Maya Secondary Center. *Ancient Mesoamerica* 13(1):41–63.

Lee, K. W., Y. J. Kim, H. J. Lee, and C. Y. Lee

2003   Cocoa Has More Phenolic Phytochemicals and a Higher Antioxidant Capacity than Teas and Red Wine. *Journal of Agricultural and Food Chemistry* 51(25):7292–7295.

Lehmann, Walther

1920   *Zentral-Amerika*. 2 vols. Dierich Reimer, Berlin.

Lentz, David L., Marilyn P. Beaudry-Corbett, Maria Luisa Reyna de Aguilar, and Lawrence Kaplan

1996   Foodstuffs, Forests, Fields and Shelter: A Paleoethnobotanical Analysis of Vessel Contents from the Ceren Site, El Salvador. *Latin American Antiquity* 3(7):247–262.

Lentz, David L., and Carlos R. Ramírez-Sosa

2002   Cerén Plant Resources: Abundance and Diversity. In *Before the Volcano Erupted: The Ancient Cerén Village in Central America*, edited by P. Sheets, pp. 33–42. University of Texas Press, Austin.

León Pinelo, Antonio de

1636   *Questión moral si la bebida del chocolate quebranta el ayuno eclesiástico*. Viuda de Juan González, Madrid.

León Portilla, Miguel

1973   *Time and Reality in the Thought of the Maya*. Beacon Press, Boston.

Lesure, Richard G.

1997   Figurines and Social Identities in Early Sedentary Societies of Coastal Chiapas, Mexico 1550–800 B.C. In *Women in Prehistory: Case Studies in North America and Mesoamerica*, edited by C. Claassen and R. Joyce, pp. 227–248. University of Pennsylvania Press, Philadelphia.

Lewis, Walter Hepworth, and Memory P. F. Elvin-Lewis

1977   *Medical Botany: Plants Affecting Man's Health*. Wiley, New York.

Lind, Michael

1987   *The Sociocultural Dimensions of Mixtec Ceramics*. Vanderbilt University Publications in Anthropology 33. Department of Anthropology, Vanderbilt University, Nashville, Tennessee.

Liogier, Alain Henri

1974   *Diccionario botanico de nombres vulgares de la Espanola*. Universidad Nacional Pedro Henriquez Urena, Santo Domingo, Dominican Republic.

Lister, Florence C., and Robert H. Lister

1987   *Andalusian Ceramics in Spain and New Spain: A Cultural Register from the Third Century B.C. to 1700*. University of Arizona Press, Tucson.

Little-Siebold, Christa

2001   Beyond the Indian-Ladino Dichotomy: Contested Identities in an Eastern Guatemalan Town. *Journal of Latin American Anthropology* 6(2):176–197.

Litzinger, William J.

1984   The Ethnobiology of Alcoholic Beverage Production by the Lacandon, Tarahumara, and Other Aboriginal Mesoamerican Peoples. Unpublished Ph.D. dissertation, Department of Anthropology, University of Colorado, Boulder.

Lloyd, Marion

2004   Elaborate Murals Paint a Different Picture of Mayas. *Denver Post*, pp. 25A and 26A. Denver.

Lockhart, James

1992   *The Nahuas After the Conquest: A Social and Cultural History of the Indians of Central Mexico, Sixteenth Through Eighteenth Centuries*. Stanford University Press, Stanford, California.

Longyear, John M.

1952   *Copan Ceramics: A Study of Southeastern Maya Pottery*. Carnegie Institution, Washington, D.C.

Looper, Matthew G.

2003   Wind, Rain and Stone: Ancient and Contemporary Maya Meteorology. In *Shamanism, Mesas, and Cosmologies in Middle America*, edited by D. Sharon, pp. 119–130. San Diego Museum Papers No. 42, San Diego, California.

López Austin, Alfredo

1988   *Human Body and Ideology: Concepts of the Ancient Nahuas.* University of Utah Press, Salt Lake City.

López Báez, Orlando

1985   Botanica y clasificacion del cacao. In *Manual sobre el cultivo de cacao*, pp. 11–28. Secretaria de Agricultura y Recursos Hidraulicos. Instituto Nacional de Investigaciones Agricolas, Centro de Investigaciones Agricolas del Pacifico Sur, Campo Agricola Experimental Rosario Izapa, México.

López Báez, Orlando, and Alfonso Sandoval Gallardo

1983   *Los sistemas de produccion de cacao en la region del Soconusco, Chiapas.* Instituto Nacional de Investigaciones Agricolas, Centro de Investigaciones Agricolas del Pacifico Sur, Campo Agricola Experimental Rosario Izapa, México.

López de Cogolludo, Diego

1957[1688]   *Historia de Yucatán.* Editorial Academia Literaria, Mexico City.

1971   *Historia de Yucatán*, 2 vols. Akademishe Druck, Graz, Austria.

López De Gomara, Francisco

1975   Historia General de las Indias (Excerpt). In *Nicaragua en Los Cronistas de Indias, Serie Cronistas No. 1*, pp. 107–25. Fondo de Promocion Cultural, Banco de America, Managua, Nicaragua.

López de Velasco, Juan

1894   *Geografía y descripción universal de las Indias.* Establecimiento Tipográfico de Fortanet, Madrid.

1975   Geografia y descripción de las Indias (Excerpt). In *Nicaragua en Los Cronistas de Indias*, pp. 171–190. Serie Cronistas No. 1. Fondo de Promocion Cultural, Banco de America, Managua, Nicaragua.

Lopez García, Julian

2000   Estética y logica social en las mesas para las almas Maya-Chortís. *Bulletin de la Societé Suisse des Américanistes* 64–65:125–130.

2003   *Símbolos en la comida indígena Guatemalteca.* Ediciones ABYA-YALA, Quito, Ecuador.

Lothrop, Samuel K.

1926   *Pottery of Costa Rica and Nicaragua.* Memoir No. 8. Contributions from the Museum of the American Indian. 2 vols. Heye Foundation, New York.

Lounsbury, Floyd

1974   On the Derivation and Reading of the "Ben Ich" Prefix. In *Mesoamerican Writing Systems,* edited by E. Benson, pp. 99–144. Dumbarton Oaks, Washington, D.C.

Lovell, W. George

1992   "Heavy Shadows and Black Night": Disease and Depopulation in Colonial Spanish America. *Annals of the Association of American Geographers* 82(3):426–443.

Lowe, Gareth W.

1975   *Early Preclassic Barra Phase at Altamira, Chiapas: A Review with New Data, Papers 38.* Brigham Young University, New World Archaeological Foundation, Provo, Utah.

Lowe, Gareth W., Thomas A. Lee, and Eduardo Martinez Espinosa (editors)

1982   *Izapa: An Introduction to the Ruins and Monuments.* New World Archaeological Foundation, No. 31. Brigham Young University Press, Provo, Utah.

Maca, Jr., Allan Leigh

2002   Spatio-Temporal Boundaries in Classic Maya Settlement Systems: Copan's Urban Foothills and the Excavations at Group 9J-5. Unpublished Ph.D. dissertation, Department of Anthropology, Harvard University, Cambridge.

Madrid Codex

1967   *Codex Tro-Cortesianus.* Akademische Druck- und Verlagsanstalt, Graz.

Marjil de Jesus, Fray Antonio, Fray Lazaro de Mazariegos, and Fray Blas Guillen

1984 [1695]*A Spanish Manuscript Letter on the Lacandones.* Translated and edited by A. M. Tozzer with additional notes by F. E. Comparato. Labyrinthos, Culver City, California.

McAnany, Patricia A.

1995   *Living with the Ancestors: Kinship and Kingship in Ancient Maya Society.* University of Texas Press, Austin.

McAnany, Patricia A. (editor)

2004   *K'axob: Ritual, Work, and Family in an Ancient Maya Village.* The Cotsen Institute of Archaeology, University of California, Los Angeles.

McAnany, Patricia A., Eleanor Harrison-Buck, and Steven Morandi

2004   Mosquito Coast Revisited: The 2003 Season of the Xibun Archaeological Research Project in Belize, Central America. *Context* 17(2):1–6.

McAnany, Patricia A., Rebecca Storey, and Angela K. Lockard

1999   Mortuary Ritual and Family Politics at Formative and Early Classic K'axob, Belize. *Ancient Mesoamerica* (10):129–146.

McAnany, Patricia A., and Ben S. Thomas (editors)

2003   Between the Gorge and the Estuary: Archaeological Investigations of the 2001 Season of the Xibun Archaeological Research Project. Submitted to the Department of Archaeology, Belmopan, Belize. Manuscript on file in the Department of Archaeology, Boston University.

McAnany, Patricia A., Ben S. Thomas, Steven Morandi, Polly A. Peterson, and Eleanor Harrison

2002   Praise the Ahaw and Pass the Kakaw: Xibun Maya and the Political Economy of Cacao. In *Ancient Maya Political Economy*, edited by M. A. Masson and D. A. Freidel, pp. 123–139. Altamira Press, Walnut Creek, California.

McBryde, Felix Webster

1945   *Cultural and Historical Geography of Southwest Guatemala.* Smithsonian Institution Institute of Social Anthropology, Publication No. 4, Washington, D.C.

McCafferty, Geoffrey G., and Larry Steinbrenner

2003   *N-RI-44-00, informe preliminar.* Report submitted to the Dirección de Patrimonio Cultural, Managua, Nicaragua.

McCafferty, Geoffrey G., Larry Steinbrenner, D. Gibson, and J. Debert

n.d.   2003 Field Season Report. Proyecto Arqueológico de Santa Isabel de Nicaragua, Municipio de Buenos Aires, Departamento de Rivas, Nicaragua.

McDougall, Elsie

1955   Easter Ceremonies at San Antonio Palopo, Guatemala. *Carnegie Institution of Washington, Notes on Middle American Archaeology and Ethnology* 5(123):63–74.

McGee, R. Jon

1990   *Life, Ritual, and Religion among the Lacandon Maya.* Wadsworth, Belmont, California.

1991   The Balché Ritual of the Lacandon Maya. *Estudios de Cultura Maya* 18:439–457.

1998   The Lacandon Incense Burner Renewal Ceremony: Termination and Dedication Ritual among the Contemporary Maya. In *The Sowing and the Dawning: Termination, Dedica-*

tion, and Transformation in the Archaeological and Ethnographic Record of Mesoamerica, edited by S. B. Mock, pp. 41–46. University of New Mexico Press, Albuquerque.

2002   *Watching Lacandon Maya Lives*. Allyn and Bacon, Boston.

McGee, R. Jon, and Belisa Gonzalez

1999   Economics, Women, and Work in the Lacandon Jungle. *Frontiers: A Journal of Women Studies* 20(2):175–189.

McKillop, Heather, and Paul Healy (editors)

1989   *Coastal Maya Trade*. Trent University Occasional Papers in Anthropology No. 8. Peterborough, Ontario.

MacLeod, Barbara

1990   Deciphering the Primary Standard Sequence. Unpublished Ph.D. dissertation, Department of Anthropology, University of Texas, Austin.

MacLeod, Barbara, and Nikolai Grube

1990   Recipes from the Royal Licuado Stand: The Prepositional Phrases of the Primary Standard Sequence. Unpublished manuscript in possession of the authors.

MacLeod, Barbara, and Dorie Reents-Budet

1994   The Art of Calligraphy: Image and Meaning. In *Painting the Maya Universe: Royal Ceramics of the Classic Period*, edited by D. Reents-Budet, pp. 106–163. Duke University Press, Durham.

MacLeod, Murdo J.

1973   *Spanish Central America: A Socioeconomic History, 1520–1720*. University of California Press, Berkeley.

MacLeod, Philip

1996   Auge y estancamiento de la producción de cacao en Costa Rica 1660–95. *Anuario de Estudios Centroamericanos* 22:83–107.

McNeil, Cameron L.

2002   Palynological Analysis of Residues from Temple Floors at Copán, Honduras and of a Sediment Core of a Local Laguna. Paper presented at the 67th Annual Meeting of the Society for American Archaeology, Denver, Colorado.

2003   Explotación ambiental en el Valle de Copán: Resultados de análisis de los columnas de sedimentos. Paper presented at the 17th Simposio de Investigaciones Arqueologicas en Guatemala, Guatemala City.

McNeil, Cameron L., W. Jeffrey Hurst, Robert J. Sharer, Ellen E. Bell, and Loa Traxler

2002   The Ritual Use and Representation of *Theobroma cacao* at Copán. Paper presented at the 100th Annual Meeting of the American Anthropological Association, New Orleans.

MacNutt, Francis Augustus

1908   *Letters of Cortes* 2 Vols. Putnam, New York and London.

1912   *De Orbe Novo: The Eight Decades of Peter Martyr D'Anghera*. Putnam, New York and London.

Marcus, Joyce

1992   Royal Families, Royal Texts: Examples from the Zapotec and Maya. In *Mesoamerican Elites: An Archaeological Assessment*, edited by D. Z. Chase and A. F. Chase, pp. 221–241. University of Oklahoma Press, Norman.

Markman, Sidney David
1968   Mudéjar Traits in the Baroque Architecture of Colonial Guatemala. *37th Congreso Internacional de Americanistas, Buenos Aires* 3:251–258.

Martin, Simon
2002a   Mortuary Themes in Maya Art and Writing. Paper presented at the 7th European Maya Conference, "Jaws of the Underworld: Life, Death and Rebirth Among the Ancient Maya," British Museum, London.
2002b   The Baby Jaguar: An Exploration of Its Identity and Origins in Maya Art and Writing. In *La organización social entre los Mayas, Memoria de la Tercera Mesa Redonda de Palenque.* Vol. 1. Coordinated by Vera Tiesler Blos, Rafael Cobos, and Merle Greene Robertson, pp. 49–78. Instituto Nacional de Antropología y Historia and Universidad Autónoma de Yucatán, Mexico City., and Mérida.
2004   Chocolate, Corn, and the Tree of Abundance: Cacao in Ancient Maya Religion. Paper presented at the 22nd University of Pennsylvania Museum Maya Weekend, "Ancient Masks and Modern Eyes: New View on Maya Traditions," March 26–28, 2004.
2005   Treasures from the Underworld: Cacao and the Realm of the Black Gods. Paper presented at the 23rd University of Pennsylvania Museum Maya Weekend, April 8–10, 2005.

Martin, Simon, and Nikolai Grube
2000   *Chronicle of the Maya Kings and Queens: Deciphering the Dynasties of the Ancient Maya.* Thames and Hudson, London.

Martinez, Maximino
1969   *Las plantas medicinales de México.* Ediciones Botas, Mexico City.

Martinez Perdomo, A.
1997   La fuerza de la sangre Chorti: Vigencia de la norma juridica tradicional. Centro Editorial, San Pedro Sula, Honduras.

Marx, F., and J. G. S. Maia
1983   Vitamins in Fruits and Vegetables of the Amazon. 1. Methods for the Determination of Beta-carotene Tocopherol and Ascorbic Acid with High Performance Liquid Chromotography. *Acta Amazonica* 13(5–6):823–830.

Marzo, Vincenzo Di, Nunzio Sepe, Luciano De Petrocellis, Alvin Berger, Gayle Crozier, Ester Fride, and Raphael Mechoulam
1998   Trick or Treat from Food Endocannabinoids? *Nature* 396:636–637.

Masson, Marilyn A., and David A. Freidel (editors)
2002   *Ancient Maya Political Economy.* Altamira Press, Walnut Creek, California.

Mata Amado, Guillermo, and Rolando R. Rubio C.
1994   Incensarios talud-tablero del lago de Amatitlán, Guatemala. In *Simposio de investigaciones arqueológicas en Guatemala,* edited by J. P. Laporte and H. L. Escobedo, pp. 35–46. Instituto de Antropología e Historia, Asociacion Tikal Guatemala, Guatemala City.

Means, Philip Ainsworth
1917   *History of the Spanish Conquest of Yucatan and of the Itzas.* Papers of the Peabody Museum of American Archaeology and Ethnology Vol. 7. Harvard University, Cambridge.

Mejia, Kember, and Else Rengifo
1995   *Plantas medicinales de uso popular en la Amazonía Peruana.* Agencia Española de Cooperación Internacional, Lima, Peru.

Mendoza, Roberto L.

1987   *El cacao en Tabasco*. Universidad Autónoma Chapingo, Texcoco, México.

Merrill, William L.

1979   The Beloved Tree: *Ilex vomitoria* among the Indians of the Southeast and Adjacent Region. In *Black Drink: A Native American Tea*, edited by C. M. Hudson, pp. 40–82. University of Georgia Press, Athens.

Meskell, Lynn M., and Rosemary A. Joyce

2003   *Embodied Lives: Figuring Ancient Maya and Egyptian Experience*. Routledge, London.

Metz, Brent

1995   Experiencing Conquest: The Political and Economic Roots and Cultural Expression of Maya-Chorti Ethos. Unpublished Ph.D. dissertation, Anthropology Department, State University of New York, Albany.

1998   Without Nation, without Community: The Growth of Maya Nationalism among Ch'orti's of Eastern Guatemala. *Journal of Anthropological Research* 54:325–349.

Miksicek, Charles H.

1983   Macrofloral Remains of the Pulltrouser Area: Settlements and Fields. In *Pulltrouser Swamp: Ancient Maya Habitat, Agriculture, and Settlement in Northern Belize*, edited by B. L. Turner II and P. D. Harrison, pp. 94–104. University of Texas Press, Austin.

1991   The Ecology and Economy of Cuello. In *Cuello: An Early Community in Belize*, edited by H. Norman, pp. 70–84. Cambridge University Press, Cambridge.

Milbrath, Susan

1999   *Star Gods of the Maya: Astronomy in Art, Folklore, and Calendars*. University of Texas Press, Austin.

2002   The Planet of Kings: Jupiter in Maya Cosmology. In *Heart of Creation: The Mesoamerican World and the Legacy of Linda Schele*, edited by A. Stone, pp. 118–142. University of Alabama Press, Tuscaloosa.

Miller, Jeffrey

1974   Notes on a Stela Pair Probably from Calakmul, Campeche, Mexico. In *Primera Mesa Redonda de Palenque, Part 1*, edited by M. G. Robertson, pp. 149–162. Robert Louis Stevenson School, Pebble Beach, California.

Miller, Mary Ellen

1997   Imaging Maya Art. *Archaeology* 50(3):34–40.

Miller, Mary Ellen, and Simon Martin

2004   *Courtly Art of the Ancient Maya*. Thames and Hudson, London and New York.

Miller, Mary Ellen, and Karl Taube

1997   *An Illustrated Dictionary of the Gods and Symbols of Ancient Mesoamerica and the Maya*. Thames and Hudson, London.

Milliken, W., R. P. Miller, S. R. Pollard, and E. V. Wandelli

1992   *Ethnobotany of the Waimiri Atroari Indians of Brazil*. Royal Botanic Gardens, Kew, England.

Millon, Rene F.

1955a   When Money Grew on Trees: A Study of Cacao in Ancient Mesoamerica. Unpublished Ph.D. dissertation, Department of Political Science, Columbia University, New York.

1955b   Trade, Tree Cultivation, and the Development of Private Property in Land. *American Anthropologist* 57(4):698–712.

Ming, Lin Chau, P. Gaudêncio, and V. P. Santos
1997   *Plantas medicinais: Uso popular na reserva extrativista "Chico Mendes"-Acre.* CEPLAM/ UNESP, Botucatu, Brazil.
Mintz, Sidney W.
1985   *Sweetness and Power: The Place of Sugar in Modern History.* Penguin, New York.
Mishler, Brent D.
1994   Cladistic Analysis of Molecular and Morphological Data. *American Journal of Physical Anthropology* 94:143–156.
1999   Getting Rid of Species? In *Species: New Interdisciplinary Essays*, edited by R. Wilson, pp. 307–315. MIT Press, Boston.
Mishler, Brent D., and Michael J. Donoghue
1982   Species Concepts: A Case for Pluralism. *Systematic Zoology* 31:491–503.
Mock, Carol
1977   *Chocho de Santa Catarina Ocotlán.* Archivos de Lenguas Indígenas del Estado de Oaxaca No. 4. Centro de Investigación para la Integración Social y Colegio de México, Mexico City.
Mock, Shirley B.
1998   Prelude. In *The Sowing and the Dawning: Termination, Dedication and Transformation in the Archaeological and Ethnographic Record of Mesoamerica*, edited by S. B. Mock, pp. 3–20. University of New Mexico Press, Albuquerque.
Moholy-Nagy, Hattula, William A. Haviland, and Christopher Jones
2003   *Tikal Report 27B: The Artifacts of Tikal: Utilitarian Artifacts and Unworked Material.* University of Pennsylvania Press, Philadelphia.
Molina, Alonso de
1571   Vocabvlario en lengva mexicana y castellana, compuesto por el muy reuerendo padre fray Alonso de Molina, de la Orden del Bienauenturado Nuestro Padre Sant Francisco; dirigido al muy excelente señor don Martin Enriquez, visorrey desta Nueua España. Manuscript at the Casa de Antonio de Spinosa, México, D. F.
Monaghan, John
1990   Reciprocity, Redistribution, and the Transaction of Value in the Mesoamerican Fiesta. *American Ethnologist* 17(4):758–774.
Mondloch, James L.
1980   K'e?s: Quiché Naming. *Journal of Mayan Linguistics* 1(2):9–25.
Montgomery, John
2002   *Dictionary of Maya Hieroglyphs.* Hippocrene Books, New York.
Morán, Francisco
1695   Arte y vocabulario de la lengua Cholti. In *American Philosophical Society*, Philadelphia. Microfilm in the American Philosophical Society, Philadelphia.
1935   *Arte en Lengua Cholti.* Facsimile of the 1695 ms. by William Gates ed. Maya Society, Baltimore.
Morandi, Steven
2004   Construction Sequences at the Group B Pyramid (Op. 56). In The Sibun Valley from Late Classic through Colonial Times, edited by P. A. McAnany, E. Harrison, and S. Morandi. Manuscript on file at the Department of Archaeology, Boston University.

Morley, Sylvanus G., and Ralph L. Roys
1941   *The Xiu Chronicle*. In Carnegie Institution of Washington, Division of Historical Research, Washington, D.C.

Morton, Julia
1981   *Atlas of Medicinal Plants of Middle America*. Charles C. Thomas, Springfield, Illinois.

Motamayor, J. C., and C. Lanaud
2002   Molecular Analysis of the Origin and Domestication of *Theobroma cacao* L. In *Managing Plant Diversity*, edited by J. M. M. Engels, V. R. Rao, A. H. D. Brown, and M. T. Jackson, pp. 77–87. CABI Publishing, Cambridge, Massachusetts.

Motamayor, J. C., A. M. Risterucci, M. Heath, and C. Lanaud
2003   Cacao Domestication 2: Progenitor Germplasm of the *Trinitario cacao* Cultivar. *Heredity* 91:322–330.

Motamayor, J. C., A. M. Risterucci, P. A. Lopez, C. F. Ortiz, A. Moreno, and C. Lanaud
2002   Cacao Domestication 1: The Origin of the Cacao Cultivated by the Mayas. *Heredity* 89:380–386.

Motley, Timothy J.
1994   The Ethnobotany of Sweet Flag, *Acorus calamus* (Araceae). *Economic Botany* 48(4):397–412.

Motolinia (Fray Toribio de Benavente)
1971   *Memoriales o libro de las cosas de la Nueva España y de los naturales de ella (ca. 1540)*. Notas y estudio análitico de Edmundo O'Gorman. Universidad Nacional Autónoma de México, Mexico City.

Muchena, Olivia N., and Eric Vanek
1995   From Ecology through Economics to Ethnoscience: Changing Perceptions of Natural Resource Management. In *The Cultural Dimension of Development*, edited by D. M. Warren, L. J. Slikkerveer, and D. Brokensha, pp. 505–511. Intermediate Technology Publications, London.

Muhs, D. R., R. R. Kautz, and J. J. MacKinnon
1985   Soils and the Location of Cacao Orchards at a Maya Site in Western Belize. *Journal of Archaeological Science* 12:121–127.

Mumford, G. K., Evans, S. M., Kaminski, B. J., Preston, K., Sannerud, C. A., Silverman, K., and Griffiths, R. R.
1994   Discriminative stimulus and subjective effects of theobromine and caffeine in humans. *Psychopharmacology* 115:1–8.

Nájera C., Martha Ilia
1987   *El don de la sangre en el equilibrio cósmico: El sacrificio y el autosacrificio sangriento entre los antiguos Mayas*. Universidad Nacional Autónoma de México, Mexico City.

Nakamura, Seiichi, and Melvin Fuentes
1999   Informe preliminar de rescate arqueológico en el cuadrante 4R en el valle de Copán. Ms. on file at the Centro Regional de Investigaciones Arqueológicas (CRIA), Copán Ruinas, Honduras.

Nash, June C.
1970   *In The Eyes of the Ancestors*. Yale University Press, New Haven.
2001   *Mayan Visions: The Quest for Autonomy in an Age of Globalization*. Routledge, New York.

National Research Council

1989   *Lost Crops of the Incas: Little-Known Plants of the Andes with Promise for Worldwide Cultivation.* National Academy Press, Washington, D.C.

Nazaré, Raimunda Fatima Ribeiro

1992   Processo de obtenção de cupulate em pó e em tabletes meio amargo, com leite e branco, a partir de sementes de cupuaçú, *Theobroma grandiflorum.* Empresa Brasileira de Agropecuária—EMBRAPA, Brazil.

Nazarea, Virginia (editor)

1999   *Ethnoecology: Situated Knowledge/Local Lives.* University of Arizona Press, Tucson.

Nee, Michael

2004   Origin and Diffusion. In *Tobacco in History and Culture: and Encyclopedia,* edited by J. Goodman, M. Norton, and M. Parascandolo, pp. 397–402. Scribner's, Farmington Hills, Michigan.

Noguera, Eduardo

1954   *La Cerámica de Cholula.* Editorial Guaranía, Mexico City.

Nuñez-Melendez, Esteban

1964   *Plantas medicinales de Puerto Rico.* Boletin del Universidad de Puerto Rico 176. Universidad de Puerto Rico Est. Exper. Agricola, Río Pedras.

Oakes, Maud

1951a   *Beyond the Windy Place: Life in the Guatemalan Highlands.* Farrar, Straus and Young, New York.

1951b   *The Two Crosses of Todos Santos: Survivals of Mayan Religious Ritual.* Bollingen Series 27. Pantheon Books, New York.

O'Brien, Karen

1998   Scales of Change: The Climatic Impacts of Tropical Deforestation in Chiapas, Mexico. In *Elements of Change,* edited by S. J. Hassol and J. Katzenberger, pp. 86–100. Aspen Global Change Institute, Aspen, Colorado.

Offner, Jerome

1983   *Law and Politics in Aztec Texcoco.* Cambridge University Press, New York.

1984   Household Organization in the Texcocan Heartland: The Evidence in the Codex Vergara. In *Explorations in Ethnohistory: Indians of Central Mexico in the Sixteenth Century,* edited by H. R. Harvey and H. J. Prem, pp. 127–146. University of New Mexico Press, Albuquerque.

Ogata, Nisao

1993   Explicación alternativa de la abundancia y *Brosimum alicastrum* (Moraceae) en el centro de la peninsula de Yucatán, México. *Biotica, nueva epoca* 1:103–107.

2002a   Studies of Mesoamerican Tropical Trees: Trees of the Maya Region and a Case Study on the Ethnobotany and Phylogeography of Cacao (*Theobroma cacao* L.). Ph.D. dissertation, University of California. University Microfilms, Ann Arbor.

2002b   Domestication and Distribution of the Chocolate Tree (*Theobroma cacao* L.) in Mesoamerica. Paper presented at the 100th Annual Meeting of the American Anthropological Association, New Orleans.

Ogata, Nisao, and Efraín De Luna

1998   Implicaciones ontológicas y epistemológicas del uso de clasificaciones en estudios ecológicos de biodiversidad. In La Diversidad Biológica de Iberoamérica 2. Volumen Especial,

492   Bibliography

Acta Zoologica Mexicana, nueva serie, edited by G. Halffter, pp. 19–33. Instituto de Ecología, A.C., Xalapa, México.

Ogata, Nisao, Arturo Gómez-Pompa, A. Aguilar, R. Castro-Cortés, and O. E. Plummer

1999   Arboles tropicales comunes del area Maya. Sistema de identificación taxonómica. CD-ROM. University of California, Riverside-CONABIO-Gestión de Ecosistemas, A. C.

Oliveira, Ana Maria de, Nadia Rosa Pereira, Antonio Marsaioli, Jr., and Fabio Augusto

2004   Studies on the Aroma of Cupuassu Liquor by Headspace Solid-Phase Microextraction and Gas Chromatography. *Journal of Chromatography-A* 1025(1):115–124.

Oliveira, M. M., M. R. P. Simpáio, F. Simon, B. Gilbert, and Walter B. Mors

1972   Antitumor Activity of Condensed Flavonols. *Anais de Academia Brasil de Ciéncias* 44:41–44.

The Olmec World: Ritual and Rulership

1995   Art Museum, Princeton University and Harry Abrams, Princeton and New York.

Orellana, Sandra L.

1981   Idols and Idolatry in Highland Guatemala. *Ethnohistory* 28(2):157–177.

Osakabe, N., M. Yamagishi, C. Sanbongi, M. Natsume, T. Takizawa, and T. Osawa

1998   The Antioxidative Substances in Cacao Liquor. *Journal of Nutritional Science and Vitaminology* 44:313–321.

Ott, Jonathan

1985   *The Cacahuatl Eater: Ruminations of an Unabashed Chocolate Addict, Replete with Diverse Historical and Scientific Discursions of Both an Entertaining and Informative Nature.*Natural Products Co., Vashon, Washington.

1993   *Pharmacotheon: Entheogenic Drugs, Their Plant Sources.* Natural Products Co., Kennewick, Washington.

Ouweneel, Arij

1990   *Altepeme* and *Pueblos de Indios*: Some Comparative Theoretical Perspectives on the Analysis of the Colonial Indian Communities. In *The Indian Community of Colonial Mexico: Fifteen Essays on Land Tenure, Corporate Organizations, Ideology and Village Politics*, edited by A. Ouweneel and S. Miller, pp. 1–37. CEDLA, Amsterdam.

Oviedo y Valdes, Gonzalo Fernández de

1851–1855   *Historia general y natural de las Indias, islas y tierra-firma del mar oceano* 4. Impr. de la Real academia de la historia, Madrid.

1959   *Historia general y natural de las Indias (1535–57).* Ediciones Atlas, Madrid.

Packaged Facts

2005   *The U.S. Chocolate Market.* Packaged Facts, New York.

Pagden, Anthony

1986   *Hernan Cortes: Letters From Mexico.* Yale University Press, New Haven and London.

Palka, Joel W.

1998   Lacandón Maya Culture Change and Survival in the Lowland Frontier of the Expanding Guatemalan and Mexican Republics. In *Studies in Cultural Contact: Interaction, Culture Change, and Archaeology*, edited by J. G. Cusick, pp. 457–474. Center for Archaeological Investigations, Carbondale, Illinois.

Paris Codex

1968   *Codex Peresianus.* Akademische Druck- und Verlagsanstalt, Graz.

Parsons, Elsie Clews
1936   *Mitla, Town of the Souls, and Other Zapoteco-Speaking Pueblos of Oaxaca, Mexico.* University of Chicago Press, Chicago and London.

Parsons, Lee Allen
1969   *Bilbao, Guatemala, An Archaeological Study of the Pacific Coast Cotzumalhuapa Region, Vol. 2.* Publications in Anthropology No. 12. Milwaukee Public Museum, Milwaukee, Wisconsin.

Parsons, Lee Allen, and Barbara J. Price
1971   Mesoamerican Trade and Its Role in the Emergence of Civilization. In *Observations on the Emergence of Civilization in Mesoamerica*, edited by R. F. Heizer and J. A. Graham, pp. 169–195. Contributions of the University of California Research Facility No. 11. University of California, Berkeley.

Paso y Troncoso, F.
1905   *Suma de visitas de pueblos por orden alfabético, anónimo de la mitad del siglo 16, Vol. 1.* Papeles de Nueva España, 2nd Ser. 1. Impresores de la Real Casa, Madrid.

Pasztory, Esther
1997   *Teotihuacan: An Experiment in Living.* University of Oklahoma Press, Norman and London.

Patiño, Victor Manual
1963   *Plantas cultivadas y animales domesticadas en América equinoccial.* 2 vols. Impr. Departamental, Cali, Colombia.
1968   Guayusa, a Neglected Stimulant from the Eastern Andean Foothills. *Economic Botany* 22:310–316.

Pendergast, David M.
1979   *Excavations at Altun Ha, Belize, 1964–1970.* Royal Ontario Museum, Toronto.
1993   Worlds in Collision: The Maya/Spanish Encounter in Sixteenth and Seventeenth Century Belize. *Proceedings of the British Academy* 81:105–143.

Pérez, Juan Pío
1843   Ancient Chronology of Yucatán; or, a True Exposition of the Method Used by the Indians for Computing Time. In *Incidents of Travel in Yucatán*, by J. L. Stephens. Appendix pp. 434–448. Vol. 1. Harper and Brothers, New York.
1877   *Diccionario de la lengua Maya*, Mérida, Yucatán, México.

Pérez Martínez, Vitalino, Federico García, Felipe Martínez, and Jeremías López
1996   *Diccionario Ch'orti', Jocotan, Chiquimula: Ch'orti'-Español.* Proyecto Lingüístico Francisco Marroquín, Antigua, Guatemala.

Pérez Romero, J. A.
1988   *Algunas consideraciones sobre cacao en el norte de la Península de Yucatán.* Universidad Autónoma de Yucatán, Mérida, Mexico.

Pérez-Romero, A., and R. Cobos
1990   Una nota arqueológica respecto a la preferencia de *Theobroma cacao* en las tierras Bajas Mayas. *Boletín de la E.C.A.U.D.Y* 17(102):33–52.

Peters, Charles M.
1983   Observations on Maya Subsistence and the Ecology of a Tropical Tree. *American Antiquity* 48(3):610–615.

Peterson, Jeanette Favrot

1993   *The Paradise Garden Murals of Malinalco: Utopia and Empire in Sixteenth-Century Mexico.* University of Texas Press, Austin.

Pinkley, Homer

1973   The Ethno-Ecology of the Kofán Indians. Unpublished Ph.D. dissertation, Harvard University, Cambridge.

Pinto, Gloria Lara

2001   Las tierras de los Indios del pueblo de Copán: Conflicto agrario y otorgamiento de justica an el siglo 17. Paper presented at the Primera Congreso Internacional de Copán, Ciencia, Arte y Religion en el Mundo de Mayas. Copán Ruinas, Honduras.

Pittier, Henri-François

1908   *Plantas usuales de Costa Rica.* Editorial Costa Rica, San José.

1926   *Manual de las plantas usuales de Venezuela.* Litografia del Comercio, Caracas, Venezuela.

1935   Degeneration of Cacao through Natural Hybridization. *Journal of Heredity* 36:385–390.

Plotkin, Mark J., Brian M. Boom, and Malorye Allison

1991   *The Ethnobotany of Aublet's Histoire des Plantes de la Guiane Francoise (1775).* Monographs in Systematic Botany, No. 35, from the Missouri Botanical Garden, St. Louis, Missouri.

Plowman, Timothy

1984   The Origin, Evolution, and Diffusion of Coca, *Erythroxylum* spp., in South and Central America. In *Pre-Columbian Plant Migration*, edited by D. Stone, pp. 125–163. Harvard University Press, Cambridge.

Pohl, John

1994   Weaving and Gift Exchange in the Mixtec Codices. In *Cloth and Curing: Continuity and Change in Oaxaca*, edited by G. Johnson and D. Sharon, pp. 3–13. San Diego Museum Papers No. 32. San Diego Museum of Man, San Diego, California.

1999   The Lintel Paintings of Mitla and the Function of the Mitla Palaces. In *Mesoamerican Architecture as a Cultural Symbol*, edited by J. Kowalski, pp. 176–197. Oxford University Press, Oxford and New York.

Pohl, Mary D.

1981   Ritual Continuity and Transformation in Mesoamerica: Reconstructing the Ancient Maya *Cuch* Ritual. *American Antiquity* 46(3):513–529.

1985   An Ethnohistorical Perspective on Ancient Maya Wetland Fields and Other Cultivation Systems in the Lowlands. In *Prehistoric Lowland Maya Environment and Subsistence Economy*, edited by M. Pohl, pp. 35–45. Papers of the Peabody Museum of Archaeology and Ethnology Vol. 77. Harvard University, Cambridge.

1994   Appendix D. Late Classic Maya Fauna from Settlement in the Copan Valley, Honduras: Assertion of Social Status Through Animal Consumption. In *Ceramics and Artifacts from Excavations in the Copan Residential Zone*. Papers of the Peabody Museum of Archaeology and Ethnology, Vol. 80. Harvard University, Cambridge.

Polanyi, Karl

1957   The Economy as Instituted Process. In *Trade and Market in the Early Empires*, edited by K. Polanyi, C. Arensberg, and H. Pearson, pp. 243–270. Free Press, New York.

Pompa, Geronimo

1974   *Medicamentos indígenas.* 41st ed. Editorial America, S. A., Miami and Panama.

Ponce de León, Luis

1961 [1574] Relacion de la provincia de Soconusco. Letter published as Appendix A. In *La Victoria: an Early Site on the Pacific Coast of Guatemala*, edited by M. D. Coe, pp. 139–140. Papers of the Peabody Museum of Archaeology and Ethnology Vol. 53. Harvard University, Cambridge.

Pope, Kevin, Mary D. Pohl, John Jones, David Lentz, Chistopher Von Nagy, Francisco J. Vega, and Irvy R. Quitmyer

2001 Origin and Environmental Setting of Ancient Agriculture in the Lowlands of Mesoamerica. *Science* 292:1370–1373.

Popenoe, Dorothy

1934 Some Excavations at Playa de los Muertos, Ulúa River, Honduras. *Maya Research* 1:62–86.

Popenoe, Wilson

1919a Batido and Other Guatemalan Beverages Prepared from Cacao. *American Anthropologist* 21(4):403–409.

1919b Useful Plants of Copan. *American Anthropologist* 21(2):125–138.

Popol vuh. Las antiguas historias del Quiche

1993 Translated by A. Recinos. Fondo de Cultura Economica, Mexico.

Porter, L. J., Z. Ma, and B. G. Chan

1991 Cacao Procyanidins: Major Flavonoids and Identification of Some Minor Metabolites. *Phytochemistry* 30(5):1657–1663.

Posada, D., and K. A. Crandall

2001 Intraspecific Gene Genealogies: Trees Grafting into Networks. *Trends in Ecology and Evolution* 16:37–45.

Pound, F. J.

1938 *Cacao and Witchbroom Disease of South America, with notes on other species of Theobroma*. Yuille's Printerie, Port-of-Spain, Trinidad.

Powis, Terry G., Fred Valdez, Jr., Thomas R. Hester, W. Jeffrey Hurst, and Stanley M. Tarka

2002 Spouted Vessels and Cacao Use among the Preclassic Maya. *Latin American Antiquity* 13(1):85–106.

Prance, Ghillean T.

1972 Ethnobotanical Notes from Amazonian Brazil. *Economic Botany* 26(3):221–237.

Prechtel, Martin

1999 *Long Life, Honey in the Heart: A Story of Initiation and Eloquence from the Shores of a Mayan Lake*. Tarcher/Putnam, New York.

2001 *The Disobedience of the Daughter of the Sun: Ecstasy and Time*. Yellow Moon Press, Cambridge, Massachusetts.

Prem, Hanns

1974 *Matrícula de Huexotzingo*. Akademische Druck-und Verlagsanstalt, Graz, Austria.

1988 *Milpa y hacienda: Tenencia de la tierra indígena y española en la cuenca del Alto Atoyac, Puebla, México*. CIESAS, Fondo de Cultura Económica, Mexico City.

Prescilla, Maricel E.

2001 *The New Taste of Chocolate: A Cultural and Natural History of Cacao with Recipes*. Ten Speed Press, Berkeley.

Price, Sally

1989 *Primitive Art in Civilized Places*. University of Chicago Press, Chicago, Illinois.

Quenon, Michel, and Genevieve LeFort

1997   Rebirth and Resurrection in Maize God Iconography. In *The Maya Vase Book: A Corpus of Rollout Photographs of Maya Vases, Volume 5*, edited by J. Kerr, pp. 884–902. Kerr Associates, New York.

Rands, Robert L.

1974   The Ceramic Sequence at Palenque, Chiapas. In *Mesoamerican Archaeology: New Approaches*, edited by N. Hammond, pp. 51–76. Duckworth, London.

Rathje, William L.

1972   Praise the Gods and Pass the Metates: A Hypothesis of the Development of Lowland Rainforest Civilizations in Mesoamerica. In *Contemporary Archaeology: A Guide to Theory and Contributions*, edited by M. P. Leone, pp. 365–392. Southern Illinois University Press, Carbondale.

2002   The Nouveau Elite Potlatch: One Scenario for the Monumental Rise of Early Civilizations. In *Ancient Maya Political Economies*, edited by M. Masson and D. Freidel, pp. 31–38. Altamira Press, Walnut Creek, California.

Rathje, William L., David A. Gregory, and Frederick M. Wiseman

1978   Trade Models and Archaeological Problems: Classic Maya Examples. In *Mesoamerican Communication Routes and Cultural Contact*, edited by T. Lee and C. Navarrete, pp. 147–175. New World Archaeological Foundation, Paper No. 40, Provo, Utah.

Recinos, Adrian

1980   *Popol Vuh:* Las antiguas historias del Quiché. In *Literatura Maya*, edited by M. de la Garza, pp. 3–99. Translated by A. Recinos. Ed. Ayacucho, Madrid.

Redfield, Robert, and Alfonso Villa R.

1934   *Chan Kom: A Maya Village*. Publication No. 448. The Carnegie Institution, Washington, D.C.

1962   *Chan Kom: A Maya Village*. University of Chicago Press, Chicago, Illinois.

Reents, Dorie

1987   The Discovery of a Ceramic Artist and Royal Patron among the Classic Maya. *Mexicon* 9(6):123–129.

Reents-Budet, Dorie

1994a   *Painting the Maya Universe: Royal Ceramics of the Classic Period*, edited by D. Reents-Budet. Duke University Press, Durham, North Carolina.

1994b   Classic Maya Pottery Painters. In *Painting the Maya Universe*, edited by D. Reents-Budet, pp. 36–71. Duke University Press, Durham, North Carolina.

1994c   Functions of Classic Period Painted Pottery. In *Painting the Maya Universe*, edited by D. Reents-Budet, pp. 72–103. Duke University Press, Durham, North Carolina.

1994d   Pictorial Themes of Classic Maya Pottery. In *Painting the Maya Universe*, edited by D. Reents-Budet, pp. 234–289. Duke University Press, Durham, North Carolina.

1998   Elite Maya Pottery and Artisans as Social Indicators. In *Craft and Social Identity*, edited by C. Costin and R. Wright, pp. 71–89. Archaeological Papers of the American Anthropological Association Vol. 8. American Anthropological Association, Washington, D.C.

2000a   Classic Maya Conceptualizations of the Royal Court: An Analysis of Palace Court Renderings on the Pictorial Ceramics. In *Royal Courts of the Ancient Maya*, edited by S. Houston and T. Inomata. Westview Press, Boulder, Colorado.

2000b Feasting among the Classic Maya: Evidence From the Pictorial Ceramics. In *The Maya Vase Book: A Corpus of Rollout Photographs of Maya Vases, Volume 6*, edited by J. Kerr, pp. 1022–1038. Kerr Associates, New York.

in press Power Material in Ancient Mesoamerica: The Roles of Cloth Among the Classic Maya. In *Wrapping Traditions in Ancient Mesoamerica*, edited by J. Guernsey and F. K. Reilly. The Center for Ancient American Studies, Washington, D.C.

Reents-Budet, Dorie, Ronald L. Bishop, Jennifer T. Taschek, and Joseph W. Ball

2000 Out of the Palace Dumps: Ceramic Production and Use at Buenavista del Cayo, Belize. *Ancient Mesoamerica* 11(1):99–121.

Reents-Budet, Dorie, Ellen E. Bell, Loa P. Traxler, and Ronald L. Bishop

2004 Early Classic Ceramic Offerings at Copan: A Comparison of the Hunal, Margarita, and Sub-Jaguar Tombs. In *Understanding Early Classic Copan*, edited by E. E. Bell, M. Canuto, and R. J. Sharer, pp. 159–190. University of Pennsylvania Museum of Archaeology and Anthropology, Philadelphia.

Reese-Taylor, Kathryn, and Debra Walker

2002 The Passage of the Late Preclassic into the Early Classic. In *Ancient Maya Political Economies*, edited by M. Masson and D. Freidel, pp. 87–122. Altamira Press, Walnut Creek, California.

Reilly, F. Kent

1994a Visions to Another World: Art, Shamanism, and Political Power in Middle Formative Mesoamerica. Unpublished Ph.D. dissertation, Department of Anthropology, University of Texas, Austin.

1994b Enclosed Ritual Spaces and the Watery Underworld in Formative Period Architecture: New Observations on the Function of La Venta Complex A. In *Seventh Palenque Round Table, 1989*, edited by V. M. Fields, pp. 125–135. Pre-Columbian Art Research Institute, San Francisco.

1996 Art, Ritual, and Rulership in the Olmec World. In *The Olmec World: Ritual and Kingship*. The Art Museum, Princeton University and Harry Abrams, Princeton and New York.

Rein, Dietrich, Teresa G. Paglieroni, Debra A. Pearson, Ted Wun, Harold H. Schmitz, Robert Gosselin, and Carl L. Keen.

2000 Cocoa and Wine Polyphenols Modulate Platelet Activation and Function. *Journal of Nutrition* 130:2120S–2126S.

Reina, Ruben E.

1966 *The Law of the Saints: A Pokomam Pueblo and its Community Culture*. Bobbs-Merrill, Indianapolis, Indiana.

Reko, Blas Pablo

1945 *Mitobotanica Zapoteca*. D.F. (Privately printed), Tacubaya, México.

Relaciones de Yucatán

1898–1900 *Colección de documentos inéditos relativos al descubrimiento conquista y organización de las antiguas posesiones Españolas de Ultamar*. 2nd Series. Real Academia de la Historia, Madrid.

Renfrew, Colin

1986 Varna and the Emergence of Wealth in Prehistoric Europe. In *The Social Life of Things: Commodities in Cultural Perpsective*, edited by A. Appadurai, pp. 141–168. Cambridge University Press, Cambridge.

Rensch, Calvin R.

1989   Etymological Dictionary of the Chinantec Languages. In *Studies in Chinantec Languages, 1*. University of Texas, Summer Institute of Linguistics, Dallas, Texas.

Restall, Matthew

1997   *The Maya World: Yucatec Culture and Society, 1550–1850*. Stanford University Press, Stanford, California.

Rice, Robert A., and Russell Greenberg

2000   Cacao Cultivation and the Conservation of Biological Diversity. *Ambio* 29(3):167–173.

Riggin, Ralph M., and Peter T. Kissinger

1976   Identification of Salsolinol as a Phenolic Component in Powdered Cocoa and Cocoa-Based Products. *Journal of Agricultural and Food Chemistry* 24(4):900.

Rimm, Eric B., Martijn B. Katan, Alberto Ascherio, Meir J. Stampfer, and Walter C. Willett

1996   Relation between Intake of Flavonoids and Risk for Coronary Heart Disease in Male Health Professionals. *Annals of Internal Medicine* 125(5):384–389.

Robertson, Merle Greene

1983   *The Sculpture of Palenque: The Temple of the Inscriptions*. Vol. 1. Princeton University Press, Princeton, New Jersey.

Robicsek, Francis, and Donald Hales

1981   *The Maya Book of the Dead: The Ceramic Codex*. University of Virginia Art Museum, Charlottesville.

Rodríguez Becerra, Salvador

1977   *Encomienda y conquista: Los inicios de la colonización en Guatemala*. Universidad de Sevilla, Seville.

Rodriguez, Dinah

1974   Aspectos socioeconomicos de la costa. In *La Costa de Chiapas (Un estudio economico regional)*, edited by A. B. Batalla and D. Rodriguez, pp. 51–94. Instituto de Investigaciones Economicas, Universidad Nacional Autónoma de México, Mexico City.

Rojas, José Luis de

1998   *La moneda indígena y sus usos en la Nueva España en el siglo 16*. Centro de Investigaciones y Estudios Superiores en Antropología Social, Mexico City.

Romanczyk, Jr., Leo J., John F. Hammerstone, Jr., and Margaret M. Buck

1998   Antineoplastic Cocoa Extracts and Methods for Making and Using the Same. Patent number: 5,712,305. MARS, Incorporated, McLean, Virginia.

Rosés Alvarado, Carlos

1982   El ciclo del cacao en la economía colonial de Costa Rica, 1650–1794. *Mesoamerica* 4:247–278.

Roth, Bryan L., Karen Baner, Richard Westkaemper, Daniel Siebert, Kenner C. Rice, SeAnna Steinberg, Paul Ernsberger, and Richard B. Rothman

2002   Salvinorin A: A Potent Naturally Occurring Non-Nitrogenous K Opioid Selective Agonist. *Proceedings of the National Academy of Sciences* 99(18):11934–11939.

Roys, Ralph L.

1931   *The Ethno-Botany of the Maya*. Middle American Research Institute, Tulane University, New Orleans.

1933   *The Book of the Chilam Balam of Chumayel*. Publication 438. Carnegie Institution of Washington, Washington, D.C.

1943   *The Indian Background of Colonial Yucatan.* Publication 548. Carnegie Institution of Washington, Washington, D.C.

1967   *The Book of Chilam Balam of Chumayel.* University of Oklahoma Press, Norman.

1972   *The Indian Background of Colonial Yucatan.* University of Oklahoma Press, Norman.

1973   *The Book of Chilam Balam of Chumayel.* University of Oklahoma Press, Norman.

Rubio Sánchez, Manuel

1977   *Historia del puerto de la Santísima Trinidad de Sonsonate o Acajutla.* Editorial Universitaria, San Salvador.

Ruz Lhuillier, Alberto

1973   El templo inscripciones, Palenque. In *Colección Científica 7.* Instituto Nacional de Antropología e Historia, Mexico City.

Ruzaidi, A., I. Amin, A. G. Nawalyah, M. Hamid, and H. A. Faizul

2005   The Effect of Malaysian Cocoa Extract on Glucose Levels and Lipid Profiles in Diabetic Rats. *Journal of Ethnopharmacology* 98(1–2):55–60.

Sabloff, Jeremy

1975   *Excavations at Seibal: Ceramics.* Memoirs Vol. 13 No. 2. Peabody Museum of Archaeology and Ethnology, Harvard University, Cambridge.

Sahagún, Fray Bernardino de

1558–1561   *Primeros Memoriales.* Paleography of Nahuatl text and English translation by Thelma D. Sullivan (1997). University of Oklahoma Press, Norman.

1950–1982   *Florentine Codex. General History of the Things of New Spain.* Translated by A. Anderson and C. Dibble. School of American Research, Santa Fe, New Mexico, and the University of Utah Press, Salt Lake City.

Saint Augustine

1950   *The City of God.* Modern Library, New York.

Salazar, Gabriel

2000   Geography of the Lowlands. In *Lost Shores, Forgotten Peoples,* edited by L. H. Feldman, pp. 21–54. Duke University Press, Durham and London.

Salgado González, Sylvia

1996   Social Change in a Region of Granada, Pacific Nicaragua (1000 B.C.–1522 A.D.). Unpublished Ph.D. dissertation, Department of Anthropology, State University of New York, Albany.

Sampeck, Katherine

2005   An Archaeology of Conquest and Colonialism: A Comprehensive Regional Survey of the Río Ceniza Valley, Department of Sonsonate, El Salvador. Unpublished Ph.D. dissertation, Department of Anthropology, Tulane University, New Orleans.

Sanbongi, C., N. Osakabe, M. Natsume, T. Takizawa, S. Gomi, and T. Osawa

1998   Antioxidative Polyphenols Isolated from *Theobroma cacao. Journal of Agricultural and Food Chemistry* 46:454–457.

Sanbongi, Chiaki, Noboru Suzuki, and Tsuyoshi Sakane

1997   Polyphenols in Chocolate, Which Have Antioxidant Activity, Modulate Immune Functions in Humans in Vitro. *Cellular Immunology* 177:129–136.

Sánchez Sáenz, M., and A. Rodríguez

1990   Aproximación preliminar al conocimiento de la clasificación botánica Muinane. *Columbia Amazonica* 4(2):67–75.

Sapper, Karl

2000[1901]   Food and Drink of Q'eqchi' Indians. In *Early Scholars' Visits to Central America: Reports by Karl Sapper, Walter Lehmann, and Franz Termer*, edited by M. Beaudry-Corbett and E. T. Hardy. Translated by T. E. Gutman. Occasional Paper 18. The Cotsen Institute of Archaeology, University of California, Los Angeles.

Saragoussi, Muriel, Jorge H. I. Martel, and Gilberto Assis Ribeiro

1990   Comparação na composição de quintais de três localidade de terra tirme do estado do Amazonas. In *Ethnobiology in Theory and Practice*, pp. 295–303. Museu Paraence Emílio Goeldi, Belém, Brazil.

Saturno, William A., Karl A. Taube, and David Stuart

2005   *The Murals of San Bartolo, El Petén, Guatemala. Part 1: The North Wall*. With a supplemental drawing by Heather Hurst. Ancient America no. 7. Center for Ancient American Studies, Barnardsville, North Carolina.

Sauer, Carl

1925   The Morphology of Landscape. In *Land and Life*, edited by J. Leighly, pp. 315–350. University of California Press, Berkeley.

Schaal, B. A., D. A. Hayworth, K. M. Olsen, J. T. Rauscher, and W. A. Smith

1998   Phylogeographic Studies in Plants: Problems and Prospects. *Molecular Ecology* 7:465–474.

Schele, Linda

1984   Human Sacrifice among the Classic Maya. In *Ritual Human Sacrifice in Mesoamerica: A Conference at Dumbarton Oaks, October 13th and 14th, 1979*, edited by E. H. Boone, pp. 7–48. Dumbarton Oaks, Washington, D.C.

1992   Sprouts and the Early Symbolism of Rulers in Mesoamerica. In *The Emergence of Lowland Maya Civilization: The Transition from the Preclassic to the Early Classic*, edited by N. Grube, pp. 117–135. Acta Mesoamericana 8, Verlag Anton Saurwein, Möckmühl, Germany.

1996   The Olmec Mountain and Tree of Creation in Mesoamerican Cosmology. In *The Olmec World: Ritual and Kingship*, pp. 105–117. The Art Museum, Princeton University and Harry Abrams, Princeton and New York.

Schele, Linda, and David Freidel

1990   *A Forest of Kings. The Untold Story of the Ancient Maya*. William Morrow, New York.

Schele, Linda, and Peter Mathews

1991   Royal Visits and Other Intersite Relationships among the Classic Maya. In *Classic Maya Political History: Hieroglyphic and Archaeological Evidence*, edited by T. P. Culbert, pp. 226–252. Cambridge University Press, Cambridge and New York.

1998   *The Code of Kings: The Language of Seven Sacred Maya Temples and Tombs*. Scribner, New York.

Schellhas, Paul

1904   *Representation of Deities of the Maya Manuscripts*. Papers of the Peabody Museum of American Archaeology and Ethnology Vol. 4, No. 1. Harvard University, Cambridge.

Schmidt, Peter

2003   *Informe del Proyecto Arqueológico Chichén Itzá, Julio 1999 a Diciembre 2002*. Centro INAH Yucatán. Instituto Nacional de Antropología y Historia, Mérida, Mexico.

Schmidt, Peter, Mercedes de la Garza, and Enrique Nalda

1998   *Maya*. Rizzoli, New York.

Scholes, France V., and Ralph L. Roys
1968   *The Maya Chontal Indians of Acalan-Tixchel*. 2nd ed. University of Oklahoma Press, Norman.

Scholes, France V., and S. E. Thompson
1977   The Francisco Pérez Probanza of 1654–1656 and the Matricula of Tipu (Belize). In *Anthropology and History in Yucatán*, edited by G. D. Jones, pp. 43–68. University of Texas Press, Austin and London.

Scholes, France V., R. Mañé, and E. Adams
1938   *La Iglesia en Yucatán 1560–1610*. Documentos para la Historia de Yucatán. 2 vols. Carnegie Institution of Washington, Washington, D.C., and Diario de Yucatán, Mérida, Mexico.

Schultes, Richard E.
1951   El género *Herrania*, pariente silvestre del cacao cultivado. *Agricultura Tropical* 7(7):43–48.
1958   A Synopsis of the Genus *Herrania*. *Journal of the Arnold Arboretum* 39:217–295.
1984   Amazonian Cultigens and Their Northward and Westward Migration in Pre-Columbian Times. In *Pre-Columbian Plant Migration*, edited by D. Stone, pp. 19–38. Papers of the Peabody Museum of Archaeology and Ethnology Vol. 76. Harvard University, Cambridge.

Schultes, Richard E., and Albert Hofmann
1979   *Plants of the Gods: Origins of Hallucinogenic Use*. McGraw-Hill, New York.

Schultes, Richard E., Albert Hofmann, and Christian Rätsch
1998   *Plants of the Gods: Their Sacred Healing and Hallucinogenic Powers*. Healing Arts Press, Rochester, Vermont.

Schultes, Richard E., and Robert F. Raffauf
1990   *The Healing Forest: Medicinal and Toxic Plants of the Northwest Amazonia*. Dioscorides Press, Portland, Oregon.
2004   *Vine of the Soul: Medicine Men, Their Plants and Rituals in the Colombian Amazonia*. Synergetic Press, Oracle, Arizona.

Schwartz, Norman B.
1990   *Forest Society: A Social History of Peten, Guatemala*. University of Pennsylvania Press, Philadelphia.

Sebastián, Santiago, M. Monterrosa, and J. A. Terán
1995   *Iconografía del arte del siglo 16 en México*. Universidad Autónoma de Zacatecas, Zacatecas, Mexico.

Sedat, David W., and Robert J. Sharer
1994   The Xukpi Stone: A Newly Discovered Early Classic Inscription from the Copan Acropolis, Part I: The Archaeology. In *Copan Note 113*. Copan Archaeological Acropolis Project and the Instituto Hondureño de Antropología e Historia.

Seler, Eduard
1902–1923   *Gesammelte Abhandlungen zur Amerikanischen Sprachund Altertumskunde, 5 Volumes*. A. Ascher, Berlin.

Sharer, Robert J.
1978   *The Prehistory of Chalchuapa, El Salvador: Pottery and Conclusions, Volume III*. University of Pennsylvania Press, Philadelphia.

2002   Early Classic Dynastic Origins in the Southeastern Maya Lowlands. In *Incidents of Archaeology in Central America and Yucatan: Essays in Honor of Edwin M. Shook*, edited by M. P.-H. M. Love and H. Escobedo, pp. 459–476. University Press of America, Lanham, Maryland.

2004   External Interaction at Early Classic Copan. In *Understanding Early Classic Copan*, edited by E. E. Bell, M. Canuto, and R. J. Sharer, pp. 297–317. University of Pennsylvania Museum of Archaeology and Anthropology, Philadelphia.

Sharer, Robert J., and Loa P. Traxler

2003   Las tumbas reales más tempranas de Copán: Muerte y renacimiento en un reino Maya Clásico. Paper presented at the Mesa Redonda de la Sociedad Española de Estudios Mayas, Santiago de Compostela.

Sharer, Robert J., Loa P. Traxler, David W. Sedat, Ellen E. Bell, Marcello Canuto, Christopher Powell

1999   Early Classic Architecture Beneath the Copán Acropolis: A Research Update. *Ancient Mesoamerica* 10(1):3–23.

Sheets, Payson, and Michelle Woodward

2002   Cultivating Biodiversity: Milpas, Gardens, and the Classic Period Landscape. In *Before the Volcano Erupted: The Ancient Cerén Village in Central America*, edited by P. Sheets, pp. 184–191. University of Texas Press, Austin.

Sherman, William L.

1979   *Forced Native Labor in Sixteenth-Century Central America*. University of Nebraska Press, Lincoln and London.

Small, Ernest, and P. M. Catling

2002   Blossoming Treasures of Biodiversity: 4. Chocolate (*Theobroma cacao*)—Sustaining the "Food of the Gods." *Biodiversity* 3(1):23–26.

Smit, Hendrik J. and Rachel J. Blackburn

2005   Reinforcing effects of caffeine and theobromine. *Psychopharmacology* 181:101–106.

Smit, Hendrik J., Elizabeth A. Gaffan and Peter J. Rogers

2004   Methylxanthines are the psycho-pharmacologically active constituents of chocolate. *Psychopharmacology* 176(3–4):412–419.

Smit, Hendrik J., and Peter J. Rogers

2000   Effects of low doses of caffeine on cognitive performance, mood and thirst in low and higher caffeine consumers. *Psychopharmacology* 152:167–173.

2001   Potentially Psychoactive Constituents of Cocoa-Containing Products. In *Food Cravings and Addiction*, edited by M. M. Hetherington, pp. 325–349. Leatherhead Food RA Publishing, Leatherhead, Surrey, United Kingdom.

2002   Effects of Caffeine on Mood. *Pharmacopsychoecologia* 15:231–257.

Smith, Mary Elizabeth

1973   *Picture Writing from Ancient Southern Mexico*. University of Oklahoma Press, Norman.

Smith, Michael E.

1986   The Role of Social Stratification in the Aztec Empire: A View from the Provinces. *American Anthropologist* 88:70–91.

1996   *The Aztecs*. Blackwell, Cambridge, Massachusetts.

Smith, Michael E., and Frances F. Berdan

2003   Postclassic Mesoamerica. In *The Postclassic Mesoamerican World*, edited by M. E. Smith and F. F. Berdan, pp. 3–13. University of Utah Press, Salt Lake City.

Smith, Michael E., Jennifer B. Wharton, and Jan Marie Olson

2003   Aztec Feasts, Rituals and Markets: Political Uses of Ceramic Vessels in a Commercial Economy. In *The Archaeology and Politics of Food and Feasting in Early States and Empires*, edited by T. Bray, pp. 235–268. Kluwer Academic Publishers, New York.

Smith, Robert E.

1952   *Pottery from Chipoc, Alta Verapaz, Guatemala*. Contributions to American Anthropology and History No. 56. Carnegie Institution of Washington, Washington, D.C.

1955   *Ceramic Sequence at Uaxactun, Guatemala*. 2 vols. Middle American Research Institute Publication No. 20. Tulane University, New Orleans.

Solano, Francisco de

1990   *Ciudades Hispanoamericanas y pueblos de Indios*. Consejo Superior de Investigaciones Científicas, Madrid.

Solorzano y Pereyra, Juan de

1952   *Política Indiana (1629)*. Atlas, Madrid.

Soltis, Douglas E., Pamela S. Soltis, Mark W. Chase, Mark E. Mort, Dirk C. Albach, Michael Zanis, Vincent Savolainen, William H. Hahn, Sara B. Hoot, Michael F. Fay, Michael Axtell, Susan M. Swensen, Linda M. Prince, W. John Kress, Kevin C. Nixon, and James S. Farris

2000   Angiosperm Phylogeny Inferred from 18S rDNA, rbcL, and atpB Sequences. *Botanical Journal of the Linnaean Society* 133(4):381–461.

Sosa, John R.

1985   The Maya Sky, the Maya World: A Symbolic Analysis of Yucatec Maya Cosmology. Unpublished Ph.D. dissertation, Anthropology Department, State University of New York, Albany.

Sotelo, A., and R. Alvarez

1991   Chemical Composition of Wild *Theobroma* Species and Their Comparison to the Cacao Bean. *Journal of Agricultural and Food Chemistry* 39:1940–1943.

Soustelle, Jacques

1935   Le totémisme des Lacandons. *Maya Research* 2:325–344.

Spencer, Jeremy P. E., Hagen Schroeter, Baskar Shenoy, S. Kaila S. Srai, Edward S. Debnam, and Catherine Rice-Evans

2001   Epicatechin is the Primary Bioavailable Form of the Procyanidin Dimers B2 and B5 After Transfer Across the Small Intestine. *Biochemical and Biophysical Research Communications* 285:588–593.

Spinden, Herbert J.

1913   *A Study of Maya Art: Its Subject Matter and Historical Development*. Memoirs No. 6. Peabody Museum of American Archaeology and Ethnology. Harvard University, Cambridge.

Spores, Ronald

1974   Marital Alliance in the Political Integration of Mixtec Kingdoms. *American Anthropologist* 76(2):297–311.

Squier, Ephraim G.

1852   *Nicaragua: Its People, Scenery, Monuments and the Proposed Interoceanic Canal*. 2 vols. Appleton, New York.

1985 [1860]   *Letter to the King of Spain, by Diego Garcia de Palacio*. Labyrinthos, Culver City, California.

Standley, Paul C.

1961 Trees and Shrubs of Mexico. In *Contributions U. S. National Herbarium.* Vol. 23. U.S. Govt. Printing Office, Washington, D.C.

Standley, Paul C., J.A. Steyermark, and Louis O. Williams

1949 Flora of Guatemala. *Fieldiana Botany* 24(6).

Stasi, L. C., E. M. G. Santos, C. M. Santos, and C. A. Hiruma

1989 *Plantas medicinais na Amazônia.* UNESP, São Paulo.

Steggerda, Morris

1941 *Maya Indians of Yucatan.* Publication No. 531. Carnegie Institution of Washington, Washington, D.C.

Steinberg, F. M., M. M. Bearden, and C. L. Keen

2003 Cocoa and Chocolate Flavonoids: Implications for Cardiovascular Health. *Journal of the American Dietetic Association* 103:215–223.

Steinberg, Michael K.

2002 The Globalization of a Ceremonial Tree: The Case of Cacao (*Theobroma cacao*) among the Mopan Maya. *Economic Botany* 56(1):58–65.

Steinbrenner, Larry

2002 Ethnicity and Ceramics in Rivas, Nicaragua, A.D. 800–1550. Unpublished Master's thesis, Department of Archaeology, University of Calgary, Canada.

Stern, William L.

1964 Anatomy of the Wood. In *Cacao and Its Allies: a Taxonomic Revision of the Genus* Theobroma, edited by J. Cuatrecasas, pp. 439–442. Smithsonian Institution, Washington, D.C.

Stone, Andrea

2002 *Heart of Creation: The Mesoamerican World and the Legacy of Linda Schele.* University of Alabama Press, Tuscaloosa.

Stone, Doris

1972 *Pre-Columbian Man Finds Central America.* Peabody Museum Press, Cambridge.

1984 Pre-Columbian Migration of *Theobroma cacao* Linnaeus and *Manihot esculenta* Crantz from Northern South America into Mesoamerica: A Partially Hypothetical View. In *Pre-Columbian Plant Migration,* edited by D. Stone, pp. 67–83. Harvard University Press, Cambridge.

Strathern, Marilyn

1988 *The Gender of the Gift: Problems with Women and Problems with Society in Melanesia.* University of California Press, Berkeley.

Stromsvik, Gustav

1941 Substela Caches and Stela Foundations at Copán and Quirigua. *Carnegie Institution of Washington Contributions to American Anthropology and History* 7(37):63–96. Publication No. 528. Carnegie Institution of Washington, Washington, D.C.

Stuart, David

1986 The "lu-Bat" Glyph and its Bearing on the Primary Standard Sequence. Paper presented at the Primer Simposio Mundial Sobre Epigrafía Maya, August 1986, Guatemala City.

1987 Ten Phonetic Syllables. In *Research Reports on Ancient Maya Writing.* Vol. 14. Center for Maya Research, Washington, D.C.

1988 The Rio Azul Cacao pot: Epigraphic Observations on the Function of a Maya Ceramic Vessel. *Antiquity* 62(234):153–157.

1989   Hieroglyphs on Maya Vessels. In *The Maya Vase Book: A Corpus of Rollout Photographs of Maya Vases, Volume 1*, edited by J. Kerr, pp. 149–160. Kerr Associates, New York.

1992   Flower Symbolism in Maya Iconography. Paper presented at the 8th Symposium on Ancient Maya Writing and Culture, "Origins: Creation and Continuity, Mythology and History in Mesoamerica," March 1992, University of Texas, Austin.

1995   A Study of Maya Inscriptions. Unpublished Ph.D. dissertation, Department of Anthropology, Vanderbilt University, Nashville.

1996   Kings of Stone: A Consideration of Stelae in Maya Ritual and Representation. *RES* 29/30:149–171.

1998   "The Fire Enters His House": Architecture and Ritual in Classic Maya Texts. In *Function and Meaning in Classic Maya Architecture*, edited by S. Houston, pp. 373–425. Dumbarton Oaks, Washington, D.C.

2000   "The Arrival of Strangers": Teotihuacan and Tollan in Classic Maya History. In *Mesoamerica's Classic Heritage*, edited by D. Carrasco, L. Jones, and S. Sessions, pp. 465–514. University Press of Colorado, Boulder.

2005   *Sourcebook for the 29th Maya Hieroglyphic Forum*. The Maya Meetings, Department of Art and Art History, The University of Texas, Austin.

Stuart, David, Nikolai Grube, and Linda Schele

1989   A Substitution Set for the "Ma Cuch/Batab" Title. In *Copán Note 58*. Copán Mosaics Project and the Instituto Hondureño de Anthropología e Historia, Copán, Honduras.

Stuart, David, Stephen D. Houston, and John Robertson

1999   Recovering the Past: Classic Maya Language and Classic Maya Gods. In *Notebook for the 23rd Maya Hieroglyphic Forum at Texas. Part 2*. Pp. 1–96. Maya Workshop Foundation, University of Texas Press, Austin.

Stuart, Gene S., and George E. Stuart

1993   *Lost Kingdoms of the Maya*. National Geographic Society, Washington, D.C.

Stuart, George E.

2001   An Inscribed Shell Drinking Vessel from the Maya Lowlands. *Research Reports on Ancient Maya Writing* 48:1–9.

Tarn, Nathaniel, and Martin Prechtel

1986   Constant Inconstancy: The Feminine Principle in Atiteco Mythology. In *Symbol and Meaning Beyond the Closed Community: Essays in Mesoamerican Ideas*, edited by G. H. Gossen, pp. 173–184. Studies on Culture and Society. Vol. 1. Institute for Mesoamerican Studies, State University of New York, Albany.

Taschek, Jennifer T., and Joseph W. Ball

1992   Lord Smoke-Squirrel's Cacao Cup: The Archaeological Context and Socio-Historical Significance of the Buenavista "Jauncy Vase." In *The Maya Vase Book: A Corpus of Rollout Photographs of Maya Vases, Volume 3*, edited by J. Kerr, pp. 490–497. Kerr Associates, New York.

Tate, Carolyn

1985   The Carved Ceramics Called Chochola. In *Fifth Palenque Round Table, 1983, Vol. 7*, edited by V. M. Fields, pp. 123–133. Pre-Columbian Art Research Institute, San Francisco.

1992   *Yaxchilan: The Design of a Maya Ceremonial City*. University of Texas Press, Austin.

Taube, Karl A.

1985 The Classic Maya Maize God: A Reappraisal. In *Fifth Palenque Round Table, 1983, Vol. 7*, edited by V. M. Fields. Pre-Columbian Art Research Institute, San Francisco.

1986 The Teotihuacan Cave of Origin: The Iconography and Architecture of Emergence Mythology in Mesoamerica and the American Southwest. *RES: Anthropology and Aesthetics* 12:51–82.

1989 The Maize Tamale in Classic Maya Diet, Epigraphy, and Art. *American Antiquity* 54(1):31–51.

1992a *The Major Gods of Ancient Yucatán. Studies in Precolumbian Art and Archaeology.* Dumbarton Oaks, Washington, D.C.

1992b The Temple of Quetzalcoatl and the Cult of Sacred War at Teotihuacan. *RES: Anthropology and Aesthetics* 21:53–87.

1994a The Iconography of Toltec Period Chichen Itza. In *Hidden among Hills: Maya Archaeology of the Northwestern Yucatan Peninsula. Contributions of the International Maler Symposium, Bonn 1989*, edited by H. J. Prem, pp. 212–246. Acta Mesoamericana 7, Möckmühl, Germany.

1994b The Birth Vase: Natal Imagery in Ancient Maya Myth and Ritual. In *The Maya Vase Book: A Corpus of Rollout Photographs of Maya Vases, Volume 4*, edited by J. Kerr, pp. 652–685. Kerr Associates, New York.

2001 Itzamná. In *The Oxford Encyclopedia of Mesoamerican Cultures: The Civilizations of Mexico and Central America*, edited by D. Carrasco, pp. 56–57. Oxford University Press, Oxford, England.

2002 Heaven and Hell: Portals, Xibalba and the Flowery Paradise. Paper presented at the 7th European Maya Conference, "Jaws of the Underworld: Life, Death and Rebirth Among the Ancient Maya," November 5–10, 2002, British Museum, London.

2003a Ancient and Contemporary Maya Conceptions About Field and Forest. In *The Lowland Maya Area: Three Millennia at the Human-Wildland Interface*, edited by A. Gómez-Pompa, M. F. Allen, S. L. Fedick, and J. J. Jiménez-Osorino, pp. 461–492. Haworth Press, Binghamton, New York.

2003b Maws of Heaven and Hell: The Symbolism of the Centipede and Serpent in Classic Maya Religion. In *Antropología de la eternidad: La muerte en la cultura Maya*, edited by Andrés Cuidad Ruiz, Mario H. Ruz Sosa, and M. Josefa Iglesias Ponce de León, pp. 405–442. Sociedad Española de Estudios Mayas, Madrid.

2003c Tetitla and the Maya Presence at Teotihuacan. In *The Maya and Teotihuacan: Reinterpreting Early Classic Interaction*, edited by G. E. Braswell, pp. 273–314. University of Texas Press, Austin.

2004a Flower Mountain: Concepts of Life, Beauty, and Paradise among the Classic Maya. *RES: Anthropology and Aesthetics* 45:69–98.

2004b Structure 10L-16 and Its Early Classic Antecedents: Fire and the Evocation and Resurrection of K'inich Yax K'uk' Mo.' In *Understanding Early Classic Copan*, edited by E. E. Bell, M. A. Canuto, and R. J. Sharer, pp. 265–295. University of Pennsylvania Museum of Archaeology and Anthropology, Philadelphia.

2005 The Symbolism of Jade in Classic Maya Religion. *Ancient Mesoamerica* 16(1):23–50.

Taussig, Michael

1993 *Mimesis and Alterity: A Particular History of the Senses.* Routledge, New York.

Tax, Sol

1949   Folk Tales in Chichicastenango: An Unsolved Puzzle. *Journal of American Folklore* 62:125–135.

Tedlock, Barbara

1982   *Time and the Highland Maya.* University of New Mexico Press, Albuquerque.

1992   The Road of Light: Theory and Practice of Mayan Skywatching. In *The Sky in Mayan Literature*, edited by A. F. Aveni, pp. 18–42. Oxford University Press, New York.

1992 [1982]   *Time and the Highland Maya.* Revised ed. University of New Mexico Press, Albuquerque.

Tedlock, Dennis

1985   *Popol Vuh: The Definitive Edition of the Maya Book of the Dawn of Life and the Glories of Gods and Kings.* Simon and Schuster, New York.

1996   *Popol Vuh: The Mayan Book of the Dawn of Life (Revised Edition).* Touchstone, New York.

2002   How to Drink Chocolate from a Skull at a Wedding Banquet. *RES: Anthropology and Aesthetics* 42:166–179.

2003   *Rabinal Achi.* Oxford University Press, Oxford.

Tello, Julio C.

1960   *Chavín: Cultura matriz de la civilización Andina.* Universidad de San Marcos, Lima.

Templeton, A. R., E. Routman, and C. Phillips

1995   Separating Population Structure from Population History: a Cladistic Analysis of the Geographical Distribution of Mitochondrial DNA Haplotypes in the Tiger Salamander, *Ambystoma tigrinum. Genetics* 140(2):767–782.

Terán, Silvia, and Christian Rasmussen

1994   *La Milpa de los Mayas: La agricultura de los mayas prehispánicos y actuales en el noreste de Yucatán.* Gobierno del Estado de Yucatán, México.

Terrio, Susan J.

2000   *Crafting the Culture and History of French Chocolate.* University of California Press, Berkeley.

2003   Chocolate: The Field Museum of Natural History. *American Anthropologist* 105(1):150–152.

Thomas, Nicholas

1991   *Entangled Objects: Exchange, Material Culture, and Colonialism in the Pacific.* Harvard University Press, Cambridge.

Thompson, Catherine

1983   Women, Fertility and the Worship of Gods in a Hindu Village. In *Women's Religious Experience: Cross-Cultural Perspectives*, edited by P. Holden, pp. 113–131. Croon Helm, London.

Thompson, J. Eric S.

1930   *Ethnology of the Mayas of Southern and Central British Honduras.* Field Museum of Natural History Anthropological Series 17, No. 2. Field Museum of Natural History, Chicago, Illinois.

1938   Sixteenth and Seventeenth Century Reports on the Chol Mayas. *American Anthropologist* 40(4):584–604.

1948   An Archaeological Reconnaissance in the Cotzumalhuapa Region, Escuintla, Guatemala.

Carnegie Institution of Washington Contributions to American Anthropology and History 9(44):1–94. Publication 574. Carnegie Institution of Washington, Washington, D.C.

1956   Notes on the Use of Cacao in Middle America. *Notes on Middle American Archaeology and Ethnology* 128:95–116.

1962   *A Catalog of Maya Hieroglyphs.* University of Oklahoma Press, Norman.

1964   Trade Relations between the Maya Highlands and the Lowlands. *Estudios de Cultura Maya* 4:13–48.

1974   *The Maya of Belize: Historical Chapters Since Columbus.* Benex Press, Belize City.

1970   *Maya History and Religion.* University of Oklahoma, Norman.

1977   A Proposal for Constituting a Maya Subgroup, Cultural and Linguistic, in the Petén and Adjacent Region. In *Anthropology and History in Yucatán*, edited by G. D. Jones, pp. 3–42. University of Texas Press, Austin and London.

Toledo, Victor M.

1992   What is Ethnoecology? Origins, Scope and Implications of a Rising Discipline. *Etnoecologica* 1(1):5–21.

Tolstoy, Paul

1989   Coapexco and Tlatilco: Sites with Olmec Materials in the Basin of Mexico. In *Regional Perspectives on the Olmec*, edited by R. J. Sharer and D. C. Grove, pp. 85–121. Cambridge University Press, Cambridge.

Tomaso, E. D., M. Beltramo, and D. Piomelli

1996   Brain Cannabinoids in Chocolate. *Nature* 382:677.

Tonkin, Elizabeth

1983   Women Excluded? Masking and Masquerading in West Africa. In *Women's Religious Experience: Cross-Cultural Perspectives*, edited by P. Holden, pp. 163–174. Croon Helm, London.

Torquebiau, E.

1992   Are Tropical Agroforestry Homegardens Sustainable? *Agriculture, Ecosystems and Environment* (41):189–207.

Torquemada, Juan de

1723   Los veinte i un libros rituales i monarchia Indiana, con el origen y guerras de los Indios Occidentales. 3 vols. Madrid.

Tovilla, Martín Alonso

1960   *Relación histórica descriptiva de las provincias de la Verapaz y de la del Manché, escrita por . . . , año de 1635.* Editorial Universitaria, Guatemala.

Tozzer, Alfred M.

1907   *A Comparative Study of the Mayas and the Lacandon.* The MacMillan Company, New York.

1957   *Chichen Itza and Its Cenote of Sacrifice; A Comparative Study of Contemporaneous Maya and Toltec.* Memoirs Nos. 11–12. Peabody Museum of Archaeology and Ethnology. Harvard University, Cambridge.

Traxler, Loa P.

1994   A New Discovery at Copan. *Expedition* 35(3):57–62.

Trotter, R. T., and M. H. Logan

1986   Informant Consensus: A New Approach for Identifying Potentially Effective Medicinal

Plants. In *Plants in Indigenous Medicine and Diet*, edited by N. L. Etkin, pp. 81–112. Redgrave Publishing Company, Bedford Hills, New York.

Turner II, B. L., and Charles H. Miksicek

1984   Economic Plant Species Associated with Prehistoric Agriculture in the Maya Lowlands. *Economic Botany* 38(2):179–193.

Turner II, B. L., William Johnson, Gail Mahood, Frederick M. Wiseman, B. L. Turner, and Jackie Poole

1983   Habitat y agricultura en la region de Copan. In *Introduccion a la arqueologia de Copan, Honduras*, Vol. 1, edited by C. Baudez, pp. 35–142. Instituto Hondureno de Antropologia e Historia, Tegucigalpa.

Turner, Victor

1967   *The Forest of Symbols: Aspects of Ndembu Ritual*. Cornell University Press, Ithaca, New York.

1982   *From Ritual to Theatre: the Seriousness of Play*. Performing Arts Journal Publications, New York.

Uphof, Johannes Cornelius Theodorus

1968   *Dictionary of Economic Plants*. 2nd ed. Verlag von J. Cramer, Lehre, Germany.

Urcid, Javier

1993   The Pacific Coast of Oaxaca and Guerrero: The Westernmost Extent of Zapotec Script. *Ancient Mesoamerica* 4(1):141–165.

Vail, Gabrielle

2002   *The Madrid Codex: A Maya Hieroglyphic Book, Version 1.0*. Dumbarton Oaks. A website and database available online at: <http://doaks.org/codex>, accessed May 1, 2005.

Valdez, Fred, Jr.

1987   The Prehistoric Ceramics of Colha, Northern Belize. Unpublished Ph.D. dissertation, Department of Anthropology, Harvard University, Cambridge.

Van Gennep, Arnold

1960   *The Rites of Passage*. Translated by M. B. Vizedom and G. L. Caffee. University of Chicago Press, Chicago, Illinois.

Van Hall, Constant J. J.

1914   *Cocoa*. Macmillan, London.

1932   *Cocoa*. 2nd ed. Macmillan, London.

Vázquez de Espinosa, A.

1942   *Compendium and Description of the West Indies*. Translated by C. U. Clark. Smithsonian Miscellaneous Collections Vol. 102. Smithsonian Institution, Washington, D.C.

Venturieri, G. A., and J. P. L. Aguiar

1988   Composição do chocolate de amendoas de cupuaçu (*Theobroma grandiflorum*). *Acta Amazonica* 18:3–8.

Verhagen, Inez L.

1995a   Excavaciones en la iglesia de San Pedro y San Pablo Caluco, El Salvador. Unpublished report to the Dirección del Patrimonio Cultural, Consejo Nacional para la Cultura y el Arte, San Salvador, El Salvador.

1995b   Investigaciones arqueológicas en las alrededores de Caluco, El Salvador. Unpublished report to la Dirección del Patrimonio Cultural, Consejo Nacional para la Cultura y el Arte, San Salvador, El Salvador.

1997   Caluco, El Salvador: The Archaeology of a Colonial Indian Town in Comparative Perspective. Unpublished Ph.D. dissertation, Vanderbilt University, Nashville.

Vickers, W. T., and T. Plowman

1984   Useful Plants of the Siona and Secoya Indians of Eastern Ecuador. *Fieldiana Botany* 15:1–63.

Viel, René

1993   *Evolucion de la Ceramica de Copan, Honduras.* Instituto Hondureño de Antropología e Historia y Centro Estudias Mexicanos y Centroamericanos, Tegucigalpa, D.C. and Mexico City.

Villacorta Calderón, José Antonio, and Carlos Villacorta

1976   *Codices mayas: reproducidos y desarrollados.* Tipografía Nacional, Guatemala City.

Villafuerte, Daniel, Maria del Carmen Garcia, and Salvador Meza

1997   *La cuestion ganadera y la deforestacion: Viejos y nuevos problemas en el tropico y Chiapas.* Universidad de Ciencias y Artes del Estado de Chiapas y Centro de Estudios Superiores de México-Centroamerica, Tuxtla Gutierrez, Chiapas, México.

Villagutierre y Sotomayor, Juan de

1933   *Historia de la conquista de la provincia del Itzá.* Sociedad de Geografía e Historia de Guatemala, Guatemala.

Villa-Rojas, Alfonso

1987 [1945]   *Los elegidos de Dios: Etnografía de los Mayas de Quintana Roo.* INI Colección No. 56, México, D. F.

Vogt, Evon Z.

1969   *Zinacantan: A Maya Community in the Highlands of Chiapas.* Harvard University Press, Cambridge.

1976   *Tortillas for the Gods: A Symbolic Analysis of Zinacanteco Rituals.* Harvard University Press, Cambridge and London.

1981   Some Aspects of the Sacred Geography of Highland Chiapas. In *Mesoamerican Sites and World-Views,* edited by E. P. Benson, pp. 119–142. Dumbarton Oaks, Washington, D.C.

1993   *Tortillas for the Gods: A Symbolic Analysis of Zinacanteco Rituals.* 2nd ed. University of Oklahoma Press, Norman and London.

1998   Zinacanteco Dedication and Termination Rituals. In *The Sowing and the Dawning: Termination, Dedication and Transformation in the Archaeological and Ethnographic Record of Mesoamerica,* edited by S. B. Mock, pp. 21–30. University of New Mexico Press, Albuquerque.

Von Nagy, Christopher L., Mary D. Pohl, and Kevin O. Pope

2001   *A Theater Community in a Theater Polity: Archaeological Research at San Andrés, Tabasco, Mexico.* Department of Anthropology, Florida State University, Tallahassee.

Voorhies, Barbara, and Janine Gasco

2004   *Postclassic Soconusco Society: The Late Prehistory of the Coast of Chiapas, Mexico.* Institute for Mesoamerican Studies, State University of New York, Albany.

Wagley, Charles

1949   *Social and Religious Life of a Guatemalan Village.* Memoirs No. 71. American Anthropological Association, Washington, D.C.

Walsh, Jane MacLaren, and Yoko Sugiura

1991   The Demise of the Fifth Sun. In *Seeds of Change: A Quincentennial Commemoration,* edited by H. J. Viola and C. Margolis, pp. 17–41. Smithsonian Institution Press, Washington, D.C.

Warren, D. Michael, L. Jan Slikkerveer, and David Brokensha (editors)

1999   *The Cultural Dimension of Development.* Intermediate Technology Publications, London.

Wasson, R. Gordon

1962   A New Mexican Psychotropic Drug from the Mint Family. *Botanical Museum Leaflets, Harvard University* 20(3):77–84.

Watanabe, John M.

1990   From Saints to Shibboleths: Image, Structure, and Identity in Maya Religious Syncretism. *American Ethnologist* 17(1):131–150.

Waterhouse, A. L., J. R. Shirley, and J. L. Donovan

1996   Antioxidants in Chocolate. *Lancet* 348:834.

Weil, Andrew T.

1980   Cocoa, Not Cocaine. *Science* 209:1182.

Weinberg, Bennett Alan and Bonnie K. Bealer

2001   *The World of Caffeine: The Science and Culture of the World's Most Popular Drug.* Routledge, New York and London.

Weisburger, J. H.

2001   Chemopreventive Effects of Cocoa Polyphenols on Chronic Diseases. *Experimental Biology and Medicine* 226:891–897.

Weitlaner, Robert J.

1952   Curaciones Mazatecas. *Anales del Instituto Nacional de Antropología e Historia* 4:279–285.

West, Robert C., Norbert P. Psuty, and Bruce G. Thom

1969   *The Tabasco Lowlands of Southeastern Mexico.* Louisiana State University Press, Baton Rouge.

Wheatley, Paul

1971   *The Pivot of the Four Corners.* Aldine, Chicago, Illinois.

Whitkus, R., M. de la Cruz, L. Mota-Bravo, and A. Gómez-Pompa

1998   Genetic Diversity and Relationships of Cacao (*Theobroma cacao* L.) in Southern Mexico. *Theoretical and Applied Genetics* 96:621–627.

Whitlock, B. A., and D. A. Baum

1999   Phylogenetic Relationships of *Theobroma* and *Herrania* (Sterculiaceae) Based on Sequences of the Nuclear Gene Vicilin. *Systematic Botany* 24:128–138.

Whitten, Norman

1985   *Sicuanga Runa: The Other Side of Development in Amazonian Ecuador.* University of Illinois Press, Urbana.

Wichmann, Søren

1995   *The Relationship among the Mixe-Zoquean Languages of Mexico.* University of Utah Press, Salt Lake City.

Wickizer, Vernon D.

1951   *Coffee, Tea and Cocoa: An Economic and Political Analysis.* Stanford University, Stanford, California.

Wiedemann, B., H. Lerche, H. Lotter, A. Neszmélyi, H. Wagner, and A. A. Müller

1999   Two Novel Triterpenoids from the Stemwood of *Herrania cuatrecasana. Phytochemistry* 52:333–337.

Wiersum, K. F.

1997   From Natural Forest to Tree Crops, Co-Domestication of Forests and Tree Species, an Overview. In Processes and Stages in the Transition from Natural Forest Ecosystems to Tree Crop Plantations. Hinkeloord Report No. 22, edited by J. F. Wienk, K. F. Wiersum, and J. J. Neeteson. Sub-department of Forestry. Agricultural University Wageningen, *Netherlands Journal of Agriculture Science* 45:425–438.

Wilk, Richard R.

1991   *Household Ecology: Economic Change and Domestic Life among the Kekchi Maya in Belize.* University of Arizona Press, Tucson and London.

Wilkerson, S. Jeffrey K.

1984   In Search of the Mountain of Foam: Human Sacrifice in Eastern Mesoamerica. In *Ritual Human Sacrifice in Mesoamerica*, edited by E. H. Boone, pp. 101–132. Dumbarton Oaks, Washington, D.C.

Willey, Gordon R.

1972   *The Artifacts of Altar de Sacrificios.* Papers of the Peabody Museum of Archaeology and Ethnology, vol. 64. Harvard University, Cambridge.

Willey, Gordon R., W. R. Bullard, Jr., J. B. Glass, and J. C. Gifford

1965   *Prehistoric Maya Settlements in the Belize Valley.* Papers of the Peabody Museum of Archaeology and Ethnology Vol. 54. Harvard University, Cambridge.

Willey, Gordon R., Richard M. Leventhal, Arthur Demarest, and William L. Fash

1994   *The Copan Residential Zone.* Papers of the Peabody Museum of Archaeology and Ethnology, Vol. 80. Harvard University, Cambridge.

Williams, Louis O.

1981   The Useful Plants of Central America. *Ceiba* 24(1–2):1–342.

Wilson, Richard

1990   Mountain Spirits and Maize: Catholic Conversion and Renovation of Traditions among the Q'eqchi' of Guatemala. Unpublished Ph.D. thesis, London School of Economics, University of London.

Winning, Hasso von

1985   *Two Maya Monuments in Yucatan: The Palace of the Stuccoes at Acanceh and the Temple of the Owls at Chichén Itzá.* Southwest Museum, Los Angeles.

Wisdom, Charles

1940   *The Chorti Indians of Guatamala.* University of Chicago Press, Chicago, Illinois.

1950   *Materials on the Chorti Language.* Middle American Cultural Anthropology Microfilm Series 5, Item 38. University of Chicago Library, Chicago, Illinois.

1961   *Los Chortis de Guatemala.* Seminario de integracion social Guatemalteca, Guatemala City, Guatemala.

Wolf, Eric

1959   *Sons of the Shaking Earth.* University of Chicago Press, Chicago, Illinois.

1966   *Peasants.* Prentice-Hall, Englewood Cliffs, New Jersey.

1982   *Europe and the People Without History.* University of California Press, Berkeley.

1999   *Envisioning Power: Ideologies of Dominance and Crisis.* University of California Press, Berkeley.

Wood, G. A. R.

1975   *Cocoa.* Longman, London.

1982   *Cacao.* C.E.C.S.A., Mexico City.

Worldaware

1994   Booker Tate Award for Small Businesses: Green & Black's. Worldaware. <http://www.worldaware.org.uk/awards/awards1994/green.html>, accessed February 3, 2004.

Ximénez, Francisco

1929   *Historia de la provincia de San Vicente de Chiapa y Guatemala.* Biblioteca "Goathemala" de la Sociedad de Geografía e Historia 1–5. Tipografía Nacional, Guatemala City, Guatemala.

1971–1975 *Historia de la provincia de San Vicente de Chiapa y Guatemala de la orden de predicadores.* 5 vols. Guatemala: Sociedad de Geografía e Historia de Guatemala, Guatemala City, Guatemala.

1985   *Primera parte del tesoro de las lenguas cakchiquel, quiché y zutuhil, en las que dichas lenguas se traducen a la nuestra española,* edited by Carmelo Sáenz de Santa María. Tipografía Nacional, Guatemala City, Guatemala.

Yamagishi, M., M. Natsume, A. Nagaki, T. Adachi, N. Osakabe, T. Takizawa, H. Kumon, and T. Osawa

2000   Antimutagenic Activity of Cacao: Inhibitory Effect of Cacao Liquor Polyphenols on the Mutagenic Action of Heterocyclic Amines. *Journal of Agricultural and Food Chemistry* 48(10):5074–5078.

Yang, H., P. Protiva, B. Cui, C. Ma, S. Baggett, V. Hequet, S. Mori, I. B. Weinstein, and E. J. Kennelly

2003   New Bioactive Polyphenols from *Theobroma grandiflorum* ("Cupuaçu"). *Journal of Natural Products* 66(11):1501–1504.

Young, Allen M.

1982   Effects of Shade Cover and Availability of Midge Breeding Sites on Pollinating Midge Populations and Fruit Set in Two Cocoa Farms. *Journal of Applied Ecology* 19:47–63.

1983   Seasonal Differences in Abundance and Distribution of Cocoa-Pollinating Midges in Relation to Flowering and Fruit Set between Shaded and Sunny Habitats of the La Loa Cocoa Farm in Costa Rica. *Journal of Applied Ecology* 20:801–831.

1984   Mechanism of Pollination by Phoridae (Diptera) in Some *Herrania* Species (Sterculiaceae) in Costa Rica. *Proceedings of the Entomological Society of Washington* 86:503–518.

1985   Pollen-Collecting by Stingless Bees on Cacao Flowers. *Experientia* 41:760–762.

1994   *The Chocolate Tree: A Natural History of Cacao.* Smithsonian Institution Press, Washington, D.C.

Young, Allen M., and D. W. Severson

1994   Comparative Analysis of Steam Distilled Flora Oils of Cacao Cultivars (*Theobroma cacao* L., Sterculiaceae) and Attraction of Flying Insects: Implications for a *Theobroma* Pollination Syndrome. *Journal of Chemical Ecology* 20:2687–2703.

Young, Allen M., B. J. Erickson, and E. H. Erickson, Jr.

1989   Pollination Biology of *Theobroma* and *Herrania* (Sterculiaceae) 3. Steam-Distilled Floral Oils of *Theobroma* Species as Attractant to Flying Insects in a Costa Rican Cocoa Plantation. *Insect Science and Its Application* 10(1):93–98.

Young, Allen M., M. Schaller, and M. Strand

1984   Flora Nectaries and Trichomes in Relation to Pollination in Some Species of *Theobroma* and *Herrania* (Sterculiaceae). *American Journal of Botany* 71:466–480.

Young, James Clay

1981   *Medical Choice in a Mexican Village*. Rutgers University Press, New Brunswick, New Jersey.

Zantwijk, Rudolf van

1985   *The Aztec Arrangement*. University of Oklahoma Press, Norman.

Zender, Marc

1999   Diacritical Marks and Underspelling in the Classic Maya Script: Implications for Decipherment. Unpublished Master's thesis, Department of Archaeology, University of Calgary, Canada.

2000   A Study of Two Uaxactun-style Tamale Serving Vessels. In *The Maya Vase Book: A Corpus of Rollout Photographs of Maya Vases, Volume 6,* edited by J. Kerr, pp. 1038–1055. Kerr Associates, New York.

Zerega, Nyree J. C., Diane Ragone, and Timothy J. Motley

2004   Complex Origins of Breadfruit: Implications for Human Migrations in Oceania. *American Journal of Botany* 91(5):760–766.

Zorita, Alonso de

1963   *The Lords of New Spain: A Brief and Summary Relation of the Lords of New Spain*. Translated by B. Keen. Phoenix House, London.

Zoumas, Barry L., and J. Frank Smullen

1991   Chocolate and Cacao. In *Encyclopedia of Food Science and Technology*, edited by Y. H. Hui. Wiley, New York.

Contributors

Manuel Aguilar-Moreno, Associate Professor, Art History Department, California State University, Los Angeles

Mario M. Aliphat F., Professor of Anthropology and Human Ecology, Laboratorio de Etnoecología y Regiones Indigenas, Colegio de Postgraduados, Puebla, Mexico

Nathaniel Bletter, Ph.D. candidate, Plant Sciences Program, New York Botanical Garden, and Biology Department, the Graduate Center, City University of New York

Laura Caso Barrera, Professor of Ethnohistory and Anthropology, Laboratorio de Etnoecología y Regiones Indigenas, Colegio de Postgraduados, Puebla, México

Douglas C. Daly, B. A. Krukoff Curator of Amazonian Botany, Institute of Systematic Botany, New York Botanical Garden

Betty Bernice Faust, Senior Researcher, Department of Human Ecology, Centro de Investigación y de Estudios Avanzados del Instituto Politécnico Nacional, Unidad Mérida, Yucatan, México

William R. Fowler, Associate Professor, Department of Anthropology, Vanderbilt University, Nashville, Tennessee

Janine Gasco, Associate Professor, Department of Anthropology, California State University, Dominguez Hills

Arturo Gómez-Pompa, Professor, Department of Conservation Biology, University of California, Riverside, and Advisor, Centro de Investigaciones Tropicales, Universidad Veracruzana, México

Michael Heinrich, Professor and Head, Centre for Pharmacognosy and Phytotherapy, School of Pharmacy, University of London

John Henderson, Professor, Department of Anthropology, Cornell University, Ithaca, New York

Javier Hirose-López, Graduate student, Centro de Estudios Mayas, Instituto de Investigaciones Filológicas, Universidad Nacional Autónoma de México

W. Jeffrey Hurst, Senior Staff Scientist, Hershey Food Technical Center, Hershey, Pennsylvania, and Clinical Professor of Comparative Medicine, M. S. Hershey Medical Center, Pennsylvania State University, Hershey

Rosemary Joyce, Professor, Department of Anthropology, University of California, Berkeley

John Justeson, Professor, Department of Anthropology, State University of New York, Albany

Terrence Kaufman, Professor, Department of Anthropology and Linguistics, University of Pittsburgh

Johanna Kufer, Ph.D., University of London Centre for Pharmacognosy and Phytotherapy, School of Pharmacy, University of London

Patricia A. McAnany, Professor, Department of Archaeology, Boston University, Boston, Massachusetts

Cameron L. McNeil, Ph.D., Department of Anthropology, the Graduate Center, City University of New York

Simon Martin, Research Specialist in Maya Epigraphy, University of Pennsylvania Museum of Archaeology and Anthropology, Philadelphia

Satoru Murata, Ph.D. candidate, Department of Archaeology, Boston University, Boston, Massachusetts

Nisao Ogata, Professor, Centro de Investigaciones Tropicales, Universidad Veracruzana, México

Timothy Pugh, Assistant Professor, Queens College, City University of New York, and the Graduate Center, City University of New York

Dorie Reents-Budet, Senior Research Fellow, Department of Anthropology, National Museum of Natural History, Smithsonian Institution, Washington, D.C.

Robert J. Sharer, holds the Sally and Alvin V. Shoemaker Professorship in Anthropology, University of Pennsylvania, and is Curator of the American Section, University of Pennsylvania Museum, Philadelphia

Larry Steinbrenner, Ph.D. candidate, Department of Archaeology, University of Calgary, Canada

David Stuart, the Linda and David Schele Professor of Mesoamerican Art and Writing, University of Texas, Austin

Karl Taube, Professor, Department of Anthropology, University of California, Riverside

Index

Pages with *f* denote figures; pages with *t* denote tables

Current Check-Outs summary for Contreras
Mon Nov 22 12:00:44 CST 2010

BARCODE: 31782003407877
TITLE: Chocolate in Mesoamerica : a cult
DUE DATE: Dec 13 2010

#1 11-22-2010 12:00PM
Item(s) checked out to Contreras, Letici

TITLE: Chocolate in Mesoamerica : a cult
BARCODE: 31782003407877
DUE DATE: 12-13-10